MATERIAL WOMEN, 1750–1950

For our mothers,
Marguerite Eichorn Daly and Royce Budge Fowkes

Material Women, 1750–1950

Consuming Desires and Collecting Practices

Edited by
Maureen Daly Goggin and Beth Fowkes Tobin

Routledge
Taylor & Francis Group
LONDON AND NEW YORK

First published 2009 by Ashgate Publishing

Published 2016 by Routledge
2 Park Square, Milton Park, Abingdon, Oxfordshire OX14 4RN
711 Third Avenue, New York, NY 10017, USA

First issued in paperback 2016

Routledge is an imprint of the Taylor & Francis Group, an informa business

British Library Cataloguing in Publication Data
Material women, 1750-1950 : consuming desires and
collecting practices.
1. Consumption (Economics)--Sex differences. 2. Women
consumers--History. 3. Women collectors--History.
4. Consumer behavior--History.
I. Goggin, Maureen Daly. II. Tobin, Beth Fowkes.
306.3'09-dc22

Library of Congress Cataloging-in-Publication Data
Material women, 1750-1950 : consuming desires and collecting practices /
Maureen Daly Goggin and Beth Fowkes Tobin.
p. cm.
Includes bibliographical references and index.
ISBN 978-0-7546-6539-7 (hardback : alk. paper)
1. Women--Social conditions. 2. Women consumers--History. 3. Material culture--History. I. Goggin, Maureen Daly. II. Tobin, Beth Fowkes.

HQ1150.M38 2009
305.409--dc22

2009026968

ISBN 13: 978-1-138-25307-0 (pbk)
ISBN 13: 978-0-7546-6539-7 (hbk)

Contents

Figures

17.2 The elaborate "South Island Pioneer" period room with the North Island "pioneer hut" just visible on the left in the women's section, at the New Zealand Centennial Exhibition, 1940. 1/2-036211-F, PAColl 3036, Eileen Deste Collection, Alexander Turnbull Library, Wellington, New Zealand.

17.3 Visitors throng the Canterbury Colonists Exhibition, 1950–51. The conventional long rectangular gallery space has a high ceiling with period room displays around the perimeter for promenade viewing. Dr Barker's roomy V-hut with vitrine and map displays dominate the center of the gallery. *Canterbury Colonists Exhibition, 1950–51*, The Friends of the Canterbury Museum, Christchurch, 1951, p. 29.

17.4 A costumed historical procession, part of the Canterbury centenary celebrations in Christchurch city, December 1950. 19XX.2.55, Leicagraph Studio photograph, Canterbury Museum.

17.5 Even men came to look at the horse and carriage in the Canterbury Street in this view from 1960. The arcade-style Costume Gallery is on the upper level. Garments similar to those on display, and the fabric and trimmings, could be seen in the shops in the street, which were based on actual stores and establishments in Christchurch city. 1990.358.902, unknown photographer, Rose Josephine Reynolds Collection, Canterbury Museum.

17.6 A female visitor prepares to be served in the J Ballantyne shop, Canterbury Street, Canterbury Museum, 1960. Ballantynes later became a well-known department store in the city. 1990.358.923, unknown photographer, Rose Josephine Reynolds Collection, Canterbury Museum.

17.7 Visitors young and old peer into the Cob Cottage, Canterbury Street, Canterbury Museum, 1960. 1990.358.950, unknown photographer, Rose Josephine Reynolds Collection, Canterbury Museum.

17.8 The Victorian Room display, Canterbury Museum, 1960. 1990.358.950, unknown photographer, Rose Josephine Reynolds Collection, Canterbury Museum.

17.9 Extensive use of elaborately dressed mannequins and mural settings were a feature of the Costume Gallery, Canterbury Museum, shown here in 1960. 1990.358.979, unknown photographer, Rose Josephine Reynolds Collection, Canterbury Museum.

17.10 Fashion show, James Smith's department store, Wellington, *circa* 1953. PAColl-3332-03-15, James Smith Ltd Collection, Alexander Turnbull Library, Wellington, New Zealand.

Contributors

Editors

Maureen Daly Goggin, Professor of Rhetoric and Interim Chair of the Department of English at Arizona State University, is the author of *Authoring a Discipline: The Post-World War II Emergence of Rhetoric and Composition* (Erlbaum, 2000); co-author with Richard Bullock of *The Norton Field Guide to Writing with Readings* (Norton, 2006) and *The Norton Field Guide to Writing with Readings and Handbook* (Norton, 2008); editor of *Inventing a Discipline* (NCTE, 2000); and co-editor with Neal A. Lester of *Racialized Politics of Desire in Personal Ads* (Rowman and Littlefield, 2008); she has also written extensively about the history and the field of rhetoric, gender and race, and visual and material culture. Currently, she is working on the gendering of creativity, a project that examines needlework among other forms of women's cultural production.

Beth Fowkes Tobin, Professor of English at Arizona State University, is the author of *Superintending the Poor: Charitable Ladies and Paternal Landlords in British Fiction, 1770–1860* (Yale University Press, 1993), the award-winning *Picturing Imperial Power* (Duke University Press, 1999), and the award-winning *Colonizing Nature: The Tropics in British Arts and Letters, 1760–1820* (University of Pennsylvania Press, 2005). She has written extensively on the art, literature, and science of colonialism. For her research on the representation of the tropics, she received a fellowship from the National Endowment of Humanities and a Caird Fellowship from the National Maritime Museum, Greenwich, and is currently studying eighteenth-century natural history collections, in particular the shell collection of the 2nd Duchess of Portland.

Contributors

ANDREA ADOLPH is an Assistant Professor of English and coordinator of service-learning at Kent State University Stark Campus. She has published essays on intersections of consumption and embodiment in modern and contemporary British women's novels, and she is currently at work on a book-length study of female desire in the age of post-war British austerity.

ARIEL BEAUJOT is an Assistant Professor of History at Laurentian University, Canada. She received her PhD from the University of Toronto in 2008. Ariel has published articles in *Oral History Forum*, and *Producing Fashion: Commerce, Fashion and Consumers*. She is currently writing a book which explores the ways in which women's accessories reveal the beliefs, values, and prejudices of Victorians in England.

EMILY BILLS received her PhD in the History of Architecture from the Institute of Fine Arts at New York University. She teaches urban studies at the University of Southern California in Los Angeles and The New School in New York. Her dissertation, entitled *The Telephone Shapes Los Angeles: Communications and Built Space, 1880–1950*, received a Graham Foundation Carter Manny Award Citation of Special Recognition and an ACLS Henry Luce Dissertation Fellowship in American Art. Emily balances her academic career with her position as Research Director of Urban Operations, an architecture and design office based in Los Angeles, California.

SHANA J. BROWN (PhD, University of California, Berkeley) is a specialist in modern Chinese cultural and intellectual history. Her interests include the significance of visual and material culture to intellectual life. Her study *Pastimes: Chinese Historical Studies at the Intersection of Art, Commerce, and Politics, 1870–1930* focuses on the relationship between turn-of-the-century historical studies and the commercial trade in art and antiquities. Current projects include the history of Chinese photography and the art of tattooing in contemporary China. She is currently an Assistant Professor in the Department of History, University of Hawaii, Manoa.

JENNIFER T. CRISS received her doctorate in Art History from the University of Pennsylvania. A specialist in late-nineteenth-century French art and culture, she has held positions at the Philadelphia Museum of Art and the Phillips Collection in Washington, DC. Among her fellowships are a Chateaubriand from the French government and a research grant from the Winterthur Museum. She has lectured widely on the topics of *japonisme* and women artists at venues including College Art Association, the National Museum of Women in the Arts. Criss is currently based in the Washington, DC area.

Ruth E. Iskin's book, *Modern Women and Parisian Consumer Culture in Impressionist Painting*, has been published by Cambridge University Press (2007). Her essays have been published in *The Art Bulletin, Discourse,* and *Nineteenth-Century Contexts,* and in exhibition catalogues and anthologies. Recently, "Was there a New Woman in Impressionist Painting?" was published in the exhibition catalogue of Women in Impressionism of the Ny Carlsberg Glyptotek Museum, Copenhagen (2007) and her "Selling, Seduction and Soliciting the Eye: Manet's Bar at the Folies-Bergère" was anthologized in *Reclaiming Agency: Feminist Art History in the Postmodern Era,* N. Broude and M.D. Garrard, eds. (University of California Press, 2005). She holds a PhD from UCLA and teaches Art History at the Ben-Gurion University of the Negev.

Angma D. Jhala is an Assistant Professor of History at Bentley University. She has taught at Tufts and Harvard Universities and has published *Courtly Indian Women in Late Imperial India* (Pickering and Chatto, 2008). She is currently writing a book on the history of aesthetics in the nineteenth- and twentieth-century Indian zenana and has published, or will shortly, articles on gender, law, and sexuality in colonial India, royal aesthetics and Bollywood film, princely education and the politics of marriage in colonial princely India. She is also working on a novel.

Ellen Kennedy Johnson's teaching and research interests at Arizona State University revolve around the rhetoric of "things"—landscape, fashion, decorative objects, needlework, and numerous other belongings—as sources of insight about the meaning of eighteenth- and nineteenth-century British literary texts. Her essay "'The Taste for Bringing the Outside In': Nationalism, Gender, and Landscape Wallpaper (1700–1825)" was published in *Women and Material Culture, 1660–1830,* edited by Jennie Batchelor and Cora Kaplan (Palgrave Macmillan, 2007).

Dior Konaté is Assistant Professor of African History at South Carolina State University in Orangeburg, where she is also teaching World History. She received her BA and MA from Cheikh Anta Diop University (Dakar, Senegal) and her PhD from the University of Wisconsin – Madison. She has written on issues of prisons in colonial and post-colonial Senegal, juvenile delinquency, women in prison, and women in politics. Currently, she is working on a number of projects on women and visual arts in colonial Senegal and Senegalese youth.

BRONWYN LABRUM is a Senior Lecturer in the School of Visual and Material Culture at Massey University – Wellington, New Zealand. A former history curator at the Museums of New Zealand Te Papa Tongarewa, she is the author of *Women's History: Researching and Writing Women's History in New Zealand* (Bridget Williams Books, 1993) and co-editor of *Fragments: New Zealand Social and Cultural History* (Auckland University Press, 2000) and *Looking Flash: Clothing in Aotearoa New Zealand* (Auckland University Press, 2007). She has published widely in the history of women, twentieth-century welfare, and material culture and museums, and is currently researching the material histories of everyday life in post-war New Zealand.

WESSIE LING's research evolves around identities, with an emphasis on the discourse of cultural identities in the production of fashion. Author of *Fusionable Cheongsam* (Hong Kong Arts Centre, 2007), she has researched extensively on the *qipao*, with articles appearing in the *Journal of the Study of British Cultures* and the *Journal of Design Culture and Criticism*. She is Senior Lecturer in the London College of Fashion at the University of the Arts, London.

ELIZABETH C. MACKNIGHT is a Lecturer in European History at the University of Aberdeen. Her research focuses on gender roles within the French aristocracy. She is currently completing a book on gendered sociability in Parisian high society, 1880–1914, and has another project underway on aristocratic education and family life in France of the Third Republic.

PAMELA CORPRON PARKER is Associate Professor of English and Director of Women's Studies at Whitworth College. She is author of numerous publications on Elizabeth Gaskell, and is currently working on a book-length project titled *A Woman's Place: Literary Tourism and the British Woman of Letters* that investigates the significance of nineteenth-century literary tourism in shaping our conceptions of the British woman of letters.

CYNTHIA PATTERSON earned her PhD in Cultural Studies from George Mason University in May 2005. She is an Assistant Professor of English at the University of South Florida – Lakeland. Her dissertation research earned fellowship support from the Smithsonian Institutions, Winterthur Museum and Library, and the Pennsylvania Historical and Museum Commission. She has published in *American Periodicals* and *The Pennsylvania Magazine of History and Biography*. Dr Patterson is currently revising her book-length manuscript, *"Exclusively from Original Designs": The Philly Pictorials and the Graphic Arts*. Her research interests include visual culture studies and nineteenth-century American art, literature, and cultural history.

Rebecca J. Pulju is an Assistant Professor of History at Kent State University in Ohio. She completed her doctorate at the University of Iowa and is revising her manuscript, *The Good Buyer: Women, the Family, and the Creation of Mass Consumer Society in France, 1944–1965,* for publication. Her work examines the changing nature of the family and home in modern France and calls attention to the place of women consumers in the cultural and social changes of the post-war years. She has published in the *Journal of Women's History* and the proceedings of the Western Society for French History.

Pamela Siska is a Lecturer in the program in Writing and Humanistic Studies at MIT. She has published papers on Percy Shelley, Tennyson, and medieval debate poetry, as well as writing pedagogy. Her other research interests include horror fiction and crime narratives. She is currently writing her dissertation on Percy Shelley.

Acknowledgements

Edited collections come to fruition through the labor of many hands behind the scenes. We want to take the opportunity to acknowledge those who made this work possible. First we want to thank Erika Gaffney, Publisher at Ashgate, for her enthusiastic support of our series on Women and Material Culture which includes two other volumes, *Women and Things, 1750–1950: Gendered Material Practices* and *Women and the Material Culture of Needlework and Textiles, 1750–1950*. Her guidance and sage advice have been invaluable. We also want to express our gratitude to Anne Keirby, Editorial Administrator in Humanities, and Meredith Norwich, Associate Editor, for their advice and assistance in helping us navigate the intricacies of the publishing process. Finally, we are grateful for the excellent staff at Ashgate, especially Patrick Cole, proofreader extraordinaire, Elizabeth Ball for her fine indexing, Jacqui Cornish, Senior Editor of Visual Studies, for her expert guidance, and to Cynthia Imogen Hammond for her thoughtful analysis and helpful critique of the manuscript.

The idea for these volumes grew out of a graduate seminar we co-taught on theories and practices of material culture studies. We are especially indebted to our students whose enthusiasm for material culture inspired us: Kelly Adams, Matt Berretta, Hedra Bledsoe, Jacqueline Brady, Regina Clemens-Fox, Lowell Duckert, Karen Engler, Valarie Fazel, Lakresha Graham, Jennifer Hagen, Amy Hann, Larry Hobson, Barbara Kirchmeier, Sara McKinnon, Amanda Owens, Lisa Ricker, and Cynthia Roses-Thema. We were further buoyed by the overwhelmingly positive response to this series, and thank all those who corresponded with us expressing their enthusiasm for this project.

Our work on these volumes was also made possible by year-long sabbatical leaves granted by the College of Liberal Arts and Sciences at Arizona State University, and fully supported by the Chair of our department, Neal A. Lester, for which we are indebted. Maureen is also grateful for the support from an Exemplary Award bestowed by Arizona State University. Beth acknowledges support from the National Science Foundation and the British

Academy. Since so many of the essays that appear here depend on the expertise and kindness of librarians, curators, and archivists, we gratefully acknowledge their critical contributions.

Convention has it that acknowledgements end with a gesture toward family support; we do so not because we are obliged to but because we really mean it. Maureen wants to express her gratitude to Peter Goggin for his unwavering intellectual and emotional support. Beth thanks Joe for his patience and wisdom.

Introduction: Consumption as a Gendered Social Practice

Beth Fowkes Tobin

The interdisciplinary and feminist essays in this collection build on the scholarly work of the past two decades, taking the topic of women and consumption into new arenas with its global perspective and its comparative framework. Exploring the connections between consumption and subjectivity, the essays expand upon and complicate the idea that consumption is key to the construction of gendered, classed, and national identities. Providing a cross-cultural perspective on consumption are essays on such topics as French women's fantasies about American kitchen appliances, the role of red dresses in Senegal's partisan politics, the similar display techniques deployed by New Zealand's museums and department stores, and the consumption of European couture fashion in India's cloistered, aristocratic zenanas. The links between print culture, taste, class, and national identity are also explored in essays on the British fashion plates from the early nineteenth century, the aspirational pictorials of an American illustrated monthly from the 1840s, and Chinese women's weekly magazines from the 1930s. In addition to examining gender and consumption, this volume also addresses gender and collecting, exploring women's collecting in Britain, France, and China as a way for them to participate in scholarly, artistic, literary, and scientific pursuits dominated by men. Also examined is the way in which the display of collected objects—in Impressionists' paintings, in autograph albums, in mass-produced illustrations, in the glass cases of museums and department stores—participates in the construction of particular identities, as well as serving as a value-producing material practice.

This volume's attention to the meaning-making potential of consuming practices owes much to current discussions of consumption within the broad field of material culture studies that posit the mutually constitutive and fluid relationship between subjects and objects. Rather than view this dyadic relation as a binary, whereby the subject in manipulating the object is the producer of meaning, we are persuaded by such anthropologists and archeologiststs as Webb Keane and Christopher Tilley that objects, even those mass-produced and consumed within the domestic sphere, can be productive of not only complex meanings but also of effects; things can influence people and "can intervene in the social world."[1] A dress, for instance, is, as several anthropologists have argued, a "mechanism" or a "technology" for producing specific identities and kinds of social interactions.[2] Ariel Beaujot's chapter in this volume demonstrates how identity is shaped by the technology of dress with her discussion of the way in which kid gloves were produced and marketed explicitly to shape and whiten the middle-class woman's hands. Ellen Johnson's chapter on the adoption of military dress by women during the Napoleonic era argues that clothing was a way for women to signal their patriotism and engagement in the political realm, while Wessie Ling's chapter on the popularity during the 1920s and 1930s, particularly in Shanghai, of the *qipao*, a hybrid dress blending Western and Chinese aesthetic elements, suggests that this dress helped Chinese women negotiate the tensions between cosmopolitanism and traditional Chinese culture.

Not only do objects, like dresses and gloves, participate in the formation of identities and the constitution of embodied subjectivities; subjects can endow objects with subjectivity, and furthermore, objects can act with a kind of agency we tend to think should be reserved for human subjects.[3] For instance, a shell lying on the beach can, with its physical attributes of delicacy, color, and shape, exert a certain power over a beachcomber and compel that person to do something, which in this case would be to pick it up. In this way an object possesses agency as if it were a subject, and when a shell is used to establish one's identity as a naturalist, an object is being enlisted in the construction of an identity. As Bruno Latour reminds us, the relationship between subjects and objects is flexible, porous, and contingent. He argues that conceiving of this relationship in simple dialectical terms is far too restrictive and challenges us to "abandon the mad idea that the subject is posed in its opposition to the object, for there are neither subjects nor objects, neither in the beginning—mythical—nor in the end—equally mythical. Circulations, runs, transfers, translations, displacements, crystallizations—there are many motions, certainly, but not a single one of them perhaps, that resembles a contradiction."[4] The essays in this volume illuminate ways in which subjects and objects mutually construct each other, attending to the role of gender in these dynamics as well as situating these dynamics within culturally, historically, and socially specific contexts.[5]

Theories of Consumption

In keeping with material culture studies' approach, this volume examines women's consumption and collecting as social practices that are productive of social and cultural meanings and effects. Too often consumption has been portrayed, especially within Marxist and neo-Marxist traditions, as the endgame of capitalism's stages of production, rather than as fertile ground for invention. According to Marxist interpretations of capitalism, the mass-produced commodity is the product of alienated labor because the producer, not in control of the means of production, is unable to recognize him or herself in the commodity he or she produces. While this may be an accurate description of production within capitalist economies—mass-produced commodities are, indeed, the product of alienated labor—it does not necessarily follow that the act of consuming mass-produced commodities partakes of that alienation. Theodor Adorno made this assumption in his (in)famous 1940 essay "The Culture Industry," in which he argued that the mass-produced products of the culture industry, in particular movies and popular tunes played on the radio, lull its consumers into a benumbed state of mild pleasure, giving them just enough satisfaction to keep them from getting frustrated with their "pathetic" little lives and keeping them in their traces obediently working so that they would be able to buy yet another sweet dose of oblivion.[6] Adorno's condemnation of popular culture, in particular American popular culture with its film stars and pop musicians, as a form of alienation from the true productive pleasure derived from actively shaping the lived-in world, grew out of a Marxian privileging of labor and production over consumption as the site of meaning making, self-expression, and human satisfaction.

Consumption, as defined in Adorno's terms, was a form of solace for or distraction from the emptiness of capitalism's non-productive and alienated labor. However, several intellectual trends within various fields of sociology and anthropology began in the late 1970s to rethink and re-examine consumption, no longer regarding it as deficient or as a lack, and instead began to see consumption as a form of expression or a means of agency for the consumer. For instance, within Britain the Birmingham Center for Cultural Studies was instrumental in redirecting thinking about consumption with its focus on youth cultures, identity formation, and social protest. Such proponents of this brand of cultural studies as Dick Hebdige in *Subculture, The Meaning of Style* (1979) interpreted youth culture's consumption practices—the punk kids' sporting of safety pins and the mods' sartorial displays—as capable of registering critique and protest of their parents' world. As such, youth culture's use of clothing was conceived of by these cultural critics as not only inventive but also as engaged in the social and political discourse. Borrowing de Certeau's ideas about making do with what was available—the mass-produced commodity as raw material for identity building and social critique—further enhanced the study of consumption and transformed the interpretation of the purchase of mass-produced commodities: no longer dupes of advertising and commercial strategies, shoppers could be conceived of as deploying tactics and engaging in practices that were in opposition to the dominant commercial forces at work.[7] Pop culture became a site for resistance, and studies flourished in the 1980s and 1990s celebrating how young people used media, space, and products as raw materials for the production of selves or discourses.[8] This kind of interpretive work, prone to caricature with its interest in Madonna and fandoms, may have run its course, exhausted perhaps by its narrow focus on pop culture and youth subcultures within contemporary US and British society. However, the interpretative strategies developed within cultural studies were to out-live the preoccupation with contemporary pop culture and were to be taken up in historical and sociological studies. Viewing consumption as a social practice that intersected with identity formation, historical studies in the 1990s began to inquire into the meanings objects held for consumers, building upon but departing from economic historians' focus on consumer behavior and the rise of the modern commercial society.[9] Indeed, the bulk of historical and sociological work on consumption continues to be dominated by this focus on identity formation and self-expression, with several essays in this volume, namely those by Siska, Macknight, Iskin, Beaujot, Johnson, and Criss, utilizing this approach to the consumption of commodities.[10]

At the same time that proponents of cultural studies were celebrating consumption as creative, anthropologists in the UK and the US were turning their attention to consumption as a topic worthy of their attention. Though archeologists, folklorists, and museum studies scholars have always attended to the meanings and relationships that objects engender,[11] anthropologists in the 1980s intensified their interest in material culture and the problem of exchange, focusing on the contexts within which consumption occurred. Various anthropological approaches to consumption emerged in the 1980s, with Daniel Miller's body of work anchoring a new appreciation of ethnography as a method for studying material culture. Positioning himself against what he has called a Marxist anti-materialist bias that he sees as seeping into humanist studies of consumption, Miller insists on taking consumption seriously as a theoretical problem and on making consumption the object of careful ethnographic study.[12] His classic essay on the consumption in Trinidad of Coca-Cola, the iconic mass-produced commodity, explodes once-dominant ideas about the corrosive power of the global circulation of mass-produced commodities on local and traditional societies.[13] His essay demonstrates how Trinidadians' consumptive practices appropriate and re-make the beverage's social significance to resonate with their own cultural needs and customs. Several essays in *Material Women* are indebted to this focus on the way in which mass-produced objects, though designed to have certain effects, can be appropriated by consumers, who redirect their use to create new meanings. This redirection and inventive use of commodities can be seen in this volume's essays by Ellen Johnson, Dior Konaté, and Rebecca Pulju, who show us the way in which mundane, domestic objects can empower women within the political arena. Rebecca Pulju demonstrates how post-war French magazine articles celebrating US kitchens laid the foundation for French women's political activism and their demands that their government provide the necessary infrastructure—gas, electricity, and water—so that the task of household management was less time-consuming and back-breaking. Konaté's essay explains how the red dresses worn by supporters of *Bloc Africain* were initially designed to signal their wearers' party allegiance and newly won enfranchisement, but because the dress gained widespread popularity beyond partisan politics, this style of dress was taken up as a fashion statement that signaled Senegalese women's participation in modernization.

Anthropology's contribution to rethinking consumption within the framework of material culture has been crucial to focusing attention on consumption as social practice, and wresting consumption away from the rational actor model (Adam Smith's self-interested individual) espoused by economists and business schools with their concerns about marketing and distribution. In addition, anthropology's long-standing interest in economic exchange and the production of value, initiated by Marcel Mauss and Bronislaw Malinowski in the 1920s, was re-energized by work in the 1980s and 1990s by such anthropologists as Marilyn Strathern, Annette B. Weiner, Fred R. Myers, and Nicholas Thomas.[14] Additionally, in a very influential essay on commodities and regimes of value, which served as the introduction to the collection of essays, *The Social Life of Things: Commodities in a Cultural Perspective* (1986), Arjun Appadurai redeployed Simmel's definition of consumption as a form of exchange to argue that objects could move in and out of the commodity function. Together with Igor Kopytoff, whose essay "The Cultural Biography of Things: Commoditization as Process" was published in *The Social Life of Things*, Appadurai laid out the theoretical stakes for studying the circulation of commodities, arguing that the meanings of objects emerged in their movement: "all efforts at defining commodities are doomed to sterility unless they illuminate commodities in motion." Rather than thinking of commodities as things produced for exchange, Appadurai broke from "the production-dominated Marxian view of the commodity" to focus "on its total trajectory from production, through exchange/distribution, to consumption." Building on Kopytoff's work on the social lives of objects, Appadurai argued that "certain things are seen as moving in and out of the commodity state." Though objects can begin their existence as commodities (think of the mass-produced Barbie dolls), they can become something else, including a gift, an heirloom, a museum piece, and as such, these objects can be described as having been diverted from the "commodity phase" into another phase through various procedures involving "enclaving" and removal from circulation.[15] This reconceptualization of the commodity as a stage through which an object can pass during its social life has been very productive: scholars in anthropology, geography, history of science, and cultural history, tracking the movement of an object through various social situations and cultural contexts, have found this approach useful for analyzing the circuits of exchange and consumption within globalized economies.[16]

Appadurai's work, with its focus on exchange as a source of meaning making, challenged prevailing notions of consumption as devoid of agency. This insistence that objects have social lives, that their meanings are derived from human interactions and are shaped by particular contexts, has been fruitful for those scholars who study collectors and their collections. Appadurai's paths and diversions can help explain how collecting takes objects out of the commercial sphere and diverts them from the market, in effect sacralizing them and imbuing them with symbolic value, which in turn can increase their monetary value in the marketplace. Collecting can be conceived of as a form of exchange if one extends the timeframe to that of the object's "life," charting its initiation into the status of a collected object and its life after the death of its collector, which often instigates the exchange process in the form of an auction or the inheritance of the collected object.[17] In her chapter on Gaskell's autograph collection, Pamela Corpron Parker traces the way in which letters signed by famous writers move in and out of differing value regimes, and how some become gifts, others commodities, and others yet are "enclaved" (to use Appadurai's term) and remain within Gaskell's private collection, now housed in a rarebook room. This instability of value is a problem central to collection studies, as Michael Thompson demonstrates in *Rubbish Theory* (1979). In the chapter on the Duchess of Portland's shell collection, Tobin attends to the way in which shells must undergo a series of operations involving gathering, cleaning, naming, and display in order to move out of the category of detritus to become scientific specimens and to accrue scientific value, which can also translate into market value.

While anthropology, with its long-standing concern with material culture, exchange, and value, has re-energized the study of consumption, taking it well beyond economists' preoccupation with consumer behavior, sociologists such as Pierre Bourdieu have, with their systematic analysis and careful fieldwork, studied the way in which consumption is connected to class and is key in establishing difference between social groups. Just as anthropologists privilege *culture*'s explanatory power, sociologists, particularly those trained in Europe, have had a long-standing regard for the utility of class analysis. Bourdieu's interrogation of those social practices engaged in the display of social status was built upon earlier work by Marcel Mauss (gift-giving as a way to show status) and Jean Baudrillard (auction as tournaments of value), and culminated in the very influential *Distinction: A Social Critique of the Judgment of Taste* (1984), which provided a finely detailed portrait of mid-twentieth-century French consumption.[18] Bourdieu's work on distinction has had an enormous effect on historical studies of consumption, in particular on studies of elite groups and their social practices. Questions about the role of taste in the formation of middle-class and aristocratic identities are fruitfully considered from Bourdieu's point of view. Contributor Elizabeth Macknight, in her study of French aristocratic women's display and arrangement of interior spaces, owes her theoretical framework to Bourdieu and his idea that consumption is a means to signal status and create differentiation. Women's consumption, often perceived as the height of frivolous and distracted non-productive activity, can be understood from a sociological perspective as engaged in display of social status and class differentiation; this idea was first imperfectly formulated by Veblen at the turn of the twentieth century, to be later articulated with greater precision and theoretical purchase by Bourdieu.[19] Ruth Iskin's chapter on French advertising posters and Cynthia Patterson's on mid-nineteenth-century women's magazines demonstrate how important taste was in marking class affiliation. In her study of women Impressionist artists, Jennifer Criss argues that Mary Cassatt's and Berthe Morisot's depiction in their paintings of Japanese objets d'art from their own collections was a way for these artists to convey their own high cultural status and social distinction. Displaying *Japonaiseries*, as we also learn from Macknight's chapter on the French aristocracy, was a way for these women artists to signal their "adherence to contemporary fashions championed by high-bourgeois society as well as the concerns of progressive culture."

Women and Consumption

Though there are various theories of consumption, those sociological and anthropological theories that explain consumption as a social practice are most useful for our purposes, which is to investigate women's consumption as a form of engagement with material culture. Of the theories canvassed above, only Veblen's possesses any specific gender analysis, and as Ruth Iskin, Ariel Beaujot, and others elsewhere have argued, Veblen's analysis of women's consumption as a form of status seeking and display of social position is insufficiently nuanced to explain women's relation to commodities, which, if one adopts a material culture studies perspective, must necessarily be a highly contingent, multiplicitous, and culturally and historically specific social process.[20] Gender analysis is also surprisingly lacking in studies of collecting practices, with a few exceptions.[21] What is needed is more work that brings together consumption with gender, such as Emma Casey and Lydia Martens' *Gender and Consumption: Domestic Cultures and the Commercialisation of Everyday Life* (Ashgate, 2007), which examines birthday parties, wedding days, and laundry practices as social practices with complex meanings that challenge traditional notions of what constitutes the domestic. Also exemplary is Erika Rappaport's recovery of the role of shopping in the construction of late nineteenth-century female urban identity; *Shopping for Pleasure: Women in the Making of London's West End* (2000) explores the merchandizing and advertising strategies that made department stores and teashops appropriate urban destinations for respectable middle- and upper-class women and established shopping as the number one leisure activity for such women. *Material Women*'s aim is to contribute to the study of consumption and gender with its historically grounded and culturally specific essays on women and the objects they purchase.

This volume's strength is its historical range and global perspective. Case studies of women's consumption in distinct time periods and locales are put into conversation with each other. A dominant theme in this book is the way in which consumption constructs subjectivity. For instance, we learn that Mary Shelley's desire for English-made objects helped her to define herself as a writer, artist, and an Englishwoman while living abroad in Italy; we learn that early-twentieth-century, aristocratic, Indian women, despite their cloistered existence within the zenana, managed to construct a cosmopolitan identity by purchasing European fashionable luxury goods; and we learn that Chinese women in the 1920s and 1930s negotiated the tensions between modernity and traditional Chinese aesthetics when they wore the hybrid dress, the *qipao*, a sleek silk sheath with a high collar. These women's purchases became ways for them to construct complex cosmopolitan identities beyond those afforded by the domestic realm. Consumption also enabled women to enter into the public realm of history, politics, and erudition, spaces usually reserved for men, such as Senegal's political arena and the elite world of Chinese scholars. From Andrea Adolph, Ruth Iskin, Elizabeth Macknight, Cynthia Patterson, and Ellen Johnson, we learn that the way in which women consume, as well as what they consume, is shaped by societal expectations concerning taste, class, and femininity. Female consumption, for the middle classes at least, is fraught with anxiety about excess and expenditure, as Andrea Adolph's study of the impact of wartime rationing on women in Virginia Woolf's and Noel Streatfeild's novels shows. Middle-class women, as Adolph contends, were expected to keep their desires under check and their consumption within moderation, and yet, as Iskin and Patterson note, they were targeted as key consumers by such commercial forces as department stores and ladies magazines, which encouraged women to consume as a path to attaining middle-class respectability.

This volume's juxtaposition of case studies from different national regions and historical eras is productive of unexpected convergences. Reading Pulju's essay on French women's fantasies about American kitchens side by side with Konaté's essay on Senegalese fashion reveals that these two seemingly unrelated forms of consumption are linked structurally in the political realm. Both authors argue that changes in the French law that gave the vote to women in the 1940s are key to understanding their consuming practices as forms of engagement with the political process. Senegalese women signaled their support for "*Bloc Africain* a political party to rally colonized peoples in French West Africa," by designing and wearing a type of dress, *robe bloc,* and in this way performed and displayed their new identities as fully fledged participants in the political process. French women's desire for electrified kitchens (refrigerators, stoves, ovens) in the post-World War II era spurred women to participate in the political process, demanding as voters that their government provide the necessary infrastructure to support an electrified home. While Pulju's essay acknowledges that French journalists exaggerated the degree to which American women's lives were made modern through the consumption of time-saving devices, Emily Bills' chapter shows how Bell Telephone managed to convey through their advertising campaigns of the 1930s through 1950s that modernity had not yet come to the American middle-class home without the installation of the telephone, featured in their advertisements as a technological force of modernization and rationalization for the American home.

The roles of elite women as keepers of their families' traditions and as inspiration for middle-class women's emulative consumption are explored in a number of essays. Providing historical background on the princely states of India, Jhala argues that the women of the courtly zenanas participated in multiple and hybrid subject positions as consumers of European design in the form of jewelry, dress, and furniture. Jhala contends that these elite women of the zenana, with their complex and eclectic patterns of consumption, challenge simplistic binaries that posit opposition between colonizers and the colonized, British and Indian, metropole and imperial periphery. This essay speaks to similarities amongst elite women across geographical divides, and their charge to maintain, indeed curate, objects that display family status and national heritage while performing their own identities as fashionable and modern women. French aristocratic women, who had to "balance family expectations regarding the display of inherited items against their own desire to create a distinctive personal space," had much in common with courtly princesses of Indian states. Indeed, class emerges in several chapters as an important category of analysis. Beaujot suggests that middle-class women emulated aristocratic women with their use of kid gloves to protect the whiteness of their hands, and Patterson shows us how middle-class women were targeted by publishers of ladies' magazines who appealed to their desire for elegance and affordable art for their homes.

The role of gender in collecting is explored across national boundaries and time periods with Tobin's chapter on eighteenth-century British collectors of natural history specimens, Criss' chapter on nineteenth-century French collectors of Japanese objects, Parker's chapter on Victorian autograph collectors, and Brown's chapter on Chinese women, who in the early twentieth century collected books, manuscripts, and calligraphy. Placing these studies next to each other with their different geographical and historical contexts allows for unexpected congruencies to emerge. Gaskell's literary autograph collecting and the Duchess of Portland's shell collecting, though distinct activities with very different sets of practices, share similar goals in that these collecting activities were ways for these two women to establish themselves in male-dominated arenas. For Gaskell, her collection enabled her to create a sense of community with other novelists, and for the duchess, her natural history collection earned her the respect and attention of Britain's scientific elite. Collecting as an entree into the educated elite and male worlds of art and science was also a strategy of several female Chinese collectors, who at the turn of the nineteenth century frequented the art and book markets of the Qing Dynasty capital, Liulichang, where they purchased books, artworks, and studio art supplies. With their expertise as book and manuscript collectors, these women, Shana Brown contends, constructed a vibrant turn-of-the-century cultural scene that was a significant precursor to the modern urban art movements of the twentieth century.

Other convergences that emerge in this volume have to do with collecting and displaying objects. We see from Elizabeth Macknight's and Jennifer Criss' chapters that Japanese objets d'art, *japonaiseries*, were popular with late-nineteenth-century France's cultural elite; they were displayed not only in aristocratic homes, as Macknight notes, but also were incorporated, as Criss points out, into Mary Cassatt's and Berthe Morisot's paintings. Criss argues that these impressionist painters included *japonaiseries* as elegant motifs within their paintings to signal their membership in the avant-garde as well as to appeal to their patrons' desire to display their own good taste and cultural capital.[22] Display as a value-producing mechanism is further explored in Iskin's study of the techniques of display that nineteenth-century Parisian department stores developed to appeal to their potential customers. What is implicit in Iskin's, Criss', and Macknight's chapters is highlighted by Labrum's contention that "the modern museum developed in tandem with the department store in the nineteenth century: architecture, styles of display and interpretation owed as much to commerce as to culture." Display techniques, involving furniture and architecture, traveled across medias and venues from the sanctity of the museum space to the bustling market-driven department store, confirming that the production of value, both monetary and non-monetary (artistic, scientific, cultural value), is intertwined and not so easily separated from commerce by vows of the disinterested pursuit of the arts, sciences, and national heritage.

Material Women is divided into four sections: "Consuming Desires," "Home and Consumption," "Dress: Gendered and Political Identities," and "Collecting, Displaying, and Creating Value." With essays written by authors from diverse disciplines—social history, literary studies, fashion studies, history of art and architecture, and urban studies—this volume has a historical sweep and a range of approaches to consumption that can only be achieved with a multi-authored collection. Yet, despite this diversity of approach and range of specialties, the essays in this volume are united in their refusal to see women's consumption as passive and as mere expenditure. Our authors argue collectively that women's consuming practices can be understood as a form of social labor, productive of social meanings and engaged in the creation, maintenance, and transformation of social relations. The contributors in this volume approach consumption as a social activity, some focusing on how clothing, furniture, and jewelry display class and rank as well as signal national identity and political allegiances. Other contributors are concerned with the intersection of print culture, taste, and conceptions of home comfort, and argue that consumption produces a combination of expected and unexpected effects through the interaction of subjects with objects. The contributors who focus on collecting suggest ways in which women's collecting practices enable complex identifications and participation in the elite scientific, literary, and artistic spheres of their societies. *Material Women* takes women's consumption seriously as a form of productive labor that possesses the potential for epistemic discovery and social significance.

Notes

1. Christopher Tilley, "Introduction: Theoretical Perspectives," in *Handbook of Material Culture*, eds. Christopher Tilley, Webb Keane, Susanne Küchler, Michael Rowlands, and Patricia Spyer (London and Thousand Oaks: Sage, 2006), 10. See also Tilley, "Objectification," in *Handbook of Material Culture*, 60–73; Janet Hoskins, "Agency, Biography and Objects," in *Handbook of Material Culture*, 74–84, and *Biographical Objects: How Things Tell the Stories of People's Lives* (London: Routledge, 1998); Webb Keane, "Introduction: Subject and Objects," in *Handbook of Material Culture*, 197–202.
2. Hoskins, "Agency," 81. See, for instance, Diana Crane, *Fashion and Its Social Agenda: Class, Gender and Identity in Clothing* (Chicago: University of Chicago Press, 2000); Wendy Parkins, ed., *Fashioning the Body Politic: Dress, Gender, Citizenship* (Oxford: Berg, 2002); and Michael Zakim, *Ready-Made Democracy: A History of Men's Dress in the American Republic* (Chicago: University of Chicago Press, 2003).
3. See, for instance, Alfred Gell, *Art and Agency: A New Anthropological Theory* (New York: Oxord University Press, 1998).
4. Bruno Latour, "The Berlin Key or How to Do Words with Things," in *Matter, Materiality, and Modern Culture*, ed. P.M. Graves-Brown (London: Routledge, 2000), 10.

5. The essays in this volume, in keeping with its material culture studies' approach, attend to the role of objects within the framework of lived experience rather than focusing the instability of the subject as it is produced within textuality, an approach which in literary studies has become known as "thing theory," with its more philosophical and linguistic preoccupations. For "thing theory," see Bill Brown, ed., "Thing Theory," *Critical Inquiry* 28 (2001): 1–22.

6. Theodor Adorno, *The Culture Industry: Selected Essays on Mass Culture*, ed. J.M. Bernstein (London: Routledge, 1990).

7. Michel de Certeau, *The Practice of Everyday Life*, trans. Steven F. Rendall (Berkeley, CA: University of California Press, 1984).

8. See, for instance, John Fiske, *Understanding Popular Culture* (Boston: Unwin Hyman, 1989), and Henry Jenkins, *Textual Poachers: Television Fans and Participatory Culture* (New York: Routledge, 1992).

9. The literature on the history of consumption is enormous and beyond the scope of this essay. For examples of economic history concerned with the development of commerce and the rise of consumer society, see Fernand Braudel, *Civilization and Capitalism, 15th–18th Century*, 3 vols. (New York: Harper & Row, 1982–84), and Neil McKendrick, John Brewer, and J.H. Plumb, *The Birth of the Consumer Society: The Commercialisation of England* (Bloomington: University of Indiana Press, 1982). For examples of social history concerned with the social meanings attached to commodities, see the essays in John Brewer and Roy Porter's *Consumption and the World of Goods* (New York: Routledge, 1994), in particular Lorna Weatherill, "The Meaning of Consumer Behavior in Late Seventeenth- and Early Eighteenth-Century England," 206–27, T.H. Breen, "The Meaning of Things: Interpreting the Consumer Economy in the Eighteenth Century," 249–60, and Amanda Vickery, "Women and the World of Goods: A Lancashire Consumer and her Possessions, 1751–81," 274–301. See also essays in Ann Bermingham and John Brewer's *The Consumption of Culture, 1600–1800: Image, Object, Text* (New York: Routledge, 1995), especially Kathleen Wilson, "The Good, the Bad, and the Impotent: Imperialism and the Politics of Identity in Georgian England," 237–62, Lawrence Klein, "Politeness for Plebes: Consumption and Social Identity in Early Eighteenth-Century England," 362–82, and Richard Leppert, "Social Order and the Domestic Consumption of Music: The Politics of Sound and the Policing of Gender Construction in Eighteenth-Century England," 514–34. For a critique of this body of work's exclusive focus on Europe's "consumer revolution," see Craig Clunas' important review, chastising scholars of British economic and cultural history for their ethnocentric assumptions about the European/British origins of modernity: "Modernity Global and Local: Consumption and the Rise of the West," *American Historical Review* 104 (1999): 1497–1511. Perhaps Brewer's response to Clunas' critique can be found in John Brewer and Frank Trentmann, eds., *Consuming Cultures, Global Perspectives: Historical Trajectories, Transnational Exchanges* (Oxford: Berg, 2006).

10. Current work on imperialism has demonstrated an interest in linking material culture with identity. See, for instance, Maya Jasanoff, *Edge of Empire: Lives, Culture and Conquest in the East, 1750–1850* (New York: Knopf, 2005) for a discussion of the role of material culture in the lives of colonial officials, as well as the essays in Tim Barringer and Tom Flynn, eds., *Colonialism and Its Objects: Empire, Material Culture, and the Museum* (New York: Routledge 1998).

11. Material culture has been the focus of such object-centric disciplines as archeology and museum studies. The text-centric disciplines of literary studies, rhetoric and communication, history, and even art history have much to learn about the study of objects from such archeologists as Christopher Tilley, *Metaphor and Material Culture* (Oxford: Blackwell, 1999), and such museum studies scholars as Susan Pearce, *On Collecting: An Investigation into Collecting in the European Tradition* (New York: Routledge, 1995). Within American studies, there has always been a strong appreciation of the material culture; see, for instance, David Kingery, ed., *Learning from Things: Method and Theory of Material Culture Studies* (Washington, DC: Smithsonian Institution Press, 1995), Jules David Prown and Kenneth Haltman, *American Artifacts: Essays in Material Culture* (East Lansing, MI: Michigan State University Press, 2000), and Robert St George, *Conversing by Signs: Poetics of Implication in Colonial New England Culture* (Chapel Hill: University of North Carolina Press, 1998).

12. Beginning with his *Material Culture and Mass Consumption* (Oxford: Blackwell, 1987), Daniel Miller has been an advocate for the importance of studying consumption as a socially and culturally significant practice. See Miller, *A Theory of Shopping* (Ithaca, NY: Cornell University Press, 1998), in which he links a particular form of shopping, provisioning, to sacrifice, arguing that shopping can have "a ritual structure" and "be involved in the creation of value and relationships" (113). See also his edited volumes *Acknowledging Consumption* (New York: Routledge, 1994) and *Material Cultures: Why Some Things Matter* (Chicago: University of Chicago Press, 1998).

13. Daniel Miller, "Coca-Cola: A Black Sweet Drink from Trinidad," in Daniel Miller, ed., *Material Cultures* (Chicago: University of Chicago Press, 1997), 169–87.

14. Bronislaw Malinowski, *Argonauts of the Western Pacific*, 1922 (Prospect Heights, IL: Waveland Press, 1984); and Marcel Mauss, *The Gift: The Form and Reason for Exchange in Archaic Societies*, 1925, trans. W.D. Hall (New York: Norton, 1990). For the reworking of exchange theory, see, for instance, Jonathan P. Parry, "The *Gift*, the Indian Gift, and the 'Indian Gift'," *Man* 21 (1986): 453–73; Marilyn Strathern, *The Gender of the Gift* (Berkeley: University of California Press, 1988); Annette B. Weiner, *Inalienable Possessions: The Paradox of Keeping-While-Giving* (Berkeley: University of California Press, 1992); Maurice Godelier, *The Enigma of the Gift*, 1996, trans. Nora Scott (Chicago: University of Chicago Press, 1999); Fred R. Myers, ed., *The Empire of Things: Regimes of Value and Material Culture* (Santa Fe: School of American Research Press, 2001); and Nicholas Thomas, *Entangled Objects: Exchange, Material Culture, and Colonialism in the Pacific* (Cambridge: Harvard University Press, 1991).

15. Arjun Appadurai, "Introduction: Commodities and the Politics of Value," in *The Social Life of Things: Commodities in a Cultural Perspective* (Cambridge: Cambridge University Press, 1986), 3–63, 16, 13. See also, in the same volume, Igor Kopytoff, "The Cultural Biography of Things: Commoditization as Process," 64–93.

16. For an excellent overview of this new field, see Robert J. Foster, "Tracking Globalization: Commodities and Value in Motion," in Tilley et al., eds., *Handbook of Material Culture*, 285–302.

17. Time, according to Bourdieu, is key in disguising the economic self-interest at work in the gift exchange: "the lapse of time interposed is what enables the gift or counter-gift to be seen and experienced as an inaugural act of generosity, without any past or future, i.e. without *calculation*"; Pierre Bourdieu, *Outline of a Theory of Practice* (Cambridge: Cambridge University Press, 1977), 171.

18. Pierre Bourdieu, *Distinction: A Social Critique of the Judgment of Taste* (Cambridge: Harvard University Press, 1984); Jean Baudrillard, "The Art Auction: Sign Exchange and Sumptuary Value," in *For a Critique of the Political Economy of the Sign*, trans. Charles Levin (St Louis, MO: Telos Press, 1981), 112–22.

19. Thorstein Veblen, *The Theory of the Leisure Class: An Economic Study of Institutions*, 1899 (New York: New American Library, 1953).

20. See, for instance, Colin Campbell, "Understanding Traditional and Modern Patterns of Consumption in Eighteenth-century England: A Character-Action Approach," in Brewer and Porter, eds., *Consumption and the World of Goods*, 40–57; Lorna Weatherill, "The Meaning of Consumer Behaviour"; and Amanda Vickery, "Women and the World of Goods."

21. See, for instance, Russell W. Belk and Melanie Wallendorf, "Of Mice and Men: Gender Identity in Collecting," in *The Material Culture of Gender: The Gender of Material Culture*, ed. Kenneth Ames and Katherine Martinez (Ann Arbor, MI: University of Michigan Press, 1997), 7–27. Susan Pearce, a leader in museum studies, raises the issue of gender difference in collecting practices in *Museums, Objects, and Collections* (Washington, DC: Smithsonian Institution Press, 1993).

22. See Marcia Pointon, *Strategies for Showing: Women, Possession, and Representation in English Visual Culture, 1665–1800* (Oxford: Oxford University Press, 1997), for a discussion of the importance of displaying strategies in constructing gendered and classed identities.

Consuming Desires

"The Things I So Indispensably Needed": Material Objects as a Reflection of Mary Shelley's Life

Pamela Siska

A striking feature of Mary Shelley's letters from Italy, as well as of her postscripts to letters of her husband Percy Bysshe Shelley, is how frequently she asks friends living in England or elsewhere in Italy to send her a variety of small, seemingly trivial, domestic items. We see this same tendency not only in her letters written from Italy but in those written while living in Marlow, which was 30 miles from London but seemed to her a world away. Why were these items so important to her that she asked for them to be sent despite the inconvenience and expense for the sender and for her? Certainly there were practical reasons related to the cost, quality, or availability of some items, but beyond these practical considerations about *why* she needed or wanted to send for some things, there remains the intriguing matter of *what* she chose to ask for.

When reading the letters, I found that most of the items she requested fell into categories: books, writing materials, art supplies, sewing paraphernalia, foodstuffs, articles of clothing, and grooming accessories. (In some cases, I needed to find out exactly what an item was, for example, a Bramah pen, hot pressed paper, a chip hat.) I asked whether the objects reflected Mary Shelley's class, gender, and nationality. Did most people of Mary Shelley's class consider such things necessities or luxuries? Were the objects especially significant to a woman? Were they particularly indicative of English taste? Finally, I asked what the items conveyed about her own unique personality and identity.

I suggest that the items she requested reflect Mary Shelley's various roles: not only a woman of letters but an artist, mother, and homemaker, as well as a fashionable and well-groomed lady. In addition, her requests reveal her behavior as a consumer: she was a product of her time, whether following the current fashions in scarves or subscribing to prevailing infant care practices, and she usually wanted the best quality items, a tendency that was often at odds with her need to be economical and to live within the Shelleys' rather limited means. Finally, the items she asked for while in Italy reveal a desire to maintain her "Englishness" while living abroad, and this desire is, I believe, a manifestation of the larger human longing for familiar things in times of anxiety or sorrow, and certainly Mary Shelley's life while in Italy was fraught with adversity.

Born in London in 1797, Mary Wollstonecraft Shelley (née Godwin) was the daughter of political philosopher William Godwin and feminist writer Mary Wollstonecraft. Young Mary's education was fairly typical of the period, although it did include some subjects that were unusual for girls to study, such as Latin. In 1814, when she was 17, Mary met poet and radical thinker Percy Bysshe Shelley, who was married to Harriet Westbrook. Less than three months after their first meeting, Mary and Shelley eloped to France (along with Mary's step-sister Claire Clairmont) and finally married in 1816, after Harriet committed suicide. They spent the summer of 1816 living near Lord Byron on the shore of Lake Geneva. It was here that Mary wrote the work for which she is best known: *Frankenstein, or the Modern Prometheus*. While in Europe, Mary created not only this "hideous progeny" (as she referred to the novel in her introduction); she also produced flesh and blood progeny: between 1815 and 1819 she gave birth to four children, only one of whom lived past the age of three. In addition to writing, she assisted Shelley with his translations of classical texts and worked as a fair copyist for both Shelley and Byron. After Shelley's drowning death in the Gulf of Spezia in 1822, Mary remained in Italy for only a year, returning to England in 1823 with Percy Florence, her only surviving child. Between 1823 and her death in 1851, along with attending to her son's upbringing and education, she edited and published Shelley's works and immersed herself in her own writing. Although *Frankenstein* is considered her masterpiece, her literary output also included six other novels, short stories, plays, reviews, biographical essays for Dionysius Lardner's *Cabinet of Biography*, and *History of a Six Weeks' Tour of France, Switzerland, and Germany* and other travel writings. Indeed, recent scholarship on Mary Shelley, especially that of Betty T. Bennett, Emily Sunstein, and Miranda Seymour, has shown her to be much more than the author of a Gothic novel and wife of Percy Shelley: she was an erudite, independent, and prolific writer. She was also an artist, mother, homemaker, and fashionable lady—a multifaceted woman whose influence on literature and culture is still felt today.

Books were a necessity for Mary in her role as writer. Much has been written about the books she read in terms of their influence on her thought and work, but if we consider books as objects, if we look at "how books convey meaning even before they are opened and read—how embedded they are in networks of family and friends, of rank and privilege,"[1] what is of interest here is how Mary acquired them. Susan Staves has identified the ways in which eighteenth-century women writers acquired books:

purchasing them, borrowing from public or private libraries, receiving them as payment for professional services, receiving them as gifts, or getting them through an informal borrowing network.[2] In the nineteenth century, women's methods of acquiring books were essentially the same, and Mary obtained them through several of these means. Her father, William Godwin, was a bookseller for most of his life,[3] and while Mary lived with him, she had ready access to books. After her marriage to Shelley, while still in England she ordered books from Hookham's Library[4] or asked Shelley when he was in London to buy books she had selected from the *Manuel du Libraire*.[5] But in Italy it was more difficult to acquire books. Soon after the Shelleys and Claire Clairmont arrived in Florence in October 1819, Mary wrote to Maria Gisborne, whom they had met five months earlier in Livorno, asking her to send "by the very first quick & sure conveyance"[6] copies of several recently published books, including *Frankenstein*. Gisborne became for Mary a steady source of books in Italy, with Mary asking her to borrow them, buy them, or retrieve her own copies from previous residences. Later in 1819 Mary asked Gisborne to borrow from a library and send to her works by Rousseau and Voltaire. In February 1820 she asked Gisborne to bargain for "a good Quarto Bible with the Apocrypha,"[7] and in April to buy her a Greek–Latin lexicon and borrow from her son Henry Reveley an encyclopedia volume containing the entry for shorthand. In early 1821 she asked Gisborne to send Sophocles and Xenophon "if you can find it among our books [at Casa Ricci in Livorno, where the Shelleys lived with the Gisbornes in the summer of 1820]."[8] Later that year, Mary found an additional book source, at least for new publications: in November she wrote to Gisborne from Pisa, where the Shelleys and Byron were living on opposite sides of the Arno: "New books we hardly want, since we get them from Ld B."[9]

Other crucial articles for Mary in her role as woman of letters were writing supplies. From Marlow[10] she wrote to Shelley, who was staying in London to conduct business, asking him to get her "a good thick book to write extracts in—ruled,"[11] an item important enough to her that she reminded him about it in another letter two days later: "remember my book for transcribing."[12] In Italy she needed more books for copying, and again Gisborne was a reliable provider. In February 1820 she wrote to Gisborne in Livorno: "Order at your Stationers a dozen plain books like that the Prometheus [Shelley's *Prometheus Unbound*] was copied in."[13] In pens, too, Mary also had a specific preference. In a letter of January 1821 to Leigh Hunt in London, she asked him to make up a parcel of items including "an excellent penknife of several blades" and "a few hundreds of Brama's pens."[14] "Brama's pens" refers to pens made by Joseph Bramah, an English inventor and one of several pen makers in early nineteenth-century London who were producing pens with steel barrels and nibs.[15] However, the fact that Mary asked for a penknife along with the pens indicates that she wanted another of Bramah's creations:

> During the time the early makers of steel pens were perfecting the article, several experimenters were offering to the public writing instruments made from various materials. Bramah patented "quill nibs," made by splitting quills and cutting the semi-cylinder into sections, which were shaped into pens and adapted to be placed in a holder.[16]

Mary's lap desk was also a writing necessity. It was left behind in Marlow when the Shelleys left England in 1818, and Mary repeatedly asked to have it sent to Italy (along with Shelley's desk). In November 1821 she wrote to Gisborne: "Every day increases my anxiety concerning the desk—Do have the goodness to pack it off as soon as you can,"[17] and in December she pleaded: "And my desk too—pray at any rate get it out of Ollier's clutches and send it to me."[18] The saga of the desk continued into the following year: "I hope, by this time, my desk is *en route*—I am anxious to hear that it is safe out of Ollier's hands,"[19] Mary wrote in January. By February she was becoming worried: "Not having heard news from you I am anxious about my desk."[20] In fact, she did not receive the desk until October 1822. Although Mary certainly wanted the contents of the desk (letters from the Marlow days and other papers), the desk itself was no doubt also valued as a familiar work space,[21] and it became a repository for her most treasured possessions: after her death in 1851, her journals, locks of her dead children's hair, and Shelley's silk-wrapped heart enfolded in pages of *Adonais* were found in it.[22]

From childhood, Mary had been steeped not only in writing but in art, like many young women at a time when "drawing, painting, and fashionable needlework demonstrated taste and 'polite' knowledge as markers of cultural distinction …"[23] When Mary was 17, her stepmother, Mary Jane Godwin, wrote to Lady Mountcashell: "Frances [Mary's half-sister Fanny Imlay] and Mary draw very well."[24] Mary's childhood exposure to art went beyond drawing instruction: her father took her and the other children on visits to artists' studios, including William Turner's, to fire their imaginations.[25] Godwin's efforts seem to have succeeded: Mary's enthusiasm for art was not just a fashionable pastime but a passion that she pursued into adulthood. In her journal from October to December 1816, "drawing lesson" appears in nearly every entry. In October 1817 she wrote from Marlow to Shelley in London:

> I want to practice drawing a little before I go to Italy—I have accordingly purchased pencils but find that it is too cold to draw from nature—could you get me a drawing or two to copy—I do not like prints … they may be either pencil drawings or water coloured.[26]

From Rome, she wrote to Leigh Hunt in April 1818: "besides our eternal visits to these divine objects [Roman ruins and artworks]—Clare [sic] is learning singing—I painting & S [Shelley] is writing a poem so that the *belle arte* take up all our time."[27] Her journal in April 1819 again records frequent drawing lessons. The fruits of these artistic efforts include what Miranda Seymour suggests may be a self-portrait.[28]

For her artistic pursuits Mary needed supplies, and here, as with her writing paraphernalia, she had very specific requests. In 1818 she wrote from Bagni de Lucca to Peacock in London: "be so kind as to send 12 Brookman & Langdon pencils, 3BB—3B—3F—3HF so marked."[29] In one of the 1821 letters to Maria Gisborne about her desk, she asked her friend to send, along with the desk, six Brookman & Langdon pencils. Brookman & Langdon, located in Piccadilly, was by 1821 well established as a premier maker of pencils. Thomas Molineux, in his 1823 edition of *An Introduction to Byrom's Universal Short-hand*, writes:

> The best lead pencils I have lately met with, are made by Brookman and Langdon, of different degrees of hardness, according to the particular purpose for which they are required. Those of the hardest quality, for Engineering, are distinguished by the mark HH, near the end of the pencil; and those for Architecture and Short-hand, being not quite so hard as the former, by the mark H.[30]

In fact, Brookman may have invented the pencil lettering system: "B standing for 'black,' H for 'hard,' with the number of repeated B's or H's indicating increasing blackness or hardness."[31]

Even with the best of pencils, Mary needed additional materials for her forays into art. In the November 1821 letter to Maria Gisborne about the desk and pencils, she also asked for "the best vellum drawing paper for miniatures" and "a cake of carmine from Smith's and Warner's."[32] Smith, Warner & Co, located, like Brookman & Langdon, in Piccadilly, was a leading purveyor of art supplies in the nineteenth century. The company's catalogue for 1811–12 featured watercolor cakes (for example, carmine), colored pencils, black lead pencils, brushes, easels, canvases, hot pressed drawing papers, and Bristol boards. The catalogue also contained endorsements of Smith & Warner's wares by well-known artists, including Turner.[33] About a month later, Mary wrote to Gisborne again, repeating her request for the Smith & Warner's carmine and adding "the finest hot Bristol pressed paper."[34] Hot pressed paper, a glazed paper made by rolling paper through hot rollers or pressing it between hot steel plates, was one of three drawing paper surfaces available in the early nineteenth century, along with cold pressed and rough. It had a smooth surface and was used mainly for watercolors.[35]

Of the triumvirate of "drawing, painting, and fashionable needlework,"[36] Mary was also accomplished at the third skill,[37] as indicated by her frequent requests for sewing paraphernalia. In March 1817 she wrote from Marlow to Marianne Hunt in Hampstead:

> Will you take the trouble to furnish me with a little stock of haberdashery as I cannot well get it here—This includes—a quantity of White Chapel

> needles—balls of cotton of all sizes tapes—some black sewing silk and silk of other colours —pins—a pair of large and one of smaller sciszars [sic] and any other articles of the same nature that you may deem necessary.[38]

From Milan in April 1818 she wrote to the Hunts in London, asking them to arrange for Peacock to send, along with some sealing wax, some pins: "these things are so bad here."[39] In December 1820, she wrote from Pisa to Hunt in London with a list of requests:

> a dozen papers of middle sized pins—an assortment of good needles—a small pointed pair of Scissars [sic] ... let the needles be in a very small morocco case such as they make on purpose for papers of needles—a steel topped thimble and some ounces of stocking cotton ...[40]

Still in Pisa in March 1821, Mary asked Maria Gisborne in Livorno to buy her a darning needle case, and, later in the month, she added a postscript to a letter by Shelley to Peacock in London, asking for "4 skeins of white netting silk, 2 green, 2 crimson, all of a size fit for purses."[41] In the November 1821 letter to Gisborne in which she inquired about her desk, she also asked for needles in a case, pins, "minnkin pins," scissors, and skeins of white netting silk "not too fine for purses."[42]

In her fascinating book on the material culture of sewing, Mary C. Beaudry offers an in-depth exploration of sewing paraphernalia throughout history. Her investigation of nineteenth-century articles provides a historical context for some of the items Mary mentions in her letters. Papers of pins were a relatively new commodity in the 1820s: prior to 1785, pins were sold loose. Whitechapel needles were embroidery needles with long eyes to allow easy passage of thread. Minnikin pins, as the name suggests, were tiny pins less than half an inch long. Thimble manufacturing in the nineteenth century was centered in Birmingham, where gold, silver, brass, steel, and steel-topped thimbles were produced. Finally, the best scissors and knives were made in Sheffield, which by the sixteenth century was already an established center of cutlery production.[43]

Some of Mary's sewing projects were for her children and the requests for items (sewing-related and otherwise) for the children reflect the concerns of an attentive mother. From Marlow she wrote in June 1817 to the Hunts in London, asking for flannel and lawn along with patterns for clothes for son, William, who was two and a half years old, and in October she wrote to Shelley, also in London, requesting eight yards of flannel for William's petticoats and for her own: "I do not want Welch flannell [sic] but it must be thick and good."[44] (Interestingly, both the transcription book and the flannel that Mary wants Shelley to purchase while in London are to be "thick and good," the substantialness of the articles apparently signifying that she was getting her money's worth.)

Little William died of malaria on June 7, 1819, at age three and a half, but at this point Mary was expecting another baby,[45] and in August 1819 she wrote from Livorno to Marianne Hunt in London that she hoped she had sent the "child's things" she had asked for in June: "for indeed I need them—if you have not slip in a pair of baby's stays for a pattern—but pray send them immediately." She adds: "I shall be in the most wretched state ever poor woman was if you do not let me have them."[46] She asked the Hunts about the box of items in September and again on November 2. The baby, Percy Florence, was born on November 12, 1819, and on November 24 Mary wrote from Florence to Marianne Hunt: "after hearing that the box you so kindly sent was shipped from Genoa, we have heard no more of it—fortunately a box from Peacock contained the things I so indispensably needed—but I am now in great want of the flannel for the child."[47] In letters to Gisborne from December 1819, there appear almost daily mentions of the Hunts' box, such as this announcement: "I am become uneasy about this felucca which seem to be above a month coming from Genoa—I am afraid that it is cast away & all the little boy's flannel petticoats are gone to the bottom."[48] When Mary finally received the box in mid-December, she complained to Gisborne: "We have received our box—it contained no books—it was a silly, expensive affair—but that was not my fault—I did the best I could and that you know is a consolation."[49] Apparently it also contained no flannel, for she wrote six months later, in July 1820, from Livorno to Gisborne in London: "do not forget to ask Mrs. Hunt for the flannel &c. that she bought for the last winter but did not send. I wish you to bring that with you."[50] What seems an obsessive concern with flannel may be more easily understood if we remember that, at this point, three of the Shelleys' children—an unnamed girl who lived less than two weeks, William, and Clara Everina—had died. Given this tragic history, Mary seems to have been taking whatever steps she could to provide her new baby with everything she thought necessary for his survival, including warm flannel clothing.

Another necessity for a growing child was stockings. In March 1820, Mary asked Maria Gisborne:

> Do you think that you cd get me some little stockings or shoes that wd wash for Percy—If not could not the Miss Riccis [daughters of the Gisbornes' landlord] manufacture some out of his old ones? ... his foot is the length of your middle finger—if it can be done, wd you set them to work?[51]

In July of the same year, she wrote from Livorno to Gisborne in London, asking for six pair of worsted stockings and twelve pair of cotton "for a babe of a year and half"[52] and in November 1821 from Pisa to Gisborne: "also send a dozen pair stockings for child 3 years old."[53] In both of these requests, Mary overstates Percy's age. In July 1820 he was eight months old, not a year and a half, and in November he was two years old, not three. Presumably she was not only requesting larger sizes so that he would grow into the stockings but also cleverly factoring in the time it would take for the parcels to reach her.

Not just clothing baby Percy but feeding him required specific goods sent from abroad. In February 1820 she wrote from Pisa to Gisborne in Livorno: "send me some Arrow root or, in default of that Tapioca."[54] In a letter about a month later, she asked Gisborne again for a pound of arrowroot, and yet again four days later she wrote: "I daily expect a parcel from you as I am in great want of the arrow root."[55] The following month she wrote to Gisborne's husband John, asking for a pound of it. Her enthusiasm for arrowroot may seem perplexing, but it can be understood if we see Mary as a woman of her time:

> Eighteenth century Rousseau-esque philosophies were changing the status of children to that of idealised, vulnerable animals and, beginning with William Buchan's medical dictionary in the 1790's, a whole repertoire of new dishes developed for the nursery and for the sickroom based on rice, sweetened sago or *salop*, arrowroot jellies, *panadas*, chicken broths, and boiled meats with mashed potatoes.[56]

Although it was later learned that arrowroot and other such starchy substances were of little nutritional value and actually contributed to infant malnutrition, by the nineteenth century they were widely prescribed by doctors for infants and invalids,[57] giving rise to the popular notion that they were good sustenance: "The universal baby food in England during the 19th century was 'pap', a nutritionally inadequate gruel made from water, broth or tea (rarely milk), mixed with breadcrumbs, arrowroot, cornflour, rice, or tapioca."[58] Tapioca, Mary's "default" for arrowroot, was also commonly used in puddings and other dishes for babies and small children in the nineteenth century; by Victorian times it had become a nursery mainstay. As with the flannel, Mary's insistence on arrowroot is understandable in light of her babies' deaths: she was trying to do all she could to ensure Percy's well-being.

Not all the items that Mary requested for her small son were as purely practical as stockings and pabulum: there were also some more frivolous things. In late December 1821 she asked Gisborne in London to send "a box of ivory letters and some picture books"[59] for Percy, who was then almost two years old, perhaps as a belated Christmas gift.

Tending to the children and the home while writing novels,[60] learning Greek, helping translate classical texts, and acting as Shelley's copyist did not mean that Mary Shelley neglected her appearance while in Italy. In addition to being author, wife, and mother, and mistress of the house, she was also a well-groomed, fashionable lady. Her "astonishing"[61] red-gold hair was considered one of her best features and, based on the grooming articles she asked for, she seems to have realized this and taken pains to care for it. In December 1818 she wrote in a postscript to a letter from Shelley to Peacock in London: "when you send another parcel I wish you would contrive to get 2 hairbrushes & a small tooth comb from Florriste hairdresser, Germain [Jermyn] St."[62] The following year Mary asked Maria Gisborne in London to enclose in a box of items bound for Florence "the very finest small tooth comb you can get and a brush for it—I can get a comb here, but it is not fine enough."[63] Mary clearly had specific criteria when it came to combs, and Shelley's selection did not satisfy them: in 1820 she wrote from Pisa to Gisborne in Livorno:

> I send the comb S [Shelley] bought for me—it is so awkwardly made, that it tears my hair to pieces—Could you contrive to exchange it for 2 or 3 small ones, three or four fingers wide and four or five or six long, you would very much oblige me.[64]

Apparently Gisborne's eye for combs was better than Shelley's: in 1821 Mary asked Gisborne for "a tortoise shell comb for combing out the hair—half dozen ditto such as you gave me."[65]

Mary also had definite tastes when it came to clothing. In a December 1819 letter to Gisborne from Florence, she asked for yards of material to match an enclosed swatch and also "a gown of close pink stripe—not like the enclosed but of good material—if it is no wider than that buy 9 brach [*bracciatura,* Italian for yards]. if wider 8. send it by the first good conveyance."[66] Although Gisborne may have chosen combs that met with Mary's approval, her judgment failed to hit the mark when it came to gown material; the following month Mary complained: "The pink is not at all the thing I mean, being both cold and ugly, and not fit for washing."[67] In shoes, too, Mary had high standards. She wrote in March 1820 from Pisa to Gisborne in Livorno: "I want a pair of black [shoes] for the house ... Will he [the shoemaker] make a slim pair of stuff kid or morocco for this they must be made on the same last as my green stuff ones."[68] His work did not please her: in a February 1821 letter to Gisborne in Livorno she asked about how much she owed various tradesmen there, including her former shoemaker, about whom she complained: "This man deserves an excessive scolding—When at Leghorn last summer I ordered 6 P. of walking shoes & he has made them of such vile leather that I can only wear them a few times—I shall have no more from him."[69]

Whether it was combs, shoes, or gown material, the items that others picked out were often found unsatisfactory, even when the buyer was guided by Mary's descriptions. She seems to have been aware that she was hard to please. Writing to Shelley from Marlow in September 1817, Mary asked him to buy a sealskin fur hat for little William. After giving him instructions about where and how to buy it and what it should be like ("it must be a fashionable round shape for a boy mention particularly and have a narrow gold riband around it—that may be taken in if too large ... let it be rather too large than too small—but exactly the thing would be best"[70]), she changed her mind and directed Shelley not to get the hat: "it may not fit him or please me."[71]

William's hat had to be of a fashionable shape, and Mary's choices in her own accessories also show that she was a product of her time and not immune to fashion trends. In March 1821 from Pisa she asked Maria Gisborne in Livorno: "I wish you could get me from Arbib's a scarf of China crêpe. I want it a light pretty color, lilac or blue but not pink."[72] Seymour tells us that "Arbib's" is actually Hadbib's,[73] and Lady Blessington offers this contemporary glimpse of the place: "The shop of a Jew named Hadbib at Leghorn, filled with shawls, and various other objects of Eastern manufacture, is much frequented, and offers an assemblage of very rich merchandise to tempt strangers."[74] Both the color of the scarf—a "light pretty" lilac or blue—and its material—China crêpe—were fashionable during the period.[75]

In February 1821 she wrote to Maria Gisborne in Livorno, inquiring about "the price of some very fine cambric pocket handkerchiefs taking a dozen of them,"[76] and the following month, after hearing their price, decided: "the handkerchiefs must be bargained for: they are too dear."[77] Apparently either Gisborne was able to strike a bargain or Mary decided they were worth the price, for in April she implored Gisborne: "I must absolutely have pocket handkerchiefs, so be so kind and get them (half dozen) as I mentioned, without delay."[78] Here again, Mary's request reflects the taste of the times. Margarete Braun-Ronsdorf notes that, in the early nineteenth century, like their Regency dandy counterparts, "increasingly ladies also regarded the handkerchief as an indispensable accessory for an elegant costume."[79] Decorated with a bit of hem stitching or embroidery, the handkerchiefs in vogue were "simple white ones, made from more or less fine linen cambric."[80]

Perhaps no articles of clothing reflect the fashions of a period as much as hats, and here Mary was also *au courant*. In April 1820 Mary wrote from Pisa to Maria Gisborne in Livorno:

> I wish for love or money to get a chip hat before you go or I much fear shall not get it [at] all—What of raw silk—perhaps your milliner or your Seraph cd tell you whether the silk I desire is used for netting if it is send a quantity—common netting silk is not the thing I want—if they do not know send me a pattern that I may get more if it is right.[81]

In letters to Gisborne in May she inquired about the status of her "bonnet" and asked about a veil for the hat: "scratch out the stockings for Shelley be so kind as to put in their place a handsome square of black net veil."[82]

It is no accident that she asked for a chip hat while Maria Gisborne was in Livorno, or Leghorn. Chip hats made from straw were widely produced in England in the eighteenth century, but the import in the nineteenth century of finer straw, Leghorn straw, from this Italian province, seriously hurt the English chip hat industry. The Leghorn became "the constant rival of the Dunstable"[83] and other domestic fibers. Responding to the crisis, the Royal Society "advertised premiums to encourage the production of both Chip and

Leghorn hats, as well as the import of the raw material from … Bermuda and the Bahamas."[84] English chip hat production revived, and in 1827 the Royal Society discontinued its premiums. Regardless of the source of their fibers, chip hats were extremely fashionable throughout the eighteenth and nineteenth centuries.[85] They may have started out as headgear for lower- and middle-class women,[86] but, in the way that the "straw hats of the peasantry were introduced at court in the reign of Anne,"[87] in the reign of the Georges, chip hats ascended from the lower classes to the upper. The enduring popularity of the chip hat on both sides of the Atlantic is attested to by its appearance in Keats' "Meg Mereilles" in 1818 and in "The White Chip Hat" by Nathaniel Parker Willis nearly 30 years later.

Whether penknives or handkerchiefs, the items Mary wanted had to be of the best quality, which sometimes meant costly brand name goods, such as Smith & Warner paint or Brookman & Langdon pencils. Yet, at the same time, we see in her requests a recurring concern with being economical and living within the Shelleys' limited means. When asking the Hunts in London to buy lawn, she cautioned them: "not too expensive."[88] After receiving the Bible from Maria Gisborne, she declared, "it appears to me you were sadly cheated,"[89] and she wanted a Greek–Latin lexicon only if it could be "got reasonably."[90] She asked Gisborne to bargain for the cambric handkerchiefs,[91] to send gown material only "if the duty is not intolerable,"[92] and to get her a darning needle case in Livorno because they were too expensive in Pisa: "I have seen one here but they cost ten pauls."[93] Of the China crêpe scarf from Hadbib's, Mary wrote to Gisborne: "I believe they ask the English six monete for them but I should think you could get it for four, or for thirty livres,"[94] and she opined that the square of black net veil for her hat would be "infinitely cheaper"[95] in France than in England (the Gisbornes would soon be passing through France on their way back to England).

Although higher cost and inferior quality may have been reasons that Mary preferred certain English goods to their Italian counterparts, her requests for some articles also reveal, I think, a desire to maintain her "Englishness" while living abroad. Perhaps no commodity is so emblematic of Englishness as tea. In August 1818, soon after arriving in Italy, Mary wrote from Bagni de Lucca to Maria Gisborne in Livorno: "if your heart should be moved to come and visit me, be so kind as to increase Mr. Dunn's debt and bring a few pounds of tea with you."[96] Italy teemed with English expatriates and tourists during the 1810s and 1820s[97] and many of them must also have wanted reminders of home: "Mr. Dunn" was Henry Dunn, an Englishman who ran a British general store in Livorno.[98] Again in October 1819 from Florence she wrote to Gisborne in London, seeking "½ lb very best green tea you can possibly get … send by very first quick and sure conveyance to Pisa … Townley tea was tried and found wanting, perhaps there is better at Dunn's."[99] Mary wanted not only this most English of beverages, but the quintessential English toiletry, lavender water.[100] A preference for English wares is evident as well in her complaint to Gisborne about a bobbin that it "is not English"[101] and her request for "a good English corkscrew"[102] (presumably she wanted her corkscrew, like her pins, thimble, and scissors, to be made of good English steel from Birmingham or Sheffield).

Although disdainful of the English tourists in Italy and contemptuous of an England that had become "Castlereagh land,"[103] Mary retained a measure of homesickness. In 1820 she wrote to Maria Gisborne, who was about to return to England: "I long for your English letters and all the queer, bad, I fear, the many disagreeable things that will strike you at first sight, in that unhappy land."[104] For all its faults, England was the devil she knew, and Italy, for all its delights, was a place of domestic discord, scandal, illness, and death. If it is true that "in crucial moments of change or frailty or expectation, people seek certainty in the material world,"[105] the familiar English things must have been a comfort to her.

A pen, drawing paper, a thimble, a scarf, and some tea—considered separately, these things could be objects in the life of nearly any woman of nearly any time. Taken together, they begin to form a picture of a certain kind of woman: a woman of a particular age, class, and sensibility. When we look at the objects closely enough to see their particulars—a Bramah quill pen, hot pressed drawing paper, a steel-topped thimble, a lilac China crêpe scarf, and the very best green tea—the woman to whom they belonged emerges clearly: an Englishwoman of many talents, a writer and an artist as well as a mother and homemaker, a woman of refined taste and a sense of style. Brillat-Savarin proclaimed: "Tell me what you eat and I will tell you what you are."[106] Not just what we eat, but what we buy, borrow, and create—the things we choose to have around us—the things we consider indispensable—tell the world what we are.

Notes

1. Jennie Batchelor and Cora Kaplan, "Introduction," in *Women and Material Culture, 1660–1830*, eds. Jennie Batchelor and Cora Kaplan (Basingstoke: Palgrave Macmillan, 2007), 6.

2. Susan Staves, "'Books without which I cannot write': How Did Eighteenth-century Women Writers Get the Books They Read?" in Batchelor and Kaplan, *Women and Material Culture*, 192–208.

3. Miranda Seymour, *Mary Shelley* (London: John Murray, 2000), 58.

4. Hookham's was a bookselling publishing firm as well as a circulating library. Percy Bysshe Shelley, *The Letters of Percy Bysshe Shelley*, ed. Frederick L. Jones (Oxford: Clarendon Press, 1964), vol. 1, 319.

5. In her excellent edition of Mary Shelley's letters, Betty T. Bennett explains that the *Manuel du Libraire*, first published in Paris in 1809, was "a compendium, by author, of rare, valuable, and unusual books in all languages, from the beginning of typography." Mary Wollstonecraft Shelley, *The Letters of Mary Wollstonecraft Shelley*, ed. Betty T. Bennett (Johns Hopkins University Press, 1980), vol 1, 52.

6. Mary Wollstonecraft Shelley, *Letters*, vol. 1, 110.
7. Ibid., 128.
8. Ibid., 184.
9. Ibid., 211.
10. Marlow was 30 miles from London, but in 1817 it was fairly isolated. In her letters from Marlow, Mary referred to the place as "the country."
11. Mary Wollstonecraft Shelley, *Letters*, vol. 1, 51.
12. Ibid., 53.
13. Ibid., 128.
14. Ibid., 173–4.
15. Henry Bore, *The Story of the Invention of Steel Pens* (New York: Ivison, Blakeman & Company, 1890), 17–34.
16. Ibid., 32–3.
17. Mary Wollstonecraft Shelley, *Letters*, vol. 1, 210.
18. Ibid., 213. Charles Ollier was a London-based publisher of several of Shelley's works, as well as writings by Keats, Hunt, and Lamb.
19. Ibid., 215.
20. Ibid., 217.
21. Mary may have written *Frankenstein* at this lap desk, but I can find no evidence in her journal, letters, or others' contemporary accounts that she either had or did not have it with her in Geneva in the summer of 1816.
22. Seymour, *Mary Shelley*, 316; Mary Wollstonecraft Shelley, *The Journals of Mary Shelley 1814–1844*, eds Paula R. Feldman and Diana Scott-Kilvert (Baltimore: Johns Hopkins University Press, 1987), 435; Emily W. Sunstein, *Mary Shelley: Romance and Reality* (Boston, Toronto and London: Little, Brown, 1989), 384–5.
23. Gary Kelly, "Education and Accomplishments," in *Jane Austen in Context*, ed. Janet Todd (Cambridge: Cambridge University Press, 2005), 257.
24. Seymour, *Mary Shelley*, 53.
25. Ibid., 50.
26. Mary Wollstonecraft Shelley, *Letters*, vol. 1, 53.
27. Ibid., 91.
28. Seymour, *Mary Shelley*, 299–300.
29. Mary Wollstonecraft Shelley, *Letters*, vol. 1, 82.
30. Thomas Molineux, *An Introduction to Byrom's Universal Short-hand*, 6th edition (London: Longman, Hurst, Rees, Orme and Browne, 1823), 35.
31. Henry Petroski, *The Pencil: A History of Design and Circumstance* (New York: Knopf, 1990), 157.
32. Mary Wollstonecraft Shelley, *Letters*, vol. 1, 211.
33. National Portrait Gallery, Research, "British Painters and Artists' Suppliers," National Portrait Gallery, <http://www.npg.org.uk/live/artistsupp.as>.
34. Mary Wollstonecraft Shelley, *Letters*, vol. 1, 213.
35. John Krill, *English Artists' Paper: Renaissance to Regency*, 2nd revised and expanded edition (New Castle, DE: Oak Knoll Press, 2001), 195, 206.
36. Kelly, "Education and Accomplishments," 257.
37. Mary C. Beaudry notes that "needlework" meant both the "everyday, 'practical' or 'necessary' work" of sewing, mending, and knitting and "fancy work" such as embroidery. *Findings: The*

Material Culture of Needlework and Sewing (New Haven: Yale University Press, 2006), 5. The needlework that was thought to demonstrate a young woman's taste and good upbringing was the "fancy" kind. Judging from the items she asked for in her letters, it seems that Mary was doing mostly the "everyday" kind.

38. Mary Wollstonecraft Shelley, *Letters*, vol. 1, 30.
39. Ibid., 65.
40. Ibid., 173.
41. Ibid., 186.
42. Ibid., 211.
43. Beaudry, *Findings*, 19, 24, 29, 54, 96.
44. Mary Wollstonecraft Shelley, *Letters*, vol. 1, 38, 51.
45. In September 1817, when William was 20 months old, Mary gave birth to a girl, Clara Everina, who died in September 1818.
46. Mary Wollstonecraft Shelley, *Letters*, vol. 1, 104.
47. Ibid., 115.
48. Ibid., 117.
49. Ibid., 120.
50. Ibid., 155.
51. Ibid., 141.
52. Ibid., 153.
53. Ibid., 211.
54. Ibid., 128.
55. Ibid., 134.
56. Kate Colquhon, *Taste: The Story of Britain Through its Cooking* (New York: Bloomsbury USA, 2007), 269.
57. John Wiltshire, "Medicine, Illness and Disease," in Todd, *Jane Austen in Context*, 310; Bee Wilson, "Thick and Thin," *New Statesman* 14, October 29, 2001: 47.
58. Nancy Scheper-Hughes, Introduction to *Child Survival: Anthropological Perspectives on the Treatment and Maltreatment of Children*, ed. Nancy Scheper-Hughes (Dordrecht, Holland: D. Reidel, 1987), 5.
59. Mary Wollstonecraft Shelley, *Letters*, vol. 1, 213.
60. While in Italy, Mary wrote *Valperga* and *Matilda*.
61. Seymour, *Mary Shelley*, 85, 260.
62. Mary Wollstonecraft Shelley, *Letters*, vol. 1, 84.
63. Ibid., 110.
64. Ibid., 128.
65. Ibid., 211.
66. Ibid., 120.
67. Ibid., 123.
68. Ibid., 135.
69. Ibid., 184.
70. Ibid., 45.
71. Ibid.

72. Ibid., 185.

73. Seymour, *Mary Shelley*, 260.

74. Marguerite Blessington, *The Idler in Italy*, vol 2 (Philadelphia: Carey & Hart, 1839), 293.

75. Antje Blank, "Dress," in Todd, *Jane Austen in Context*, 236; C. Willett Cunnington, *English Women's Clothing in the Nineteenth Century* (London: Faber & Faber, 1937), 49.

76. Mary Wollstonecraft Shelley, *Letters*, vol. 1, 184.

77. Ibid., 185.

78. Ibid., 198.

79. Margarete Braun-Ronsdorf, *The History of the Handkerchief* (Leigh-on-Sea, England: F. Lewis, 1967), 36.

80. Ibid.

81. Mary Wollstonecraft Shelley, *Letters*, vol. 1, 142.

82. Ibid., 145.

83. Cunnington, *English Women's Clothing*, 54.

84. Royal Society for the Encouragement of Arts, Manufactures & Commerce, "The British Empire and Commonwealth Museum," Item 5: Chip Hats, <http://www.rsa.org.uk/250/empire.asp>.

85. Cunnington, *English Women's Clothing*, 64, 69, 95.

86. Kirstin Olsen, *Daily Life in 18th-Century England* (Westport, CT: Greenwood Press, 1999), 99.

87. Frederick William Fairholt, *Costume in England: A History of Dress from the Earliest Period Till the Close of the Eighteenth Century* (London: Chapman and Hall, 1846), 375.

88. Mary Wollstonecraft Shelley, *Letters*, vol. 1, 38.

89. Ibid., 129.

90. Ibid., 143.

91. Ibid., 185.

92. Ibid., 122.

93. Ibid., 132. (A paul is a *paolo*, an Italian silver coin named after Pope Paul III. Oxford English Dictionary 2nd ed., s.v. "paul.")

94. Ibid., 185.

95. Ibid., 145.

96. Ibid., 78.

97. Benjamin Colbert, *Shelley's Eye: Travel Writing and Aesthetic Vision* (Aldershot, Hants, England; Burlington, VT: Ashgate Publishing, 2005), 124–5.

98. Mary Wollstonecraft Shelley, *Letters*, vol. 1, 78n.

99. Ibid., 110.

100. Ibid., 287.

101. Ibid., 143.

102. Ibid., 140.

103. Ibid., 137.

104. Ibid., 145.

105. Editors' Preface, *Journal of Material Culture* 8, no. 3 (2003): 243–4.

106. Jean Anthelme Brillat-Savarin, *The Physiology of Taste: Or, Meditations on Transcendental Gastronomy*, trans. M.F.K. Fisher (New York: Harcourt, 1978), 3.

2

Material Women: The Department-Store Fashion Poster in Paris, 1880–1900

Ruth E. Iskin

Department-store posters constituted a significant part of poster production in the late nineteenth century. Jules Chéret alone made over 160 such posters.[1] However, late nineteenth-century department-store posters have elicited relatively little scholarly interest.[2] Scholarship on French fashion has tended to focus primarily on paintings and fashion plates, which preceded posters as a form of fashion advertising.[3] The fashion poster was an invention of the large stores that sold ready-to-wear clothes and other goods appealing to a broad market, primarily of the middle classes. The *magasins de nouveautés* (drapery and fancy goods stores) were relatively large stores, revolutionizing shopping habits and paving the way for the truly gigantic department stores.[4] They were already commissioning posters in the 1840s and 1850s. The department stores developed this advertising strategy further beginning in the 1860s and 1870s.

This essay focuses on a particular genre of department-store posters—those that advertised women's fashions.[5] During the last decade of the nineteenth century, many posters commissioned by Parisian department stores to promote women's mass produced ready-to-wear clothing were designed according to a formula developed in the 1880s and early 1890s. I investigate this formula, scrutinizing a selection of posters made by known and anonymous artists. The selection is not based on an aesthetic criterion or on the oeuvre of a specific artist, since my objective is to understand how the visual design and iconography of fashion posters were motivated by the department store's advertising goals. For this reason, I pay attention to the innovative strategies by which posters were designed to appeal to their target consumers. Did posters merely echo other fashion advertising, particularly fashion plates, or did the formula and specificities of the medium have a different kind of impact? I argue that posters developed modern fashion advertising both by using a distinctive formula and through their public urban presence. In order to place the department-store poster within its immediate historical and theoretical context, I begin with introductory comments on advertising and nineteenth-century department stores, and continue with a discussion of late nineteenth- and turn-of-the-century theories of consumption, in particular Veblen's theory on conspicuous consumption and Simmel's "Philosophy of Fashion."[6] I go on to an analysis of the department-store poster formula that promoted feminine fashions by juxtaposing images of women with prices of items, concluding with comments on the function of posters advertising fashions—prompting a material and imaginary consumption—and on the impact of posters in comparison to other contemporary fashion advertising.

Advertising the Department Store

Like many businesses in France during the second half of the nineteenth century, department stores commissioned large-scale outdoor posters. Although major stores had in-house publicity departments, large-scale lithographic posters were commissioned from outside artists and printing firms. Posters advertising feminine fashions featured women in ready-to-wear clothes and accessories. Furthermore, they highlighted two of the most important innovations of the department store: low and fixed prices and special promotions, referred to as *expositions* (huge seasonal displays) to which potential consumers were invited with no obligation to buy. Posters had a specialized role within the broader advertising strategies of department stores, which included sales catalogues, agendas, illustrated cards and other graphic materials, press advertisements and self-promotional articles.[7]

Department stores devoted enormous budgets to advertising.[8] In an extensive 1893 study on department stores, Georges d'Avenel estimated that the largest stores, the Grands Magasins du Louvre and Bon Marché, spent two to three million francs annually on advertising.[9] Somewhat earlier, Zola's novel on the department store, *Au Bonheur des Dames* (*The Ladies' Paradise*), observes that the department store spent "nearly six hundred thousand francs annually on posters, advertisements and appeals of all sorts."[10] It is not clear what part of this budget went to posters, but Zola's well-researched realist work tells us that a major advertising campaign of stores such as the Bon Marché included ten thousand posters.[11] This large print run was significantly higher than that of many other posters promoting other venues or goods.

Advertising was crucial for department stores because they had to attract very large numbers of consumers for their mass-produced goods and depended on a high turnover. Their sales revenues kept growing; for example, in 1876–77 the annual sales volume of the Bon Marché was 72,693,993 francs and by 1895–

96 it had reached 159,420,596 francs.[12] Georges d'Avenel estimated that each day between 15,000 and 18,000 shoppers entered the largest stores in Paris, the Bon Marché and the Grands Magasins du Louvre.[13] The special sales drew even larger crowds. According to Zola, nearly 100,000 shoppers constituted "the afternoon crush" on the opening day of an *exposition* of white goods.[14] As Zola's novel shows, women were the typical consumer of the department store and thus constituted the majority of these vast shopping crowds. Before examining the formula of the department-store fashion poster, let us ask, with the aid of two major theorists of the late nineteenth- and turn-of-the-century, why did women consume fashion?

Veblen's Vicarious Consumption versus Simmel's Fashion Supplement

Thorstein Veblen and Georg Simmel developed different theories on women's consumption. Veblen's influential book, *The Theory of the Leisure Class: An Economic Study of Institutions*, first published as a volume in 1899, distinguished women as the main consumers, but argued that women's consumption was vicarious. Women did not seek to attain their own social status, but rather to establish and sustain the reputation of their husbands—men who were making fortunes but lacked the time to display them.[15] The wife who used to be "the drudge and chattel of the man … the producer of goods for him to consume,—has become the ceremonial consumer of goods which he produces."[16]

Veblen's theory reinforces the stereotype of woman/consumer versus man/producer. But his understanding of women consumers was not quite as monolithic as is often assumed. He recognized a change in the status of women, noting that they no longer performed vicarious leisure simply on behalf of a husband, but for "the reputability of the household taken as a corporate unit—a group of which the housewife is a member on a footing of ostensible equality."[17] However, despite this recognition of women's changing roles, Veblen dismissed the possibility that women consumed to establish their own status, maintaining that it was still a vicarious undertaking, "although in a slightly altered state." It was "performed for the quasi-personal corporate household, instead of, as formerly, for the proprietary head of the household."[18] Thus, though Veblen perceived the emerging role of women as co-heading their household, he did not adapt his theory accordingly.

Cultural historians of nineteenth-century France have criticized Veblen's theory on women's consumption, arguing that women consumed to establish their status and identity. Whitney Walton demonstrated that middle-class women increased their spending on personal goods such as clothes and jewelry over items for the home such as linen and silver during 1869–70 as compared with 1828–30. Her study suggests that women's spending patterns developed so as to give priority to asserting their class and identity by emphasizing "the style, taste, and richness of a bourgeois woman's appearance over the amount and value of her household linen and silver."[19] Leora Auslander further rejects Veblen, proposing that late nineteenth-century French women's consumption included the representation of the "self," and that this change occurred during the 1880s.[20] This is significant for the present study because it was during the 1880s that posters advertising department stores as selling women's ready-to-wear clothes began to flourish, reaching a high point in the 1890s. It is thus very likely that posters, along with other department-store advertising, played a significant role in this change by encouraging women to consume mass-produced fashion and accessories to establish their status and identity.

Although print media in general and advertising in particular were soaring during the years Veblen wrote his book, he overlooked their role. For example, he did not consider advertising or other media images in discussing emulation, which based on a comparison "prompts us to outdo those with whom we are in the habit of classing ourselves."[21] Before the development of the department-store poster, fashion plates were used to advertise fashions in France, the United States, and other countries, presenting women wearing the promoted designs, and thus encouraging emulation. The acute observer of modernity, Charles Baudelaire, recognized that contemporary young men and women imitated the print media images with which they identified: "many people force themselves into the likeness of fashion-plates."[22]

Although Veblen notes that the exhibition of class became more important during the modern period in large anonymous metropolitan centers where one is seen by many "transient observers," he did not comment on the importance of media images in this context. He writes that "[t]he means of communication and the mobility of the population now expose the individual to the observation of many persons who have no other means of judging of his reputability than the display of goods ..."[23] Had Veblen recognized the role of advertising and media images, he might have remarked that those who lived in the modern metropolis found models for emulation in the advertisements which stimulated their conspicuous consumption.

Georg Simmel's 1905 essay about fashion did not agree with Veblen's theory of women's vicarious consumption as establishing men's status, but rather proposed that women consume fashion to establish their own identity and status. Simmel probed why women placed priority on fashion by considering their social standing and psychological demands. He proposed that fashion was a supplement for unfulfilled desires, "a compensation for their [women's] lack of social position in a professional group."[24] Fashion "supplements a person's lack of importance, their inability to individualize their existence purely by their own unaided efforts ..."[25] Each person has both a drive "towards individualization" and "immersion in the collectivity."[26]

> [I]f the satisfaction of one of these drives is denied in a certain field of life, it seeks another, in which it then fulfills the amount that it requires. Thus, it seems as though fashion were the valve, as it were, through which women's need for some measure of conspicuousness and individual prominence finds vent, when its satisfaction is more often denied in other spheres.[27]

Simmel explains the role of fashion for women as related to the traditional social and psychological constraints on women's status and subjectivity. Women use fashion because of its social function as "connection and differentiation."[28] Fashion provides a means of belonging to an approved collectivity while establishing particularity and demarcation. It serves to express "the impulse towards equalization and individualization" and "the allure of imitation and conspicuousness."[29] Simmel notes that fashion suited women because it "elevates even the unimportant individual by making them the representative of a totality, the embodiment of a joint spirit" and facilitates "a social obedience," while providing "a form of differentiation:"[30] "Out of the weakness of the social position to which women were condemned throughout the greatest part of history there arises their close relationship to all that is 'custom', to that which is 'right and proper' …"[31] Fashion suits women's needs since it offers "a sphere of general imitation, the individual floating in the broadest social current" along with "a certain conspicuousness, an individual emphasis, an individual ornamentation of the personality."[32]

According to Simmel, fashion operates by maintaining the unity of a "social circle and their class" while closing the latter off from "those standing in a lower position which the higher group characterizes as not belonging to it."[33] The lower classes "strive towards the upper" using fashion for this purpose. They "encounter the least resistance in those fields which are subject to the whims of fashion, because it is here that mere external imitation is more readily accessible."[34] Simmel does not discuss department stores in this context, yet clearly such stores provided the conditions through which women could use fashion to establish their middle-class status and femininity through ready-to-wear fashion.

Simmel's theory advances the understanding of women's consumption of fashion beyond Veblen because he recognizes that women use fashion to establish their own status, not merely that of their household or husband. Furthermore, by addressing specifically women's use of fashion, rather than consumption in general, as Veblen did, Simmel is able to define specific characteristics of women's consumption of fashion as striving to establish their collective identity and individual differentiation. His theory of fashion as supplement proposes that women's consumption of fashion is impelled by their lack of social and professional standing and serves their need for status. Based on the social, professional, and political status of women during the late nineteenth century, Simmel's theory of fashion as supplement throws light on women's consumption of fashion as an arena in which they could gain access and belong to a gendered and classed collectivity.

It could be argued that women had additional aims and motivations in consuming fashion beyond those articulated by Simmel and that, furthermore, by the late nineteenth century new educational and professional avenues opened up for some women, enabling their establishment of status and identity in realms other than the consumption of fashion. It could also be argued that not only women, but also men, established class status and social belonging, at least in part, through the consumption of fashion. My interest here, however, is not to refute or modify Simmel's notions but rather to use his theory in order to explain how posters appealed to women to consume fashion on the basis of historically constituted social and psychological needs, which Simmel's theory identifies. I shall propose that the department-store fashion poster exploited women's wish to belong to a specific gendered and classed social group by establishing and widely diffusing an image of a "type" of the middle-class consumer of department-store fashion.

Simmel's ideas are especially pertinent to the changed conditions brought about by the accessibility of relatively low-priced ready-to-wear department-store fashions and the increased pace of fashion change. As we will see, for large numbers of women who could not afford one-of-a-kind items but could purchase mass-produced clothing, the department-store fashion poster provided a picture of a "collective" identity to which they could aspire. The wider affordability of mass-produced clothes was a necessary condition, but not a sufficient one. Department stores had to create a perception that women's ready-made clothing met needs or desires that women associated with the consumption of fashion. Chief among the strategies adopted was an advertising icon of the fashionable bourgeois woman in ready-to-wear clothes.

As d'Avenel's study of department stores confirms, it was the "feminine public that formed the large troops" of the department-store clientele.[35] Moreover, posters promoting feminine fashions were designed primarily to appeal to women's gazes since they advertised products that women bought and only they could wear. Many scholars have fruitfully used the influential early insights of John Berger and Laura Mulvey about the male gaze and the objectified image of women.[36] The case of advertising images that promote gender-specific goods such as fashion complicates a binary division of a masculine active gaze versus woman as passive image.[37]

The investigation of posters promoting feminine fashions necessitates asking not only how they turn women into objects but also how they address women's gazes. As Judith Williamson points out, signs must mean something to someone: "He or she is not a simple receiver but a creator of meaning … because he/she *has been called upon to be so.*"[38] Department-store fashion posters featured images of women in which the potential woman consumer could "recognize" herself. How did they accomplish this? In what follows I investigate the iconography of the department-store fashion poster in light of the conflicting notions of Veblen and Simmel. Did this iconography call on the middle-class woman to establish the status of her husband/household? Did it appeal to women consumers to use fashion as a supplement to shore up their own social status?

The Iconography of the Department-Store Fashion Poster

The iconography of many late nineteenth-century posters commissioned by large Parisian stores to promote ready-to-wear clothes is remarkably consistent despite the fact that these posters advertised different establishments. Most posters feature a large image of a generic woman, sometimes accompanied by a generic female friend or daughter, posed against a blank flat background, or sometimes within a representational context such as the urban environment near the department store. This use of a formula was economical, but there were additional reasons for it, arising in the historical moment at which the department store and its ready-to-wear fashions and mass-produced accessories were still relatively new and needed to become acceptable.

In the second half of the nineteenth century the wealthiest women ordered their wardrobes from elite fashion designers, and well-to-do women frequented department stores to purchase various goods but still had most of their clothes made individually. Women of lesser means began to purchase clothes in department stores, had their clothes made by inexpensive seamstresses or sewed their own clothes.[39] The department store diffused middle-class fashion at relatively accessible prices. Yet, as Michael Miller notes, the acceptance of ready-made clothes was gradual and required the overcoming of consumer resistance: "Women's fashions ... were an especially difficult market to penetrate."[40] Work clothes and army uniforms were the first to be mass-produced but "well into the century, ready-to-wear for women remained confined primarily to less fashion sensitive items like coats, dressing gowns, and dress accessories."[41] It was only from 1889 onwards that the full range of women's ready-to-wear fashions became available and was sold in department stores.[42]

The department stores diffused mass-produced clothing at affordable prices, enabling the middle classes, including the petit bourgeoisie, to emulate the upper classes.[43] As Philippe Perrot suggests, the ready-to-wear industry "became crucial in spreading bourgeois norms, for those ready-to-wear copies became pedagogical instruments of deportment and morality."[44] Posters of department stores promoting such fashions played an important role in popularizing the ready-to-wear "look" and in establishing its status.

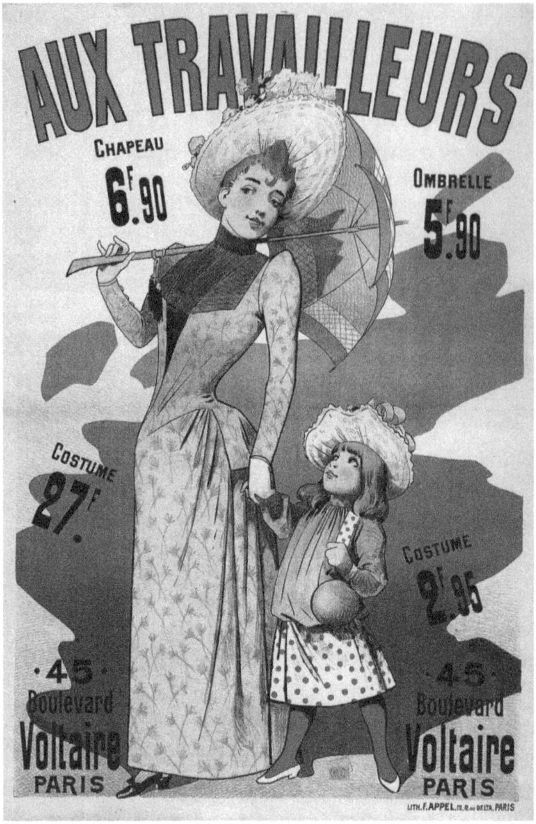

2.1 Alfred Choubrac, *Aux Travailleurs*, *circa* 1890. Poster, Imprimerie F. Appel, Paris. 100.6 × 141.6 cm. The Poster Photo Archive, Posters Please

Department stores targeted the growing middle classes and some stores set low prices, appealing to petit-bourgeois and working-class consumers, as in the case of La Belle Jardinière (which had branches in Lyon, Marseille, Nantes, and Angers), La Samartaine and Ville Saint Denis.[45] Les Grands Magasins Crespin-Dufayel catered to this part of the market by enabling the purchasing of a wide range of items on credit.[46] The poster *Aux Travailleurs* is evidence that stores appealing to working-class and petit-bourgeois women used a similar cliché image of a woman wearing ready-made clothes as a respectable mother with her nicely dressed daughter (Figure 2.1).

By the 1880s and 1890s many department stores were using similar iconography and images of women wearing mass-produced clothing as an icon of fashionability that denoted bourgeois class and femininity. The central figure was presented alone or accompanied by her young daughter, a female friend, or both (Figures 2.1, 2.2, 2.3, 2.4). Most often these posters were gender segregated. Rather than merely conforming to the conservative ideology of separate spheres, which was being challenged in the second half of the nineteenth century, gender-segregated iconography in poster advertising became an early version of what was established later as market segmentation.

In featuring gender-segregated figures, department-store fashion posters were modeled on the precedent of the fashion plate, whose iconography was in harmony with the ideology of gendered spheres of public versus private and probably motivated by it. It should be noted, however, that the strict divisions advocated by the ideology of separate spheres did not correspond to actual practices established by the late nineteenth century. Women were already working in production and services outside the domestic environment, while middle-class women were ardent consumers, all activities conducted in

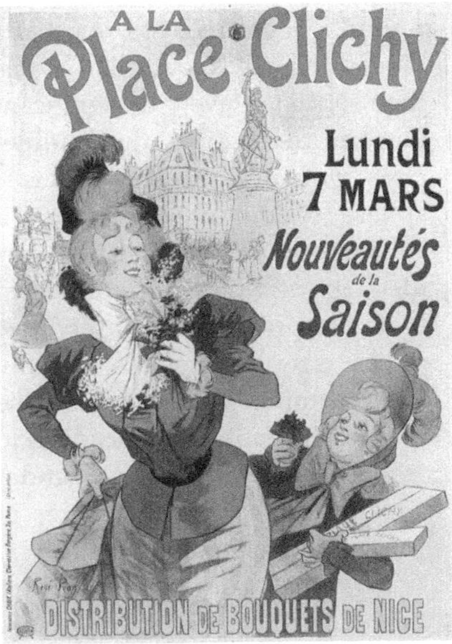

2.2 René Péan, *A La Place Clichy, Nouveautés de la Saison*, 1898. Poster, Imprimerie Chaix, Paris. 86.4 × 125.7 cm. The Poster Photo Archive, Posters Please

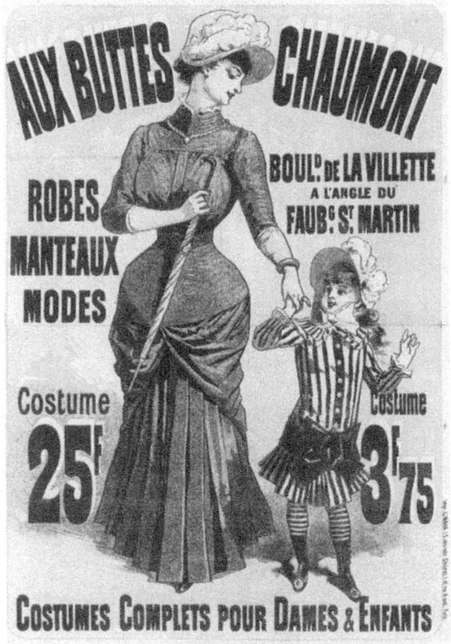

2.3 Jules Chéret, *Aux Buttes Chaumont*, *circa* 1881. Poster, Imprimerie Chaix, Paris. 114.4 × 165.2 cm. The Poster Photo Archive, Posters Please

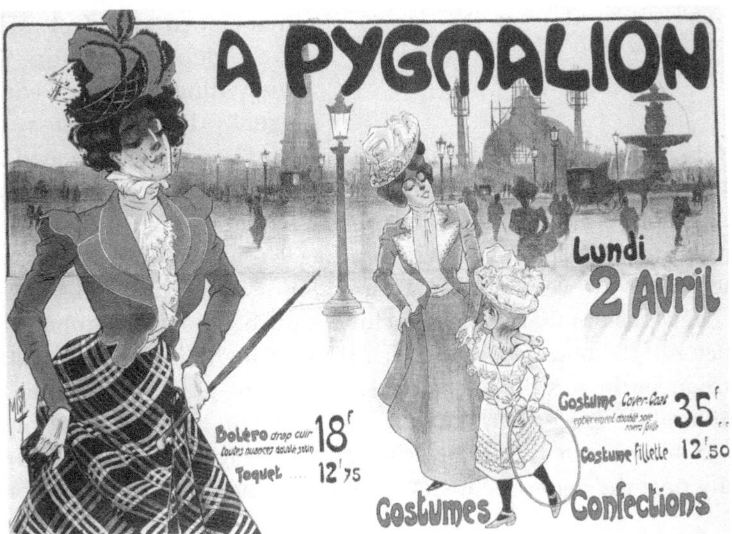

2.4 Misti, *A Pygmalion*, 1900. Poster, Imprimerie B. Sirven, Toulouse. 301 × 228.7 cm. The Poster Photo Archive, Posters Please

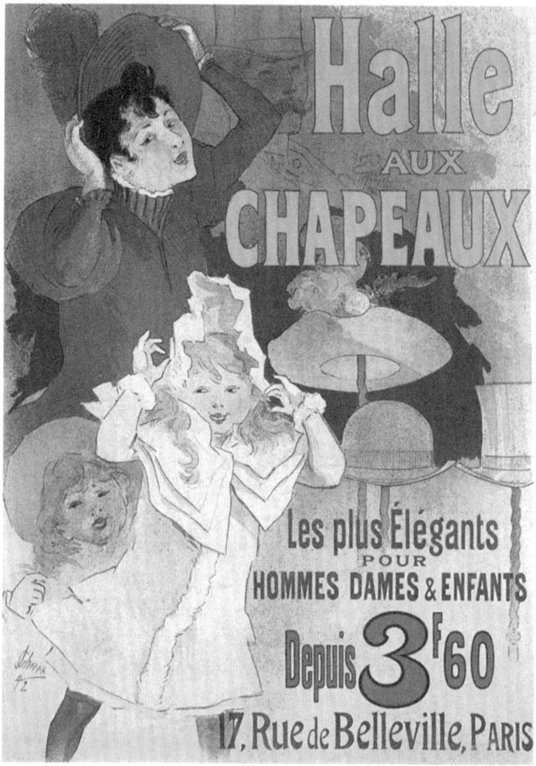

2.5 Jules Chéret, *Halle aux Chapeaux*, 1892. Poster, Imprimerie Chaix, Paris. 85.8 × 123.9 cm. The Poster Photo Archive, Posters Please

public.[47] Department-store posters (and of course department stores themselves) played a significant part in re-situating the middle-class woman from the domestic sphere to the urban sphere of consumption, countering the ideology of women's domesticity. Not surprisingly, conservative critics saw "women's mobility and seeming autonomy in the commercial public" as leading to "their claims for greater gender equality in the public spheres of work and education."[48]

In *Au Bonheur des Dames*, Zola described the space of the department store as a gigantic palace for women, which made shopping a new kind of leisure activity. The department store deployed some characteristics of domesticity, constituting a new kind of urban space for women that helped them feel "at home."[49] Yet department-store posters promoting ready-to-wear fashions usually did not situate women in a domestic space. Rather, their gender-segregated iconography created images of idealized public spaces that appeared congenial to women.[50] The department-store fashion poster represented women as confident in urban space, whether returning from shopping carrying packages (Figure 2.2), walking in the city in their ready-to-wear clothes (Figure 2.4) or shopping in the store (Figure 2.6). Even posters that did not include an urban context implied the urban character of the bourgeois consumer by showing her dressed in outfits worn on urban outings, fully accessorized with hat, gloves, purse, and parasol or umbrella (Figures 2.1, 2.2, 2.3, 2.4, 2.5, 2.6). Some posters highlighted fashionable women's urban presence by depicting women walking in the city, usually near the department store that had commissioned the poster (Figures 2.2, 2.4).

Many posters assured the respectable status of women of the middle-classes by showing them with their young daughters (Figures 2.1, 2.2, 2.3, 2.4); in some cases the petit-bourgeois woman also appears with her daughter

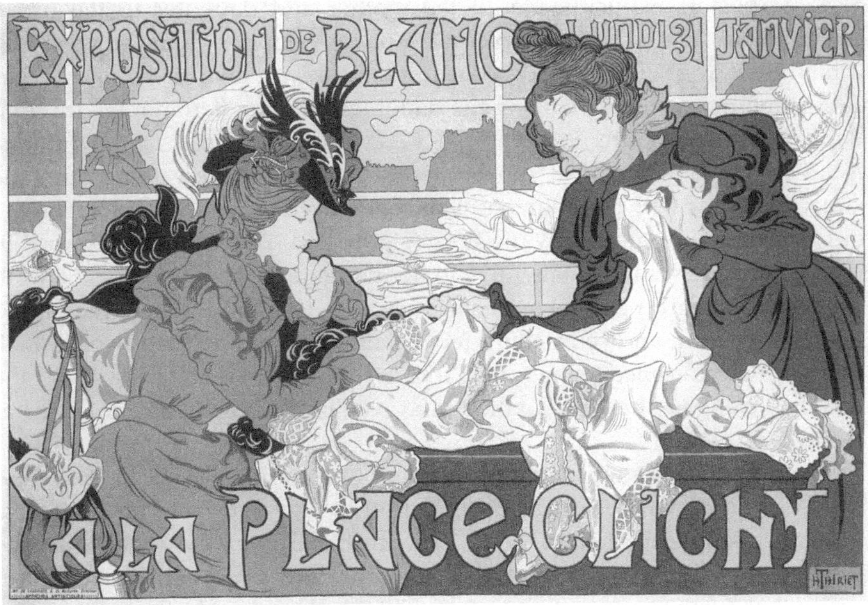

2.6 Henri Thiriet, *A la Place Clichy, Exposition de Blanc*, 1898. Poster, Imprimerie De Vaugirard, G. De Mallherbe, Paris. 132.1 × 92.1 cm. The Poster Photo Archive, Posters Please

(Figure 2.1). Combining images of mothers and daughters in a single poster was economical since it advertised clothing both for mature women and for young girls.[51] It is noteworthy that these posters usually did not depict the mother and daughter inside the home in the tradition of many earlier fashion plates. Rather, they affirmed the woman's middle-class, married, and motherhood status outside the private sphere, thus focusing more on the status of the woman than on the absent household or husband.

Posters tended to represent the bourgeois and petit-bourgeois mother as a mature female figure at the top of the familial hierarchy, with the young girl in her charge (Figures 2.1, 2.2, 2.3, 2.4). Lisa Tiersten has demonstrated that the women's press explicitly reconciled women's role as consumers for domestic products and for their own elegant appearance with their duties as wife and mother.[52] Department-store poster images featuring single women and mothers in department-store clothing usually represented them away from the domestic context and focused on the fashionability of the figures. Furthermore, the type of fashions worn by the women implied a public rather than private context. Posters depicting mothers and daughters dressed for urban outings participated in reconfiguring the image of motherhood from mandatory domesticity to modernized motherhood in public spaces.[53]

Some posters explicitly placed the mother and daughter in the urban environment partaking of the pleasures of consumption. They suggest that a bourgeois woman can enjoy consumption on her own or as part of her role as mother, while socializing the daughter into her "femininity" through department-store attire. For example, René Péan's poster, *A La Place Clichy, Nouveautés de la Saison*, 1898, shows a mother and daughter walking along the street, returning with their purchases and enjoying the scent of the violets given out as a spring promotion by the store (Figure 2.2). This woman, absorbed in the pleasurable scent, is inattentive to her daughter. Were it not for the well-dressed young girl next to her, the heavily corseted slim-waisted, red-haired woman, wearing an eye-catching red jacket and a plumed hat, would look more like a café-concert singer than a bourgeois mother. The presence of the daughter mitigates her presentation as a sexualized woman, safeguarding her respectable status.

Some posters juxtaposed the mother with another woman. Péan's *A La Place Clichy*, which foregrounds a mother and daughter, also shows a miniature single woman walking by with her dog at the back. Misti's *A Pygmalion* presents a single woman in front, and a mother and daughter somewhat further away (Figure 2.4). This poster gives both types status, depicting them showing off their fashionable appearance in urban space. They are walking on the Place Châtelet in Paris, near the Pygmalion department store (which was located on the Boulevard Sebastopol), thus associating the bourgeois woman's fashionability with urban shopping. The single woman attracts the eye with her bright red hat and jacket. Nonchalant, her face is seen through a transparent veil stretched from a decorated hat. She is walking in Paris self-contained, fully aware of her urban performance. She is contrasted with the elegant bourgeois mother who is paying close attention to her well-dressed daughter. Including both types, the poster caters to a larger target group and calls on each type to "recognize" herself in one of them.

Chéret's *Halle aux Chapeaux* (Figure 2.5) is a rare instance of a French fashion poster showing father along with mother and daughters. The bourgeois man with his top hat is peripheral. Barely visible at the back, the faint contours of his upper body fade into the bluish background. The pastel monochromatic color dematerializes him. His ethereal hovering contrasts with the material presence of the woman and daughters. The colors of the mother's and daughters' clothes, along with their position in front, call attention to them—the mother's bright red dress and matching hat, one girl's red stockings against her white dress. The man maintains his authority through his distance in the background, as if he were not quite part of the consumption scene. Mother and daughters, on the other hand, are avid consumers who display the goods they are wearing. While partially absenting the bourgeois man from a role as full-fledged consumer, the poster visualizes the message that the store caters to consumers of both genders through the prominent display of hats for both men and women in the foreground.

Typecasting women as consumers, this unusual poster corresponds to the practices of, and discourses on, women as primary consumers in Paris during the second half of the nineteenth century. Chéret's representation of the man with the woman and girls does not adhere to the common formula presenting a woman alone, with a friend, a daughter, or both. Nonetheless, it coheres with the main tenet of the formula by placing a marked emphasis on the woman and girls and visually separating the man's airy presence from them. Although this particular poster may agree with Veblen's theory of women's vicarious consumption, it is an exception that proves the rule. The formulaic iconography of the French department-store poster that features the fashionable woman consumer, sometimes with other women consumers or her daughter, does not support Veblen's theory of women as consuming vicariously on behalf of their husband.

Such posters were part of a larger arena of print media that promoted consumer culture, each with its own emphasis. Studying the iconography of this type of poster, although essential, does not in and of itself provide a full answer to the question of what made the formula of the department-store fashion poster successful or effective in the eyes of the poster designer, printing firm/publisher and ultimately the commissioners of the posters—the department stores. To tackle this question, the next section considers another important part of the formula, the prominence of price indications in the department-store fashion poster.

Prices, Status, and Affordability

A key element in the formula of the department-store fashion poster was the juxtaposition of prices next to specific items such as costume, hat, parasol, and a child's dress (Figures 2.1, 2.3, 2.4, 2.5). This was a striking innovation of the poster compared with its predecessor, the fashion plate. The latter did not include the prices of the items it depicted. The prominence of the prices shown next to items on the poster turned the products into merchandise. The nineteenth-century *Larousse Grand Dictionnaire Universel*'s entry for "*Marchandise*" says that although economists distinguish only between product and capital, merchandise is "a particular state of things," which is neither product nor capital. Products become merchandise by being put on the market and brought before the consumer.[54] The large figures denoting prices were blatant announcements that the items on view were merchandise.

In proclaiming prices, posters may have been influenced by sales catalogues, which were published in small, slim booklet formats and developed around the same time as posters.[55] (In turn, covers of late nineteenth- and turn-of-the-century catalogues borrowed some conventions from posters.) Although both posters and sales catalogues announced prices, they used different formulas. During the late nineteenth century, sales catalogues tended to maintain a clearer division of image and text in their page design than did posters. Prices and descriptive information were kept distinct from the illustration. This can be seen, for example, in a page from the winter catalogue of the Grands Magasins du Printemps, 1894–95 (Figure 2.7). The image is separate from the block of text in three columns, which describes the fabrics and features of each of the three dresses, and lists prices. The formula of the department-store poster advertising fashion excluded lengthy descriptive information and included relatively large price statements integrated into the image space. Moreover, the highlighting of a few prices, as in posters, had a different function from that of the extensive price lists in sales catalogues. The former had primarily a symbolic value connoting affordability, whereas the latter had a more practical and informative function. As d'Avenel observed in the early 1890s, women "incessantly" compared prices in catalogues of different department stores.[56]

Printing prominent prices on posters next to the image of a fashionably dressed woman had several functions. It called attention to the fixed price policy of the department store, which was a central feature of its new retailing strategies, replacing the practice of individually negotiated prices in small shops. Moreover, placing a chic woman next to relatively large price statements contextualized her within the public space of the marketplace. Shifting focus from the whole image of the woman to discrete parts of goods for sale singled out by price, the poster implied that consumers could acquire the sartorial status of the fashionable bourgeoise. It promised that a woman could become as fashionable as the poster icon by buying such items. However, all this could create the impression that the woman herself was on display for sale. Zola emphasizes this effect in *Au Bonheur des Dames*, describing a display in a department-store window that features mannequins whose heads are replaced by price tags:

> The well-rounded neck and graceful figures of the dummies exaggerated the slimness of the waist, the absent head being replaced by a large price-ticket pinned on the neck; whilst the window reflected and multiplied the forms without end, peopling the street with these beautiful women for sale, each bearing a price in big figures in the place of a head.[57]

Zola takes some literary license in describing a window display in which heads are replaced by price tags, but he captures the new regime of merchandise display that gave the price unprecedented visibility. His description stresses another important facet of department-store displays of ready-to-wear fashion, namely their construction of a standardized woman entirely composed of department-store goods.

GRANDS MAGASINS DU PRINTEMPS — PARIS

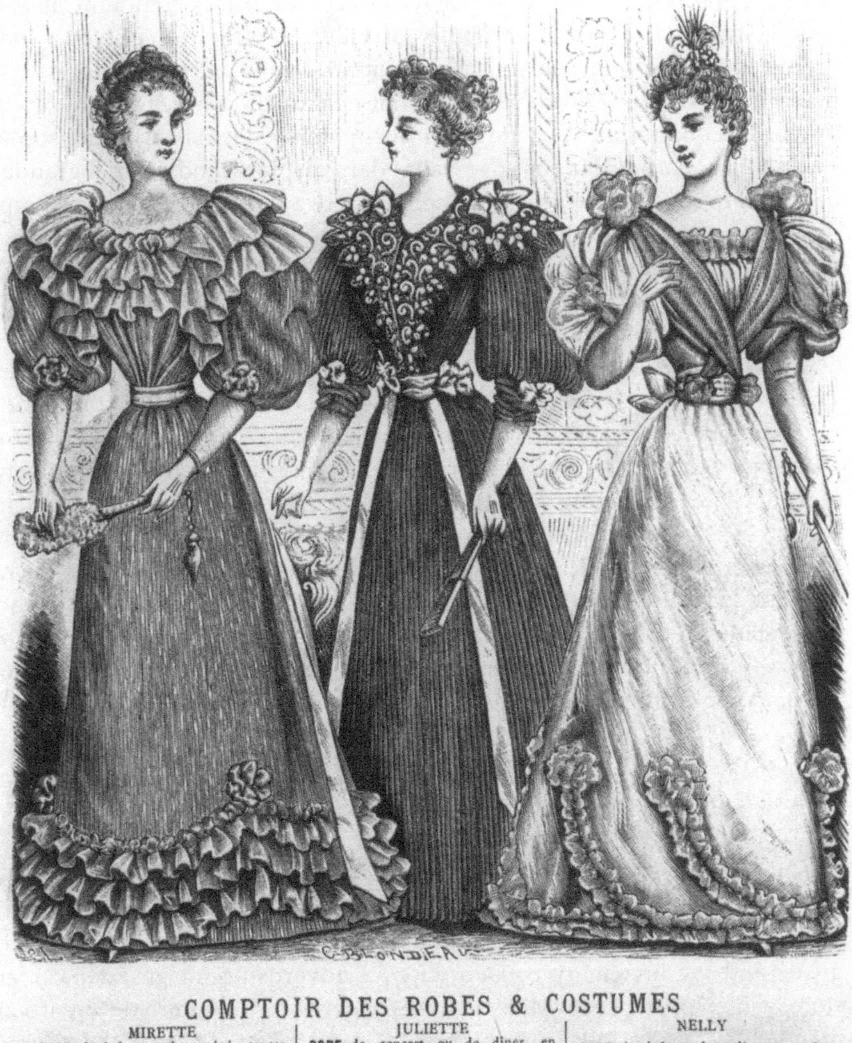

COMPTOIR DES ROBES & COSTUMES

MIRETTE

ROBE de bal en crêpe crépé, toutes nuances claires, jupe doublée garnie tout autour de trois volants en crépon et choux en ruban, corsage décolleté garni d'une mousseline de soie assortie, manches demi-longues, ceinture en ruban de satin . **69.»**

Avec les trois volants de la jupe en mousseline de soie. . . . . **92.»**

En surah toutes nuances claires, mousseline de soie au corsage, volants de la jupe en pareil, nœuds de ruban et ceinture longue belle qualité . . . . **125.»**

Avec mousseline de soie au corsage et à la jupe . . . . **145.»**

JULIETTE

ROBE de concert ou de dîner, en voile plissé royal, jupe ronde plissée, corsage rentré dans la jupe, grand col en guipure écrue, nœuds et ceinture en ruban belle qualité.

Prix. . . . . **68.»**

En nuances plus foncées : marine, vieux-rouge, beige, noir et capucine, robe montante et manches longues, guipure noire ou écrue.

Prix. . . . . **75.»**

En surah toutes nuances . . **140.»**

NELLY

ROBE de bal en bengaline ou satin merveilleux, nuances : crème, argent, rose, ciel, maïs, nil, lilas, cardinal et vieux-rose ; jupe doublée garnie tout autour de ruches de tulle assorti avec choux, corsage décolleté garni de tulle formant bretelles, ceinture en ruban.

Prix. . . . . **120.»**

En moire belle qualité, mêmes nuances. **190**

2.7 A page from the winter sales catalogue of Grands Magasins du Printemps, 1894–95. Bibliothèque Forney, Paris. All rights reserved

From the advertiser's viewpoint, the cumulative effect of juxtaposing the image of the fashionable woman with large-scale prices communicated the overall message of the affordability of ready-to-wear fashions and mass-produced accessories, sold in large quantities in department stores.[58] The poster's message of affordability did not negatively affect its claim of class status. The environment of the department store established the consumer's status through a sumptuous space, abundant displays, and palatial grandeur. In addition, congenial service affirmed the bourgeois standing of the shopper. As a sales catalogue of the Petit Saint-Thomas explained, "knowing very well that low prices do not entirely suffice to satisfy" consumers, the store needs to show an attitude of "complaisance and politeness," along with "the freedom to view the merchandise without being harassed to buy it."[59]

Some posters indicated the attentive attitude of the sales-person. Henri Thiriet's Art Nouveau-style poster *A la Place de Clichy* represents a bareheaded saleswoman serving the elegant consumer (Figure 2.6). While both women share in a "collectivity" (to use Simmel's term) of the feminine fashion style of the late 1890s, wearing similar dresses with puffed sleeves, the higher class consumer is distinguished by her sumptuously decorated hat and purse as well as her refined gestures. She is represented as an individual distinguished by class, taste, and a contemplative attitude towards the merchandise whose fine details she is examining. Such scenes of the process of consumption are relatively rare in department-store fashion posters, which typically show a woman displaying her outfit against a blank background amidst prices.

Material and Imaginary Consumption

The images of fashionable women in posters were constructed on an anonymous formula. How could women be motivated to consume by such images in order to further their status? Forging a link between the consumption of material goods and the imaginary consumption of advertising images, department-store fashion posters provided vicarious experiences in quite a different sense than Veblen's "vicarious consumption." They prompted potential consumers to establish their classed and gendered identity by converting the vicarious experience of looking, an imaginary consumption, into acquiring material goods. In the subjective encounter with the formulaic image of posters and the ready-to-wear fashions they promoted, women could imagine themselves gaining status and a collective identity.

During a time when opportunities in higher education and professional careers had not yet reached large numbers of women, the department store and its representation of women in late nineteenth-century fashion posters offered a symbolic value of bourgeois status to women of the middle classes. Department stores encouraged emulation by presenting women as displaying ready-made clothing and accessories on their bodies. Showing that class, femininity, and fashionability could be acquired at affordable prices required addressing consumers as subjects who could imagine using fashion as a supplement to gain status and a sense of belonging.

Women who could afford to shop vicariously consumed images of "themselves" as a prelude and after-effect to the perpetual process of looking at images and buying the kind of clothes and accessories featured in images. Posters, window displays, and various kinds of print-media images all evoked fantasies of seeing oneself in the featured items. Women who could not afford department-store goods could only "consume" images as a substitute. In his 1873 novel *Le Ventre de Paris*, Zola describes a young working-class woman, Cadine, lingering in front of a shop-window display. In "moments of vanity and coquetry ... she bought herself in imagination some of the magnificent dresses displayed in the windows of the 'Fabriques de France.'"[60] His description of Cadine's imaginary consumption shows how it was prompted by visual display:

> ... amid the crowd of market women in dirty aprons gazing at future Sunday dresses, the girl would feel the woolens, flannels, and cottons to test the texture and suppleness of the materials; and she would promise herself a gown of bright-colored flannelling, flowered print, or scarlet poplin. Sometimes even from among the pieces draped and set off to advantage by the window-dressers she would choose some soft sky-blue or apple-green silk and dream of wearing it with pink ribbons.[61]

The woman who could not buy in small shops or large department stores (not even in those that established new practices of selling on credit) had no possibility of materializing the imaginary consumption evoked by ubiquitous images of women in fashionable clothing. On the other hand, for consumers who could afford to shop, imaginary consumption and material consumption reinforced each other. If imaginary consumption never fully materializes, neither does material consumption. The power of the imaginary persists beyond the momentary act of material consumption. The women who bought department-store fashions and accessories consumed not merely those mass-produced objects but the images of chic women in posters and other print media.

What was the effect of the ubiquitous images of fashionable women circulating in the mass media of the time, and especially of their presence in large-scale posters in public spaces? Commissioned by department stores, fashion posters had a specific function within a wider advertising program. They not only taught women how to sport the current fashionable look, as intimate-size fashion plates did; nor did they merely persuade women that the components of this look were affordable, as sales catalogues demonstrated in detail. Posters provided an additional dimension not present in hand-held fashion plates or illustrations in catalogues. They coined a large-scale icon of the fashionable woman wearing affordable mass-produced clothing that embodied middle-class status. Furthermore, they lent this icon a new public status by making it visible in urban space. This helped to secure the supplemental power of department-store ready-made fashion for women. Unlike fashion plates and journal illustrations, the prominently visible department-store poster beckoned women to identify with icons whose symbolic power was augmented by scale, outspoken presence in public space, and association with the modern urban experience of shopping in department stores. In posters pasted on boulevard hoardings, women could see images of fashionable women mirrored within the urban spaces that they increasingly inhabited.[62] While serving its own promotional needs, the department-store fashion poster thus played a role in materializing modern women's visibility.

Notes

Author's note: My thanks to Cristina Cuevas-Wolf, Jacki Feldman, Relli Shechter, and Kerri Steinberg for stimulating comments that contributed to the revision of this article and to Beth Tobin for careful reading and editorial suggestions.

1. On Chéret, see Lucy Broido, *The Posters of Jules Chéret,* Catalogue Raisonné 2nd ed. (New York: Dover, 1992); Bradford R. Collins, "The Poster as Art: Jules Chéret and the Struggle for the Equality of the Arts in Late Nineteenth-Century France," *Design Issues* 2 (1985): 41–50.

2. An exception is a recent article by Françoise Tétart-Vittu, which includes a brief but informative discussion on department-store posters, "Catalogues et Affiches," in *Les Cathédrales du Commerce Parisien: Grands Magasins et Enseignes,* eds. Béatrice de Andia and Caroline François, 135–42 (Paris: Action Artistique de la Ville de Paris, 2006). The scholarly examination of the history of consumption in nineteenth century France is indispensable to work on department-store posters. Some studies present various images of department stores, including posters, while the primary focus has been on textual sources. See Whitney Walton, *France at the Crystal Palace: Bourgeois Taste and Artisan Manufacture in the Nineteenth Century* (Berkeley: University of California Press, 1992); Philippe Perrot, *Fashioning the Bourgeoisie: A History of Clothing in the Nineteenth Century,* trans. Richard Bienvenu (Princeton, NJ: Princeton University Press, 1994); Michael Miller, *The Bon Marché: Bourgeois Culture and the Department Store, 1869–1920* (Princeton, NJ: Princeton University Press, 1981); Rosalind Williams, *Dream Worlds: Mass Consumption in Late Nineteenth-Century France* (Berkeley: University of California Press, 1982); Leora Auslander, "The Gendering of Consumer Practices," in *The Sex of Things: Gender and Consumption in Historical Perspective,* eds. Victoria de Grazia with Ellen Furlough, 79–112 (Berkeley: University of California Press, 1996), and idem, *Taste and Power: Furnishing Modern France* (Berkeley: University of California Press, 1996); Lisa Tiersten, *Marianne in the Market: Envisioning Consumer Society in Fin-de-Siècle France* (Berkeley: University of California Press, 2001).

3. For major contributions in this area, see Valerie Steele, *Paris Fashion: A Cultural History* (New York: Oxford University Press, 1988); Aileen Ribeiro, *The Art of Dress: Fashion in England and France 1750 to 1820* (New Haven: Yale University Press, 1995); Marie Simon, *Fashion in Art: The Second Empire and Impressionism,* trans. Edmund Jephcott (London: Zwemmer, 1995).

4. *Magasins de nouveautés,* such as the Petit St Thomas and the Hotel de Ville, revolutionized retail shopping in the 1840s through their groupings of goods, ready-to-wear clothes, fixed and low prices, high turnover, free entry, and exchange or reimbursement of purchases. Miller, *The Bon Marché,* 25–6. On the development of *Magasins de nouveautés,* see Piedade da Silveira, "Les magasins de nouveautés (1800–1850)," in de Andia and François, eds., *Les Cathédrales du Commerce,* pp. 33–43; on the history leading up to them, see de Andia, "Introduction," ibid., 10–31.

5. According to Tétart-Vittu, *magasins de nouveautés* were called Grand Magasins from 1860; "Catalogues et Affiches," 135. I use the term "department-store poster" both for posters of department stores (*grands magasins*) and for posters of their predecessors, *magasins de nouveautés.*

6. Simmel's article, "The Philosophy of Fashion," was first published in 1905; Simmel's "Psychology of Fashion" was published in 1895. Georg Simmel, "The Philosophy of Fashion," [1905], trans. Mark Ritter and David Frisby, in *Simmel on Culture, Selected Writings*, eds. David Frisby and Mike Featherstone, 187–205 (London: Sage Publications, 1997); see Frisby, "Introduction to the Texts," in ibid., at 13.

7. During the 1870s and 1880s *L'Illustration* and *Le Monde Illustré* published articles describing new or enlarged store premises and new departments. Miller notes that the staff of the Bon Marché probably prepared the self-promotion articles, Miller, *The Bon Marché*, 173, 222; Erika D. Rappaport discusses the close relationship of department store and press, and the press advertising of Selfridge's in London, in "'A New Era of Shopping': The Promotion of Women's Pleasure in London's West End, 1909–1914," in *Cinema and the Invention of Modern Life*, eds. Leo Charney and Vanessa R. Schwartz, 130–55 (Berkeley: University of California Press, 1995).

8. On the earlier limited promotion of old style boutiques, see Miller, *The Bon Marché*, 22–4. On traditional small stores versus new retailing, see Philip G. Nord, *Paris Shopkeepers and the Politics of Resentment* (Princeton, NJ: Princeton University Press, 1986). Extensive advertising became common as early as the 1840s, including full-page examples. Miller, *The Bon Marché*, 26–7, 173–5.

9. Vicomte Georges d'Avenel, "Mécanisme de la vie moderne: Les Grands Magasins," *Revue des Deux Mondes* (July 1, 1894): 329–69, at 350.

10. Emile Zola, *The Ladies' Paradise*, trans. Henry Vizetelly's firm, 1886, intro. K. Ross (Berkeley: University of California Press, 1992), 348. *Au Bonheur des Dames* was first published as a volume in 1883.

11. Ibid., 237.

12. Miller, *The Bon Marché*, 62.

13. d'Avenel, "Mécanisme de la vie moderne," 354.

14. Zola, *The Ladies' Paradise*, 349. Zola's research notes indicate that 70,000 people came to the special sale days at the Louvre department store; Miller, *The Bon Marché*, 53.

15. Thorstein Veblen, *The Theory of the Leisure Class: An Economic Study of Institutions* (New York: Vanguard Press, 1899), 179.

16. Ibid., 83.

17. Ibid., 66.

18. Ibid., 66–7.

19. Walton, *France at the Crystal Palace*, 98–105, at 101.

20. Auslander includes women's participating in the nation among the later functions of women's consumption, in "The Gendering of Consumer Practices," 79. See also Tiersten's critique of Veblen, in *Marianne in the Market*, 8–9.

21. Veblen, *The Theory of the Leisure Class*, 103.

22. Charles Baudelaire, "Some French Caricaturists," in *The Painter of Modern Life*, ed. and trans. J. Mayne, 166–86 (London: Phaidon, 1965), at 183. This is discussed in Ruth E. Iskin, "Popularizing New Women in Belle Époque Advertising Posters," in *A Belle Époque? Women and Feminism in French Society and Culture 1890–1910*, eds. Diana Holmes and Carrie Tarr, 95–112 (Oxford and New York: Berghahn Books, 2006).

23. Veblen, *The Theory of the Leisure Class*, 86–7.

24. Simmel, "The Philosophy of Fashion," 197.

25. Ibid.

26. Ibid., 196.

27. Ibid.

28. Ibid., 189.

29. Ibid., 196.

30. Ibid., 194.

31. Ibid., 196.

32. Ibid.

33. Ibid.

34. Ibid., 190.

35. d'Avenel, "Mécanisme de la vie moderne," 347.

36. John Berger, *Ways of Seeing* (New York: Penguin, 1973), 45–64; Laura Mulvey, "Visual Pleasure and Narrative Cinema," [1975] in *Art after Modernism: Rethinking Representation*, ed. Brian Wallis, 360–73 (New York: New Museum of Contemporary Art; Boston: D.R. Godine, 1984).

37. Recent studies that focus on consumption and images in the context of consumption have increasingly paid attention to the representation of, and appeal to, women's gazes. See, for example, Alexandra Keller, "Disseminations of Modernity: Representation and Consumer Desire in Early Mail-Order Catalogs," in Charney and Schwartz, eds., *Cinema and the Invention of Modern Life*, 156–82; Rappaport, "'A New Era of Shopping';" Tiersten, *Marianne in the Market*, 26; Ruth E. Iskin, "The Pan-European *Flâneuse* in Fin-de-Siècle Posters: Advertising Modern Women in the City," *Nineteenth-Century Contexts* 25 (2003): 333–56; Sharon Marcus, "Reflections on Victorian Fashion Plates," *Differences: A Journal of Feminist Cultural Studies* 14, no. 3 (2003): 4–33; Ruth E. Iskin, *Modern Women and Parisian Consumer Culture in Impressionist Painting* (Cambridge: Cambridge University Press, 2007).

38. Judith Williamson, *Decoding Advertisements: Ideology and Meaning in Advertising* [1978] (London: Marion Boyars, 1990), 41.

39. On classes of female consumers of department stores, see Tiersten, *Marianne in the Market*, 215–19.

40. Miller, *The Bon Marché*, 34. On the gradual development and acceptance of ready-to-wear for women see, Perrot, *Fashioning the Bourgeoisie*, chapters 4 and 5.

41. Miller, *The Bon Marché*, 34.

42. Florence Brachet Champsaur, "Les Grands Magasins et la mode," in de Andia and François, eds., *Les Cathédrales du Commerce*, 143–8 at 146.

43. On the evolving relationship between ready-made department-store fashion and elite fashion, see ibid.

44. Perrot, *Fashioning the Bourgeoisie*, 72.

45. Ibid., 77.

46. On Crespin-Dufayel, see Bruno Centorame, "Les Grands Magasins Crespin-Dufayel," in de Andia and François, eds., *Les Cathédrales du Commerce*, 81–4.

47. Walton discusses shopping as requiring women to enter the marketplace, in *France at the Crystal Palace*, 16.

48. Tiersten, *Marianne in the Market*, 23.

49. The department-store edifice included amenities such as a buffet, a well-stocked reading and writing room, and convenient bathrooms for women, which were still a rarity in other urban spaces at the time. On the relationship of "home" and public space in the department store in France and England respectively, see Tiersten, *Marianne in the Market*, 188–99, and Rappaport, "'A New Era of Shopping'," 144–7.

50. See Iskin, "The Pan-European *Flâneuse*."

51. Some department-store posters advertising male clothing (which are outside the scope of this article) juxtaposed mature men and boys in ready-made garments. For a rare discussion of issues pertaining to men as consumers in the second half of the nineteenth century in the context of Victorian and Edwardian social life, see Christopher Breward, *The Hidden Consumer: Masculinities, Fashion and City Life 1860–1914* (Manchester: Manchester University Press, 1988).

52. Tiersten, *Marianne in the Market*, 190.

53. On the change in attitude towards mothers in public space from mid to late nineteenth century, see ibid., 188–99.

54. S.v. "*Marchandise*," Pierre Larousse, *Grand Dictionnaire Universel du XIXe Siècle*, vol. 10, reprint (Geneva and Paris: Slatkine, 1982), 1142.

55. See Tétart-Vittu, "Catalogues et Affiches," on the evolution of early French sales catalogues; Rappaport, "'A New Era of Shopping'," on sales catalogues of the English department store Selfridge's; and Keller, "Disseminations of Modernity," on the US Sears catalogues.

56. d'Avenel, "Mécanisme de la vie moderne," 347.

57. Zola, *The Ladies' Paradise*, 8.

58. For example, Chéret's *circa* 1881 *Aux Buttes Chaumont* inscribes the woman's costume as 25 francs and the girl's dress at 3.75 francs (Figure 2.3). Almost a decade later Alfred Choubrac's *circa* 1890 poster for the store *Aux Travailleurs* (At the Workers), whose name indicates its appeal to working-class consumers (Figure 2.1), announces relatively low prices that remain close to those in the 1881 poster—27 francs for the woman's dress and 2.95 francs for the girl's.

59. Cited in Miller, *The Bon Marché*, 26.

60. Emile Zola, *The Belly of Paris*, trans. Ernest Alfred Vizetelly (Los Angeles: Sun and Moon Press, 1996), 245.

61. Ibid., 243.

62. As Elizabeth Wilson notes, "the department store assisted the freeing of middle-class women from the shackles of the home." Department stores provided reading rooms, as well as tearooms or restaurants, where women could meet each other on their own in a public space at a time when a respectable woman still had to be accompanied by a male family member in most restaurants. Elizabeth Wilson, *Adorned in Dreams: Fashion and Modernity* (London: Tauris, 2005), 150.

3

Nostalgic Appetites: Female Desire and Wartime Rationing in Virginia Woolf's *Between the Acts* and Noel Streatfeild's *Saplings*

Andrea Adolph

It is difficult to discuss the era of World War II in Britain without acknowledging the significant impact of wartime rationing on the everyday lives of Britons. Social historians and writers drawn to gastronomy are beginning to outline for later generations the myriad ways in which rationing and ongoing austerity affected those left to defend the Home Front, and even the basics of the rationing policies seem compelling in their contrast to contemporary affluence. With regard to food and food rationing, the limitations that were placed upon British diets almost from the moment when war was declared on Germany can be hard to fathom from nearly 70 years down the road, when food shortages, at least in developed nations, are more likely discussed as a choice made by those attempting to slim down. From March of 1940, the meat ration was set at an amount that allowed the average Briton not quite three ounces per day, less than the serving size recommended today by dieting gurus. Staples of pre-war diets such as bacon and butter were under siege as soon as war was underway, even before rationing was official in early 1940, and war often directly affected the importation of food. In the words of one woman interviewed in May 1940 by Mass Observation, "We have bugger all to cook."[1]

Although the harshness of wartime food consumption was softened somewhat by the nationalism that accompanied its necessity, over time, many Britons envisioned pre-war meals as part and parcel of the Britain others were fighting for. In 1944, a fed-up James Devon decried ongoing food rationing and linked his meals to his other inalienable rights: "… the heritage of freedom resides as much in the domain of food … as in the sanctions of Habeus Corpus or the Great Charter … the freedom for which we are fighting includes the right to the kind of meals we remember from pre-war days."[2] Popular memory allowed for those pre-1939 meals to stand in metonymically for a pre-war Britain that was all but lost by the time the war was over, particularly for the British middle classes, whose lives in large part would never again see pre-war standards of living. Connections between the impact of austerity in Britain and nostalgia for a general pre-war way of life can easily be drawn, but food shortages also intersect with other forms of cultural nostalgia, and in this essay I will illustrate how these links can be further examined to elucidate how austerity impacts issues of female desire, how going without perhaps ironically enhances an awareness of one's ability to desire, and how this new form of desirous female agency during World War II engendered a nostalgia for normative sexual and gender prescriptions. Policies made necessary by the fact of war were also enmeshed with the ways in which women were directed to perform their feminine roles.

Beyond sexual desire, though, I claim that women's recognition of their ability to want, as opposed to need, is central to the desire that emerges in the cultural and literary texts here examined, and that this formulation of subjective desire subverts traditional ways in which women have been trained to conceive of themselves as desiring subjects. Muriel Dimen writes that "[w]anting, associated with adulthood, active will, and masculinity" has been privileged in modern cultures as "better than need, linked to infancy, passive dependency, and femininity."[3] Wanting is perceived as purposeful, willful, and masculine; the desire that arises from wartime scarcity pushes the limits that have traditionally defined women as needy, and thus as passive. In a culture of nationalism that allowed women vocational and other freedoms, but simultaneously demanded of them allegiance to specific domestic roles in the name of Britain, this kind of desire is both a natural extension of those new roles and anathema to the interests of the nation. As Nicola Humble has pointed out: "Where people's choice of food had previously involved issues of tradition and habit, social status and style, it was now hedged about with questions of patriotism and morality, the subject of a continued barrage of propaganda."[4] In order for a woman to conform not only to the roles historically on offer to her, but simultaneously to those roles tailored to wartime, she must strike an impossible balance between the good of the family and the nation, on one hand and, on the other, her own good.

Women have been inundated for centuries with mandates for proper consuming habits and for the boundaries that tightly circumscribe feminine appetite. The mouth and the vaginal cavity are linked as twin creatures of transgressive desire—one for gluttony, the other for lust—and this conflation of female desires results in a policing of what enters the mouth as a way to proactively defend the genitals, that biological center of femaleness. As Julia Kristeva reminds us, "… orality signifies a boundary of the self's clean and proper body ... all food is liable to defile."[5] There is a historical investment in ensuring that the body—particularly the female body—is not defiled, even symbolically. Reina Green notes that this caution appears in writing as early as 1581: women should "'not eate openly ... lest shee see such meats as she might desire and lust after'" [sic].[6] Admonitions such as this one emerge time and again in conduct literature, and while current readers might find quaint, even laughable, such prescriptions for female consumption, they should see how significant that discourse remained within twentieth-century modernity (and remains still). The ongoing equation of lust with hunger has resulted in what is now considered a normative, "feminine" interest in self-denial—of food, of sex, of embodiment—whether that be denial masquerading as diet or standing in for the kinds of nurturing to which women are still expected to attend. Regardless of the fact that humans are, it would seem, insatiable, we readily adopt the notion that controlling this urge is somehow a native ability, when what is truly human—for men and for women—is to want, to go on wanting.[7]

The World War II era in Britain presented no exception to this rule; indeed, the fact of scarcity only increased the ways in which women were figured as icons of self-denial. Although scarcity was a fact for nearly everyone, women were at the center of the Ministry of Food's marketing of wartime policies. For even as women donned uniforms and became important to continuing industry, they still remained in charge of feeding families, of "making do" in the kitchen after queuing for whatever was on hand on a given day. Lord Woolton, who was made Minister of Food in early 1940, appealed to women during his first official broadcast: "I tell you in plain and direct language that you are risking the lives of our fighting men if your waste of food takes up extra shipping space."[8] It was expected that women with families would ensure that others had as much to eat as possible, and this idea trumped any notion of women's hunger or appetite. The periodical *Woman's Own*, in September of 1940, encourages: "What a test of affection to lay down your sugar ration for your husband-son-boy friend! Yet who wouldn't if it meant he was going to get a really good package from home."[9] By the time the war ended, one woman asserted: "Frankly, I think the women of this country are half-starved."[10] A particularly feminine brand of asceticism was enhanced by nationalism and the urgency brought about by war's other realities, such as evacuations, labor shortages, and the Blitz. To appear desirous during wartime meant not only that a woman was not living up to her feminine duty, but also that she was lacking in the moral fiber necessary to win the war.

The impact of wartime food rationing on how women were viewed with regard to their consumption practices is evident in women's writing of the period, as well as in artifacts from British women's culture. An exemplary piece of this narrative of scarcity is Virginia Woolf's final novel, *Between the Acts*. Although the novel itself is situated in June of 1939, when Europe was on the brink of a war that had not yet manifested, and although Woolf began composing this novel in 1938, she began revising the manuscript's earliest scenes during the summer of 1940, just as the "Phoney War" had come to an end and the German bombs began to fall, making Woolf's pre-war narrative almost a palimpsest as the realities of World War II made their ways into her novel.[11] Woolf's narrative reflects her overwriting of the present day onto the idyllic past: "The future shadowed their present, like the sun coming through the many-veined transparent vine leaf."[12] "For all its 'airy' atmosphere," Sallie Sears points out, "the novel sees this 'future' everywhere implicit in the quality of its present existence."[13] While much of the scholarship that examines *Between the Acts* has addressed the novel in the quite significant contexts of Woolf's pacifism and of the impact of the war on her creativity and even her mental stability, here I turn to a cultural narrative that is woven into the novel, a narrative that increased in significance the everyday lives of those left on a Home Front that came to be defined by lack.

Woolf's novel, while ostensibly a pre-war narrative, is stocked with references to the kinds of goods that were no longer available while Woolf completed the drafting of and subsequently revised the text. The presence in the novel of the very foodstuffs that were in short supply during the early war years are at the very least prescient and are likely no accident, and the everyday realities of wartime rationing policies and practices, evident in Woolf's letters and diary entries of the period, also infuse the narrative of *Between the Acts*. In "Luncheon at 'The Leaning Tower': Class and Consumption in Virginia Woolf's *Between the Acts*," I have discussed Woolf's deployment of food and food imagery in this novel, particularly with regard to her use of food to drive home issues of gender and sexuality for two of her female characters, Isa Oliver and Mrs Manresa.[14] Further assessment, however, specifically in the context of the realities of rationing, illuminates how what might appear to be surface-level ephemera can actually add to our considerations of Woolf's ambivalence about the war and, importantly, also illuminates a narrative ambivalence with regard to female sexual agency. As the narrative posits a longing for pre-war ways of eating, significant of pre-war middle-class existence, it engenders a concurrent nostalgia for other aspects of pre-war life that signify social and cultural stability: namely, the heterosexual marriage union.

When rationing was announced in September of 1939, items initially controlled included "butcher's meat (i.e., beef, mutton, lamb, pork and veal), bacon and ham, butter and margarine, cooking fats … and sugar."[15] Rationing of sugar, bacon and ham, and butter actually began in January of 1940, while meat rationing followed in March. In our present-day world of low-fat recommendations, it might not seem all that bad to limit one's intake of things such as bacon and butter, but these were staples of British diets, and there is no denying that people were affected by the cutbacks. Butter, especially, at ¼ pound per week, was one rationed good that people did not look forward to going without. A woman interviewed by Mass Observation in November of 1939 stated: "I should probably be able to eat the whole of my week's ration of butter in one day"[16]; a man exclaimed: "it's damned silly. Why[,] we use 1 lb. a day!"[17] It comes as no surprise, then, to find Woolf herself exclaiming in a letter over a gift of butter when Vita Sackville-West sent a pound to Monk's House in November of 1940: "Never never Never have we had such a rapturous astounding glorious … I broke off a lump and ate it pure."[18] This kind of delight in something as pedestrian as butter indicates the state of Woolf's own larder, but also her interest in appetite, an interest that many critics have been too quick to dismiss. In her diary entry for December 16, 1940, Woolf is weary, with "so little fat to cook with. And so much shopping to do. And one has to weigh and measure. Then Kingsley comes & devours sugar & butter."[19] For Woolf, as for virtually all of Britain, "making do" was an onerous, though necessary, part of daily life.

In 1941, a Mass Observation poll indicated the foods that were missed most: fruit, butter, eggs, and sugar topped the list.[20] But in June of 1939, when Woolf's narrative is set, food exists in abundance; in fact, Woolf has filled her novel with the very foods that were most scarce and most missed after rationing began. Harriet Blodgett metaphorically reads the dislocated community members in Woolf's novel as "*orts* … morsels left at the end of a feast,"[21] but for the novel's author—and, later, for its readers—morsels are all that remain of the meals known before wartime. Food in this novel is part of the re-creation of an earlier and soon-to-be-lost way of life, and for Woolf's contemporaries, it would also have had a very specific cultural resonance. Alex Zwerdling has pointed out that, in part, the novel "is obviously and deliberately timebound" and "is rooted … in an acute longing for an earlier, more civilized phase of English culture."[22] While I will not attempt to assess here Woolf's own degree of longing or its presence in the novel, what her inclusion of pre-war edibles into her narrative does accomplish is the creation of a narrative of nostalgia: food shortages were such a ubiquitous cultural fact for Britons that the abundance of food in the novel becomes metonymic for a way of life that quickly disappeared after the onset of war.

In the world occupied by the Oliver family, food is plentiful—indeed, sacred. The Pointz Hall larder was originally a chapel, and although in 1939 old Bart takes visitors there to view the architecture, readers in 1941 would at least be as aware of other items therein: "the hams that hung from hooks … the butter on a blue slate … the joint for tomorrow's dinner."[23] The most basic items on what were known as "straight" rations are invested in the novel with a degree of rarity, as they would soon be in real time. Because in 1939, "everyone in the house is sick of beef and mutton" (15), Isa Oliver orders fish for luncheon, but her choice of fish is also indicative of pre-war luxury. When ordering, she asks, "What fish have you this morning? Cod? Halibut? Sole? Plaice?" (18)—her ability to choose from among several fish, rather than take what is on offer and "make do" as wartime housewives would have done, underscores this aspect of pre-war existence. But the fact that all of these types of fish are indigenous to the sea also indicates how changed life will become soon after this one June day. The sea during wartime is full of submarines rather than fish, and the choice that Isa finally makes, sole—actually "Dover sole" in Woolf's Early Typescript[24]—comes from waters that separate Woolf and her British readers from the primary scene of war and that help to mitigate possible Nazi occupation. Because fish was unrationed during wartime, it never disappeared, and indeed, consumption of fish rose among all classes during wartime,[25] but fish was expensive and difficult to come by. According to Ina Zweiniger-Bargielowska, one of the "most persistent grievance[s] concerned ... the uneven distribution of fish and fresh fruit ... Discontent about fish was expressed continuously."[26] The surplus of fish in Woolf's narrative, both literal and metaphoric, is in this cultural context a recurring reminder of pre-war meals.

There is evidence, too, that as she revised her early drafts into the Later Typescript, Woolf made adjustments that reflect ongoing food shortages. When "Eliza Clark, licensed to sell tobacco" takes the stage as Queen Elizabeth, she is described as able to "reach a flitch of bacon or haul a tub of oil with one sweep of her arm in the shop"[27]; however, the Early Typescript instead describes her as dexterous with candles and oranges and, while oranges would have been scarce, oil and bacon were first among rations, and both were sorely missed when Woolf made this textual change.[28] Already in November of 1939, a Mass Observer reported that interviewees "had got tired of asking for [bacon], so now didn't bother,"[29] and the shortage of cooking oil meant that baking was nonexistent for many households during the war years.

The novel contains several references to this lack of baked goods. In addition to the lack of cooking fats, powdered egg replaced the "brown basket full of eggs" so easily reached for in Mrs Sands' kitchen below stairs[30]; without "shell eggs" and cooking fats, cakes became easier to buy than to bake. When Mrs Manresa, during the tea interval, derides the refreshments—"so many bought cakes, so few made at home"—she alludes to a choice that can no longer be made during wartime without compromised results (117). And, well, without sugar, the consumption of which was slashed right from the start of the war, a cake is rather a moot point, and along with fish and fruit and ham and cream and any number of other consumables that populate Woolf's novel, but not the table of its author (nor of its readers), sugar is a central metaphor of *Between the Acts*. In the text, words are "like sweets ... pink, green, and sweetness" (10), and near the novel's end, Lucy dips her fresh raspberry into sugar, doubly decadent in a time when both are hard to come by (212–13).

But sugar in the novel is most evident when it is entering the mouth of the seductive Mrs Manresa, which it does frequently. Her consumption of sugar—at one point of a "shovelful of brown sugar candy" (55)—only adds to her transgressive nature. The policies of rationing and the propaganda machine that was Britain's Ministry of Food together codified a model for consumption that made excessive eating not only unethical, but unpatriotic. Wartime slogans such as "Better Pot-Luck with Churchill today than humble pie under Hitler tomorrow ... Don't waste food!" indicate the important link between what Britons were eating and what might transpire if the Home Front were weakened.[31] Thus Woolf's characterization of Mrs Manresa, who for George Ella Lyon "reeks sex,"[32] is enhanced by the conflation of her questionable morality and the eating habits that would appear to wartime readers as bad for Britain. Woolf even worked on this emphasis between the Early and final typescripts: prior to wartime, Mrs Manresa longs to leave the luncheon party and "curl up ... with a paper and a cigarette," but in the published novel, she dreams of "a cushion, a picture paper, and a bag of sweets."[33] Because, as discussed above, sugar is not meant to be consumed by British women, but instead by British men off fighting the war in Europe, in the novel it stands as a reminder of how to (or not to) properly conform to standards for femininity.

Each time Mrs Manresa is found putting sweets into her mouth, she solidifies the place of gluttony on the list of her sins and thus magnifies the lust that is already a part of her composite, an aspect of her character that Giles notes as he makes his way toward the infamous choking snake in the grass.[34] Woolf uses eating as a trope that increases the undesirable qualities of Mrs Manresa, and her disgust with people like "the Manresa" is echoed in her diary entry of February 26, 1941, when she recalls a "fat, smart woman, in red hunting cap, pearls, check skirt, consuming rich cakes. Her shabby dependent also stuffing ... The fat woman had a louche large white muffin face. T'other was slightly grilled. They ate & ate."[35] But this same diary entry also indicates an ambivalence about wartime consumption that makes its way into the text of *Between the Acts*. In the same diary entry, Woolf admits: "Food becomes an obsession. I grudge giving away a spice bun."[36] While she cannot tolerate gluttony in others (perhaps especially in those who already exhibit a singular vulgarity), neither can she escape the very real fact that food is scarce and that her own appetite must be acknowledged. "How one enjoys food now," she writes in December 1940. "I make up imaginary meals."[37]

Given the connections that historically have been made between women's gustatory and sexual appetites, and given the way in which those two aspects of desire are bound together in the form of Mrs Manresa, it is difficult to avoid the cultural unease that such "food lust" calls up. Woolf's illustrations of overindulgent female consumers are in line with Susan Bordo's assessment that "frequently ... female hunger as sexuality is represented by Western culture in misogynist images permeated with terror and loathing rather than affection or admiration."[38] Woolf's use of this Western tradition in *Between the Acts*, however, stands in contrast to the evocative nostalgia of food in the novel. There is a distinct conflict between the tender recollections of food gone by and the wartime impulse to limit food consumption. Scholars including Phyllis Lassner and Karen Schneider have pointed out Woolf's ambivalence in this novel when it comes to the war, and Gill Plain writes that Woolf "was, in a sense, the last person to believe in the possibility of a consistent, effective strategy" for her novel, "and it is therefore not surprising that she should undermine the one she hoped to create."[39] Conceiving of food as a key to pre-war nostalgia strengthens the case for a fundamental ambivalence in the novel that looks backward even as it must move forward into the violence of world war.

In addition to Woolf's own contradictory impulses, the novel's ending has also been the root of conflicting evaluations by critics: some see in the final silhouette of Isa and Giles a return to primitivism, whether as a positive rejection of the war machine, or as Woolf's fear of annihilation by Nazi Blitzkrieg, a view suggested by Nancy Topping Bazin and Jane Hamovit Lauter. Christine Froula has read the ending as a re-casting of the Genesis myth, and Evelyn Haller imagines the novel's final scene as inclusive of "sex as life-renewal."[40] Woolf's use of rationed goods to make her final point as the family ends their collective day with a dessert of fruit and sugar, however, brings back to the narrative the conflicts found in previous passages that explore the issues surrounding food consumption. The penultimate scene exhibits how while Isa on one level rejects her feminine role and, to some degree, her husband, she also rejects alternative forms of female desire that are on offer in the text. Isa finally says no to the wanton sexuality of Mrs Manresa, although she has lusted in her heart after gentleman farmer Rupert Haines all afternoon; she also seems in no way inclined to follow the path of the lesbian Miss LaTrobe. Instead, the final scene is one that relies upon a heteronormativity that falls short of what might be expected from such an otherwise unconventional narrative.

Turning to the Early and Later typescripts, as well as to the final, published version, one can see what Hana Wirth-Nesher notes as "an increased emphasis on both a movement toward collective origins and a denial of origin."[41] The narrative's reification of heterosexual marriage seemingly affirms the status quo and the "natural" order of regeneration, but the narrative's varied reactions to the confines of history and to masculine social orders call such a reading into question. Even as Isa becomes a part of this old, old story, she stands up to her husband, fighting like a "vixen, in the heart of darkness," recalling Conrad's "savage and superb" African woman who emerges from the jungle dressed for combat.[42] Just prior to the final tableau, however, while the family is assembled at the dinner table, there is the fact of Giles' banana to be considered. By asking readers to revisit the nostalgic aspects of food as she prepares to close her novel, Woolf reasserts the qualities associated with food and consumption earlier in the novel. In the published text, when Giles offers his wife a banana, "she refused it."[43] Interestingly, in the Early typescript, when offered the same banana, "Isa took it," and in the Later typescript, she "took it; but laid it down."[44] Woolf also deleted another sentence from the Later typescript that indicates Isa's full rejection of the banana, a sentiment that she would ultimately restore to the final manuscript (435). This deletion follows Isa's "Yes, yes, yes … No, no, no" deliberation,[45] which is a critical moment leading up to her final choice to join with her husband, even as she admits to hating him on some level.

While the phallic possibilities of Giles' banana are obvious, and while they perhaps should not be completely ignored, the historical context of wartime rationing should also remind readers of the banana's other capacities. By the end of 1940, the importation of bananas had been abolished by the British government,[46] making this particular fruit a distinct symbol of what was lost, what was, at least in the present time of the novel's creation, relegated to a former way of life. Isa's rejection of her husband's banana can be read as a rejection of the strictures of interwar life and all that it encompassed, including its prescriptions for femininity. Given the strong rhetoric of the time period, though, rhetoric that encouraged female self-denial for the good of the nation, what Isa may actually be rejecting is a food that has been banned from Britain, something that she is not meant to desire if her heart and her sense of national duty are in the right places. By rejecting the transgression of actually eating the banana, Isa is rejecting the sexual alterity of Mrs Manresa, leaving the fruit untouched just as she leaves Rupert Haines, always cast in shades of gray, untouched. Haines is a catalyst for Isa's sexual desire in a way that her husband is not: "the presence of his body in the room last night could so affect her … the words he said … could so attach themselves to a certain spot in her; and thus lie between them like a wire, tingling, tangling, vibrating."[47] Instead of asking, along with Mrs Manresa, "why waste a single drop that can be pressed out of this ripe, this melting, this adorable world?" (56), Isa remains at the end of the novel a vascillator who plays the part of the ür-woman even as she has spent a full day resisting its limitations. By adhering to feminine propriety, Isa accepts the discourse of wartime England, ultimately choosing to support its struggle as she rejects a taste of its past.

The assertive qualities that are embodied by Mrs Manresa, who is depicted as excessive, especially during wartime scarcity and in opposition to the self-denying Isa, illustrate the associations between female appetite and female agency. Mrs Manresa is not merely a sexual aggressor who follows another woman's husband into the conservatory while no one is watching. She is a woman whose very nature pushes her beyond the traditional mode of feminine behavior altogether, and Woolf's use of food consumption as a way to emphasize this nature is furthered by the context of scarcity from which her original readers would have understood the novel. Readers going without would recognize Mrs Manresa's appetite not as profligate, but as a natural result of human desire. Even if readers might be able to castigate her for gluttony, their ability to desire vicariously through her would allow for her appetite to emerge as complex, as both suspect and envied. Her announcement to all present at luncheon that when in the country, she removes her stays and rolls in the grass (42) indicates that she allows herself (at least when in the country, underscoring the performative quality of feminine garments) to shed the constructs, the confines, of feminine culture. Her behavior is not typically masculine, but by virtue of having eschewed a feminine code, she becomes masculinized. This gendering follows Dimen's understanding of human impulse to divide want from need: Mrs Manresa is a desiring subject who *wants* and who moves herself toward what William B. Irvine discusses as "terminal desires" that are fulfilled for the sake of pleasure or other specific outcome.[48] Likewise, Mrs Manresa "absolutely refuses" old Bart Oliver when he offers her a chair, and "she pressed him down again."[49] Her actions are direct and circumvent the possibility of accepting, along with a kindly gesture, a gendered obligation. Her potentially physical interaction with Bart (physically pressing him back into his chair) also suggests how her masculinization manifests on the same physical plane where other aspects of the physical body exist: hunger, sexual expression. Dimen explains that "*feeling need* is not the same as *being needy*,"[50] and Mrs Manresa expresses want that is aware of its roots in a brand of need that is not feminized, but that is the unconscious "other half" of her conscious wanting. "When gratification is foreseeable," Dimen writes, "longing, and therefore need, is as welcome as the hunger that rises with the smell of dinner cooking on the stove, as reassuringly exciting as sexual desire for a tried-and-true lover."[51] Mrs Manresa is a comfortable composite, an example of androgynous desire because she is not (yet) forced to encounter the scarcity that would push her into neediness.

This kind of explicit desire—wanting, defining, and pursuing a specific, terminal need—is evident in many interviews performed by Mass Observation during the early hours of World War II. The idea of rationing that was to come only encouraged British women to assert their wills to consume in a way that would have made Woolf's Manresa proud. The theme in many of these interviews is "get what you want," and while later shortages would thwart even some of the most consciously projected desires for food, the attitude that many women discovered within them defied those social and political rhetorics of sacrifice for the good of men, of nation. In October of 1939, a 25-year-old woman remarked: "I've taken to using sugar in my tea lately. I didn't used to, but I thought I might as well get what I can. While I can." "They can fine you for hoarding," her contemporary, 22, concurred, "but they can't fine you for hoarding inside your inside. I've eaten more in the last week than ever before in a month." A Mass Observer reported: "The general attitude appears to be that the housewife will get what she can, where she can, when she can." The instincts of these women led them to approach their desires head-on rather than to follow that path more expected of women. "My

Mother has given up bacon for herself," another woman explained, "so as to be sure that my father shall not go without"; this more stereotypical response to lack was prevalent, but it was hardly the only way to deal with wartime shortages.[52] The diary entries that Woolf penned, as well as these replies to Mass Observation inquiries, exhibit the very real ways in which scarcity can clear the way for a particular brand of female agency. Denial is often the product of plenty; one has to have in order to deny. From within the midst of rationing practices, denial was a luxury that few could afford. Instead, food became a site from which women learned to negotiate desire in ways that they might have overlooked in less lean times.

As the war drew on, most Britons grew somewhat accustomed to the shortages, but the juxtaposition of scarcity's stringent feminine ideal against the increasing autonomy of the nation's women meant that any complacency with regard to gender roles was much less attainable. Increased concerns over women's activities, including their sexual activities, added to gendered wartime rhetoric, and this further scrutiny of women in the public sector lay at odds with the idea of the freedom women seemed to have gained during the war years. The issues that arose from the nexus of female consumption and desire became intertwined with multiple social discourses about women and their acceptable places in wartime culture. First published in 1945 and spanning the years from 1939 until about 1944, Noel Streatfeild's *Saplings* brings together the threads of a larger wartime examination of female desire. This little-known novel continues the themes begun in earlier works such as Woolf's and builds upon those themes to include issues that arose from concerns that emerged as the war crisis accelerated. Streatfeild is recognized more as a writer of children's books than of literature for an adult audience, but this novel rests upon real adult themes that affect adults and children alike. As Jeremy Holmes notes in his afterward to Persephone Books' reissue of the novel, Streatfeild "takes a happy, successful, middle-class pre-war English family ... and then tracks in miserable detail the disintegration which war brought to tens of thousands of such families."[53] Written during the centerpiece years of wartime destruction, the novel chronicles the decline of one family largely as it is written upon the person of its mother, Lena Wiltshire. Lena is a beautiful, frivolous, and passionate woman whose maternal side is always lacking, but pre-war affluence allows her to purchase what she lacks in this way—nannies, governesses—and pre-war gender norms allow for her position as wife to provide her with a stable identity. Once the war shifts the foundation of her pre-war existence, however—her family is separated and relocated, her husband succumbs to the Blitz—the social and familial orders that once reined in Lena's "true" desiring self are destroyed, and her transgressive nature is all that is left. Of course, that nature cannot survive in a wartime ethos so intolerant of female excess.

When the novel opens in the same summer of 1939 in which Woolf's novel is set, the Wiltshire family forms an exceptionally English family unit. Lena and her husband, Alex, are raising four children in their London home, and together this group is the picture of an interwar middle-class ideal, the very ideal that many imagined Britain was fighting for against the Axis powers. The internal make-up of the family unit, however, is imbalanced: Lena's maternal instincts are sorely lacking. For Lena, her children are "charming decorations, not interfering with the original portrait of two people"[54]; children fill out the portrait, but she will not allow them to get in the way of her direct and deeply sexual connection to her husband. "The children were darlings," but Lena "was not a family woman, she was utterly wife, and, if it came to that, a mistress too ..." (17). She is described as "all impulses" (20) and as direct: "she stated what she wanted, and then she withdrew" (21); like Mrs Manresa, Lena's nature is assertive, masculinized. The frankness with which Lena's passionate nature is expressed is a direct contrast to the image of the perfect English family, which would trigger in popular imaginations an image of quite a different mother figure from Lena. In a reversal of traditionally gendered sexuality, Lena is the aggressor, and she works hard against the fact that her husband's passion for her has cooled as fatherhood has shifted his efforts toward family and children, away from her.

Like Woolf, Streatfeild capitalizes on the ways in which food can signify gender, but unlike the wanton sensuality that appetite emphasizes in Mrs Manresa, Lena's frivolity and her surface-level maternal identity are underscored by the ways in which food becomes associated with her character. Although Streatfeild's narrative is not as redolent with edible goods as is Woolf's, in *Saplings*, food is mentioned strategically, especially in the pre-war chapters that help to construct what the war will dismantle as the novel progresses. The food that signifies Lena's mothering recalls a level of affluence that the war and its effects (and later, austerity and the welfare state) have rendered anachronistic by the time Streatfeild's readers would have picked up her book. Hotel meals, with the family circling the table and the children in matching blue suits, involve strawberry ice cream. The seaside holiday, a last idyll before the effects of war commence, includes fresh prawns eaten on the sand because Lena "saw a picnic fire in her mind's eye ... if a saucepan had to be borrowed she was the one to do it, charm got that kind of thing. She saw herself standing on a cottage doorstep" (39–40). Lena planned trips to Fortnum and Mason (known for its prepackaged delicacies), where she chose things to send away to school with her eldest son. Lena performs maternal nurturing through charming gestures rather than through the kind of attention to health and nutrition for which wartime mothers were held accountable. While Streatfeild's readers would have been inundated with informative radio talks showcasing the vitamin content of vegetables and the availability of no-cost cod liver oil for children, Lena prepares for war by purchasing "three months' supply" of goods that include a box of Elva plums for the children (60). As in Woolf's novel, the food here helps to create a sense of pre-war lifestyles, but in this case, the emphasis is on fanciful, extravagant desires rather than on mere excess. Lena is created, in part, from this affiliation with impractical, ephemeral consumable goods, the kinds of food that are enjoyable in the moment, but that do not provide true sustenance. Lena's anti-maternal qualities come to the forefront through her disparate appetites.

As long as Lena can exist within the confines of her marriage to Alex and of her duties—however skewed—as a mother, Lena's passionate nature can be held in check. If her libido appears to be active beyond a typically acceptable, "feminine" level, then it is nonetheless justified within the parameters of the marriage union because her desire has an object, is terminal in its pursuits. But with war as its backdrop, the narrative cannot guarantee this safety to Lena and her predilections. Alex is taken from his family early in the blitzing of London, and at this point, Lena loses the stability that keeps her desires in check. Without a terminus, her desires eventually become diffuse and even more hedonistic than they appear to be when she is able to focus them upon an appropriate target. Widowed, Lena takes up drinking and a clandestine love affair almost simultaneously, and her taste for neither is readily held in check. Upon her first meeting with Walter, an American in England for the war effort, they "drank a great deal of whiskey," and her "eyes ran over him. Her thoughts made shivers run up and down her spine. Her cheeks burned" (204). Lena is depicted as a cavern of desire: she is seemingly unable to adhere to any of the mandates for feminine behavior, instead succumbing to her "nature" at the first opportunity. Although Walter is up for the challenge, he also thinks how there "was something lewd in a mother pushing her children off to bed so that she might be made love to on the drawing-room sofa" (213). The double-standard here indicates how far Lena's impulses carry her. She is beyond the masculinity embodied by Walter; by contrast, her sexuality is almost grotesque.

Lena's behavior exemplifies an age-old conflation of women's appetites that emerged during World War II in the form of multiple governmental discourses that, while meant to help women deal with some of the more problematic aspects of wartime living, ultimately codified female behavior and reinforced misogynist understandings of female sexuality. While the Ministry of Food was carefully leading Britain's women to defend the Kitchen Front at the expense of their own appetites, another crisis created a need for additional prescriptions to be handed down to women, this time from the Ministry of Health. Venereal disease (primarily gonorrhea and syphilis) became a domestic issue that threatened to demand more attention than did ongoing food shortages—plus, it was much more difficult to talk about, to broadcast information about, and so it created much concern while the trouble lasted. Memoranda from the Ministry of Health indicate that in 1941, diagnoses of sexually transmitted diseases were up 70 percent from pre-war data, and by 1943, occurrences had risen 139 percent from 1939 statistics.[55] In a throwback to Victorian-era Contagious Disease Acts, many Britons were accepting of the notion that "certain women should be examined periodically."[56] The sexual expression of now-public women at work in the auxiliary military and in factories became suspect, and a new campaign was waged to stop the spread of disease. In the minds of most, the problem stemmed from several other sources—women, foreigners, soldiers—but great pains were taken to reach women through BBC broadcasts, as well as through newspaper and magazine advertisements.

Much of the discourse that surrounded this issue linked together distinct parts of a "problem": newly autonomous women, alcoholic beverages, and unsuspecting men (often Americans or soldiers from other allied forces). This vision persisted even at ministerial levels and fuelled the production of new discourse that drew even tighter the boundaries for gendered desire and behavior. In a letter from Wilson Jameson of the Ministry of Health to Sir Richard Maconachie of the BBC, Jameson states: "venereal diseases are being spread in the neighborhood of camps and ports more by young girls who throw themselves at any man in uniform willing to buy them a couple of drinks … than by any other single class in the community."[57] (Fortunately, an internal memo from Janet Quigley, a talks producer, helped to balance this view: "… I think we should avoid seeming to put too much of the responsibility on the young girls."[58]) Not that it was new to decry the deterioration of female chastity and sobriety, but this very public conversation brought these issues to the forefront of wartime culture, and new forms of public education were created that paralleled the rhetorics of female appetite that were brought about by food rationing. Consumption of alcohol joined the nexus of female appetite and desire during the latter half of the war years.

Into this discourse comes a fictional character such as Lena Wiltshire, to whom readers would undoubtedly have brought a certain amount of this ongoing conversation about female sexual desire. Although the war, the bombing, is what literally dismantles this family when its home and its patriarch are destroyed, cultural sentiments allow for the onus of accountability to shift instead to Lena's improper appetites for men and for alcohol. "There's a certain type," one middle-aged woman told a Mass Observer for the "Women in Pubs" report, "who just go in to pick up men. Get what they can sort of thing … They're the ones who go after Canadians and Americans and spread disease."[59] Cultural anxieties about sexually transmitted diseases—ultimately, about newfound female empowerment—are embodied in Streatfeild's Lena. She should be cast as a tragic figure, a victim of wartime tragedy; nearly any other woman in her position would be portrayed in that way. Lena's tastes, however, along with her already problematic position on the gender spectrum, disallow her that privilege.

From within her own particular cultural and historical context, Lena signifies the changes wrought by war upon those left at home, particularly upon women; she also represents the collective interest in a return to the known quantity of traditional female desire tucked safely away within the folds of matrimony. Nancy Huse writes of Lena that "her eroticism devalues sacrifice and transcendence, implicit to the mystique of war."[60] The instability found in Lena's characterization is created from the same cultural anxiety that fuelled an interest in women's return to the domestic sphere after the war was over.

Lena's intemperance and inability to maintain a widowed chastity result in a threat by Alex's family to remove her children—the last remnants of her respectability—from her care. While the narrative seems to demand that readers acknowledge the manifold ways in which war wreaks havoc on all whom it touches, including women and children, this threat stands as a significant indictment of Lena's "nature," of an innate sexuality that was still feared, as evident in the discourse that surrounded the mid-war venereal disease question. It is difficult to speculate whether Streatfeild herself is passing judgment, or whether she is merely harnessing a point of view that many would have recognized in order to illustrate the fall of the representative Wiltshire clan, but in any case, Lena's fate is sealed when the boundaries drawn by the social order close around her. Rather than capitalize upon the dual gifts of her own assertive qualities and the cultural moment that offered women more latitude than they had seen prior to wartime, Lena receives the message clearly that in order to survive, she must conform. She turns from the tempestuous affair with her American and decides to remarry, and chooses a man who sees her as "so lonely, so pathetic, needing a strong man to look after her, to spoil her, to order her about."[61] The narrative mirrors social responses to women's increased autonomy during wartime and to a very public version of female sexuality that was reined in as soon as the need for women's public participation lessened and post-war homemaking replaced wartime service as a woman's national duty.

Lena is among the first wave of British women to be cajoled back into normative gender relationships and domestic roles in a post-war landscape that promoted heavily the opportunities that lay in "the supremacy of [women's] biological role to bear children, their emotional role as caretakers and nurturers, and their spiritual role to act as the upholders of moral values."[62] The ending of this novel, as with the final pages of Woolf's last fiction, is unsettling: it neither makes attractive the resolution that Lena reaches, nor does it pronounce her fate to be anything but inevitable. At the end of the war years, as in their beginning, female appetites simultaneously fascinate and provoke those who consider their origins. In both Woolf's novel and Streatfeild's exist strong impulses to move forward into the revolutionary territory of female agency; however, both narratives also contain almost reflexive responses to the appetites of the women within. Perhaps the uncertainty of war created unconscious desires for codes that could be counted on as formerly level terrain began to shift. Although the kind of social and sexual power suggested in these two novels did not die on VE Day—feminist historians have been careful to document the ongoing changes in post-war British women's lives—the discomfort created by these new modes of femininity explains, in part, the slow pace of change in the post-war epoch.

Notes

1. Mass Observation Archive, Topic Collection 67/2/C (Cafés 1940), University of Sussex. All future references will refer to the Archive as MOA. All quotations are reproduced with the permission of Curtis Brown Group Ltd., London on behalf of the Trustees of the Mass Observation Archive Copyright © The Trustees of the Mass Observation Archive.
2. James Devon, *Let's Eat!* (London: War Facts Press, 1944), 4, 12.
3. Muriel Dimen, *Sexuality Intimacy Power* (Hillsdale, NJ: The Analytic Press, 2003), 212.
4. Nicola Humble, *Culinary Pleasures: Cookbooks and the Transformation of British Food* (London: Faber and Faber, 2005), 83.
5. Julia Kristeva, *Powers of Horror: An Essay on Abjection*, trans. Leon S. Roudiez (New York: Columbia University Press, 1982), 75.
6. Reina Green, "Open Ears, Appetite, and Adultery in *A Woman Killed with Kindness*," *English Studies in Canada* 31, no. 4 (December 2005): 56. Green quotes a translation by William Lowth of Barthélmy Batt's *The Christian Mans Closet*.
7. Irvine takes for granted this fact of humanity in his survey of desire. William B. Irvine, *On Desire* (Oxford: Oxford University Press, 2005), 104, 285.
8. Lord Woolton, "The Minister of Food Talks to Housewives" (radio transcript, Monday, April 8, 1940), BBC Written Archives Centre, microfilm T664.
9. *Woman's Own*, September 14, 1940: 24.
10. MOA, Topic Collection 67/6/A (Food Questionnaire 18.2.46), University of Sussex.
11. Virginia Woolf, *Pointz Hall: The Earlier and Later Typescripts of* Between the Acts, ed. Mitchell Leaska (New York: University Publications, 1983), 29. Leaska's extensive work with the extant typescripts of Woolf's novel allow for careful, if sometimes still speculative, dating of her writing and revision.
12. Virginia Woolf, *Between the Acts* [1941] (New York: Harcourt Brace Jovanovich, 1985), 114. All future references will identify the text as *BA*.
13. Sallie Sears, "Theater of War: Virginia Woolf's *Between the Acts*," in *Virginia Woolf: A Feminist Slant*, ed. Jane Marcus (Lincoln: University of Nebraska Press, 1983), 215.
14. Andrea Adolph, "Luncheon at 'The Leaning Tower': Class and Consumption in Virginia Woolf's *Between the Acts*," *Women's Studies: An Interdisciplinary Journal* 34, no. 6 (2005): 439–59.
15. Ministry of Food (Great Britain), *Food Control (National Rationing); Instructions to Food Control Committees; Part I; October 1939*.
16. MOA, Topic Collection 67/1/E (Food Shortages), University of Sussex.
17. MOA, Topic Collection 67/1/B (Introduction of Rationing, 1939–40), University of Sussex.
18. Virginia Woolf, Letter to Vita Sackville-West (Letter 3662), in *The Letters of Virginia Woolf, Volume Six, 1936–1941*, eds. Nigel Nicholson and Joanne Trautmann (New York: Harcourt Brace Jovanovich, 1980), 447–8. The third of the underlined "never"s, as well as the underlined word "glorious," are both underlined a third time in the original.
19. Virginia Woolf, *The Diary of Virginia Woolf, Volume Five, 1936–1941*, ed. Anne Olivier Bell (New York: Harcourt Brace Jovanovich, 1984), 343. All future references will refer to this as *Diary*.

20. MOA, Topic Collection 67/2/C (Cafés 1940), University of Sussex.

21. Harriet Blodgett, "Food for Thought in Virginia Woolf's Novels," *Woolf Studies Annual* 3 (1997): 57.

22. Alex Zwerdling, "*Between the Acts* and the Coming of War," *NOVEL: A Forum on Fiction* 10, no. 3 (Spring 1977): 221, 225.

23. Woolf, *BA*, 32.

24. Woolf, *Pointz Hall*, 47. Leaska calls the two extant versions of the novel the Early and Later typescripts. I retain his capitalization in my discussions.

25. Ina Zweiniger-Bargielowska, *Austerity in Britain: Rationing, Controls, and Consumption 1939–1955* (Oxford: Oxford University Press, 2000), 40–41.

26. Ibid., 77.

27. Woolf, *BA*, 83.

28. Woolf, *Pointz Hall*, 99.

29. MOA, Topic Collection 67/1/E (Food Shortages), University of Sussex.

30. Woolf, *BA*, 33.

31. This and other wartime propaganda posters are on exhibit at the Imperial War Museum, London.

32. George Ella Lyon, "Virginia Woolf and the Problem of the Body," in *Virginia Woolf: Centennial Essays*, eds. Elaine K. Ginsberg and Laura Moss Gottleib (Troy, NY: Whitson, 1983), 121.

33. Woolf, *Pointz Hall*, 85; *BA*, 66.

34. Woolf, *BA*, 99.

35. Woolf, *Diary*, 357.

36. Ibid., 357.

37. Ibid., 347.

38. Susan Bordo, *Unbearable Weight: Feminism, Western Culture, and the Body* (Berkeley: University of California Press, 1993), 117.

39. Gill Plain, *Women's Fiction of the Second World War: Gender, Power and Resistance* (New York: St Martin's, 1996), 134. See also Phyllis Lassner, *British Women Writers of World War II: Battlegrounds of Their Own* (New York: St Martin's, 1998); and Karen Schneider, *Loving Arms: British Women Writing the Second World War* (Lexington: University Press of Kentucky, 1997).

40. Nancy Topping Bazin and Jane Hamovit Lauter, "Virginia Woolf's Keen Sensitivity to War: Its Roots and Its Impact on Her Novels," in *Virginia Woolf and War*, ed. Mark Hussey (Syracuse: Syracuse University Press, 1991), 39; Christine Froula, "Rewriting Genesis: Gender and Culture in Twentieth-Century Texts," *Tulsa Studies in Women's Literature* 7, no. 2 (Autumn 1998): 197–220; Evelyn Haller, "The Anti-Madonna in the Work and Thought of Virginia Woolf," in Ginsberg and Moss, eds., *Virginia Woolf: Centennial Essays*, 104.

41. Hana Wirth-Nesher, "Final Curtain on the War: Figure and Ground in Virginia Woolf's *Between the Acts*," *Style* 28, no. 2 (Summer 1994): 183–200, Academic Search Complete, accessed November 23 2007, par. 42.

42. Woolf, *BA*, 219; Joseph Conrad, *Heart of Darkness* (Harmondsworth: Penguin, 1988), 101.

43. Woolf, *BA*, 213.

44. Woolf, *Pointz Hall*, 177, 178, 434.

45. Woolf, *BA*, 215.

46. Sir Thomas G. Jones, *The Unbroken Front, Ministry of Food, 1916–1944: Personalities and Problems* (London: Everybody's Books, 1944), 153–4.

47. Woolf, *BA*, 14–15.

48. Irvine, *On Desire*, 56.

49. Woolf, *BA*, 108–9.

50. Dimen, *Sexuality Intimacy Power*, 213.

51. Ibid., 213.

52. MOA, Topic Collection 67/1/E (Food Shortages), University of Sussex. All of these interviews are from the same topic collection file.

53. Jeremy Holmes, Afterword to *Saplings*, by Noel Streatfeild (London: Persephone Books, 2000), 364.

54. Noel Streatfeild, *Saplings* (London: Persephone Books, 2000), 14.

55. Great Britain, Ministry of Health, "Campaign Memorandum of V.D. Propaganda for the Ministry of Health," January 25, 1943; April 3, 1944; BBC Written Archives Centre, File R51/225/1 (Venereal Disease 1A 1942–43).

56. MOA Topic Collection 12/1/B (First V.D. Survey, November–December 1942), University of Sussex.

57. Wilson Jameson, letter to Sir Richard Maconachie (February 5, 1944), BBC Written Archives Centre, File R51/225/2 (Venereal Disease 1B 1944–45). Crown copyright material is reproduced with the permission of the Controller of HMSO and the Queen's Printer for Scotland.

58. Janet Quigley, memo to A.C. (February 16, 1944), BBC Written Archives Centre, File R51/225/2 (Venereal Disease 1B 1944–45). Reproduced with permission of the BBC and their Written Archives Centre.

59. MOA File Report 1611 (Women in Pubs), University of Sussex.

60. Nancy Huse, *Noel Streatfeild* (New York: Twayne Publishers, 1994), 66–7.

61. Streatfeild, *Saplings*, 333.

62. Naimh Baker, *Happily Ever After? Women's Fiction in Postwar Britain 1945–60* (New York: St Martin's, 1989), 17. In this passage Baker discusses a 1954 treatise, *The Natural Superiority of Women*, by Ashley Montagu.

Home and Consumption

4

A Touch of Distinction: Furnishing French Aristocratic Homes in the Nineteenth and Twentieth Centuries

Elizabeth C. Macknight

It is our noticing them that puts things in a room, our growing used to them that takes them away again and clears a space for us.[1]

Proust's Narrator took pleasure in noticing things in a room. Invited to dine at the home of the aristocratic Guermantes family, he becomes absorbed in looking at paintings by Elstir and loses track of time.[2] Like a curious visitor, this essay sets out to observe the ways in which French aristocrats furnished and decorated their homes in the nineteenth and twentieth centuries. Châteaux and *hôtels particuliers* varied in architectural design and there was change as well as continuity in the arrangement and use of rooms. Some of these properties were transformed by the installation of electric lighting and plumbing at the turn of the century; others retained a more stable internal appearance dating back hundreds of years. The focus is on noble women's engagement with the task of interior decorating, a task they normally carried out in consultation with their husband, in discussion with artists under commission, and with the help of hired workmen. Personal preferences played a role in decision making, but noble women had to balance these with family expectations regarding the display of inherited items to create a distinctive space.

Class, Space, and Habitus

Proust knew the value of time spent in a room surrounded by familiar things. The process of "growing used to them that takes them away again and clears a space for us" may be understood in Bourdieu's terms as the conditioning that produces a person's "habitus." Bourdieu's work on "distinction" underlines the ways in which the production of living spaces and the production of bodily practices are interrelated and informed by class.[3] A person's "taste" says much about his or her place in society, for choices in furniture and decoration, like choices in food and clothing, indicate not only a level of income but also the enjoyment of or aspiration to a particular lifestyle.

In nineteenth-century France people were intrigued by the notion of "distinction." When a female admirer asked the Comte Robert de Montesquiou: "'Master, what is distinction?' he replied: 'The first thing is never to think of it.'"[4] Distinction, it seemed, was something one had to be "in the know" about and that required being born into the aristocracy. Distinction may be understood as the type of code Georg Simmel described in "The Secret and the Secret Society": that is, "a secret doctrine, some theoretical, mystical, or religious knowledge." Members of a "secret society" believe "certain insights must not penetrate into the masses; those who know form a community in order to guarantee mutual secrecy to one another."[5] Curiosity about distinction and the possibility of achieving it were fuelled by social fluidity at the top rungs of French society. Despite the creation of imperial titles under Napoleon I, and the intermarriage of wealthy commoners and aristocrats that expanded the post-revolutionary social elite, the middle class continued to revere the aristocratic way of life and to judge what was "bourgeois" as inferior. Theodore Zeldin observed: "Noble exclusiveness was a matter of show. It strongly resembled the *distinction* the bourgeoisie cultivated. And the bourgeoisie adopted many of the ideals associated with the aristocracy."[6]

The essence of distinction, which is embodied in Proust's aristocratic characters, resided in a person's physical behavior and demeanor: that is, ways of speaking, moving, acting, and interacting that evinced a whole set of attitudes and beliefs about the social world. "Blue-blooded" nobles resisted the ascension of *haut bourgeois* into their ranks by promoting themselves guardians of these "ideal" bodily practices and attitudes. Through impenetrable codes of etiquette they exerted, in Elias' terms, "reciprocal supervision" of behavior in order to retain the "important instruments of their dominance," the "marks of distinction and prestige."[7] Elegant living spaces were key to this strategy for distinction, producing an atmosphere so refined and so familiar that, to borrow Montesquiou's phrase, one had "never to think of it." The popular success of etiquette, hygiene, and home decorating manuals published under noble pseudonyms at the turn of the century shows how the notion of distinction, as something contained in the "ideal" bodily practices and attitudes of the aristocracy, exerted its grip on the imagination of the middle class. For the authors of such works, a noble pseudonym was a lucrative marketing tool.

Like bodily practices, the production of living spaces was informed by gender as well as by class.[8] Leora Auslander argues that in the era of absolutist monarchy in France, *style* in French furnishing was an "affair of state," but after the 1789 Revolution *taste* became "an affair of elite women."[9] The nineteenth century saw the emergence of taste professionals, mostly men, who gave advice to bourgeois wives on the manner in which they should adorn themselves, as well as the goods they should purchase and arrange within the home to represent the family's social position. Bourgeoises were producers as well as consumers whose social, business, and domestic activities bridged the private sphere of the home and the public sphere of the marketplace.[10]

Noble women also fulfilled the roles of producer and consumer by participating in the rituals of high society. Dressed in luxurious toilettes, they engaged in a broad array of activities designed to reproduce social networks and enhance family status. Noble women hosted dinners, garden parties, salons, soirées, and balls. They attended concerts, theater, opera, and exhibitions. They chaired fundraising committees for the arts and charities, and they invited guests to their country estates and seaside villas. The homes of the nobility were designed less for privacy and intimacy than they were for entertaining on a grand scale. Châteaux and *hôtels particuliers* were spacious dwellings with multiple salons and personal apartments for each spouse. Noble families hired up to 30 servants to tidy, light fires, cook, carry, scrub, polish, and prepare.

If the creation of a beautiful home was important to all elite women in post-revolutionary France, why study noble women separately? Some historians argue that the early decades of the French Third Republic (1870–1940) witnessed the triumph of the bourgeoisie and that the increased social, political, and economic power of this class was evident culturally, for instance, in what Auslander calls a "bourgeois stylistic regime" in furnishing.[11] Under the Ancien Régime, new styles had been identified with successive kings and some items were so expensive as to be available only to the court aristocracy. From the 1880s to World War I, however, the bourgeoisie drove consumer demand in France for "historicist pastiche" furniture. Through home furnishing, according to Auslander, the bourgeoisie signaled that it was "the dominant social group behind and within the [republican] regime."[12]

This essay will argue that, although the aristocracy lost much of its political influence in France by 1914, it maintained its social and cultural authority by setting the benchmark of "distinction." Since the production of living spaces was tied to bodily practices, the aristocracy was understood to have "naturally" superior taste in home furnishing and decoration that the wealthy bourgeoisie could emulate but never quite attain; distinction remained more than a sum of material possessions. Nobles were also disposed to hold certain attitudes toward home furnishing and decoration, particularly in regard to inherited items, that for historical reasons were different from the attitudes of the bourgeoisie. To investigate those attitudes, and the practices that stemmed from them, a historian cannot rely on prescriptive manuals written for a bourgeois readership; my approach is to draw on the private archives of noble families as well as on published memoirs, paintings, and photographs.

The essay is divided into three sections: the first explains the significance of rural and urban property ownership to nobles and the link between family possessions and noble identity; the second looks at the social spaces of an aristocratic home where guests were entertained; and the third looks at the personal apartment of a noble woman where she slept and performed the daily rituals that served to restore and prepare her for sociability.

Living "Nobly"

Land was the primary investment from which all nineteenth-century nobles drew status. For relatively poor nobles this amounted to one estate with a large residence that was not impressive enough to call a château, so known as a *maison de maître, gentilhommière,* or, in the south-west, a *castel.* Rich nobles, however, owned several estates including at least one with a château. Rural property ownership was of symbolic importance for the nobility, for it signified their original separateness from the bourgeoisie or town dwellers. In addition to rural property, however, most nobles owned or rented an urban residence, in a provincial town or in Paris, and chose to live part of the year on their country estate and part of the year in an apartment or *hôtel particulier.* They spent winter and spring, the social "Season," in town, and summer and autumn in the country. Parisian nobles, those who lived part of the year in the capital, faced higher expenses for food and leisure than nobles in the provinces, and the resources to own or pay rent on property in Paris set the Parisian nobility apart from most provincial nobility.

David Higgs has argued that, during the nineteenth century, a powerful ideology of family developed among the French nobility. "Above all," he argues, nobles "inculcated in their progeny the importance of visualising their world as a network of families rather than of individuals. Egalitarianism and individual accomplishment could never outweigh a society based on distinguished families that preserved the values of the past."[13] For the aristocracy one way to preserve the values of the past was to live surrounded by tangible reminders of the privileged social position it had long enjoyed. To occupy the same property, and make use of the same objects as their ancestors, helped nobles to create a sense of family unity. Boni de Castellane, born in 1867, wrote of his ancestral home, the Château de Rochecotte in the Loire Valley: "Each generation served there as a link in the chain of the line. In the styles of furniture one saw what united them all, one to another."[14]

Inherited items featured in rural and urban residences and were a source of pride to aristocrats. This was especially true of family portraits that were generally commissioned from leading artists, making them valuable works of art in monetary terms, not to mention the additional sense of attachment they commanded in relatives. The Abbé Mugnier of the Parisian parish of

Sainte-Clotilde took the opportunity, on a visit to the Prince de Chalais' home, to view and discuss the family portraits. Madame Julia Daudet, wife of the writer Alphonse Daudet, had no choice but to admire the Comte Robert de Montesquiou's array of ancestral likenesses; he made a point of showing them off to visitors.[15] Nobles also preserved in the home papers and artifacts testifying to their family's aristocratic status. René de La Croix de Castries, born in 1908, wrote a book *Papiers de famille* to accompany an index of 1,720 dossiers conserved at the Château de Castries.[16] François-Charles d'Harcourt recalled that in 1944, when a fire broke out in the family château, hundreds of linen items embroidered with the Harcourt coat of arms were destroyed, but a servant managed to save "a small case containing an admirable Saxon fountain" as well as "the large gold medal that the pope gave my great-grandfather, the French ambassador to Rome, to thank him for the help he had given him in 1849."[17]

The preservation of family patrimony had aesthetic and financial implications. Adeline Daumard has shown through her research into death inventories that bourgeois home furnishing was characterized by homogeneity, and that in the late nineteenth century bourgeois couples did not live surrounded by their parents' furniture but rather purchased their own.[18] By contrast, aristocratic couples felt compelled to live with the belongings of previous generations in addition to items they bought themselves. This produced greater eclecticism in the furnishing of an aristocratic home. For example, in 1879 the Baron and Baronne Picot d'Aligny inherited family portraits, paintings, and furniture from the Baronne's rich uncle Gluflet who had been a collector. These came to the couple's château, Montmirey-la-Ville in Franche-Comté, and over the years new purchases and gifts were added including tapestries in the style of Louis XV, Arab curios sent from Algeria by their cousin Hubert Lyautey, and a Louis XVI iron screen given to them by the Baronne's mother.[19] Not all nobles necessarily wanted to live with their parents' furnishings. The Comtesse Anna de Noailles, born in 1876, recalled that as a child she did not like her parents' home on the avenue Hoche with its gilt chairs, Oriental carpets, and round divans with puffed-up Turkish gauze cushions. Her ideal space was a leafy garden.[20]

The distribution of family patrimony created potential for dispute among siblings. In post-revolutionary France all children, regardless of sex, had the right to inherit an equal share of family property. There were subtle variations in the way that "right" was interpreted by different groups in society, and noble families preferred to maintain the integrity of the principal estate by making the eldest son its inheritor through negotiation with other brothers and sisters. Rural residences in particular contained some very large pieces of furniture such as chests and cupboards, known in French as *meubles meublants*, that were normally included with the building in wills. Where there was disagreement over property division, noble women were more likely than men to renounce a strictly equal share of inheritance in order to keep the peace and avoid a legal battle. One female aristocrat, born in 1924, gave a frank account of the problem:

> For people of my generation, all the parents who are not dead are in the process of dying; half my friends have quarrelled with their brothers and sisters due to matters of inheritance which used to be managed a bit better whereas now people demand the furniture. I'll admit upfront that, in order not to fight, my sister and I left the two châteaux entirely furnished to our two brothers and we shared the remainder between ourselves, which was the furniture from my parents' Parisian apartment. If we want to get along, there needs to be some who are prepared to relinquish their part of the heritage. ... But my sons reproach me for it now and that's the difficulty.[21]

From the late nineteenth century, when an agricultural crisis in France led to a decline in land values, many aristocratic families had to find ways to cut expenditure and diversify their sources of income. One option for a noble man was to marry a rich heiress. Most of the really big fortunes in Parisian high society at the turn of the century belonged to industrial and banking families whose origins were non-French but whose members became French citizens. Schneider and Wendel, who manufactured cars and military equipment; Say and Lebaudy, who owned sugar refineries; Ephrussi and Kann, who were bankers; and Porgès, who ran a diamond company, established a branch of their families in Paris and, within a generation or two, their offspring married into the French nobility.

The Say sisters, Jeanne and Marie, who became respectively the Marquise de Brissac and the Princesse Amédée de Broglie upon marriage, used their wealth to undertake extensive restoration and refurbishment of noble properties. Jeanne installed a private theater on the top floor of the Château de Brissac and had a new stable block built as a Christmas present for her son. In 1875 she encouraged her younger sister, Marie, to purchase the Château de Chaumont, then to look for an aristocratic husband to go with the property. Marie wed the Prince Amédée de Broglie and soon afterwards the couple hired architect Ernest Sanson to design extensions to Chaumont; these included a new basement kitchen, to replace the kitchen formerly located on the ground floor, as well as a large stable block and *basse-cour*. Chaumont became one of the first châteaux in France to have electric lighting put in to replace oil lamps.

For women of aristocratic birth it was difficult not to resent the capacity of rich commoners to invest "new money" in ancient properties. The Duchesse Élisabeth de Clermont-Tonnerre, for instance, never forgave her father and stepmother, who were trying to save money, for selling the estate Mangé which had belonged to her real mother's family and been promised to her when she married. Nor did Élisabeth forgive a rich American couple, the Mackays, for buying Mangé. Recalling a visit to "[her] old property," she wrote:

> The Mackays had completely distorted the relationship between the château and the land. The costs had been exorbitant, the savings ridiculous. The house itself, stripped of its paintings and Renaissance cabinets that had been its ornament, seemed sordid to me. The drapes were full of holes and dirty, the carpets were worn out.[22]

To the Duchesse, the broken link between the château and land (*pays*) was a reflection of how broken she felt at having her mother's family estate removed from her possession. Empty, soiled, and damaged were words to describe what she observed, as well as what she felt inside.

It is possible to read the grudge that the Duchesse de Clermont-Tonnerre held against the Mackays into a caricature she made, further on in her memoirs, of the American heiress, Anna Gould:

> I saw this one [Miss Gould] on her first arrival in Paris. It was said that she was ugly, and she was by comparison with the aesthetic of Paris, but perhaps not according to that of her country. ... She was small, thin, her face entirely taken up by a large nose and two enormous black eyes, her complexion was yellow; her hair pinned up into wings like an aeroplane made her shorter, and her back was strewn with long black hairs. Boni de Castellane, whom she subsequently married, was to transform her. He had her plucked, shampooed, made-up, [and] styled.[23]

The "transformation" that Boni performed on Anna, as it is detailed by the Duchesse in a description that contains many stereotypes of the Jewish body, functioned in reverse to the changes made at Mangé.[24] Élisabeth aligned her perception of the château interior, after the property's sale, as "sordid," with the "ugly" appearance of an American Jewish heiress, a woman with plenty of money. A French aristocrat, Boni, was cast in the role of raising the Jew's external presentation up to the aesthetic of Paris; one racial standard was exchanged for the other. Despite the work to improve Anna's appearance, in the Duchesse's eyes, this American heiress did not belong to Parisian high society any more than the Mackays belonged on her land.

The Comtesse de Mirabeau-Martel, known to contemporaries by her pseudonymn Gyp, used references to furnishing in her work to underline differences of class and race. Gyp penned several anti-Semitic novels in the late 1890s, at the height of the Dreyfus Affair, in which Jewish characters grow rich by dubious means and accumulate impoverished nobles' property. M. Dampyré, for example, obtains for a "derisory sum" the tapestries of an old Breton noble family which impress an aristocratic visitor.[25] Gyp portrayed Jews as scheming and underhand, attributes that in her eyes made the "Jewish race" a greater threat to the aristocracy than the bourgeoisie whom she scorned for its clumsy efforts to emulate the aristocratic lifestyle. In *The Ancestors*, Gyp satirized a bourgeois character "of old [French] stock" trying to find appropriate portraits to grace the walls of his newly purchased country home. The hastily purchased fakes fail to disguise the stains on the wood panelling identifying where the portraits of the "real" owners had previously hung.[26]

Entertaining Company

The Comtesse de Mirabeau-Martel was herself the subject of various portraits, including a literary one made by a bourgeoise, Julia Daudet, after a visit to Gyp's home in the Parisian suburb of Neuilly in March 1894. Julia described her hostess, "the writer of great talent, the woman of malicious spirit," receiving guests in her salon:

> Charming Gyp, so very clearly Gyp by her indefinable smile … and so very clearly Mirabeau-Martel by the originality of her whole person. … Her salon at Neuilly, which is light and brightened by its drapes and by the white dress of the mistress of the house, shows taste for the distinctive curio, not the craze for artists' *bric-à-brac*. And sunk in her low chair, in a familiar pose that brings her eyes to the same level as your own, she chats away, this Gyp, about everything and everyone.[27]

Here living space and bodily practices are portrayed in complete harmony. Gyp, in her white dress, blends seamlessly into her surroundings, contributing to the brightness of the salon and displaying her personal charms as well as her Mirabeau-Martel ancestry. Taste for things original ("the distinctive curio") is manifest within the space and reflects the "originality of her whole person."

What kind of a space was a salon? The term originates from the French translation of the Italian word *salone*.[28] During the second half of the seventeenth century it came to be applied to a room designed for the reception of guests; this room normally featured a ceiling that was higher than that in other rooms and that was domed and decorated with paintings and architectural ornaments. The architect Louis Le Vau introduced the salon into his château designs from the 1640s and the results so impressed contemporaries that demand arose to make such a room a standard feature in the homes of the elite. Gradually the salon took over from the dining room (*la salle à manger*) as the principal room in a noble residence and the one most used for receiving guests. Many homes had more than one salon, for instance, a *salon d'été* for summer entertaining and a *salon d'hiver* for winter receptions.

In the nineteenth century the term salon also came to be applied to a type of social gathering that in the eighteenth century had been called a *société*. Such an occasion was principally designed for guests to engage in conversation under the skilful direction of the hostess. Accounts of such occasions often contain small details about furnishing and decoration that serve to personalize the hospitality of the hostess and to evoke the atmosphere in the room. At the home of the Princesse Mathilde Bonaparte, for instance: "The palms, that give an air of a winter garden to the largest salon, overhear noisy and interesting conversations when Taine and Renan reply to one another or when Pailleron and Dumas discuss theatre."[29]

Some women invited artists to their salon and art historians have shown the way in which commissions from the elite helped to further artists' careers, expand their oeuvre, and drive the market for new aesthetic tastes forward. Natalie Adamson, in her article on Odilon Redon's commissioned decorative screens, identifies this process as the production of Bourdieu's "circles of belief."[30] Upper-class patrons "consecrated" the value of works within the market by buying and exhibiting them in their salons, which led to further commissions and sales for the artist when friends and relatives were invited to admire the work at special inauguration viewing parties.[31] Gloria Groom has documented the commissions received by Édouard Vuillard from patrons including the Princes Emmanuel and Antoine Bibesco. She points out that because upper-class patrons changed address frequently, Vuillard was called upon to install and reinstall panels many times and in the process adapt them to different architectural settings. The consequences for the artist were positive in that he had relations over a long period of time with some patrons and opportunities arose to create new works for them.[32] Dealers like Georges Petit, Paul Durand-Ruel, Siegfried Bing, and the Bernheim brothers performed a crucial role in the art world by putting patrons in touch with artists. At dealers' galleries, nobles could purchase works direct or make arrangements for a commission; most auctions took place at the Hôtel Druout.

Patronage relationships were often characterized by considerable warmth. Eisenschitz, the Murats' secretary, received a letter from Émile Adam dated January 29, 1903 in which the artist declared: "It gave me great satisfaction that the Princesse [Murat] found my painting [*Le cheval Général*] handsome and well done." Similarly, in a note addressed to the Princesse on February 15, 1902, Gérôme thanked her for purchasing a small statue entitled *Campagne d'Egypte* for 6,000 francs. "I am eager to forward to you the expression of my contentment for I am extremely satisfied to have one of my children so well placed."[33]

Collecting was a popular hobby among noble women and men. The Princesse Mathilde Bonaparte, mourning the fate of her Saint-Gratien home in the aftermath of the Franco–Prussian War of 1870–71, told her nephew, the Comte Primoli: "It must have been ransacked by the Prussians! My furniture, which I collected piece by piece!"[34] Many nobles were interested in Oriental artwork during the late nineteenth century, although few could rival the formidable collection assembled in Paris by Henri Cernuschi.[35] The Comte Robert de Montesquiou and Edmond de Goncourt were avid collectors of Japanese *objets d'art* and the Princesse Cécile Murat commissioned a kimono from Babani.[36] The Princesse Berthe de Wagram incorporated Chinese elements into her decorating scheme by purchasing fans, umbrellas, jade tobacco pots, and porcelain vases.[37] Part of the joy of collecting lay in showing the collection to others. Gustave Schlumberger recalled that the Comtesse de Béarn gave "large, very interesting dinners for archaeologists, members of the Academy of Inscriptions, amateurs and great collectors" who were invited to admire her "wonderful collections of books, paintings, antiques and medals."[38]

A passion for collecting made the hall in many a French château look overcrowded during the nineteenth century. In the 1850s the Baron James de Rothschild asked English architects to design a hall for the Château de Ferrières, which he filled with his collections of antique furniture, sculpted busts, porcelain vases, and paintings. At the turn of the century, the hall in the Château de Grosbois owned by the Wagrams contained a grand piano, divans, at least one writing table, and a table piled with books. The latter was probably a sign of anglophilia, for book-covered tables were considered an example of English comfort and were uncommon in French châteaux where books were normally shelved in the library.[39]

When guests were invited to an aristocratic home for dinner they were usually received first in the salon or hall before moving into the dining room (*la salle à manger*). In Paris a noble woman typically held one large dinner party per week, to which up to 40 people were invited; after the meal the salons were thrown open to guests and it was traditional to pay a call on the woman in whose home one had dined the previous week. Proust depicted the moment of anticipation before dinner at the home of the Guermantes when:

> with a vast gyratory whirr, multiple and simultaneous, the double doors of the dining room swung apart; a butler with the air of a court chamberlain … announced the tidings "Madame is served," in a tone such as he would have employed to say "Madame is dead," which, however, cast no gloom over the assembly.[40]

Guests then processed into the dining room in order of seniority. The Comtesse de Pange describes a similar type of procession taking place at every family meal: "my grandmother walked at the head enveloped in her shawls and black lace. Then my mother, my father, and I would follow in order."[41] The dining room of an aristocratic home often featured in-built decoration such as wood or marble paneling and sculpture. Typically a large sideboard dominated one wall with an extendable dining table and chairs in the center of the room and additional chairs positioned against the walls. Large tapestries were hung such as the Gobelins tapestry representing Vincennes in the seventeenth century at the *hôtel particulier* once owned by the Comte and Comtesse Potocki.[42]

After dinner, men and women separated into the men's smoking room (*le fumoir*) and the ladies' sitting room (*le petit salon*). These rooms had distinct types of interior furnishings and decoration because they were gendered spaces where men and women engaged in sex-specific activities: smoking for men and embroidery for women. The *fumoir* was lent a "masculine" air through dark shades of wall coloring and an assembly of smokers' armchairs, cabinets, and glass-topped collector showcases. In contrast, the *petit salon* was a lighter, brighter space with a *chaise longue*, ladies' easy chairs, and sewing tables. At the Musée Jacquemart-André, the *fumoir* is decorated with Chinese and Japanese decorative objects, rugs, and eighteenth-century portraiture. The room is reached by passing through the leafy winter garden (*le jardin d'hiver*). The *fumoir*, like the *petit salon*, was not an especially large space, and after a *grand dîner* younger men must have stood unless extra chairs were brought in. Liqueurs were savored and cigars were smoked. After a dinner for men (*un repas d'hommes*) hosted by the Murats on July 4, 1912, 31 guests, plus the host, smoked a total of 28 cigars. The following evening, on July 5, after a dinner for 62 male and female guests, the men smoked 37 cigars.[43] Card games were often played when men and women reunited in the salon unless other entertainment was planned. André de Fouquières recalled the Princesse de Broglie's habit, at Chaumont, of beginning a game of bridge at midnight and continuing till dawn. Liqueurs, syrups, and fruit jellies were left out for the players and the *valet de pied* went to sleep in the library.[44]

Her Own Space

A noble woman began and ended each day in her personal apartment that was a unique and gendered space; she had complete control over who was admitted there and how the apartment was furnished and decorated. A typical apartment comprised three rooms: a bedroom (*la chambre*), a dressing room (*le cabinet de toilette*), and a sitting room (*le petit salon*, often "*petit*" only in name). In a *hôtel particulier* these rooms were located on the first floor and had windows overlooking the garden. In an apartment building the rooms faced on to an inner courtyard. The bedroom and *petit salon* were adjacent on either side of a shared chimney. Oil or gas lamps provided lighting throughout the home until electricity began to be installed from the 1890s.

The suite can be understood diagramatically as concentric rings whose radius passed through the spectrum of a noble woman's intimate relations. A noble woman chose who entered each ring according to the degree of intimacy she shared with them. The outer ring represented the *petit salon* where a noble woman received close friends and relatives. Sometimes she might hold her afternoon reception (known as a *jour*) in this room or adjourn there to chat or play cards with guests after dinner. A noble woman also used her *petit salon* as a place to read, write, sew, paint, play the piano, converse tête-à-tête, and enjoy the company of pets. It was a room for individual pursuits, companionship, and sociability. A second ring of much smaller circumference represented a noble woman's *chambre*, where her husband, children, and very intimate friends could join her at her discretion, and where servants could enter when summoned to perform a task. The Baronne Mathilde de Mackau, for example, wrote to her friend Constance asking her to ensure that the servant Martin lit a fire in the bedroom on the date of her return from Villepatour.[45] The central ring in the diagram represented the *cabinet de toilette* to which a noble woman admitted only her maid (*la femme de chambre*). "The *cabinet de toilette* requires absolutely closed doors," wrote the Comtesse de Tramar. It was "a woman's holy of holies," affirmed the Baronne de Staffe.[46]

The apartment belonging to a noble man comprised a *chambre, cabinet de toilette,* and study (*le cabinet de travail*). A noble man sometimes received people in his study but less often than his wife did in her *petit salon* since he spent the afternoon at his club or calling on female friends at their homes. After dinner he might invite male guests to the *fumoir* or return to his club after attending the opera.

To have a personal apartment within one's residence was extremely rare in the nineteenth century when the working class occupied cramped living quarters with family or fellow servants and bourgeois couples shared one bedroom. Personal apartments affected the dynamics of power in upper-class marriages. Separate sleeping spaces meant that a noble woman could retire to her *chambre* to abstain from sex that might lead to pregnancy or to sleep alone during times of marital tension or crisis. The *petit salon* and *cabinet de travail* enabled husband and wife to receive friends separately and to carry out activities like reading and writing without disturbance. Personal apartments went some way towards fostering balance in the relationship between a noble woman and her spouse. They promoted autonomy and independence in married life.

A feature of this independence was a noble woman's ability to furnish and decorate her personal apartment as she wished. Of course, her husband had the same right to furnish and decorate his apartment. When electricity was installed in the Harcourt family home, the Marquis continued to use the oil lamp in his study since he preferred its soft glow to the harsh electric light that he said ruined the eyes.[47] Noble children had little say in what went into their bedroom, and there were items there that would not normally be found in an adult's bedroom, such as a nurse's bed. Adolescents, however, were given some freedom to choose the items they liked to have around them. The Prince Alexandre de Wagram, for example, born in 1884, had a glass fishbowl in his bedroom at the turn of the century.[48]

How did a noble woman personalize her space? In her apartment she decided the arrangement of purchased and inherited items as well as gifts. Essential pieces of furniture for a *chambre* and *petit salon* were a bed, several large closets or cupboards, some chairs and small tables, a writing desk, and some bookshelves and footstools. These items in the Art Nouveau style featured at the 1900 Paris Exposition and were sold to elite customers at Galérie Bing. A noble woman often introduced exotic pieces such as a Japanese screen, a Turkish ottoman, a Spanish chest, or a Chinese lacquered chair into her furnishing scheme.[49]

To decorate her apartment a noble woman displayed paintings, tapestries, small sculptures, and busts that she had commissioned, received as gifts, or bought at auction. Framed photographs of friends and family stood on a dresser or small table alongside knick-knacks and curios brought back from travels. In her *chambre* the Princesse Berthe de Wagram kept a Punch doll at the end of her bed and photographs of her immediate family on the commode and desk.[50] The Comtesse Anna de Noailles and her sister, the Princesse Hélène de Caraman-Chimay, had mementos of their holidays at the Palazzo Dario in Venice. A noble woman also had items of religious or spiritual significance in her personal apartment since this was where she prayed early in the morning or late at night. The Princesse Mathilde Bonaparte kept a copy of *The Christian Day* at her bedside.[51]

What about the *cabinet de toilette*, the room that the Baronne de Staffe described as "a woman's holy of holies"? It was here that every morning a noble woman had her hair brushed and arranged by her maid who also assisted her to dress. This process was repeated several times per day, for a noble woman changed her garments to suit her morning, afternoon, and evening activities. Chairs, stools, cabinets, and a dressing table with mirror bore witness to a noble woman's preparation for sociability. In her *cabinet de toilette* at the Château de Serrant, the Duchesse de La Trémoille had pale wood furniture, a palm, and silver candelabras in the 1920s. The room's appearance changed little through the twentieth century except for the insertion of a portrait of the Duchesse over the white mantelpiece.[52]

Beauty and hygiene manuals published under noble pseudonymns at the turn of the century emphasized that care for the body was not only beneficial to health and well-being but also a sign of virtue. Around 1900 noble women purchased beauty products from Rose-Bertin (59 rue Boissière), where they could also have a manicure and pedicure, and they were perhaps massaged by Durville, director of the School of Magnetism and Massage (23 rue St Merri), who obligingly offered treatment at home.[53]

Bathing was considered to be of medical benefit to invalids in the nineteenth century and in some households it was also recognized to be a pleasurable activity. People generally washed their body using a shallow round tub placed on the floor and filled with water; for those who could afford it, however, a more pleasant experience could be achieved by installing a bathroom with a permanent tub. In an extension to the Château d'Armainvilliers, built in the 1880s, the Rothschilds had bathrooms connected to each bedroom, seven on one floor alone. Another Rothschild property, the Château de Ferrières, had a bathroom with a tub when it was built in the late 1850s, and in 1925 Clément More was hired to make the room over in the Art Deco style for the Baronne Édouard de Rothschild. The alcove above the bath was freshly decorated with images of peacocks flying through clouds. Since plumbing was expensive it remained uncommon in French homes well into the twentieth century; in 1954 only half of French homes had running water and half of rural homes still had no running water in 1962.[54] There were certainly some aristocratic properties where facilities remained basic. In the 1960s, when the English wife of the Vicomte de Baritault arrived at the Château de Roquetaillade, she found one bathroom, no water closets, and 60 chamberpots.[55]

Conclusion

Up until 1914 the aristocracy retained its social and cultural authority because the haute bourgeoisie, despite its wealth, could never attain "distinction." After World War I, however, class relationships changed and a new emphasis on "chic" meant that money became more important than birth for entry into upper-class circles. One of the main drivers for change to the aristocratic lifestyle, and its decline after 1914, was the cost of maintaining and staffing urban and rural residences. Historians have traced a shift that occurred in nobles' pattern of investment across the second half of the nineteenth century. The trend in response to falling rents and the agricultural crisis was to move money away from land and into the stock market. Under the July Monarchy 60 percent of noble wealth was found in property, compared with only 38.8 percent in 1911.[56] Gérard Rousset-Charny has documented the varied destinies of 30 upper-class residences in Paris. During the Belle Époque these sumptuous homes located in the eighth and sixteenth *arrondissements* had been commissioned from leading French architects; in the twentieth century, all but three passed out of private ownership.[57] A similar pattern unfolded in the countryside. André de Fouquières remarked that his great nephews believed him to be the last of their family for whom the word château was synonymous with residence.[58] The expense and responsibility of maintenance made ownership impractical and the rate of occupation even at holidays declined. Consequently many châteaux were converted into reception centers or museums.

Living with inherited items continued to be important to nobles with the result of eclectic interior decorating.[59] One nobleman, born in 1934, described his home this way: "The furniture and paintings are, for the most part, items with family associations [*les souvenirs familiaux*] through force of circumstance, and among them some, exceptional ones, are just as familiar in character as the most up-to-date items."[60] Of course, "exceptional" furniture and paintings were usually valuable and represented a considerable tax burden for their owners. At an extreme, the effort to keep such pieces in the family rather than sell them could result in a sense of "privation." As one noble woman, born in 1924, put it: "I think that it is all this education we received, my husband and

I—happily the same education—and all this past we hold on to, that makes us cling to our property. We are deprived—that's the word—because of this property."[61]

When nobles wrote about their homes in nineteenth- and twentieth-century France, they did so with an awareness of change as well as a desire to emphasize continuities and to preserve memories. In furnishing and decorating, the French aristocracy showed commitment to past heritage but also a capacity for adaptation that has long been one of its strengths. At the turn of the century Julia Daudet wrote admiringly of the Comtesse de Mirabeau-Martel and her light, tastefully furnished salon devoid of *bric-à-brac*. The Comtesse, it seemed, had adapted, as old ways were being superseded by new:

> Despite all the precaution taken by the vigilant women who galvanized their servants, or took the care of the most valuable objects into their own hands, the dust got into the multitude of nooks and crannies already known to it in the confused jumble of the shops, crept into the mouldings, the carvings, the inlays, the many folds of the fabrics, and into the threadbare tapestries. To track and get rid of it became a chore and a concern until the day when, as sheer French common sense recovered its courage and its need for order and clarity, the furniture got cleared, with the useless cluttering objects put in the display cabinet and the ill-assorted collection of things set on one shelf leaving the place more open and free.[62]

Notes

1. Marcel Proust, *In Search of Lost Time*, vol. 2, *Within a Budding Grove*, trans. C.K. Scott Moncrieff and Terence Kilmartin, revised by D.J. Enright (London: Vintage, 1996), 282.
2. Marcel Proust, *In Search of Lost Time*, vol. 3, *The Guermantes Way*, trans. C.K. Scott Moncrieff and Terence Kilmartin, revised by D.J. Enright (London: Vintage, 1996), 483–8.
3. Pierre Bourdieu, *Distinction: A Social Critique of the Judgement of Taste*, trans. Richard Nice (London: Routledge, 2000).
4. Christian de Bartillat, *Histoire de la noblesse française: de 1789 à nos jours*, vol. 2, *Les nobles du Second Empire à la fin du XXe siècle* (Paris: Albin Michel, 1991), 85.
5. Georg Simmel quoted in Daphne Spain, *Gendered Spaces* (Chapel Hill: University of North Carolina Press, 1992), 18.
6. Theodore Zeldin, *France 1848–1945*, vol. 1, *Ambition, Love, and Politics* (Oxford: Oxford University Press, 1973), 17. On "bourgeois" as a pejorative term, see Béatrix Le Wita, *French Bourgeois Culture* (Cambridge: Cambridge University Press, 1994), 26–7, 53–6.
7. Norbert Elias, *The Civilising Process*, vol. 2, *State Formation and Civilisation*, trans. Edmund Jephcott (Oxford: Basil Blackwell, 1982), 254.
8. Pierre Bourdieu, *Masculine Domination*, trans. Richard Nice (Cambridge: Polity Press, 2001).
9. Leora Auslander, *Taste and Power: Furnishing Modern France* (Berkeley and Los Angeles: University of California Press, 1996), 174–5.
10. Auslander, *Taste and Power*, 220–24; Bonnie G. Smith, *Ladies of the Leisure Class: The Bourgeoises of the Nord in the Nineteenth Century* (Princeton: Princeton University Press, 1981), chapters 3–4.
11. Auslander, *Taste and Power*, part 3; Charles Sowerwine, *France since 1870: Culture, Politics and Society* (New York: Palgrave, 2001), 40–54.

12. Auslander, *Taste and Power*, 255–6.

13. David Higgs, *Nobles in Nineteenth-Century France: The Practice of Inegalitarianism* (Baltimore: Johns Hopkins University Press, 1987), 222.

14. Boni de Castellane, *Mémoires* (Paris: Perrin, 1986), 23.

15. Journal entries May 21, 1880, September 25, 1881, April 10, 1883 in *Archives Privées* Mugnier, 238/1; Julia Daudet, *Souvenirs autour d'un groupe littéraire* (Paris: Charpentier, 1910), 190–94.

16. René de La Croix de Castries, *Papiers de famille* (Paris: Éditions France-Empire, 1977), 26.

17. François-Charles d'Harcourt, *Regards sur un passé* (Paris: Robert Laffont, 1989), 47–8.

18. Adeline Daumard, *Les bourgeois et la bourgeoisie en France depuis 1815* (Paris: Aubier, 1987), 22–7, 73–4.

19. Mark Girouard, *Life in the French Country House* (London: Cassell and Co., 2000), 328.

20. Anna de Noailles, *Le livre de ma vie* (Paris: Mercure de France, 1976), 12–15.

21. Éric Mension-Rigau, *Aristocrates et grands bourgeois: education, traditions, valeurs* (Paris: Pluriel, 1994), 115.

22. Élisabeth de Clermont-Tonnerre, *Au temps des équipages* (Paris: Grasset, 1928), 81.

23. Clermont-Tonnerre, *Au temps des équipages*, 151.

24. The stereotypes have been applied to a Jewish female body but some derive from stereotypes of the Jewish male body. The way gender operates in the passage is significant because the process Anna undergoes is designed to make her look beautiful or feminine. See Sander Gilman, *The Jew's Body* (New York: Routledge, 1991), 5, 172–3, 179–93, 203, 205; Linda Nochlin and Tamar Garb, eds., *The Jew in the Text: Modernity and the Construction of Identity* (London: Thames and Hudson, 1995), 83–96, 97–120.

25. Willa Z. Silverman, "Gyp et l'Affaire Dreyfus,"' *Modern and Contemporary France* 43 (1990): 5–16.

26. Gyp, "Les ancêtres," in *Les moins de vingt ans* (Paris: Calmann-Lévy, 1930), 95–126.

27. Daudet, *Souvenirs*, 185–6.

28. Girouard, *Life in the French Country House*, 132.

29. Daudet, *Souvenirs*, 73.

30. Natalie Adamson, "'Circles of Belief': Patronage, Taste and Shared Creativity in Odilon Redon's Decorative Painting," *Studies in the Decorative Arts* (1996): 107–30; Pierre Bourdieu, "The Production of Belief: Contribution to an Economy of Symbolic Goods," in *The Field of Cultural Production: Essays on Art and Literature* (New York: Columbia University Press, 1993), 74–80.

31. Bourdieu, "The Production of Belief," 78.

32. Gloria Groom, *Édouard Vuillard Painter-Decorator: Patrons and Projects, 1892–1912* (New Haven: Yale University Press, 1993), 2–3, 36–9, 59–65, 95–6, 113–19, 139–43, 162–4, 175–7, 195–9.

33. Letter January 29, 1903 and letter February 15, 1902 in *Archives Privées* Murat 31/78.

34. Joanna Richardson, *Portrait of a Bonaparte: The Life and Times of Joseph-Napoleon Primoli 1851–1927* (London: Quartet Books, 1987), 57.

35. The Musée Cernuschi was inaugurated in 1898.

36. *Japonisme et mode* Exhibition Catalogue (Paris: Les Musées de la Ville de Paris, 1996), 140.

37. *Archives Privées* Maréchal Berthier 173 bis/426.

38. Gustave Schlumberger, *Mes souvenirs 1844–1928* (Paris: Plon, 1934), 120.

39. Girouard, *Life in the French Country House*, 308–9, 330–31.

40. Proust, *The Guermantes Way*, 501.

41. Comtesse Jean de Pange, *Comment j'ai vu 1900* (Paris: Grasset, 1962), 25.

42. Marc Gaillard, *Les belles heures des Champs-Élysées* (Amiens: Martelle, 1990), 132.

43. *Archives Privées* Murat 31/95.

44. André de Fouquières, *Cinquante ans de panache* (Paris: Horay, 1951), 256.

45. Letter December 19, 1864 in *Archives Privées* Mackau 156 (I)/315.

46. Comtesse de Tramar, *Le bréviaire de la femme: pratiques secrètes de la beauté* (1903) quoted in Françoise de Bonneville, *Le livre du bain* (Paris: Flammarion, 1997), 109; Baronne de Staffe, *Le cabinet de toilette* (Paris: Havard, 1903), 1.

47. Michel Chabot, *Histoire de Jean et Yvonne domestiques en 1900, Racontée par Paul, leur fils, à Michel, son petit-fils* (Paris: Les Editions 1900, 1988), 84.

48. *Archives Privées* Maréchal Berthier 173 bis/408.

49. *Archives Privées* Murat, 31/77–9; *Archives Privées* Maison de France 300 (III)/712; Nancy J. Troy, *Modernism and the Decorative Arts in France: Art Nouveau to Le Corbusier* (New Haven: Yale University Press, 1991), 7–51.

50. *Archives Privées* Maréchal Berthier 173 bis/408.

51. Henri de Régnier, *Images Venitiennes* (Paris: Fontemoing, 1912); Richardson, *Portrait of a Bonaparte,* 57.

52. Girouard, *Life in the French Country House,* 304–5.

53. "Liste des maisons recommandées," in *Livre d'or 1900* (Paris: Bender, 1900), 765–86.

54. Susan K. Foley, *Women in France since 1789* (New York: Palgrave, 2004), 244.

55. Girouard, *Life in the French Country House,* 237.

56. Christophe Charle, "Noblesse et élites en France au début du XXe siècle," in *Les noblesses européennes au XIXe siècle* (Milan: Università di Milano and Rome: École Française de Rome, 1988), 407–33; Adeline Daumard, *Les fortunes françaises au XIXe siècle* (Paris: Mouton, 1973), 257–67.

57. Gérard Rousset-Charny, *Les palais parisiens de la belle époque* (Paris: Délégation à l'Action Artistique de la Ville de Paris, 1990), 64, 69, 75, 91, 93, 101, 109, 113, 119, 123, 129, 137, 144, 149, 152, 158, 163, 167, 169, 173, 176, 180, 185, 187, 192, 199, 215, 217, 224, 232. The Camondo and Jacquemart-André residences were converted to museums that can be visited today.

58. Bartillat, *Les nobles du Second Empire,* 159–61.

59. Jean-Bernard Naudin and Christiane de Nicolay-Mazery, *Visite privée: hôtels particuliers de Paris* (Paris: Chêne, 1999).

60. Mension-Rigau, *Aristocrates et grands bourgeois,* 109.

61. Mension-Rigau, *Aristocrates et grands bourgeois,* 110.

62. Julia Daudet, *Journées de femme* (Paris: E. Fasquelle, 1898), 78.

5

"Novel and Ingenious": Innovative Graphic Arts in the Women's Magazines of the 1840s and the Construction of Middle-Class Taste

Cynthia Patterson

In his "Editor's Book Table" column for November 1843, Louis A. Godey promised the fair readers of his illustrated monthly magazine a special treat for the next month's holiday issue:

> The December Number will contain the greatest novelty ever yet offered in a Magazine, THIRTY-ONE COLOURED EMBOSSED MEDALLION SEALS, with every variety of design, and with beautiful and appropriate Mottoes, ready for immediate use. These cannot be had separately for less than seventy-five cents. They are offered by the publisher as a holiday present to his fair patrons. This has never before been attempted by a Magazine, and is only another instance of what may be effected by good taste and an expensive outlay of capital.[1]

This full-page embellishment, designed for pull-out and immediate use, drew the label "die-sink cameo stamp" as it utilized a method of textured embossing that left the raised surface in white relief, because during printing the relief remained untouched by the colored ink surrounding it.[2] Godey's friendship medallions feature not only small engraved emblematic figures, but also verbal insignias such as "Time Will Unite Us," "We Part To Meet Again," and "Forget Me Not" (Figure 5.1).

Since most of the *Lady's Book*'s full-page embellishments—fashion plates, floral prints, art reproductions, fancy needlework patterns, and the like—were designed for framing and display, Godey evidently found it necessary to instruct his readers on the proper use of these novelty medallions. "A little gum Arabic dissolved in water, and applied to the back of any of the seals in [the] December number, will cause them to adhere firmly to a letter," Godey advises in his February 1844 "Editor's Book Table" column (104). Notably, Godey conflates the medallions' value with both their expense and their utility.

He notes the "expensive outlay of capital" required to present this gift to his readers. Godey further insists that while his medallions are "appropriate" and "useful," they are also "novel," "beautiful" and indicative of "good taste." In presenting them to his readers, Godey also enabled his readers to participate in ritual commodity exchange with their social intimates—friends and family members—for the purpose of cementing social ties and promoting cultural refinement (see Figure 5.1).

Louis Godey thus schooled his readers to associate their patronage of his magazine with the consumption of fine art, the exchange of commodity goods (in this instance, his friendship seals), and the display of refined taste. However, Godey was not the only publisher of a ladies' monthly magazine to connect subscription to his magazine to utility, consumption, commodity exchange, and refined taste. In fact, the publisher's lavish holiday present to his readers was specifically designed to stave off challenges to *Godey's* nearly 15-year reign as the nation's leading ladies' magazine. While *Godey's Lady's Book* steadily improved in print quality and increased in circulation throughout the 1830s, by 1843 three new arrivals to the Philadelphia magazine scene threatened *Godey's* supremacy—*Graham's Lady's and Gentleman's Magazine; The Ladies' National Magazine* (*Peterson's*), and *Miss Leslie's Magazine: Home Book of Fashion, Literature and Domestic Economy*.

Frank Luther Mott, the great historian of periodical literature, referred to these magazines collectively as the "Philadelphia picture periodicals."[3] In this chapter, I employ a short-hand designation "Philadelphia pictorials," to refer collectively to these magazines. As Mott points out, in the decade of the 1840s, the combined circulation of the Philadelphia periodicals surpassed those of any other American city.[4] Newspaper and magazine columnists from the major eastern seaboard cities routinely recognized the supremacy of these magazines—*Godey's* and *Graham's* in particular—over their Boston and New York counterparts. As one reviewer wrote: "Our sister city of Philadelphia has long been famous for the number of family newspapers and pictorial magazines which she annually pours forth over the country in regularly increasing supplies."[5]

While established rival magazines like New York's *Knickerbocker* targeted an aristocratic elite, and largely featured reprints of continental, often British, authors and artwork, the Philadelphia pictorials promoted original American art and literature, targeting the burgeoning middle classes. In this chapter, and the larger project from which it is taken, I argue that these magazines did more to democratize and commodify American art in the 1840s than any other medium.[6]

The early decades of the nineteenth century witnessed an explosion in textual and visual materials, as improved technologies of reproduction, coupled with increased literacy and improved methods of distribution (canals, railroads, turnpikes) permitted more widespread dissemination of print and visual

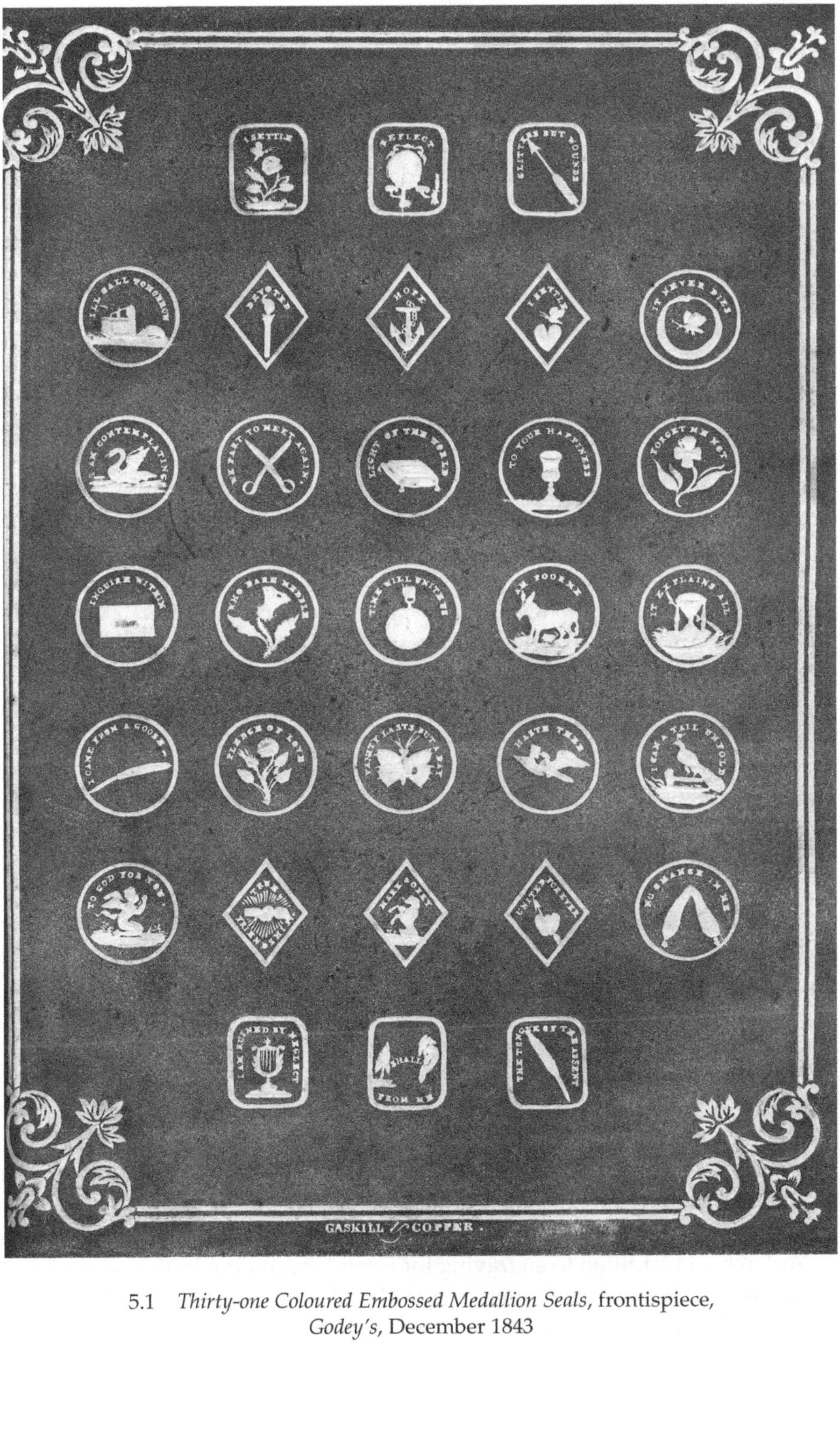

5.1 *Thirty-one Coloured Embossed Medallion Seals*, frontispiece, *Godey's*, December 1843

media.[7] The American reading public in the major cities faced a cornucopia of available reading material, including occasional pamphlets, daily and weekly newspapers, monthly magazines, gift books, annuals, serialized novels, and books.[8] Additionally, with the rise of the American Art-Union and other art organizations, mass-reproduced engravings of both the work of European masters and original American artists became widely available to the urban citizenry.[9] In major metropolitan areas like New York, Boston, and Philadelphia, American audiences faced a dizzying display of visual culture, in newly opened museums, on billboards, in storefront displays, banners, daguerreotype studios, street signs, and even on banknotes.[10]

Yet the Philadelphia pictorials were the first to target a national reading audience of moderate means, and to penetrate widely to markets outside the eastern seaboard cities, bringing "original" American art into the hands of ordinary citizens. In towns too small to support art galleries and print shops, middle-class readers who could not afford the more expensive annuals and gift books could nonetheless sample the latest in American graphic art via the pullout embellishments in the monthly magazines.[11] As a result, these magazines were extremely popular and widely circulated in their era. *Graham's* boasted a circulation of 40,000 in 1842—at a time when the US population hovered around 17,000,000.[12] By 1850, Godey advertised a print run in excess of 80,000, at a time when the American Art-Union membership rolls ran to only 16,500.[13]

By the late 1830s, the demand for visual and material goods linked to cultural refinement and "good taste" created an economic climate favorable for a challenge to *Godey's* decade-long virtual monopoly of the market for monthly magazines of literature and art. The first serious challenge came from a young George Rex Graham. In 1839, at the age of 26, Graham, newly admitted to the bar, had abandoned the law profession to buy a struggling Philadelphia monthly magazine, the *Casket*. Within a year, he also purchased *Burton's Gentleman's Magazine*, combining the two into one publication which he titled *Graham's Lady's and Gentleman's Magazine (the Casket and Gentleman's United)*. While Graham maintained a commitment to the gentleman readers he inherited from *Burton's* subscription list, he also sought to compete with *Godey's* by offering the fashion plates and "elegant embossed work" popular with lady readers.[14]

Graham's fashion plates in the early 1840s, however, nearly always featured a nattily dressed gentleman, in addition to the female figures. By 1842, *Graham's* fashion plates also occasionally appeared with a beautifully embossed lace border. From the signature beneath the May 1842 yellow-trimmed lace fashion plate, it is clear that Graham's "elegant embossed work" was being designed by Frederick Quarre, a French artist and designer living in New York who, in addition to engraving for *Godey's* beginning in 1839, also owned his own magazine, *Artist*.[15] Between 1841 and 1843, *Graham's* featured a series of novelty lace embellishments clearly crafted by Quarre (see Figure 5.2),

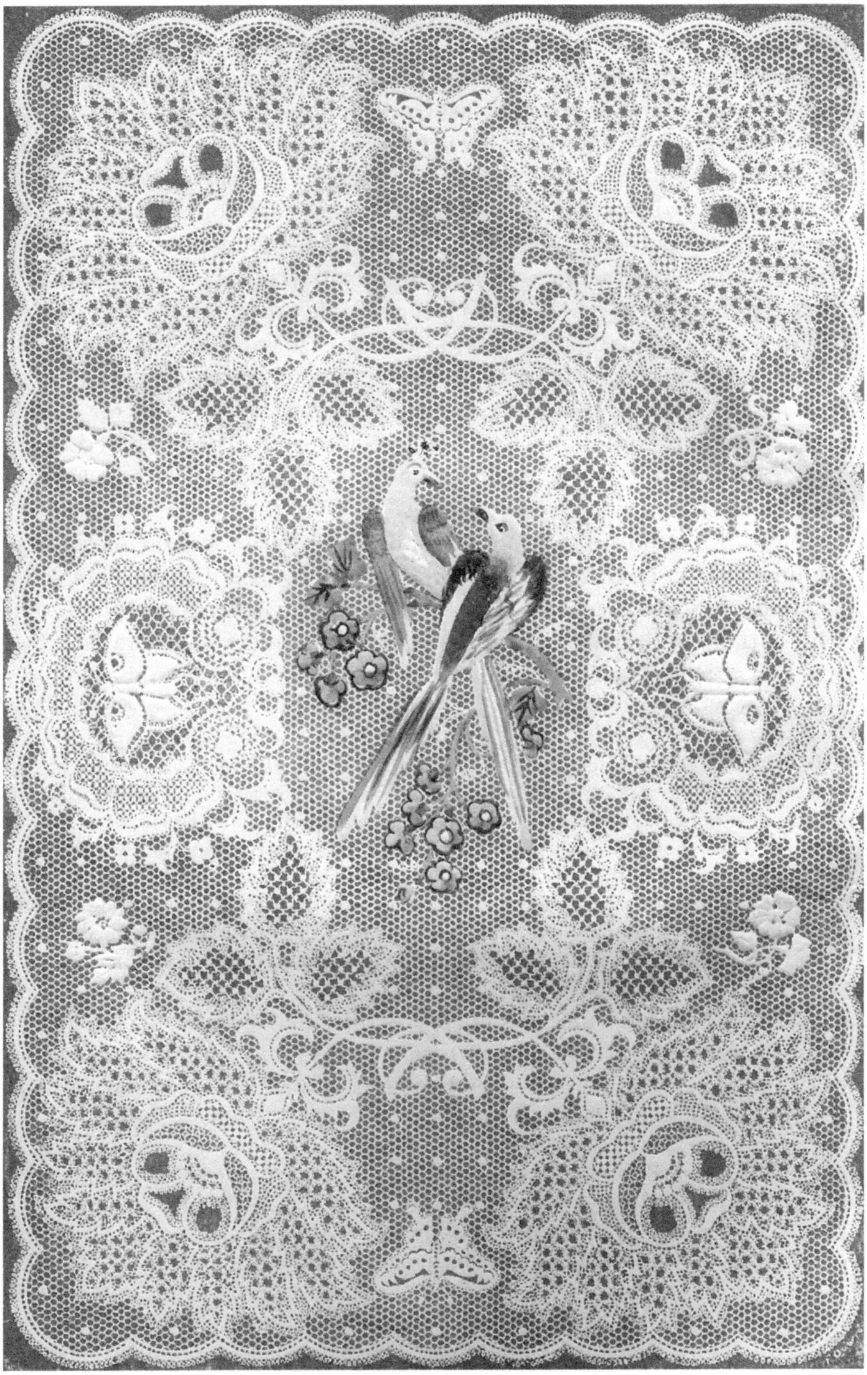

5.2 *Lace and Birds*, frontispiece, *Graham's*, January 1842

although Graham did not capitalize rhetorically on Quarre's achievements by "puffing" his art work in the editorial spaces of the magazine. However, *Graham's* lady readers could thus "own" and display the equivalent of fine Irish lace, in the embossed embellishments offered in his magazine.

Puffing Quarre's skill would fall to Charles J. Peterson, a friend of Graham's. Three years after Graham launched his challenge to *Godey's*, Peterson plotted with Graham to publish a cheaper $2.00 per year competitor to Godey's popular $3.00 per year magazine. Peterson and Graham also engaged the writing and editorial services of the well-known writer, Ann S. Stephens, foil to *Godey's* popular lady-editor, Sarah Josepha Hale. Although the new magazine featured fewer pages than *Godey's* (36 to *Godey's* usual 48–72), Peterson prided himself on featuring a minimum of three engravings in each issue to *Godey's* two, and in offering reduced price incentives: $1.25 per year for a club of eight subscribing simultaneously.[16] In 1843, Peterson also purchased Quarre's New York magazine, *Artist*, securing both his subscription list and the artistic services of Quarre.

Peterson lost no time in broadcasting news of his prized purchases. In the June 1843 issue of *The Lady's World*, he announced that the next volume, beginning July 1843, would feature the combined artistic talents of mezzotinter John Sartain, and artwork from the burin of Frederick Quarre (see Figure 5.2). In a special column entitled "Embellishments in this Number," Peterson crowed:

> THE COLORED PLATE engraved by F. Quarre for this number is an earnest of what he can do now that his undivided attention is bestowed on his art. In this unique design he has embodied no less than three illustrations. The first outline is that of a sea-shell. In this is placed a lace pattern, corresponding to the shape of the shell, and embodying a rare and elegant style. For the third illustration we have a miniature wreath of morning glory, surrounding the shell, while the same flower appears, of a more natural size, in the interior. Altogether the plate is unrivalled by anything Monsieur Quarre has hitherto produced. (192)

However, Monsieur Quarre and his subscription list proved to be only two of Peterson's prized quarry in the purchase of the *Artist*—Madame Quarre also contributed her services to the newly merged magazines. Peterson notes in his column on the fashions for October 1843:

> Our fashion plate, this month, is one of Madame Quarre's best; and is engraved in a new style, and printed in violet. It is even more elegant than the one printed in blue, published in our August number. We challenge, for it, a comparison with any fashion plate which may appear for this month. (139)

Peterson further notes, in the same month's column entitled "Publisher's Gossip," that by means of Madame Quarre's "correspondent in Paris," the magazine is able to "get out the correct fashions, *a month in advance of our contemporaries*" (140).

Clearly, the standard for "style" and "taste" in women's fashions in the early 1840s seems to be all things "French." The American women's monthly magazines that carried fashion plates—*Godey's*, *Graham's*, *Peterson's*—looked to the French to establish the fashion trends, and until the watershed year of 1843, often imported used plates directly from France. So in securing the services of Monsieur and Madame Quarre, Graham, and later Peterson, cornered a "commodity" that Peterson wisely promoted in attempting to establish the superior artistic "taste" of his magazine. In 1843, Godey went one step further, challenging the supremacy of the French plates by "Americanizing" the fashion plates, and arguing that his magazine offered "refinements" not even the French had seen fit to circulate to eager consumers. As Godey boasts to his readers in presenting his holiday friendship medallions: "The French, who embrace almost every novelty in their various works of fancy, have not yet hit upon this idea of offering to the fair sex in remote places the luxuries and elegances of the larger cities."[17]

At $3.00 per year, *Graham's* and *Godey's* targeted slightly more affluent, but still predominantly middle-class readers, offering those of modest means in "remote places" the "luxuries and elegances" previously restricted to the wealthy elite living in the eastern seaboard cities.[18] *Graham's* styled itself as a more "literary" magazine that balanced the fashion plates and sentimental tales, with descriptions of gentlemanly sporting activities and biographies of male author/contributors and statesmen. With its reduced subscription fees, *Peterson's* appealed to a more cost-conscious feminine readership, with poetry and serialized sentimental novelettes in addition to its French fashions. These three Philadelphia magazines—*Godey's*, *Graham's*, and *Peterson's*—began targeting national audiences by the early 1840s, and soon established a rhetoric of nascent nationalism and American exceptionalism, in counterpoint to their New York and Boston contemporaries.

In January 1843, a small but attractive little monthly entitled *Miss Leslie's Magazine: Home Book of Fashion, Literature and Domestic Economy* had entered the Philadelphia magazine fray to challenge the established triumvirate. Financed by the "ample means" of publisher Morton McMichael (an old school friend and former partner of Godey), and edited by popular recipe book and gift book editor, Eliza Leslie, *Miss Leslie's* displayed from its inaugural issue a commitment to push magazine embellishment to new artistic heights.[19] It was McMichael and Leslie who first emphatically employed the rhetoric of novelty, utility, taste, and refinement to the consumption of their artistic wares, in an attempt to lure readers away from their longer established competitors.

McMichael, educated as a lawyer, and having served as a Philadelphia sheriff and alderman, had earlier put his oratorical skills to use in an 1839 address on "Public Education" before the Philadelphia Lyceum. In that address, McMichael argued for America's supremacy as the "pinnacle of civilization," citing three necessary precursors for this distinction: widespread public education, supremacy in the "mechanical arts," and art that contributed to the moral education of the populace.[20] In linking the "mechanical arts" to moral education through "art," McMichael foreshadowed in this address the impetus for launching *Miss Leslie's* in January 1843. Inspired by recent exhibitions of the Franklin Institute, McMichael cast his fledgling magazine as the popularizer and democratizer of American mechanical and artistic innovations.

In his "Publisher's Table" for the magazine in February 1843, McMichael puffs his magazine as both "useful" and "decorative." He argues that the magazine will be both "pleasant and practical," and will shun the "mawkish sentimentality" and "hacknied" prose of its competitors. He particularly touts the magazine's innovative embellishments, remarking, "Imitation may be practiced by any body, but how few are there who possess the skill to originate." He promises his readers only "that which is novel and attractive," pointing out that the first "decoration" for the present issue was "raised from a die which took the premium at the recent exhibitions of the Franklin Institute." McMichael also opines: "few publishers would have ventured to give [the embellishment], even if they had the sagacity to perceive its practicability."[21]

Although the magazine lasted just 12 months with McMichael and Leslie at the helm (magazinist Timothy Arthur Shay took it over in January 1844), it featured a series of "firsts" to magazine embellishment that capitalized on the latest innovations in the graphic arts. In addition to the "raised impression from a die" highlighted previously, the magazine also featured a host of other firsts: colored mezzotint; lithotint; steel engraving using colored inks; embossed engravings; die-cut-out fashion plates layered one on top of the other; and the art of medal ruling. Moreover, in introducing each innovative embellishment, McMichael and Leslie touted them as both "novel" and "ingenious."

The staple of the illustrated magazines had long been woodcuts and line engravings. Newspapers and book illustrations tended to utilize woodcuts, due to the cheapness and greater ease of production of this method. The oldest form of embellishment, woodcuts relied on a relief process whereby a wooden block is carved to leave a flat, raised surface that is then inked and pressed onto paper. However, woodcuts could not deliver the same artistic sophistication as newer methods, and although used by the Philadelphia pictorials, they were not favored. Line and stipple engraving on steel, according to art historian Wendy Wick Reaves, had become the "respected medium for reproduction" by the 1840s,[22] and the annuals and illustrated monthly magazines (including the Philadelphia pictorials) touted "steel engravings" as the principal method used to furnish readers the popular "fashion plates."[23]

Louis Godey boasted that he kept 150 young ladies in work hand-coloring his famous fashion plates.[24] As was true of the other engraving techniques featured in the Philadelphia pictorials, 1843 proved to be a watershed year for the ubiquitous fashion plates. The principal improvements involved three distinct strategies, the first of which *Godey's* and *Graham's* had engaged in prior to 1843 as well. First, the magazines shed their reliance on recycled French and English fashion plates, hiring engravers to prepare original plates, though, of course, based on the fashion trends in Europe. Both *Godey's* and *Graham's* used this technique before 1843. Godey added a second innovation to his magazine in 1843—engaging illustrators to show feminine figures free of the "tight-lacing" associated with the European styles, thereby creating "Americanized" fashions.[25] Finally, *Miss Leslie's* used the fashion plates to create new novelty embellishments for its readers, again relying on both printing innovations and an emerging cult of the celebrity.[26]

Godey started boasting of "entirely original contents" and improved paper quality as early as January 1840, although at that time, his fashion plates appear to be printed from woodcuts and on the same paper as the textual material.[27] By April 1840, touting a circulation of 17,500 subscribers, *Godey's* offered hand-colored fashion plates printed on higher quality paper. In the "Editors' Table" for April he noted: "We have advanced with a steady step, and now compare with the best French or English periodicals that are devoted exclusively to this subject—which, as everybody knows, the Lady's Book is not."[28] Thus, Godey reminded his readers both that his magazine is *more* than just a guide to fashions, and that his *American* fashion plates now compete with their European counterparts. By December 1840 he groused that "exchange papers" fail to distinguish between borrowed and original plates: "Exchange papers in noticing the embellishments in the various magazines should make a distinction between those engraved expressly for a work and second hand plates. We give two engravings in each number from steel plates engraved expressly for the Book."[29]

Godey used these American-engraved fashion plates as an early form of "product placement," advertising his magazine and instructing readers how and where to read it. His hand- colored fashion plates for both January and February 1841 feature conspicuously placed bound volumes of the magazine. The January number reveals a parlor scene with a mother surrounded by her children, one daughter playing a piano with a bound volume clearly titled "Ladies Book" resting on the piano top. Wanting to assure his readers that his magazine should serve more than ornamental purposes, his February plate shows four female figures, one of whom appears to be reading to her companions out of a bound volume of the *Ladies Book*. An April 1841 fashion plate targets readers who may have subscribed too recently to have collected a year's worth of the magazine for binding—this plate shows a reader leafing through a single-copy number of *Godey's*. Not to be outdone, George Graham offered similar fashion plates in September and November 1841, adding a male fashion figure. Both publishers thereby schooled their captive readers to connect consumption of their magazines with other genteel parlor activities.

Meanwhile, as noted earlier, *Miss Leslie's* stressed "novelty" and "innovation" in the fashion plates, offering the celebrity plate of Princess Esterhazy (then touring America), and a novelty plate never before featured in a monthly illustrated magazine. In January *Miss Leslie's* led off with a die-cut technique featuring two fashion plates layered on top of each other, with an oval hole cut out of the face of the top plate so that the face of the bottom figure served both, an innovation repeated in the May issue. This costly process was generally reserved for expensive gift books and children's paper dolls and books. The publisher boasts of these fashions: "Our plates of the fashions, it will be observed, are not mere mechanical copies from indifferent French engravings, but they are original pictures drawn and executed by artists of the first eminence." In stressing the originality and uniqueness of their embellishments, McMichael and Leslie encouraged their readers to consider them as precious commodities offered for their readers' consumption.

Peterson's tried to compete with these innovations, offering a fashion plate printed in blue ink. Peterson's blue-inked plate appeared along with a second specially prepared gift plate, a hand-colored floral entitled *Peony and Butterfly* that Godey groused editorially had been a concept prepared first for his magazine.[30] In offering both the blue-inked fashion plate and the colored floral, Peterson crowed: "We call particular attention to the peony and butterfly in this number. This embellishment was got up under the supervision of Mrs. Hill, a celebrated teacher of painting in water colors." Peterson continued: "The execution of the flower will bear the closest examination, and is equal to anything in the most expensive drawing-books; and yet this embellishment is furnished to our subscribers in addition to the two other costly illustrations which adorn the number."[31]

Peterson also notes the markers of status implied by consumption of these fashion plates, described as "costly," "novel," and "equal to anything in the most expensive drawing-books." Like *Miss Leslie's* and *Godey's*, *Peterson's* adopted the strategy of linking consumption of his innovative embellishments to aspirations of upward mobility and gentility. Middle-class magazine readers could imitate the consumption patterns of the cultural and economic elite via the purchase and display of fashion and novelty plates from these illustrated monthlies. The blue ink, the die-cut overlaid figures, the raised embossed celebrity embellishments—these were just the innovations to the fashion plates!

Miss Leslie's choicest work for 1843 focused on what were already the most costly and time-consuming engraving methods: mezzotint and lithography. The leading mezzotint engraver in Philadelphia in the 1840s, and indeed in the entire country, was the English emigrant, John Sartain. As Sartain scholar Katharine Martinez notes, few American engravers before 1830 had attempted the technique of mezzotint, though artists and collectors admired and purchased English mezzotints. Mezzotint uses intaglio printing techniques—

"intaglio," the Italian word for "incised," indicated the techniques relying on the use of a burin to incise lines on metal plates.[32]

Sartain spent the decade of the 1830s perfecting this technique, which involved roughening up the metal surface (a process Sartain called "preparing the grounds"), and dampening the paper in the printing process, costly and time consuming. To increase the number of imprints from one plate, Sartain switched from a copper to steel plate, trained his own printer in the technique, and arranged for the construction of a suitable press to produce the prints.[33] Because mezzotinting had long been connected with the successful reproduction of portraits for mass distribution, Sartain quickly befriended prominent Philadelphia portrait painters. By 1840, he was already producing mezzotints for a variety of sources, including individual print sales, art associations, and magazines.[34]

In their March 1843 issue, Leslie and McMichael pushed magazine mezzotint embellishment to a new height by offering their readers *The Pets,* a "coloured mezzotint," engraved by Sartain from a picture by English artist, Edwin Landseer. Sartain had earlier engraved an identical mezzotint, though uncolored, for the May 1839 issue of *Burton's Gentleman's Magazine.* In the "Publisher's Table" for the March 1843 issue, McMichael described his version of the embellishment to his readers:

> The principal plate is a mezzotint by Sartain, from one of Landseer's finest pictures; and to give to it the highest possible effect and finish, we have had it coloured in the richest style by the most skilful artist, in his line, to be found in this country. No other publisher has ventured to give a *coloured mezzotint;* and no coloured print of any description at all approaching this of ours, has ever before been furnished to the subscribers of a monthly magazine.[35]

The publisher's rhetoric here clearly displays the status meant to be conveyed to the owner of this embellishment. By insisting that it is taken from one of Landseer's "finest" paintings, engraved by the best-known engraver of the era, and finished in the "richest style" and with the "highest possible effect and finish" by the "most skillful artist, in his line," the publisher elevates the value of the embellishment. Instead of mere "picture," a light and superfluous addition to the serious literary matter, it becomes the magazine's *raison d'etre.* Cast as a prized "commodity," the embellishment distinguishes its consumer from subscribers to *other* illustrated magazines.[36] Indeed, the embellishments featured in *Miss Leslie's* in 1843, and soon matched by *Godey's* and *Peterson's,* surpassed those found previously only in the expensive annuals, that generally sold for two to three times the price of an entire year's subscription to one of the Philadelphia pictorials.[37]

In April 1843, *Miss Leslie's* offered to its readers another first, a lithotint, *Grandpapa's Pet,* prepared by John H. Richards of the P.S. Duval firm.[38] Lithography, a technique of printing from stone, appeared in the Philadelphia pictorials before 1843. Cephas Childs, a Philadelphia printer and publisher, specialized in lithography in the 1820s and 1830s, believing it to be the print medium closest to painting, and ideal for engraved portraits.[39] Childs employed the deaf-mute Alfred Newsam, and recruited from France the young lithographer, Peter S. Duval.[40] Lithography, a planographic method of printing, works on the natural repulsion of grease and water. Lithographers employed a greasy pen, drawing on the surface of a dry stone.[41] Color, if desired, could be added by hand, after printing. By 1843, Duval had started his own lithography business, specializing in colored lithographed prints. His strategy involved painting in colors directly on the stone.[42] Print historians generally distinguish between "lithotints" (tonal lithography using colors on one stone only) and "chromolithography" (the successive use of multiple stones to build up color).[43] Regardless of the method used, adding colors aimed at achieving the effect of watercolor painting in a print medium.[44] Duval prepared elaborate chromolithographed covers for *Godey's* in the 1840s.

Miss Leslie's devoted the front page article of the April 1843 issue to a detailed description of this "new art." Reminding readers that they were promised "whatever novelties in the way of embellishments we could procure," the publisher assured his audience that he has "not hesitated either to incur expense" in so doing. He identified lithotint as "an art hitherto unknown in the United States," and traced its invention to a London lithographer "of rare skill," Mr Hullmandel. He noted that his own engraver saw several productions by Hullmandel prepared in this manner, and working in conjunction with Duval, experimented with achieving like results. The publisher predicted that lithotint would "effect a revolution" in print publishing."[45] Although print historians point out that lithotint never really caught on in America, they also recognize *Grandpapa's Pet* as the first lithotint produced in America.[46] In the same April 1843 issue, the publisher presented a fashion plate prepared in "chalk-tints on stone," also claiming it to be the first time that this technique had been applied to a magazine embellishment.

In August 1843, *Miss Leslie's* featured yet another "first" in magazine embellishments, introducing the plate with another front-page article beginning: "Our readers will have noticed that it is a part of the plan of our Magazine, to present whatever is new and attractive in the graphic art." She continued with a description of that month's plate, entitled *Belisarius*, engraved by A. Spencer (see Figure 5.3), identifying it as "the art of *medal ruling*, executed by the original inventor of the medal ruling machine." While print historians contest the assertion that Asa Spencer was the first to perfect the art of medal engraving, they do acknowledge his contribution to the process.[47] Medal engraving relies on what is known as a "pantographic device" that utilizes two needles to trace the surface of a coin, medal, or small relief and transfer the image to metal plates, preserving areas of light and shadow to reproduce the quality of relief (see Figure 5.3). An earlier version

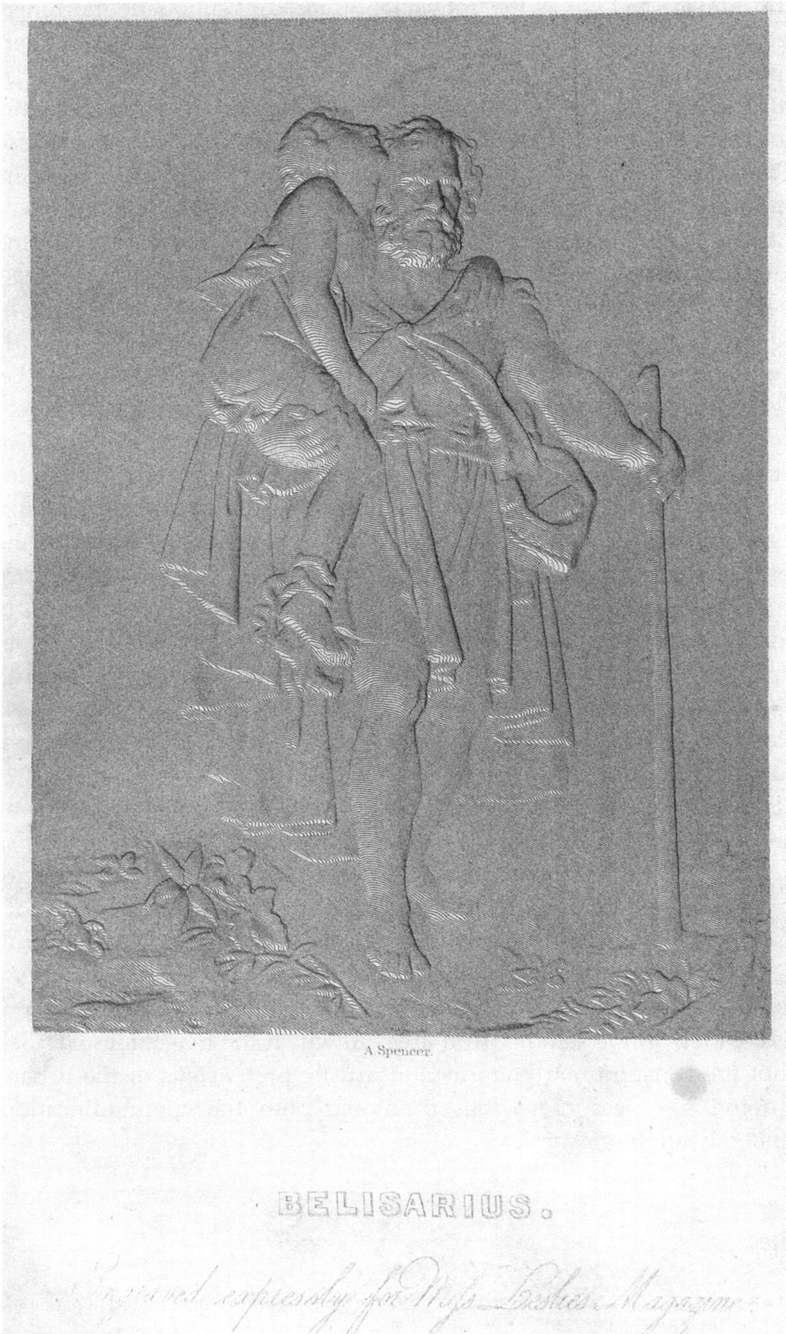

5.3 *Belisarius*, frontispiece, *Miss Leslie's*, August 1843. Courtesy the Winterthur Library: Printed Book and Periodical Collection

of this device, known as the "physiognotrace" or "silhouette machine," was used to trace a person's profile. In introducing the engraving to readers, the publishers reminded those who might have forgotten their history lessons that Belisarius was the "great general" who protected the emperor Justinian.[48] In offering their subscribers *Belisarius*, Leslie and McMichael enabled readers to consume and display the middle-class equivalent of the classic marble sculpture—in the form of an engraved bas relief art reproduction.

As the year drew to a close, one surmises that McMichael's "ample means" proved insufficient to sustain continued production of these costly engravings, for after this beautiful plate, *Miss Leslie's* embellishments noticeably fell off in quality. *Graham's*, meanwhile, failed to engage rhetorically in the degree of one-upmanship evident between *Godey's*, *Peterson's*, and *Miss Leslie's*, relying instead on tried-and-true mezzotints and Quarre's richly colored lace patterns for the bulk of the magazine's pictorial matter. While *Godey's*, *Peterson's*, and, most particularly, *Miss Leslie's* promoted innovations to American graphic arts, and attached clear signifiers of taste and upward class mobility to consumption of these new commodities, the publishers of these illustrated monthly periodicals still needed to contend with market forces that circumscribed the limits of their innovations. In an era before widespread use of advertisements, embellishments that were expensive to produce required a large enough audience to support their continued production. In the case of *Miss Leslie's*, lack of a substantial enough subscription base likely contributed to the discontinuation of the expensive and innovative embellishments.

However, in one short, watershed year, *Miss Leslie's* challenged the artistic superiority of her established male competitors, *Godey's*, *Graham's*, and *Peterson's*. By linking innovations in the mechanical arts with artistic novelty, Eliza Leslie and Morton McMichael presented to the subscribers of their monthly magazine costly embellishments never before provided to a middle-class audience. Employing rhetoric clearly linking the embellishments' value to both utility and to cultural refinement, these publishers encouraged middle-class readers in the remote rural areas to which the magazines circulated to adopt the consumption patterns and artistic pretensions of the urban elite. In doing so, these magazines promoted both the commodification and democratization of American art.

Notes

1. *Godey's Lady's Book*, November 1843, 240. Citations to magazines will be placed in parentheses after the quoted passages.
2. Thomas Beckman, the leading scholar of this graphic art, dates the first widespread use of die sink cameo stamps to the mid 1850s, and notes that blue ink, like that used for the *Godey's* medallions, was the color of choice in the early years of this art form. Diesinking was used most frequently

on business cards, company letterheads, and envelopes. Godey's holiday present to his readers pre-dates the earliest examples catalogued by Beckman by nearly a decade. See Thomas Beckman, "American Diesinkers and Their Cameo Stamps, 1850–1880: A Researcher's Discoveries and Survey," *Maine Antique Digest* (May 1999): 44b–46b.

3. Frank Luther Mott, *A History of American Magazines, Volume I: 1741–1850* (Cambridge: Harvard University Press, 1957), 520.

4. Mott, *A History of American Magazines, Volume 1*, 378.

5. See, for example, "Parlor Periodicals," *Democrat's Review*, January 1852, 76. Retrieved from American Periodical Series Online.

6. This chapter is a reorganized version of chapter 2 of my book-length manuscript, *Art for the Middle Classes*, to be published by The University Press of Mississippi.

7. For more on these technological changes, see Ronald J. Zboray, *A Fictive People: Antebellum Economic Development and the American Reading Public* (New York: Oxford University Press, 1993).

8. For a discussion of this "explosion" in print culture in America, see Isabelle *Lehuu, Carnival on the Page: Popular Print Media in Antebellum America* (Chapel Hill: University of North Carolina Press, 2000). For a similar discussion focused on Britain, see Patricia Anderson, *The Printed Image and the Transformation of Popular Culture 1790–1860* (Oxford: Clarendon Press, 1991).

9. For information on the American Art-Union, see Mary Bartlett Cowdrey, *American Academy of Fine Arts and the American Art-Union 1816–1852* (New York: New York Historical Society, 1963). Heidi Nichols discusses the relationship between the American Art-Union and *Sartain's Union Magazine* in chapters one and three of her book. See Heidi Lynne Nichols, *The Fashioning of Middle-Class America: Sartain's Union Magazine of Literature and Art and Antebellum Culture* (New York: Peter Lang, 2004).

10. On early American museums, see David R. Brigham, *Public Culture in the Early Republic: Peale's Museum and Its Audience* (Washington, DC: Smithsonian Institution Press, 1995); James W. Cook, *The Arts of Deception: Playing with Fraud in the Age of Barnum* (Cambridge: Harvard University Press, 2001). On the importance of window displays to American consumer culture, see Leigh Eric Schmidt, *Consumer Rites: The Buying and Selling of American Holidays* (Princeton: Princeton University Press, 1995). For a discussion of mid-nineteenth-century methods of self-imaging, see Shawn Michelle Smith, *American Archives: Gender, Race, and Class in Visual Culture* (Princeton: Princeton University Press, 1999). For a discussion of billboards, banners, signs, and currency, see David M. Henkins, *City Reading* (New York: Columbia University Press, 1998).

11. The illustrated gift books and annuals that peaked in popularity a decade earlier, in the 1830s, served as the first major venue for the distribution of original American art reproductions. For an excellent discussion of the historical context for the emergence of American gift books and annuals, see Stephanie Mayer Heydt's dissertation "The Art of *The Gift*: William Sidney Mount, Daniel Huntington and the Antebellum Gift Book Industry," particularly Chapter 1, "'The Age of the Annual': The Gift Book in its Social Context," PhD Dissertation, Boston University, 2008. Heydt does a particularly nice job of tracing the increasing importance of the role of women in promoting consumption of the fine arts via their involvement in the annuals and illustrated magazines, and the link between "pious consumption" and an emerging consumer culture targeting women. For more on "pious consumption," see Lori Merish, *Sentimental Materialism: Gender, Commodity Culture, and Nineteenth-Century American Literature*(Durham: Duke University Press, 2000).

12. James Playsted Wood, *Magazines in the United States* (New York: The Ronald Press Co., 1971), 47. Louis Godey claimed 100,000 readers early in the decade (from readers sharing with family and friends) and he stated that he had printed 40,000 copies of the July 1849 number (*Godey's*, July 1849, p. 82). Mott asserts that by just before the Civil War, *Godey's* subscription list topped out at 150,000 (see Mott, *A History of American Magazines, vol. 1*, 181).

13. See *Godey's*, December 1850, p. 384. On Art-Union figures, see Cowdrey, *American Academy*, 243.

14. *Graham's* began to advertise "elegant embossed work" on the title page as early as July 1841, as well as the "Finest Mezzotinto and Steel Engravings." In fact, in enumerating the embellishments in each issue, this genre of "Lace Work and Flowers" appears repeatedly between 1841 and 1843.

15. For biographical information on Quarre, see George C. Groce and David H. Wallace, *The New-York Historical Society's Dictionary of Artists in America 1564–1860* (New Haven: Yale University Press, Sixth Printing, 1979), 520.

16. For background on *Peterson's Magazine*, see Frank Luther Mott, *A History of American Magazines, Volume II: 1850–1865* (Cambridge: Harvard University Press, 1957) 306–7. For more on the life of Charles Peterson, see Karen Nipps, "Charles Jacobs Peterson," in *Dictionary of Literary Biography, Volume 79: American Magazine Journalists, 1850–1900*, ed. Sam G. Riley, 236–41 (Detroit: Gale Research Co., 1989).

17. "The Embellishments," *Godey's Lady's Book*, December 1843, 240.

18. As noted previously, the established New York monthly, *The Knickerbocker*, targeted the aristocratic old elite, featuring primarily the work of continental writers and artists. The Philadelphia illustrated monthly magazines, on the other hand, targeted a decidedly more middle-class audience, and boasted of American ingenuity, and mechanical and artistic achievements.

19. Eliza Leslie was a sister to the painter, Charles Leslie, and her sister Anne married into the Philadelphia publishing dynasty of the Carey family. For biographical details on Leslie, see *Godey's* January 1846, page 1 article, "Our Contributors, Miss Eliza Leslie." Also see Alice B. Haven, "Personal Reminiscences of Miss Eliza Leslie," *Godey's Lady's Book*, April 1858, 344–50; Pennsylvania Academy of the Fine Arts, *Catalogue of the Exhibition of Paintings and Drawings* (Philadelphia: T.K. and P.G. Collins, Printers, 1843); Elisa E. Beshero-Bondar, "Eliza Leslie," in *Dictionary of Literary Biography, Volume 202: Nineteenth-Century American Fiction Writers*, ed. Kent P. Ljungquist, 166–72 (Detroit: Gale Research Co., 1989); John S. Hart, *Female Prose Writers of America* (Philadelphia: E.H. Butler, 1852), 26–32; Mott, *A History of American Magazines, Volume I*, 534 and 733–4; Ophia Smith, "Charles and Eliza Leslie," *Pennsylvania Magazine of History and Biography*, 1950, 512–27.

20. For McMichael's lyceum address, see Morton McMichael, "An Address Delivered before the Northern Lyceum of the City and County of Philadelphia," in the *Historical Society of Pennsylvania Closed Stacks* under "McMichael" (Philadelphia, 1839). The question of tax-supported public high school education was a source of public debate in this era. The Franklin Institute had sponsored a series of successive high schools beginning in 1826, and by 1836, the Pennsylvania state legislature had passed legislation to fund public high schools. Philadelphia's Central High School opened in 1839, the same year as McMichael's address. See Bruce Sinclair, *Philadelphia's Philosopher Mechanics: A History of the Franklin Institute 1824–1865* (Baltimore: Johns Hopkins University Press, 1974), particularly chapter five.

21. "Publisher's Table," February 1843: 76.

22. Wick Reaves is particularly concerned with portrait prints, and the challenges faced by Cephas Childs in trying to introduce consumers to lithographed prints of their painted portraits, for distribution to a wider circle of friends, when line and stipple engravings on steel had been the preferred method for portrait prints previously. See Wendy Wick Reaves, ed., *American Portrait Prints: Proceedings of the Tenth Annual American Print Conference* (Charlottesville: University Press of Virginia, for the Smithsonian Institution, 1984), 97.

23. Bamber Gascoigne, *How to Identify Prints: A Complete Guide to Manual and Mechanical Processes from Woodcut to Inkjet*, 2nd ed. (London: Thames & Hudson, 2004), sec. 13a.

24. Mott, *A History of American Magazines, Volume I*, 591.

25. It is difficult to determine which of Godey's several "editors" was behind this drive. As Sarah Josepha Hale's biographer Patricia Okker notes, Godey reminded readers in 1859 that Hale was not the fashion editor; see Patricia Okker. *Our Sister Editors: Sarah J. Hale and the Tradition of Nineteenth-Century American Women Editors* (Athens: University of Georgia Press, 1995), 231. The title page for January 1843 lists Hale, McMichael, and Godey as editors, with Sedgwick, Leslie, and Willis as regular contributors. Since Leslie and McMichael had, in fact, defected to start their own monthly and it is unlikely Godey suggested the changes in the fashion style, that leaves Hale and Sedgwick. While it is possible that Sedgwick drove the reform, it seems rather in keeping with Hale's forceful presence at the magazine to have pushed through the changes to the fashions and then to have turned her attention to the literary matter she so clearly preferred to direct.

26. On the rise of a celebrity culture in America, see Thomas N. Baker, *Sentiment and Celebrity: Nathaniel Parker Willis and the Trials of Literary Fame* (New York: Oxford University Press, 1999); and David Haven Blake, *Walt Whitman and the Culture of American Celebrity* (New Haven: Yale University Press, 2006).

27. See "Publisher's Notice," page 48, and fashion plate, page 49, *Godey's Lady's Book*, January 1840.

28. See "Editors' Table," *Godey's Lady's Book*, April 1840, 191.

29. "Editors' Table," 285.

30. The September 1843 number of *Godey's* contained a "Coloured Rose and Butterfly" that Godey claimed to have commissioned before the *Peterson's* August "Peony and Butterfly." He huffs that his magazine for July featured an uncolored version of the rose embellishment, *before Peterson's* August "Peony and Butterfly."

31. See "Publisher's Table," *Peterson's Magazine,* August 1843, 72.

32. Gascoigne, *How to Identify Prints,* sec. 1b.

33. Basil Hunnisett notes that even with steel plates, Sartain needed to engrave four plates of each subject to meet the circulation demands of 40,000 for *Graham's Magazine* in the early 1840s. See Hunnisett, *Engraved on Steel: The History of Picture Production Using Steel Plates* (Aldershot: Ashgate, 1998), 336. For these reasons, publishers frequently used the editorial spaces of their magazines to encourage subscribers to be the first to re-subscribe. Charles Peterson, in particular, claimed that the earliest imprints (and therefore the crispest) went to the earliest re-subscribers. See "Publisher's Card," *The Ladies National Magazine,* December 1848, 216.

34. On Sartain's career, see the excellent collection edited by Katharine Martinez and Page Talbott, *Philadelphia's Cultural Landscape: The Sartain Family Legacy* (Philadelphia: Temple University Press, 2000). See also Katharine Martinez, "John Sartain (1808–1897): His Contribution to American Printmaking," *Imprint* 8, no. 1 (1983): 1–12. Finally, see Martinez's essay, "Portrait Prints by John Sartain," in Reaves, ed., *American Portrait Prints,* 135–93.

35. See "Publisher's Table," *Miss Leslie's Magazine,* March 1843, 112. In that same issue Leslie and McMichael also offered their readers a plate of "Berlin worsted patterns for Slippers," also proclaiming that this embellishment is "an entirely new one ... as this is the first time any thing of the kind has been attempted in this country."

36. For a discussion of "commodity fetishism," see Sut Jhally, *The Codes of Advertising: Fetishism and the Political Economy of Meaning in the Consumer Society* (New York: Routledge, 1990); Judith Williamson, *Decoding Advertisements: Ideology and Meaning in Advertising* (London: Marion Boyars, 1978).

37. Indeed, as a reviewer for the *Southern Chronicle* noted of *Godey's* early issues for 1845, the magazine had become "as ornamental as an annual" (*The Editors' Book Table, Godey's,* March 1845, 144).

38. Nicholas B. Wainwright notes this about Duval: "Duval came into his own as a lithographer in 1835, when the partnership of Lehman & Duval moved into attractive quarters in a new four-story building on the southeast corner of Dock Street and Bank Alley. This was an excellent business location, for it faced the Merchant's Exchange in the heart of the commercial district." See Nicholas B. Wainwright, *Philadelphia in the Romantic Age of Lithography* (Philadelphia: The Historical Society of Pennsylvania, 1958), 30.

39. For a discussion of lithography as a "fine art," see Janet Flint, "The American Painter-Lithographer," in *Art and Commerce: American Prints of the Nineteenth Century* (Charlottesville: University Press of Virginia, 1978), 127–8. See also Antony Griffiths, *Prints and Printmaking: An Introduction to the History and Techniques* (New York: Alfred Knopf, 1980), 101–2.

40. For more on Cephas Childs and Alfred Newsam, see Reaves, ed., *American Portrait Prints,* 83–134.

41. Gascoigne, *How to Identify Prints,* sec 19a.

42. Gascoigne, *How to Identify Prints,* sec 19d.

43. See Peter C. Marzio, "The Democratic Art of Chromolithography in America: An Overview," in *Art and Commerce: American Prints of the Nineteenth Century* (Charlottesville: University Press of Virginia, 1978), 92.

44. See Michael Twyman, *Lithography 1800–1850* (London: Oxford University Press, 1970), 147–50.

45. See "The New Art of Lithotint," *Miss Leslie's Magazine,* April 1843, 113–14.

46. Marzio, "The Democratic Art," 92; Karen Nipps, *Naturally Fond of Pictures: American Illustration of the 1840s and 1850s* (Philadelphia: Library Company of Philadelphia, 1989), 2.

47. See Arthur H. Frazier, "Joseph Saxton and His Contributions to the Medal Ruling and Photographic Arts," ed. Smithsonian Institution (Washington, DC: Smithsonian Institution Press, 1975), 2–8; Groce and Wallace, *New-York Historical Society's Dictionary of Artists;* Elizabeth M. Harris, *The Art of Medal Engraving: A Curious Chapter in the Development of 19th Century Printing Processes* (Newtown, PA: Bird & Bull Press, 1991), 7–12.

48. *Miss Leslie's Magazine,* August 1843, 33.

6

The Women's Paradise: The American Fantasy, Home Appliances, and Consumer Demand in Liberation France

Rebecca J. Pulju

There is no place where the position of women is more enviable than the United States. There, she holds an important place in the couple. He works for her. She works for him. Liberated from her domestic cares by her mechanical servants, she is free to justify her superiority in culture and refinement.

So declared journalist Merry Bromberger in the women's weekly *La Femme* in 1945.[1] The American way of life figured prominently in the French women's periodical press of the post-war period. While elite intellectuals often belittled the standardization and mechanization of American culture and life, women's journals celebrated American modernization as a means of liberating women from onerous domestic chores. Claiming that American mechanization had all but eliminated housework in the United States, journalists championed American mass consumer society with its apparent prosperity, leisure, and gender equality.

The American lifestyle portrayed in French women's magazines in the post-war period contrasted starkly with French poverty. In truth, it also contrasted with the reality of life in the United States, where leisure, prosperity, and equality had certainly not been attained by most American women. Regardless of their inaccuracy, the stories and images disseminated by these magazines are valuable for providing insight into the hopes, desires, and fantasies of French women in the post-war period. They also lend insight into how mass consumer society was created in post-war France. During the Cold War, the American government would actively advertise its "way of life" in France and throughout Europe.[2] In response, French intellectuals, in particular those on the political Left, would feel compelled to defend French culture against the American onslaught.[3] Despite the influence of these post-war intellectuals, the French path to mass consumer society was more convoluted than this model of domination-resistance would suggest. As historians of Europe and North America have shown, the United States did not simply impose mass consumer society on Europeans after the war.[4] A survey of articles in the women's press following the Liberation reveals the complexity of transatlantic exchange and suggests that at least some women hungered for aspects of American mass culture long before they existed in France. Communist poet Louis Aragon could derisively label the United States a "civilization of bathtubs and fridgidaires," but women journalists pitched their message to an audience that likely found those same bathtubs and fridgidaires quite attractive.[5] By the end of the 1950s, the consumer durables and new furnishings that women journalists described would be labeled simply "modern." At the moment of the Liberation, however, with France impoverished and American troops a common sight in France, these goods, and the "way of life" associated with them, were decidedly American, and decidedly appealing.

In the mid 1940s, mass consumer society had not yet arrived in France. The consumer goods lauded in the women's press were not available in France, and the nation teetered between poverty and plenty before the war years led eventually into the period of prosperity known as the "*trente glorieuses.*" At the Liberation, the need for reconstruction, fascination with American standards of living, and the recent enfranchisement of French women all shaped journalists' demands for change. Despite the rapid return of partisan politics after the war, French leaders agreed on one principle: France needed to modernize if it wished to maintain its status as a world power.[6] In the late 1940s, as the economic plans of the Fourth Republic began to solidify, French women journalists insisted that modernization should extend to the home. They looked to the United States as a model for France and cajoled their readers into making demands, as consumers and newly enfranchised citizens, for change.

While French women struggled with the burdens of daily life during reconstruction, they were barraged with images of America in the journals they consumed. Living conditions in France made the United States look like a consumer paradise. Nearly two million French homes had been damaged by World War II, and standards of comfort in French housing had been far behind the United States even before the war.[7] As late as 1954, only 26.6 percent of French homes had a private, indoor toilet, 58.4 percent had running water, and 10.4 percent had a bathtub or shower.[8] These living conditions greatly affected women, as they were responsible for caring for home and family. A 1948 study of urban women found that married women without children dedicated more than 56 hours a week to domestic work; those with children averaged over 80 hours a week.[9] Housework without modern amenities was not only time consuming, it was hard labor. Washing clothes, for example, often entailed running up and down stairs to a water tap in the courtyard, a chore that made running water and washing machines particularly attractive innovations.[10]

The popular women's press was one of the most important purveyors of images of American home comfort in France following the war. Women's magazines featuring the home and practical advice, and addressing themselves to wives, mothers, and homemakers, had developed rapidly, along with the rest of the popular press, after 1870.[11] The interwar years saw the introduction of a number of fashion journals that grew in popularity with the spread of high fashion to the streets and the increasing use of cosmetics.[12] The image of the managerial housewife overseeing a home replete with consumer durables was born in the interwar women's press, but never became a reality, due to depression economics and the continued reluctance of the French middle-class to buy mass-produced goods.[13] After the war, women journalists would take advantage of the national discourse on reconstruction to promote the kinds of homes, and goods, that French women needed. Their demands were spread by a women's press that steadily increased in popularity. In the post-war years, the national press printed about 70 million journal issues per month; in 1948, 24 million of these issues were women's publications. This number reached 29 million in 1950 and 31 million in 1951. In 1952, the number of issues of women's journals sold in France equaled that of the political, economic, technical, financial, agricultural, union, artistic, and sporting press combined.[14]

The appearance of women's journals changed with the conditions of the post-war years. Immediately following the Liberation, journals were nearly devoid of ads, were printed on poor quality paper, and were usually under 20 pages long in keeping with government restrictions on paper. Modern advertising stimulated consumer demand, but it is revealing that demands for American-style consumer durables predated the glossy and intrusive ads that would become popular over the course of the 1950s.[15] In the late 1940s, there were very few large, colored ads, suggesting that despite the power of modern advertising, it was not the only force driving demand for change.[16] Despite the restrictions facing journals in the immediate post-war period, dozens of them appeared each week at a price low enough for women to buy several at once. Not only did their short stories and photos offer an escape from reality, but most articles were short enough to be read in breaks from attendance to domestic chores and family responsibilities.

The journals of the immediate post-war years also differed slightly in their content from their successors. Written in the earliest phases of reconstruction, many devoted ample space to advice for women trying to create a comfortable home life amidst poverty and destruction. Journalists also wrote in the wake of emancipation, as French women went to the polls for the first time. Several women's journals of the immediate post-war period, started by women formerly active in the Resistance, explicitly encouraged women's political participation.

Resistance hero Lucie Aubrac served as director of the short-lived *La Femme*. Resisters and representatives of the *Mouvement Républicaine Populaires* (MRP) in the constituent assemblies of the Fourth Republic, Germaine Peyroles and Solange Lamblin, started *Marie-France*.[17] However, the political content of women's journals was not usually their selling point. This is apparent in the short life-span of *La Femme*, as well as in the gradual depoliticization of *Marie-France*, which remained a big seller through the 1950s.[18] It is clear, however, that the political issues of the war years influenced the journals of the immediate post-war period and that women's new citizenship responsibilities, as well as the national focus on reconstruction, inspired calls for women's political participation and consumer demands.

Following the Liberation, national attention was focused on the problems of rebuilding, and women's primary responsibility in this process was child-bearing and rearing. Women's journals never denied the need for a pronatalist drive and even stressed the importance of population growth for building a strong France. At the same time, journalists encouraged women to take advantage of their new political rights and criticized the government for failing to support women in their efforts to feed, clothe, and shelter their children, activities that were generally believed to be essential to national reconstruction. Journalists pushed "private" issues into the public sphere to politicize both their demands and their readers. They encouraged women to vote to improve their own living conditions. Another feature of the immediate post-war years was the place of the United States in these demands. Oftentimes, journalists used the example of America and American home modernization as a model for the future of French society. The American woman, with her mechanized home in the consumer's paradise, provided an attractive vision of the future.

America was a constant source of interest in the women's press and articles abounded examining various aspects of life in the United States. Depictions were not always flattering, in particular when they dealt with American contributions to fashion and food. *Elle* observed, for example, in a 1946 article on Hollywood starlets on a shopping expedition, that French women dreaming of these shopping opportunities "could console themselves by seeing how people dress in Hollywood."[19] But on the whole, the United States emerged as a young, vigorous nation unbridled by custom, class tension, or a complicated past. Though it lacked French culture and civilization, the United States was comfortable and wealthy. These qualities may have inspired derision among French intellectuals, as well as fears for the future of French culture, but in the women's press they often evoked envy and longing for a life of comfort and ease in place of the heavy burdens of housework and child-rearing common in post-war France.

The presence of young American men in France during and after the Liberation added an interesting dimension to portrayals of the United States.

Many articles described the strength and physical fitness of these young men, in comparison to the French population. In *La Femme Nouvelle*, a woman described introducing her parents to "her" American: "In our little dining room, I saw Herbert, jammed between the table and the piano. He seemed to be of another race, from another world, in his impeccable uniform. Papa and Mama looked, next to him, little, shriveled, and poor in their clothes from before the war."[20] The stories often had ambivalent messages—in this case, the kind young GI eventually stops writing his French sweetheart, suggesting that he romanced her only to pass the time before returning to the United States. Even when ambivalent, these physical descriptions of Americans implicitly condemned French men, who clearly had not prepared French women for the hyper-masculine American male. The same condemnation was present in articles about how the "American boy" was raised. One journalist noted that American boys had a more practical education than French children, were more independent than French children, and were infused with "team spirit" from a young age (this was reinforced by the importance of sports in American schools).[21]

GIs also represented American consumer society, and their physical health was only one sign of the wealth of the United States. The French, and other Europeans, were shocked by the wealth of the US Army. French people in liberated territories literally supplied themselves with goods the American army left behind, and the image of the GI offering gum, candy, and other goods to French children was ubiquitous.[22] Journals told stories of GIs buying dinner for young girls in restaurants, some noting the "purity" and "sweetness" of the relationship between two young people unable to understand each other's language.[23] Less sympathetic views and stories also circulated, owing to the heavy involvement of GIs in the black market and their trading of goods for alcohol or sex.[24]

Occasionally, journalists expressed frustration at the inability of these young Americans to understand the French situation. In a bittersweet story about a charming and genuine GI stationed in a Biarritz family's home, the "hostess," a bit saddened by the GI's intention to leave Europe and never return, reminded him of the fact that the horror of war was a menace for him, but was, for her family, "the bread and water of each day" and was in no small part due to the fact that an ocean separated the United States from Japanese imperialism; France had no such barrier against Hitler.[25] In 1946, *La Femme* reported on a brochure printed by the United States Army in response to GIs' complaints about the French. It seems the GIs found the French pretentious, lazy, and dirty. The American army had been forced to explain to its troops that French women did not smile at GIs in the street because they were not prostitutes, that the French did not all dream of becoming millionaires, and that French homes and people were dirty because France was a poor country with a shortage of soap and modern conveniences.[26]

Despite remarks on the lack of comprehension and empathy of some GIs, the images of American men, couples, and homes in women's magazines were decidedly positive. The American couple living in the consumer paradise was egalitarian, comfortable, prosperous, and, above all, modern. Stories of young French women following their GI husbands home to America were frequent, and these French women served as witnesses to the condition of women and the standard of living in the United States. In 1946, *La Femme Nouvelle* printed extracts of a letter ostensibly submitted to the magazine by a GI bride. The bride was most amazed by "the incredible comfort of the kitchen" which was not only practical "but so pretty and agreeable to live in that one never wants to leave."[27] Articles included frequent references to the dearth of consumer goods in France. American kitchens were modern, efficient, and rational, "considering that cooking is a job like any other."[28] After describing the dimensions of the kitchen workspace and the arrangement of the cupboards, appliances, and dishes, she concluded that: "Finally, all of this is created according to scientific calculations in order to eliminate any useless movement, any waste of time and energy. With this goal in mind, housewives are advised to use both of their hands, which is easy when one possesses furnishings of this kind."[29] Modern consumer goods had clearly simplified the lives of American women.

At this stage, while consumer goods were most noteworthy, the poverty in France made even the food available in the United States appear glamorous. *La Femme* followed several GI brides to their new homes and commented on the great abundance that obviously was lacking in France. The journalist visited the grocery store with the young bride, Monique, and noted: "Her purchases at the grocery store are a true test for her vocabulary, but the abundance here is such that all one needs, most of the time, is to point a finger at the object one desires."[30] The image that epitomized abundance, equality, and the absence of class tension, in part because of the success of American motion pictures, was that of California.[31] In 1946, *La Femme* printed an article titled, "The Land of the Stars is also an Earthly Paradise: The Life of Three Households in California." The article described the lifestyles of three families at different income levels who had also been featured in the American review, *Life*. The article began: "Life in the open air, in an eternal summer, high salaries combined with low priced merchandise, urbanism and ultramodern comfort in a new country unencumbered by its past, these are the characteristics of life in California, the ideal life for every American."[32] The article portrayed the life of each family, including that with the smallest budget, the family of a firefighter, as comfortable and modern.

La Femme reported that the firefighter, who was married with two children, lived in a six-room house that he owned. His wife, Mrs Loeffler, had a refrigerator and a washing machine. The family went "everyday, in their Dodge, to swim in the ocean, forty kilometers away."[33] Like the Loeffler family, a sales director's family had no domestic servants, but had eliminated most housework through the acquisition of domestic appliances. *La Femme* reported that Nancy and Betty Campbell "accomplish in three hours and thirty minutes the washing of the entire household: two hours in the washing machine and one hour and thirty minutes of drying in the sun."[34] Only the richest family, that of a famous composer, had domestic servants; "their life differs very little, however, from that of all the other Californians."[35] The portrayal of the United States as a society devoid of class differences and tensions was common in the French women's press, and the absence of domestic servants in well-to-do families drew comment here and in other articles.[36] According to women journalists, modern consumer goods, and labor-saving domestic appliances in particular, had an equalizing effect.

Life in the consumer paradise was characterized not only by social equality, but by gender equality, especially within marriage. In "24 Hours with Barbara and Teddy in Paris (Texas)," Merry Bromberger described the life of a fictional American couple. She used Barbara and Teddy's upbringing to extol the greater racial, class, and gender equality in the United States. The assertion that: "They were students together in high school, the most beautiful building in town, in the middle of the park, where all of the town's children, girls, boys, black, or white are raised," is evidence of the idealism of the journalist's evaluation of the American South in 1945.[37] Clearly, descriptions of the United States emphasized what women found lacking in French society, rather than providing an accurate image of life in America.

Bromberger and other journalists repeatedly emphasized the gender equality of American marriages. Consumerism was central to this image, as women's power as domestic consumers justified their equality, and consumer durables gave them the free time to enjoy their social position. After Teddy leaves for work, Barbara listens to the daily radio program for practical information about purchases. She was attentive because "she is the one who spends, as American wives do, the money that her husband earns, and she must make wise purchases."[38] Economic power underlay women's strength in American society, but the domestic appliances women bought with their money led to other liberties as well. In the story, Barbara throws her laundry in the washing machine and leaves to do her shopping and meet her friends for ice cream. She returns only at 5:00 pm to prepare dinner before Teddy returns at 6:00 pm to eat and to inform her that they will be going to the opera that evening. That the young couple in Paris, Texas was spending the evening at the opera reveals both the particularly French nature of this fantasy and contradicts the assertion that the United States was a cultural wasteland. French journalists clearly embraced the aspects of American society that they wanted applied to France. Women journalists were not, however, alone in making this connection between consumer goods and cultural development. French intellectuals and sociologists who advocated the rationalization of the home often argued that reducing women's household labor would give them a more fulfilling intellectual and cultural life.[39]

In the article, Barbara's life is made easier and more fulfilling by the charming manners of her husband and by her household appliances, both of which Bromberger explicitly claimed were better than in France. Bromberger wrote that: "Her women's magazines had warned Barbara that her husband could return with many European mannerisms, among which his habit of smoking in bed is not the most exasperating."[40] Journalist Henriette Pierrot also cited the fear that European habits might have rubbed off on the American GI in an article about French GI brides called "Three Thousand French Women in the Women's Paradise."[41] Again, a reduction of household labor allowed for cultural and intellectual growth as Pierrot explained that "in the United States, it is the women that read while the men work. They are the ones that hold literary, artistic, and worldly reputations."[42] Economic power as domestic consumers undergirded their position as "it is the woman who makes purchases" and women "who have in hand all of the money on the continent that never ceases to roll."[43] "Life," according to Pierrot, "is organized for women, and men find it perfectly natural that women should be in control. She is the motor of their ambition. It is to satisfy women's desires that Americans work so hard."[44]

Modern consumer goods were, of course, essential for creating this situation as:

> Mechanical progress has made the American a free woman. It has freed her of all domestic cares. She devotes hardly one hour to her kitchen each day because all her purchases are made by telephone, the grocery store delivers everything to the home, canned and frozen foods allow for instant meal preparation, and the dishwasher operates on its own.[45]

The contrast with France in material terms is clear, but Pierrot also emphasized gender equality and the fear of American women that GIs would bring home European habits. In Europe: "They [the GIs] have above all discovered, on the other side of the ocean, women who do not believe themselves superior to men, spouses, fiancés, and attentive friends who are complaisant, admiring, and have sewn on their buttons, cooked tasty dishes for them, and have listened to their talk and treated them like men. And this European experience has caused an uproar in the United States."[46] For Pierrot, gender roles and the standard of living were connected and consumer goods were the answer to problems with both.

Through portrayals of the United States, the journalists for French women's magazines created the image of a woman's paradise in which domestic cares were eliminated by consumer durables and modernization, and women were not servants of their husbands. Women's roles were more complementary than equal, as in this paradise women did not pursue careers, but rather, while their husbands worked, enjoyed the ability to stay home and read and socialize, carving out literary and artistic reputations in the process. To celebrate women's power as household managers and consumers recognized their intellect and ability, but did not challenge gender roles within the household or society. These recurring images are an important indication of what journalists found lacking, and desirable, in French women's lives, and the popularity of the journals reveals the attraction these images held for French women in general. Women journalists did not limit themselves to fanciful description, however, but also made active demands for a change in living conditions in France and prompted their readers to do the same. These demands for change in the lives of wives and mothers focused on domestic responsibilities, but also took on a decidedly political character as women exercised their new right to vote.

Historians have shown that French women did not immediately become active in formal politics with enfranchisement, but this does not mean that women passively accepted the status quo with the beginnings of the Fourth Republic.[47] In fact, while most of society, including the journalists writing for women's magazines, accepted the notion that women ideally belonged in the home, and not in formal political roles or in the professional world, this did not preclude the possibility of making political demands and, as exhibited in the above articles, wielding economic and social influence. Housewives' demonstrations both during and after the war had frightened public figures with their dangerous influence on public opinion and proved that women's demands as consumers had social, economic, and political effects.[48] In the post-war period, women's journals also focused on demands from within and about the household in their attempts to prompt women into political action.

Identifying their readers as wives, mothers, and consumers, the journalists in women's magazines often stressed the responsibilities inherent in these roles as a basis for political demands. As women exercised political power for the first time, journalists tried to awaken political interest by showing their readers how family and material concerns were linked to national politics. As a journalist for *La Femme Nouvelle* wrote in 1945: "If we want France to live and to regain its place as a great nation, it is necessary that our institutions are rebuilt taking account of, even functioning for, the family.[49]

Population growth was necessary, she acknowledged, but impossible without state support of families. Given the importance of natalism in French political discourse since the late nineteenth century, this acknowledgement is unsurprising. In fact, the constitution of the Fourth Republic would state that "the nation guarantees to the individual and the family the conditions necessary for their development."[50] The author placed herself within this discourse, but in her call for a "politics of the family," linked this national goal to improving housing conditions and ameliorating household labor.

Stating that, "In today's society, the family with many children cannot live without the heroism of the mother," she pointed out the problems posed by "pitiable" and "anachronistic" housing.[51] Only the introduction of electricity could ameliorate domestic labor and "we [the French] must modernize our homes quickly by equipping them with electric appliances, thereby transforming our kitchens."[52] She tied this situation to national political issues by pointing out that these domestic concerns were "dependent, in large part, on our industrial possibilities."[53]

Journalists pointed out how national political issues and reconstruction plans influenced living conditions, often citing women's natural practicality and family experience as justification for their political influence. In *Marie-France*, Marthe Doutreuve recounted the story of a woman who had spent some time in a charming rural village whose only water supply was 500 meters from the homes and often polluted by the animals that also used it. When she asked the mayor why a better supply was not possible, he laughingly showed her a huge dossier containing the history of water supply problems in the village, explaining that the issue had caused so many disputes no action had ever been taken. "Well," exclaimed the friend, "if there had been women on the municipal council of X, the problem would have been solved long ago!" Doutreuve went on to state that:

> We want municipalities to feed us, to house us comfortably ... When peace returns and our prisoners are home, we will be asked to send deputies into power. We will demand of them actions and guarantees that will safeguard the interests of the family ... This will be our "politics". A true, sane politics.[54]

Both women's inherent good sense and their role in the family would be a benefit to future politics and national reconstruction. That said, women were clearly more fit to speak on some issues than others, and despite encouraging women to exercise new rights, journalists consistently stressed the connection between the family and national politics when addressing women.[55]

Women's specific knowledge of the home and family was especially important in this time of reconstruction and rebuilding. Almost every article urging women to participate in politics called for some type of home modernization or increased production of consumer durables. The recurrence of these demands for modernization, along with the many articles describing the American way of life that filled the pages of women's magazines, reveal the level of dissatisfaction with the standard of living in France and the desire to choose elements of the American system and apply them to France. In 1946, an article in *La Femme* made explicit the contrast between France and the United States while also calling on women to use their political power to lighten their domestic burdens. The author of "That perfect domestic servant: electricity" noted that in 1939, 24,550 electric cookers were sold in France, as compared to 275,000 in the United States, despite the fact that the American population was only three times larger than the French. She cited a 1944 study that found that about one-third of French households which needed a kitchen appliance would like to buy an electric one, and noted that: "For all women, electric household appliances represent a veritable liberation."[56] Despite that, the washing machines found in one out of two American households were strangers to France. In 1938, while 1,031,000 machines had been sold in the United States, only 4,200 were sold in France.[57]

The author described to the readers of *La Femme* many of the electrical appliances available in the United States and how they functioned, demonstrating that in construction and utilization "the Americans are far ahead of France."[58] Further, the use of these machines was often not possible with the current distribution and price of electricity in France. Hence, the final message of the author:

> *Conclusion*: our domestic comfort will be, in the years to come, a direct result of our economic policy. Ah! yes, these great problems of importation and exportation, these electrification plans, these new service plans, all of these questions that seem to be above your head, Madame, have an important direct influence on the agreeability or difficulty of your daily life, and no small influence on the happiness of the home that is so important for making you smile. So? Do not be disinterested in politics. France is you, because we are a democracy, the French polity is you. And you see how important that is ...[59]

She called women to join the national debate surrounding reconstruction, if only as a means of attaining home comfort.

At the Liberation, knowledge of the home comfort available in the United States, the nascent political rights of French women, and living conditions in France prompted journalists to make demands that were political in nature, but based on women's position as domestic consumers, wives, and mothers. The image of American life so present in the women's press is important not for understanding America in the 1940s, but for understanding what women journalists found lacking in French society in the same period, and for learning what French women encountered in the magazines they consumed weekly and monthly. The United States was not a classless society of egalitarian marriages and domestic comfort, but this was the image that French women consumed in the years following World War II. Journalists lauded this fantasy lifestyle at the same time as they demanded changes in the French way of life. Women had specific reasons for welcoming consumer durables, despite the opinions of French intellectuals, and these demands and desires must be considered when examining how consumer society emerged in post-war France. As efforts for national reconstruction got underway, journalists prompted women to use their power as citizens to ensure the modernization of their homes and the amelioration of their daily burdens. Essentially, they were calling for the creation of a mass consumer society, in which all families would have access to the living conditions that made American women's lives appear so comfortable and fulfilling.

Notes

1. Merry Bromberger, "24 heures avec Barbara et Teddy à Paris (Texas)," *La Femme* 11 (1945): 2.

2. See Robert Haddow, *Pavilions of Plenty: Exhibiting American Culture Abroad in the 1950s* (Washington, DC: Smithsonian Institution Press, 1997); Walter Hixson, *Parting the Curtain: Propaganda, Culture, and the Cold War 1945–1961* (New York: St Martin's Griffin, 1997); Richard Kuisel, *Seducing the French: The Dilemma of Americanization* (Berkeley: University of California Press, 1993); Richard Pells, *Not Like Us: How Europeans Have Loved, Hated, and Transformed American Culture Since World War II* (New York: Basic Books, 1997). For images of women in propaganda and advertising, see Emily Rosenberg, "Consuming Women: Images of Americanization in the 'American Century'," *Diplomatic History* 23 (1999): 479–97. Kuisel notes that the American State Department began its cultural and informational campaign on the United States in 1948. It reached a peak in 1952, and included press releases, radio programs, and documentary films, among other media. Kuisel, *Seducing the French*, 25.

3. For the reaction of French intellectuals to American culture, see Kuisel, *Seducing the French* and Philippe Roger, *The American Enemy: The History of French Anti-Americanism* (Chicago: University of Chicago Press, 2005).

4. See Jessica C.E. Gienow-Hecht, "Shame on US? Academics, Cultural Transfer, and the Cold War—A Critical Review, *Diplomatic History* 24 (2000): 465–94; Richard Kuisel, "Americanization for Historians," *Diplomatic History* 24 (2000): 509–15; Mary Nolan, "Consuming America, Producing Gender," in *The American Century in Europe*, eds., R. Laurence Moore and Maurizio Vaudagna, 243–61 (Ithaca: Cornell University Press, 2003); Pells, *Not Like Us*; Uta Poiger, "Beyond 'Modernization' and 'Colonization'," *Diplomatic History* 23 (1999): 45–56; and Vanessa Schwartz, *It's So French: Hollywood, Paris, and the Making of Cosmopolitan Film Culture* (Chicago: University of Chicago Press, 2007).

5. Aragon quoted in Kuisel, *Seducing the French*, 38.

6. Historian Michael Bess has coined the term "Technological Darwinism" to describe the sense that France needed to modernize in order to maintain its autonomy and independence. Bess, *Ecology and Technological Modernity in France, 1960–2000* (Chicago: University of Chicago Press, 2003).

7. For reconstruction and housing, see Louis Houdeville, *Pour une Civilisation de l'Habitat* (Paris: Éditions Ouvrières, 1960); W. Brian Newsome, "The Struggle for a Voice in the City: The Development of Participatory Architectural and Urban Planning in France, 1940–1960," PhD Dissertation, University of South Carolina, 2002); Peggy A. Phillips, *Modern France: Theories and Realities of Urban Planning* (Landham: University Press of America, Inc., 1987); and Danièle Voldman, *La Reconstruction des Villes Françaises de 1940 à 1954: Histoire d'une Politique* (Paris: Éditions l'Harmattan, 1997). For a comparison of American and European pre-war living standards, and ideas about a "standard of living," see Victoria de Grazia, *Irresistible Empire: America's Advance through Twentieth-Century Europe* (Cambridge: The Belknap Press of Harvard University Press, 2005).

8. Houdeville, *Pour une civilisation*, 143.

9. Mattei Dogan and Jacques Narbonne, *Les Françaises Face à la Politique* (Paris: Cahiers de la Fondation Nationale des Sciences Politiques, 1955), 35–6.

10. Women's historians have shown that the time women spent in domestic work did not decrease with mechanization. See Ruth Schwartz Cowan, *More Work for Mother: The Ironies of Household Technology from the Open Hearth to the Microwave* (New York: Basic Books, Inc., 1984). This does not negate the fact that the kind of labor involved changed, especially in the case of washing clothes.

11. See Samra-Martin Bonvoisin and Michèle Maignien, *La Presse Féminine* (Paris: Presses Universitaires de France, 1986).

12. See Bonvoisin and Maignien, *La Presse Féminine*. On interwar fashion, see Mary-Louise Roberts, *Civilization without Sexes: Reconstructing Gender in Postwar France, 1917–1927* (Chicago: University of Chicago Press, 1994).

13. See Robert L. Frost, "Machine Liberation: Inventing Housewives and Home Appliances in Interwar France," *French Historical Studies* 18 (1993): 109–30.

14. Dogan and Narbonne, *Les Françaises Face à la Politique*, 67.

15. In 1963, more than 50 percent of an issue of *Elle* was dedicated to advertising; advertising in *Marie-France* varied between 40 and 45 percent; and in fashion magazines like *Vogue* it could reach 60 to 70 percent. Evelyn Sullerot, *La Presse Féminine* (Paris: Armand Colin, 1963), 232.

16. By the mid-1950s, *Marie-Claire*, *Marie-France*, and *Elle* published issues that were over 100 pages long, on good quality paper, and with high-quality color photographs. Lazareff pioneered the glossy photos in her work at *Elle*, importing the necessary equipment, and her first 15 covers, from the United States. Françoise Giroud with Claude Glayman, *Si je Mens ... Conversations avec Claude Glayman* (Paris: Société Express-Union et Éditions Stock, 1972), 120; Sullerot, *La Presse Féminine*, 68.

17. "De la Resistance à la Reconstruction," *Marie-France* 4 (1944): 1; Sullerot, *La Presse Féminine*, 67.

18. *Cahiers de l'Institut Français de Presse* (Paris: Institut Français de Presse et des Sciences de l'Information, 1989), 56–85. In 1958, *Marie-France* printed over 755,000 copies per month, *Cahiers*, 85.

19. "Voila comment on s'Habille à Hollywood," *Elle* 18 (1946): 6.

20. Claude Martine, "Histoire de Thé," *La Femme Nouvelle* 10 (1945): 11.

21. Cécile Agay, "Le Boy Américaine à l'Ecole," *Marie-France* 8 (1945): 5.

22. See Elizabeth Coquart, *La France des G.I.'s: Histoire d'un Amour Déçu* (Paris: Albin Michel, 2003); Marc Hillel, *Vie et Mœurs des GIs en Europe: 1942–1947* (Paris: Balland, 1981); Lee Kennett, *GI: The American Soldier in World War II* (New York: Charles Scribner's Sons, 1987), 199; and Dominique Veillon, *Vivre et Survivre en France, 1939–1947* (Paris: Éditions Payot et Rivages, 1995), 306.

23. For example, René Lehmann, "Elle et Lui," *La Femme Nouvelle* 1 (1945): 2.

24. Kennett, *GI*, 201–2; and Veillon, *Vivre et Survivre*, 307–12.

25. Marguerite Lichtenberger, "Notre ami Jack," *Marie-France* 77 (1946): 12–13.

26. "Les GIs Adressent 112 Reproches aux Français," *La Femme* 36 (1946): 8–9, 19.

27. Carine, "Le système Taylor à La Cuisine," *La Femme Nouvelle* 27 (1946): 15.

28. Ibid., 15.

29. Ibid., 15.

30. "Premières Images de la Nouvelle Existence de Mesdames GIs, Le Bonheur à l'Américaine," *La Femme* 46 (1946): 4.

31. Richard Pells explains that by the mid-1920s, about 70 percent of films shown in France were American. *Not Like Us*, 15. Victoria de Grazia explains that the 1946 Blum-Byres agreement that ended the pre-war import quota on American films in France by replacing it with a screen time quota helped American filmmakers to overrun the French industry by 1947. Victoria de Grazia, "Mass Culture and Sovereignty: The American Challenge to European Cinemas, 1920–1960," *Journal of Modern History* 61 (1989): 53–87.

32. "Le Pays des Stars est aussi le Paradis Terrestre: La Vie de Trois Ménages en Californie," *La Femme* 30 (1946): 4.

33. Ibid., 4. The family's home ownership was notable, as in the mid-1940s, in Paris, its suburbs, and the 28 largest cities in France, only an average of 23.3 percent of the population owned homes. Newsome, "The Struggle for a Voice in the City," 63.

34. "Le Pays des Stars," 4.

35. Ibid., 5.

36. See, for example, Berthe Bernage, "Recevrons-nous Quand Même?" *Le Petit Echo de la Mode* 40 (1947): 2.

37. Bromberger, "24 heures," 2.

38. Ibid., 2.

39. See, for example, Jean and Françoise Fourastié, *Histoire du Confort*, 2nd edition (Paris: Presses Universitaires de France, 1962). Jean Fourastié was an economic advisor at the Commissariat du Plan who championed modernization in France and, in this work, the home.

40. Bromberger, "24 heures," 2.

41. Henriette Pierrot, "Trois Mille Françaises au Paradis des Femmes," *La Femme* 41 (1946): 3.

42. Ibid., 3.

43. Ibid., 3.

44. Ibid., 3.

45. Ibid., 3.

46. Ibid., 3.

47. See Dominique Veillon and Éric Alary, "L'Après-guerre de Femmes: 1947, un Tournant?" in *L'Année 1947*, eds. Serge Bernstein and Pierre Milza, 487–511 (Paris: Presses de la Fondation Nationale des Sciences Politiques, 2000); Hanna Diamond, *Women and the Second World War in France, 1940–1948: Choices and Constraints* (Essex: Pearson Education Unlimited, 1999), and "Gaining the Vote: A Liberating Experience?" *Modern and Contemporary France* 3 (1995): 129–48; Claire Duchen, *Women's Rights and Women's Lives in France, 1944–1968* (New York: Routledge, 1994), and "Une Femme Nouvelle pour une France Nouvelle," *Clio* 1 (1995): 151–64; and Jane Jenson, "The Liberation and New Rights for French Women" in *Behind the Lines: Gender and the Two World Wars*, eds. Margaret Randolph Higgonet et al. (New Haven: Yale University Press, 1987), 272–84.

48. Rebecca Pulju, "Consumers for the Nation: Women, Politics and Consumer Organization in France, 1944–1965," *Journal of Women's History* 18 (2006): 68–90.

49. C.D., "Une Politique de la Famille est Nécessaire," *La Femme Nouvelle* 10 (1945): 4.

50. Claire Duchen, *Women's Rights*, 30. On natalism, see Kristen Stromberg Childers, *Fathers, Families, and the State in France, 1914–1945* (Ithaca: Cornell University Press, 2003); Susan Pedersen, *Family, Dependence, and the Origins of the Welfare State: Britain and France, 1914–1945* (Cambridge: Cambridge University Press, 1993); and Miranda Pollard, *Reign of Virtue: Mobilizing Gender in Vichy France* (Chicago: University of Chicago Press, 1998).

51. C.D., 4.

52. Ibid., 4.

53. Ibid., 4.

54. Marthe Doutreuve, "Politique Féminine," *Marie-France* 19 (1945): 5.

55. The political messages of women's journals, though fairly similar, did vary according to the political positions of their directors. *La Femme*, which only lasted through 1947, was more overtly political than *Marie-France*, which was close to the *Mouvement Républicain Populaire*, a Christian Democratic party. See Jenson, "The Liberation and New Rights," and Duchen, "Une Femme Nouvelle," on the place of women in political ideology. Duchen points out that even the Communist Party had difficulty conceiving of women as mothers and workers at the same time.

56. "Cette Parfaite Domestique: l'Electricité," *La Femme* 64 (1946): 4.

57. Ibid., 4.

58. Ibid., 5.

59. Ibid., 19.

7

Talking Points: Advertising Female Telephone Identity

Emily Bills

In 1928 Arthur W. Page, the Bell Telephone Company's Vice President for Publicity, announced that the company was going to take a radical new turn in its approach to telephone marketing by promoting residential subscriptions.[1] Up to that point Bell was preoccupied with obtaining a monopoly over the country's long-distance system and, to promote this goal, Bell advertisements regularly suggested that the smooth functioning of American business depended on that corporate consolidation. Businessmen were therefore presented as Bell's primary subscribers and the telephone device as an apparatus used exclusively for the efficient perpetuation of commercial pursuits. As such, it was routinely pictured grasped in the hand of powerbroker, industrialist, and farmer, the active male participants in the country's economic advancement. The telephone, Bell's advertising imagery made clear, was an obligatory tool for facilitating the serious, masculine business of corporate endeavor.

Page's announcement marked a radical shift in that approach. Influenced by a commercial environment increasingly focused on mass consumption, Page declared that Bell would now promote telephone use for the completion of a variety of daily tasks by a wider spectrum of consumers. To ensure broad usage, Bell redirected its own self-perpetuated perception of telephone service as a "must-have" business necessity to a "would-like-to-have" common convenience. It then set its sights on the largest market for telephone use still left untapped: the residential sphere.

This new focus on residential telephone use completely reshaped the visual and written content of Bell marketing material. While histories of technology note that women had always used the telephone for everything from social calls to ordering goods, for over 25 years the only women to appear in Bell advertisements were switchboard operators, that is, those providing telephone service, not utilizing it.[2] Now, with the help of N.W. Ayer and Sons, the company's favored advertising agency, and its own in-house marketing division, Bell produced print advertisements, pamphlets, fliers, and other material in which homemakers were routinely depicted as telephone users.[3]

This essay explores through a close reading of the company's marketing material between the late 1920s and 1950s, how Bell sought to shape the nature of that use. First, with reference to Roland Marchand's analysis of twentieth-century American advertising strategies, I identify how Bell promoted maximum telephone use as a means for women to obtain "comfort and convenience" in the residence.[4] In these advertisements, telephony sheds its association with the stiff, regimented world of the modern office and reemerges as a softer, more accommodating service "befitting" the ambiance of the modern home. The inferred goal is to transfer telephony's masculine associations to those traditionally aligned with femininity: a smoothly functioning, stylish home orchestrated—via telephone use—with skillful ease.

Second, I illuminate the class and space-based imperatives inscribed in the promotional material. Pre-World War II, Bell primarily advertised the telephone as a tool utilized by the wealthy homemaker to dictate tasks to her household staff. Post-World War II, Bell focused on the servantless household and a homemaker who uses the telephone to more efficiently complete tasks herself. In both cases, however, the advertisements promote a spatial interpretation of calling activity in which access to telephone extensions throughout the house facilitate the efficient completion of a variety of household responsibilities. Whether large or modest, the house was depicted as a kind of domestic landscape with each room possessing its own telephone use functions (in the boudoir to call her maid, in the kitchen to call repairmen). In the post-war period, women are even instructed to work directly with architects to include wiring plans throughout their homes.

This spatial interpretation is important, I suggest throughout the chapter, because although telephone use has been the subject of numerous studies that are particularly occupied with social relations within the community, almost none of these conversations consider the ways in which telephone companies encouraged, and possibly shaped, that use as a factor of the physical space of the home. For over 30 years, however, Bell advertisements consistently encouraged women to transform their homes into totally wired environments and suggested how those wired environments negated their need for physical contact with the outside world. Through word and image, homemakers were told that the social and commercial space of the community was most effectively accessed via telephones in the residence, not face-to-face contact in real space. Women, these advertisements suggested, must be recognized as capable household executives, but executives whose activity is almost entirely relegated to their domestic surroundings.

Queen of her Castle: Telephone Convenience for the Gracious Home

"Picture yourself at 9 o'clock on a busy morning," a Bell brochure begins. "Your breakfast tray has been removed. In the kitchen, Cook is busily clearing up the dishes ... It is, we have said, 9 o'clock. And at 9:30 you have an appointment. Thirty minutes in which to arrange your day!"[5]

In "New Convenience for the Fine Home," a wealthy homemaker is confronted by what is a woefully inadequate amount of time to fulfill her morning tasks, at least by traditional methods. "But note, if you please, that a telephone is upon the table beside you." We turn the page and find our troubled star happily wielding the receiver of a fancy French telephone with advanced dial system. Within 15 minutes, we learn, she has approved the day's meals with Cook, arranged for the butler to prepare a guest room, asked the gardener to tend the flowers, and called for Bob, the chauffeur, to bring the car around. Just in time! With a final turn of the dial, she telephones Mrs Brown to affirm a punctual arrival for their meeting.

Starting with a flurry of advertisements and informational material released in the late 1920s, Bell advanced several themes that helped to significantly increase telephone awareness among its prospective residential clientele. These ranged from time-saving applications for more efficient home management, to scheduling appointments, to facilitating a teenager's social life. Telephone use, these advertisements explain, is a lifestyle choice that makes the business of running a home much easier. Furthermore, that ease is directly proportional to the number of extensions in the home. In advertisement after advertisement, Bell strove to make it "the style" for an average home to have two or three telephone extensions and an affluent home to have a seemingly unlimited number. As Bell informs the reader in another pamphlet, "Modern Telephone Service for the Home": "The modern concept of comfortable living requires a logical relationship between the interests and activities of the household and the number of telephones it should have."[6]

These two pamphlets reflect Bell's commitment to promoting its new "comfort and convenience" campaign, an approach to mass merchandising that promoted telephone service as an attractive accessory to gracious living. Yet the company never felt the same competitive pressure as other corporations to pursue broad consumption of its product. By the 1920s AT&T, the parent company of the Bell System, possessed a near monopoly over the country's telephone service, devices, and accessories. Still, as Roland Marchand explains: "So pervasive was the notion that the public must be reeducated to imagine how much it might pleasurably consume, rather than how little it might get by on that even AT&T glimpsed the possibilities of expanding its sales."[7] At the crux of that campaign was the notion, advanced by Page, that: "The power of advertising to change public habits and ideas should now be employed to transform the consumer image of the telephone from that of a necessity to that of a convenience, even a luxury."[8] This "changed psychology" would ideally lead residential subscribers to seek "all the telephone facilities they can conveniently use, rather than the smallest amount they can get along with."[9]

Maximum telephone saturation, Bell advertisements counseled, signals a contemporary household, one run by a savvy homemaker dedicated to the creation of an organized, accommodating, and elegant domestic environment. No longer a tool of necessity, the telephone was now to be understood as a tool of convenience, and as such it was entirely appropriate to have as many telephone extensions as one desired. The difference between necessity and convenience may seem subtle, but this softer, more accommodating telephone identity served to transfer its distinctly masculine, commercial association to a feminine, domestic one. Whereas multiple extensions in the modern office contribute to an atmosphere of hustle and bustle, in the residence they were said to facilitate an atmosphere of refined efficiency.

The telephone's new feminized persona was immediately palpable in the company's marketing material. From the moment Bell targets the residential subscriber, the female figure becomes a kind of Bell mascot. As early as 1928, she appears on the cover of a regional Bell magazine, her chiseled, geometric face rendered in deco style, the radiating curves of her flower broach mirrored in the telescoping waves emanating from the telephone receiver. Sharp, jagged lines indicate in graphic form the processes of electrical speech; the razor-sharp lines of her own visage attract the magnetic sound waves, achieving a stylized merging of woman and telephone (see Figure 7.1).

This visual assimilation signals what was clearly Bell's larger commercial project: to find a way for the whole of a woman's routine to be organized around telephone use. But not any woman would do. During the first two decades of Bell's residential marketing campaign, telephones are primarily characterized as delegation tools wielded by wealthy homemakers. This was largely because they were more likely to own homes large enough to accommodate all the telephone accessories and extensions Bell could think to sell and, as the United States entered the Depression, the only demographic with dispensable income. Indeed, the focus on convenience over necessity was primarily intended to raise Bell's profit margin through increased calling activity and the sale of telephone accessories.

Still, Bell was reluctant to extend this "feminization" of telephone use to the device itself and did not promote a range of telephone colors and styles until the late 1950s (Bell's depiction of the French model in "New Conveniences" was fairly uncommon at the time). According to Marchand, one Bell official said that if the company had competitors who marketed "beautifully decorated hand sets," they would undoubtedly join in the competition.[10] Instead, women were asked to embrace Bell's black, standard issue models as appropriate additions to their interior décor. Thus, for the period of time covered by this

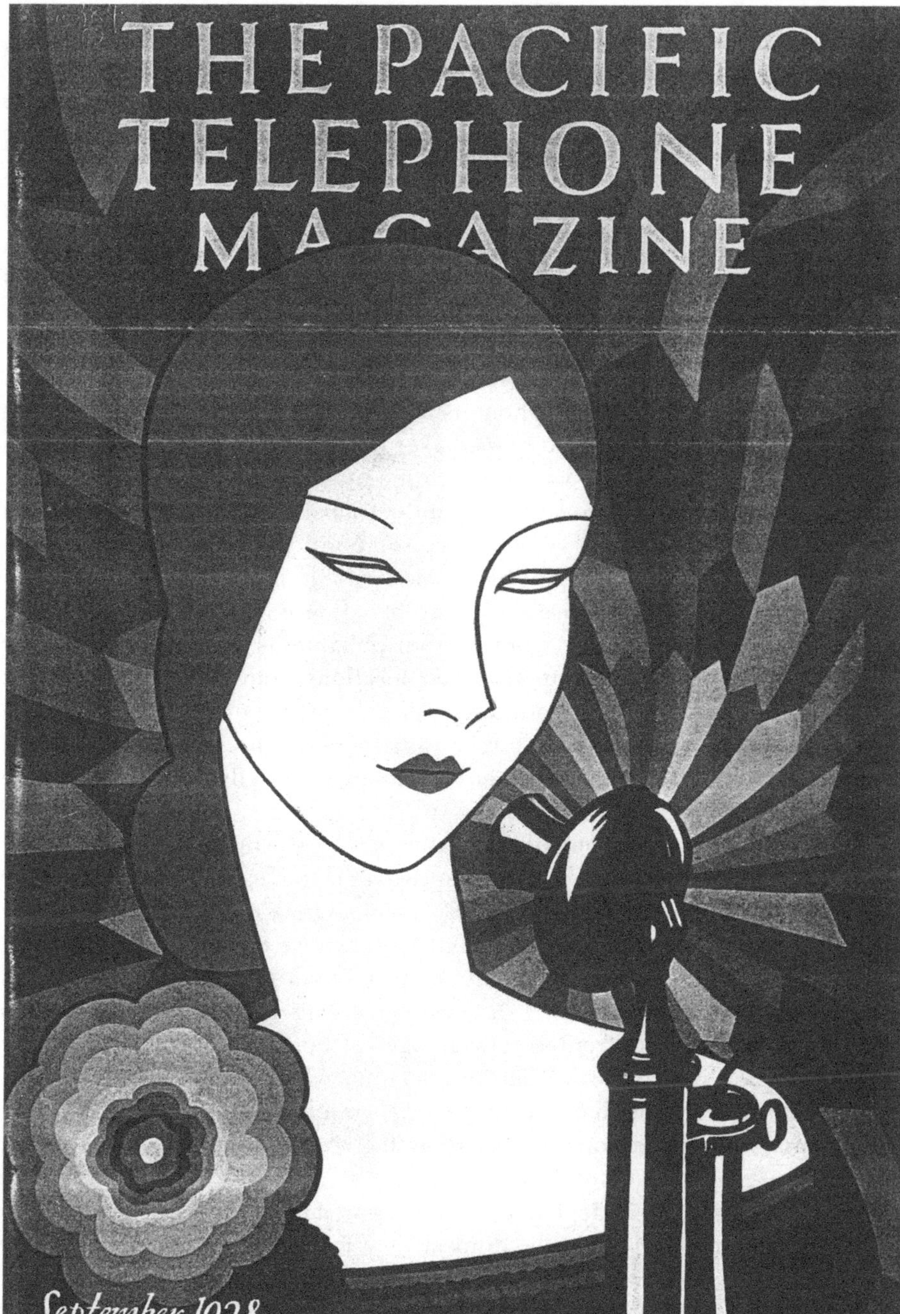

7.1 Journal cover, *The Pacific Telephone Magazine*, September 1928

essay it is the integration of telephone use into the domestic lifestyle, and not "personalized" telephone devices, that Bell promoted as feminine in its residential advertisements.

Merchandising remained a central part of Bell advertisements for wealthy homemakers, however, particularly in the form of multiple telephone extensions. For women running an estate, Bell suggested an interhome telephone system with extensions in every room to facilitate communication with her household staff. They also suggested lines to the community to help fulfill obligations outside of the home. A woman's work is never done, was the unspoken theme, for as long as there was work, there was a need for the telephone.

Work, needless to say, has a loose connotation in this formulation. As a tool for the wealthy, the telephone is marketed as a means of merging the daily duties of the privileged homemaker with the leisure lifestyle to which she is accustomed. There was a masculine model for this characterization: earlier advertisements show the busy industrialist conducting business from his country home, or the Washington, DC politician communicating with his office while vacationing at his seaside retreat. But Bell's representation of a woman's telephone use is discernibly different from a man's. While telephones ostensibly free women from obligations within the home, or enable correspondence from removed locations, they are never pictured outside their domestic surroundings. Bell's imagery empowers its female consumers to negotiate the public sphere through the use of modern technology, but then negates their ability to physically enter that sphere themselves.

This domestic entrapment is further solidified through imagery that depicts women as models of graciousness in the home, not masculine power on the job. In material from the 1920s and 1930s, telephones are consistently promoted as organizational tools, but tools whose use function is merged with a kind of relaxed respectability pictured as appropriate for a woman's home, social station, and sex. While women are instructed to use telephones to work, they are confronted with images of homemakers who somehow attend to domestic duties while simultaneously engaging in a life of repose. This contradiction often found its pictorial counterpart in the image of elite homemaker as glamorous flapper type, the embodiment of both decorum and devil-may-care. As the well-heeled star of "Modern Telephone Service for the Home," she is depicted sporting diaphanous daywear, a pixie bob hairdo, and a telephone in the domestic environment of her choice.[11] Once again, however, that choice is strictly limited to the spaces of the home. We find her reclining on a cheerful window seat wielding the popular candlestick model; she is spotted later in the bedroom gabbing on a chaise longue, or in the parlor talking in a flowered wingback (see Figure 7.2). Trusty Bell-issued equipment is a constant companion. Not yet rendered in

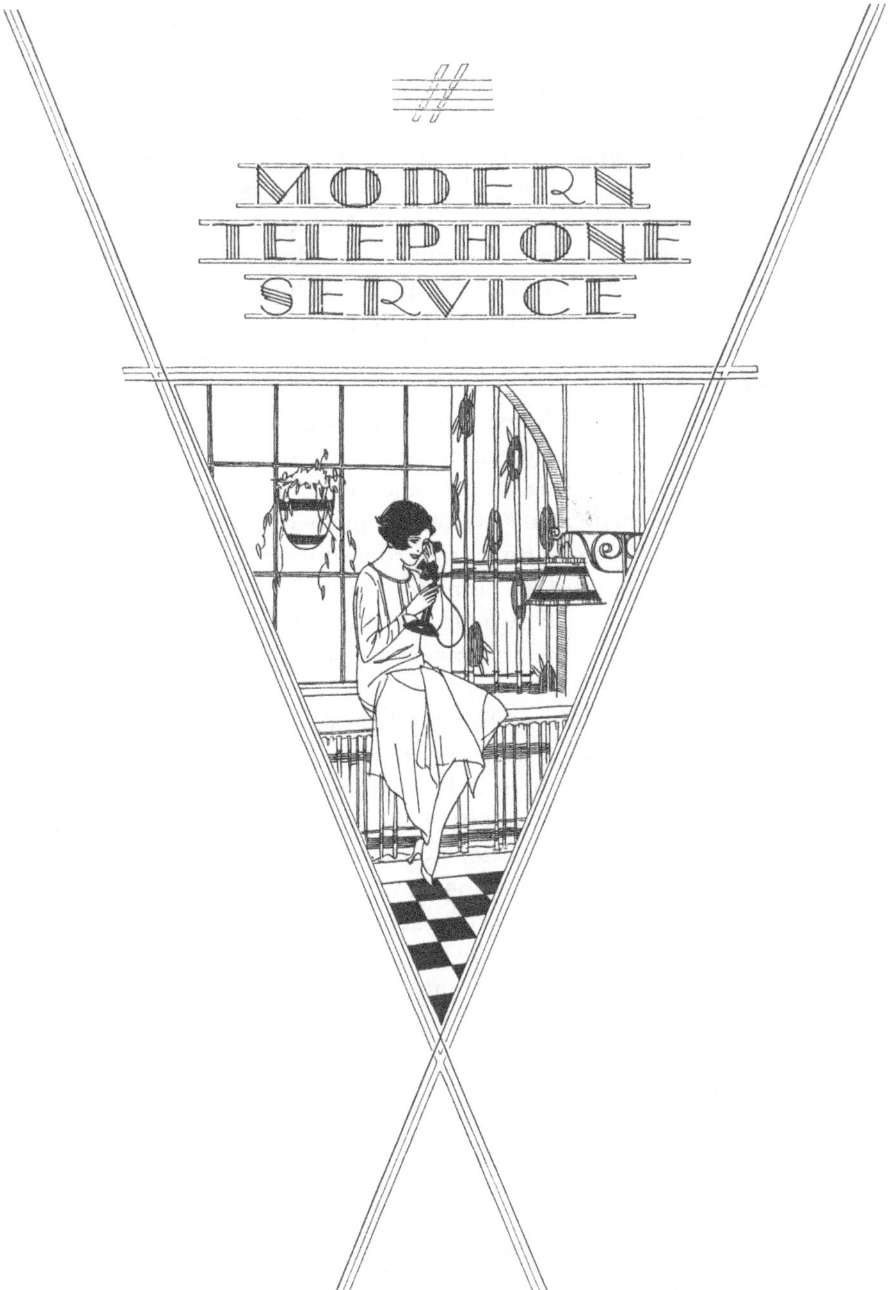

7.2 Pamphlet, "Modern Telephone Service for the Home," frontispiece (1920s). Collection 6: Bell System/Record Group 6, Book 5: Publications—Non-Periodic, AT&T Publications and Vertical Files Collections, AT&T Archives and History Center

fashion colors, it is like the little black dress of communications devices, an accessory to her wardrobe and her interior décor, which in turn reflect the limited boundaries of her prescribed experience.

Frequent telephone use, the consumer is led to believe, makes the completion—or delegation—of a homemaker's work so easy that her lifestyle reflects one of tranquility more than toil. This impression is further cultivated in advertisements that align telephone accessibility with the projection of a serene, sophisticated domestic environment. Just as a man's identity is associated with his financial success, a woman's identity is bound to the physical appearance and efficient operation of the domestic sphere. Bell utilizes this social convention to add ammunition to its campaign. Again and again, the homemaker is told that the telephone will help her to run her home with perfect precision, making it both a pleasure to live in and a pleasure to visit. Interhome communications between "the queen of the castle" and her household staff ensure the facilitation of a sophisticated "subtle management" in which there was "no bustling confusion, no shouting from room to room, no scurrying to and fro."[12] If "interesting homes are mirrors of those who live in them," one advertisement instructs, "they have a subtle air of charm and graciousness ... in their furnishings ... their arrangements for living comfort ... especially telephone convenience."[13]

Importantly, for each domestic activity assigned to the telephone comes a corresponding spatial environment with its own social associations. While these spatial meanings will eventually shift after World War II, when the company began to target the servantless household and the small house type, in these earlier examples they reflect the organization of domestic space in which owner and servants traditionally occupied different parts of the house. In the advertisement "Boudoir to Kitchen ... to guest Room," for example, the telephone replaces the system of bells and buzzers that previously facilitated correspondence in the vast social separation between the "upstairs" and "downstairs" quarters. Pictured in her boudoir, the lady of the house retains the dress and posture of repose while utilizing her interhome telephone to pass instructions to the kitchen staff. The advertisement's layout reinforces this distinction, the spaces of recline separated in vertical space from the spaces of toil, the two brought together "by merely pushing a button"[14] (see Figure 7.3).

The gracious home, the advertisements from this period suggest, is one that is so well managed that the "home administrator" never has to leave those quarters favorable to her social station. The telephone facilitates this separation, and in so doing also acts as an extension of the staff: an inanimate in-house messenger. Similarly, just as the homemaker bases the size of her staff on the size of her home, so too does she base the number of telephone extensions. "Telephone service should be one of your greatest household conveniences—

Boudoir to Kitchen . . . to guest Room

. . . *or across the Continent*

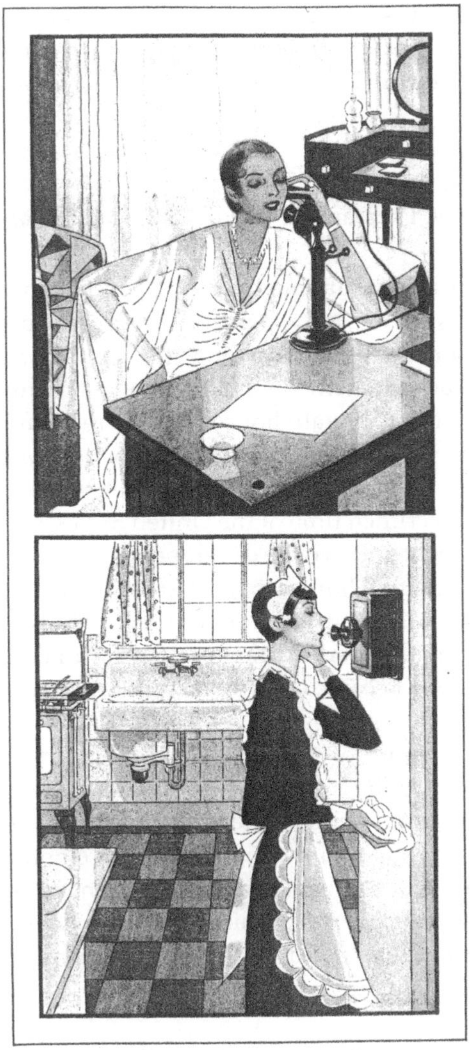

Your Bell telephones can be intercommunicating within the home—yet bring neighbors, cities and continents within instant call

Boudoir to kitchen . . . living-room to nursery . . . sun parlor to garage . . . or to London! Over the same telephones.

Here is a feature of modern telephone convenience and comfort within the home. At moderate cost you can have telephone service in nearly every room . . . and have some instruments connected with certain others. By merely pushing a button you are able to converse with other people in the house—yet from these same telephones you can talk halfway round the world.

It is such a convenience to be linked by telephone with selected parts of your house. And to have telephones in whatever rooms you need them. It saves so many steps, and enables you to carry on the household routine efficiently and with a minimum of effort.

Telephone service should be one of your greatest household conveniences—and it can be. Your local Bell Company will be glad to have a representative show you how *enough telephones* will contribute to your ease and comfort. Just telephone the Business Office, today.

7.3 Advertisement, "Boudoir to Kitchen … to guest Room … *or across the Continent*," AT&T, 1930. Warshaw Collection of Business Americana—Telephone, Archives Center, National Museum of American History, Smithsonian Institution, Washington, DC

and it can be," Bell counseled readers. "Your local Bell Company will be glad to have a representative show you how *enough telephones* will contribute to your ease and comfort."[15]

For the majority of residential subscribers of more modest means, these advertisements most likely served to reinforce modern communications as an instrument of bourgeois privilege. In fact, when Bell changed its focus to the wiring of smaller homes in the 1940s and 1950s, it necessarily toned down the push for an interhome system. However, the essence of its marketing message never wavered. "Only a few people ... have estates," Bell explained as early as 1930, "but everyone can enjoy true *telephone convenience*."[16]

Micromanaging the Modern Midget: Preplanned Wiring as Home Decor

Although the Bell Company never fully abandoned its focus on telephone use by the elite, by the mid-1940s there was a perceivable switch in its marketing material from the servant-filled mansion to the servant-less minimal house type. The exact moment of this switch is not fully discernable (Bell occasionally included small houses in its residential wiring campaign before the 1940s) but an attention to more modest homes began appearing with growing frequency as the belt-tightening days of the Depression transitioned into the crunch time of the United States' entry into the war. As the federal government and private developers increasingly promoted the mass production of minimal homes to meet growing housing shortages, residential utility providers of all types took notice. The same was true of Bell. By V-J Day, the company had seemingly turned full circle: convenience in the "modern mansion" became convenience in the "modern midget."

This change did little to rock the core of the company's "comfort and convenience" campaign. The size of the target home shrank, but the discursive rules for speaking about residential telephone use remained highly conventionalized. The micromanager of the minimal house embraces telephone use because it is indicative of a broader household management policy predicated on ease. The homemaker recognizes the telephone as a convenient tool for running her household efficiently and, as mistress of refined living, knows frequent telephone use helps to maintain the comfort and beauty of her surroundings.

This advertising message jumped from the 1930s to the mid-1940s relatively unscathed despite changes to traditional gender roles during the war, when working- and middle-income women were widely encouraged by the popular media to enter the workforce.[17] In fact, Bell never depicted women as breadwinners during the war, likely due in part to the elevated economic class of their target audience. However, even Bell's depiction of middle-income female consumers continued to ensconce them within the constraints of the home. The advertisements from that period mainly addressed the country's military engagement by celebrating telephony as a means of keeping families connected. In these images, telephone and homemaker are pictured at the center of the family that has gathered around the receiver. It is her stable presence in the home, constantly accessible by telephone, these advertisements suggest, that is her contribution to the war effort.

Furthermore, while Bell changed the size of its target home, the economic class of the homemaker remained of central importance. This consistent focus is likely due to a shift after the war in which the company's residential advertisements actively promoted prewiring plans as part of the homebuilding process. The upsurge in prefabricated housing production after World War II undoubtedly encouraged Bell's efforts in this direction. Just as home construction started to include fully integrated environmental systems, such as heating and lighting, Bell believed they should also include a telephone system. Much of the company's post-war residential marketing material focused on this goal by asking homebuilders and homebuyers to install telephone conduit in new homes or incorporate hidden wiring into remodeling plans. This meant, however, that while Bell's target post-war subscriber resides in a modest home, they still have the means to either commission the construction of a new home or finance a major remodel.

Women, this marketing campaign made clear, are the supervisors of those homebuilding or remodeling plans. The idea was not new. Bell had encouraged female clients to work with their architects to install tracks behind walls and indicate outlet locations in the construction of new homes for about two decades.[18] After all, women were most likely to understand where outlets were useful and how exposed wires (the ugly result of homes that were not prewired) could ruin the beautiful environment they worked so hard to maintain. In the post-war period, Bell increasingly encouraged women to embrace their home-planning skills so that they might approach the builder-buyer relationship with confidence, particularly if that confidence meant they demanded prewired homes. In turn, Bell also asked the architectural community to recognize the homemaker's administrative powers and consult her when preparing building plans. "Every woman wants telephone outlets in her new home," the builder is reminded, and it is to her that the architect will likely have to cater.[19]

The home is clearly women's business, and Bell wants to show it respects her position as manager, mother, and hostess by including her in the wiring decision-making process. As such, Bell advertisements often

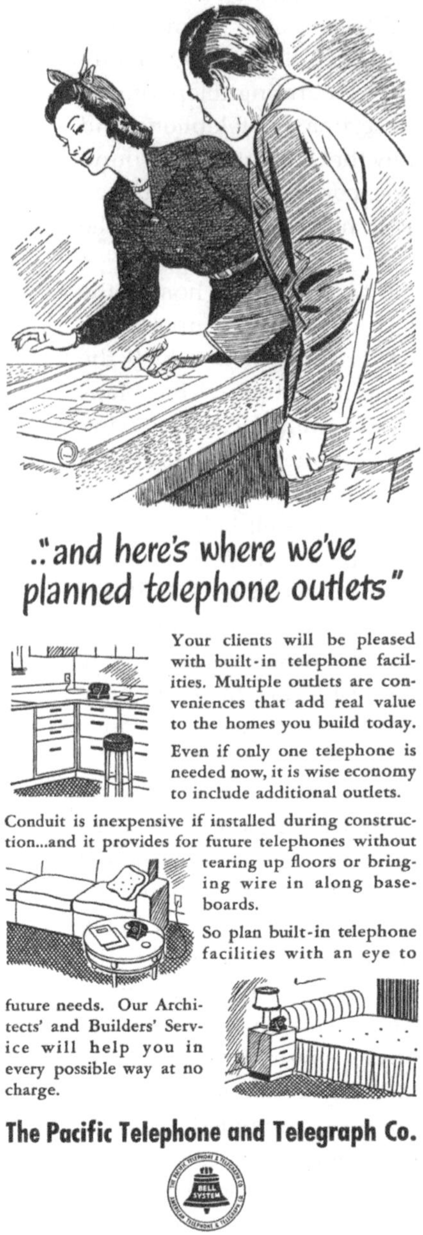

7.4 Advertisement, "... and here's where we've planned telephone outlets," Pacific Telephone, *Architect & Engineer*, January 1946

picture the homemaker working with her architect as he explains the location of telephone conduit in building plans (see Figure 7.4). In effect, the homemaker becomes a surrogate architect, an image Bell perpetuated through its "prewiring ads" run in national magazines of interest to architects and their female clientele, such as *Architectural Record* and *Ladies' Home Journal*. They also mounted displays at home-planning events promoted by women's magazines. In the summer of 1954, for example, *Better Homes & Gardens* teamed with Bell to produce a nationwide model home show. *Better Homes & Gardens* showcased "new trends" in home construction and decoration, while Bell exhibited an array of telephone services and administered advice about telephone preplanning.[20]

That summer, an article in *Bell Telephone Magazine* reported that over one million prospective homebuyers visited 100 locally built models in which they could observe first hand how preplanned telephone conveniences were integrated into the average-sized home.[21] There are no corroborating sources for these statistics and, in fact, it is even difficult to assess the number of homes with telephone connections at the time. The United States Housing Census does not distinguish between business and residential subscriptions until the 1970s and, while some records were kept at the company or exchange level, according to sociologists Claude Fischer and Glen Carroll, most of the macrostructural variables charting the number of business versus residential subscriptions are simply unavailable.[22] Nevertheless, it is clear from reviewing Bell's marketing material that its post-war merchandising remained focused on residential telephone use and deferred to the homemaker as executive of the domestic sphere.

Bell's conceptualization of homemakers as home planners took the form of both interior designer and housecleaner. Both interpretations are of central importance, but Bell's marketing material in the post-war period often sought to engage the homemaker as decorator first and worker second. This is not to say that Bell stopped presenting the telephone as a means to complete household chores, and the concluding section of this essay discusses how that objective was marketed to middle-income women. A good number of the advertisements, however, were geared toward convincing women that hiding the unsightly mechanics that contribute to a home's ideal functioning was the most proactive way to manage the visible aesthetic environment. In a way, the framing of the argument was not unlike Bell's approach to selling telephony to wealthy homemakers: using telephones to complete daily tasks, elite women were instructed, ensures the maintenance of a smoothly functioning and thus pleasantly appearing domestic environment. Bell's attention to preplanned wiring, moreover, shifts the emphasis from the completion of household duties as a means of obtaining pleasing interiors to controlling the telephone's own physical incursion on those interiors.

This changed emphasis was part of Bell's broader attempt to make telephone installations an inherent part of the homebuilding industry, which would ostensibly increase residential subscriptions. Bell advertisements geared toward women and their architects, however, remain silent about the company's larger financial goals and instead related preplanning to the physical nature of the minimal house type itself. The advertisements emphasize how "modern" interiors, characterized by prefabricated building components, simple materials, and the absence of decorative elements, such as moldings and baseboards, do not lend themselves readily to attached wires. Whether a simple Cape Cod or a streamlined glass-and-steel model, exposed wiring, Bell advertisements suggest, can easily mar such homes with their sparse detailing.

In other words, planning the inside made for the most appealing outside. The telephone's working parts, women were told, no more belong on the surface of a home's interior walls than do pipes and electrical wires. Bell even asks the homemaker to turn the home inside out in her imagination; in many advertisements, walls are peeled away to reveal the location of conduit and outlets. "To be really complete in every detail," a 1952 advertisement instructs the homemaker, she must recognize that telephone raceways in the walls are as "fundamental as kitchen cabinets."[23] Whether hiding dishes behind cabinets, pipes under floors, or telephone wires behind walls, it is the appearance of the homemaker's surroundings, and not the work that takes place in them, that is the primary subject of the preplanning credo. "Beauty is as beauty does," she is reminded in innumerable advertisements that feature harmonious combinations of interior décor, homemaker, and "machine."

Thus, much like her elite counterpart, these women are rarely pictured in either a state of complete repose or concerted effort. We find her leaning against her wood-paneled living room wall, a roaring fire illuminating with its romantic glow her special "telephone corner." She is pictured elsewhere in a flawlessly tailored suit, ankles demurely crossed, telephone in hand. Home and person are perfectly tended, the inner workings of her telephone system tucked away behind drywall, much like her undergarments are hidden under her Dior Tulip skirt. These outward appearances signify domestic bliss and, in advertisements like "As fundamental as hidden pipes …," the signs of her success are easily identifiable: perfectly orchestrated modern décor, check; stylish automobile in the garage, check; white-gloved hand casually cradling telephone receiver, double-check (see Figure 7.5).

Marketing a Telephone Community

There is a final point to be made about Bell's marketing message for telephone use in the minimal home: the management of domestic duties. The middle-income household is almost assuredly a servantless household, and thus there is no separation of domestic space based on class divisions as seen in advertisements featuring elite homemakers. This housewife gets her hands dirty and, as a result, is doubly in need of time-saving devices (although as refinement demands, she is never actually pictured elbow high in dirty dishwater or scrubbing the kitchen floor). The telephone is therefore no longer a tool used primarily for delegating tasks to a household staff but for direct engagement with a myriad of household duties: she uses it to call repairmen, order goods, and so on. Thus, while Bell still presents the minimal home as a landscape comprised of different environments with different potential calling requirements, the advertisements now concentrate on calls placed by the homemaker to outside locations.

This project is framed as a component of the organization of labor in the minimal home, and it appropriately applies the language of scientific management to calling practices. For example, the company informed homemakers that they could defeat the inconveniences of space and time by installing extensions in every room of the house, which would ostensibly "contribute to labor saving and step saving … in the same ways as can a 'science kitchen.'"[24] A Bell cartoon from 1955 declares that telephones help busy women "take the 'run' out of running a home."[25] In another, a tuxedo-clad groom innocently carries his new bride into her modern, state-of-the-art kitchen, only to hear her cry out, "What! No Kitchen Telephone?"[26] (see Figure 7.6).

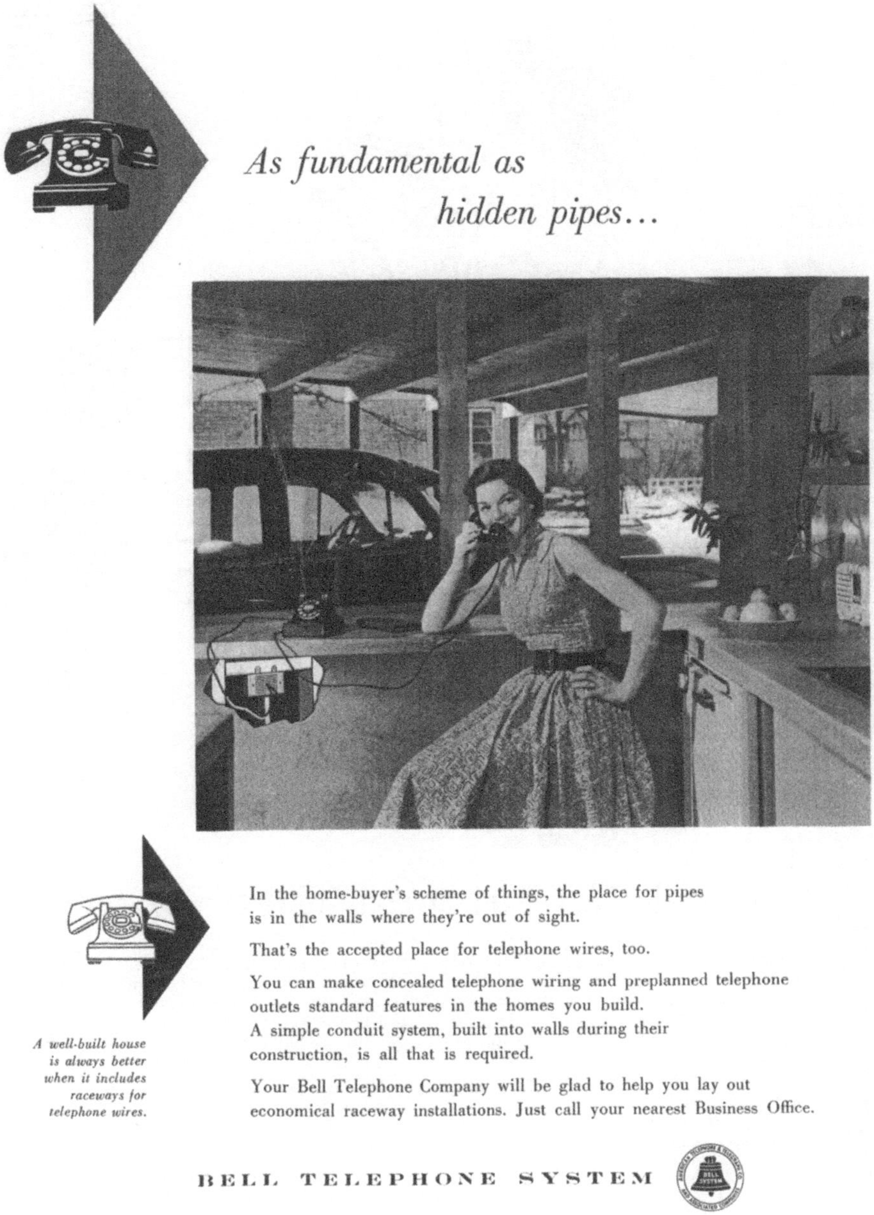

7.5 Advertisement, "As fundamental as hidden pipes ...," AT&T, *circa* 1951. N.W. Ayer Advertising Agency Records, Archives Center, National Museum of American History, Smithsonian Institution, Washington, DC

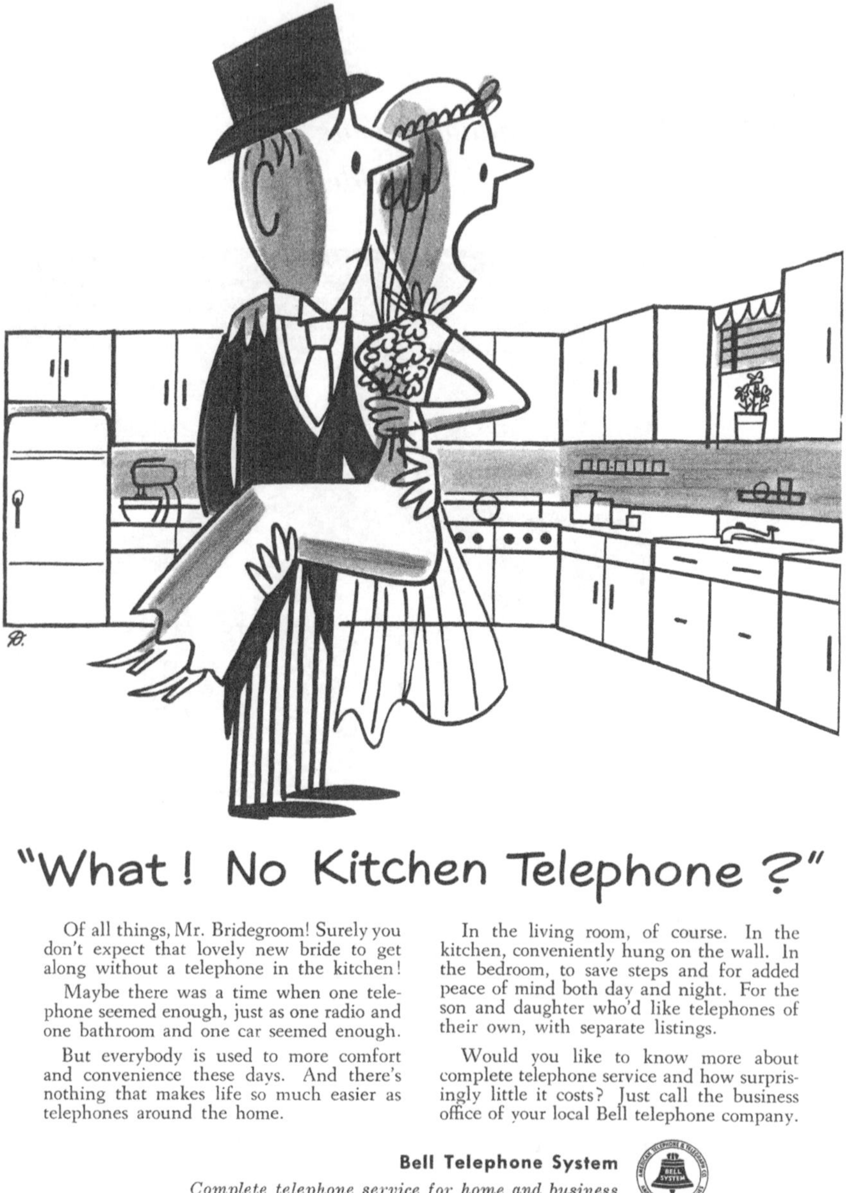

7.6 Advertisement, "What! No Kitchen Telephone?" AT&T, 1955. N.W. Ayer Advertising Agency Records, Archives Center, National Museum of American History, Smithsonian Institution, Washington, DC

The general intensification of housewares consumption after World War II created the ideal climate for Bell's time-saving marketing campaign, as the *Better Homes and Gardens* partnership suggests. However, the theme of the "technologically liberated housewife" was not unfamiliar to a mid-century audience: architectural historian Gwendolyn Wright points out how, since the 1890s, women had been coached in the ways utilities like gas and electricity—and the products that utilized these services—could help them become expert home administrators.[27] For example, domestic scientists like Lillian Gilbreth applied Frederick Winslow Taylor's time-motion principles for production in the factory to production in the home.[28] This is not to say, however, that Gilbreth and other early home economists embraced telephones themselves. For example, according to Claude Fisher's study on telephone use before 1940, almost none of the path-breaking advice books on household management favored using the telephone for shopping.[29] The popular Christine Frederick even recommended against it because, according to her: "The telephone habit encourages the lack of knowledge of conditions and prices."[30]

Yet while some home management educators remained leery of the telephone as a space-time-crunching tool for chores like shopping, as technology historians Carolyn Marvin, Lana Rakow, and Michèle Martin have noted, from the time of its inception women's magazines and merchandisers advanced ideas about how the telephone might contribute to better home management.[31] For example, advertisements encouraging women to order goods by telephone appeared as early as the 1880s.[32] In the 1930s, *Sunset Magazine* advice columnist Genevieve A. Callahan included the telephone as an important aspect of the larger project to reeducate housewives in the lessons of scientific home management. Her article, "Fourteen Pages of Household Helpfulness," called for a "right-about-face" in the mental attitude and self-discipline of her readers that included "the cultivation of open-mindedness toward new equipment and new methods of working."[33] Callahan introduced the article by chastising the homemaker for not using her telephone to call repairmen and other service providers for assistance.

Nor was the subject new to Bell's residential advertising campaign. Marketing material in the 1930s, such as the advertisement "In Just 30 Minutes," emphasized telephone use as a way to beat the clock.[34] As the language of time-motion principles gained mainstream appeal after World War II however, promoting telephones as time-savers converged neatly with the growing tide of consumer culture, particularly shopping. In fact, advertisers of all types increasingly embraced female telephone use for ordering goods and word-of-mouth advertising. In so doing, they projected an illusion of technological liberation said to free women from the physical activity of traveling to the marketplace, but which ultimately served to further remove them from the commercial sphere. In a 1940 M-J-B coffee advertisement, for example, a homemaker finds she is out of coffee, a real problem since her husband has invited his boss—a "real *nut* on coffee"—to dinner. The problem is easily solved: she dials her local grocer to place the order, and the product is delivered without the homemaker ever having to leave the house.[35]

Women, these examples suggest, were encouraged to view the community as a space of consumption, and the telephone as a tool with which to more efficiently navigate it. As such, the telephone shapes the production of domestic labor as a function of the homemaker's ability to access desired products and services without leaving the residence. This external focus encourages the homemaker to imagine the space of her house as a totally wired environment in which readily available telephones diminish her need to physically engage with the outside world. As Raymond Williams' discourse on mid-century America observes, the perception of the telephone as arbiter between indoor, private space and outdoor, public space has further implications in the context of a growing suburban culture. Here, the outside world is increasingly brought into the home through the expanding communications complex. In this atmosphere of insularity, Williams suggests, taking a trip to the outside world becomes an antiquated exercise.[36]

The telephone, Bell advertisements similarly suggested, plays a central role in facilitating that physical disconnect with the outside world. To be sure, the message was an inherent part of promoting all forms of telephone use; inscribed in the very action of communicating via telephone is the negation of interaction in real space. In the period covered by this essay, however, it is homemakers whom Bell regularly asked to fundamentally rethink how they conceived communication by utilizing the telephone to navigate the space outside their front door. Therefore, while it was sometimes marketed as a space-crunching tool that frees the businessman from the constraints of his office (important calls can be made from a summer retreat), or as a time-crunching tool that frees women from the constraints of the home (by providing extra time to attend social activities), its ultimate function was to reduce a homemaker's interaction in the public realm to those contacts made from the privacy of her domestic surroundings.

In reality, there is no conclusive documentation of the degree to which residential subscribers around the country utilized their telephone as mainline to the public sphere.[37] In fact, it is likely that the popular conception of the telephone as replacement for face-to-face contact was largely perpetuated through Bell propaganda, which consistently marketed telephony as a surrogate for actual movement between the home and spaces of community interaction, like shopping districts. Nevertheless, the spatial messages in Bell's telephone marketing material are important because they reflect a long-term corporate advertising policy predicated on a three-part connection between woman, home, and telephone, a connection that mandated women remain in their homes as an essential aspect of their engagement with its product. Yet while most analyses of telephone use discuss its impact on social relations in the community, almost none specify how Bell related that use to the domestic sphere. The oversight is surprising because most other household conveniences have been analyzed in terms of their aesthetic contribution to, and shaping of activity within, their physical surroundings—from the way television encourages family togetherness in particular rooms in the house to the introduction of electrical appliances as features in the scientific management of kitchen chores.[38]

Yet as this review of Bell marketing material reveals, between the late 1920s and 1950s the company was fully dedicated to inserting its product into the physical space and daily activity of the home. Moreover, the marketing of telephone use to women differed in significant ways from the marketing of other home products, particularly by asking women to perceive their homes as totally wired environments, themselves as architectural planners, and their communities as entirely telephone accessible. It is in this context that the company's conceptualization of homemaker-as-telephone-user—whether wealthy or of average income—should be understood. Bell persistently engaged women in a popular dialogue about the telephone's relationship to the organization of everyday endeavors within the residence. Furthermore, they addressed them not as passive consumers but active producers within the household. Bell's formulation of female "telephone identity" was thus one of authority, but an authority that was ultimately limited to the domestic sphere.

Notes

1. A.W. Page, "Public Relations and Sales," General Commercial Conference (Bell System), Shawnee-on-Delaware, PA, 1928, Microfiche 368B, IBIC. Cited in Roland Marchand, *Advertising the American Dream: Making Way for Modernity, 1920–1940* (Berkeley: University of California Press, 1985), 117; see also Claude S. Fischer, *America Calling: A Social History of the Telephone to 1940* (Berkeley: University of California Press, 1992), 79.

2. See Carolyn Marvin, *When Old Technologies Were New: Thinking about Communication Technologies in the Late Nineteenth Century* (New York Oxford University Press, 1988); Lana F. Rakow, *Gender on the Line: Women, the Telephone, and Community Life* (Champaign: University of Illinois Press, 1991); Michèle Martin, *"Hello Central?" Gender, Technology, and Culture in the Formation of Telephone Systems* (Montreal: McGill-Queen's University Press, 1991).

3. Bell formed a "literary bureau" to supervise company publicity in 1890 and hired N.W. Ayer and Sons in 1908.

4. Marchand, *Advertising the American Dream.*

5. Collection 2: SBC Communications Inc./Record Group 5: Predecessor and Subsidiary Companies/ Southwestern Bell Telephone Company/Publications—Non-Periodic/"New Convenience for the Fine Home" (1930), AT&T Archives (hereafter ATT).

6. Ibid.

7. Marchand, *Advertising the American Dream*, 120.
8. Ibid.
9. Ibid.
10. Ibid.
11. Collection 6: Bell System/Record Group 6, Book 5: Publications—Non-Periodic/"Modern Telephone Service for the Home" (1920s), ATT.
12. Bell advertisement, quoted in Marchand, *Advertising the American Dream*, 119.
13. "Interesting Homes," Bell advertisement, 1930, Warshaw Collection of Business Americana—Telephone, Archives Center, National Museum of American History, Smithsonian Institution, Washington, DC (hereafter WC).
14. Ibid.
15. Italics in original. "From Boudoir to Kitchen," Bell advertisement, box 26, 1930, WC.
16. Italics in original. "In the Smooth Functioning of an Estate Telephones Play a Particularly Important Role," Bell advertisement, 1930, box 26, WC.
17. For depictions of women as war workers, see Maureen Honey, *Creating Rosie the Riveter: Class, Gender, and Propaganda During World War II* (Boston: University of Massachusetts Press, 1985); and Susan M. Hartmann, *The Home Front and Beyond: American Women in the 1940s* (New York: Macmillan, 1982).
18. The earliest example I have found is a 1929 mock article: R.T. Barrett, "Jack and Jill Build a Home," *Pacific Bell Magazine* 22 (January 1929): 8–9.
19. "Every Woman Wants Telephone Outlets in her New Home," Bell advertisement, *circa* 1946–49, box 10, N.W. Ayer Advertising Agency Records, Archives Center, National Museum of American History, Smithsonian Institution, Washington, DC. (hereafter AC).
20. R.S. Callvert, "Telephone Conveniences in Your New Home," *Bell Telephone Magazine* 33, no. 3 (Autumn 1954): 165–6.
21. Ibid.
22. Claude S. Fischer and Glenn Carroll, "Telephone and Automobile Diffusion in the United States, 1902–1937," *American Journal of Sociology* 93 (March 1988): 1158. Similarly, I did not find statistics charting residential telephone subscriptions in the AT&T Archives.
23. "As fundamental as kitchen cabinets ...," Bell pamphlet, *Electrical Construction and Maintenance*, 1952, WC.
24. Adolph F. Michel and T. Hunt Clark, "Advance Arrangements for Telephone Convenience," *Bell Telephone Magazine* 28, no. 4 (Winter 1949–50): 217.
25. "How to take the 'run' out of running a home," Pacific Telephone advertisement, *Architect and Engineer* (April 1955): 45.
26. "What! No Kitchen Telephone?" Bell advertisement, 1955, box 17, AC.
27. Gwendolyn Wright, *Building the Dream: A Social History of Housing in America* (Cambridge: MIT Press, 1983).
28. Lillian Gilbreth, *The Home-maker and Her Job* (New York: D. Appleton, 1927).
29. Fischer, *America Calling*, 233.
30. Christine Frederick, *Household Engineering: Scientific Management in the Home* (Chicago: New School of Home Economics Press, 1915), 329.
31. Marvin, *When Old Technologies Were New*; Rakow, *Gender on the Line*; Martin, *"Hello Central?"*.
32. WC, coll. 60, box 5.
33. Genevieve A. Callahan, "Fourteen Pages of Household Helpfulness," *Sunset* 72, no. 3 (March 1934): 18.
34. "In Just 30 Minutes," Bell advertisement, n.d., box 9, AC.

35. "M-J-B *Why?*" MJB advertisement, *Sunset* 84–85 (May 1940): 46.

36. Raymond Williams, *Television, Technology and Cultural Form* (New York: Schodken, 1975). See also Harry Henderson, "The Mass-Produced Suburbs, I," *Harpers* 207, no. 1242 (November 1953): 26.

37. Fischer, *America Calling*.

38. For a discussion of television and family life, see Lynn Spigel, *Make Room for TV: Television and the Family Ideal in Postwar America* (Chicago: University of Chicago Press, 1992).

Dress: Gendered and Political Identities

8

Trans-coding Nationalism: Subjectivity and Military Themes in Regency Women's Dress

Ellen Kennedy Johnson

In *Persuasion*, Jane Austen posits alternative social roles for women apart from the ideology claiming their suitability only for matters concerning the private sphere. Mrs Croft, wife of naval hero Admiral Croft, is presented as her husband's equal, his confidant, and moreover, his ship mate as she traveled with him "four times across the Atlantic," "once to the East Indies," to "Cork, and Lisbon, and Gibraltar," never "suffering in body or mind." While Austen models an enlarged view of female liberty in Mrs Croft, the reality of life for middle-class women in Regency England was more constrained, and most could only dream of living such a noteworthy civic existence.

At the time Austen was writing *Persuasion*, British women appropriated military themes into their fashions, accessorizing the simple, white muslin under-dress with accoutrements à la militaire, such as frogs, epaulets, braided trims, tassels, and feathers. They added overcoats called spencers and redingotes, which mimicked the shape and style of British and French military uniforms. They wore Mamalouc turbans, Russian cloaks, Wellington boots, Cossack mantles, and Trafalgar dresses, named after the revered military heroes of the Napoleonic Wars. Together with the fabrics, beads, and exotic furs gleaned from the Indian subcontinent and other imperial endeavors in Egypt, Africa, and Eastern Europe, women created a visual record of their engagement with national and international events.[1] In this essay, I argue that women's commitment to this trend goes beyond the mere outward signifiers of nationalism and patriotism. As the military uniform signified authority, activity, and the opportunity for men to earn rank and fortune by merit, women, too, desired to write these narratives of adventure, social mobility, and comradeship onto their bodies in a subtle and acceptable form of cross dressing.

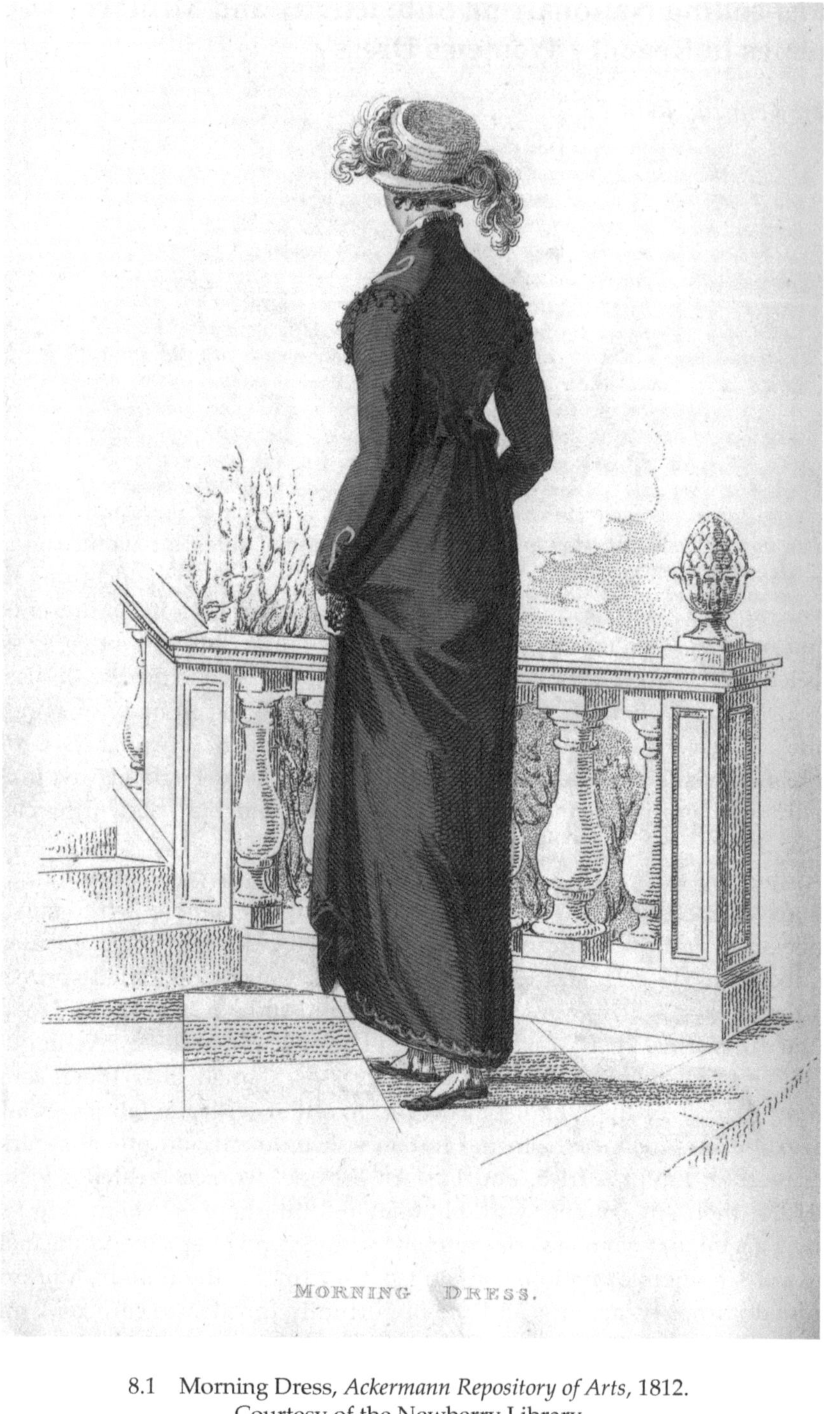

8.1 Morning Dress, *Ackermann Repository of Arts*, 1812. Courtesy of the Newberry Library

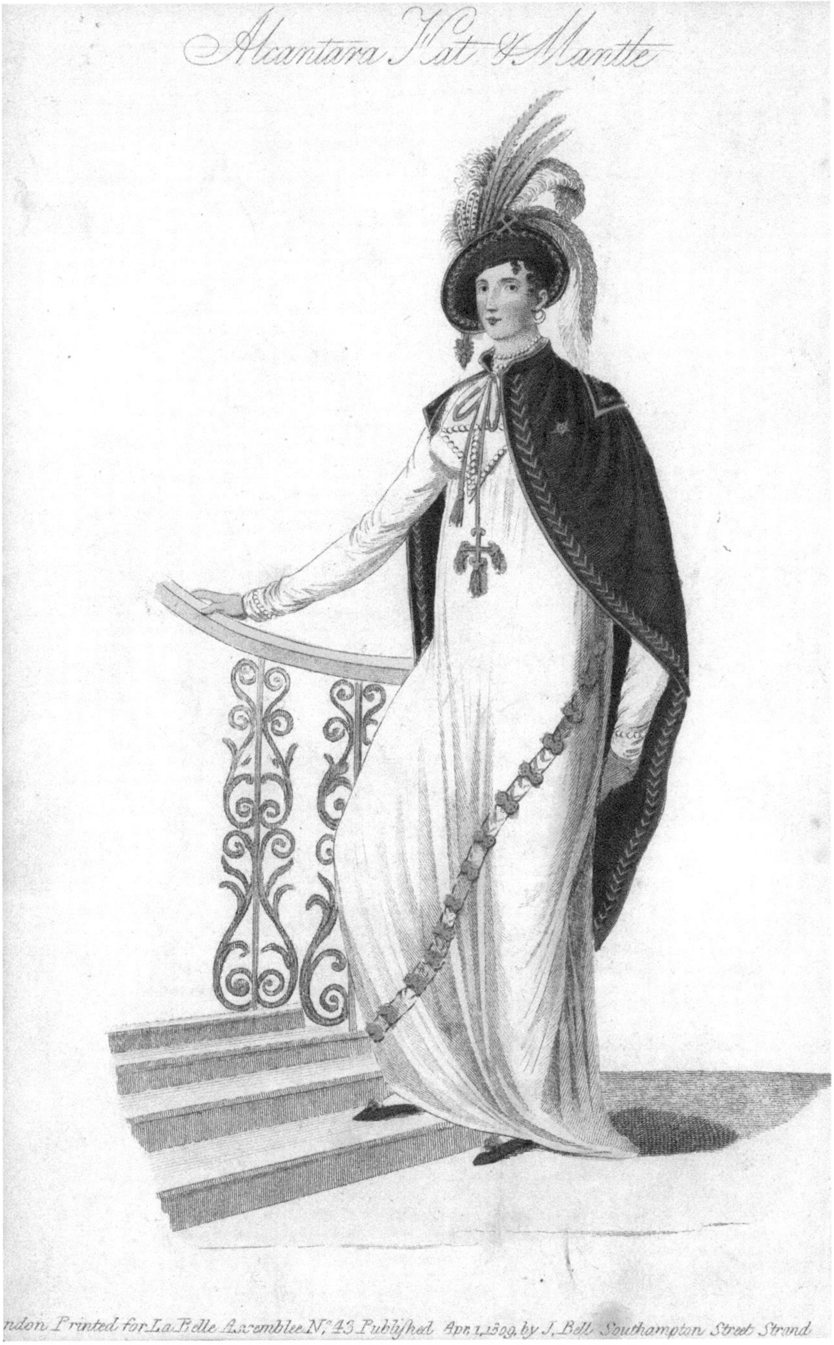

8.2 Evening Dress and Mantle, *La Belle Assemblée*, 1809. University of Washington Libraries, Special Collections, UW28224z

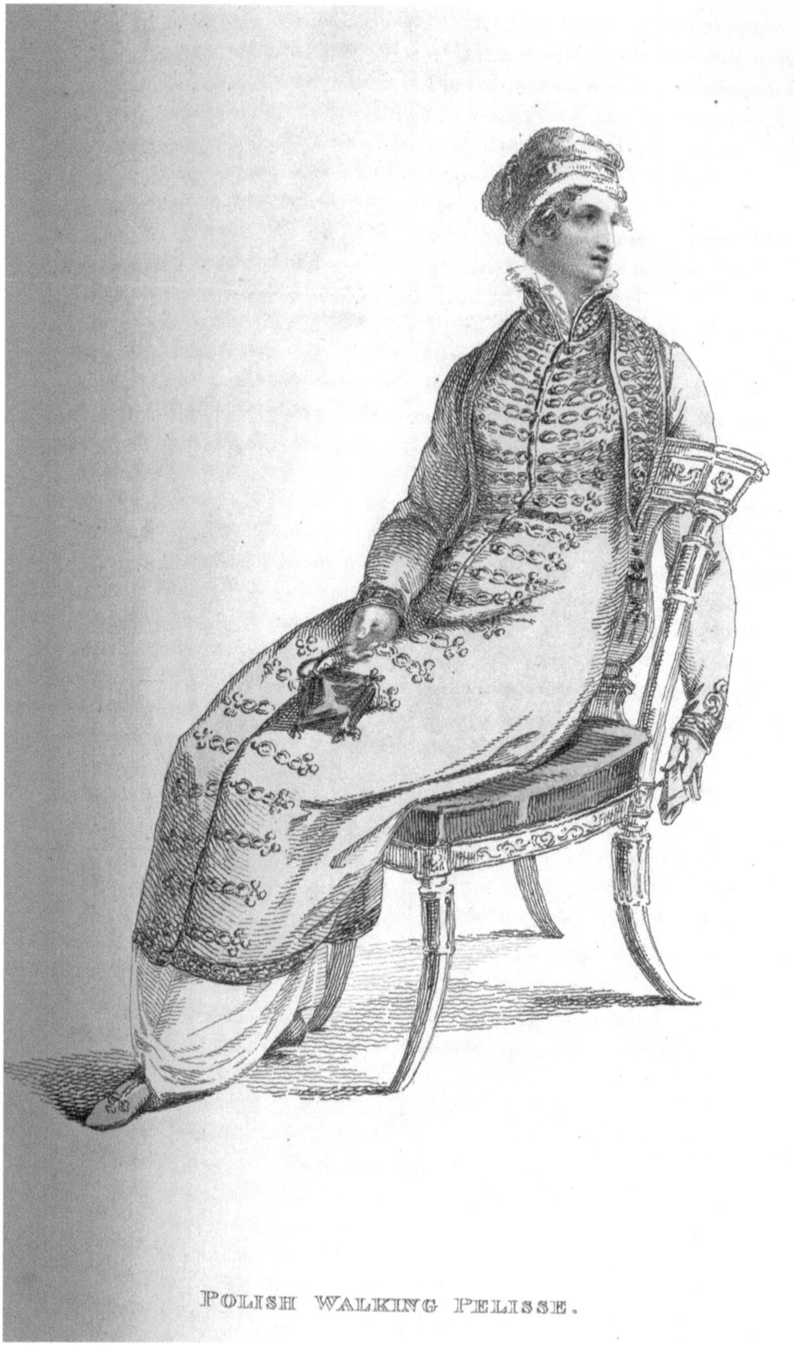

8.3 Polish Walking Pelisse, *Ackermann Repository of Arts*, 1809.
Courtesy of the Newberry Library

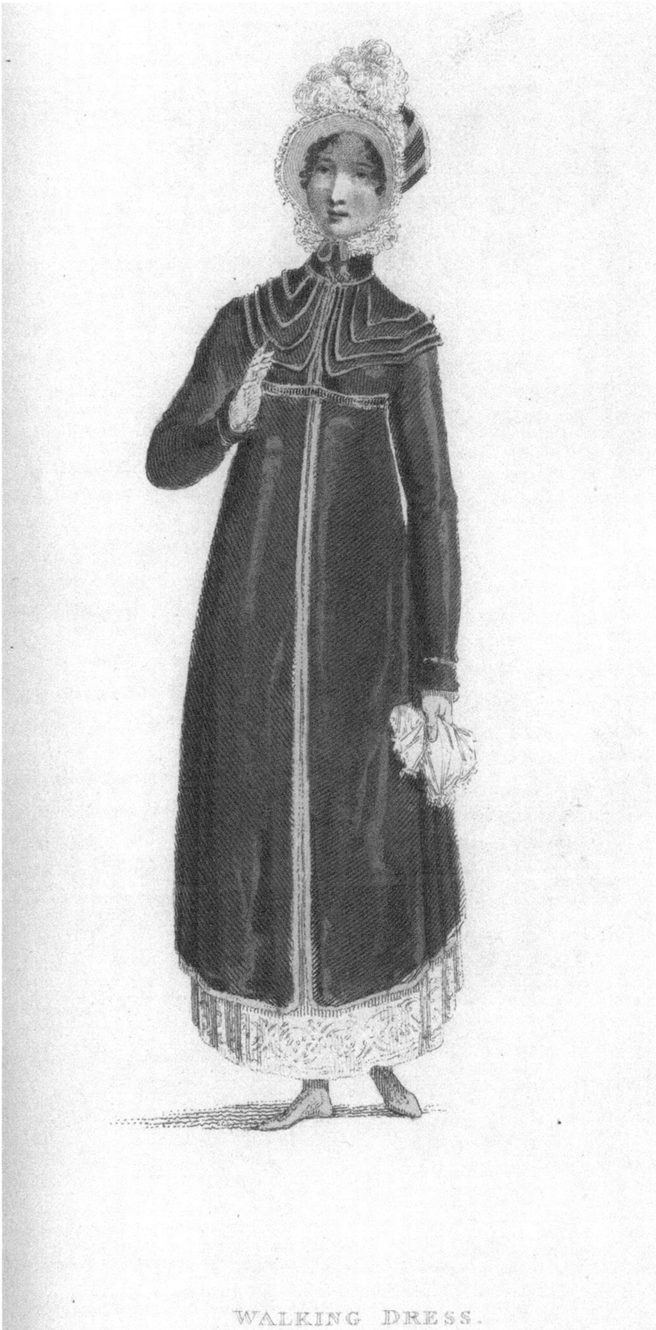

8.4 Walking Dress, *Ackermann Repository of Arts*, 1815.
Courtesy of the Newberry Library

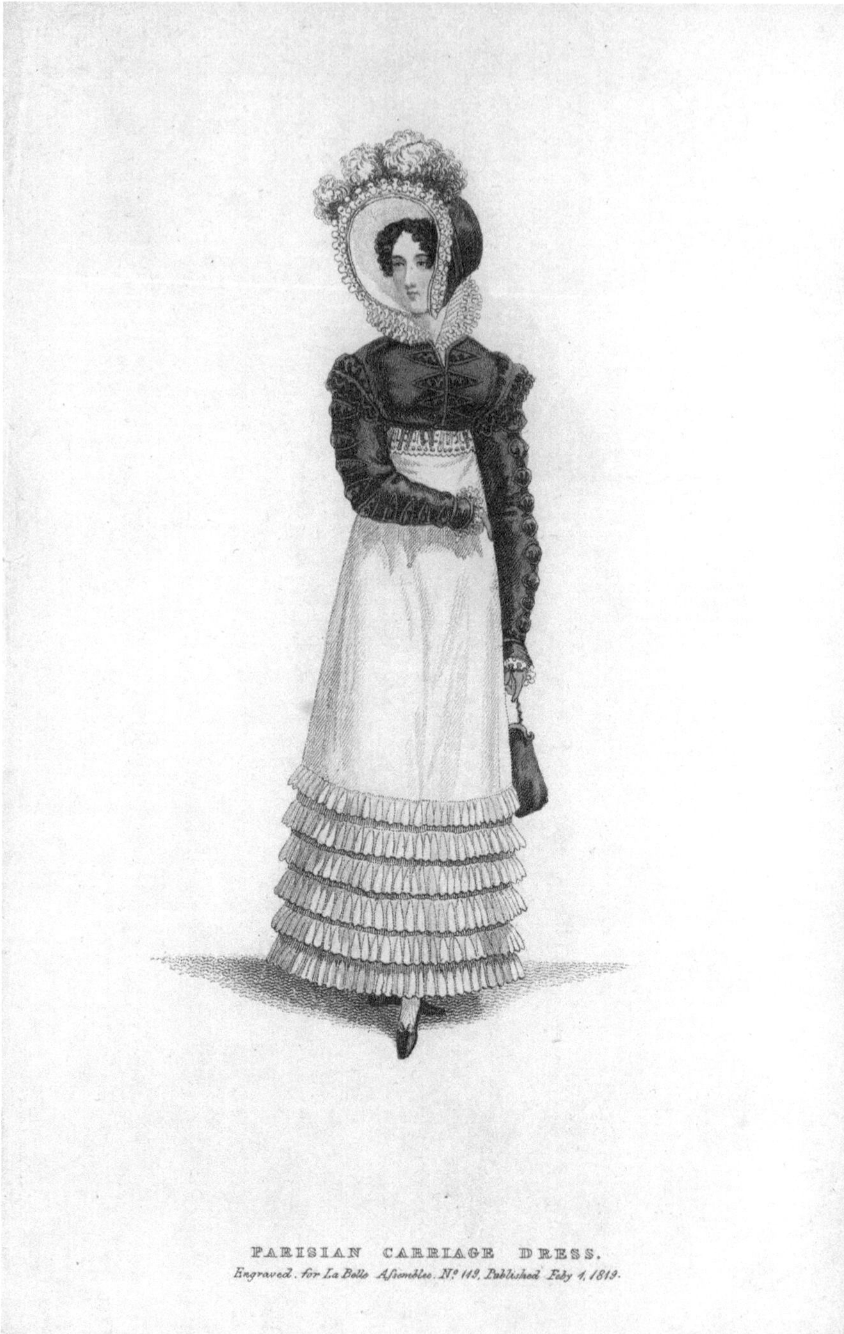

8.5 Parisian Carriage Dress and Military Spencer, *La Belle Assemblée*, 1815. University of Washington Libraries, Special Collections, UW28225z

Theorizing the significance of women's designing of clothes, Cheryl Buckley writes, "dress and dressmaking are cultural sites where identity, place, and memory figure."[2] Military and imperial motifs in women's dress in the first two decades of the nineteenth century represent a unique and historically specific performance of female subjectivity, where appropriating military modes of dress deemphasized sexual difference and perhaps hinted at the possibility of an egalitarian social system. Without dispute, fashions of the day serve as a visual tableau of larger historical and cultural events, and war has often been a catalyst for changes in fashion trends. In general, fashions during wartime tend to be more practical for obvious reasons: the need to conserve fabric for making military uniforms, women having less time to construct, clean, and afford elaborate designs due to the expansion of their duties in the absence of men in the household, and the psychological desire to appear less frivolous in times of national crisis.

However, in England at the end of the eighteenth and the beginning of the nineteenth centuries, many other social factors specific to the time may have contributed to the rise of this trend toward women's fashion à la militaire. First, government contracts given to manufacturers in Northern England stimulated an unprecedented growth in the industry by the end of the eighteenth century and were integral to the growth of the civilian market for textiles.[3] When the expanding middle-class population demanded affordable, ready-made clothing, these thriving cotton mills were already configured to produce homogeneous-styled garments to the masses. The abundance of slopworkers willing to sew in their homes meant low overheads for the industry and allowed for greater profits. The prevalence of drab-colored blue, gray, and greens used in women's spencers and redingotes reflects the mass production of similarly colored uniforms for men. In fact, in "Guide to Good Taste and Dress," published in 1808, "London Dust" and "Dust of Ruins" (or as we call them, muted blue and grey) were considered the two most tasteful colors for garments.[4] By the beginning of the nineteenth century, there was a fairly successful distribution network in place supplying massive amounts of fabric in these colors to keep up with the demand for military uniforms. Since the cut of women's jackets in this period were not so dissimilar from men's, using these stock colors and converting a rudimentary pattern to fit the smaller physique of a woman would have been a simple procedure. Many women, too, sewed their husbands' and brothers' military clothes to save on the cost of labor. Jane Austen discusses making a dozen shirts for her brother when he was on shore leave, and in her novel *Mansfield Park*, she describes how her heroine, Fanny Price, sews and mends her sea-faring brother William's uniforms before he sails to the East Indies. We can assume, then, that when women during this period decorated their clothes with military buttons, furs, braids, and other trims used on military uniforms, they were utilizing surplus materials in a practical way.

Beyond these obvious considerations though, the civilians' embracing of military themes in their dress most often represents a show of patriotism and support for the nationalist cause. The sailor suit, worn by young boys and girls of all classes in England and the United States from the late nineteenth century until the years following World War II, is a good example of civilians adopting military themes in their dress, as is the appearance of the bomber jacket in the United States after World War II, camouflage jackets and prisoner of war bracelets in the Vietnam era, and most recently, the ubiquitous presence of the American flag on sweaters, jackets, scarves, and numerous other fashion items, designed to show support for the United States in the aftermath of the September 11th attack. Most contemporary theories about the importance of clothes to the reading of significant cultural events is easily applied to the late eighteenth and early nineteenth centuries, when the British middle-class, en masse, embraced the institutions of emerging capitalism, private property, and the nuclear family. In the service of these ideals, the fashion magazine burst on the scene and the latest styles were displayed in stunning aquatint and meticulous sartorial detail. French and English fashion magazines such as *Ackermann Repository of Arts*, *La Belle Assemblée*, and the *Lady's Magazine* flooded the British market by the end of the eighteenth century and both British and French women, despite the political turmoil between the two countries, shared an affection for similar fabrics, perfumes, trimmings, dress, and hair styles. By the end of the eighteenth century, France was both recovering from a revolution and building up their military might to fight the English. These important events were reflected in fashion trends away from the extravagant silks and brocades worn by the aristocracy to the more affordable cottons provided by trade with the Indian subcontinent and the burgeoning home-grown textile industries. France, too, was rapidly establishing manufacturing facilities to compete with foreign trade, and fabric mills reproducing lighter cambrics and calicos sprung up all over.

During the French Revolution, French citizens, both male and female, donned patriotic garb as propaganda for the new regime. In fact, by 1792, a decree was passed that the cockade, a ribbon rosette of red, blue, and white pinned on the hats of both sexes, be worn by every citizen. In "Costume in the Age of Napoleon," Philippe Seguy describes the significance of costume as a political tool:

> For the first time in the history of costume, a social and political category was asserting itself by the conspicuously external means of dress … Politics thus created fashion. It was the one and only source of inspiration. People no longer stated their opinion; they also displayed them. In fact, a collective hysteria to do so prevailed for the first time in history. Not only was there a definite iconography and ideology reflected in the republican costume, but former high fashion came to be seen as the unique and futile occupation of the idle rich.[5]

In the light of the long-standing competition between France and Great Britain, the proliferation of military conflict between the two nations, and the ubiquitous presence of men in uniform throughout England, it is easy to assume that British women would also want to stage a show of patriotic fervor through their dress and other fashion accessories. Since we have the benefit of looking at this question about women's choice of dress from an historical perspective, we can see that while men have always claimed the prerogatives of nation building, women have always taken on the obligation of sustaining national identity, both symbolically, as women in need of defense by the nation's sons, as mothers who reproduce its citizens, and wives who remain faithful to its protectors, and practically, by sustaining the war efforts through sewing uniforms, knitting socks, filling jobs, nursing the wounded, and keeping up morale. The cultural politics of the emerging middle class, as Andrew McCann asserts, created an "internal colonization" of marginalized subjects, such as women, "functioning as a way of integrating diverse communities into the infrastructures of both a national collective and a capitalist economy."[6] Along with other cultural markers, like language and deportment, dress was an important staging arena for the performance of British womanhood and wearing patriotic dress was a way in which she could signal her approval of national ideologies.

From the end of the eighteenth century, through the first decade of the nineteenth, when some of the most significant battles of the Napoleonic Wars were fought and won by Britain and its allies, the trend toward naming women's attire in honor of prestigious British military heroes, their allies, and the defeated was commonplace. In a letter to her sister Cassandra in January of 1799, Jane Austen writes: "I will not wear my white sattin cap tonight after all; I am to wear a Mamalouc cap instead,"[7] a style made popular after the recent defeat of the French at the Battle of the Nile and named for the hero of the HMS Aboukir.[8] The fashion section of *Ackermann Repository of Arts* in 1809 introduced "the Nelson," in honor of the fallen Vice Admiral, which consisted of the padding used as a bustle pinned to the lower edge of the bodice, near the derriere,[9] and women wore "Nelson Rose feather[s]"[10] in their hats. In that same year, the Trafalgar dress, a white satin gown trimmed in gold lamé, made its debut, followed by the Platoff costume, named for the Cossack commander Count Platoff who offered his daughter's hand in marriage to anyone who would bring him Napoleon's head.

Wellington mania lasted for several years after the Battle of Waterloo in 1815; women proudly wore Wellington boots, Wellington hats, Wellington slippers, and Wellington mantles. In a letter to the editor of the *Repository*, John Alfred Parnell, having recently been on his European tour, wrote on September 2, 1815, just three months after the Battle of Waterloo, that women on the continent were imitating English fashion by donning Wellington military boots of "fine red kid and Morocco leather ... with very small yellow gilt buttons at the side … and a star of royal purple embroidered on the instep," as well as Prince Blucher demi-boots with "red covered buttons" on the instep, honoring the Prussian general whose army was invaluable to Wellington, and spencers à la militaire in "Prussian blue kerseymere."[11]

While little has been written about the embracing of military themes in women's dress in England in the first quarter of the nineteenth century, much has been written about how men's dress moved away from the lavish display of silks and brocades worn in the sixteenth and seventeenth centuries, meant as a marker of nobility and high birth, to the less ostentatious modern three piece-styled suit made of cloth from local mills. By the end of the eighteenth century, the spirit of revolution permeated the English psyche: having lost its colonies in North America, and witnessing the fate of the monarchy in France, England embraced the change in men's fashion as imperative to the safety of the aristocracy, but it also served to set a new standard for masculinity, away from the foppish display of wealth to the more understated show of politeness and industriousness.[12] As the war between Britain and France intensified, so did the need for men on both sides of the channel to prove their superiority in might, and the emerging men's styles of the period accentuated their virility. The insouciant folly of dress worn by the Macaronis at the end of the eighteenth century was replaced by costumes accentuating masculinity and man's active participation in world events, and away from what many considered the passive greediness of the aristocracy. Military costume, most specifically, exemplified this new masculinity. A uniform dripping with medals, trims, gold braids, and shiny brass buttons, signifying individual achievements on the battlefield, verified a man's dynamic role in shaping the nation. More important, class distinctions were less apparent in the ubiquity of the uniform, and courageous deeds recorded on jackets and coat sleeves now had little to do with one's birthright or social rank.

Along with the usual reports of battles lost and won, tales of exotic foreign lands and heroic encounters with pirate ships kept soldiers' family and friends enthralled. Jane Austen, for example, "flew as usual to the ship news"[13] every chance she could, according to her friend Sarah Spencer, which one can assume would be the natural inclination of a sister whose two brothers, Frank and Charles, were engaged in military endeavors in far away lands and also served as a respite from the usual doldrums of country living. In 1800, Austen writes enthusiastically to her sister Cassandra about a piece of information she read recently about their brother who "secur[ed] a Turkish ship from the French" and was "forced to burn her."[14] Austen's relationship to the navy also finds expression in many of her novels, but mostly in *Persuasion*, where even the silly Musgrove sisters had the navy list nearly memorized and charm Captain Wentworth with their sincere enthusiasm for "finding out the ships which [he] had commanded"[15] and listening intently to his stories about his adventures on the high seas.

Juxtaposed against Anne's father, the morally lax and sartorially effeminate Sir Walter Eliot, are the naval heroes, Admiral Croft and Captain Wentworth, whose robust endeavors in the Napoleonic Wars portend a new moral order—a meritocracy. By including the story of the failed sailor Dick Musgrove, the novel's narrator implies that military rank and power are earned by hard work, integrity, and the desire to raise oneself above their assigned social status. Anne's usual silence is broken when she defends military men against her father's charge that their "obscure birth and undue distinction"[16] disqualify any one of them from leasing Kellynch Hall: "The navy," she retorts, "who have done so much for us, have at least an equal claim with any other set of men, for all the comforts and the privileges which any home can give."[17] She ends with a jab at Sir Walter's inherited wealth and fiscal negligence, necessitating their removal to less expensive lodgings, claiming "sailors work hard enough for their comforts, we must allow."[18]

Therefore, if men used fashion as a way to express national goals and announce their active participation in the building of the great nation, could not women mimic these same goals by inscribing onto their bodies a new model of femininity, in which women had both a public and a private function? If men could transcend class barriers by wearing military uniforms, could not women transcend gender barriers by adopting similar democratically styled dress? By looking at the fashion periodicals of the first quarter of the nineteenth century, such as *Ackermann Repository of Arts*, *The Lady's Magazine*, or *La Belle Assemblée*, women's dress, and more so, casual day dress, became more masculinized as flounces and longer skirts were replaced with plain, shorter hemlines more suitable to walking and horseback riding. By the turn of the nineteenth century, women "bid adieu to steel busks, long stays, and all the torturing compression under which British beauty has so long laboured."[19] The looser fitting, plain muslin gowns served as the perfect palette for writing on the social imperatives of the day. Accessorizing with spencers, redingotes, curacos, hats, and accoutrements such as frog closures, braided trims, and military style buttons are shown frequently in the fashion plates from *circa* 1800 to 1820. All of these additions were adaptations of men's military-style dress, and in addition to the usual accessories of fashion signifying bravery in battle or one's participation in important military operations, women's dress also accentuated the spoils of war—the furs, muffs, turbans, feathers, and shawls brought back from successful endeavors in battlefields and English colonies around the globe.

Many military features added to women's dress served practical purposes, too, and accentuated a growing freedom of movement, which might be attributed to their middle-class status, as the complex set of rules governing social interaction prohibited aristocratic women from traipsing through the countryside muddying their garments. By 1805, the train at the back of the dress was completely gone and hems were cut right above the ankle, allowing for more freedom of movement. A small slit at the elbow of the riding jacket, similar to those seen on men's military uniforms, served as a mini-pocket allowing women to forgo carrying a ridicule while horseback riding or engaging in other active sports. In the first 20 years of the century, the "classical" or "Empire" dress dominated the fashion scene, emphasizing vertical lines, lightweight fabrics, and high waists, allowing women to abandon their corsets and layers of petticoats, granting them more freedom of movement, and at the same time, deemphasizing both the hip and the bust. Aileen Ribeiro explains the significance of the classical form adopted in the late eighteenth and early nineteenth centuries in both France and England as a way to comfort the citizenry by drawing parallels between the "startling political developments" of the time and "the heroic days of Greece and Rome."[20] This trend, beginning in the 1780s merely as masquerading for the upper classes, evident in Vigee-Lebrun's paintings of Marie Antoinette in pastoral settings and loose fitting gowns, or Angelica Kaufmann's paintings of women in Turkish costume, eventually filtered down to the middling classes. By the first decade of the nineteenth century, women used this basic tunic form as a template, creatively adding fabrics, colors, and accoutrement inspired by military uniforms to invent unique adaptations of the conventional classical fashions of the day.

Furthermore, the accelerated growth of the cotton industry allowed the factories for the first time to produce fabrics that actually competed in quality with the Indian trade. Trade journal publisher and domestic connoisseur Rudolf Ackermann wrote in 1810 about the impressive muslin goods coming out of northern England, enabling "many persons to substitute British [cloth] for India, and so well have they been imitated, that experienced vendors themselves have not been able to distinguish them."[21] Because of this, the middling classes donned garments nearly indistinguishable from the upper class, improving the appearance of the lower and middle classes and effectively disabling a reliable marker for class differentiation. Because middle-class women could purchase or make staple garments like spencers and redingotes inexpensively, this allowed them to spend more money on stunning accessories to distinguish themselves from the masses and exercise their creative spirit. A coqulicot feather in a hat or ermine cuffs are examples of this trend. Where a jacket made in a mill would have cost a mere 2/-d (and even less if the fabric was purchased and sewn at home), the feather donning the hat would have cost 8/-d. Twenty years earlier, the muslin under-dress would have cost 14/-d alone.[22]

Both the trend toward democratization of dress and the lack of feminine features in the newer fashions was disturbing to many. In *Letters from England,* Robert Southey laments the loss of the feminine-styled fashions, such as the wasp-waisted dress, writing: "All these fashions went like the French monarchy, and about the same time; but when the ladies began to strip themselves they did not know where to stop. And these follies travel where the science and literature and domestic improvements of the English never reach!"[23] In the introduction to *Modes and Manners of the Nineteenth Century*, published in 1909, and at the time considered the definitive text about the social and cultural trends of the preceding century, Grace Rhys characterizes English dress styles in the first two decades of the nineteenth century as having a "socialist tendency," where "the lower ranks of society are being leveled up [and] distinctions in dress are being done away with."[24] M. Edwardes, the author of the three-volume text, describes this fashion trend in negative terms and laments the infiltration of styles from foreign lands into the wardrobes of "healthful and robust" English ladies. About women's fashion between the years 1811 and 1817, he writes:

> Women certainly never dressed to less advantage. Taking it for granted that the woman's chief object is to make herself beautiful and to please, it is incomprehensible that fashions so highly unbecoming should have lasted so long; perhaps if it was with the idea of providing an extra enticement to men to seek more closely the jewel that lay hidden in such a strange and unattractive casket. Anyhow, no woman was found at that time to draw the attention of her sisters to the inharmonious and grotesque appearance she presented.[25]

Rhys describes seeing two girls—"pure English types"—walking in the Welsh mountains "dressed in gowns fashioned after the model of Arab dress first brought to London dusty and blood stained, after the Soudan war." She writes: "How narrow the world's limits are growing when Saxon maidens in Arab dress can be found straying by a Celtic fastness."[26] Rhys, Edwardes, and Southey's criticisms involve the public performance of women's bodies during a time when the definition of middle-class women's role in public society was, purportedly, narrowing, prompting us to question to what extent middle-class women internalized and adopted the tenets of domestic ideology in an era when the majority of them had a vested interest in understanding the daily movements of war campaigns, as few families did not have a brother, father, son, or neighbor involved in the protracted wars with France and other countries. Through military publications like the shipping news and the proliferation of newspapers, magazines, and other up-to-date publications, along with women's donning of pseudo military dress and wearing the spoils of the Empire, critics like Rhys, Edwardes, and Southey may also have been concerned with what they perceive as the interruption of the homo-social nature of military culture.

Furthermore, these criticisms do not seem to reflect the real material practices of women in the decades of the nineteenth century. While both the British and French economies were gearing up to what would become fashion as the kind of industry we know now, complete with competition, advertisements, and psychological drama, most middle-class British women were discriminating in the type of clothes they wore, and chose outfits based on social standing and age appropriateness. As clothing historian Diana Donald points out in *Followers of Fashion: Graphic Satires of the Georgian Period,* clothing was not treated as expendable, but more as "possessions [or] personal investments of sentimental value," evidenced by the "re-making and refurbishment of garments at every level of society."[27] English women were more concerned with dressing "tastefully," rather than following every fashion trend reported in the fashion periodicals of the day, and as Donald goes on to say, "taste was given a moral dimension."[28] Yet, a vast majority of women's day dresses worn between 1800 and 1820 reveal a full-scale acceptance of military and imperial themes, which indicates that the styles were well accepted and considered tasteful, despite the androgynous or unisex-like cut of the clothing. Fashioned after men's military uniforms, women wore similarly styled redingotes (riding coats), pelisses and spencers à la militaire, Wellington slippers, Mameluke robes, Cossack hats, Witzchour mantles, and Blucher boots. The Kutusoff hat and mantle, named for the style worn by the Russian general who commanded the Allies against Napoleon, was worn by both men and women.

The addition of men's styles to women's fashion did not go without notice from the establishment, prompting an elderly woman to write into the *Lady's Museum* that when she sees a young lady "shew a fine ankle" because "the petticoat is shortened until half the leg is exposed—I blush for her indelicacy."[29] Like Edwardes, Rhys, and Southey, this editorial seems to be a response to the de-feminizing of women's garments, as before and certainly after the first quarter of the nineteenth century, women's clothing was used to mark the body as innocent/not innocent, pure/impure, healthy/unhealthy, and fruitful/barren, à la the tenets of domestic ideology. More to the point, de-sexing the female body vexes the overarching political goal of mobilizing the population to fight a war by drawing on the mythology of the female body in need of protection and women as the caretakers of the nation. In this sense, clothing à la militaire changed woman's role in the body politic both literally and figuratively. Military and imperial motifs in dress allowed women to occupy a liminal space between the public and the private world, where the acceptable display of patriotic fervor in dress was a welcome part of England's nationalist agenda, but at the same time, the androgynous nature of the clothing deemphasized women's sexuality and, perhaps, implicitly suggested the possibility of a more egalitarian existence.

For example, in *Persuasion,* Anne claims that Admiral and Mrs Croft were the happiest married couple she had ever seen, "who seemed so particularly attached and happy ... [their] two hearts so open, no tastes so similar, no feelings so in unison, no countenances so beloved."[30] This companionate model of marriage was rare for the time and must have intrigued Austen, as she uses the couple to level a critique of the prevailing nature of middle- and upper-middle-class courting rituals. The Croft marriage mirrors the solidarity developed between servicemen and one that often transcended class boundaries. Mrs Croft's active support of her husband's military career allows her to be a player in both the public and private realms: by taking a more active role in her husband's military service, she contributes to what the British considered the most important public role a citizen can play—that of defending your country, while simultaneously, she performs her duties in the private sphere—that of creating domestic harmony. The manner in which Mrs Croft relays the story of her life at the Musgrove dinner party comes in between Anne's musings about her and Captain Wentworth's "perpetual estrangement"[31] as the antithesis of the Croft's indissoluble alliance. In Sophie Croft's narrative about "the happiest part of her life [spending] time on board a ship,"[32] Austen uses Frederick Wentworth's distaste for allowing women on board to highlight the conventional wisdom about the nature of women's role in the nationalist cause.[33]

Frederick promotes the standard gender role division when he compares a captain's feeling toward a favored ship to "the passion [ladies] would have as to the fashion and strength of an old pelisse, which [was] lent about among half your acquaintance, ever since you could remember, and which at last on some wet day, is lent to yourself."[34] Clearly, at this point in the novel, Austen seems to connect Frederick's view of female/male roles as a roadblock to the kind of companionate marriage the Crofts enjoy. His understanding of separate spheres ideology is typical for the time. As Sean Nixon remarks, "the centrality of being able to provide for a household of dependants—in particular a wife—manifested a fierce independence that was important to middle-class men," whose authority was defined "through their power over a range of dependants in the territory of the Empire, as well as the home."[35] Yet, Austen challenges these notions in the character of Mrs Croft, whose "only suffering in body or mind" occurs "when on land,"[36] or in other words, when she was forced to operate in the domestic sphere and deprived of the company of her companion and best friend—her husband, Admiral Croft. While Austen's *Persuasion* rarely discusses the details of her characters' dress, her personal letters impart a keen understanding of the styles of the day and the joy she finds in constructing new outfits and discussing the current fashion trends with her sister, Cassandra. We can imagine, though, how Mrs Croft might have looked and what she wore; and indeed, in the 1996 film version of Persuasion, produced by the BBC, Fiona Shaw, playing Mrs Croft, is a tall, vigorous woman, whose face might also show a hint of the "weather-beaten," as Sir Walter scornfully depicts the visages of naval officers who, by virtue of their active participation in the defense of the nation, spend too much time in the sun. Mrs Croft wears a double-breasted scarlet mantle with epaulets, a turban made of silk with a long gold tassel at the side, and cameos dangle from her pierced ears, presumably purchased during her voyages with her husband to Gibraltar, Lisbon, or other ports of call. In effect, she is wearing the nation and not dressed in pure white like the Musgrove sisters, hoping to catch the eye of Captain Wentworth; nor is she pretty like the prolific Mary, or quiet and self-effacing like Anne. But her energy and enthusiasm are attractive to her dining partners and clearly to her husband, Admiral Croft, who blushes and must avert his eyes from hers when she talks about all the things they missed when forced to be apart. Indeed, the hint here is that Mrs and Admiral Croft, as the alternate model of womanhood and the model of active masculinity, respectively, have it all: companionship, mutual admiration, shared goals, and, judging from the glow on Admiral Croft's face, a hearty sexual relationship.

Corporeal inscription through the art of fashion undoubtedly mandated that women in early nineteenth-century Britain adopt military and imperial themes in their dress as a display of national cohesion and, unconsciously, women participated in the homogenization of British middle-class culture, as the purpose of the fashion magazine is not to promote individuality, but to solidify cultural mores. However, this is not to imply that women were blind followers of fashion. Although they appeared to adopt uniformity in dress, their creative innovations and styling of hats, coats, dresses, and shoes revealed continuous, novel reinventions of what the fashion industry meant to convey about women's roles in private and public life. This practice delineated a certain historically specific performance of femininity that had never been before or would be again repeated on as grand a scale. By the third decade of the nineteenth century, women's dress would again become highly sexualized, as waists grew narrower and hiplines grew wider with each succeeding decade that passed, until the classic vertical dress-line was replaced by garments designed with angles and curves. Undoubtedly, the mind often acts in accordance with the social actions we are scripted to perform. Elizabeth Grosz points out that culture and nature often twist into each other and origins are not so easily traceable, whereas "the psyche can be a projection of the body's form."[37] While the practice of wearing nationalist dress can be easily written off as a typical show of patriotic fervor, and all the related psychology that goes along with it, I contend that, through the actual performance of this fashion trend, women trans-coded its meaning, from the expected show of patriotism by Britain's dutiful daughters, to a practice in which women could rehearse new subjectivities.

Notes

1. See Figures 8.1–8.5 for examples of these trends in women's fashion. A frog is an ornate, ornamental fastener used in place of buttons or as a decorative piece used on the cuffs of a riding coat. An epaulet is a shoulder ornament most often constructed of cording and tassels. Spencers and redingotes, adapted for women and used as overcoats, were inspired by men's military uniforms: a spencer is a short double-breasted jacket with wide labels and a redingote, which is the French word meaning "riding coat," is a longer version of the spencer. A pelisse is an empire-

styled overcoat extending to the bottom of the hip or the knee, belted with a high waist and a military style broad collar. The fashion for spencers and redingotes decorated with military braids, trims, and frogging were inspired by the uniforms worn by Polish Hussars, one of Britain's most loyal allies in the Napoleonic Wars. Additionally, accoutrements such as fur, beads, and feathers used in coats, hats, dresses, and shoes represented the spoils of war gleaned from the unique textiles, gemstones, fabrics, and ornaments of both allied and conquered lands.

2. Cheryl Buckley, "On the Margins: Theorizing the History and Significance of Making and Designing Clothes at Home," in *The Culture of Sewing: Gender, Consumption and Home Dressmaking*, ed. Barbara Burman (Oxford: Berg Press, 1999), 58.

3. Beverly Lemire, *Dress, Culture, and Commerce: The English Clothing Trade Before the Factory, 1660–1800* (Basingstoke, Hampshire: Macmillan, 1997), 40.

4. C. Willett Cunnington, *English Women's Clothing in the Nineteenth Century* (New York: Dover Publications, 1990), 14.

5. Philippe Seguy, "Costume in the Age of Napoleon," in *The Age of Napoleon: Costume from Revolution to Empire*, ed. Katell le Bourhis (New York: The Metropolitan Museum of Art/Harry N. Abrams, 1989), 49.

6. Andrew McCann, *Cultural Politics in the 1790s: Literature, Radicalism, and the Public Sphere* (New York: St Martin's Press, 1999), 31.

7. Jane Austen, *Jane Austen's Letters*, ed. Deirdre Le Faye (Oxford: Oxford University Press, 1995), 33.

8. Constance Hill, *Jane Austen: Her Home and Her Friends* (Whitefish, MT: Kessinger Publishing, 2004), 76. Hill explains this fashion trend in detail: "The word *Mamalouc* is given as *Mamalone* in Lord Brabourne's 'Letters of Jane Austen,' which is evidently a clerical error; the letters *uc* in the MS. having been mistaken for *ne*. The battle of the Nile, fought in the preceding August, had set the fashion in ladies' dress for everything suggestive of Egypt and of the hero of Aboukir. In the fashion-plates of the day we find Mamalouc cloaks and Mamalouc robes of flowing red cloth. Ladies wear toupées, somewhat resembling a fez, which we recognise as the 'Mamalouc cap,'[and] their dainty feet encased in 'green morocco slippers bound with yellow and laced with crocodile-coloured ribbon.'"

9. *Ackermann Repository of Arts, Literature, Commerce, Fashions, and Politics* (London: Rudolf Ackermann, Vol. I, January 1809), 52.

10. Hill, *Jane Austen*, 76.

11. *Ackermann Repository of Arts* (London: Rudolf Ackermann, Vol. XIV, September 1815), 305.

12. Anne Hollander, *Sex and Suits* (New York: A.A. Knopf, 1994); David Kutcha, "The Making of the Self-Made Man: Class, Clothing, and English Masculinity, 1688–1832," in *The Sex of Things: Gender and Consumption in Historical Perspective*, eds. Victoria de Grazia and Ellen Furlough (Berkeley: University of California Press, 1996). Both Hollander and Kutcha offer a detailed analysis of the politics of English men's fashion in the late eighteenth and early nineteenth centuries.

13. Jane Austen. *Letters 1796–1817*, ed. R.W. Chapman (Oxford: Oxford University Press, 1978), 87.

14. Ibid., 117.

15. Jane Austen, *Persuasion*, ed. Linda Bree (Ontario, Canada: Broadview Literary Texts, 2000), 97.

16. Ibid., 59.

17. Ibid.

18. Ibid.

19. Cunnington, *English Women's Clothing*, 73.

20. Aileen Ribeiro, *Dress in Eighteenth Century Europe 1715–1789* (New Haven: Yale University Press, 2002), 273–5.

21. Michael M. Edwards, *The Growth of the British Cotton Trade* (New York: A.M. Kelley, 1967), 45.

22. Werner Schlote, *British Overseas Trade from 1700 to the 1930s* (Oxford: Blackwell, 1952), 114, 116, 118. Symbols are for shillings and pence.

23. Robert Southey, *Letters From England: By Don Manuel Alvarez Espriella*, 3 volumes (London: Longman, 1808), 2: 276.

24. Grace Rhys, "Introduction," in *Modes and Manners of the Nineteenth Century*, by M. Edwardes (London: J.M. Dent and Company, 1909), xv.

25. M. Edwardes, *Modes and Manners of the Nineteenth Century* (London: J.M. Dent and Company, 1909), 116–17.

26. Rhys, "Introduction," xvi.

27. Diana Donald, *Followers of Fashion: Graphic Satires of the Georgian Period* (London: Hayward Gallery Publishing, 2002), 13.

28. Ibid., 15.

29. Phillis Emily Cunnington, *The History of Underclothes* (London: Courier Dover Publications, 1992), 108.

30. Austen, *Persuasion*, 97.

31. Ibid., 97.

32. Ibid., 103.

33. Ibid., 103. Bree writes: "the rules were officially that only the captain could bring his wife on board ship, though in practice others of the officers did so, and some ships accommodated wives and mistresses of men of other ranks." Not all married captains were accompanied by their wives. Of Jane Austen's two sisters-in-law married to navy officers, only one accompanied her husband on many of his tours of duty.

34. Ibid., 98.

35. Sean Nixon, "Exhibiting Masculinity," in *Representation: Cultural Representations and Signifying Practices*, ed. Stuart Hall (London: Sage Publications, 2000), 299–300.

36. Austen, *Persuasion*, 300.

37. Elizabeth Grosz, *Volatile Bodies: Toward a Corporeal Feminism* (Bloomington: Indiana University Press, 1994), 27.

9

"The Beauty of her Hands": The Glove and the Making of the Middle-Class Body

Ariel Beaujot

In the Victorian and Edwardian periods women used gloves not only to cover their skin as a protection from the elements but also as a defense from the gaze of others. What lay beneath the glove, in the case of the middle and working classes, was the hand of someone who labored—more often than not these women dusted, gardened, scrubbed, shook, painted, and handled large objects. In other words, the glove hid the hands of women who exposed their bodies to the elements and got dirty. The glove was an open secret—it was a well-known way to hide one's labor, and to level the hierarchy of classes in Britain. To put on a glove was to participate in an act that likened the middle class to the aristocracy and the working to the middle class. To adorn one's self in this accessory was a way to prevent class slippage. As the practice of wearing gloves became standardized, however, people found new ways of distinguishing the minutiae of class hierarchy; now they looked to the glove itself, reading class through fit, fabric, cleanliness, repair, and color.

The theoretical background for this essay draws on the work of Michel Foucault who asserts that "one of the primordial forms of class consciousness is the affirmation of the body."[1] In this instance, it is a specific part of the body—the hands—that affirm the woman's status as part of the "leisured" middle class. Following upon Foucault's insight, Wai Chee Dimock and Michael T. Gilmore suggest that classes "become 'real'—become solid, integral, and perhaps even acquirable—to the point where they appear entirely objective and self-evident," once they are inscribed on the body.[2]

Along the same lines, Judith Butler argues that gender is also an acquired state. Butler suggests that femininity is an identity constructed through a series of gestures and movements that come to represent "womanhood."[3] In

Butler's work the female body "becomes its gender through a series of acts which are renewed, revised and consolidated through time."[4] Prescriptive literature must be read against these frameworks, which suggest that class and gender are performed on a day-to-day basis, to find instances of the middle-class body "made-real" through use of gloves, creams, posture, diet, and exercises.

Apprehension surrounding social rank was pervasive among the middle classes. They were anxious that if they failed to represent their class correctly, they would not only be seen as working class, they would also be seen as having a characteristic of a different race: a darkened complexion. Class, race, and nation were imbedded into the practice of wearing gloves, which protected white skin. According to the narratives of scientific racism that abounded in the period, whiteness represented a racially superior complexion. In the age of Darwin, science could justify linking skin color with the "civilizing" practices of imperial rule. It was imperative that women, especially, maintained their pale skin tone because they were highlighted as representatives of the British race.[5] The whiteness of English women's complexion, sustained by glove wearing, symbolized not only their leisured class status, distancing them from the working class, but also symbolized the superior racial status of their nation on the world stage.

As well as acting as a protective cover for the skin and helping women to maintain the important distinction between the white races and other conquered races, the glove was involved in the performance of femininity. The varying shapes of the hands in this period were thought to represent different types of womanhood, and it was the tight, well-fitted, and easily moldable glove that helped women to create the hand shape required for the proper middle-class lady. This essay is a response to Judith Butler's call for scholars to "describe the mundane manner in which [gender] constructs are produced, reproduced, and maintained within the field of bodies."[6] I use Jules Prown's material culture methodology along with written sources such as prescriptive literature, etiquette manuals, advertisements, women's magazines, fashion plates, and dance hall music, to find instances of how the middle-class, female body was "made-real" through the use of gloves.[7]

This essay will show how two small pieces of fabric can illuminate the values, attitudes, assumptions, and ideas of an entire culture. Gloves are important objects of study because they help us to understand the way that the Victorian middle classes "performed" their classed, raced, and gendered identities. But before we move on to discussing the glove, let us first look at the meaning of what lay beneath it—the hand. In her 1908 etiquette guide, *Every Woman's Toilet Book,* Mrs Noble offered her commentary on the place of hands in the overall perception of a British woman. "One of woman's greatest charms," Noble claims, "is in the beauty of her hands, members which are truly adorable when their smallness is combined with other indications of fine breeding; but," she insists, "even if they are large they may still be beautiful if they are shapely, finely made, and white, with blue veins, taper fingers, and rosy nails, slightly arched."[8] Noble's observations make evident that there was more at stake in the perfect hand than simple physical traits; hands were a manifestation of class and gender written on the body. In the Victorian and Edwardian periods the ideal hand was thought to be particular to the middle class and was often cited in opposition to working-class hands which were "large and strong and coarse"[9] and aristocratic hands which were "long and sometimes too thin."[10] Throughout the nineteenth century delicate white hands were considered a primary indicator of women's "fine breeding" as well as a corporal expression of their detachment from manual labor. Mrs Noble's observations, then, were a reflection and a reaffirmation of the bodily identity that came to distinguish the middle-class women's physique from other social classes.

Leonore Davidoff and Catherine Hall's foundational study, *Family Fortunes,* demonstrates that the Victorian ideal for the middle-class household was one that had a working husband and a leisured wife.[11] Women were supposed to establish their family's status via the conspicuous consumption of dress and fashion accessories as well as through sustaining a leisured lifestyle. However, necessity dictated that many middle-class women had to do housework and gardening to keep up the appearance of another marker of middle-classness—the home.[12] The bind in which women found themselves—acting leisured while participating in unpaid work—created great anxiety that surfaced in etiquette manuals and fashion plates, and played out across the bodies of women. On promenade and at dinner parties women presented the silhouette of the perfect hand to friends, neighbors, and strangers; as such, they became walking advertisements for the benefits of gloves and other related paraphernalia.

Gloves were essential props for middle-class women who attempted to conform to the separate sphere ideology. To glove the hand was an important part of the process that middle-class women used to achieve small white hands which showed an absence of labor. However, a woman's soft white appendages were not natural but had to be kept up on a daily basis as an indication of her leisured status. Throughout the Victorian period, it was thought that class was marked on the body and that middle- and working-class women could be identified by their skin color, the size of their hands, and the appearance of their gloves. Here I map the story that was sold to women about the importance of maintaining small, soft, white hands.

This story, which ends in the later 1920s when leisure became represented by sunny vacations and tanned skin, begins in the 1830s when various phenomena coalesced to provide the pressure and the means to compel middle-class women to consider white hands as an indication of their class status. At this time etiquette manuals made a transition from conduct-oriented to consumption-oriented, women's magazines began to proliferate, and the glove industry started to standardize their wares, increasing production and ensuring a snug fit. I will consider how all of these factors worked together to create an unsettled sense of self which surrounded the middle-class hand.

Constructing the Middle-Class Body: The Glove and the Maintenance of the Perfect Hand

Middle-class women of the Victorian period would have the public believe that within their gloves lay hands that were never subjected to labor; however, real women did not always have the luxury of complete idleness and they worked hard at creating the illusion of pristine hands. Fortunately for the historian, prescriptive literature can provide insight into the time and energy that was spent on the creation and preservation of delicate white hands. This literature encouraged women to present a standardized body that came to be understood as specifically middle class. Consider, for example, a quotation from *The Woman's Book* (1911) which suggested that women's work could be hidden by cleaning their hands: "with little care the busy housewife can keep her hands in as good condition as the lady of leisure."[13] Here we see that the look of the middle-class leisured wife was not natural but took constant "care." In other words, ideal hands had to be cultivated and maintained.

Leather gloves made from young goats (kids, hence "kid gloves") were considered best for hiding imperfect hands. It was thought that cotton and silk conformed to a woman's hand too readily, making them a real "test of shapely knuckles and tapering finger tips."[14] In comparison to other fabrics the soft leather of kid was more likely to preserve its shape than cotton or silk, and could even be manipulated to emulate tapered fingertips using glove stretchers. Furthermore, women were advised to change their gloves numerous times a day in order to retain the well-shaped appearance of their hands.[15] Women also purchased gloves that were too small to create the appearance of tiny hands.[16] These practices deliberately rendered women's hands non-usable, signaling that they did not participate in labor.

Before placing their hands into gloves in the evening, women were known to actively shape hands into forms they did not take on naturally. Mrs Noble explains that when women's fingers did not meet the right standards, they could be coaxed into the resemblance of a point with a few simple exercises. "In addition to capping the fingers at bedtime," she suggests, "the woman whose bump of vanity is abnormally developed can materially improve the appearance of her hands when a dinner or bridge-party is contained in the evening's program, by wearing her black velvet 'strait-jackets' for a couple of hours previously, and molded tips preserving their acquired shape in a satisfactory manner throughout the evening."[17] Middle-class women born with the unfortunate defect of dull fingertips, or alternatively having dulled their pointy fingers through housework, could still shape their appendages so that they fit the standards of the day.

But the shape of a woman's hand was not all she had to be concerned about; women were cautioned that they must wear clean, well-fitted, kid gloves if they were to be considered middle class. The author of *Etiquette for Ladies and Gentlemen* (1876) warns against wearing "soiled or ripped gloves" when attending a public event: "With regard to dress itself, the first things a lady ought to think about are her gloves and shoes; for soiled or ripped gloves, or shabby boots, will destroy the effect of the most elegant gown ever worn."[18] Class is made visible not only by a woman's primary covering, which indicates wealth, but also through the accessories worn with the dress. This advice suggests that if a woman was unaware of, or could not afford, the right accessories, she would not be considered a proper lady.

Fabrics other than kid were considered vulgar and could be used as a way to recognize the lower classes.[19] In the comedic song "Rotten Cotton Gloves," a would-be lady sports a pair of cotton gloves that are described as misshapen, dirty, old, torn, and seam-stripped:

Gloves always add a finish
And they make you look a don
I think these gloves were finished
Long before I put them on,
There's an openwork arrangement
Round the finger tips,
It comes in ve'ry handy
When you're eating fish and chips …

I'm wearing rotten cotton gloves;
Can't afford fur ones got no quids,
Can't afford a pair of "kids."[20]

Though they were worn in the hopes of class passing, the cotton gloves became an indication of the poverty of the woman singing the song. The rotten cotton glove is an object of mockery as it so clearly shows the owner as a working-class up-start.

Gloves themselves were often stand-ins for the hands that middle-class women coveted. Good quality white kid gloves were desirable because they made hands appear small and soft while hiding any imperfections.[21] The backs of gloves were generally decorated with three lines of "pointing" which is a technique of stitching creating a raised design on the back of the hand. The pointing may have acted as a reminder of the ideal hand underneath, emphasizing the blue veins that were essential elements of the perfect Victorian hand.[22] Furthermore, during the nineteenth century the glove industry began to mechanize, ensuring middle-class women that their hands would be hidden in gloves that acted like a second, more perfect, skin. Various inventions of the early and mid-nineteenth century helped improve the fit of gloves. Before the mechanization of the industry, kid gloves were either made-to-order for wealthy women or the sizing was decided at random by the glove-cutters working on ready-made gloves for the middle class. In the 1830s, Xavier Jouvin, a French medical student, had a profound effect on the mechanization of glove production by determining that hands could be classified into 320 shapes and sizes.[23] Jouvin patented a series of tempered steel blades in the shape of each possible hand size. This allowed glove cutters to punch gloves with more precision so that they could fit a variety of different hand shapes. Other inventions that improved the snugness of gloves included elasticized wrists, glove fasteners, and the "looper" that ensured that the entire glove was machine-stitched, including the fingertips.[24] The mechanization of the glove industry standardized the shape of gloves, making them one of the first ready-made clothing items for middle-class women. Mechanization made kid gloves more affordable for those less likely to buy gloves made-to-order.

Gloves that had become too shabby to be worn in public were often used as a way to protect and rejuvenate the hands. Women who engaged in housework or gardening that was likely to stain, roughen or redden hands wore loose gloves with the tips of the fingers cut off.[25] Women also used old gloves at night; they were filled with cream and worn while sleeping in order to ensure that hands remained pristine. Gloves were filled with various skin-improving recipes that were extolled in fashion magazines, advice manuals, and encyclopedias as both preventative measures and remedies for freckled, tanned or burnt skin. These creams were concocted from ingredients readily available in the household, and were typically some combination of soap, buttermilk, lemon juice, vinegar, rainwater, rosewater, glycerin, horseradish, and oatmeal.[26] As well as domestic remedies, commercially made beauty recipes were also advertised in women's magazines. One such complexion bath was "Bridal Bouquet Bloom," advertised as a "lovely milky and hygienic liquid." Commercial cosmetics and creams were advertised as healthy and wholesome, but in reality they contained chemicals that were unsafe.[27] Advertising copy for "Bridal Bouquet Bloom" claims that it "imparts exquisite Beauty to the Face, Neck, Arms and Hands ... It never fails to remove Freckles, Sunburn, and prevents all Roughness and Wrinkles."[28] This cure-all medicine was advertised both as a way to uphold the exquisite beauty of the white skin, and as a remedy for women whose skin was rough or sun damaged. These skin creams were designed to maintain "a white, soft hand ... without marring its usefulness."[29] While advice literature did not pretend that middle-class women could live their lives devoid of housework and gardening, they still provided skin-care advice that helped hide this work, distinguishing them from the tanned and freckled hands of the working class.[30]

The process of creating a distinct middle-class hand went beyond conventions of glove wearing; women were also advised to alter their posture in order to portray themselves as leisured women.[31] The respectable upright pose of middle-class women had practical consequences for the middle-class arm: by avoiding leaning women could circumvent rough elbows. For Victorians, the ideal arm was smooth with dimples in the place of the elbow.[32] Women whose elbows were "coarse and scaly" were chastised in women's magazines for "leaning the elbows upon desk or table."[33] Instead, they were to keep their postures straight with elbows free from contact. The upright posture suggested in the articles of women's magazines and prescriptive literature was visually represented in popular fashion plates.

The primary purpose of fashion plates in weekly and monthly periodicals was to disseminate knowledge quickly about the latest couture.[34] These drawings consistently showed stylized female bodies with extremely small waists, hands, and feet. The bodies in fashion plates were models displaying the approved gestures, skin color, and posture that were held up as ideals to be emulated by the middle-class woman. Though the dress and female silhouette of fashion plates were ever-changing, the hand gestures and arm movements of the women in these images remained remarkably constant.[35] The hands in fashion plates had a set amount of gestures, all of which were inactive. Arms and hands were arrested in mid motion: gently reaching for objects, calmly gesturing towards items of interest, and holding accessories insecurely within their gloved hands. As can be seen in the fashion plate from *The Queens, the Lady's Newspaper* (1871), women's small hands hold parasols and fans at the end of their tapered fingertips (Figure 9.1). None of these objects are grasped firmly; in fact, most accessories depicted in women's hands are barely held at all. The fans are not being waved, nor are the parasols positioned directly over heads or leaned on for support.

A study of middle-class portraiture shows that the conventional poses of fashion plates were reproduced in photographs of real men and women (Figure 9.2). The semi-bent arm of the wife holding gloves, and a little girl with lax hands holding a basket of flowers, are gestures replicated over

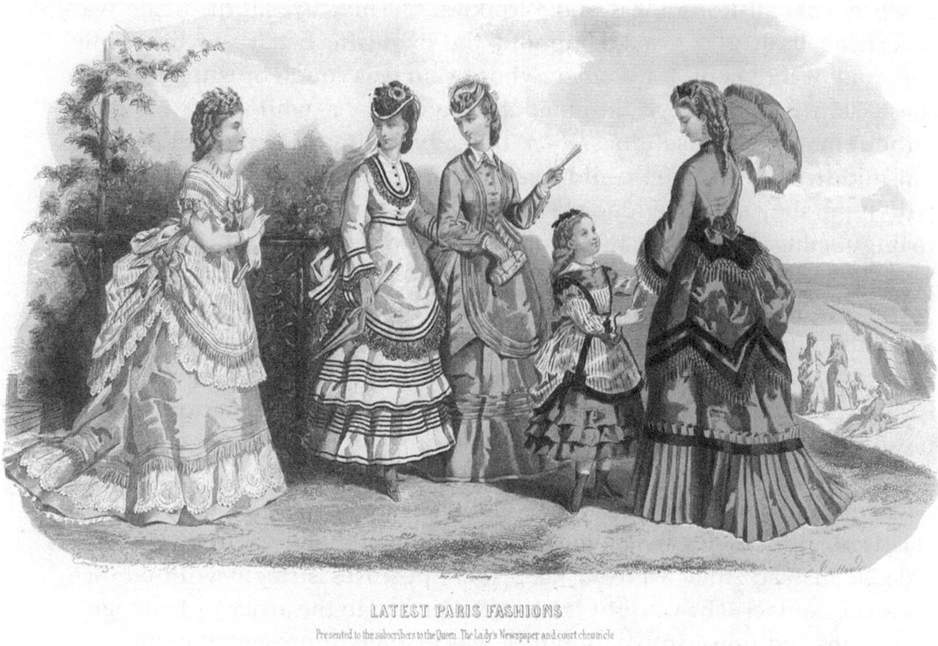

9.1 Fashion plate in *The Queens, the Lady's Newspaper*, July 1, 1871, page 12. Courtesy of Mary Evans Picture Library

and over again in professional photographs. This demonstrates, at least in a formalized setting, that average women emulated the poses and gestures of fashion plates. The constant and consistent repetition of movements depicted in fashion plates, photographs, and etiquette manuals worked in unison to create the conventional poses that helped to produce a collective middle-class body.[36]

The middle-class body was not only cultivated by a series of postures and gestures but also by eating habits. Plump, well-fed women tended to exhibit dimpled elbows; the layer of fat under a lady's skin helped to generate the perfect arm.[37] Throughout history there has been a strong association between wealth and weight. The dimpled elbow is a direct reflection of the foods that a woman ate, as well as the wealth of her husband's household. Plump women with dimpled elbows were viewed as child-bearing women who could uphold the tenets of domestic motherhood and would reproduce the British race. Victorians often placed these women in opposition to the image of the emaciated infertile working-class spinster. Dimpled elbows, therefore, were not only associated with middle-class leisure, but also with the role of the woman as mother prescribed by the separate sphere doctrine.

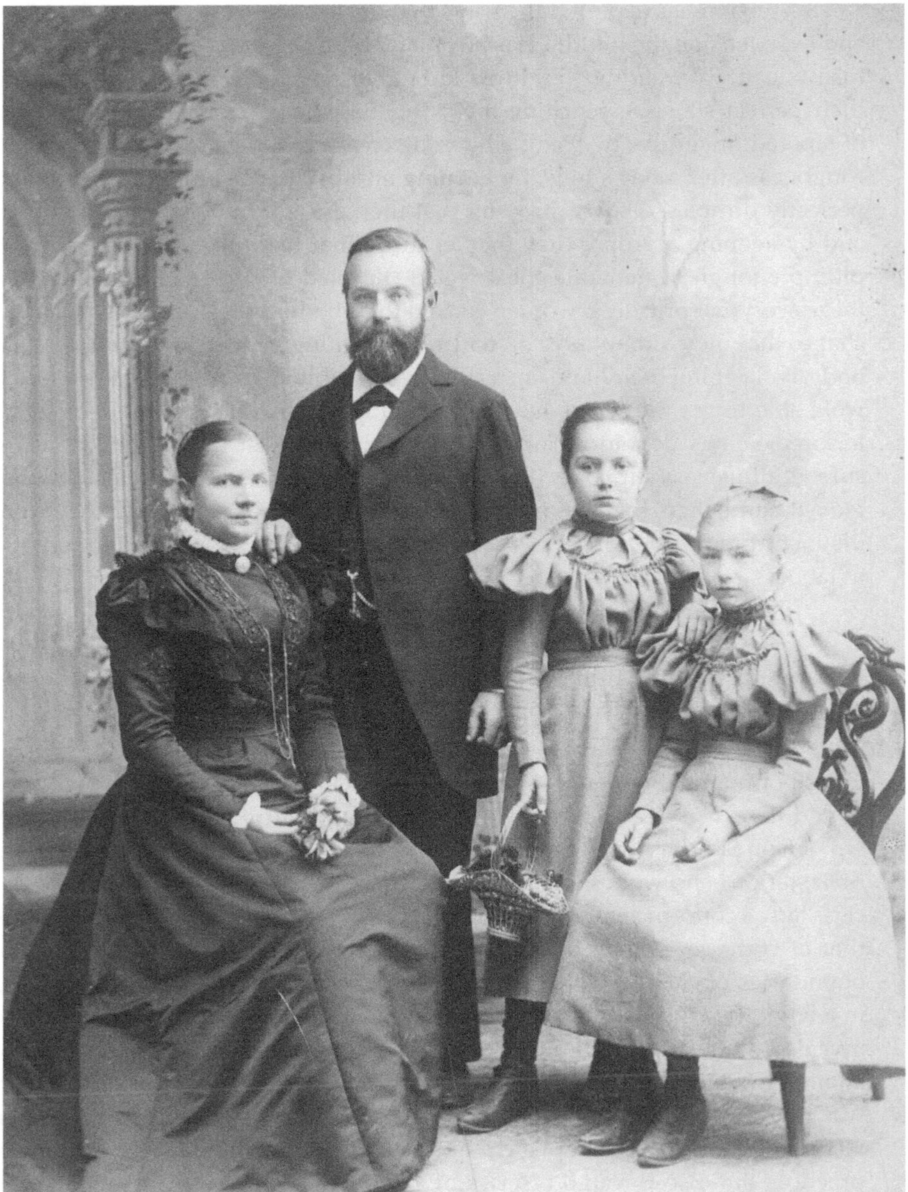

9.2 Family photo, 1897. Courtesy of Mary Evans Picture Library

This section has explored the ways that the middle-class woman's hands—and by extension the middle-class woman's body—were created, enacted and maintained. By wearing well-fitted kid gloves, hands were immobilized into their perfect state; by pinching their fingers, women created the semblance of tapered fingertips; by using whitening creams, women erased the dirt and roughness after a day's toils; by keeping an upright posture, they preserved perfectly dimpled elbows, proving that they did not hunch or lean in labor; and by keeping a proper diet, they ensured that their arms and hands were plump enough to generate the coveted dimpled elbows and knuckles. Via these everyday practices, women coaxed their bodies into culturally ordained shapes that they did not take on naturally, creating a formalized middle-class body. By keeping their hands in a state of soft whiteness, middle-class women were able to get the sense that they upheld the separate sphere ideology as leisured beings devoid of labor. This illusion in turn helped quell unease surrounding class slippage. It was partially by maintaining a perfect-looking gloved hand, then, that the middle-class convinced themselves that they were distinct from the working class, whose hands were large, rough, and red due to labor.

Differentiating the Middle-Class Body: The "Large and Red" Hands of the Working Class

Class boundaries were not as firm as etiquette manuals and popular songs would have us believe. Working-class maids, who dressed like middle-class women on Sundays or to shop at markets, were warned that they must "dress their station" and were sometimes fired for their cross-dressing.[38] The middle-class lady's concern surrounding the appearance of her social inferiors reveals that at some level they understood that class was a performance and the boundaries of class were permeable. Middle-class women found themselves in a bind: they insisted that their "snowy white" complexion was natural but revealed that their anxieties were well founded by insisting their servants not attempt to have white skin themselves. Middle-class women's primary concern was that they could be visually differentiated from working-class servants, factory workers, and shop girls not only through different consumption practices but also through a series of clues that appeared on their physical bodies. In the Victorian period advice literature encouraged women to look for actual changes in the body such as skin color and hand size as indications of who was middle class and who was working class.

The hand was such an important site for the production of class identity that the laborer was referred to as the "hand."[39] In the Victorian vocabulary, the word "hand" was synonymous with the word worker, and the worker was identified by their hands. In the nineteenth century, class was defined by its proximity to labor. If a person worked with his/her hands in a factory, farm or domestic service, they were considered working class; if a person owned or managed a business or home, they worked with their minds and were considered to be middle class. In this context the hand, or the worker, does the will of the mind, or the middle class.[40] In other words, working-class hands make the lifestyle of the middle classes possible, enabling the middle classes to show little to no effect of this labor upon their bodies. For those many middle-class women who did work, the glove acted as a concealer, covering over the close proximity between the middle and working classes.

The Victorian vocabulary that equated workers and hands had a visual component that associated large hands and laboring hands. The best and most elaborate examples of this type of thinking are contained within the diaries of Arthur Munby, an eccentric Victorian gentleman. A minor poet and civil servant, Munby had a fascination with working-class women. His diaries reveal the secret life of a voyeur who got a sexual thrill out of watching women get dirty and do physical work.[41] Though his obsession with dirt and working-class women's bodies may be atypical of the era, Munby's fixation with women's hands spoke to prevalent concerns of the time. Munby's diaries are littered with descriptions connecting women's large, red, raw hands with their working-class status. To get a sense of the extraordinary strength of Munby's obsession, I will quote an entry from August 21, 1860 at length:

> I passed a tallish young woman, evidently a servant, who was noticeable for the size of her gloveless hands … I looked at her hands, and spoke my opinion of them. "How can you like them?" she says, like Margaret in the garden; "they are so large and red, I'm ashamed of them." "They are just the hands for a servant," say I: "They show you are hardworking, and you ought to be proud of them. You wouldn't wish them to be like a lady's?" "Yes I should!" said she, bitterly: "and I should like to be a lady, and I wish my hands were like yours!" And she looked enviously at my hand, which was quite white and small by the side of hers. I could not then understand her vehemence: but remembering the difference between my fist and those small taper lady hands one sees in drawing rooms, it did seem pathetic that this poor wench should envy my hands, and fancy that if her own were like them, she would have reached a ladylike pitch of refinement.[42]

This chance encounter between a gentleman and a servant girl plays upon fears of gendered cross-dressing and class impersonation that both concerned and thrilled the Victorians. In Munby's insistence on praising the working woman's hands, he reverses their gender roles, placing the servant as manly worker and himself as leisured lady. At the same time, the maid, who wishes her hands were like Munby's, expresses her desire to masquerade as part of a class other than her own. The concept that class and gender were performative acts, made real by how one's hands were used and through the comparison of one hand to another, generated a considerable amount of anxiety for middle-class women who were led to believe that their status was in constant danger of erosion.

Etiquette manuals warned that if a lady neglected to sustain the proper appearance of her hands, they would physically change—eventually becoming red, raw, and enlarged to the point where they looked like the hands of a laborer rather than the hands of a proper lady. Manuals such as *Every Woman's Toilet Book* suggested that hands could become enlarged with too much physical labor: "You may lead an active, energetic life, or rather, you should lead such a life," suggests the author, "and yet not enlarge your hand; but even in domestic duties or exercise you can take certain care. For instance, try never to stretch wide your hand by carrying more than you conveniently can, or doing man's carpenting, or lifting heavy weights. Of course, often we are powerless to avoid such work, but when possible think of your hands." She goes on to suggest that: "Our grandmothers would not row, golf was unheard of, and fine ladies would not even carry their prayer-books to church for fear of ruining their hands. In the eighteenth century pages were employed to open doors and handbooks, etc., to save their mistresses' fine delicate hands."[43] This manual proposed that an active middle-class lifestyle could change the size of women's hands. Carrying too much weight, stretching the fingers, cleaning too vigorously, participating in sport, and doing men's work all had the potential of enlarging the hands. The idea that one's daily routines became physically apparent was part of the nineteenth century's concept of the self. It was believed that a woman's character—her inner thoughts, her private daily routines, even her soul—was manifested physically upon her body.[44] In other words, the inner self was put on public display to be read by those who knew how.

Etiquette manuals shared with practitioners of phrenology the belief that a person's temperament "is depicted in legible characters upon the external countenance."[45] Phrenology theorized that the brain shaped the physical body. In scientific circles this type of knowledge was largely replaced with Darwinism by the middle of the nineteenth century; however, phrenological assumptions continued to have cultural resonance until the turn of the century.[46] Prominent scientists such as J.C. Lavater posited that the head, and secondly the hands, could be studied to understand a person's intellectual and moral character.[47] In *The Psychonomy of the Hand; or, the Hand an Index of Mental Development* (1865), Richard Beamish indicates that a woman's hands can tell onlookers what sort of wife and mother she might be: "The square fingers represent more delicacy, symmetry, arrangement, punctuality, and deference to precedent and authority than the spatulous" (or spread-out fingers). Beamish further proposes: "Where the thumb is small, there is the index of gentleness and love; where large, of precedent and legality, and a tendency to social and domestic harshness and despotism."[48] Using a similar index to the hand as does phrenology, etiquette books suggest that a woman's disposition became apparent through her hands: "Character, again, is largely to be determined by the hands," explains Noble. "You hear people say she is neat-handed, or has such strong, kind capable hands, or the sensitive hand of an artist … No woman should ever allow hands to get rough, even in the coldest and most severe weather, it is always a sign of carelessness."[49] This passage reads as a phrenological explanation of women's natures: artistic women have sensitive hands and careless women have rough hands. There are obvious class biases in this statement. As we have seen, rough hands tended to be working-class hands; and the quoted passage ignores the necessity of work, instead suggesting that working-class women are careless rather than responsible and hard working.

The use of the science of body shapes in etiquette manuals, with their focus on the appearance of hands, helped women to identify the class of those around them. However, such advice also reaffirmed that middle-class women must uphold the tenets of the domestic sphere—they must remain kind and sensitive in order to appear as such. Alternatively, if a woman acted inappropriately for her station—if she worked, exercised, or carried too much—this would be represented physically through the increased breadth of her hands. The discourse of phrenology was used by etiquette manuals as a scare tactic to ensure that middle-class women remained idle.

From the 1830s until just after the turn of the nineteenth century, women took great pains to preserve their hands in a state of small, soft whiteness. Fashion plates and etiquette manuals stressed the importance of the perfect hand to their middle-class consumers, who in turn purchased such objects as gloves, creams, and washes. Together, these elements constitute what Judith Butler has identified as "the mundane way in which social agents *constitute* social reality through language, gesture, and all manner of symbolic social sign."[50] The hand gestures depicted in fashion plates, the erect posture encouraged by etiquette manuals, and the exercises used to create tapered fingertips, can all be considered mundane, everyday practices. Put together with the maintenance of the skin through the use of gloves and creams, one can see that the obsession with perfect hands created a regimented daily routine focused on the management of the body. Through these daily rituals, women styled their bodies into a femininity that was particular to the middle class. Once this performance was accomplished, white middle-class women used their constructed identity as the norm against which to judge all other classes and femininities. Aristocratic women's over-indulgent leisure, for example, was represented in their fingers that were considered "too thin," presumably because of their total lack of engagement with the physical environment. At the other end of the spectrum, working-class women's need to labor was considered unwomanly and was reflected in hands that had "nothing feminine about [them] in form or texture."[51] This essay expands upon Michel Foucault's belief that class consciousness had its origins in the differentiation of the body. With this in mind I have suggested that the literature, images, and corrective devices intended to distinguish the middle-class hand helped to produce a particular kind of body which was associated with a middle-class identity in the nineteenth century.

Notes

Author's note: I am grateful to several people for their assistance. Initial encouragement came from the Women, Gender and Sexuality Reading Group at the University of Toronto where I delivered an early draft of this essay. I am indebted to my supervisor, Lori Loeb, who offered encouragement and organizational advice for the essay. For their useful suggestions, constructive criticisms, and much appreciated editorial help, I would also like to thank Amanda Irvine, Tim Blackmore, and Amy Milne-Smith.

1. Michel Foucault, *The History of Sexuality: An Introduction* (New York: Pantheon Books, 1978), 126.
2. Wai Chee Dimock and Michael T. Gilmore, *Rethinking Class: Literary Studies and Social Formations* (New York: Columbia University Press, 1994), 3.
3. Margaret Beetham, *A Magazine of Her Own? Domesticity and Desire in the Women's Magazine, 1800–1914* (London and New York: Routledge, 1996), ix; Judith Butler, *Bodies That Matter: On the Discursive Limits of Sex* (New York: Routledge, 1993); Judith Butler, *Gender Trouble: Feminism and the Subversion of Identity* (New York: Routledge, 1990); Judith Butler, "Performative Acts and Gender Constitution: An Essay in Phenomenology and Feminist Theory," in *Performing Feminisms: Feminist Critical Theory and Theatre*, ed. Sue Ellen Case (Baltimore: Johns Hopkins University Press, 1990). For a sociological perspective on gender performance, see Candace West and Don H. Zimmerman, "Doing Gender," *Gender and Society* 1, no. 2 (1987).
4. Butler, "Performative Acts," 274.
5. For nineteenth-century examples of British middle-class women as representatives of the nation, see Eliza Lynn Linton, *The Girl of the Period and Other Social Essays*, 2 vols., Vol. 1 (London: Richard Bentley & Son, 1883), 1–9; and Mrs Robert Noble, *Every Woman's Toilet Book* (London: George Newnes, Limited, 1908), 63. For a discussion of fashionable women as representatives of the nation, see Kristin Hoganson, "The Fashionable World: Imagined Communities of Dress," in *After the Imperial Turn: Thinking with and through the Nation*, ed. Antoinette Burton (Durham and London: Duke University Press, 2003), 216; and Anne McClintock, *Imperial Leather: Race, Gender and Sexuality in Colonial Conquest* (New York: Routledge, 1995).
6. Butler, "Performative Acts," 276.
7. Jules Prown, "Mind in Matter: An Introduction to Material Culture Theory and Method," *Winterthur Portfolio* 17 (1982): 1–19.
8. Noble, *Every Woman's Toilet Book*, 56.
9. Arthur Munby, "Munby Diary," in *Munby, Man of Two Worlds: The Life and Diaries of Arthur J. Munby, 1812–1910*, ed. Derek Hudson (Cambridge: Gambit, 1974), 72.
10. Noble, *Every Woman's Toilet Book*, 56.
11. Leonore Davidoff and Catherine Hall, *Family Fortunes: Men and Women of the English Middle Class, 1780–1850* (Chicago: University of Chicago Press, 1987). The idea of separate spheres has been contested by many. Historians of consumerism such as Erika Rappaport, Thomas Richards, and Bill Lancaster have challenged the separate sphere doctrine by demonstrating how department store managers, women shoppers, and advertisements created a home away from home in nineteenth-century shopping centers. The department store effectively turned the separate sphere doctrine onto itself, granting women a place in the public sphere by equipping it with domestic necessities. Historians of feminism such as Lisa Tickner, Barbara Caine, and Linda Colley show how women manipulated the domestic ideology to gain access to the public sphere by presenting themselves as respectable women who were concerned with issues that were traditionally part of the woman's sphere of influence. Historians have also shown how female philanthropists accessed the public sphere by negotiating the boundaries of public and private to their own ends. See, for

instance, William Lancaster, *The Department Store: A Social History* (London: Leicester University Press, 1995); Erika Diane Rappaport, *Shopping for Pleasure: Women in the Making of London's West End* (Princeton: Princeton University Press, 2000); Thomas Richards, *The Commodity Culture of Victorian England: Advertising and Spectacle, 1851–1914* (Stanford: Stanford University Press, 1990); Barbara Caine, *Victorian Feminists* (Oxford: Oxford University Press, 1992); Linda Colley, *Britons: Forging the Nation, 1707–1837* (New Haven: Yale University Press, 1992); Lisa Tickner, *The Spectacle of Women: Imagery of the Suffrage Campaign, 1907–14* (London: Chatto & Windus, 1987); Gareth Stedman Jones, *Outcast London: A Study in the Relationship between Classes in Victorian Society* (London: Penguin Books, 1992); Ellen Ross, *Love and Toil: Motherhood in Outcast London, 1870–1918* (New York: Oxford University Press, 1993); Judith R. Walkowitz, *City of Dreadful Delight: Narratives of Sexual Danger in Late-Victorian London* (Chicago: University of Chicago Press, 1992), 52–8; Amanda Vickery, "Golden Age to Separate Spheres? A Review of the Categories and Chronology of English Women's History," *The Historical Journal* 36, no. 2 (1993): 383–414.

12. Looking at the question of women's housework, historians Anne McClintock and Patricia Branca suggest that women did not cease to work once the domestic ideology took hold; instead their work was denied by the culture at large. McClintock, *Imperial Leather*, 216; John Tosh, "New Men? Bourgeois Cult of Home," in *Victorian Values: Personalities and Perspectives in Nineteenth-Century Society*, ed. Gordon Marsden (London: Longman, 1998), 80; Patricia Branca, "Image and Reality: The Myth of the Ideal Victorian Woman," in *Clio's Consciousness Raised: New Perspectives on the History of Women*, ed. Mary S. Hartman (New York: Octagon Books, 1976), 179–90.

13. Florence B. Jack and Rita Strauss, *The Woman's Book: Contains Everything a Woman Ought to Know* (London: T.C. & E.C. Jack, 1911), 461.

14. William M. Smith, *Gloves Past and Present* (New York: The Sherwood Press, Inc., 1917), 106.

15. Anon, *The Ladies' Hand-Book of the Toilet: A Manual of Elegance and Fashion* (London: H. Gt. Clarke and Co., 1843), 34.

16. Valerie Cumming, *Gloves*, ed. Aileen Ribeiro, *The Costume Accessories* series (London: B.T. Batsford Ltd., 1982), 60.

17. Noble, *Every Woman's Toilet Book*, 65.

18. Anon, *Etiquette for Ladies and Gentlemen* (London: Frederick, Warne and Co., 1876), 12.

19. Cumming, *Gloves*, 19; Smith, *Gloves Past and Present*, 108.

20. Harry Gifford, Fred E. Cliffe, and George Arthurs, "Rotten Cotton Gloves" (London: Montgomery & Company, 1928).

21. Philippe Perrot, *Fashioning the Bourgeoisie: A History of Clothing in the Nineteenth Century*, trans. Richard Bienvenu (Princeton: Princeton University Press, 1981), 120.

22. For a description of the perfect hand emphasizing blue veins, see Noble, *Every Woman's Toilet Book*, 56.

23. Xavier Jouvin won medals at French, English, and American exhibitions for his invention. B. Eldred Ellis, *Gloves and the Glove Trade* (London: Sir Isaac Pitman & Sons, Ltd., 1921), 66; Jouvin's Glove Manufactory, "Jouvin's Glove Manufactory," in *Women's Clothes and Millinery Box 3; Advertisements–Gloves*, ed. John Johnson Collection (Paris: Jouvin's Glove Manufactory, 1862); Smith, *Gloves Past and Present*, 72, Cumming, *Gloves*, 17.

24. Cumming, *Gloves*, 62, Ada Heather-Bigg., "Women and the Glove Trade," *Nineteenth Century* 30, no. 178 (1891): 941; Smith, *Gloves Past and Present*, 77.

25. Anon, *Etiquette for Ladies and Gentlemen*, 11.

26. Noble, *Every Woman's Toilet Book*, 52, 53, 58, 61; Jack and Strauss, *The Woman's Book*, 450.

27. Valerie Steele, *Fashion and Eroticism: Ideals of Feminine Beauty from the Victorian Era to the Jazz Age* (New York: Oxford University Press, 1985), 126.

28. Bridal Bouquet Bloom, "Bridal Bouquet Bloom," in *Beauty Parlour Box 1, Advertisements Beauty Parlour-Hair-dressers' Advertisements*, ed. John Johnson Collection (1892).

29. Anon, *Etiquette for Ladies and Gentlemen*, 11.

30. By the turn of the nineteenth century, middle-class denial of women's work was perceived to be so all-encompassing that the American Victorian social critic Thorstein Veblen wrote a book analyzing the social significance of the ornamental lives of middle-class women. In his work

Veblen outlines the extent that women would go to sustain the semblance of leisure. Thorstein Veblen, *The Theory of the Leisure Class: An Economic Study of Institutions* (New York and London: The Macmillan Company, 1899).

31. For a discussion of furniture, seating, and the maintenance of genteel posture, see Katherine C. Grier, *Culture and Comfort: Parlor Making and the Middle-Class Identity, 1850–1930* (Washington and London: Smithsonian Institution Press, 1988), 117–42.

32. Noble, *Every Woman's Toilet Book*, 49.

33. Jack and Strauss, *The Woman's Book*, 450.

34. Vanda Foster, *A Visual History of Costume: The Nineteenth Century* (London: B.T. Batsford, 1984), 16; Vivian Holland, "On Collecting Fashion Plates," *The Book-Collector's Quarterly* 2 (1951): 13–18; Shanon Marcus, "Reflections on Victorian Fashion Plates," *Differences: A Journal of Feminist Cultural Studies* 14, no. 3 (2003): 10–11; Doris Langley Moore, *Fashion through Fashion Plates, 1771–1970* (New York: Clarkson N. Pooter Inc., 1971), 13–19.

35. The magazines that were consulted are *Townsden's Monthly Selection of Paris Fashions* (1832–52), *Ladies' Cabinet* (1832–52), *Ladies' Magazine* (1828–69), *The Queen* (1847–1900), *Le Journal des Demoiselles* (1880–90), *The Tailor and Cutter* (1870–90).

36. For a similar interpretation of pose, see Richard L. Bushman, *The Refinement of America: Persons, Houses, Cities* (New York: Random House Inc., 1993), 63–9; Andrea Volpe, *The Middling Sorts: Explorations in the History of the American Middle Class* (New York: Routledge, 2001), 159.

37. Anne Hollander, *Seeing through Clothes* (New York: Penguin Books, 1988); Susan Bordo, *Unbearable Weight: Feminism, Western Culture, and the Body* (Berkeley: University of California Press, 2003); John Crowley, *The Invention of Comfort: Sensibilities and Design in Early Modern Britain and Early America* (Baltimore: Johns Hopkins University Press, 2001).

38. The phrase "cross-dressing" is used by Anne McClintock to specify the substitution of one woman's garments for another woman's garments across class lines. Although typically cross-dressing refers to transgressing gender barriers, here it is not about gender so much as it is about class.

39. For a popular Victorian novel that plays upon the connection between hands and workers, see Charles Dickens, *Hard Times* (New York: Pearson Longman, 2004).

40. Leonore Davidoff, "Class and Gender in Victorian England: The Diaries of Arthur J. Munby and Hannah Cullwick," *Feminist Studies* 5, no. 1 (1979): 89.

41. For further information on Arthur Munby's life, see: Diane Atkinson, *Love and Dirt: The Marriage of Arthur Munby and Hannah Cullwick* (London: Macmillan, 2003); Davidoff, "Class and Gender,"; Derek Hudson, *Munby, Man of Two Worlds: The Life and Diaries of Arthur J. Munby 1828–1910* (London: William Clowes & Sons, 1972); McClintock, *Imperial Leather*; Barry Reay, *Watching Hannah: Sexuality, Horror and Bodily De-Formation in Victorian England* (London: Reaktion Books Ltd., 2002).

42. Munby, "Munby Diary," 71.

43. Anon, *The Ladies' Hand-Book of the Toilet*, 18, Noble, *Every Woman's Toilet Book*, 59.

44. The anonymous author of *The Ladies' Hand-Book of the Toilet* reassured women that they could improve their external beauty by simply cultivating a good character. Along the same lines, Mrs Noble suggests that one must only "be nice to look nice." The concept that the innermost character of a woman could be read in her "external appearance" was a throwback from conduct manuals of the eighteenth-century, which relied on the concept of inner character rather than external appearance as the marker of a person's social class. Anon, *The Ladies' Hand-Book of the Toilet*, vii; Noble, *Every Woman's Toilet Book*, 80; Michael Curtin, *Propriety and Position: A Study of Victorian Manners* (New York: Garland, 1987); Nancy W. Ellenberger, "The Transformation of London 'Society' at the End of Victoria's Reign: Evidence from the Court Presentation Records," *Albion* 22 (1990); Marjorie Morgan, *Manners, Morals and Class in England, 1774–1858* (Houndmills: Macmillan, 1994). For examples of American women also believing that inner character is reflected on the physical body, see Kathy Peiss, *Hope in a Jar: The Making of America's Beauty Culture* (New York: Metropolitan Books, 1998).

45. Anon, *The Ladies' Hand-Book of the Toilet*, vii.

46. Roger Cooter, *The Cultural Meaning of Popular Science: Phrenology and the Organization of Consent in Nineteenth-Century Britain* (Cambridge: Cambridge University Press, 1984); Cynthia Eagle Russett,

Sexual Science: The Victorian Construction of Womanhood (Cambridge: Harvard University Press, 1989), 22–4. Cooter's work, *The Cultural Meaning of Popular Science*, demonstrates how phrenology became important for reforms in prisons, schools, and insane asylums throughout the nineteenth century.

47. Joanne Finkelstein, *The Fashioned Self* (Cambridge: Polity Press, 1991), 18; John Casper Lavater, *Essays on Physiognomy: Designed to Promote the Knowledge and the Love of Mankind*, trans. Thomas Holcroft, 12th ed. (London: William Tegg, 1862), 180; Paolo Mantegazza, *Physiognomy and Expression* (London: Walter Scott, 1890), 257.

48. Richard Beamish, *The Psychonomy of the Hand; or, the Hand an Index of Mental Development* (London: Frederick Pitman, 1865), 85.

49. Noble, *Every Woman's Toilet Book*.

50. Butler, "Performative Acts," 270.

51. Munby, "Munby Diary," 72.

10

Made for Maharanis: Aesthetics of Courtly Women in Colonial Princely India

Angma D. Jhala

In 1902, Maharani Sunity Devi sat for a formal state photograph at the Lafayette Studios in London. The young Hindu queen of the eastern Indian kingdom of Cooch Behar was richly decked out in the apparel she had worn earlier that year for the coronation of King-Emperor Edward VII. Her self-fashioned style reflected both the aesthetic norms of Empire and indigenous courtly Indian traditions of ornamentation. On her head she wore a diamond-encrusted tiara made by a European jeweler, which at that time Indian rulers wore in lieu of formal crowns. She complemented it with a high-collared, white satin gown designed by a French dressmaker, embroidered in gold thread, which she wrapped around her body like a *sari*. As for jewels, she radiated diamond and pearl encrusted bangles, rings, and a heavy necklace that combined European and Indic motifs. Most significantly, she displayed prominently the Badge of the Imperial Order of the Crown of India on her chest—an honour given to esteemed Indian men and women for their service to the colonial Raj.[1]

Sunity Devi herself was a woman who bridged various identities, western and eastern, dynastic and cosmopolitan. She was born into a prominent Hindu family of Calcutta intellectuals, the Sens, who were advocates of women's education, widow remarriage, and increasing the age of marital consent for boys and girls. Her father Keshub Chandra Sen, the leader of the Brahmo Samaj, founded by Raja Ram Mohun Roy, was considered to be the Martin Luther of Hinduism. He advocated a dynamic policy of social reform and a "superstition-free" version of Hindu spirituality, which endorsed monogamy, a theistic view of divinity that emphasized a belief in one God who was omniscient and omnipresent, the eradication of caste distinctions, a critique of vedic ritual, and greater education for women. His philosophy was neatly encapsulated in his lifelong mantra: "One God, One Life, One Wife."

Sen argued that women who were learned would make better spouses and mothers, and in 1872 urged the British government to pass legislation, known as the Brahmo Marriage Act, which increased the minimum marital age for girls to 14 and boys to 18.[2] The Sens were part of a lively circle of scholars, poets, artists, and political and religious thinkers, most famously the family of the Bengali poet and Nobel Laureate, Rabindranath Tagore.

Sunity Devi's state marriage in 1878 to the Maharaja of Cooch Behar, who counted several members of the English royal family and the British aristocracy as close associates, was in part "arranged" through the intervention of local British political officials, who sought a westernized, educated, upper caste Hindu bride from a progressive family for the young ruler they wished to modernize. Sunity Devi would become the first Indian woman to write her autobiography in English,[3] travel to Europe,[4] and openly socialize in British high society, both in India as well as the metropole.[5] One of her sons, conceived during her first visit to England in 1887,[6] was named in honor of his godmother, Queen Victoria, and her daughters, daughter-in-law, and granddaughter would have lavish courtships in Europe.

Royal and aristocratic Indian women, like Sunity Devi, were part of an engaged culture of imperial patronage, which reflected hybrid, colonial identities. Just as she lived within multiple worlds, between the semi-autonomous princely state and the British Indian capital of Calcutta, as well as between the colony and the metropole, so did a number of her contemporaries. At this time, most Indian courtly households had separate spaces for women, the zenana, and for men, the mardana. The zenana was the "female quarters" of the palace, where women lived behind *pardah* (literally translated as the "veil" or "curtain") within the *antahpura* or interior compartment. Socio-politically, the zenana refers more broadly to the women's spheres of governance and power, distinct from a male arena of authority, within the royal court. The tradition of the zenana entered medieval India during the thirteenth century with the spread of Islam and was eventually adopted by Hindu, Muslim, Sikh, and Buddhist ruling dynasties in the subcontinent.

During the late nineteenth and early twentieth centuries, the ateliers of the zenana courts created many beautiful *objets d'art,* which reflected the cultural hybridity of princely India during the height of the British Raj, introducing radical new forms of jewelry, fashion, and architecture which juxtaposed conventional elements with hitherto unknown Occidental trends. Sunity Devi's daughter-in-law, Maharani Indira Devi of Cooch Behar (1892–1968) would be the first woman to incorporate French chiffon fabrics for elegant, summer evening saris in India. It was a revolutionary fashion choice in her day, for chiffon was still considered lingerie and not outerwear.[7] The princely courts were also formidable patrons of the European jewelry houses, such as Boucheron, Chaumet, Cartier, Harry Winston, and Van Cleef & Arpels, and their creations reflect an amalgamation of both European and Indic styles, from the Edwardian to the Art Deco. These pieces were often made for Indian royal and aristocratic women, who were active in choosing the settings for the gems. Such elaborate jewels would be worn both for state occasions, such as coronations, marriages, and vice-regal visits, as well as for private functions.

Exploring the zenana ateliers reveals a fascinating glimpse into the lives of courtly women, who have been largely neglected in the study of Empire history and colonial South Asia. Mythologized by Orientalist literature as lascivious and sensual, and reconstructed by nationalist discourse as silent and secluded, the zenana woman has invariably been depicted as the object of male desire and devoid of agency. A dependent and victimized creature, bejeweled and dressed gorgeously only for the eyes of her male kin, she is the screen upon which both colonial and nationalist imaginary longings play themselves out in forming conceptions of the Indic "traditional" or indigenous. Indian women who practiced the customs of the zenana and the veil were believed to be "confined to a life of languid idleness in closed rooms, hidden from view ... suffused with an unhealthy sexuality and a disabling passivity."[8]

Such Orientalist portraits of the material opulence of the zenana fueled perceptions of a passive, despotic, "timeless" India and its barbaric rulers, in opposition to an active, rationalist, "modernizing" West. In contrast to this simple binary deconstruction of the relationship between the Occident and the Orient, where the West recreated the East in its own eyes,[9] zenana women were themselves discerning connoisseurs, designers and patrons of art, fashion, and architecture, who were innovators of a novel hybrid cultural expression. They interfused elements both of the West and the East, the modern and the pre-colonial, the religious and the secular, and their histories reflect a story of the colonial encounter, which was not one-sided but in several instances resulted in a dialog of reciprocal rapport between the colonizer and the colonized. These were not veiled women who remained "trapped" by the dictates of custom, but adventurers and entrepreneurs, who saw the possibility for creating eclectic new visual products, which emerged out of a catholic aesthetic sensibility.

Contrary to the supposition that a zenana lifestyle enclosed Indian women from the public sphere of ideas or cultural exchange, their lives were inherently transnational. Despite the secluded boundaries of *pardah,* late nineteenth- and twentieth-century courtly Indian women lived within three spheres, crossing the divide between home and the world, the public and the private, the domestic and the political. They navigated between the inner realm of the family and the wider arena of the royal court; they crossed between the regional seclusion of what was termed the "native" or "princely states" and the major cities of metropolitan, British India such as Calcutta, Bombay, and Delhi; and they traveled between Europe, America, and Asia in an era when few Indian women (or men, for that matter) made such journeys, crossing the breadth of Empire. In contrast to arguments that the colonized woman literally "disappears" and is precluded agency from lived historical experience between the forces of patriarchy and imperialism, tradition and modernity,[10] or that the public and private spheres of male and female discourse are separated through a construction of an "outer world" and an "inner home" in colonial India,[11] these examples bring out of the archives life histories of women who actively crossed both the inner and the outer spaces of family and the wider court, the colony, and the metropole. It thus complicates the historical discourse on the relationship between tradition and modernity in colonial India, suggesting that zenana women were carriers of both.

This chapter seeks to complicate the current historiography on imperial collecting and royal patronage in colonial India, through an emphasis on the role of women. How did the contact zone between indigenous South Asian leaders and Euro-American designers, jewelers, and craftsmen create new visual products? How did a late imperial style influence concepts of beauty and aesthetic production in both the metropole and the colony? How did women in seclusion, who practiced the traditions of *pardah* and the zenana, influence a wider sphere of cultural production and perceptions of visual culture? Incorporating biographies, memoirs, colonial design diaries, and the records of American and European designers and auction houses, this chapter attempts to "mine" the imperial archive as much as it can.

Building upon the work of David Cannadine, Durba Ghosh, and Maya Jasanoff, this research argues that there was a vibrant cross-cultural exchange between imperial actors and colonized subjects in India. As Cannadine has argued in relationship to class and Ghosh in terms of domesticity and family, the colonial encounter was often a conversation of reciprocal rapport, exchange, and influence based on the diversity of particular life histories, which cannot be neatly encapsulated into monolithic paradigms.[12] These findings critique the earlier Orientalist thesis introduced by Edward Said of a binary paradigm, where a hegemonic Europe recreated a distinct and "inferior" East in its own words and image.[13] In particular, this chapter furthers arguments introduced innovatively by Maya Jasanoff in *Edge of Empire: Lives, Culture, and Conquest in the East, 1750–1850* on the nature of colonial collecting and connoisseurship.[14] As Jasanoff notes, instead of a dominant British Empire, which imposed its own cultural markers globally in a unilateral manner, the colonial project accommodated difference. Indeed, there was a steady exchange of ideas from East to West and vice versa as well as the creation of new, hybrid products. This chapter argues that an exploration into the material culture of the zenana complicates current readings regarding gender, class, and colonialism in late imperial India.

This essay will begin with a brief introduction to the general history of the Indian princely states during the late colonial period and the hierarchy of the imperial zenana. It will then explore the production of items for visual consumption, such as clothing, jewelry, and architecture, for courtly women, both as consumers and as designers.

Princely India: Indian Kingship and British Paramountcy

Princely India, and the zenana ateliers within it, was historically a heterogeneous entity, which encompassed some 600 semi-autonomous kingdoms that existed alongside British India until 1947. These "native" or "princely" states, as they were termed, formed a diverse and powerful polity. Indian kingship itself was not static or homogenous, and each princely state had its own history, culture, religion, language, and kinship groupings, which differentiated it from other "little kingdoms," as did the zenanas within them. They ranged from the Hindu Rajput and Maratha states of western India, the Sikh kingdoms of the Punjab in the north, the Muslim states of Bhopal and Hyderabad which had Mughal, Persian, and Afghan antecedents, the Buddhist tribal kingdoms of eastern Bengal, such as the Chakma Raj which had ties with Burma, and the powerful southern states of Travancore and Mysore. As an entity, princely India was by no means a homogenous whole to be classified with sharp, defining brushstrokes. Some states were as large as European countries and as wealthy, such as Kashmir and Hyderabad.[15] Some upheld primogeniture; others were matrilineal in succession, such as the South Indian kingdoms of Travancore and Cochin.[16]

The conquest of Bengal in the mid-eighteenth century by the British East India Company augured the subsequent spread of British imperial power within the subcontinent. By the time of the treaties of 1818 and the defeat of the Marathas and the Pindaris during the decline of the Mughal Empire, the East India Company had emerged as the single paramount power on the Indian subcontinent in the early nineteenth century. The aim of British paramountcy, however, was not to directly rule the whole of India, but rather only those areas which were financially profitable and politically expedient, such as Bengal and the presidencies of Bombay and Madras. For the remaining "terra incognita," the British implemented a policy of "indirect rule," which provided "a cheap means of pacifying and subordinating regions not under their own direct control" by forming subsidiary alliances and treaties with the native rulers.[17]

Under the umbrella of the Pax Britannica, the princes held full authority in internal matters of state governance such as taxation, state revenue collection, criminal and judicial law and the development of educational and cultural institutions.[18] However, they could not conduct foreign policy and were obliged to maintain a body of Company troops, which would be stationed in their kingdoms under the control of a British political officer.[19]

By the mid-nineteenth century, the crisis of the 1857 Mutiny, which threatened to topple British colonial rule in the subcontinent, highlighted the vital role of the Indian princes in Britain's policy of "indirect rule."[20] During the revolt, certain princes in the native states, such as Gwalior, Hyderabad, Patiala, Rampur, and Rewa, proved to be "breakwaters in the storm" which would have otherwise "swept away" the British, in the words of the first Viceroy Lord Canning.[21] Thereafter, the princes were "accorded a permanent position as part of the British Empire."[22] The Queen's 1858 Proclamation, which was announced shortly after the events of the Mutiny, sought to "respect the rights, dignity and honour of native princes as our own," because they were the quintessential "'natural leaders' of South Asian society."[23] In shifting from Company to Crown rule, the statement aimed to establish a new social order with the British monarchy as the focus of sovereignty, capable of structuring into a single hierarchy all its subjects, Indian and British.[24] It encouraged and embellished a "language of feudal loyalty" among the Indian princes.[25]

In 1876, Prime Minister Benjamin Disraeli proclaimed Queen Victoria Empress of India during an opening of Parliament. In his speech, Disraeli emphasized the heterogeneity of the princes in regards to race, religion, and legal tradition, and eulogized their rare histories as "highly gifted and civilized." He claimed that the lustre of these royal lineages rivaled the antiquity of the English monarchy itself. The princes, he intoned, "occupy Thrones which were filled by their ancestors when England was a Roman Province."[26] Disraeli suggested that these kingdoms represented India's extraordinary cosmopolitanism, which could have no "coherent community" unless it was incorporated into the "integrating systems" of the Empire.[27]

The Delhi Imperial Assemblage, held one year later in 1877 to officially crown Victoria "Empress of India," served even further to associate the Empress's authority and that of the British with India's "traditional" rulers.[28] Lord Lytton, the newly appointed Viceroy and Governor-General, orchestrated the highly ornate ceremony. His hope was that the public pageantry would establish the Queen's authority by placing her rightfully "upon the ancient throne of the Moguls."[29] Lytton believed that the strong support of the Indian princely order was crucial to the interests of the Crown. The "native aristocracy of the country," he wrote to Queen Victoria, "whose sympathy and cordial allegiance is no inconsiderable guarantee for the stability ... of the Indian Empire."[30] Those who attended, some 300 princes, were seen as the "flower of the Indian nobility," thanked for their participation in the suppression of the Mutiny and awarded new honours for meritorious service in a similar tradition of "nazar" or fealty as that which was performed earlier at Mughal darbars.[31] The ceremony combined both Anglo-Norman and Mughal conceptions of royalty and visual display, which would be mirrored in the ateliers of the princely courts.[32]

In the subsequent period, a system of "personal" relationships between the Indian rulers and their British sovereigns, as romantically portrayed in the literature of the late nineteenth and early twentieth centuries, began to emerge. The British realized that they had to woo their princely allies if they wished to protect and strengthen this symbiotic relationship. In return for services rendered during the Mutiny and with the hope for continued future partnership, the Crown devised a system of gifting honors to Indian dignitaries, such as gun salutes, knighthoods, and titles, in a similar manner to that with which it favored its own aristocracy and gentry in England. Royal Indian women, such as wives and other female relatives of Indian rulers, were included in this process of "ornamentation" and were awarded the Order of the Crown of India for meritorious acts of service, as Sunity Devi proudly displayed in her 1902 portrait.[33] The jewel aesthetically represented the marriage of the Crown with its Indian colony. With an image of the Queen in its centerpiece, the necklace interspersed Tudor roses with the Indian symbol of lotuses.[34]

The ceremonial of the darbar, where members of the British administration officially met native princes, was perhaps the most telling public display of the Raj's incorporation of the symbols of indigenous leadership. Such grand occasions reflected the theatricality of imperial power and the relationship between the Crown and its subsidiary allies, which was in emulation and imitation of the pageantry of both Mughal and European royalty. In such settings, appropriate etiquette and deportment were essential elements of political dialogue and exchange. Seating placements, ceremonial dress, and stylized modes of speech between Indian royals and British proconsuls were all of great importance.[35] The 1877 Delhi Darbar, where Viceroy Lytton officially declared Queen Victoria Kaiser-I-Hind or Empress of India, was expressive of this trend of visual ornamentation, replete with both Anglo-Saxon and Indic symbols of kingship.[36]

The Viceroy, as a Crown representative, transplanted the majesty of the Queen or King-Emperor to India and effectively symbolized the British monarch's suzerainty over India's own "native" leaders. Curzon, who served as Viceroy from 1899 to 1905, took Lytton's concept of pageantry to a more ornate level. He was a man who epitomized his historical age; he thrived on spectacle and was captivated by the aristocracies of the East.[37] While on tour in Asia, he wrote detailed descriptions of royal palaces and royal etiquette. In his opinion, India's grandeur lay in its princes and titled wealth, which made England, in comparison, appear "dingy and unimaginative."[38] Curzon particularly appreciated pomp in the display of the Raj, which he believed would preserve India's princes from the diluting influence of the West.

In 1903, he personally organized and orchestrated the imperial darbar at Delhi to announce the coronation of Edward VII. He wrote to a friend that it would be the "biggest show that India will ever have had."[39] He believed it would bring together people from all over the subcontinent and radiate the glory of the Empire outwards through the unity of India. The symbolism of kingship was forefront in his pageantry and he wanted the princes to be "prominent actors in the ceremony," not "mere spectators at it."[40] He invited twice as many princes as had arrived for Lytton's 1877 assemblage, and his festivities lasted two weeks, with around 150,000 people gathered.[41] The Duchess of Marlborough, who was present, described the occasion as something out of the *Tales of the Arabian Nights*.[42] These were markers of a clear link between the traditions of monarchy and the power of Empire: "the relationships between the aristocracies of the metropolis, and the aristocracies of the periphery ... [are] integral to our understanding of any patrician order and any imperial system."[43] In such a manner, the Raj manufactured a hierarchy along British lines and transported it to India, while simultaneously incorporating local elements. Princes mingled easily with members of the Raj bureaucracy, as social equals through the honors system, which tied them with the British.[44] Several of the ornaments designed by zenana ateliers, such as costumes, jewelry, and footwear, would have been fashioned for such ceremonial occasions and reflected these political relationships of shared power and mutual ornamentation.

Acquiring the support of India's traditional leadership helped to legitimize Britain's paramountcy in South Asia. As Michael Fisher observes: "by ensuring the loyalty of India's 'princes' and the continuity of its traditional institutions—primarily through the careful guidance of the Resident—the British Empire was intended to be eternal."[45] In her famous proclamation, Queen Victoria emphasized her hopes for indirect rule by underlining the Crown's tolerance towards the religious traditions and customs of the princes:

> We hereby announce to the native Princes of India that all treaties and engagements made with them by or under the authority of the Honourable East India Company are by us accepted, and will be scrupulously maintained, and we look for the like observance on their part. We desire no extension of our present territorial possessions ... We shall respect the rights, dignity and honour of native Princes as our own; and we desire that they, as well as our own subjects, should enjoy that prosperity and that social advancement which can only be secured by internal peace and good government.[46]

Queen Victoria herself was fond of her Indian subjects. Indeed, it has been argued that she was more "passionate" about India than any earlier British monarch. In particular, the Queen was enamored by the princes, whom she regularly invited to Windsor and Sandringham, and incorporated them into her larger kinship networks, in several cases acting as godmother to the children of rulers and their wives.[47]

The princes were accepted as integral elements into this larger project of paramountcy for several reasons. Indigenous leadership was an inexpensive method for the British to patrol and administrate large areas of land, which were often inaccessible: an essential element of indirect rule. The princes were also important contributors to the British imperial military by financing campaigns and providing recruits, not only for battles on Indian soil but also overseas. They symbolized the grandeur of the Empire and the eloquence of ancient monarchies, when played out in the setting of "public consumption" such as darbars, vice-regal visits, and tours by the English royal family when visiting the crown colony. Lastly, the princes provided support at the all-India level and in British wars abroad, particularly in the global conflicts of the early and mid-twentieth centuries.[48]

To European observers, their martial prowess, at "once fierce and outlandish," added to their glamor as rulers.[49] The customs of the native courts appeared to the "untutored gaze of English romantics, immensely old," leading Disraeli to admiringly reflect that their dynastic lineages were far older than that of the English monarchy itself.[50] The lifestyle of pageantry appealed to certain European travelers as well. During Lord Irwin's 1929 vice-regal visit to the kingdom of Kolhapur, a *Times* correspondent described the zenana ladies as adorned in gorgeous saris, peering through "nebulous curtains," and the courtiers as dressed in "vivid sashes and pagris and jeweled swords."[51]

Outside the perimeters of their kingdoms, native princes could not hold diplomatic ties with other states or countries.[52] While they could maintain standing armies, they could not exceed a predetermined number, nor employ Europeans, Americans or members of other Asiatic countries in their ranks.[53] They were also barred access to foreign capitalists. Rulers themselves could not leave their kingdoms without first informing their Residents and Political Officers of their travel itineraries.[54] Paramountcy effectively stripped the princes of external influence outside their kingdoms, and they were dependent upon the Crown in matters relating to foreign policy and defense of their states.

At the same time, many of the princely states were internally autonomous, and the presence of the paramount power was rarely felt within their borders. As William Lee-Warner noted: "In a Native State, large or small, the Queen's writ does not run; that is the main point: it is foreign territory in the midst of the Queen's dominions."[55] The nineteenth-century treaties allowed the princes to maintain a fair degree of autonomy within their principalities, and by the early twentieth century, they pushed for greater visibility in all-India affairs. As Vijaya Raje Scindia, Rajmata (Dowager Queen) of Gwalior suggested, it was in this period that in many ways "the princes had become real kings."[56]

However, due to a lack of unanimity among the princes, they were unable to maintain a unified front, divided by divergent loyalties on the lines of religion, language, ethnicity, and culture.[57] Often personal rivalries negatively affected hopes for political cooperation. This inability to maintain cohesion arguably led to the wane of the princely order and its weakened place in Indian politics by the mid-twentieth century. The period of rapid metamorphosis, which brought modernization, independence, and democracy to the new nation of India, can be interpreted as the twilight years for princely India. The princes were generally characterized as the losers in the battle for power between the British Empire and the Indian nationalists with independence and the resolution of partition in 1947.[58] In the nearly 30-year period from 1919 to 1947, the lives of the Indian princes were forever altered. At the end of World War I, the princely states were still relatively secure, having been active in providing war aid, particularly in the form of troops. Indian rulers were admired by their subjects and even by nationalists. In the 1920s, Mahatma Gandhi, whose father and grandfather had served as chief ministers under Indian princes, was himself "positive" towards the states, which were close to his ideals of Ram Rajya, the "acme of swaraj."[59] Yet, a few decades later they were virtually extinct and non-existent players in the construction of the Indian republic.[60]

While the nation won independence from foreign rule, the princely states lost their autonomous identities. Rulers were stripped of their executive rights, and their territories merged with the new democratic republic. In 1971, under Prime Minister Indira Gandhi, the erstwhile princes lost their last major entitlement, their constitutionally granted incomes, the "Privy Purse," which was based on an annual percentage of the revenue from their former kingdoms. With the absorption of the princely states, their systems of administration and land tenure were gradually abolished. Nonetheless, many of these erstwhile sovereigns remained active in the public life of the nation, and continued to engage in politics and influence the aesthetics, fashion, and arts of Indian popular culture.

The Imperial Zenana

Just as the princely states were diverse as a group, the zenana itself housed women from several kingdoms, regions, and religions, serving as what can be described as a microcosmic "united nations" within the sphere of the court. Originally a Persian institution, which entered India with Muslim invasions, the zenana altered local customs as Hindu dynasties emulated the mannerisms of the Muslim court. Although the concept of gender-segregated living spaces was ancient to India, finding reference in the Sanskrit epics and the *Kamasutra*, as well as classical Hindu architecture, such as the Rajput fort of Chittor in Rajasthan, it was not rigidly enforced until the arrival of Islam.[61] During Mughal Emperor Akbar's reign in the latter half of the sixteenth century, there was a marked move towards the confinement of women and the creation of a harem structure.[62] As he and a number of his descendants married Hindu Rajput princesses, Mughal courtly life and architecture was in turn imitated by non-Muslim royal elites.[63]

As the exclusively female quarters in the ruler's palace, each zenana had its own unique history and socio-political identity. During the colonial period, it brought together women with different religious, caste, regional, linguistic, aesthetic, and clan affiliations, creating a heterogeneous, cosmopolitan world within the already cosmopolitan universe of princely India. Hierarchical and polygamous institutions, Hindu Rajput zenanas, for example, were presided over by predominantly Kshatriya women who were supported by females from Brahmin, Sudra, and Vaisya castes, as well as Muslims and Jains. The royal household could hold as many as 30 or more wives, as well as female relations, serving women, and attendants.[64] In 1940, when Maharani Gayatri Devi of Jaipur first arrived in the Jaipur zenana as a young bride, she was amazed by the sheer number of women:

> In the year of my marriage, there were still 400 women living in the Zenana. Among them were widowed relatives and their daughters as well as their servants and attendants; the Dowager Maharani and her retinue of ladies-in-waiting, maids, cooks, and other servants; comparable retinues for each of [my husband's] three wives and all the retainers of the late Maharaja's other wives. Presiding over them was the only one of the late Maharaja's wives who was still alive. She was known to us as Maji Sahiba and we treated her with the utmost deference. As one of Jai's wives, I could almost never uncover my face in her presence and always had to be seated a few places to her left.[65]

In addition to the wives, mothers, sisters, female relations of the dynastic family, and the aristocracy, the zenana also included courtesans (which often exceeded the number of royal wives), women in service capabilities, such as maids, cooks, dyers, weavers, astrologers, musicians, and singers, as well as eunuchs. During the twentieth century, Christian women also entered the zenana as wives and mistresses of Indian rulers and the courtly aristocracy, and as governesses, nurses, and teachers for the children of the household. Until the middle of the twentieth century, many royal Indian women still continued to live within the bounds of the palace zenana.

During the colonial period, the traditions of the zenana, such as *pardah* and pre-colonial attitudes towards dress, toilette, jewelry, and architecture, increasingly were being modified by exogamous influences. As several scholars have argued, colonial domesticity combined elements of the modern and the traditional.[66] As Sanjay Joshi has noted: "'traditional' ideas played a role in the construction of 'modern' ideas about religion, community, gender relations, and the nation."[67] In many ways, the zenana ateliers themselves produced items, which were literally a hodge-podge of Indic and European elements.

For Love of Jewels: European Jewelry Houses and the Princely Indian Patron

> Princess Brinda of Kapurthala, daughter-in-law of the Maharaja, had every woman green with envy. Her collection of jewels would make Tiffany and Cartier turn in their vaults. Emeralds the size of walnuts hung from her ears and diamond necklaces by the yard circled her throat.
>
> Vanity Fair, 1936[68]

At the height of the British Raj, during the second half of the nineteenth century, a steady flow of European jewelry, which combined Western and Indian elements, was being sent to India for its elite consumers, often to be worn for coronations, imperial darbars, and vice-regal visits. Indian princes were particularly receptive to European jewelers and eager to reset their ancestral gems in the latest Western styles. The first commissions by princes for foreign jewelers began with the early virgin trips of the royal families of Bahawalpur, Cooch Behar, and Patiala to England and the continent during the 1880s.[69] Indian princes were regular clients of European couture houses.[70] They were most feted in France and were also well received in Switzerland, Italy, and Germany where they were treated often on "par in essence ... with the surviving crowned heads of Europe," in contrast to their reception in Britain, where they were still reminded of their subordinate position in the imperial hierarchy.[71] Parisian jewelers, outfitters, portrait painters, hoteliers, and purveyors of luxury goods responded favorably towards the Indian princes as if to compensate for the loss of their own royalty.[72] Three Indian dynastic families, from the states of Baroda, Indore, and Kapurthala, eventually bought residential properties in France.[73]

In 1911 Maharaja Sayajirao III of Baroda purchased jewelry from Chaumet and Boucheron for the engagement of his daughter, Indira Devi (1882–1968) to Maharaja Madho Rao Scindia of Gwalior (r. 1886–1925). Indira herself picked out the jewels.[74] His wife Chimnabai of Baroda, a spirited and adventurous woman, was also a great patron of European and Indian jewelers. She was known as a crack shot while being a "tactful opponent" of *pardah*, even though she practiced it when at home in Baroda, and was a passionate advocate of women's education. Chimnabai was fond of jewels and gems, even if her husband Sayajirao was more abstemious by nature. She allegedly bought jewelry that had earlier belonged to Russian grand dukes after the revolution, mostly large emeralds.[75] She was particularly adept at outsmarting top European jewelers in her knowledge of diamonds, a skill which even amazed her husband.[76]

During her trips to Europe, Chimnabai moved around freely and comfortably, and began to frequent the ateliers of Cartier, whom she invited to Baroda in 1911.[77] Not only did she frequent European jewelers, but she was careful to keep an Indian craftsman with her at all times, taking Baroda's senior court jeweler with her on her European visits to advise her on purchases from European firms.[78] The Reverend Weeden described Chimnabai as a woman of exquisite taste and looks during a visit to Baroda:

> The Maharani is of middle height, but carries her head so proudly and yet so gracefully that she appears taller than she really is. Her carefully kept and abundant hair is hidden by a *sari* of white silk shot with gold, which falls over the perfect outline of her exquisite figure and is gathered between the knees, showing the ankles circled with pearls and the small bare feet, which are as beautifully kept as her hands. She has two features which distinguish her beyond all other women: her magnificent teeth, revealed within the firm mouth by her rare and charming smile, and her arms, which are the most comely in the world. It was not till I had been with her for some time that I noticed the collar of emeralds as large as pigeons' eggs round her neck, and the chain of priceless pearls that falls from her shoulders to the waist.[79]

The jewels commissioned by zenana women and Indian princes correlated with a pre-war wave of Western jewelry and fashion design. This new style "reveled in a pick-and-mix appropriation of designs and inspiration from any number of societies situated beyond the Bosphorus, weaving them together in a style that came loosely to be termed 'Persian.'" These design motifs were "an Asian mélange, which saw differences between Hindus and Muslims, Arabs and Persians, Turks and Indians, sultans and maharajas, and ancient and modern brushed aside in the creation of a colourful fantasy world, which would ever after be known as the land of a '*thousand and one nights*.'"[80] A piece illustrative of this style was an early aigrette made by Boucheron for the royal family of the Francophile Sikh kingdom of Kapurthala. The ruler and his family spoke French and regularly visited Paris, where they maintained a residence. The aigrette included ribbons, bows, and garlands reminiscent of Louis XVI as well as a "gentle, spray-like droop" of a traditional *jigha*. At first the cataloguer at Boucheron could not classify the piece, mistaking it for a corsage, and labeled it in the company's file book upside down.[81]

From 1911 onwards, Cartier, with its lengthening list of Indian clients, ensured that its Oriental Jewellry collection had more recognizable Indian influences than Persian ones. Smooth, cabochon-cut stones replaced the conventionally heavily faceted stones of European jewelry, and were often set in the red, green, and white enamel work of the Jaipuri style.[82] In 1911, the Sikh Maharaja of Patiala, Bhupinder Singh, had a traditional forehead ornament made for his wife, which was unusual as it incorporated the use of platinum, much in vogue with European jewelers, but only beginning to gain appeal with Indian clients, who historically preferred gold for the setting of precious stones.[83] Later, in 1935, he had another pair of earrings commissioned for his wife, which combined new European jewelery trends with Indic ones. He also had a pair of ruby and diamond "chandelier-style" earrings made in Indian stylized settings in platinum rather than enameled or filigreed gold, as well as a ruby, diamond, and pearl tasseled necklace which was inspired by Art Deco but had a north Indian *buta* motif with a traditional silk-cord tie.[84]

After India's independence in 1947, the wife of Maharaja Sayajirao of Baroda's grandson, Maharaja Pratapsinhrao of Baroda, Sita Devi, would be an avid collector (and patron) of jewelry.[85] From the late 1940s to the 1960s, she gave thousands of stones from the family vault to be set by the New York and Paris branches of Van Cleef and Arpels[86] and had several of the Baroda jewels reset.[87] Famously, she is known to have sold a pair of emerald and diamond anklets to Harry Winston in 1953. Later, the jeweler reconfigured them into a necklace for the Duchess of Windsor, the former Mrs Wallis Simpson, who wore it to a New York party where Sita Devi was also present. Allegedly, the princess had quipped to guests admiring the jewels that they had looked as good when worn on her feet as on the duchess's throat! It is no surprise that the duchess soon after returned the necklace, and Harry Winston had to find another buyer.[88] Sita Devi also had a necklace and earrings of diamonds and emeralds made for her by Van Cleef & Arpels in 1949–50, as well as a bracelet with five rows of pearls, diamonds, and an emerald in platinum.[89]

Similarly, in 1928 Maharaja Bhupinder Singh of Patiala had his jewels reset by the Parisian jeweler Bucheron. Allegedly, Bhupinder Singh brought six iron chests of precious stones, which included sapphires, rubies, and pearls, as well as over 7,000 diamonds and more than 1400 emeralds to Europe. While certain traditional objects such as *bazubands* (armlets) and *sarpeches* (turban ornaments) were designed, there was a fair amount of objects, including necklaces, earrings, and *nath*s (nose rings), which, while having "clear Indian references," was in the Art Deco style.[90] Many of these pieces would have been purchased for the women of the Patiala zenana. One ornate *nath* had a string of pearls and diamonds encrusted in platinum.[91] Another dramatic ruby necklace had more than 14 strands of rubies alongside diamonds and pearls in an ornate geometric design.[92] Another two necklaces designed in 1935 by Cartier comprised of 834 diamonds, 1,159 pearls, and 355 rubies; and 85 emeralds (1,117.25 carats) and 1,369 diamonds (124.48 carats).[93]

These opulent pieces would have been worn for both European and indigenous audiences at coronations, royal weddings, vice-regal visits, and, most significantly, all-India-level darbars, where they would be seen by British dignitaries as well as fellow princes, who were competing with each other for ascendancy within the imperial hierarchy. At the same time, many of these pieces would also have been worn for smaller courtly domestic occasions such as birthdays of the ruler and his family, minor weddings of family relations, and for daily wear, but still with the knowledge that they were on display for the eyes of state ministers, the indigenous aristocracy, and the many retainers within the zenana.

Chiffon in the Evening: New Fashion Trends

In the colonial context, choice of dress marked the social and political status of the wearer. Popular British attitudes premised the superiority of all things European, including garments, in part due to the belief that the "highly structured dress" of the Occident reflected "moral rectitude" in contrast to the loose, unstitched Indian clothing of the morally lax and lazy colonized peoples.[94] For some Indian princes, wearing European stylized dress expressed their sense of modernity and pro-British sentiments.

Sunity Devi's dress which she wore for the coronation of Edward VII in 1902 was designed for her by a French milliner, although she normally used the London dressmaker Madame Oliver Holmes.[95] Indian princes and zenana ladies were keen patrons of European tailors and couturiers. Whether in *pardah* or semi-*pardah*, Indian princesses began wearing Western garments and adding them to their wedding trousseaus. The Muslim regnant queen, Begum Sultan Jahan of Bhopal (r. 1901–26), invariably wore European clothes under her full-length *burkha*.[96] Sunity Devi's daughters were equally comfortable in European and Indian dress, as they "danced through the ball-rooms of London and Calcutta in the smartest Parisian toilettes, and were as much at home in the Park or at a gala night at the Opera as in their own country."[97]

Royal Indian women commissioned some of the most celebrated fashion designers of their day as well. Indira Devi of Cooch Behar ordered more than 100 shoes from Salvatore Ferragamo, including one pair ornamented with pearls and diamonds from the Cooch Behar treasury. Ferragamo noted that he made one set of shoes in green velvet with a spiral of pearls running up the heels and a second pair in black velvet with a diamond buckle.[98] The Australian-born Maharani of Puddukkotai (1894–1967), Molly Fink, and Rani Sita Devi of Kapurthala (1915–2002) commissioned clothes from the leading French couture houses, including Callot Soeurs, Jean Patou, Madeleine Vionnet, Jeanne Paquin, Elsa Schiaparelli, Edward Molyneux, Coco Chanel, and Jeanne Lavin.[99] Rani Sita Devi in particular worked with the choicest chiffon materials of the period.[100] She also commissioned a silver fox coat from Mainbocher, an American couturier who designed the wedding dress worn by Wallis Simpson in 1937 for her marriage to the Duke of Windsor.[101]

Indira Devi was the first woman to use chiffon for her saris. She designed fashionable patterns with the French textile maker Monsieur Erigua, as well as the Paris-based firm Sarees Inc. which specialized in using the latest Western fabrics for the Indian market.[102] Her signature look, a floral colored chiffon sari coupled with a string of pearls, has become the iconic image for sophisticated Indian women worldwide. The use of "racy" material such as chiffon delighted Indira Devi who thought it novel to wear "underpants as saris."[103] She coupled stunning, light chiffons with traditional heavy gold or silver thread borders.[104]

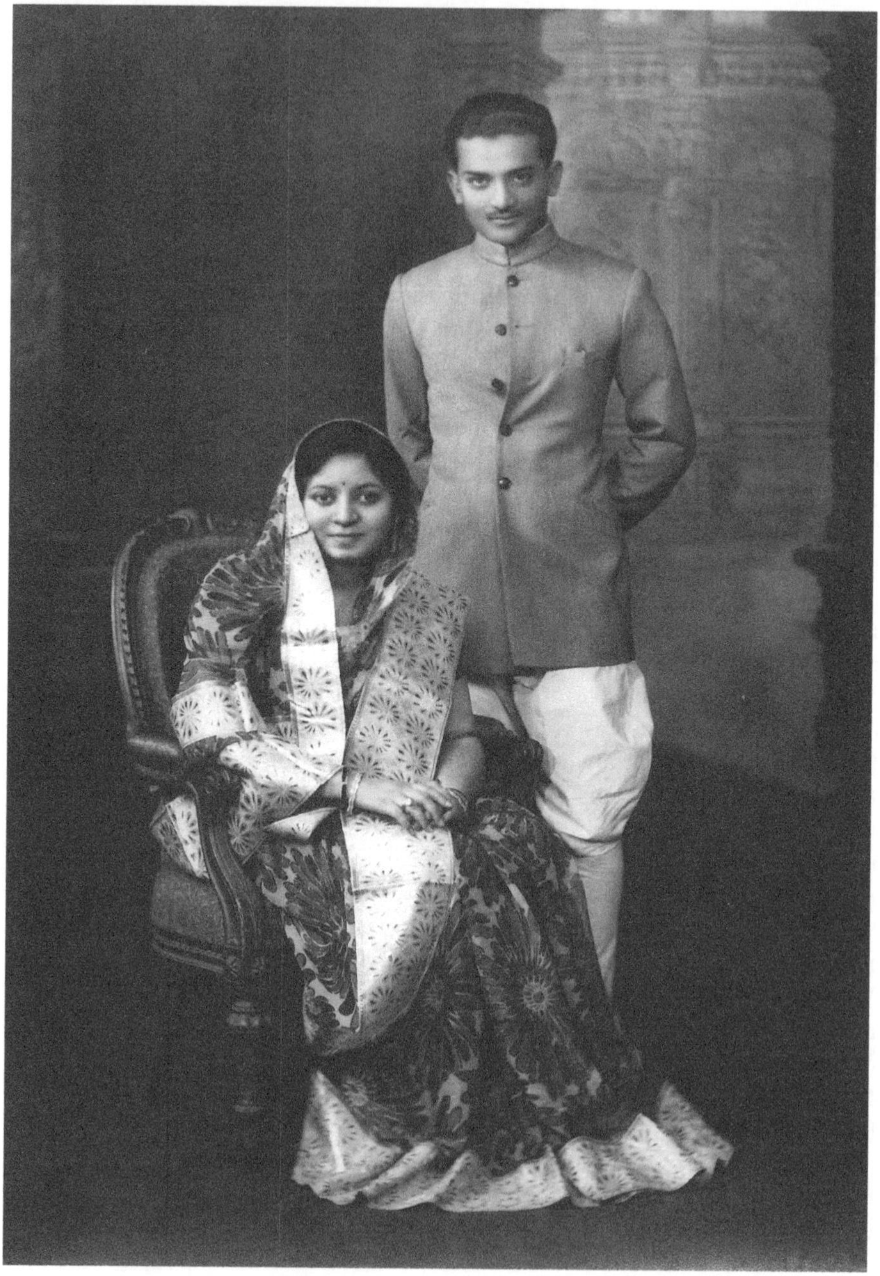

10.1 Maharani Brijraj Kumari and her husband, Maharaja Meghrajji III of Dhrangadhra, soon after their wedding in 1943. Here the Maharani is wearing a chiffon sari with a silkscreen floral pattern and a heavy silk border. This elegant dress style came into vogue with Maharani Indira Devi of Cooch Behar's earlier fashion innovations. Private Collection

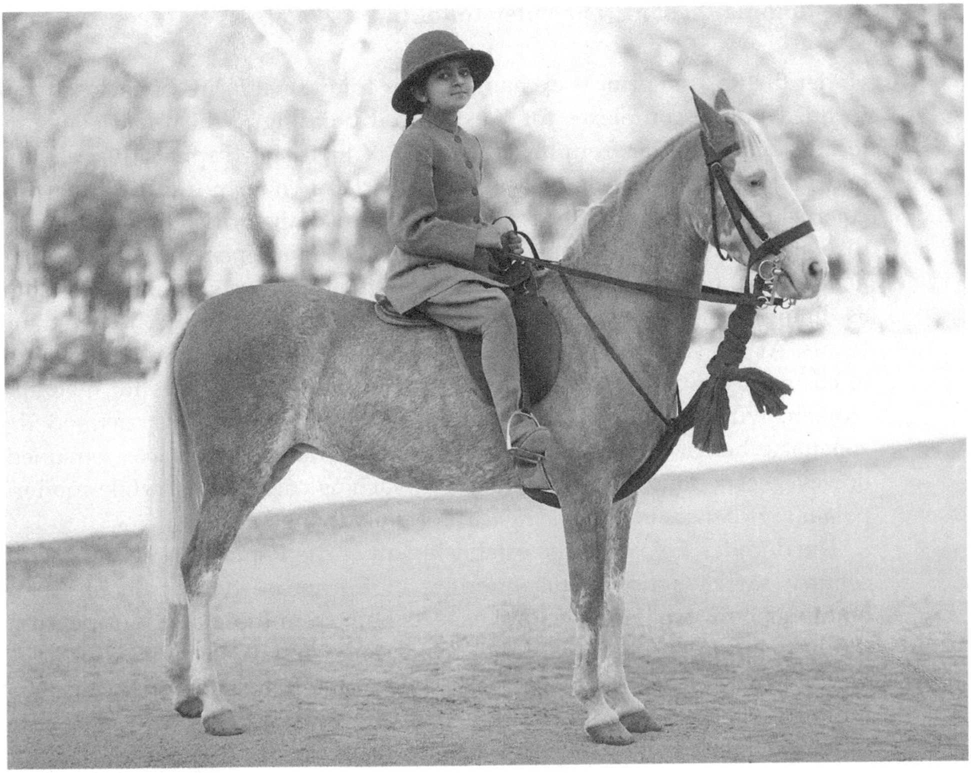

10.2 Maharani Brijraj Kumari of Dhrangadhra as an unmarried princess of Jodhpur in the 1930s. Here she is dressed in jodhpurs before her morning ride. Private Collection

Some royal women, such as Maharani Sanyogita Raje of Indore, wife of Yeshwant Rao Holkar, had formal photographs taken with the photographer Man Ray, dressed both in saris and Western clothing,[105] and they entertained in India and Europe, equally comfortable in both forms of attire. Maharaja Tukoji Rao Holkar had purses of gold and enamel handles made in the latest Art Deco styles for the women of his zenana.[106]

Indian maharanis also made unusual commissions from European designers for items to be used as part of their Eastern-styled toilette. Maharani Sita Devi of Baroda ordered a gold tongue scraper from Val Cleef & Arpels, which she requested "tres urgent" for her daily use.[107]

While fashion and jewelry saw the development of new trends and objects to be worn as part of a late imperial style, it was architecture which would most dramatically display this cultural conversation on a large scale. The palaces of the Indian princes would rival any of their compatriots in Europe, and sometimes outshine them.

The Colonial Zenana: The Splendor of India's Palaces

Under the Raj, the princes exchanged their traditional forms of enclosed and fortified palace complexes for Westernized buildings, which had elaborate facades and were far from the city center of their state capitals. Just as they had incorporated aspects of Mughal imperial architecture during the pre-colonial period, Indian princes adopted aspects of the British Indian imperial display. For many European-educated courtly Indian men and women, they now wanted palaces which accommodated their more modern lifestyles such as dining at table, entertaining European guests, and playing billiards and tennis. At the same time, these newer palaces still had to maintain aspects of customary practice such as gender-segregated living spaces for men and women, with strict divisions between public entertainment areas and the zenanas where women still practiced *pardah*. Traditional palaces remained, however, especially for ceremonial use, such as coronations, while modern palatial residences became *de rigueur* for daily living.[108]

The decades following the establishment of the Raj in the late nineteenth century saw a boom in the building of European-styled palaces. These buildings borrowed architectural aspects both from India and Europe, from the baroque to the baronial. The palace of Maharaja Jayajirao Scindia of Gwalior (r. 1843–86) was built in the style of the Italianate Renaissance just in time for the royal visit of Prince Albert Edward of Wales in 1875–76. The British architect commissioned for the project, Sir Michael Filose, was told to study the great palaces of Europe in detail, from the materials, furniture, and carpets, to the pictures and the plumbing used, and to recreate them in Gwalior, with no expense spared.[109] A renaissance style was also used in the palace at Cooch Behar, which was built in 1887. It had a dome modeled on that of St Peter's in Rome and a darbar hall fashioned in the style of Raphael.[110]

In 1878, Maharaja Sayajirao III of Baroda began work on what would become his new Indo-Saracenic palace of Laxmi Vilas. It was built in a 700-acre park and was considered at the time the most expensive building for a private residence constructed during the long nineteenth century. Employing two British architects, Major Charles Mant of the Royal Engineers and Robert Fellowes Chisholm, who had earlier been a director of the Madras School of Art, it incorporated a hybrid late imperial style, fusing together Mughal, Rajput, and various European motifs alongside a Western floor plan. The interiors of the palace were a mixture of marble columns from Carrara, Venetian mosaic floors, stained glass windows from Germany, and moldings from England. The grounds of the palace were also of British design by William Goldring, who had earlier trained at Kew Gardens. In many ways, this new style reflected the roles of Indian princely men and women in identifying themselves as simultaneously traditional leaders and modern Western dynasts.[111]

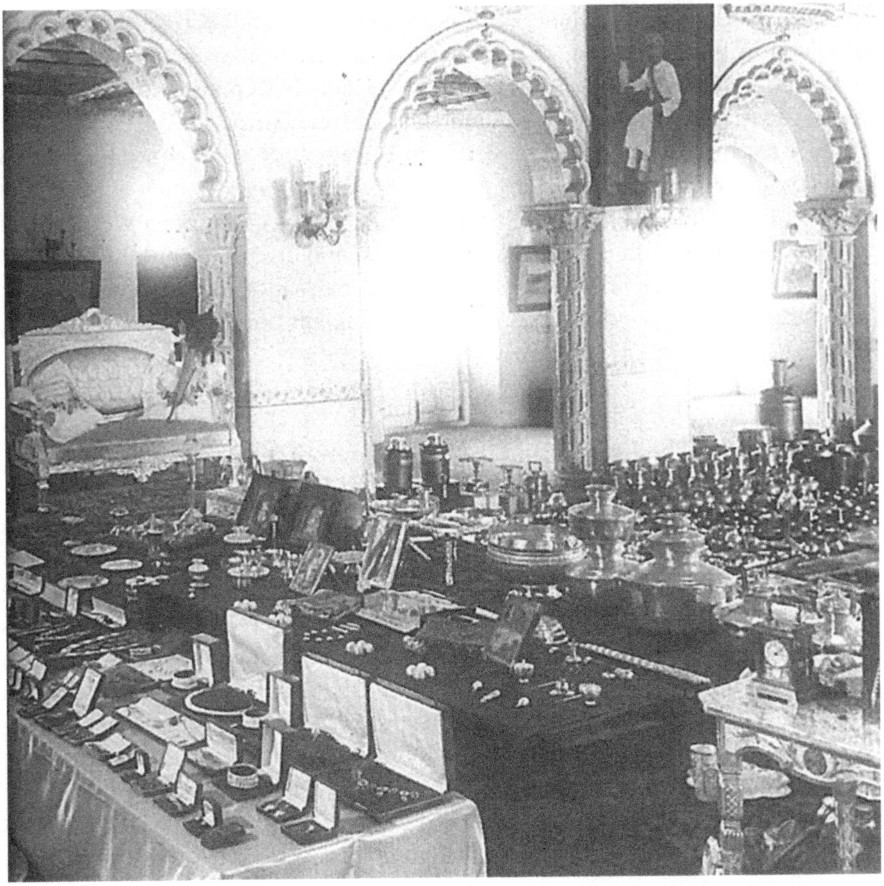

10.3 *Daija* (dowry) of a princess from Dhrangadhra. Note that the items showcased include jewelry, hair ornaments, clocks, furniture, bathing vessels, and *puja* paraphernalia. They are an eclectic assortment of both Indian and European objects and several are of a hybrid aesthetic. Private Collection

In the twentieth century, Indian royal architecture adopted elements of the Art Deco and Machinist fashions. In Jodhpur, Umaid Bhawan Palace was constructed in a high Deco style, under the direction of Polish artist Stephan Norblin, by local artisans and carpenters during World War II. In Indore, the Oxford-educated Maharaja Yeshwant Rao Holkar, who was keen on the avant-garde, commissioned Eckart Muthesius to build a palace for him and his female relations in a contemporary style.[112] Most of the furniture and furnishings were also made in a similar style, from tubular chairs to light fixtures of then fashionable materials such as chrome, lacquer, and tinted glass from Germany. Yeshwant Rao Holkar also bought three versions of *Birds in Space* by Constantin Brancusi. In particular, Maharani Sanyogita Raje was involved in the fashioning of her apartments. The Maharani's bedroom was designed by Georges Djo-Bourgeois with carpets by Ivan da Silva Bruhns in the most modern style of sleek lines and chrome furnishings. Her writing room was finished in colors of silver and gray, with a metal secretaire and chair by Louis Sognot and Charlotte Alix based on a model they exhibited at the Salon D'Automne in 1930.[113] Indeed, not only were zenana women and princes engaging with British-based architects and designers, but their eclectic taste ranged farther afield to incorporate Renaissance, Baroque, Machinist, and Art Deco styles, serving as patrons to English, French, German, Italian, and Polish designers.

In Conclusion: The Implications of Late Imperial Zenana Aesthetics

This colonial aesthetic mélange sheds light on a world that straddles various cultural and political identities, which break neat binary paradigms. In many ways, the designing women of the colonial zenana embodied a paradoxical existence. While they practiced seclusion, they themselves saw their world as porous and constantly changing. Although it was a removed, bounded, and isolated environment, it was simultaneously heteroglossic, defined through generations of women who had come from disparate places, were navigating new geographic localities and cultural identities, and whose allegiances were continually being (re)negotiated.

The material culture of the zenana demonstrates the cosmopolitanism of Indian courtly women during the height of Empire and provides a richer portrait of domestic life in colonial India as well as female homosocial spaces generally. These were products, and women, who crossed the boundaries of India and Britain, Europe and Asia, and antiquity and the modern. The making of goods for zenana ateliers highlights a relationship between various colonial actors: craftsmen from Britain, the continent and the United States, princely Indian men and women from various different religious, ethnic, and regional backgrounds, and local Indian artisans, who served these indigenous courts. The history of these objects and the women who made them or for whom they were made contributes to complicating the transnational nature of imperial historiography and colonial aesthetics.

Notes

1. Russell Harris, *The Lafayette Studio and Princely India* (New Delhi: Lustre Press/Roli Books, 2005), 71.
2. Lucy Moore, *Maharanis: The Lives and Times of Three Generations of Indian Princesses* (London: Viking, 2004), 55–8.

3. Sunity Devi, *Autobiography of an Indian Princess: Memoirs of Maharani Sunity Devi of Cooch Behar* (New Delhi: Vikas Publishing House, 1995), 11.
4. Moore, *Maharanis*, 101.
5. Ibid., 69.
6. Ibid., 106.
7. Ibid., 187.
8. Thomas Metcalf, *Ideologies of the Raj* (Cambridge: Cambridge University Press, 1995), 94.
9. Refer to Edward Said, *Orientalism* (New York: Vintage Books, 1979).
10. Gayatri Spivak, "Can the Subaltern Speak?" in *Marxism and the Interpretation of Culture*, eds. Cary Nelson and Lawrence Grossberg (Champagne-Urbana, IL: University of Illinois Press, 1988), 306.
11. Partha Chatterjee, *The Nation and Its Fragments: Colonial and Postcolonial Histories* (Princeton: Princeton University Press, 1993), 120.
12. David Cannadine, *Ornamentalism: How the British Saw Their Empire* (Oxford: Oxford University Press, 2001); Durba Ghosh, *Sex and the Family in Colonial India* (Cambridge: Cambridge University Press, 2006).
13. Said, *Orientalism*.
14. Maya Jasanoff, *Edge of Empire: Lives, Culture, and Conquest in the East, 1750–1850* (New York: Knopf, 2005).
15. Ian Copland, *The Princes of India in the Endgame of Empire, 1917–1947* (Cambridge: Cambridge University Press, 1997), 8.
16. Barbara Ramusack, *The Indian Princes and Their States* (Cambridge: Cambridge University Press, 2004), 34.
17. S.R. Ashton, *British Policy Towards the Indian States, 1905–1909* (London: Curzon Press, 1982), 7.
18. Ramusack, *The Indian Princes*, 2.
19. Ashton, *British Policy*, 7.
20. Ramusack, *The Indian Princes*, 87. She suggests that the Indian rulers are thus "an excellent prism" to view the complex hierarchies of the British Raj in India. It was a system of indirect rule, which served as a model in other areas of the Empire, including Malaya and Africa.
21. GOI, Foreign Department, Despatch No. 43A to S/S, April 30, 1860, PCI, 1792–1874, Vol. 85.
22. Ashton, *British Policy*, 17.
23. Cannadine, *Ornamentalism*, 44.
24. Bernard Cohn, "Representing Authority in Victorian India," in *An Anthropologist among the Historians and Other Essays* (Delhi: Oxford University Press, 1987), 648.
25. C.A. Bayly, *Indian Society and the Making of the British Empire* (Cambridge: Cambridge University Press, 1988), 197.
26. Hansard's *Parliamentary Debates* (3rd Ser.ccxxvii, 1876), 409.
27. Cohn, "Representing Authority," 653.
28. Mridu Rai, *Hindu Rulers, Muslim Subjects: Islam, Rights and the History of Kashmir* (Princeton: Princeton University Press, 2004), 89.
29. Lytton to Queen Victoria, April 21, 1876, I.O.L.R., E218/518/1.
30. Lytton to Queen Victoria, May 4, 1876, I.O.L.R, E218/518/1.
31. Cohn, "Representing Authority," 660.
32. Bayly, *Indian Society*, 197.
33. Cannadine, *Ornamentalism*, 90.
34. Ramusack, *The Indian Princes*, 92.

35. Ibid., 90.

36. Cohn, "Representing Authority," 656–61.

37. David Cannadine, *Aspects of Aristocracy* (New Haven: Yale University Press, 1994), 78–9.

38. Ibid., 79.

39. Ibid., 83.

40. Ibid., 85.

41. Ibid.

42. Ibid., 88.

43. Ibid., 110.

44. Cannadine, *Ornamentalism*, 89.

45. Michael Fisher. *Indirect Rule in India: Residents and the Residency System, 1764–1858* (Delhi: Oxford University Press, 1991), 32.

46. *Queen Victoria's Proclamation*, November 1, 1858, in *Imperialism and Orientalism: A Documentary Sourcebook*, by Barbara Harlow and Mia Carter (New York: Methuen, 1987), 210.

47. For example, Queen Victoria served as godmother to the son of Maharaja Nripendra of Cooch Behar in 1888, being a close friend of his wife, Maharani Sunity Devi. Their son, Victor, was named in honor of the Empress. Moore, *Maharanis*, 106–7.

48. Ramusack, *The Indian Princes*, 130–31; Copland, *The Princes of India*, 33.

49. Copland, *The Princes of India*, 24.

50. Ibid., 22.

51. Ibid., 24; *The Times of India*, November 19, 1929.

52. L.P. Mathur and Laxmi Sukhwal, "British Interference in the Internal Sovereignty of Princely States (1858–1885)," in *British Policy Towards Princely States of India*, ed. R.P. Vyas (Jodhpur: Rajasthan-Vidya Prakashan, 1991), 28.

53. Ibid., 31.

54. R.P. Vyas, "Introduction," in *British Policy Towards Princely States of India*, xii.

55. William Lee-Warner, "The Native States of India," in *British Empire Series, Volume 1: India, Ceylon, Straits Settlements, British Northern Borneo, Hong-Kong* (London: Kegal Paul, Trench, Trubner & Co, 1899), 271.

56. Vijaya Raje Scindia, *The Last Maharani of Gwalior: An Autobiography* (Albany: State University of New York, 1987), 144.

57. Copland, *The Princes of India*, 10.

58. Barbara Ramusack, *The Princes of India in the Twilight of Empire: Dissolution of a Patron–Client System, 1914–1939* (Columbus: University of Cincinnati Press, 1978), xv.

59. Lloyd Rudolph and Susanne Rudolph, *Essays on Rajputana* (New Delhi: Concept Publishing Company, 1984), 18.

60. Copland, *The Princes of India*, 2.

61. Varsha Joshi, *Polygamy and Purdah* (Jaipur: Rawat Publications, 1995), 87–8.

62. Ruby Lal, "The 'Domestic World' of the Mughals in the Reigns of Babur, Humayan and Akbar, c. 1500–1605," unpublished PhD Thesis, University of Oxford, 2000, 179.

63. Ibid., 123–7.

64. Joshi, *Polygamy and Purdah*, 24.

65. Gayatri Devi, *A Princess Remembers* (Calcutta: Rupa & Co., 1995), 167–70.

66. Dipesh Chakrabarty, *Provincializing Europe: Postcolonial Thought and Historical Difference* (Princeton: Princeton University Press, 2000); Saurabh Dube, *Stitches on Time: Colonial Textures*

and Postcolonial Tangles (Durham: Duke University Press, 2004); Lloyd I. Rudolph and Susanne H. Rudolph, *The Modernity of Tradition: Political Development in India* (Chicago: University of Chicago Press, 1967).

67. Sanjay Joshi, *Fractured Modernity: Making of a Middle Class in Colonial North India* (New Delhi: Oxford University Press, 2001), 8.
68. Amin Jaffer, *Made for Maharajas: A Design Diary of Princely India* (New Delhi: Lustre Press/Roli Books, 2007), 57.
69. John Adamson and Katherine Prior, *Maharajas' Jewels* (New York: Vendome Press, 2000), 122.
70. Jaffer, *Made for Maharajas*, 58.
71. Adamson and Prior, *Maharajas' Jewels*, 134.
72. Ibid., 135.
73. Ibid.
74. Ibid., 110.
75. Charles Allen and Sharada Dwivedi, *Lives of the Indian Princes* (New York: Crown Publishers, 1984), 205.
76. A. Monnickendam, *Secrets of the Diamond* (London: Frederick Muller Ltd., 1941), 138–9.
77. Adamson and Prior, *Maharajas' Jewels*, 116.
78. Jaffer, *Made for Maharajas*, 58, Adamson and Prior, *Maharajas' Jewels*, 110–16.
79. Adamson and Prior, *Maharajas' Jewels*, 110–16.
80. Ibid., 135.
81. Ibid., 123.
82. Ibid., 137.
83. Ibid., 168.
84. Ibid., 171.
85. Jaffer, *Made for Maharajas*, 61.
86. Adamson and Prior, *Maharajas' Jewels*, 200.
87. Jaffer, *Made for Maharajas*, 61.
88. Ibid.
89. Ibid., 88–90.
90. Ibid., 59.
91. Ibid., 71.
92. Ibid., 77.
93. Ibid., 79, 84.
94. E.M. Collingham, *Imperial Bodies: The Physical Experience of the Raj, c.1800–1947* (Cambridge: Polity Press, 2001), 186.
95. Jaffer, *Made for Maharajas*, 98.
96. Yvonne Fitzroy, *Courts and Camps in India, Impressions of Viceregal Tours, 1921–1924* (London: Methuen & Co., 1926), 290.
97. Moore, *Maharanis*, 127.
98. Jaffer, *Made for Maharajas*, 98–9; Salvatore Ferragamo, *Shoemaker of Dreams* (London: George G. Harrap & Co., 1957), 217.
99. Jaffer, *Made for Maharajas*, 99.
100. Ibid., 114.

101. Ibid., 116.
102. Ibid., 99.
103. Moore, *Maharanis*, 187.
104. Jaffer, *Made for Maharajas*, 125.
105. Ibid., 99.
106. Ibid., 118.
107. Ibid., 138.
108. Ibid., 228.
109. Ibid.
110. Philip Davies, *The Penguin Guide to the Monuments of India* (Middlesex: Penguin, 1989), II, 300.
111. Jaffer, *Made for Maharajas*, 228–9.
112. Ibid., 229.
113. Ibid., 264–5.

11

Harmony and Concealment: How Chinese Women Fashioned the *Qipao* in 1930s China

Wessie Ling

In the vain hope of overturning authority, certain social behavior by ordinary people can reclaim autonomy from pervasive forces, and at times challenge the legitimate power.[1] This chapter considers women's consumption as a way to negotiate the tensions between political power and individual identities. Through Chinese women's adaptation of the *qipao* in 1930s China, it demonstrates how modernity and traditional Chinese culture intervene, through which a new set of Chinese aesthetics emerged for Chinese clothes.

From a background of political chaos, the *qipao*[2] rose in an effort to survive and negotiate with uneven power and desire. Following its emergence in mid-1920s China, the *qipao* gained immediate currency as standard wear for Chinese women until the early 1940s. Despite numerous regulations on dress and women's bodily appearance in the Republican Era (1911–49), the *qipao* has been constantly revamped through new styles and cuts. Its most feminine form in the 1930s was as a fashionable dress favored by women of the emerging middle class in modernizing and booming cities. Then, from the 1930s, the *qipao*'s hemlines, collar, patterns, colors, and cut varied from season to season, but retained its Chinese sartorial tradition.

At a time when nationalism conflicted with the influx of imported goods and Western-style garments, wearing Chinese clothes like the *qipao* was often seen as cultural resistance to Westernization. However, the widespread adaptation of the *qipao* in the 1930s cannot be reduced to a result of nationalism. Rather, its adaptation reveals Chinese women's resistance to the Nationalist agenda for their bodies and appearance. Fashioning the *qipao* became a silent tool for Chinese women to struggle against state regulation of their bodies. Through changes in style and responses to Western fashion trends, Chinese women tactically intervened, in Certeau's term, using the *qipao* to rebel against the nation's authority, challenging the dominant Western aesthetic standards. The social practice involved in wearing and developing the *qipao* manifested a set of aesthetic judgments that was unique to Chinese clothes at that time.

This chapter examines how the *qipao* was employed in order to resist and to negotiate with institutional repression, through the study of *Linglong*, a popular women's magazine in 1930s China. Chinese women's attitudes towards Western-style fashion and aesthetic judgment, mediated through resistance and negotiation, will be analyzed.

Linglong

A weekly women's magazine, *Linglong* was published in Shanghai from 1931 to 1937. It was primarily concerned with women's matters and represented women's voice in the nation. The first half of the magazine contained sections on personal hygiene, sex, marriage, contemporary women's life, and practical knowledge, such as modern interiors, world news on women, and legal issues. The second half reviewed films and reported on Hollywood gossip, local movie news, and home-grown and Hollywood film stars. *Linglong*'s readers were female students and urban women in major cities such as Shanghai, Beijing, Tianjin, and Hong Kong. Apart from wide coverage in China, its distribution stretched to other parts of Asia such as Singapore and Indonesia, where Chinese populations were concentrated.

The study of *Linglong* in this discussion of the *qipao* is twofold. Firstly, *Linglong* is fairly representative of Chinese women of the time, and offers a realistic account of the *qipao* in the 1930s. The most eye-catching *qipao* in the Republican Era was perhaps in *Yuefenpai* (calendar posters), which is primarily illustrative and does not represent how the *qipao* was worn in reality. While celebrity- or dress-oriented magazines showed only exquisite *qipao* and fashions that were worn either in show business or by the decadent "Modern Girl,"[3] *Linglong* was down to earth, presenting real-life Chinese women wearing real *qipao*. Unlike other women's magazines of the same period where male writers were dominant, women's voices were prevalent in *Linglong*, largely because of its female editor and interactivity with its readers. Chen Zhenling was the chief editor who contributed to commentaries on women's issues and advice. The magazine's disproportionate popularity has much to do with its interactivity. Famous illustrator Ye Qianyu also contributed fashion drawings, and a substantial portion of each issue comprised readers' articles and photos. Almost every front cover was a reader's photo, while the back cover was of a Hollywood star. The magazine provided a platform for readers to launch their views on everyday life, beauty, sport, and children. *Linglong* was critical of, yet sympathetic to, the "Modern Girl."[4] It demonstrates women's rational views on the nation's restrictions on their body and their anger and resistance to the New Life Movement.[5] It reflects New Women's attitudes towards gender relationships in 1930s China, and Shanghai moviegoers' taste in films at home and aboard.[6] Not only are its views and published photos fairly representative of literate young women in China's cities, but it also presents a realistic representation of the clothes worn by Chinese women in 1930s China.

Secondly, the short life-span of *Linglong* coincided with the widespread adaptation of the *qipao*. During the 1930s, the *qipao* was developing, with Western-style fashion blossoming into many different styles, all influenced by the modernity and nationalism of the time. How was the *qipao* worn? How did Western-style fashion influence the *qipao*? Through studying Ye's fashion illustrations, readers' photos, and readers' views on Chinese women's bodies and clothes, *Linglong* helps us to understand Chinese women's attitudes towards the *qipao* and their relationship with Western-style fashion.

I begin by discussing the emergence of the *qipao* alongside Chinese women's fight for gender equality and nationalism. This is followed by discussion of the various restrictions upon women's bodily behavior and the *qipao*. How Chinese women intervened with their *qipao* under institutional repression will also be discussed, with the aid of *Linglong*. Through the materials in the magazine, I will demonstrate how a set of aesthetic judgments about Chinese clothes gradually emerged to equate the *qipao* with Western-style clothing.

Gender Equality and Nationalism

The origin of the *qipao* is closely associated with the Chinese menswear of the time. The early-1920s *qipao* had a wide, "angular and puritanical" cut, resembling the men's *changpao* and worn by women advocating gender equality.[7] At the peak of women's emancipation in the early 1920s, women's cross-dressing reflected their desire for equal rights and respect for their individuality. Chinese women began to wear the *changpao* "because they wanted to look like men."[8] Dressing in men's clothes gave the impression that they could perform male duties in society, including saving the nation, which had much to do with nation building at that time.[9] However, China's reformist intellectuals in the modern metropolis were engaged in a discourse on gender issues that was almost entirely dominated by men, with the majority more concerned with advancing their political power than advocating women's role in politics.[10] In the fight for equality, Chinese women were increasingly repressed and politically marginalized. Their disillusionment turned to cross-dressing in order to obscure their womanhood. However, those that wore the 1920s angular *qipao* were not limited to women activists[11] and students who had returned from studies aboard, but also trendy women who followed new ideas.[12] Despite many suggested names to differentiate the dress from Manchu ladies' wear of the

Qing dynasty—for instance, *changsan, changyi, changpao, zhonghua pao*[13]—none were adopted. The name *qipao* was eventually accepted, but its style bore little resemblance to the indigenous Manchurian costume.[14]

At a time when Chinese women were the subjects of social progress, their bodies became symbols of the nation. The angular and puritanical *qipao* led the transition towards the adoption of women's national dress. As part of the New Women discourse, external manifestations of modernity such as clothing, hairstyles, and footwear were frequently discussed in women's magazine columns and forums in newspapers.[15] Male writers dominated the press during that time, and their criticism of women's appearance in many publications resulted in more confusion than useful advice for Chinese women. Some men complained about women wearing men's clothing, while some preferred the *qipao* for Chinese women. The turning point for the *qipao* came with the May Thirtieth Movement in 1925, when anti-Western demonstrations raged across the nation.[16] Nationalism was fuelled all over the country, and Chinese clothes were called for to replace Western garments.[17] Given that the *qipao* was already worn by some women who were seen as open-minded reformers and advocates of strengthening the nation, its adoption seemed to answer the Nationalist cry.

Nationalism hastened the *qipao*'s popularity, but not as a distinct factor in its widespread adaptation. Chinese women who refused to totally submit to Western culture saw the *qipao* as an alternative to the country's intensified nationalism. Those who were attracted to Western-style garments but found the sizing and styling a poor fit chose the *qipao* as a comparable fashionable dress. The *qipao* accompanied Chinese women under political and social hardship, and its early adaptation filled the yawning gap between the genders. It marked an end to "hair in three tufts, clothes in two pieces,"[18] by which traditional Chinese women had been identified for dynasties. Its acceptance signaled a farewell to the past.

National Dress Versus Everyday Dress

An official declaration in the Clothing Regulations of 1929[19] finally announced the *qipao* as the accepted formal dress for women. The Nationalist government's declaration was not an attempt to force its adoption, but partly to address the chaos of women's cross-dressing,[20] and partly to encourage the *qipao* in order to strengthen the nation's integrity. Despite the inclusion of regulations on length, the use of materials, and matching accessories for the *qipao*, none of these regulations were followed. Not only did Chinese women not wear pants beneath their *qipao*,[21] which was one of the requirements in the regulations, but silk stockings were worn or bare legs were revealed under the slits, and high heels replaced flat-sole cotton shoes.[22] Chinese women made no distinction between the *qipao* as a national and an everyday dress. The dress as a national symbol clashed with its everyday usage. Chinese women did not respect the 1929 Clothing Regulations, nor did they accept a unifying style for the *qipao*. The *qipao* of *Linglong*'s readers was not uniform, and variations in style, length, and material flourished. The style of the *qipao* changed based on the season and function.

When the *qipao* became women's standard wear, it began branching out into a diverse range of styles. Most of Ye's illustrations in *Linglong* featured dresses, seldom tops and bottoms. Almost every new style in the illustrations revolved around the *qipao*. No matter whether the dress was flared, slit-less, or waist-joint, it was still considered a *qipao*. The "collarless *qipao*" "symmetric-yoke *qipao*," and "puff-sleeve *qipao*" all included non-standard features.[23]

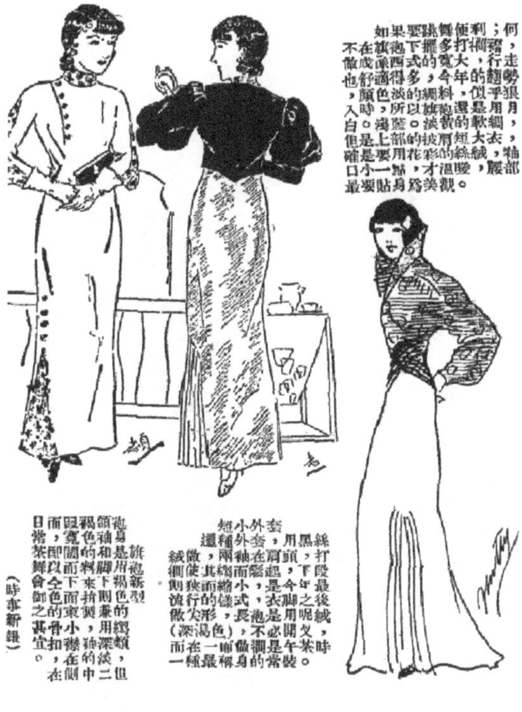

11.1 *Qipao* in a variation of styles, cut, and interpretation. *Linglong* 131 (1934): 355. From the collection of the C.V. Starr East Asian Library, Columbia University

Note: The description above refers to the top right of Figure 11.1.

Although the dresses were not restricted to the *qipao*'s "usual" features, their form and silhouette had a resemblance, allowing comprehension of how the new style of dress could be made. The drawings included instructive details such as "adding one-inch of black fur along the hem and slits," and "the dress to be three-inches below the knee with trumpet-style sleeves."[24] Apart from the use of Western-inspired clothing features, none of the drawings proposed distinctive Western-style garments. The dress illustrations in *Linglong* included the *qipao* with matching coats and accessories. Far from uniformity, the *qipao* illustrations in *Linglong* varied greatly, with timely styles. Adjacent to one drawing, the instructions read:

For the sake of convenience in dancing, why not apply pleats on the bottom part of the *qipao* making it flare like in Western-style, that would make it easier to walk. This year's trend includes light colored satin. Moon white, light blue, pale yellow satin can be used for the *qipao*.[25] (See Figure 11.1)

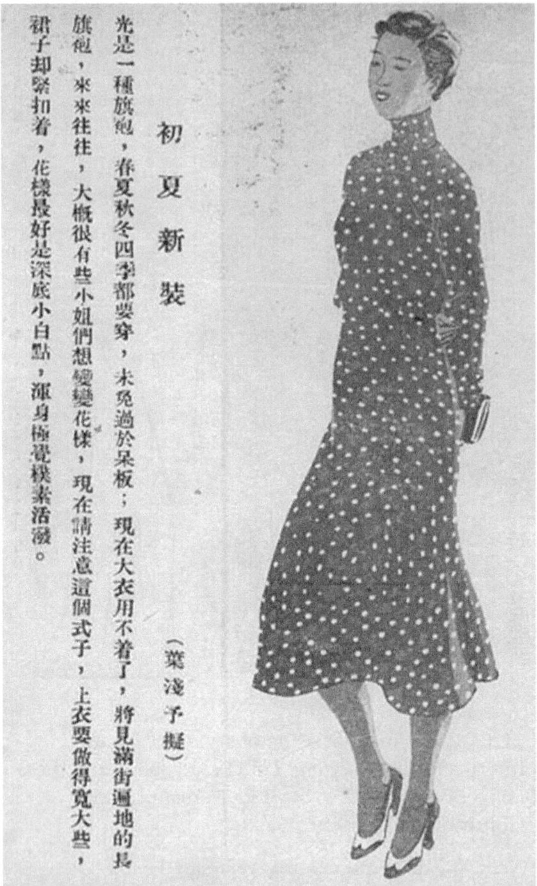

11.2 Spring/Summer new style. *Linglong* 75 (1932): 1172. From the collection of the C.V. Starr East Asian Library, Columbia University

Such instructions gave Chinese women immediate access to dressmaking knowledge. Following the abolition of foot- (1911) and breast-binding (1928), Chinese women's bodies experienced a transformation that required a new wardrobe. Besides these changes, variations in the size and form of Chinese women across the country were another issue. The sizing and fitting of most ready-made and Western-style garments remained a problem for many Chinese women. The *qipao* emerged at the right time in order to address the problem of bodily change and size variations, and the dilemma that many fashion-trend followers were unable to fit into ready-made or Western-style garments. The *qipao* was a custom-made dress, which required fitting to an individual body. Chinese women played an active role in fashioning their *qipao*. At a time of political and social upheaval, where visiting the tailor remained an occasional treat for many,[26] it was not uncommon for Chinese women to hand-sew their *qipao*.

The *qipao* in its most basic form comprised two pieces (front and back) of fabric, with no darts or complicated fastenings, which made it economical to make and easy to sew. Choices of cut, fit, materials, colors, and trimmings were often based on the wearer's personal preferences. Chinese women made their *qipao* according to the taste of the time, their needs, and "their own judgment on color matching."[27] An illustration on an "early summer new style" in *Linglong* reads:

> It would be rather dull to wear the same style of *qipao* for four seasons; heavy coat was the past when only long *qipao* filled the streets, came and went. Some ladies may want to have a change, now please pay attention to this style: Upper top to be made looser, the rest of the dress remained tight. Small white Pokka dots as pattern would be nice. The complete look would appear dynamic.[28] (See Figure 11.2)

The illustration, together with the instructive details, generated imagination among Chinese women, who were both consumers and producers of their own *qipao*. The *qipao* became the foundation for both a new style of dress and for Chinese women to implement stylistic changes in their clothing. Irrespective of its national status, Chinese women embraced its stylistic changes that made it part and parcel of the fashion cycle, in tune with Western trends and influences. The adaptability and versatility of the *qipao* made it ideal for style changes. Authenticity was never called into question thanks to the dress's hybrid origins[29] and the failure for it to be used in its intended national symbolic role. The dynamic of the *qipao* saw it in tune with Western fashion. The 1930s *qipao* was a fashionable dress that had already experienced "numerous stylistic changes, from loose to tight, tight to short, short to long."[30]

Modernity and Consumer Culture

After the 1930s, the *qipao* became tighter fitting year after year, emphasizing Chinese women's demure curves, and gradually becoming a dress symbolizing Chinese femininity. Its silhouette was in line with the trendy H-line Western-style clothes of the time. The materials (fabric, color, pattern), key to the stylistic character of the dress, were in the hands of the wearers, who were then able to determine their choice of Chinese or Western style. Yet, the *qipao* had an indissoluble link with the capitalist drive for Western modernity and commercialization. Its Chinese sartorial tradition can hardly be considered distinct. Reformers in the Republic period sought to combine the strengths of both Chinese and Western cultures, promoting the co-existence of both worlds. Modernity became one of the nation's goals, along with the desire to pursue the new and progressive in building a stronger nation. At the same time, Western powers had long imposed modernity on China via an ever-widening and interactive network of communication and exchange with the capitalist West.

Western and Chinese merchants cooperated in the move towards capitalism, promoting a leisure and consumer culture in Shanghai. The movement towards modernization fostered acknowledgement of the significance of Western cultures and ideas, underscoring the hybridity of Chinese modernity.[31] Both the *qipao* and its wearers were stitched into the rubric of such modernity. The 1930s *qipao* expressed a newness in response to the Republican search for the New Woman, the growing industrial complex, and consumer culture. The *qipao*'s perceived Chinese sartorial tradition, materiality, and wild partnership with Western-style accessories prevailed. Its wearers in the 1920s and 1930s represented an emerging middle class with some education, financial independence, and social and cultural awareness: they were the signifiers of the hegemony of the modern. Those women wearing their *qipao* were significant in the creation of a progressive China and were co-opted by the state as Republican icons.[32]

The Republican endorsement of the *qipao* underlined the dress's iconic status. Although the growing consumer culture slowed down the consumption of Western imports, Western influence upon Chinese women's dress continued. Opinions about women's consumption of imports and the pursuit of Western fashion reflected nothing more than the anxiety to open up the nation's economy. Fearful for the nation's wealth and of competition from Western goods, Chinese merchants accelerated the rapid growth of nationalism by promoting national products. However, Chinese manufactured goods were encouraged, not Chinese-styled products.[33] Imports from the West had already spread like wildfire as Shanghai opened up more and more trade routes after the 1920s. Cosmopolitan Shanghai was marked by the influx of Western cultures, where people appropriated Western ideas and lifestyles. While Western goods were not foreign to Chinese women, they were customized to suit their lifestyle.

Qipao with Western-inspired Features to Progress and Improve

At a time when Paris fashion arrived in Shanghai three to five months after its release, getting rid of Western garments and accessories was a hard task for nationalism. For those in major cities, the visibility of Western products spread from consumer magazines to department stores. When discarding Western imports was a target for the Nationalist, wearing the *qipao* became a desirable choice.[34] The influx of Western fashion soon saw the incorporation of Western-style clothing features into the *qipao*. The use of Western elements (such as fabrics and accessories) in the *qipao* became a prevailing trend in 1930s China. Chinese women embraced their new-found democracy in the *qipao*, making it a tool for a fashionable look; tailors merely followed the masses leading the trend.[35] The *qipao* provided Chinese women with an autonomous territory from which to silently rebel against the nation's betrayal of their body. Hence, Western puffed sleeves, slits split higher to the thigh, the collar modified or removed, matching scarves, long fur coats, and leather heels—the *qipao* held hands with Western fashion (see Figure 11.3). Those keeping up with the fashion trends—movie stars, students, and prostitutes—determined new styles for the *qipao*, which were quickly circulated among, and adopted by, the masses. It is debatable how far the dress departed from Chinese sartorial tradition; the whole point was to be desirable in the new-style *qipao*.

The practice through which Chinese women incorporated Western-inspired clothing features into their *qipao* was paralleled by the nation's desire for modernization. To *Linglong* readers, including Western influences in the dress was born out of the nation's drive for progression and improvement rather than a submission to Western culture and ideas. The pursuit of the new was the result of the nation's drive to modernity. Western-style garments were new to Chinese women, so were adapted through the *qipao*. One article in *Linglong* reminded readers that "not everything from Europe and the States is new … [and] everything Chinese is old," as "new" and "old" were based on Chinese people's "thoughts, action and speech."[36] In its puritanical form, the *qipao* could hardly be considered new vis-à-vis Western-style garments in 1930s China. However, its style-changing nature was the manifestation of newness to Chinese women's wardrobes. Overwhelmed by the visibility of Western imports, Chinese women took inspiration from features of Western-style clothing. The trend of ankle-length H-line dresses in the West coincided with the popularity of the *qipao*, which further facilitated the adoption of Western-inspired elements in *qipao*-making. The *qipao* shortened with the trend for short skirts in Europe,[37] then in later years the length dropped to the ankle, corresponding with the trend in European fashion. Many photographs of *Linglong* readers in their *qipao* reveal a great deal of innovation and creativity (see Figure 11.4).

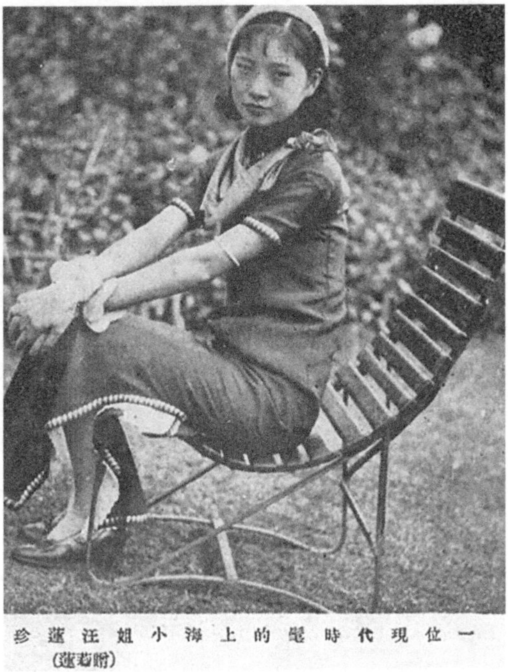

11.3 A stylish *qipao* partnered with a belly hat, scarf, and a pair of leather heels. *Linglong* 95 (1933): 651. From the collection of the C.V. Starr East Asian Library, Columbia University

Note: A Linglong reader in a stylish *qipao* partnered with a belly hat, scarf, and a pair of leather heels. Note the slit opened to the thigh.

However, not all fashionable *qipao* received praise. Those worn by the "Modern Girl" were criticized by *Linglong* readers. One *Linglong* writer considered the inconvenient "maxi-length *qipao*" with "high and stiff collar" in "high heels" to be a decadent look for the "Modern Girl."[38] The widespread adaptation and versatility of the *qipao* flourished in numerous styles for a diverse range of women in society, ranging from prostitutes to teachers, students to housewives. The question was not about wearing or not wearing

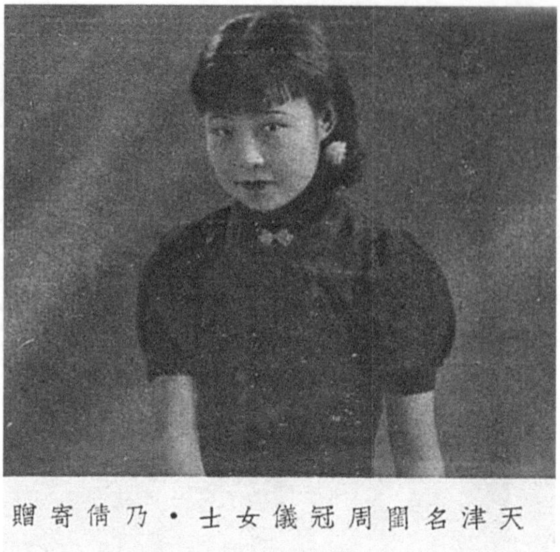

11.4 Western-style puff sleeves of a *qipao*. *Linglong* 241 (1935): 1740. From the collection of the C.V. Starr East Asian Library, Columbia University

Note: Photo from a *Linglong* reader. Note the Western-style puff sleeves of her *qipao*.

the *qipao*, but about what made it acceptable yet pretty, stylish, and trendy.

Harmony and Concealment Amid Style Change

What were the criteria for a decent *qipao*? This was a much discussed topic in the pages of *Linglong*, with most commentators agreeing that functionality and appropriateness were necessary elements in the dress's design. For a *qipao* to be functional, it had to be adaptable to different occasions such as work, parties, dancing, and shopping, and for it to be appropriate, the dress had to appeal to women of different ages, occupations, roles in society, as well as be adaptable to different types of bodies.[39] One article in *Linglong* categorized Chinese women into nine different styles: posh, sporty, cute, motherly, comical, household, boyish, elegant, and mysterious.[40] For each type of woman, the article proposed a particular clothing style along with matching accessories. Articles also addressed the *qipao*'s role in displaying women's new-found individuality while balancing this individuality with Chinese cultural beliefs about harmony. According to *Linglong* writers, what constituted a desirable women's dress was the use of harmonious colors, materials, patterns, and accessories, all based on the style, figure, and role of the wearer.[41]

Uniquely Chinese qualities were featured in the new-style *qipao*. Wang observed that the harmony embedded in Chinese women's clothing was linked to Chinese ideas about nature. For the Chinese, explained Wang, humans and nature were believed to be inseparable, and because they were seen as a single entity, Chinese clothing was expected to display patterns and colors inspired by nature. Women's clothing often featured patterns made from images of the moon, birds, flowers, and mountains, and colors were borrowed from seasonal palates.[42] Chinese women's clothing reflected culturally specific expectations about women and their harmonious relationship with nature.

The commentaries on women's dress style in *Linglong* were based on the assumption that women's clothing was custom-made. Thus, materials, colors, and patterns were the ingredients for harmony when designing their *qipao*. Chinese women exercised their full capacity to adjust these elements to their own standard, which ready-made and imported Western-style garments could not reach. The fact that many Western-style garments did not comply with the Chinese standard of harmony meant that they became unappealing in terms of Chinese women's taste and aesthetics.

Another function of clothing for Chinese women, according to *Linglong*'s commentary, was concealment. One article pointed out that clothes were used to hide bodily weaknesses such as a flat or full chest, or a disproportionate figure, and to avoid the exaggeration of nice bodily features, adopting a posture of modesty instead.[43] The characteristics of Chinese clothing outlined in *Linglong* echoed those proposed by the Chinese scholar Lin Yutang (1895–1976). Lin encouraged Chinese people to wear Chinese clothes, and stressed the dichotomous aesthetic of Chinese and Western clothing—the former served to conceal, the latter to reveal the body.[44] Accordingly, Western clothes suited only the young and beautiful; it would be cruel to those old and fat. In contrast, Chinese clothes offered equality to wearers: beauty could be revealed and ugliness could be concealed. Lin's point about the concealing nature of Chinese clothes is their ability to accommodate varied bodily features, whether desirable or undesirable. While Western-style garments present the body only in a flattering light, Chinese clothing remains neutral to all bodily shapes and forms. The concealing nature of Chinese clothes encompasses a duality that implies hiding defects and revealing appealing features. The beauty of Chinese clothes lies in their adaptability and inclusiveness.

Although Lin's article was published in the heat of nationalism, these features of Chinese clothing were picked up by *Linglong* writers, not as a resistance to Western culture and ideas, but as a point of departure in perceptions of clothing and beauty. The question of whether Western-style garments could be worn by Chinese women was asked repeatedly in *Linglong*. The differences in bodily features and aesthetic standard between Western and Chinese women discriminated against Chinese women wearing Western-style garments.[45] The common notion that the "chest-exposed style of clothes was not suitable for Chinese women due to their bodily development" acutely pointed to the inadaptability and exclusiveness of imported Western-style garments.[46]

Body Liberation in the New-style *Qipao*

The discussion of women's wardrobes in *Linglong* further emphasized the presence of harmony and concealment in Chinese clothes. They became prime considerations when a new *qipao* was made. When style change became the norm for the *qipao*, any new style was meant to "enhance natural

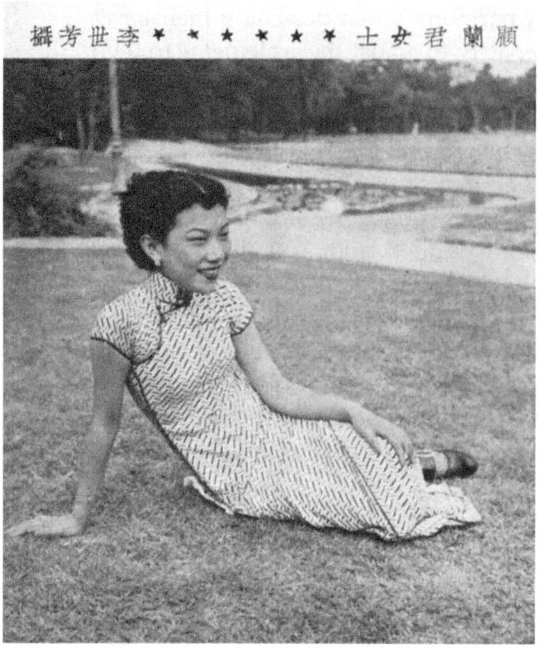

11.5 *Qipao* with cap sleeves. *Linglong* 192 (1935): 1647. From the collection of the C.V. Starr East Asian Library, Columbia University

Note: In the new form of femininity: a *Linglong* reader in a figure-hugging *qipao* with cap sleeves.

beauty,"[47] hence the "collarless *qipao*" was proposed as a result of the popularity of physical exercise that led to *jianmei* (healthy beauty). Chinese women could finally show off their chest in this new style of *qipao*, as suggested alongside one *Linglong* dress illustration.[48] Sports and swimming were enthusiastically promoted under the state's New Life Movement in 1932, which aimed to replace Chinese women's weak and fragile image with one of strong and healthy beauty. *Linglong*'s women readers welcomed this image of healthy beauty as a move towards personal achievement. Tanned skin, a strong and robust body, and a tall and sporty figure were all considered healthy and beautiful.[49] Special sports issues and photos of women's nudity were seen in *Linglong*. Chinese women felt increasingly confident with their strong and healthy figures. *Linglong* readers were not ashamed to publish their photos in swimsuits, T-shirts, and shorts, and many bare legs were displayed in sporty outfits. Shapely figures were eventually shown through the tighter-fitting *qipao*, with a longer slit to reveal bare legs (see Figure 11.5).

Given the result of the abolition of foot- and breast-binding and the goal to acquire healthy beauty, Chinese women found a new form of femininity. The *qipao* provided a means for them to celebrate their bodies. It was a natural progression for the "revealing of the legs" to be the focus of the *qipao*.[50] The figure-hugging *qipao* underwent an inevitable evolution from Chinese modernity and the immersion of Western culture, overshadowed by political movement.

A ban on *qizhuang yifu* [strange and outlandish clothes], in 1934, including restrictions on *qipao*'s length and measurement,[51] only highlighted the social oppression of women and the double standard of male authority on women's bodily appearance and behavior: on one hand, Chinese women were encouraged to wear the *qipao*; on the other hand, unreasonable impositions kept being placed on their *qipao* and appearance. No discussion on the regulations for the *qipao* was found in *Linglong*, though resistance to the ban on other items such as hairstyle and accessories was widely recorded.[52] The 1934 regulation on the *qipao* was unlikely to have been in full force, as *Linglong* readers' photos only demonstrated its varied and unaffected styles.

Conclusion

In the wake of the collapse of imperial power, Chinese women underwent clothing reforms in the Republican Era, during which the *qipao* emerged out of women's emancipation. Adaptability, versatility, and inclusiveness were the backbone of the *qipao*, whose popularity was facilitated by nationalism and the growing consumer culture. At the same time, the Nationalist government's crusade for national salvation made Chinese women's bodies a target for social progress. Their bodily appearance and the *qipao* were at the top of the agenda of the Nationalist government. Despite various attempts to nationalize their bodies and the *qipao*, Chinese women defeated the authorities by tactically intervening through adopting prevailing trends in the design of their *qipao*. The *qipao* became an autonomous territory from which to discard the label of women as weak and bearers of the tradition. Style change and the inclusion of Western-inspired elements characterized the 1930s *qipao*. Irrespective of the national symbolic role and restrictions upon the dress, Chinese women fashioned the *qipao* according to their will.

Modernity engineered both the nationalization of women's bodily appearance and the rise of the *qipao*. However, a divided view of modernity set the Nationalist government apart from *Linglong*'s female readers. Both sides demonstrated progression and improvement: the conservative government fostered the outcome of nation building; *Linglong* female readers adopted individuality, the incorporation of Western ideas, and emancipation from the ills of tradition. The inevitable clash between the two further marginalized Chinese women in society. At the same time, women's bodily reform saw the birth of a new form of femininity. The Nationalist government failed to accommodate their liberated body, while the figure-hugging *qipao* with its Western-inspired elements succeeded. Chinese women increasingly turned to fashioning their *qipao*, their imagined space for freedom and individuality.

In the great leap from dynasty to contemporary clothes, Chinese women faced a double challenge: firstly, they were exposed to uncompromising Western aesthetic standards; secondly, they were challenged by the changing function of clothes from concealment to form-revealing. Harmony and concealment set the benchmark for a trendy *qipao* that *Linglong* readers could wear rather than Western-style garments. Concealment by their *qipao* performed a dual function: hiding bodily weaknesses yet highlighting

Chinese women's new form of femininity. The 1930s *qipao* gently outlined Chinese women's slender figures. It digested Western aesthetic standards in its making. The embedded Chinese standard of harmony and concealment that outlined the characteristics of Chinese clothes resonated with a strong proportion of Chinese women.

Notes

1. See Michel de Certeau, *The Practice of Everyday Life*, trans. Steven Rendall (Berkeley and London: University of California Press, 1984).
2. Commonly known as the Chinese dress, the *qipao* is a one-piece characterized by an asymmetric yoke and stand-up collar. The term is often associated with the Manchu who are from today's northeast China. They overthrew the Ming Dynasty (1368–1644) and founded the Qing Dynasty (1644–1911). *Qi* refers to the Banner system of the Manchu; *qi* people refer to the Manchu. *Pao* is the gown worn by the Manchu.
3. It is not the aim of this chapter to discuss the *qipao* or fashion worn by the "Modern Girl" or trend-followers. This chapter aims to discuss how Chinese women negotiated their bodily appearance through the *qipao* under institutional repression from which a set of aesthetic judgments on clothes was established. The Modern Girl's look, appearance, and aesthetic standard were rather different from that of ordinary Chinese women.
4. Andrew Field, "Selling Souls in Sin City: Shanghai Singing and Dancing Hostesses in Print, Film and Politics, 1920–49," in *Cinema and Urban Culture in China, 1922–1943*, ed. Zhang Yingjin (Stanford: Stanford University Press, 1999), 114–16.
5. Hsiao-pei Yen, "Body Politics, Modernity and National Salvation: The Modern Girl and the New Life Movement," *Asian Studies Review* 29 (2005): 165–86.
6. See Barbara Mittler, "Of Elegance and Eloquence: *Linglong* and the Art of Being a 'New Woman' in 1930s China," paper presented at the AAS Annual Conference. San Diego, March 12, 2000; Leo Oufan Lee, *Shanghai Modern: The Flowering of a New Urban Culture in China 1930–1945* (Cambridge, MA: Harvard University Press, 1999), 86–8.
7. Eileen Chang was the first to write about Chinese women cross-dressing in *qipao*. Her point was later taken up by Antonia Finnane, *Changing Clothes in China* (New York: Columbia University Press, 2008), and "What Should Chinese Women Wear? A National Problem," *Modern China* 22, no. 2 (1996): 99–131; and by Hao Ng, *Duhui yunshang. Xishuo zhongguo funü fushi yu shenti geming (1911–1935)* (Hong Kong: Joint Publishing Co. Ltd, 2006), 100–101. See Eileen Chang (Zhang, Ailing), "A Chronicle of Changing Clothes," trans. Andrew F. Jones, *Positions: East Asia Cultures Critique* 11, no. 2 (2003) [1943]: 427–41.
8. Chang, "A Chronicle of Changing Clothes," 435.
9. Elisabeth Croll, *Changing Identities of Chinese Women: Rhetoric, Experience, and Self-Perception in Twentieth-century China* (Hong Kong: Hong Kong University Press, 1995), 40.
10. See Louise Edwards, "Policing the Modern Woman in Republican China," *Modern China* 26, no. 2 (2000): 115–47; and Christina Kelly Gilmartin, "Gender in the Formation of a Communist Body Politic," *Modern China* 19, no. 3 (1993): 299–329.
11. Soong Ching-ling, wife of Revolutionist Sun Yatsen, was believed to have popularized the angular *qipao* in the mid-1920s. One of the most photographed women of the time, she was spotted wearing the *qipao*, but no other kinds of dress, from then to after the liberation. In the early 1920s, women's cross-dressing, bound breast, and short hair were apparent, particularly with those who joined the army. Ng noted that during this time, women with short hair, bound breast, and in men's clothes was a strong trend. It was rather difficult to differentiate them as women or men, reserved or provocative; Ng, *Duhui yunshang*, 101.
12. Ng, *Duhui yunshang*, 272–4; A.C. Scott, *Chinese Costume in Transition* (Singapore: Donald Moore, 1958), 81–3; Yuching Wong, *Lidai funü paofu kaojiu* [*The Research and Examination of Chinese Women's Gown in Successive Dynasties*] (Taipei: *Zhongguo qipao yanjiu xiehui* [Chinese Chi Pao Research Association], 1975), 98.

13. *Minguo ribao* (February 27, 1926), cited in Ng, *Duhui yunshang*, 274, pointed out the fact that mid-1920s' *qipao* was different from that worn by the Manchu and proposed to call it *zhonghua pao* instead of *qipao*.

14. The assured survival and popularity of Manchu wear in the social and political turmoil in the early Republican era was slim against the anti-Manchu tenor of the time. Instead, Chinese women were seen in a jacket and skirt; see Verity Wilson, *Chinese Dress* (London: The Victoria and Albert Museum, 1996); Valery M. Garrett, *Chinese Clothing: An Illustrated Guide* (Hong Kong: Oxford University Press, 1994); and Mingxin Bao, "Chinese Lady's Daily Wear in Late Qing Dynasty and Early Republic Period," *Journal of China Textile University* (English edition) 8, no. 3 (1991): 9–21. Finnane noted that no hint of the *qipao* was mentioned in the Chinese press in 1925, but in 1926, it was featured massively. She argued that its rise had much to do with the national crisis of the May Thirtieth Movement. Bian further noted that only a small proportion of Shanghai women wore the *qipao* in 1923; see Xiangyang Bian, "Origin of Qipao Fashion in Early Republic Period," *Journal of Donghua University* (English edition) 20, no. 4 (2003): 21–6, 22. Newspapers showed no sign of it before March 1925, and only in the second half of the year did they mention its appearance. Also see Ng, *Duhui yunshang*.

15. Amongst these publications, *Funü zazhi* [The Ladies' Journal], the most influential and widely circulated mainstream women's magazine following the New Culture fad, was staid in fashion choices and women's social outlook. Another magazine, *New Youth*, anticipated the radical challenge to notions of "traditional women." *Liangyou Huabao* [The Young Companion] derided outlandish clothing for flappers and prostitutes. Writers for these magazines were predominantly men; see Kristine Harris, "The New Woman: Image, Subject, and Dissent in 1930s Shanghai Film Culture," *Republican China* 20, no. 2 (1995): 55–79.

16. Finnane, *Changing Clothes*, 115; Hanrietta Harrison, *The Making of the Republican Citizen: Political Ceremony and Symbols in China, 1911–1929* (Oxford and New York: Oxford University Press, 2000), 177.

17. Intense Nationalist feeling during that time saw men wearing *Sun Yatsen suit* (commonly known as the *Mao suit* outside China) and women wearing the *qipao* (Ng, *Duhui yunshang*, 268).

18. Chang, "A Chronicle of Changing Clothes," 435.

19. Announcement of the Nationalist Government: "1. Clothes: Matched collar, right yoke covers front bodice, dress length falls on the mid-point between knee and ankle, inner-pants' length matches that of dress, sleeves below the elbow, to the mid-point of the wrist; in silk, linen, cotton, blue in color; six buttons on the side. 2. Shoes: In cotton, silk or black leather." See *Clothing Regulations*, April 16, 1929 (cited in Ng, *Duhui yunshang*, 270–71).

    Translation is author's own. Regulations for the *Sun Yatsen suit* were also included as it was declared to be men's formal wear. (*"Announcement of the Nationalist Government" 1929: 3*, cited in Ng, *Duhui yunshang*, 270–71). At about the same time, the Education Department established the *qipao* nationwide as the girls' uniform for primary and secondary schools and tertiary institutes (ibid., 271).

20. Both Ng, *Duhui yunshang*, 274, and Ellen Johnston Laing, "Visualising Evidence for the Evolution of 'Politically Correct' Dress for Women in Early Twentieth Century Shanghai," *Nan Nü* 5, no. 1 (2003): 69–114, 101–2, documented that in 1926 General Sun Chuanfan called for a ban on women wearing the *qipao*. Finnane discussed its clause as a strong belief that clothing for men and women should differentiate the sexes; Finnane, *Changing Clothes*, 110–15. Also see: *Liangyou huabao* (1926).

21. Bian noted that traditionally Chinese women wore pants underneath the garment and argued that bare-legs or silk stockings under a *qipao* were not Chinese tradition but a Western influence; Bian, "Origin of Qipao Fashion," 23. Ng documented that the *qipao*'s length became shorter under the influence of the Western fashion for short skirts in 1928, and noted that women had already abandoned the pants underneath for silk stockings before the government released the *Clothing Regulations of 1929*; Ng, *Duhui yunshang*, 279.

22. High heels were widespread in 1925 and became worn by the majority of women; Ng, *Duhui yunshang*, 132.

23. *Linglong* 54 (1932): 167; *Linglong* 60 (1932): 454; *Linglong* 55 (1932): 213; *Linglong* 131 (1934): 355; *Linglong* 129 (1934): 228.

24. *Linglong* 45 (1932): 1816; *Linglong* 57 (1932): 310.

25. *Linglong* 131 (1934): 355.

26. Finnane observed that only one in four used a tailor while one in five bought ready-to-wear. Unaffordable and problem of fit were the major obstacles to marketing international fashion, which also explained the predominance of home- and tailor-made over imported ready-made clothes; Finnane, *Changing Clothes*, 115.

27. *Linglong* 43 (1932): 1710.

28. *Linglong* 75 (1932): 1172.

29. Wessie Ling, *Fusionable Cheongsam* (Hong Kong: Hong Kong Arts Centre, 2007).

30. *Linglong* 75 (1932): 1172.

31. Peter Carroll, "Refashioning Suzhou: Dress, Commodification, and Modernity," *Positions: East Asia Cultures Critique* 11, no. 2 (2003): 443–78, 445.

32. The featuring of Chinese women as Republican icons in desirable and exquisite *qipao* was typified in *Yuefenpai* [calendar posters]. These posters were first produced by foreign and Chinese companies in 1900s Shanghai, Guangzhou, and Hong Kong. They depicted elegant Chinese women in the latest *qipao* fashion promoting an array of consumer products (including tobacco, wine, cosmetics, and so on) and were also known as *meinu yuefenpai* [beautiful lady calendar posters]; see Pak-Tong Cheuk, "A History of the Calendar Poster," in *Chinese Women and Modernity: Calendar Posters of the 1910s–1930s*, eds Ng Chun Bong, Cheuk Pak-Tong, Wong Ying, and Yvonne Lo, 8–15 (Hong Kong: Joint Publishing Co. Ltd, 1996), 9. They were circulated within and outside China where Chinese populations were present.

33. See Ng, *Duhui yunshang*, and Laing, "Visualising Evidence."

34. It was recorded that an unofficial gang, *Modeng pohuai tuan* [Modern destructive gang] attacked and destroyed women's Western-style clothes in public. Those wearing Chinese-style clothes were not the targets; *Linglong* 11 (1934): 643.

35. Chang noted the "unaccountable waves of communal fancy that become apparent from time to time" and considered that Chinese fashions during the Republican period could be "read as representing the will of the people"; Chang, "A Chronicle of Changing Clothes," 439.

36. *Linglong* 43 (1936): 3329.

37. Ng, *Duhui yunshang*, 279.

38. *Linglong* 30 (1933): 1593.

39. *Linglong* 25 (1935): 1621–2.

40. *Linglong* 25 (1935): 1619–20.

41. *Linglong* 42 (1936): 3283–4; *Linglong* 25 (1935): 1621–2.

42. Xing Wang, *Bainian fushi chaoliu yu shibian* (Hong Kong: Commercial Press, 1992),18–22.

43. *Linglong* 9 (1937): 683–5.

44. Yutang Lin, "*Lun xizhuang*," in *Lin Yutang zuanza, Shangjuan* (Fuzhou: *Haixia wenyi chubanshe*, 1988 [1934]), 351–4.

45. *Linglong* 3 (1936): 169.

46. *Linglong* 54 (1932): 167.

47. *Linglong* 9 (1937): 683.

48. *Linglong* 54 (1932): 167.

49. *Linglong* 71 (1932): 1006.

50. Scott, *Chinese Costume in Transition*, 84.

51. "The length of the *qipao* was not to be shorter than one Chinese inch above the ankle; the sleeves were not to be above the elbow; the slits of the *qipao* were not to be more than three inches above the knee; hair was not to be below the collar line unless it was tied in a knot; and no feet and legs were to be exposed except when engaging in manual labor"; Jonathan Spence, *The Search for Modern China* (New York: W.W. Norton & Co., 2000), 357; cited in Yen, "Body Politics," 173.

52. Yen, "Body Politics," 173–4; Spence, *The Search for Modern China*, 357.

12

Women, Clothing, and Politics in Senegal in the 1940s–1950s

Dior Konaté

In Senegal, allegiance to political parties has been expressed in a variety of ways, and fashion has not been an exception to this desire to display party allegiance. Take, for example, a dress, which motivated Senegalese women to involve themselves in politics during the 1940s and 1950s. In 1945, the Senegalese Lamine Guèye, leader of the *Bloc Africain,* a political party that rallied colonized peoples in French West Africa, won voting rights for women. To Senegalese women, the motto *bloc* reflected their determination to win the right to vote, leading to their participation in the colony's political life. They expressed their growing political involvement through the medium of clothing, adopting a dress, the *robe bloc,* which, as we will see, was pregnant with meanings. This chapter examines the extent to which the *robe bloc,* a dress worn by Senegalese women during that time, forged an intimate connection between women and politics. As will be shown, the *robe bloc* conveyed a number of meanings in the Senegalese political arena. Yet apart from being considered primarily as a political emblem, the *robe bloc* also became an important new consumer item especially for urban women, sparking a fashion phenomenon during the 1950s. This chapter will explore the social and political contexts in which the *robe bloc* took place, to illuminate some of ways in which clothing can function as a political tool and symbol.

Women and Politics in Senegal: Winning the Right to Vote

Women's participation in the Senegalese political scene is most visible in political parades where women engage in folkloric displays of singing and dancing and wear colorful clothing, upon which is emblazoned party slogans and depictions of political leaders' faces. In fact, in Senegal as elsewhere in Africa, women constitute today a sizeable voting number; yet, they are still under-represented in the political decision-making process. But women, who are politically conscious and committed to transformation, mobilize themselves in creative ways to make an impact on politics.

Since the 1990s, several African countries have resorted to a quota system for women.[1] In this fight for gender representation in politics, Senegal made a big move on Friday March 23, 2007, when the National Assembly passed and approved a parity law. The law calls for equal access of men and women to electoral mandates and elective functions and holds political parties responsible for facilitating equal access. Abdoulaye Wade, Senegal's newly elected President, announced that lists that did not comply with the new parity law would be barred from participation in elections. For women in Senegal, the year 2007 was as significant as the year 1945 when they gained the right to vote for the first time.

Senegalese women have a long history of political involvement. Their ability to act or organize politically goes back to the first half of the nineteenth century, thanks to Senegal's exceptional status in politics in French-speaking West Africa. "Senegal was not only France's oldest possession, but until the early 1950s it was politically the most important member of the French West African Federation,"[2] noted H.O. Idowu. It has a long tradition of politics that can be traced back to 1848, when France granted the right to vote to the male inhabitants of the major settlements of Dakar, Saint-Louis, Rufisque, and the Gorée Island.[3] In these cities, known as the Four Communes, the French applied an assimilation policy.

Assimilation entailed the notion that France's colonial possessions should become integrated into the *métrople,* the mother country. As a result of the assimilation policy, the Four Communes were granted the same rights as their counterparts in the metropolis. Full citizenship was extended to their inhabitants[4] while elective institutions were created to give them a participation in the management of local affairs, a political assimilation to France, and an administrative decentralization.[5] Africans from the Four Communes who were able to pursue higher education could rise to be termed *évolué* or evolved, while the rest of the Senegalese population remained French subjects. These privileges put Senegal ahead of the other colonies of French West Africa[6] and as one commentator put it, writing in 1901, France's policies in Senegal made it the "aristocratic colony."[7] Yet, according to Frederic Schaffer, "though this enfranchised population voted often their numbers were small."[8] Moreover, "it was a male franchise."[9] Women in the Four Communes were not allowed to vote, but they were actively involved in the political associations.[10] Still they had to wait another 70 years before being able to vote for the first time.

Senegalese women's access to universal rights followed the French's government implementation of reforms that shifted the terrain of colonial politics. Constrained by a changing world context to reorganize the political structures of their colonies in the wake of nationalist demands that emphasized certain goals such as the right to education and improving economic standards of living, the French issued the decree of April 21, 1944 signed in Algers. With this law, French African colonies were called upon to elect new representatives to the Constituent Assemblies and to participate in municipal elections. However, Article 17 of the decree gave a new category of voters, Frenchwomen, the right to vote and be eligible under the same conditions as men. On February 19, 1945, it was decreed that women of French citizenship residing in French West Africa and Togo were excluded from the vote, while all Frenchwomen living in the same regions could participate in all elections.[11]

For Senegalese women in the Four Communes, they were being discriminated against; their citizenship was also being called into question. The response to the exclusion was immediate and intense, particularly when additional limitations were introduced to support that ban. The question of women's voting rights then became linked to the ability to read and write in French and being *évolué,* the French for evolved. To the authorities, women not knowing how to read or write French could not write on the bulletin the candidate of their choice.[12] The true reason was that despite their assimilation policy, the "French people evidenced anxiety over the prospect of being outnumbered in their own polity by Africans."[13] To the Senegalese who had a long history of electoral politics, barring women from participating in elections was an outrage. In March and April 1945, Cournarie's arbitrary decision forced the Senegalese onto the path of protest, putting on the forefront Lamine Guèye, a Paris-trained lawyer and the first West African to hold a French Doctorate in Law (Figure 12.1).

Concerned with gaining control over local politics in Senegal, "Lamine Guèye, a player in communal politics since 1910s, made the quest for political assimilation, the leitmotif of this political career, establishing for himself an unassailable position in the political world of the Four Communes."[14] With emerging leaders such as Guèye, signs that African citizens in the Four Communes were seeking to consolidate themselves into a status-group were clear. Leading the local branch of the *SFIO,*[15] as well as being Senegal's deputy to the French Parliament after World War II, Guèye was also the leader of the *Bloc Africain,* "the name of the *SFIO* proposed by its citizen-Socialist members."[16] Made up of diverse political forces, the *Bloc Africain* was also the first African political party to rally all colonized peoples in French West Africa. Guèye's political background allowed him to take the lead in the fight for women's voting rights. Believing

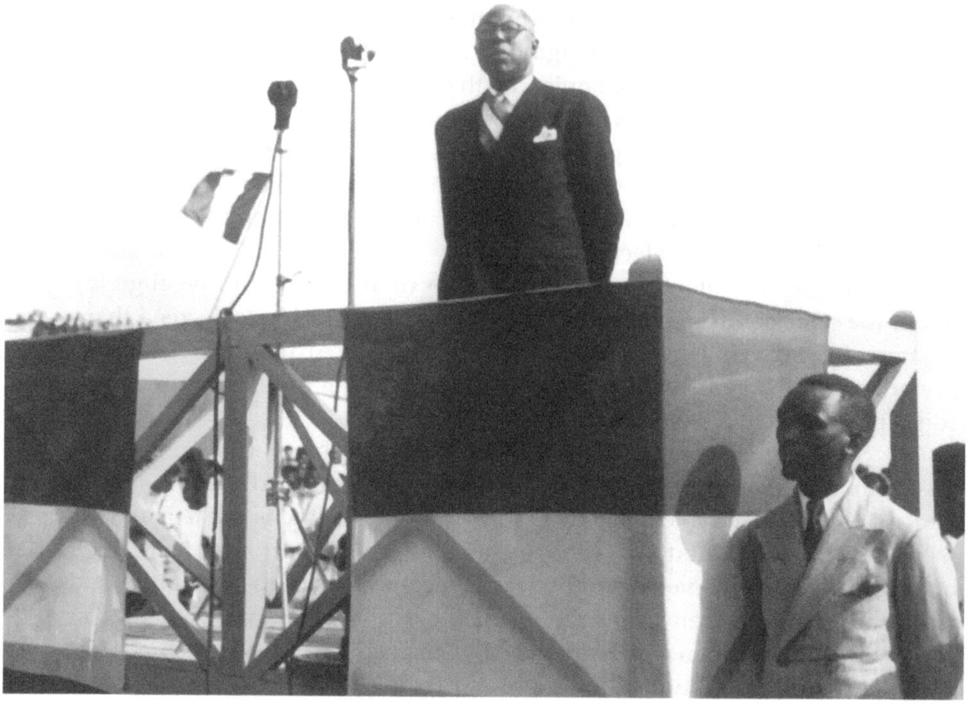

12.1 Lamine Guèye making a speech in Dakar, Senegal, 1947.
Image IFAN-CAD. Picture G. Labitte

that political assimilation meant that any group should not be left out of electoral processes, women in particular, Guèye took the fight to France. His intervention in Paris led consequently to the decree of April 17, 1945, issued by Giaccobi, Minister of Colonies, to overturn that of February 19, 1945.[17] The new decree ultimately gave women in the Four Communes the opportunity to exercise the same electoral rights as French women. For Senegalese women, the credit goes to Lamine Guèye and it was clear that he was their favorite politician.

The political achievements carried out by his party, the *Bloc Africain*, were of such great significance that the "slogan *b'loc, b'loc* came to symbolize change, and opposition to the French system."[18] The motto *b'loc* symbolized their victory and, with the right to vote, women were ensured of now playing a much greater role in politics. With strong convictions to achieve that goal, women conveyed their victory through the medium of clothing, adopting a particular cloth style, the *robe bloc*, a dress pregnant with meanings. Yet, to address the importance of the *robe bloc* as a lens through which to look at the connections between women and politics in

Senegal, a discussion on what makes clothing a tool and symbol of political struggle is needed.

Clothing: A Tool and Symbol of Political Struggle

A conceptual definition of clothing would be useful to start the discussion. Here I define clothing as any look that includes clothes, hairstyles, jewelry, and ornamentation accessories. Armed with this definition, it becomes possible to assess more critically the degree to which and why clothing is a powerful tool and symbol of political struggle and how Senegalese women used clothing as an instrument of political identity in the 1940s–1950s. Clothes have been described as readable texts that convey clear messages and alternatively, clothing has been described as a "bundle of cultural symbols."[19] Both concepts draw discussions across disciplines that provided multiple views of cloth as commodity, an object of social exchange, and a vehicle of symbolic meaning as well. In those discussions, clothing practices, clothing behavior, materials of which clothes are made, fabrication techniques, the utility and properties of clothes, the labor of their production, clothes and identities, are among other themes analyzed.[20] These analyses draw attention to the fact that while clothing shapes, encloses, protects, exposes, and interacts with the body, it is also "an indication of how people in different eras have perceived their position in social structures and negotiated status in boundaries."[21] Making choices about what to wear can reveal much about people and communicate messages about their identity. Answering the question of why people wear clothes, Leenhardt responds that: "it is neither the cold nor the nudity that prompts men to wear clothes, but desires to endow themselves with anything that help affirm themselves."[22] Thus, clothing plays a crucial role in defining and expressing social, economic, and moral identities. However, "clothing speaks not only of status, wealth, beauty,"[23] and identity. It performs a major role in political choices as well.

Clothing is also an instrument of political power. In his treatise on elegance, Honoré de Balzac wrote: "the costume being the most powerful symbols, the (French) Revolution was a debate between the silk and the sheet as well."[24] This dimensional aspect of clothing enhances its function as a visual medium of politics, allowing it to convey messages that words cannot. The significant role of clothing in the dynamic of political processes and struggles has been discussed in several studies. In the introduction of *Cloth and the Human Experience*, Jane Schneider and Annette B. Weiner suggest the importance of cloth to the making and transformation of political and social meanings in human societies.[25] Hilda Kuper makes a similar argument, stressing how clothing is an index of social, economic, and political direction.[26]

Several studies have shown that printed cloth in African societies has long been used to advertise political affiliations, choices, and slogans. Some authors note that in the task of nation-building, clothing plays a highly visible role in spreading the political messages of Africa governments, while the achievements of many African nations are given "concrete expression on cloth."[27] Others show the importance of clothing to support independence movements. In Swaziland, traditional clothing assumed a new significance with the development of movements for independence from colonial rule, as parties and supporters conveyed their awareness of national interests and cultural identity through the medium of clothing.[28] In her study of politics in Ivory Coast, Mona Etienne discussed how "cloth has become a prime motivation of party support and a focus of attention for the recipients."[29] Kathleen E. Rickford reinforces this statement, stressing that "the capacity of factory cloth to elicit strong emotional responses is vital to its use as a political tool."[30] In Ivory Coast, she wrote, "wax and roller print textile were used in rallying popular support and influencing public opinion."[31] Patterns reflected political trends, events, and personalities.

Elsewhere in Africa, clothing could crystallize and express frustration and could become a popular form of political protest, as was, for instance, the case of the *Sape* phenomenon in Congo: "The *sapeurs,* as they call themselves used fashion as a way of disengaging themselves from those in power."[32] Created in a context of political turmoil, the *sape* remained a refuge for young Congolese to express their social alienation. For instance, Charles D. Gondola argues that "the Congolese sapeurs have created with elegance what the sans-culottes developed with rags: an instrument of protest and an emblem of political rallying."[33] Although the language of clothing speaks of political choices or aspirations and provides some groups with a means to voice their frustrations and anxieties, political issues and well-known leaders have sometimes inspired clothing, as will be discussed later in this chapter.

In her study of jewelry styles in Senegal, Marian Johnson shows that inspiration came from political events and leaders. Especially popular was Lamine Guèye, who not only inspired the *robe bloc,* but also a bracelet style that captures the imagination: the *balmarqué de Lamine Guèye.*[34] Another earring called *wow ou dede* ("yes or no" in Wolof) carried a political message as it was created as a kind of campaign button for the election of 1960, asking whether Senegal should become independent from France.[35] The power of politics to influence clothing styles in Senegal was in evidence in the 1930s, when a headscarf style named *Popular Front*[36] became a popular item among women.[37] Yet, the *robe bloc* was among the many clothing styles inspired by Senegalese politicians, the one that captured the imagination as it bonded women, clothing, and politics in a meaningful way.

The *Robe Bloc*: Connecting Women and Politics

Though Senegalese historians have not ignored the political significance of clothing during the colonial era, I argue that they have overlooked an important phase of the history of women in Senegal by providing only a slight understanding of the link between female political activism and cloth styles. Therefore the connections between cloth choices and women's identities in Senegal in the 1940s–1950s will help us to understand their concerns and struggles during that time.

The history of clothing in Senegal has begun to be investigated. The primary focus of early studies has been on cloth styles and accompanying accessories,[38] fashion and clothing styles among young girls in Dakar,[39] and on public opinion and political life in Dakar with a focus on clothing, dances, and music as traditional means to express activism.[40] No full-length studies of the history of clothing with connection to women's political activism have yet been attempted. This chapter aims to fill that gap.

Cheikh Faty Faye's pioneering contribution cleared the path of studies of clothing and political activism in Senegal. He investigated clothing among the Senegalese and demonstrated how it accounted for a vibrant political life in the colonial cities as styles were inspired by parties and politicians and also as vehicle for political messages. Faye mentioned the importance of the *robe bloc* among women as inspired by Lamine Guèye and his party; however, he failed to further his analysis. Ousseynou Faye's study of cloth styles and accessories in Dakar provides a historical perspective on clothing and its importance among Africans. The focus was mainly on traditional clothes, but Faye argues that the Senegalese were forced to adapt to new styles thanks to the availability of new fabrics and styles brought by French merchants and to the influence of French fashion. Likewise, the *robe bloc* was mentioned at the end of the paper. Recently, Djibril Seck has documented clothing and fashion among girls in Dakar from 1945 to 1960. His study looks at clothing in a much wider context by investigating different styles that emerged in Senegal and relates them to Senegalese girls' preference for new styles. Seck shows how the creation of multiple fashion designs in Senegal fit into the economic, political, and social context of the colonial period in the region. Yet, he offers insights on the creativity and active input of girls in always adopting new styles that reflected their economic, social, cultural, and political dynamism. These pioneer studies shed light on a number of characteristics and issues of clothing in colonial Senegal, but do not provide a detailed description of the relations between women's political activism, clothing, and identity in Senegal.

According to Ann Smart Martin, "material things are functional and utilitarian: they work. Material things are also evocative and emotional: they mean."[41] What material things come to mean, and how to interpret meaning, are things not to overlook. So, this section provides a solid basis for broad questions about the meanings of clothing among women in Senegal, especially as clothing can be "an important marker of time"[42] and of political identity. But let us briefly outline the theoretical edifice upon which our analysis is built.

This analysis of the *robe bloc* is about what our clothes say about us and how our choice of specific clothes speaks volume about our identity. Clothing as subject parallels the academic interest in the issues of identity. Scholars in a variety of disciplines, including anthropology, sociology, ethnology, and the humanities, have contributed to the long intellectual history of the study of clothing and the ways in which it is used to articulate and project identities. In that body of literature, the role of clothing in the construction of personal, cultural, social, and political identity has been fully addressed. Malcolm Bernard, in *Fashion as Communication*, argues that fashion, style, clothing, and dress and the sphere of activity that they represent are "pre-eminently among the ways subordinate groups contest and challenge prevailing identities and positions."[43] Many scholars have also taken an interest in the connections between clothing and identities in recent years. Hilda Kuper, for example, has written recently on the use of clothing (dress, costume, and uniform) to demonstrate status and identity at different levels and at different times. In her study of costume, cosmology, and identity among the Swazi of Swaziland, southeast Africa, she explains that "both power and relationships are revealed in dress, uniforms, and costume as well as other social goods."[44] Other studies have analyzed the use of clothing and body symbolism in the articulation of different identities. The work of Hildi Hendrickson interprets the use of flags and bodies in the Hereros' efforts to represent their identity in colonial Namibia. According to her, "the use of colored cloth to express national political affiliation is the direct extension of its use in this context to express local, gendered and historical identities."[45] Moreover, the importance placed on clothing as a visible expression of identity and its role as an agent of change in social and political relationships have been well researched by Annette Weiner, Jane Schneider and others in the book, *Cloth and the Human Experience*. Throughout the book, cloth provides the ability to understand what Weiner and Schneider, in the introduction, called "the otherwise overlooked"[46] activities and identities of women.

Yet, this essay draws heavily on the edited book by Hildi Hendrickson, *Clothing and Difference*. Topics such as body coverings as essential in the constitution of social identities, the role of clothing to articulate differences in gender, age, and religion, to create female identity, and as a principal medium of communication, are this book's focus. Hendrickson explains how "bodies and dress help to express and shape ideas about the most potent kinds of political and spiritual power thought to be available to human beings."[47] This rich body of literature offers an interesting framework in which to examine the use and significance of the *robe bloc* (Figures 12.2 and 12.3) among Senegalese women in mid-twentieth century Senegal.

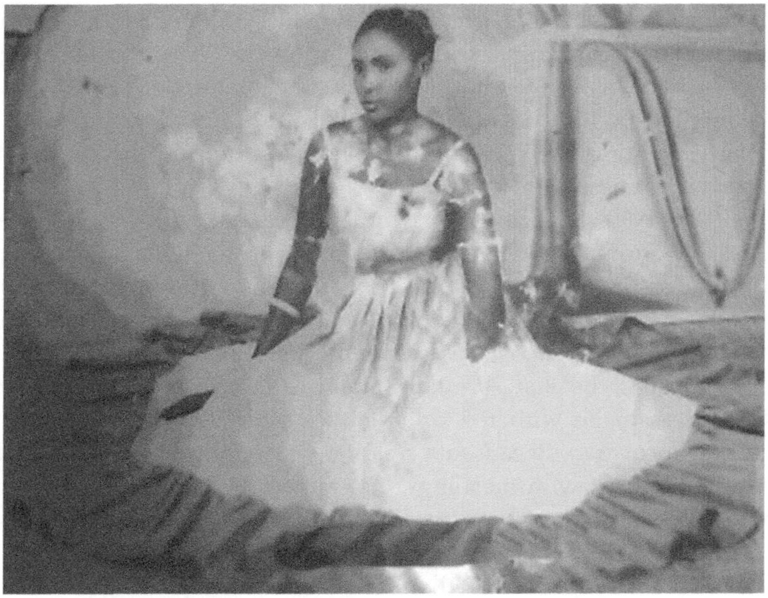

12.2 Example of *robe bloc* with layers of fabrics worn by Maguette Hane, Dakar, Senegal, 1948. Courtesy Moussa Diagne

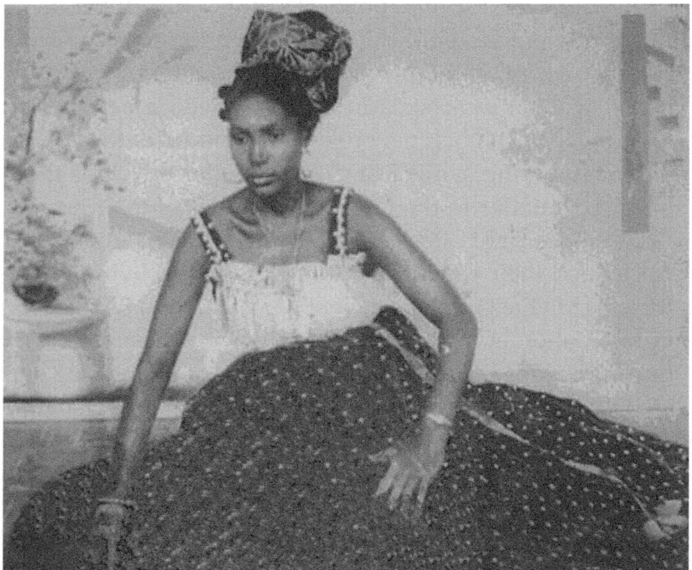

12.3 Another example of *robe bloc* with a different type of fabric worn by the same person, Dakar, Senegal, 1950. Courtesy Moussa Diagne

The *robe bloc* has been a particularly powerful symbol of Senegalese women's political identity and consciousness in the 1940s–1905s. In that context, the *robe bloc* offers an avenue for interrogating the intersections between women, clothing, and political identity in colonial Senegal with reference to recent scholarly works for reassessing the role of clothing in the construction of different identities.

In 1940s–1950s Senegal, townswomen developed their own conventions of dress by adopting the *robe bloc*. Like the short hairstyle among women in 1920s France, the *robe bloc* "was not only a fashion, it was an epoch. It was a particular sign of a time."[48] A form of political commentary, the *robe bloc* has much to tell us about Senegalese women's connection to politics.

Named after the *Bloc Africain*, Lamine Guèye's party, the *robe bloc* was a long dress made with red color fabrics which sometimes left the right shoulder uncovered. Because its creation was politically motivated, the *robe bloc* was pregnant with meanings. The appeal of the *robe bloc* as a political cloth related to the fact that it served as a visual and political language of signs. For instance, it was a highly symbolic act for Senegalese women to show allegiance to Lamine Guèye. In other words, women turned the *robe bloc* into an individual statement of political loyalty to their favorite politician. Moreover, as they asserted their status as new voters, townswomen adopted the *robe bloc* to communicate their new positions and accentuate their new political role.

The *robe bloc* assumed several political significances. It became one avenue of expression of women's political involvement in the Four Communes and their changing perceptions of themselves as new voters. Furthermore, the *robe bloc* endowed women in Senegal in the 1940s with a new political identity and acted as the focus of their new role in the politics of the Four Communes. It was also the unifying symbol of their struggle as well as that of the *Bloc Africain*, and a reminder to the French authorities of their arrogant decision to deny them those rights. The spread of the *robe bloc* among women in the towns proclaimed their equality with Frenchwomen living in the colony, as well as their right to act as respectable French citizens. So, the *robe bloc* was a visual representation of a grammar of politics in which actors invented and improvised in response to a new reorganization of political power relations.

Additionally, the *robe bloc* served as an important and visually immediate sign of appurtenance to the *Bloc Africain*. For women wearing the *robe bloc* was an expression of political affiliation to the *Bloc Africain* and a public demonstration of the acceptance of the party's principles. The number of female militants of the *Bloc Africain* could be measured by the number of women wearing the *robe bloc*. The dress was worn at all political meetings from the 1940s to the 1950s.[49]

Additionally, the movement to wear the *robe bloc* drew its strength from the broader political context of the 1940s: women winning the right to vote for the first time. Thus by choosing this dress, they viewed it as a self-conscious move toward political change and a gesture of political autonomy. At this point, the *robe bloc* served as a reminder to the wearer of her commitment to be a good citizen and fulfill her political duties. In adopting the *robe bloc* as the unifying symbol of their political victory, Senegalese women viewed themselves as a part of the mainstream of French political assimilation. Thus, the *robe bloc* could be interpreted as evidence of a refusal among women in the Four Communes to lose rights granted to them by their French citizenship.

The creativity in the use of the *bloc* style among the Senegalese during the 1940s and 1950s was, though, gender-centered. "Throughout history and across the globe men and women have consciously manipulated their material world in order to fabricate their identities physically and to differentiate themselves from each other."[50] In Senegal, although both men and women adopted the *bloc* fashion, they attached different meanings to it. During the same period of time, the *caftan bloc* was popular among Senegalese men. However, women were more creative in their interpretation of the *bloc* style than men because they were able to distinguish themselves with the style by bringing more political meanings to it.

The *caftan bloc,* a long costume with long sleeves and a front opening below the belly button, was more traditional in its cut. In contrast, the *robe bloc* was European in its design, breaking with traditional women's clothes in Senegal. Yet, the dress "remained local in conceptualization."[51] Women's loyalty to Lamine Guèye was so deep that they copied through the *robe bloc* the European style of their preferred politician. Lamine Guèye, "used to living in the towns, traveled in the interior dressed formally in well-pressed suit and tie."[52] Recognizing the colonial cultural context of the time and the dominance of its assimilation policy is necessary in order to understanding the clothing choices in Senegal.

The *évolué* and the *citoyen français* labels influenced tastes in European clothes for townspeople but also for leaders such as Lamine Guèye and his supporters. In Senegal, "the citizens showed great pleasure at any indications of acceptance as equals by Europeans."[53] Townswomen, in choosing the *robe bloc,* wanted to "dress as much like a European as possible, for this was the mark of an évolué."[54] Dressing well in European clothes, "achievement in western education, knowledge of European manners and sophistication as a townsman" were signs of somebody being an *évolué,* "a label once carried consciously and proudly."[55] For women, the choice of a European style could be interpreted as a way to imitate the elegance of their preferred politician who, it was said, "used his Europeanization as a good asset in the electoral business."[56] One might say that the adoption of the *bloc style* by Senegalese men could be interpreted as a way to support women for winning the right to vote or just as a fashion phenomenon among men. Also regarding the gendered differences in the use of the *bloc* style, women had more room to express how valuable to them was the right to vote. For instance, they looked for anything that made the *robe bloc* politically visible. Appropriate colors were indicated precisely. In addition to the name, also politically meaningful was the color of the *robe bloc*, which was made with red color fabrics. The red color, the most distinctive part of the dress, was the party color of the *Bloc Africain*. This color symbolizes many meanings including power, progress, and change.

The style of *robe bloc* has tended to be very distinct and unique. Senegalese women were and are used to wearing clothes that incorporated yards of fabrics, but nothing like the *robe bloc*, a style that broke with traditional women's clothes. A salient characteristic of the *robe bloc* was the quantity of fabric used to make it. Most *robes bloc* required more than twelve meters of fabric (Figures 12.2 and 12.3). Perhaps the main reason why women used a large amount of fabrics has to do with their desire to enhance the symbolism of the dress. That symbolism became much more pronounced as the red color was "expressed over all the ten or more meters of fabric used to make the dress."[57] It was later when the *robe bloc* became a consumer item among urban women in the 1950s that new fabrics with printed patterns replaced the red color fabrics.

In her study of used clothing practices in Lusaka, Karen T. Hansen argues that "clothes are not worn passively but require people's collaboration."[58] The reputations of Senegalese women as highly fashion conscious, always searching for more grace and sophistication, added more meanings to the *robe bloc*. For instance, "Senegalese women considered gold of any quality a necessity for their costume"[59] as "gold jewelry has long been a source of feminine empowerment in Senegal."[60] The appeal and popularity of the *robe bloc* among urban women in Senegal as a political cloth was evident in the 1940s as they combined it with several gold jewelry items of different sizes and shapes, all named after the *Bloc Africain*. *Bracelets bloc*,[61] *bagues bloc*,[62] and *colliers bloc*[63] were commissioned by women to match the *robe bloc*.

The last element that enhanced the *robe bloc* was the creation of a hairstyle type called *Jamano Coura*.[64] There is a debate about the person behind the inspiration of this hair-braiding style. Some Senegalese argue that it was named after Coura Waly Cissé, Lamine Guèye's mother; the politician was most known as Lamine Coura Guèye. Others, however, argue that Coura Thiaw, a famous Senegalese dancer, inspired the *Jamano Coura* hairstyle.[65] What we know for sure is that this hairstyle was widespread among urban women at the time of the *robe bloc*.

It was this combination of elegance, creativity, novelty, and Senegalese women's desire to negotiate the transition to their new political roles that infused the *robe bloc* and *bloc* accessories with specific meanings. Its political significance was so deep that it became so popular, shifting from a political cloth to a fashion phenomenon, as well as a marker of woman as fashionable.

The *Robe Bloc:* From Political Cloth to a Fashion Phenomenon

The Senegalese appear to have derived considerable pleasure from and pride in the display of fashions. Their reputations as highly fashion conscious is not of recent origin. Travelers to Senegal in the nineteenth century reported on the Senegalese's preference for European styles. Describing Dakar in 1892, the Duc d'Uzès wrote a letter stating that "some Senegalese are dressed in latest Paris fashions, with hats, jackets, shirts, ties, trousers, belts, shoes and canes."[66] Already in 1892, African born in the Four Communes were "citizens" of France. The French citizen label mentioned earlier entered their dictionary to mean also dressing in the nicest and latest European fashions. Taste for European styles also rested on the fact that Dakar, Senegal's capital, was given the name "The Paris of Africa."[67]

Visitors also remarked about the power of fashion and the importance of dress as an indicator of wealth, class, and status differences among women in particular. "The ability of Senegalese women to absorb the slightest changes in style is legendary. The reputation for style and elegance that they have nurtured through the years begins with the *signares*."[68] In fact, "women in Senegal, more than most women in Africa, have been preoccupied with manipulating their personal funds to finance the enhancement of their beauty,"[69] noted Marian Ashley Johnson. It was with this background that the *robe bloc* became an important new consumer item among urban women. But its fame was rested primarily on a culture of consumption.

From 1946, the *robe bloc* grew in popularity and by the early 1950s was sending shock waves throughout Senegal. Significant to the popularity of the *robe bloc* as a new fashion was the end of World War II, a period of change in Senegal's economy with an availability of fabrics of all qualities on the market. Between 1945 and 1950, enormous increases in fabric imports had already occurred, while the fashion industry in Senegal increased, thanks to a proliferation of fashion journals, beauty stores, textile factories, shoemakers, barber shops, and tailors (see Figure 12.4).[70] The appeal and popularity of the *robe bloc* were also to some extent influenced by changes in fashion as well.

Over the years, Dakar continued to be the "Paris of Africa," and by the mid-1950s was a place of "fantasy and novelty."[71] Furthermore, the Senegalese woman was referred to as the "Parisian woman of the Black continent"[72] (see Figure 12.5). In addition, "popular magazines with clothing tips for French women in the tropics"[73] and local magazines printed in Senegal, such as *Paris-Dakar* and *Bingo,* featuring fashion tips from France, also influenced changes in fashion. Yet, new trends initiated by women designers increased the appeal of the *robe bloc* as a consumption item. Among them was Fatou Wade, owner of the beauty shop *Au Paradis des Dames*, who first started her career making *robes bloc* in 1946.[74]

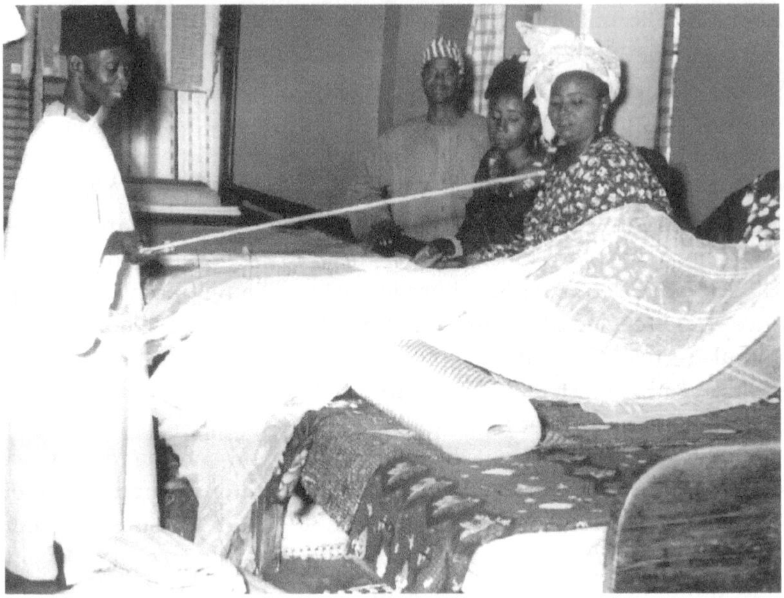

12.4 Pierre Grosse's fabric shop, Dakar, Senegal, 1950.
Image IFAN-CAD. Picture Chérif

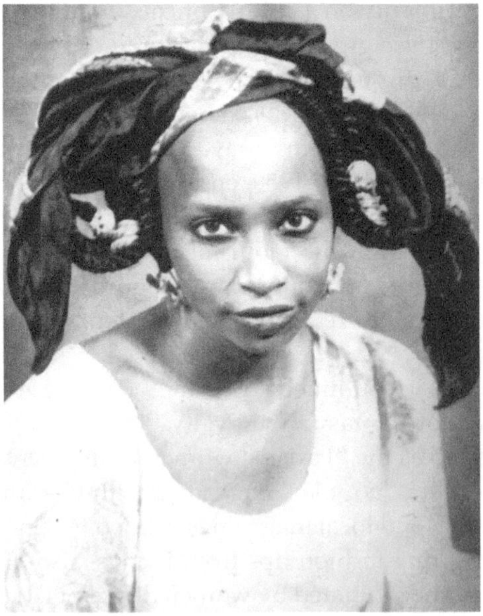

12.5 Wolof woman with Gossi hairstyle, Dakar, Senegal, 1948.
Image IFAN-CAD. Picture Cocheteaux

As the *robe bloc* shifted from political cloth to fashion item, it was associated particularly with the young, urban, and educated. Most educated women, who craved for European clothes, immediately turned to the *robe bloc.* A Senegalese woman writer who lived her childhood in Tilène, a populated neighborhood of Dakar, in the 1950s explained in her biography how as a school student she felt desperate for not wearing any European clothes and complained loudly until her grandmother decided to make a dress for her.[75] In sum, there were many reasons for Senegalese women's fascination with and desire for the *robe bloc*. The dress was favored for its simplicity. Made in one piece, the *robe bloc* was more comfortable than many traditional women's clothes like the wrap and the *grand boubou*, "a long billowy costume with huge sleeves that incorporates yards of colorful fabric."[76] The simplicity of the *robe bloc* offered even more comfort because it eased dance motions for women who wore it and "attended the 'bal poussière,' a mid-1950s' cultural phenomenon that itself was a factor in the popularity of the dress."[77] The *robe bloc* became more attractive when women started to replace the original red color fabrics with a new variety of printed fabrics that flooded the market. So, a woman wearing the *robe bloc* was immediately seen as fashionable.

Wearing the dress also marked a Senegalese woman as *civilisé*, the French for civilized, another label of the French assimilation policy. In Senegal, "the epitome of *civilisé* is the elegant fashionable woman with her carefully tended and adorned body"[78] with European accessories or styles like the *robe bloc*. Finally, the *bloc* style was also associated with married woman status. In his study of jewelry in Senegal, Bodiel Thiam shows that any Senegalese woman married legitimately should have in her jewelry box a *bracelet bloc* and a *ring bloc* that weighed 60 and 8 grams respectively.[79]

The *robe bloc*'s popularity grew as a new consumption item among women as the *Bloc Africain* continued to "attract support mainly in the towns and among many who had no franchise."[80] Two of my informants for this chapter told me that the popularity of the *robe bloc* went beyond the limit of the Four Communes. My own mother, Oulimata Diop, a native of Thiès, recalled having four or five *robes bloc* made with non-red color fabrics. At the question why four dresses of the same style, her answer was because of the popularity of such a style. She told me that the *robe bloc* was so fashionable that on one of her annual visits to her family in the village, her cousins and childhood friends borrowed her *robes bloc* to imitate the fashion.[81] My second informant, Seynabou Diagne, a native of Dakar, told me that the *robe bloc* was more popular in Dakar than anywhere else in Senegal. Her explanation rested on the fact that all new styles or fabrics were first enjoyed by the populations of Dakar, but also because of Dakar's place in the Senegalese political scene of the 1940s–1950s and beyond. She remembered attending with friends almost all Lamine Guèye's meetings in Dakar, all of them wearing *robes bloc*.[82] The popularity of the *robe bloc* in connection to Lamine Guèye and his party, the *Bloc*

African, was so profound that when Guèye left his own party to consolidate the SFIO, women from the Four Communes followed their favorite leader.[83] Later, Lamine Guèye followed his dream to reach a real assimilation with a new decree on his political records: the 1946 Lamine Guèye Law that extends French citizenship to all Africans. Women celebrated this victory as well with another hairstyle called *Kaadu Lamine*, or the Speech of Lamine.[84] Yet, the *robe bloc* remained the most powerful symbol of women's political activism in 1940s–1950s Senegal, as well as a phenomenal consumer item during the same time.

Conclusion

This study opens up clothing to multiple readings and offers readers a deeper understanding of the role played by the *robe bloc* in the political choices of women in 1940s–1950s Senegal. During these decades, Senegalese urban women in particular used clothing to reinvent themselves in powerful new ways. The study also suggests the rich possibilities found in linking material culture to processes of political choices. The example of the *robe bloc* illustrates how a single item or object carried many layers of meanings, with a more flexible symbolic system than even language. Not only did it serve as the unifying symbol of Senegalese women's political victory after winning the right to vote in 1945, but the dress played a significant role in allowing them to express in a powerful way their political roles. Here a cloth is invested with a specified intention, namely the shaping and solidification of political identity, and an effort to influence the political space. Its appeal as political cloth led consequently to its popularity as a new fashion phenomenon, supported by a strong culture of consumption among the Senegalese.

Notes

1. Aili M. Tripp, Dior Konaté, and Colleen Lowe-Morna, "Sub-Saharan Africa: On the Fast Track to Women's Political Representation," in *Women, Quotas and Politics*, ed. Drude Dahlerup, 112–37 (Oxon and New York: Routledge, 2006).
2. H.O. Idowu, "The Establishment of Elective Institutions in Senegal," *Journal of African History* IX (1968): 261.
3. Frederick C. Schaffer, *Democracy in Translation: Understanding Politics in an Unfamiliar Culture* (Ithaca: Cornell University Press, 1998), 14.
4. Alice C. Conklin, *A Mission to Civilize: The Republican Idea of Empire in France and West Africa, 1895–1930* (Stanford: Stanford University Press, 1997), 76–7.
5. Idowu, "The Establishment of Elective Institutions," 268–70.
6. Ibid., 274.

7. Pierre Mille, "The Black Vote in Senegal," *Journal of African Sociology* 1 (1901): 64–79.

8. "For instance in 1922, only about 18,000 voters, 1.5 percent of the indigenous enjoyed full citizenship," in Schaffer, *Democracy in Translation*, 14.

9. Idowu, "The Establishment of Elective Institutions," 274.

10. Jean-Bernard Lacroix and Saliou Mbaye, "Le vote des femmes au Sénégal," *Ethiopiques* 6 (1976): 27. Lacroix and MBaye note "that already in 1871, women showed support to Lafon de Fongauffier, elected Senegal's deputy to the French Parliament, by organizing dance parties and creating songs in his honor, some of them being still remembered today." See also Niang Fatou Siga Niang, *Reflets de modes et traditions Saint-Louisiennes* (Dakar: Editions Khoudia, 1990), 133–5.

11. Lacroix and MBaye, "Le vote des femmes," 29.

12. Ibid., 29.

13. Schaffer, *Democracy in Translation*, 67.

14. Catherine Boone, *Merchant Capital and the Roots of State Power in Senegal, 1930–1985* (New York: Cambridge University Press, 1992), 82.

15. SFIO: French Socialist Party. In Senegal a section of the SFIO had been created during the Popular Front period before World War II.

16. Ruth S. Morgenthau, *Political Parties in French-Speaking West Africa* (Oxford: Clarendon Press, 1964), 137.

17. Lacroix and MBaye, "Le vote des femmes," 34.

18. Morgenthau, *Political Parties*, 137.

19. Hilda Kuper, "Costume and Identity," *Comparative Studies in Society and History* 15 (1973): 348.

20. For more information on textiles, clothes, and clothing, refer to Ruth Barnes and Joanne B. Eicher, eds., *Dress and Gender: Making and Meaning* (New York: Berg, distributed by St Martin's Press, 1992); Annette. B. Weiner and Jane Schneider, eds., *Cloth and the Human Experience* (Washington, DC: Smithsonian Institution Press, 1989).

21. Diana Crane, *Fashion and Its Social Agenda: Class, Gender and Identity in Clothing* (Chicago: University of Chicago Press, 2000), 1.

22. M. Leenhardt, "Pourquoi se vêtir?" *L'Amour de l'Art* 1 (1952): 14.

23. Adeline Masquelier, "Mediating Threads: Clothing and the Texture of Spirit/Medium Relations in Bori (Southern Niger)," in *Clothing and Difference: Embodied Identities in Colonial and Post-Colonial Africa*, ed. Hildi Hendrickson, 66–94 (Durham and London: Duke University Press, 1996), 78.

24. Honoré de Balzac, "Traité de la vie élégante," in *Oeuvres complètes, oeuvres diverses, Paris*, vol. 2 (Paris: Louis Conard, 1938), 105. "Le costume étant le plus énergique symbole, la Révolution fut also un débat entre la soie et le drap."

25. Jane Schneider and Annette B. Weiner, Introduction to *Cloth and the Human Experience*, eds. A. Weiner and J. Schneider (Washington, DC: Smithsonian Institution Press, 1989).

26. Kuper, "Costume and Identity," 364–5.

27. Anne M. Spencer, "In Praise of Heroes: Contemporary African Commemorative Cloths," *African Arts* 16 (1982): 84.

28. Kuper, "Costume and Identity," 358–9.

29. Mona Etienne, "Women and Men. Cloth and Colonization: The Transformation of Production Distribution Relations among the *Baule* (Ivory Coast)," *Cahiers d'Etudes Africaines* 65 (1999): 61.

30. Kathleen E. Rickford, "The ABC's of Cloth and Politics in Ivory Coast," *Afrika Today* 41 (1994): 6.

31. Ibid., 6.

32. Phyllis M. Martin, "Contesting Clothes in Colonial Brazzaville," *Journal of African History* 35 (1994): 423. See also Charles D. Gondola, "Dream and Drama: The Search for Elegance among Congolese Youth," *African Studies Review* 42 (1999): 36.

33. Gondola, "Dream and Drama," 36.

34. Marian A. Johnson, "Gold Jewelry of the Wolof and Tukulor of Senegal," *African Arts* 27 (1994): 48.

35. Ibid., 49.

36. The Front Popular was a coalition of left-wing French parties (Communist Party, SFIO, radical party) that won the 1936 elections. Its achievements in improving social conditions were numerous: union rights, a work shift of 40 hours a week, and paid leaves drew it the support of populations.

37. Adja N'Deye B. Ndiaye, *Collier de Cheville* (Dakar: Nouvelles Editions Africaines, 1983): 67.

38. Ousseynou Faye, "L'habillement et ses accessoires dans les millieux Africains de Dakar, 1857–1960," *Revue Sénégalaise d'Histoire* 1 (1995): 69–86.

39. Djibril Seck, "Histoire des modes vestimentaires chez les jeunes filles à Dakar 1945—1960," Mémoire de Maîtrise, Université Cheikh Anta Diop, 2000.

40. Cheikh F. Faye, "Opinion publique et animation politique: permanence des moyens traditionels dans un contexte colonial," *Historiens Géographes du Sénégal* 6 (1991).

41. Ann Smart Martin, "Material Things and Cultural Meanings: Notes on the Study of Early American Material Culture," *The William and Mary Quarterly* 53 (1996): 12.

42. Phyllis Martin, *Leisure and Society in Colonial Brazzaville* (Cambridge: Cambridge University Press, 1995), 154.

43. Malcolm Bernard, *Fashion as Communication* (London and New York: Routledge, 1996), 6.

44. Kuper, "Costume and Identity," 348.

45. Hildi Hendrickson, "Bodies and Flags: The Representation of Herero Identity in Colonial Namibia," in *Clothing and Difference: Embodied Identities in Colonial and Post-Colonial Africa*, ed. Hildi Hendrickson (Durham and London: Duke University Press, 1996), 215.

46. Schneider and Weiner, "Introduction," in *Cloth and the Human Experience*, 4.

47. Hendrickson, *Clothing and Difference*, 3.

48. Marie-Louise Roberts, "Samson and Delilah Revisited: The Politics of Women's Fashion in 1920s France," *The American Historical Review* 98 (1993): 660.

49. Faye, "Opinion publique," 61.

50. Laura Fair, "Dressing up: Clothing, Class and Gender in Post-Abolition Zanzibar," *Journal of African History* 39 (1998): 93.

51. Johnson, "Gold Jewelry," 38.

52. Morgenthau, *Political Parties*, 138.

53. Ibid., 129.

54. Martin, "Contesting Clothes," 408.

55. Ibid., 408.

56. Seck, "Histoire des modes," 91.

57. Hildi Hendrickson, "Bodies and Flags," 224.

58. Karen T. Hansen, "Transnational Biographies and Local Meanings: Used Clothing Practices in Lusaka," *Journal of Southern African Studies* 21 (1995): 136.

59. Johnson, "Gold Jewelry," 39.

60. Ibid., 39.

61. Bracelet bloc.

62. Rings bloc.

63. Necklaces bloc. For more information on *the bijoux bloc* or *jewelry bloc*, refer to Bodiel Thiam, "La coiffure 'gossip' et les bijoux qui lui sont assortis," *Notes Africaines* 45 (1950): 9–11.

64. The *Jamano Coura* meant literally the Epoch of Coura.

65. Niang, *Reflets de modes*, 33.

66. Duchesse D'Uzès, *Le voyage de mon fils au Congo* (Paris, 1894, 15) quoted by Martin, "Contesting Clothes," 406.

67. Hudita Nura Mustapha, "Portraits of Modernity: Fashioning Selves in Dakarois Popular Photography," in *Images and Empires: Visuality in Colonial and Postcolonial Africa*, eds. Paul S. Landau and Deborah D. Kaspin (Berkeley and Los Angeles: University of California Press, 2002), 177.

68. "*Signares* is a Portuguese name that was given to the *métisse*, women entrepreneurs (mostlyWolof) who contracted marriages with Europeans and who had virtually controlled the coastal trade for several years, beginning in the sixteenth century. Some of these women displayed great wealth in their dress, especially their jewelry, and became arbiters of taste," in Johnson, "Gold Jewelry," 38.

69. Ibid., 38.

70. In his study of fashion trends in colonial Senegal, Djibril Seck shows that "the number of textile factories just in Dakar rose from 7 in 1947 to 12 in 1950 because of the delocalization of some of French factories in Senegal. Also the number of tailors and designers increased from 8 in 1948 to 20 in 1950, while beauty shops were also on the rise with 7 in 1947 to 30 in 1948 due to a high demand in European industrial goods," in Seck, "Histoire des modes," 48.

71. *Bingo* 63 (1958): 20.

72. Ibid., 20.

73. Martin, "Contesting Clothes," 409.

74. Seck, "Histoire des modes," 59.

75. Nafissatou Diallo, *De Tilène au Plateau: une enfance dakaroise* (Dakar: Les Nouvelles Editions Africaines du Sénégal, 1997), 74.

76. Johnson, "Gold Jewelry," 40.

77. Seck, "Histoire des modes," 69.

78. Mustapha, "Portraits of Modernity," 178.

79. Bodiel Thiam, "Coloration des bijoux ouolof en or de basse qualité," *Notes Africaines* 46 (1950): 45.

80. Morgenthau, *Political Parties*, 138.

81. Interview with Oulimata Diop, 72 years old, Thiès, Senegal, December 17, 2008.

82. Interview with Seynabou Diagne, 70 years old, Dakar, Senegal, December 29, 2008.

83. Faye, "Opinion publique," 61.

84. Niang, *Reflets de modes*, 39.

Collecting, Displaying, and Creating Value

13

The Duchess's Shells: Natural History Collecting, Gender, and Scientific Practice

Beth Fowkes Tobin

Born in 1715, Margaret Cavendish Holles Harley inherited her mother's vast fortune and her father's passion for collecting. Her father was Edward Harley, the 2nd Duke of Oxford, and his huge collection of books and manuscripts now make up a significant portion of the manuscripts in the British Library today. Margaret, who married William Bentinck, the 2nd Duke of Portland, was a collector of fine arts, such as drawings by Leonardo da Vinci and Rembrandt, decorative arts such as Italian cameos and French snuffboxes, and antiquities, such as the Portland Vase now housed in the British Museum. But her great love was natural history specimens, which included insects, birds, plants, and above all, shells.[1] According to Thomas Martyn in *The Universal Conchologist* (1784–92), the duchess had the largest and finest shell collection in Britain, if not all of Europe:

> [T]he first praise is confessedly due to the superb collection of the Dutchess Dowager of Portland; so rich a display in the number as well as rarity and perfection of these subjects, together with species of marine productions, perhaps is not to be equalled. In this branch of science her Grace's superior knowledge is as well known as it is eminently demonstrated, in the critical arrangement of this immense cabinet, which altogether justifies the very great expense of time and money employed in the formation of it.[2]

When she died, her collections of shells, coins, art, classical statuary, and other antiquities, including the Portland Vase, were sold at auction, her shells constituting the majority of the items for sale. At this auction, which lasted 38 days, were collectors and their agents from Britain and Europe, who bought her shells as they were eager to possess her conchological treasures, some of which were very rare, including those she acquired from Cook's voyages to the Pacific.[3]

Not only did she amass and organize one of Britain's most important shell collections, she also collected plants, birds, and insects, and she oversaw the construction of a botanical garden, a hot-house, a menagerie, and an aviary at Bulstrode, her country house in Buckinghamshire, which became, like the British Museum, an important center for the study of natural history. At the center of a network of naturalists and collectors, she welcomed to Bulstrode Sir Joseph Banks, the President of the Royal Society, Daniel Solander, premier taxonomist and British Museum curator, and several other important figures including the famed botanical illustrator, Georg Dionysis Ehret, naturalist Thomas Pennant, the author of *British Zoology*, and Dr Thomas Shaw, professor at Oxford.[4]

How did the Duchess of Portland acquire her magnificent shell collection? What were the means by which she accumulated her shells? Answering these questions is no simple matter since she was relatively silent on the matter; methods for collecting shells are infrequent topics in her letters. However, there are clues to her collecting and classifying practices in her correspondence with three of her friends and fellow collectors: Richard Pulteney, a provincial doctor, amateur botanist, and author of a book on botany; Henry Seymer, a country gentleman, amateur natural history artist, and an avid collector of natural history specimens; and John Timothy Swainson, an amateur conchologist and customs official, whose bureaucratic assignments on the seacoast suited his hobby perfectly. Also helpful in reconstructing the culture of shell collecting and its material practices are the letters of Mary Delany, the duchess's dearest friend.[5] Since they spent much of their widowhood together, Mrs Delany was in a position to observe the duchess, and as Mrs Delany was also a shell worker, we can extrapolate from Mrs Delany's techniques and practices to glimpse the duchess's engagement with the material culture of shell collecting.

Gender and Science

Margaret Cavendish Bentinck's method of acquiring shells has been described by David Elliston Allen, a prominent historian of science, as "purely monetary in character, inasmuch as her activities did not extend beyond employing people herself or making payments for specimens."[6] Although Allen is right that she did purchase shells from dealers such as George Humphrey and had agents and acquaintances who collected on her behalf, he is wrong to conclude that these were her only methods of acquiring shells. To complicate our understanding of the duchess's collecting practices, I examine in this chapter what has been completely overlooked by historians of science: the fact that she was herself a specimen hunter. Her shell-hunting expeditions, given the limitations of her position in society, were confined to England; she journeyed not like James Cook to the South Pacific, but to the south coast of England, where she collected several new specimens, which were eagerly sought after when she died. Several of these English shells were purchased at the Portland auction by other collectors, finding their way into Edward Donovan's collection. Donovan's five-volume catalog, *Natural History of British Shells* (1799–1803), contains illustrations of some of the duchess's domestic shells.

In addition to suggesting that there is much more to the duchess's collecting activities than merely purchasing specimens, this chapter will also argue that the duchess's involvement with her collection went well beyond an exclusive concern with acquisition. She was actively engaged in the classification of her shells, and, having mastered the principles of Linnaean taxonomy, was quite adept at identifying her specimens' taxon. Far from evincing a "bowerbird mentality," as Allen writes, the duchess was a systematic collector who was deeply earnest about organizing and arranging her collection along scientific principles.[7] Allen's unfortunate bird metaphor, combined with his statement that she was an "inveterate collector of almost everything,"[8] conveys the notion that she was indiscriminate, thoughtless, and instinctive in her collecting—as if she were feathering her nest with flashy, shiny, bright objects. Allen's statements imply that she was an accumulator and not a collector. Women have often been characterized as accumulators since proper collecting involves organization, system, and arrangement, cognitive capabilities sometimes thought to be beyond women's abilities.[9] This chapter is an attempt to refute these disparaging characterizations of the duchess's collecting practices to argue that not only did she go out into the field to collect natural history specimens, she also worked at classifying her collections, and in the process of doing both of these activities, she was engaged in creating new knowledge about nature.

To support my assertion that she was a naturalist, I attempt in this chapter to recover her activities as a shell collector, focusing on the minutia of shell collecting. The material culture of shell collecting, I contend, contains the traces of an epistemology built upon specific material-based activities located at the intersection of touch and sight, where the tangible was as central as the visible in the production of knowledge about nature. For late eighteenth- and early nineteenth-century naturalists, description and classification of nature were their goals. Central to these activities were the physicality of the specimen, its visual and verbal representation in a book, and the process of moving back and forth between the specimen in one hand and the reference book in the other hand; this was the period's techne—the triangulation of eye, book, and object—that produced natural knowledge.[10] In documenting the material culture of shell collecting, I am trying to recover an embodied form of knowledge making, in short, a scientific praxis that belonged to a period and ethos that was dominated by the talented amateur who was not a professionalized or specialized technician or scientist. Also, in detailing the duchess's activities and those of her fellow collectors, I also hope to convey the amount of energy, movement, and activity that went into shell collecting. This is important to keep in mind as this flies in the face of the supposed indolence and physical passivity of the interred life of middle- and upper-class women of this period. And lastly, in detailing the material practices of shell collecting, this chapter will provide an outline of the processes by which a shell became a natural history specimen, charting the physical transformations it underwent and the conceptual categories it transversed as it moved from the out of doors—the seashore, the pond, or some soggy pasture—to the cotton-lined drawers of the collector's mahogany cabinet, a process by which it accrued value as an object of beauty, curiosity, and scientific inquiry.

Since science tends to forget its material and social origins,[11] my goal here is to recover the body's engagement with the making of natural knowledge: the soggy socks and shoes damp from walking in the squishy mud flats and sandy stretches left exposed by the ebbing tides as one searches for clams buried beneath the surface; the snails, not dead yet, that try to crawl out of the wicker basket into which they were dropped; the feel of the bristles of the boar's brush as one scours the shell's epidermis; the burn of the acid solution used to remove debris from shells as it splashed on one's hands; the smell of the putrid bodies of mollusks that waft off of shells and the sight of maggots as they crawl out of shells not thoroughly cleaned; the commandeering of playing cards to serve as the cardboard from which little boxes are made to house one's shells; the careful packing of specimens in boxes, embedding them in sawdust or sand so they will not break; and the tricky business of gluing tiny labels onto shells.

Collecting in the Field

As a field collector, the duchess went out into the countryside in Buckinghamshire to look for land and freshwater snails. Gathering specimens unknown to her and returning home to Bulstrode to clean the shells, she then sorted and arranged them, putting them in cabinets and eventually classifying them. She performed these activities sometimes with the help of other visiting naturalists and interested members of her household, including Rev. John Lightfoot, J. Agnew, her gardener turned illustrator, and Georg Ehret, the great botanical artist, who lived at Bulstrode in the late 1760s where he drew hundreds of plant illustrations. Gathering, arranging, classifying, and displaying botanical and zoological specimens were activities that were an important part of the duchess's life at Bulstrode. As a witness to these botanizing and conchilizing activities, Mrs Delany describes how the duchess's passion for natural history transformed space at Bulstrode, turning "her Grace's breakfast room" into a "repository of sieves, pans, platters, and filled with all the productions of *that* nature, [which] are spread on tables, windows, chairs, which with books of all kinds, (opened to their useful places) make an agreeable confusion; sometimes, not withstanding twelve chairs and a couch, it is indeed a little difficult to find a seat."[12]

Land and freshwater mollusks were found on the grounds of Bulstrode, the duchess finding a *Tellina lacustris* in a river nearby. Canals, rivers, marshes, ponds, and the ditches of a wet and soggy countryside were popular places for conchologists to search for new specimens, and Bulstrode proved to be as productive as any place in England to collect freshwater mollusks. In a river near Bulstrode, J. Agnew, her gardener, found a *Patella oblonga*, a freshwater limpet, "adhering to the leaves of the *Iris pseudacorus*,"[13] and Lightfoot wrote a paper on it, publishing it in the *Philosophical Transactions of the Royal Society*.[14] Evidently John Timothy Swainson, father of the naturalist and author William Swainson, was invited to Bulstrode to participate in a collecting expedition as he found a snail "in a canal at Bulstrode," a *Helix polita*, very rare, as he notes in his manuscript catalog.[15] Land snails were also found at Bulstrode, hiding often in "humid spots covered by herbage, rank grass, &c.; beneath the bark, or within the hollows of old trees, crevices of rocks, walls, bones, &c."[16]

How did the duchess and her naturalist colleagues collect these land and freshwater shells? What kind of tools—nets, shovels, baskets—did she take with her as she rambled over the countryside, stopping at ditches and ponds to look for mollusks? This information is not laid out explicitly in her letters and Mrs Delany does not mention anything more explicit than "bags" and "boxes," nor do her correspondents explain in any detail about what kind of equipment might have been needed for such collecting expeditions. However, we can turn to several eighteenth- and nineteenth-century guides to collecting and preserving natural history specimens for detailed accounts of the material culture of natural history collecting. In a pamphlet entitled "Short Instructions for Collecting Shells," written early in the nineteenth century to teach prospective collectors where to find shells and how to gather them, the author suggests that early mornings in rainy weather are best for land snails, and rivers, lakes, brooks, and canals are best for freshwater snails, often found under vegetation. As for bivalves, "muscles and such like," they can be found "under the mud." For snails, which might cling to plants in the water, the author recommends using a net, "such as used to land fish with," offering advice on ways to make this net transportable: "by having four joints to the hoop of this net, it may be folded up, so as to go into the pocket; and by a stout screw, may be fixed to the end of a thick walking stick." For the freshwater bivalves, he states: "it will be necessary to employ a boy, or other person, to wade for them, as they are often a foot or more under the mud."[17] Writing in the 1820s, William Swainson, the son of the duchess's friend and fellow collector, details what he regards as the proper implements for collecting shells:

> The principal of these [implements] is a ladle or spoon, made of tin or thin iron, 5 inches long and 3½ wide, with a rim about an inch in height: it should have a short hollow handle, by which it may be fixed to the end of a long walking stick; the middle should be perforated with holes, no larger than is sufficient for the passage of water. This instrument is very useful in fishing for small river shells, or for sifting fine sand on the sea-shore … In searching for the larger freshwater bivalves, a landing net, with very small meshes, is of great service, and it may be made to fit upon the same stick as that which receives the spoon already described.[18]

In addition to nets and spoon-like shovels, also necessary were "small tin boxes and bags for containing specimens."[19] One pamphlet suggests that "[w]hen collecting, it will be proper to have with you a covered basket to put the shells in, to prevent their getting broke, and some of them, particularly the land shells, from creeping away."[20]

Like the duchess, John Timothy Swainson was an enthusiastic field collector, and fortunately for us, his record, in the form of a small notebook, with notations in various ink colors, which functioned as a catalog of where and when he found his British shells, has survived and is now at the Natural History Museum in London.[21] Proud that many of his British shells were "principally of my own collecting," Swainson found many of his land and freshwater snails when he was stationed as a customs officer in London.[22] He and the shell dealer George Humphrey (G.H. in this manuscript) would go out together to Battersea, then undeveloped wetlands, in search of shells. Referring to a *Turbo bidens*, he says he "found them with G.H. in an Osier Ground near the Mills [an inn] in Battersea fields." He also notes that he found a *Sabella dentale-formis* "in a pond in the Garden of an Inn before the ascent into Barnet Midd[lesex] on the left hand in 1783," a *Nerita fluviatilis* "in the Thames adhering to Stones & old Tiles above Kingston," and a *Helix contorta* "in the ditches in Rotherhith Marshes with G.H." Swainson's notebook of his British shells states not only where he found shells but also where his friends found the shells that they then gave to him. For example, next to *Turbo bidens*, he comments: "found many years ago by G.H.'s sister on the N side of the Serpentine in Hyde park," and next to *Helix octona*, he notes "found by G.H. near Elms Battersea." It is in Swainson's notebook that we find more information about the duchess's field collecting.

From the elder Swainson's notebook, we learn that not only did the duchess find land snails and freshwater mollusks on the grounds of her country estate, but she also spent time at the seashore collecting specimens. Of the several shells he received as gifts from her, many were from Weymouth, on the south coast of England. He notes in his catalog that his specimen of the *Trochus papillosus* was "found by the D: of Portland at

Weymouth & had from her," his *Strombus pespelecani* was found "at Weym: by the D. of P.," his *Bulla patula* was "given me by the D of Pd found by her at Weym," *Venus undata* was "found by Dss. Portland off Weymouth," his *Patella groeca* was "found by the D of P off Weymouth," his *Mya declivis* was "found by the D of P off Weymouth," and of his *Cardium tuberculatum*, he writes: "my large specimen given me by GH/ found at Weym by the D. of Portland, escaped Dr. Solr. most probably found after his disease." The last entry conveys the complexity of the shell exchange circuit with Humphrey either giving or selling this shell to Swainson, a shell which Humphrey most probably had bought at the Portland auction, this shell having been found by the duchess at Weymouth sometime between 1782 and 1785, the year she died.

The majority of the shells the Duchess of Portland discovered came from Weymouth, a place she went to visit often as it was near her married daughter's residence (she married Thomas Thynne, 3rd Viscount Weymouth, who eventually became 1st Marquess of Bath). She was one of several naturalists who frequented Weymouth, which was rich in shell and fossil specimens.[23] In one of the few statements issued by the duchess about her own collecting practices, she wrote to the naturalist Thomas Pennant about two shells she had collected herself. As usual, she is always polite and even deferential to her correspondents in her shell network:

> I am always glad of an opportunity of Obeying your Commands as my stay in Town will be very short I sent to Mr Brown & gave him the two Shells you desired to have drawn & a new Solen or mytilus which I found last year at Weymouth which they tell me has not been described but if you don't chuse to take the drawing of that shell I told Mr Brown I wou'd have it.[24]

Brown was illustrating Pennant's *British Zoology*, and the duchess had given him a few of her very rare shells to draw and engrave for Pennant's volume on shells.

The duchess's visits to Weymouth were opportunities for her to indulge her love of natural history, to collect specimens, and to experience freedom from the demands and restraints of her social rank as she wandered for hours along the shore. While visiting Weymouth in 1771, she received a letter from Rev. Lightfoot, stating how glad he was to hear that she was in good health and to hear "that Weymouth had wonderfully recovered your Grace's Health & Spirits … Three or four hours daily Exercise or Motion in the open Air, your wholesome sea Breezes, your Sand Grottos, but above all the odoriferous Fragrancy of sea … & sea shells, cannot fail to brace up the languid System … ."[25] The duchess's love of the seashore continued well into her late sixties, though Weymouth's pleasures diminished with the death of her friend Mrs LeCoq, an expert specimen hunter, who had resided in Weymouth. In 1782 she wrote: "I propose setting out for Margate next week to try if the sea air has still the same Efficacy, for alas, I can never think of Weymouth again since the loss of my kind affectionate Friend Mrs. LeCoq."[26]

The shells that the Duchess of Portland found at Weymouth were accumulated in a variety of ways. She sometimes found shells by walking the beach, often accompanied by Mrs Le Coq. Describing an excursion to the beach to look for specimens, the duchess wrote to Mrs Delany:

> The other day I was on the beach, the wind blew a brisk gale; I got into a little sand grotto, and read your charming letter over and over while Mrs. Le Cocq (sic) was traveling about in search of shells, butterflys, and plants. Mr. Lightfoot desires his best compts; he goes away on Monday, and I hope to set out next Thursday. He has traversed all the island of Portland in search of plants, but has met with nothing new, neither animals nor vegetables—and has been very seasick, but he will give you a better history of his adventures than I can do, for I have no time as I expect visitors … .[27]

The duchess's fondness for Weymouth as a place to hunt for shells continued until the death of Mrs LeCoq, after which she substituted Margate for Weymouth. Even with this shift in location, the duchess continued her practice of walking the shoreline in search of shells in the summers of 1782 and 1784. Here she was sometimes not as successful finding shells as she wished: "This air is very good & I have found great benefit from it but by way of amusement[.] except very pleasant airings there is none[,] not a shell to be met with tho' I have been very diligent in my searches."[28] Perhaps such disappointments were offset by meeting, in Margate, J.T. Swainson, someone who shared her passion for collecting shells. She gave him shells, went to his apartments to examine his shell collection, and it is possible that they went out together to comb the shoreline for new specimens, the duchess writing to Mrs Delany that "he will be a good acquisition" to her community of natural history enthusiasts.[29]

This sociability of shell collecting that we glimpse in the duchess's correspondence is conveyed in greater detail in Mrs Delany's letters from the 1750s when she was an avid shellworker in Ireland:

> Yesterday at five o'clock in the afternoon we took a boat and went to a shore about a mile off to gather shells, where we found a vast variety of beauties. We were very merry in our work, but much merrier in our return home, for five of us, viz., Phill, Mrs. Don, Mr Lloyd, and a young clergyman (who is here very often, one Mr Langton), and Penelope all mounted a cart, and home we drove as jocund as ever five people were.[30]

She traveled modest distances to gather shells: "The coach is at the door, and we are going to Burdoyl, a strand about six miles off, in search of shells" for making "festoons of shell flowers in their natural colours, that are to go over the bow window."[31] The pleasures of travel to the seashore and of walking the beach in search of seashells were heightened and intensified by sharing the experience with others who were also passionate about collecting natural history specimens, a practice that appealed to fancy workers as well as collectors.

Walking on the beach at low tide or after a storm were popular ways of finding shells. William Swainson, J.T. Swainson's son, suggested that the "best time" to find marine shells was at "the lowest ebb of the tide":

> The rocks, corals and stones, which are then left exposed should be carefully examined for chitons, limpets, ear-shells, and other adhesive tribes, which are fixed upon the surface, or shelter themselves in the crevices: they are detached by suddenly passing a knife between them and the substance they are upon. Muscles, and other gregarious bivalves, furnished with a byssus, likewise occur in such situations. Whereever the rock, mud, or sand is pierced with round holes, the collector may be tolerably sure of finding bivalves: they are procured either by breaking the rock with a hammer, or digging into the sand or mud with a spade. The little puddles of salt water, left by the tide, are the habitations of many univalve shells; and other will be found beneath loose stones and sea-weeds.[32]

At low tide, those collectors and their assistants who were inclined to dig in the sand and mud would have found at "the depth of two or three feet ... many various tribes of Cockles, Clams, Razors, Purrs, and other double shells, many of which spirit up the water, or sink the surface of their beds, by which they may be discovered." In addition to examining tide pools and the mud flats that are exposed by the receding tide, collectors could explore in the shallow water the sand banks that were too deeply submerged at high tide and which were full of "thorny and other oysters, worms, Suns, Purples, and various other kinds of Shells."[33] Also recommended as a good time to search for shells on the beach was after a storm, for "[a]fter a gale of wind, or violent storm, the shore should be immediately visited, as fine shells are frequently to be met with: if the line of coast is extensive, a few boys should be engaged to assist in the search. This must be done quickly; for it not infrequently happens, that the next flow of the tide takes away every shell."[34]

In addition to looking for shells on her own and in the company of Mrs Le Coq and Rev. Lightfoot, the duchess must have employed others, fishermen most likely, to dredge for shells just off the coast of Weymouth. Several of the shells she discovered at Weymouth were found with dredging, for as J.T. Swainson's notebook testifies, his *Tennens fausta* was "dredged up at Weymouth, under the inspection of the late duchess dowager of Portland," and his *Mya pubescens* was "first noticed by the last duchess-dowager of Portland" and "Dredged up at Waymouth" (sic). His *Venus undata, Mya declivis pubescent,* and *Patella groeca* were found "by Dss. Portland off Weymouth," the word "off" suggesting dredging, a technique adapted from the way in which fishermen would use a drag-net or trawling net to gather oysters and scallops.[35] A dredge, basically a net on an iron frame or bucket, would be lowered to the sea floor and dragged to gather shellfish that rarely made it to shore alive or intact. If using a dredge with a net, larger shells would be captured while the sand and other small debris sifted back down to the seabed floor. Dredging was an effective method for harvesting live shellfish and could yield high quality specimens for collectors. J.T. Swainson dredged for shells, noting this activity in his manuscript catalog and stating, for instance, that his *Patella ungarica* was "got by dredging off Fowey" and his *Murex dispectus* was "dredged up off Margate in 1783," this perhaps occurring during the duchess's visit to Margate that summer. Though his biographer Nora McMillan suggests that Swainson may have been the first conchologist to use dredge and trawl for obtaining marine specimens,[36] dredging was a technique that the duchess had employed with great skill and success well before Swainson did.

Emanuel Mendes da Costa, Edward Donovan, John Mawe, William Swainson, and other authors of instructional pamphlets and collecting guide books cautioned their readers that most shells when found on the beach were "dead shells," often discolored by the sun, fragmented or distorted, having been pecked by birds and agitated by waves, and suggested dredging as a remedy for this problem as the best way to insure perfect specimens and, even better, shells with their animals live in them. Da Costa explained how important the live animals were, not only for classifying the shell, but also for keeping the shell at its best:

> It is always necessary, if possible, to get them alive, or with the animals in them. It not only instructs us in the natural history of the very animals, a part extremely useful to a thorough knowledge of Shells … but it also preserves the Shell in its perfect nature and beauty; for only live Shells bear the full glow of their colours.[37]

The younger Swainson advises prospective shell hunters to use "the *trawl*, or dragging net, upon a productive coast," as it "will generally bring up a variety of living shellfish." However, before trawling, Swainson cautions that it is important to ascertain whether the seabed contains live shellfish, and the best way to tell if a coast is productive is to examine the beach for dead and broken shells, which will indicate what species might be found beyond the shoreline. "The trawl should be tried in every direction, both in deep and shallow water; and when once the shelly ground has been discovered, the collector may calculate upon procuring a variety of species peculiar to such waters."[38] Trawling or dredging required the collector to be able to read the shoreline for indications of the kind of shells that might have been located off the shoreline. The duchess was regarded an expert on dredging; Thomas Pennant, author of *British Zoology*, referred an amateur naturalist, a Dr Cordiner, to her so that she could answer his questions about the various ways to dredge. As an experienced field collector, the duchess was an able interpreter of shell matter strewn across the beach, and a capable director of dredging activities since she was the first to discover many offshore species this way.[39] The fact that the duchess was a field collector and the discoverer of many unknown and unnamed specimens testifies to her knowledge of conchology and to her very high level of engagement with scientific collecting, a commitment to scientific praxis that went well beyond fashionable consumption and polite science, and which, I believe, should earn her the appellation of naturalist.

Classification

Since most commentators describe the duchess as a connoisseur, meaning someone with a bit of knowledge, much money, and an abundance of good taste, it is important to complicate this picture by pointing out not only her activities as a field collector but also her engagement with classifying her own collection. To understand her relationship to her collection and to glimpse her ambitions for it, we need to take a look at how she thought about the process of classifying her collection and examine the principles of arrangement that she employed to give it coherence and order.

The duchess's letters to Pulteney are full of concern over proper classification of her shells. Though she acknowledges that she was dependent on Lightfoot, and later Solander, to name new shells, she did the work of sorting and identifying her shells more than competently and was able to recognize what was a new shell. She used Linnaean nomenclature, following his system and checking her shells against those described and illustrated in such "authorities" as Martin Lister, *De cochleis tam terrestribus quam fluviatilibus exoticis, seu, quae non omnino in Anglia inveniantur, liber* (1685) and Dezillier d'Argenville's *L'Histoire Naturalle Eclaircie dans … la Conchyliologie* (1742). We can see how she used her natural history reference books to classify specimens (she owned copies of Lister's and d'Argenville's books) in the following passage, which was quoted in the beginning of this essay, about the way in which "her Grace's breakfast room" was turned into a "repository of sieves, pans, platters, and filled with all the productions of *that* nature, [which] are spread on tables, windows, chairs, which with books of all kinds, (opened to their useful places) make an agreeable confusion; sometimes, not withstanding twelve chairs and a couch, it is indeed a little difficult to find a seat."[40] She also used shell books written by contemporaries, many of whom she knew personally; she knew more than enough to recognize and correct their mistakes. Though she did not confront Pennant with his errors, she confided in Pulteney that Pennant had made some mistakes in the fourth volume of *British Zoology*. Writing to Pulteney, she asked him: "have you seen Pennants book of shells I think it will be of use tho' there are mistakes, & some might be added to it."[41] She complained to Pulteney on another occasion that Humphrey and da Costa's series, *Conchology*, was full of errors.

In the following letter, which I quote at length, we see how she approached the problem of classification, how committed she was to proper Linnaean terminology, and how she was politely and subtly critical of dealers like Humphrey who labeled shells using such common names as "poached egg," "Rockbead," or "Midas's Ear"[42]:

I am not sufficiently acquainted with the names the Dealers give to Shells but the only long shaped patella I recollect is not the same as the Patella unguis of Lin. & which I have sent you. Humphreys and da Costa give strange names to the Shells the latter shou'd know better but he is being Inaccurate in his descriptions ... I have sent you a Box of Shells according to the inclosed Catalogue by the Blandford Waggon Car. pd. which set out at this day April 9th & I hope will arrive safe. I fear you will find I have made many mistakes for want of assistance but hope you will pardon it. You will observe some Chasms but my Solens Tellina's have not been named; when Mr Lightfoot was in Town before Xmas he intended putting the Linnaean names to them but the Asterias took up so much time that it was not in his power. I have stuck on the names to each shell but the small ones are put in separate papers with the name of each Shell, that you will be carefull in unpacking the little Boxes. I hope the tender ones will not be broke & you will have as much amusement in looking them over as I had in sorting them.[43]

In another letter, sent in June the same year, she wrote to Pulteney with her usual mix of self-deprecation and polite criticism, lodged this time at Linnaeus, in her attempt to clear up some confusion over identifying shells Pulteney had sent her to classify. She mentions that there is a problem with classifying the *Mytilus frons* as such, and hopes that Solander will have time to deal with finding the proper class for this shell, something that he did eventually get to and which became a part of his larger project to revise and expand upon Linnaeus's categories. Linnaeus presented problems as a guide to nomenclature because, as she argues, he based his categories on a collection that was too small. The duchess's letters subtly critique Linnaeus's shortfalls while managing to maintain a proper feminine demeanor.

I have endeavoured to follow your directions & am sorry I have been able to mark so few in the Linnaeus but there are many hundreds he has not seen & consequently made many mistakes in his annotations ... I am very sorry I made a blunder in arranging my list of Volutes ... It is probable there may be a mistake in the Mytilus Frons which when free Dr. Solander will enquire into. The Murex serobilalor [?] is a very rare shell tho' mediterranean. I go to Bullstrode on Monday. I hope next winter to have another Cargo of Shells for you & if Dr Solander don't go a voyage [sic] it will be a great service in the Science of Shells[.] I shou'd not image the Strombus tuberculaby & the new Zealand Shell called Hercules Club the same[;] it is quite a new shell to me & above thirty others from new Zealand.[44]

Though she is quite modest about her knowledge and quite open about what she did not know, Pulteney often defers to her expertise, as does Henry Seymer, another one of her correspondents and a shell collector. In the 1770s, he wrote to Pulteney about his failed efforts at classifying his shells and his hopes that the duchess would help him with the Linnaean system: "If the Ds does not assist me greatly, I shall jumble them together as formerly."[45] Pulteney would often send her boxes of shells for her to examine and compare with those in her cabinet, hoping she would catch whether he had made any mistakes classifying these shells. He writes:

> I have packed up in a Box, and sent by the Coach today as single Valve (for I have not a pair) of that Shell which I have always taken for the Venus pensylvania; and I shall be glad to have it determined from your Grace's Cabinet ... but as your Grace can ... recollect such, from having several times honoured my Cabinet with your Inspection, you will easily correct such Errors where they occur.[46]

On another occasion, Pulteney sent the duchess 98 shells and a numbered list, ranging from 1 to 98, asking questions about each shell, to which the duchess replied, writing on the right-hand side of the list, what she knew about these shells. For example, Putleney wrote: "If this shell is named Dr P will be obliged to the Duchess of Portland, for the general term." The duchess replied on the same sheet of paper right next to this query, "Mya" and "not described," meaning that Solander had named the shell's genus, but had not written a description of it yet.[47] Though Solander (and Lightfoot on occasion) did the work of naming the shells, the duchess was involved enough in the process to know what shells had been named, how much Solander had done, and how much was left to do. Pulteney was always writing to her and sending her his lists of unidentified shells. Though she might have just passed them on to Solander to work on when he came to Whitehall on his weekly visit, the duchess was in charge of this flow of information and was clearly up-to-date on Solander's progress in classifying her collection.

Pulteney would also send her wish lists—shells he wanted—with the idea that she would locate the duplicates in her collection and send them to him. "I take the liberty to trouble your Grace with a list of those Sea Shells mentioned by Mr. Pennant in his Book & not referred to Linnaeus by him. If Duplicates of any of these should occur to Your Grace may I beg the favour of a Duplicate."[48] He also sent her shells that he could not name himself, hoping that Solander might find them interesting and name them for him, and he loaned her shells to fill out the few "chasms" she had in her collection so that Solander could have as complete as range of shells as possible, as he was engaged in a significant recalibration of Linnaean taxonomy, a project that was left unfinished by his untimely death in 1782.

The Duchess of Portland's commitment to the science of her shells can be seen most clearly in her ambition to publish a catalog of her shell collection. Not content to merely possess the collection, but to produce a catalog with the most up-to-date descriptions and names based on one of the largest and (at that time) most complete collections of shells, she employed Solander to name and to help arrange her collection with the idea that they were working collaboratively toward the goal of publishing the definitive shell catalog. By publishing a catalog of her collection, she intended to make her collection available to the world for consultation, hoping that others would benefit from the massive scale of her collection and its most complete-to-date series of species within the classes laid out by Linnaeus. Solander's death in 1782 and hers in 1785 put a stop to these ambitions. What would have been the definitive shell catalog of the era became a sales catalog. In her will she had stipulated that all her natural history specimens were to be sold at auction, and Solander's descriptions of her shells were what Lightfoot worked from when he wrote the auction catalog, *Portland Museum*.[49]

Conclusion

Long overlooked within the fields of history of science, women's history, cultural history, and museum studies, Margaret Cavendish Bentinck, the 2nd Duchess of Portland, merits our attention for her activities as a collector and as a naturalist.[50] Too often natural history collecting has been dismissed as an exercise in privilege and connoisseurship. With the exception of Paula Findlen's masterful study of late Renaissance Italian naturalists and Marjorie Swann's engaging examination of seventeenth-century English collecting, natural history collecting practices have not received the scholarly attention that early modern experimental science has received. In particular, shell collecting, perhaps because of its conflation with the aesthetic presentation of objects, has been largely overlooked as scientific praxis. As Emma Spary has argued, the material culture of natural history collections has yet to be fully explored as a mechanism for producing scientific knowledge.[51] It is important to recognize that natural history collectors, such as the duchess, were engaged with foundational questions concerning the organization of the natural world. Collectors of natural history specimens were ultimately exploring the tension between order in nature and the variety of life, testing systems based on Linnaean taxonomy against the plentitude and variation of life. These activities were at the heart of the Enlightenment's project of bringing concepts of systematic order to bear on the natural world.[52]

Notes

Acknowledgements: The National Science Foundation's support of a Scholars Award made writing this essay possible. The librarians at the Linnean Society and at the Zoology and General libraries of the Natural History Museum in London have been most helpful, encouraging, and generous with their time and materials. The British Academy also provided a fellowship which enabled research in England.

1. Peter Dance's work on shells is invaluable to understanding the history of shell collections. See *Shell Collecting: An Illustrated History* (Berkeley: University of California Press, 1966), and the revised version, *A History of Shell Collecting* (Leiden: Brill, 1986).

2. Thomas Martyn, *The Universal Conchologist* (London, 1784–92), 10.

3. For shells from Cook's voyages, see P.J.P. Whitehead, "A Guide to the Dispersal of Zoological Material from Captain Cook's Voyages," *Pacific Studies* (1978): 52–93, and "Zoological Specimens from Captain Cook's Voyages," *Journal of the Society for the Bibliography of Natural History* 5 (1969): 161–201. See also G.L. Wilkins, "A Catalogue and Historical Account of the Banks Shell Collection," *Bulletin of the British Museum of Natural History* 1 (1955): 71–119, and "The Cracherode Shell Collection," *Bulletin of the British Museum of Natural History* 4 (1957): 121–84.

4. She also met the philosopher Jean-Jacques Rousseau during his stay in Britain, and he wrote about how much he enjoyed botanizing with her.

5. For women's friendships, see Lisa L. Moore, "Queer Gardens: Mary Delany's Flowers and Friendships," *Eighteenth-Century Studies* 39 (2005): 49–70, and Sylvia H. Myers, *The Bluestocking Circle: Women, Friendship, and the Life of the Mind in Eighteenth-Century England* (Oxford: Oxford University Press, 1990).

6. David Elliston Allen, "Naturalists in Britain: Some Tasks for the Historian," XVI in *Naturalists and Society: The Culture of Natural History in Britain, 1700–1800* (Aldershot: Ashgate Variorum, 2001), 97.

7. David Elliston Allen, *The Naturalists in Britain: A Social History* [1976] (Princeton: Princeton University Press, 1995), 25.

8. David Elliston Allen, "Tastes and Crazes," in *Cultures of Natural History*, eds. N. Jardine, J.A. Secord, and E.C. Spary, 394–407 (Cambridge: Cambridge University Press, 1996), 397. For feminist work on women and science, see Ann Shteir, *Cultivating Women, Cultivating Science: Flora's Daughters and Botany in England, 1760–1860* (Baltimore: Johns Hopkins University Press, 1996), and Londa Schiebinger, *Nature's Body: Gender in the Making of Modern Science* (Boston: Beacon Press, 1993). See also Sally Festing, "Rare Flowers and Fantastic Breeds: The 2nd Duchess of Portland and Her Circle," *Country Life* 12 (June 1986): 1684–6, and 19 (June 1986): 1772–4.

9. Susan Pearce, a leader in museum studies, critiques this prevalent notion concerning the difference between men's and women's collecting practices in *Museums, Objects, and Collections* (Washington, DC: Smithsonian Institution Press, 1993). See also Russell W. Belk and Melanie Wallendorf, "Of Mice and Men: Gender Identity in Collecting," in *The Material Culture of Gender: The Gender of Material Culture*, eds. Kenneth Ames and Katherine Martinez, 7–27 (Ann Arbor, MI: University of Michigan Press, 1997).

10. See Bruno Latour, "Visualization and Cognition: Thinking with Eyes and Hands," *Knowledge and Society* 6 (1986): 1–40, and John Law and Michael Lynch, "Lists, Field Guides, and the Descriptive Organization of Seeing; Birdwatching as an Exemplary Observational Activity," *Human Studies* 11, nos. 2/3 (1988): 271–304.

11. For the link between disembodiment and scientific value, see Steven Shapin and Christopher Lawrence, "Introduction: The Body of Knowledge," in *Science Incarnate: Historical Embodiments of Natural Knowledge*, eds. Christopher Lawrence and Steven Shapin, 1–19 (Chicago: University of Chicago Press, 1998).

12. Mary Delany, *The Autobiography and Correspondence of Mary Granville, Mrs. Delany, [first series]: with Interesting Reminiscences of King George III and Queen Charlotte*, ed. Lady Llanover (London: R. Bentley, 1862), IV: 238.

13. Edward Donovan, *Natural History of British Shells*, 5 volumes (London, 1799–1803), vol. 5., Plate CL, n.p.

14. John Lightfoot, *Philosophical Transactions of the Royal Society* 76 (1786): 160–70, 167.

15. John Timothy Swainson, "MS Catalogue of British Shells in the Possession of J.T. Swainson," Natural History Museum, London (hereafter NHM), Zoology Library, Mollusca 1, n.p.

16. William Swainson, *Taxidermy: Bibliography and Biography* (London: Longman, 1840), 25.

17. Anon. (George Annesley, Earl of Montmorris?), "Short Instructions for Collecting Shells" [1815?], 4.

18. Swainson, *Taxidermy*, 20–21.

19. Ibid.

20. "Short Instructions," 5.
21. J.T. Swainson's manuscript catalog, n.p.
22. Transcript of J.T. Swainson's will, *Swainsoniana*, NHM, MSS 89 f S 1.
23. William Swainson writes: "the coasts of Exmouth, Sandwich, and Weymouth are particularly productive"; *Taxidermy*, 23.
24. Duchess of Portland (hereafter Dss) to Thomas Pennant, Whitehall, February 26, 1778. Pennant Correspondence, CR 2017/TP 172/2, Warwickshire County Record Office, England.
25. Lightfoot to Dss, Uxbridge, August 31, 1771. Portland Papers, Longleat House, England, vol. 14, f. 153.
26. Dss to Richard Pulteney (hereafter RP), July 6, 1782, Pulteney Correspondence, Linnean Society, London.
27. Dss to Mrs Delany, Weymouth, August 23, 1776, Delany, *Autobiography and Correspondence* (1862), V: 253–4.
28. Dss to RP, Margate, August 21, 1784, Pulteney Correspondence, Linnean Society.
29. Delany, *Autobiography and Correspondence*, VI: 223.
30. Angélique Day, ed., *Letters from Georgian Ireland: The Correspondence of Mary Delany, 1731–68* (Belfast: Friar's Bush Press, 1991), 249. "Do you not wish yourself extended on the beach gathering shells, listening to Phill [Miss Donnellan] while she sings at her work, or joining in the conversation, always attended with cheerfulness?" (246). See Allen, "Tastes and Crazes," for a discussion of Victorian codes of propriety concerning shell and seaweed collecting on the shore.
31. Delany, *Autobiography and Correspondence*, III: 542–3.
32. Swainson, *Taxidermy*, 21.
33. "Short Instructions," 3.
34. Swainson, *Taxidermy*, 21–2.
35. Edward Donovan, *Instructions for Collecting and Preserving Various Subjects of Natural History* (London, 1794), 59.
36. Nora F. McMillan, "William Swainson (1789–1855) and his Shell Collections," *Journal of the Society for Bibliography of Natural History* 9 (1980): 427–34, 432.
37. Emanuel Mendes da Costa, *Elements of Conchology: Or, an Introduction to the Knowledge of Shells* (London, 1776), 64.
38. Swainson, *Taxidermy*, 22.
39. She wrote in response to Pennant's query about dredging: "the Dss of P is extreamly obliged to Mr Pennant for Mr Cordiners Letter she will make an enquiry if there are different ways of dredging & will let him know but that she will not be able to learn till she gets to Weymouth" (Dss to Pennant, Whitehall, June 26, 1778, Pennant Correspondence, CR 2017 149/5b). The duchess, however, was not always successful dredging up new specimens: "I … am very sorry to inform [you] of the very indifferent success I have had in dredging that I fear there is not any you wish for. I have put up a few which I shall bring to Blandford with me next Thursday …" (Dss to RP, Weymouth, August 25, 1777, Pulteney Correspondence, Linnean Society).
40. Delany, *Autobiography and Correspondence*, IV: 238.
41. Dss to RP, undated letter, Pulteney Correspondence, Linnean Society.
42. *Mss Relative to British Testacea*, Zoology Library, NHM, 89 q P, f. 156.
43. Dss to RP, Whitehall, April 9, 1772, Pulteney Correspondence, Linnean Society.
44. Dss to RP, June 8, 1772, Pulteney Correspondence, Linnean Society.
45. Henry Seymer to Richard Pulteney, Fall 1772?, Pulteney Correspondence, Linnean Society.
46. RP to Dss, March 24, 1779, Portland Papers, Longleat, vol. 14, f. 148.
47. "Dr.P.s duplicates of Shells," *Mss Relative to British Testacea*, NHM, vol. 2 of 89 q P, f. 148.

48. RP to Dss, August 13, 1777, *Mss Relative to British Testacea*, NHM, vol. 2, f. 134.

49. These descriptions became what are known by historical taxonomists as Solander's "slips," now housed in the Natural History Museum. He had been using the duchess's collection to work on his own project which would have been a book revising Linnaeus's categories. These slips were consulted by malacologists throughout the nineteenth and even into the twentieth century, though Solander's failure to publish them has resulted in the diminishment of his legacy as a taxonomist. See Ilya Tëmkin's unpublished paper, "Linnaeus, Solander, and Conchology" (2006).

50. Until very recently, little scholarly attention had been focused on the duchess with the exception of Peter Dance's treatment of her shell collecting; Dance, *A History of Shell Collecting*. So far the most intensive treatment of the duchess's accomplishments has been Stott's booklet accompanying the exhibition at Harley Gallery. Opening in 2006, the exhibition focused on the Duchess of Portland's fine art and natural history collections. See Rebecca Stott, *Duchess of Curiosities: The Life of Margaret, Duchess of Portland* (Welbeck: Pineapple Press for the Harley Gallery, 2006).

51. See Spary's work on how the physical arrangement of natural history specimens stressed their materiality: Emma C. Spary, "Codes of Passion," in *Wissenschaft als Kulturelle Praxis, 1750–1900*, eds. H.E. Bodecker, P.H. Reill, and J. Schlumbohm (Gottingen: Vandenhoeck and Ruprecht, 1999).

52. The literature on the relationship between science and the Enlightenment is vast and beyond the scope of this chapter; however, in addressing the key issues concerning the relationship between science and the Enlightenment as cultural context, very helpful material can be found in the introduction to the collection of essays edited by William Clark, Jan Golinski, and Simon Schaffer, *The Sciences in Enlightenment Europe* (Chicago: University of Chicago Press, 1999); see also Jan Golinski, *Science as Public Culture: Chemistry and Enlightenment in Britain, 1760–1820* (Cambridge: Cambridge University Press, 1992); John Gascoigne, *Joseph Banks and the English Enlightenment: Useful Knowledge and Polite Culture* (New York: Cambridge University Press, 1994); Dorinda Outram, *Enlightenment* (Cambridge: Cambridge University Press, 1995); and Geoffrey Sutton, *Science for a Polite Society: Gender, Culture, and the Demonstration of Enlightenment* (Boulder, CO: Westview Press, 1995). For early modern concepts of order in nature, see Lorraine Daston and Katharine Park's volume of essays, *Wonders and the Order of Nature 1150–1750* (New York: Zone Books, 1998). For the British engagement with Enlightenment natural history, see Kim Sloan, ed., *Enlightenment: Discovering the World in the Eighteenth Century* (London: British Museum Press, 2003) and K.G.W. Anderson, ed., *Enlightening the British: Knowledge, Discovery and the Museum in the Eighteenth Century* (London: British Museum Press, 2003), both published in conjunction with the opening of the British Museum's Enlightenment Gallery. For a lucid explanation of natural classification as scientific praxis, see Peter Dear, *The Intelligibility of Nature: How Science Makes Sense of the World* (Chicago: University of Chicago Press, 2006), 53, in which Dear suggests that: "Classification was not just cataloguing, the imposition of arbitrarily selected ordering principles; it was not mere 'natural history' in the usual sense of the straightforward description of nature's contents. Eighteenth-century taxonomists generally aimed at being natural philosophers who could provide the conceptual understanding that would raise the status of their work and establish it as philosophically meaningful, not simply as useful."

14

Woman of Letters: Elizabeth Gaskell's Autograph Collection and Victorian Celebrity

Pamela Corpron Parker

Between 1836 and her death in 1865, Victorian author Elizabeth Gaskell published seven novels, the first biography of Charlotte Bronte, and dozens of short stories, sketches, and periodical articles. With Britain's expanding print culture, Gaskell's works soon found an international reading audience. To some of her contemporaries, it seemed that she, like Byron, had become famous overnight. Yet Gaskell cultivated her professional career with the same care she did her personal life. In a culture still uneasy with female public figures, she negotiated the perils and privileges of her literary acclaim through advancing the respectable public persona of "Mrs Gaskell": minister's wife, mother of four daughters, and literary activist. Her growing prominence brought with it numerous requests for patronage, professional advice, and autographs. By the mid-nineteenth century, autograph collecting became a fashionable sideline of literary culture. Indeed, collecting had become so popular that autograph historian A.N.L. Munby described it as "a cult of staggering dimensions,"[1] and critics called it "autographomania." Beleaguered by the intrusive tactics of autograph seekers, some writers disparaged them as "autographic fiends," "Albumites,"[2] and the "mosquitoes of literature."[3] Though her relationship with her reading public was not without conflict, Gaskell responded amiably to requests for her autograph, and she typically signed herself by her professional moniker, E.C. Gaskell.[4] She told one supplicant: "I am very fond of collecting autographs myself, so I can enter into the feeling which makes you wish for mine."[5]

Elizabeth Gaskell's fondness for autographs was well known by her family, friends, and professional associates, many of whom shared her enthusiasm for this popular pastime and even supplied her growing collection. Eventually these letters, autographs, and writing samples were gathered into five leather-bound volumes and several miscellaneous boxes now housed in the John

Rylands Library in Manchester, England.[6] As both a signer and collector of autographs, Elizabeth Gaskell participated in one of Victorian Britain's most popular forms of literary consumption. An 1854 letter to collector Henry Bright reveals her preference for authors' signatures:

> I don't much care for statesmen and have a handsome quantity of unknown peers at your disposal … (don't think me saucy) only I like having people I really *do* care for; I myself personally, either in the way of like or dislike,—and not people I am perfectly indifferent to. I should \rather/ like Washington Irving … DeQuincy I shall obtain for you some time. When I have a little morsel of leisure I will look over my letters, & send you word what duplicates I have *and* what I want.[7]

In an 1860 letter to her publisher at Chapman and Hall, Gaskell requested an autograph of Anthony Trollope and asserted: "I am an autograph collector, as I wish all my friends to know."[8] She also regularly supplied autographs to her admirers (both her own and other famous writers), such as in the following letter: "Will *this* note do for an autograph? If not, I will gladly send you another, and if I can send Miss Egerton Leigh any more that she will care to have (of *living* authors I have good store,) I shall be very glad indeed to send her any {of what I have}."[9] Her letters frequently referenced her "book," as she called her collection, and she pursued every opportunity for expanding it through corresponding to her literary peers, exchanging duplicate autographs with fellow collectors, and purchasing others. Gaskell's engagement with the material practices of nineteenth-century autograph collecting represents more than the passing fancy of an amateur hobbyist or the competitive accumulations of a crass materialist, however. The bulk of Gaskell's collection is gathered from her extensive correspondence with the leading literary figures of the day. As such, her album acts as an epistolary dossier of her literary credentials. Through an appropriately amateur and privatized form, Gaskell's collection performs an important self-authorizing function that marks her place as a British Woman of Letters.

Critics and collectors alike have sometimes apologized for their fascination with and acquisition of the material remnants of those figures that haunt us, inspire us, and inscribe our histories. Literary scholars routinely privilege primary textual analysis and relegate autograph collections to the category of literary ephemera. Yet albums of any kind, whether photo albums or family scrapbooks, provide illuminating representations of their creators' self-fashioning, and thus provide productive sources of analysis. For autograph albums are not only objects of perception, they also structure perception.[10] As a framework for interpretation then, autograph albums have their own syntax and contextual histories, their own hierarchies of meaning and value established by the collector. Though sometimes indecipherable, these meanings relied upon complex negotiations of values and identities at work in nineteenth-century literary culture.

Gaskell's collection—or any collection for that matter—gathers things that are organized around personal and aesthetic frameworks of meaning. In this way, Gaskell's albums provide an interpretive project that traverses the boundaries between popular and intellectual cultures, as well as private and public arenas of material practice. This study considers Gaskell's album as an oblique form of autobiography, displaying her professional alliances with the leading cultural figures of the day. Her album is both selective and purposeful in its representation of her epistolary community and the esteem of her literary peers.

In 1935, Ross D. Waller provided the first and only other survey of the Gaskell albums in *Letters Addressed to Mrs. Gaskell by Celebrated Contemporaries*, written shortly after the John Rylands Library received the collections from the estate of Gaskell's last surviving daughter, Meta. Waller's overview is more perfunctory than precise, and his lack of enthusiasm for the project becomes apparent in this rather cryptic comment:

> The collection as a whole, while on the one hand it displays the great variety of Mrs. Gaskell's friends and well-wishers, and the general respect in which she was held by her contemporaries, obliges one to recognize on the other that a temperament and outlook such as hers, however gracious and noble, does not stimulate its correspondents to the most spontaneous self-expression.

By characterizing Gaskell as appropriately "gracious and noble," though limited and limiting, Waller reveals his own conventional assumptions. His emphasis on the canonical male writers of the Victorian period replicates the prejudices of many early twentieth-century critics. He slighted or ignored completely numerous women writers included in the collection with the following dismissal: "A number of other women writers are represented in the collection, no others so eminent but all of them of some repute in their day."[11] Unfortunately, his representation of "this gallery of Victorian ladies" distorts and diminishes Gaskell's epistolary community in favor of "the less effusive gentleman."[12] Yet for those interested in women's literary history, Gaskell's collection documents a formative period of British literature when women writers participated in unprecedented numbers. Furthermore, Gaskell's album provides invaluable insights into the personal relationships and professional negotiations existing between many key contributors to Victorian literature, both male and female.

As the record of a woman writer navigating her way through the first era of mass consumption of literary culture, Gaskell's album also exhibits some of the problems inherent for female celebrities in the rising cult of personality. Shortly after the publication of her first novel, *Mary Barton*, Gaskell received a letter containing a well-intentioned warning against the dangers of being "lionized" during a trip to London. Lionization, at least as the Victorian's understood it, described the head-turning aggrandizement showered on authors when they were introduced to London literary society. While Gaskell understood the potential hazards of fame, particularly for women, she also resented the implied limitations imposed on her by her correspondent:

> It would ill become me to say I might not be materially altered for the worse by this mysterious process of "lionizing." How am I to help it? There really are people I want to see as well as things. I do think praise to one's face is a greater impertinence than blame; and either, with reference to a book published anonymously, a most under-bred thing.[13]

Gaskell found the first flush of literary fame uncomfortable, but she clearly relished the greater access to "people" and "things" her publishing success allowed her. She wrote enthusiastic letters to her friends about the dinner parties, lectures, exhibits and literati of London in 1848, yet she still tried to maintain her anonymity in her publication of *Mary Barton*. As she tells her publisher, Edward Chapman: "Hitherto the whole affair of publication has been one of extreme annoyance to me, from the impertinent and unjustifiable curiosity of people, who have tried to force me either into an absolute denial, or an acknowledgement of what they must have seen the writer wished to keep concealed."[14]

Gaskell and other women writers rarely enjoyed the full rewards of their professional achievements, either in remunerative or social terms. Their earnings were, by law, not their own, and their authorial identities were fraught with social anxieties regarding feminine privacy and bourgeois respectability. Like George Eliot and the Bronte sisters, Gaskell initially sheltered herself behind anonymity and pen names, both to avert the critical double-standards of the periodical press and to avoid intrusions on their privacy. Others, such as Elizabeth Barrett Browning and Florence Nightingale, took to their couches as celebrity invalids, controlling their exposure through emphasizing their physical frailty. Though rarely seen, women writers were certainly heard about, since they were subject to insistent and curious speculation. The reading public clamored for biographical information, portraits, and literary gossip—all eagerly supplied through the growing periodical industry supporting book publishing, such as *The Bookman*.[15] Some critics have suggested that women writers even capitalized on the interest surrounding their masked identities as clever marketing devices.[16] Though overtly cultivating a public presence retained an unseemly quality for women writers, their male peers enjoyed and even promoted their celebrity. For example, William Makepeace Thackeray and Ralph Waldo Emerson gave well-attended public lectures in London and Manchester, respectively; Charles Dickens augmented his income and received thunderous applause for his dramatizations during his 1867 and 1868 reading tours of the North of England and North America. Crowds feted him with banquets and balls: 200 invited guests came to his farewell dinner in New York, and a gigantic public banquet was held in his honor in Liverpool in 1869.[17] Even the most famous women writers limited their appearances to private dinner parties or entertained visitors in their homes. Rather than promote their careers through public lectures and performances, women writers relied on letters as their primary means for communicating with their reading public

Elizabeth Gaskell was by all accounts a prolific correspondent; she wrote hundreds—perhaps thousands—of letters. Books, stories, articles, reviews, sermons, lectures, and literary gossip—these were the *lingua franca* of her letters and the adhesive of her social world, both personal and professional. Her sloping, scurried penmanship and dash-filled, detailed prose display a life crammed with both the prosaic and profound aspects of mid-Victorian literary culture. Her correspondence with friends, family members, professional associates, and admirers occupied much of her time, perhaps even the greater portion of her written labors. She frequently complained of this pressing responsibility to her intimate friends and daughters, who sometimes acted as her amanuenses: "I've half a hundred letters to write";[18] "I have written many letters this week & have many more to write ..."[19] Like most women of her time, Gaskell used letter-writing as a means of narration and self-construction. Her letters solidified and extended her relationships beyond her Manchester community and confirmed her business relations with precision and charm. Studied alone, these letters allow a reader to eavesdrop on a delightful, if rather one-sided, conversation. When they are read alongside Gaskell's autograph album, however, a more nuanced, intertextual discussion emerges to reveal a far-flung community of writers eager to correspond with like-minded professionals. In addition to her famous friendship and correspondence with Charlotte Bronte, she exchanged letters with Anna Jameson, Florence Nightingale, George Eliot, Caroline Norton, Harriet Martineau, Harriet Beecher Stowe, and many others. Of course, many of her correspondents were celebrated literary men, as well, including Charles Dickens, Thomas Carlyle, John Ruskin, Leigh Hunt, Matthew Arnold, and Dante Gabrielle Rossetti.

Most of the items in Elizabeth Gaskell's autograph collection were drawn from her extensive epistolary community and reflect her intentional cultivation of professional associates, particularly among women writers. She was generous with her introductions among literary acquaintances. She sometimes sent signed editions of her books as an entrée to other authors and was not above writing unabashed fan letters to writers she admired. One such exchange occurs shortly after the publication of *Adam Bede* in 1859. With all positive reviews the novel received, the mystery surrounding the author's gender and identity fomented even greater public interest. Gaskell initially denied that the author was Marian Evans, because "Miss Evans' life taken at the best construction, does so jar against the beautiful book."[20] No doubt Gaskell's curiosity was heightened by the novel's occasional attribution to her, but her dogged attempts to uncover the identity of "Madam Adam"[21] humorously reveal her appetite for literary gossip. For months, she wrote a series of earnest, detective-like letters, marshaled her evidence, and followed several false leads. One long letter to fellow author Harriet Martineau relays her daughter's interrogation of an unsuspecting Blackwood's clerk through theatrical dialogue: "'Who wrote Adam Bede' 'I do not know. But I know it was not written by a lady—' (observe this last clause was volunteered.) Meta said, 'Do you *know* it was not written by a lady?' 'Yes, I do.'"[22] Despite the clerk's unequivocal response, Gaskell concludes: "I am quite convinced Miss E[vans] wrote it."[23]

When Gaskell finally received confirmation of George Eliot's identity from her publisher George Smith, she promptly initiated a correspondence with Marian Evans to congratulate her: "Since I heard, from authority, that you were the author of Scenes from 'Clerical Life' & 'Adam Bede', I have read them again, and I must, once more, tell you how earnestly fully, and humbly I admire them. I never read anything so complete, and beautiful in fiction, in my whole life before."[24] Gaskell's praise prompted an immediate response from her fellow novelist, who signed herself Marian Evans Lewes. The letter was given a prominent position in the first volume of Gaskell's autograph collection and movingly testifies to the woman writer's need for validation from her peers. Eliot muses:

> Only yesterday I was wondering that artists, knowing each other's pains so well, did not help each other more, &, as usual, when I have been talking complainingly or suspiciously, something has come which serves me as a reproof. That "something" is your letter, which has brought me the only sort of help I care to have—an assurance of fellow feeling of thorough trustful recognition from one of the minds which are most capable of judging as well as being moved. You know, without my telling you how much the help is heightened by it coming to me afresh, now that I have ceased to be a mystery & am known as a mere daylight fact.[25]

Eliot's pleasure and gratitude at being acknowledged by a respected peer are palpable. She interprets Gaskell's letter as "an assurance of fellow feeling of thorough trustful recognition" and articulates her mutual respect as one "most capable of judging" her work fairly. Though they are separated by geography, religious views, and domestic arrangements, Eliot recognizes Gaskell's validation of their shared vocations as *women writers*:

> I shall always love to think that one woman wrote to another such sweet encouraging words—still more to think that you were the writer and I the receiver ... I have indulged the idea that if my books turned out to be worth much, you would be among my willing readers; for I was conscious while the question of my power was still undecided for me, that my feeling towards Life & Art had some affinity which inspired *Cranford* and the earliest chapters of *Mary Barton*.[26]

As fiction writers engaged with similar subjects—social fiction, provincial life, and women's gendered lives—their artistic "affinity" bridges other significant differences. Like most artists, Eliot craved affirmation for her work, and Gaskell's professional regard mitigated her sense of marginalization, particularly in a male-dominated publishing industry given to holding critical double standards for women writers.

Benedict Anderson's theory of "imagined communities" may be helpful in explaining George Eliot's unlikely affiliation with Elizabeth Gaskell and Gaskell's desire to give Eliot's letter a place of honor in her autograph album. Their community is *imagined*, or figurative, because it is grounded in psychic "affinities" rather than physical or local proximities. Anderson has argued that the concrete forms of print capitalism played a significant role in forging an imagined community among the nineteenth-century British reading public through appealing to their shared linguistic, social, and literary histories. In Anderson's words, the community is imagined "because the members of even the smallest nation will never know most of their fellow members, meet them, or even hear of them, yet in the minds of each lives the image of their communion."[27] While Anderson makes an argument specific to national identity, his theory extends to other forms of imagined communities, such as Eliot's assumption of their shared "feeling towards Life & Art." Eliot and Gaskell's literature and letters provide the medium for articulating that sense of community, even as it also creates and solidifies it. Though they never met in person, their shared national, professional, and gender identities allow them to imagine each other as comrades in a figurative community of artists, even when other categories of identity diverge.

By Anderson's explanation, the popularity of British histories, biographies, anthologies, periodicals, and collected works can be understood in part as a form of literary nationalism or a performance of cultural imperialism still enacted in Britain's successful national heritage industry. (Think of the recent Dickens' Theme Park, Shakespeare's Stratford, or tours to Bronte Country, for example.) A shared literary heritage, however arbitrary or constructed, provides a figurative convergence for individuals of vastly differing material realities to imagine a "deep, horizontal comradeship" with other readers and writers.[28] Likewise, the literary consumer, and the autograph collector in particular, imagined herself within a community of like-minded compatriots, fellow citizens of a newly created urban public whose reading consumption was indicative of Britain's greater affluence, literacy, and cultural dominance. The proliferation of print media in nineteenth-century Britain marked the shift away from the small, elite publishing houses to a highly commercialized industry engaged in the mass marketing of the literary personality.[29] The practice of autograph collecting thus embodied larger changes in nineteenth-century culture, pitting the Romantic values of the creative genius against the rising spirit of commercialism that threatened to commodify the authorial image.[30]

Early in her career, Gaskell recognized the intrinsic value of letters written by famous writers, both as a personal keepsake and as an artifact of literary history. *The Life of Charlotte Bronte* (1857) drew substantially from her nearly ten-year correspondence with Bronte, much of which rehearsed her later role as Bronte's biographer. After Bronte's death in 1855, Gaskell received numerous requests for samples of Charlotte Bronte's handwriting, as the following letter highlights:

> I have been looking over my letters from Miss Bronte; and I am sorry to say that *all* the notes, & shorter letters have been weeded out for the purposes of autographs. There are absolutely none left, but long & characteristic letters, which I shall require for the purposes of biography. If, after that is written, you will remind me again I will see if I can not spare you one. I have been more entreated for her autograph tha[n] for that of any other person. Who else do you want? Send me a list, please, & I will look & see that *you* have them, if *I* have duplicates. Or come & see my book—that would be best of all.[31]

Gaskell's "book" thus provided both social and material capital confirming her association with one of Britain's most famous authors. With professional foresight, Gaskell retained the items she needed for what she called "the purposes of biography," even before she began her sidelong negotiations to write the "memoir" of her "dear friend, Charlotte Bronte."[32] Her "book" attracted the interest of friends, affirmed her status as Bronte's intimate associate and biographer, and provided a medium of exchange for acquiring additional items for her collection. She frequently donated her autographs (both her own and those of her famous peers) to charitable organizations for benefit sales.

Despite—or perhaps because of—her role as the author of one of the nineteenth century's most successful biographies, *The Life of Charlotte Bronte*, Gaskell grew increasingly anxious about the fate of her own letters. Though Gaskell routinely saved, transcribed, exchanged or gave away the letters of her famous correspondents, she just as routinely cautioned her family, friends, and publishers to use discretion in disposing her letters. She frequently instructed her publisher George Smith and her daughters to destroy her letters, and she forbade any biography to be written about her during her life.[33] She consistently resented unwanted publicity, particularly negative criticism, and usually left the country when her books were released. Throughout her life, Gaskell refused to cooperate with interviewers engaged in "the impertinent custom" of "writing 'notices' or 'memoirs' of living people."[34] In one letter refusing an interview, she complained: "I do not see why the public have any more to do with me than to buy/or reject/ the wares I supply them."[35] Gaskell represented her literary products in strictly economic terms here, but she clearly understood (as did her early editor, Charles Dickens) that increasing literacy and mass-marketing rendered the production of authorial image an important commodity. Her letters trace her efforts to guard her privacy and shape her professional image, sometimes without success. She wrote ironically of unauthorized biographies: "I always let people *invent* mine, & have often learnt some curious peculiars about myself from what they choose to say."[36] Gaskell understood the double standards alloted to famous female authors, but she also preserved a record of her professional accomplishments in her album, following nineteenth-century norms for autograph collecting.

Though autograph historians are not certain exactly when the practice of collecting the signatures of notable public figures began, they generally agree that a significant predecessor to autograph collecting surfaced during the sixteenth century as young gentlemen traveled to various continental universities to further their education. The Germans called this practice *wanderjahren*, a kind of educational tourism we might now call a gap year. Unlike the British university systems of Oxford and Cambridge, where students remained in residential colleges for the duration of their studies, European youths moved from one mentor to the next, compiling albums of signatures and letters of introduction as a means of establishing their credentials as "men of letters." In addition to providing mementos of their travels and acquaintances, these albums served as epistolary resumes similar to contemporary *curricula vita* that incorporated the album holder into a community of notable scholars and students.[37] The British Museum holds numerous examples of these *Album Amicorum* or "Book of Friends," with dates as early as 1554 and 1579. In his study, *A Guide to the Collector of Historical Documents* (1891), Henry Scott described the original albums as:

> a paper book in octavo, bound long-wise, being one of those which the Germans call *Albums*, and are much used by the young travelers of that nation, who commonly ask a new acquaintance (even at the first meeting) to write some sentence, therein, with a complement to the owner's learning, good sense, &c—which done the young man upon all occasions, especially at his return, by these hands demonstrates what good company he has kept.[38]

By the eighteenth century, persons of leisure and means throughout Europe were assembling collections of correspondence and literary manuscripts written by the religious, political, and cultural leaders. The 1789 publication of John Thane's *British Autography* testifies to the growing interest in autograph collecting throughout the century. As both a record of history and status symbol, autograph collections preserved original manuscripts, shored up Britain's national identity, and displayed the collector's social status through their association with famous personages or their financial means to purchase such artifacts. As early as 1822, private transactions involving the sale and transfer of autograph collections gave way to a commercial market for autographs. London booksellers and auctioneers began holding sales specifically containing books and autographs. Overzealous collecting led to misattributions, forgeries, and thefts. By the beginning of the nineteenth century, book manuscripts and letters of living authors and statesmen had become the targets of ambitious collectors.[39]

The characterization of autograph collectors as zealous amateurs has dogged autograph historians and literary critics since the nineteenth century. Nearly every publication regarding autograph collecting anxiously differentiates the author from amateur hobbyists of the Victorian period. Munby included himself among other "palaeographists" who, like himself, took a more scholarly interest in autographs.[40] Accordingly, the experts indicate that the most zealous practitioners came from upwardly mobile mercantile families and much of the early literature suggests that it was also a largely female activity.[41] As albums became objects of conspicuous consumption, lavishly bound and inlaid with engraved portraits of the authors, the popular rhetoric surrounding them became more critical. British poet Robert Southey expressed his abhorrence of autograph seekers by giving the following notice: "I have entered into a society for the discouragement of autograph collectors; which society will not be dissolved till the legislature in its wisdom shall take measures for suppressing that troublesome and increasing sect."[42] Harriet Martineau routinely refused all requests for autographs, and to frustrate their desires further, she had her sister pen her peremptory refusal letters for her.

The oddly feminized pathology of "autographomania" points to the excesses of autograph hunters in general and "lady collectors" in particular. Dubbed "autograph harpies," women collectors received sharp criticism for their aggressive and duplicitous tactics for acquiring autographs. In a letter in 1814, Emily Eden mocked the developing "fashion" of autograph collecting, stating that "it was quite ridiculous to see Lady Jersey and Lady Cowper and Lady E. Fielding and two or three others coming down of an evening at Middleton with their great books in satchells [*sic*], like so many little schoolboys, and showing each other their 'little treasures.' ... Afterwards," she explained, "the books are all locked up again," and each woman "wore the key of her manuscript book at her side, in case the others should get it by fair means or foul."[43] Eden ridicules the crass materialism and self-aggrandizement of the lady collectors and darkly hints at the libidinous excesses of their desire. Likewise, James Fennimore Cooper joked: "I have done a good deal of work in that way, my female correspondents, in particular, being as numerous as, I dare say, they are handsome and agreeable."[44]

As artifacts of a particular time, place, and individual, the autograph letter constitutes one of the most significant fetish objects of literary culture, the author's signature. The author's signature held special significance in Victorian culture, particularly as a marker of historical authenticity, originality, and legitimacy. Autographs simultaneously gave their collectors a tangible link to the past and a specific location for the fleeting signifiers of identity. Victorians believed a person's "hand," or penmanship, revealed the writer's gender, class, education level, and spiritual soundness. A writer's signature thus became a kind of semiotic for the individual artist's celebrity, historical specificity, and genius. For authors such as Gaskell, the autograph may have offered a kind of talisman of the writer's genius. A writer's signature not only refers to the physical existence of the writer with pen in hand (that is, "the hands ... now moldered away"), but it also suggests that some essence of that creative imagination may become accessible through the material practices of the collector. In autograph collecting, the material acquisition merges with the writer's own ineffable desires to leave her mark on literary history.

Ironically, the signature did not gain acceptance as a valid form of legal authentification until the thirteenth century and was not common until the sixteenth century, when literacy spread beyond aristocrats, the clergy, and professional scribes. In preliterate societies, the seal was preferred as the authentic marker of personal identity. In fact, the etymology of the word signature derives from *signum*, Latin for the wax impression made by the seal. In his study of the cult surrounding the signers of the Declaration of Independence, Josh Lauer explains that sealing or signing one's name performs and preserves the moment the signature is given. In this sense the signature *embodies* the signer, providing material evidence of the writer's existence and reenacting the moment when the written act is materialized and made permanent.[45] In Lauer's words: "Whereas writing makes language visible, signing renders the author present and, under the proper conditions of textual belief, immortal."[46]

In "Signature Event Context," Jacques Derrida has argued that a "written signature implies the actual or empirical nonpresence of the signer. But ... it also marks and retains his [*sic*] having been present in the past now, which will remain a future now."[47] Ironically, Derrida denies the signature's evocation as a unique marker of identity and place, only to grant the individual signature an "enigmatic originality" that conveys a "transcendental form of presentness."[48] By their very nature then, autograph albums reenact the commemorative and performative function of the signature. In Lauer's commentary:

> It might be said that every signature is a memorial, an act of self-declaration performed in some present with an eye to the future. As legal evidence or an informal mark of self-attribution, the signature is a socially-binding token of remembrance ... to sign is to commit oneself to history, to recollection—or at least its possibility. But the signature itself is a social construction, and the process by which any given autograph becomes socially valuable is, like history itself, selective and purposeful.[49]

If the narrative of history is both "selective and purposeful," then the autograph album becomes even more so as signatures are, as Pierre Nora has argued, "sites of memory."[50] Likewise, the writer's autograph served as both a material artifact and social mnemonic of British literary heritage. Collecting autographs of literary celebrities thus parallels many of the material practices of literary tourism. Autograph collectors are much like the literary pilgrim who visits the author's grave and hopes the epitaph inscribed on the tombstone will provide some understanding, connection, or insight into the "real" author.[51] The writer's home or grave offers material evidence of the author's existence, as well as affirmation of the visitor's relationship to that absent author. Likewise, autograph albums provide a concrete place for recollection and imaginative engagement with the writer, a mark of human accomplishment and relationship, and a physical location for enacting the contingent relationship between the reader/collector and the author.

Autograph albums have the uncanny ability to conjure a sense of intimacy with the past and provide a living memorial. If the signature revealed the body in the process of writing itself, it also, in Lauer's words, "served as a bridge between time and space, offering a medium through which one could commune with one's forbears and kindred spirits."[52] Like most collectors, Gaskell relished the physical connection that autographs allowed her to have with writers living and dead. In her letter to Henry Bright, she vividly describes her pleasure in handling "real identical yellow ragged letters that had been touched with the hands, right royal hands, now moldered away."[53] Her gothic overtones, however ironic, are reminiscent of the ghost stories that permeate her short fiction. Many of these stories are filled with letters lost, found, and stolen—letters that interpolate the voices of the past into the present and inscribe themselves onto the narratives of their readers. These stories mark the illusive nature of the past, while also insisting that the past is always with us.

Though she resisted all contemporary efforts by others to write her biography, Gaskell's autograph collections may represent a thwarted autobiographical impulse. Her album commemorates her successful career and offers material proof that she was in the good company of the leading figures of nineteenth-century literature. Gaskell's autograph albums represent a form of professional assertion, albeit in a privatized and feminized form. As one of Victorian Britain's most celebrated literary figures, she collected and exchanged autographs, arranging and giving precedence to those that testified to her significant contributions to British literary history. In doing so, Gaskell enacted a ritual of connection that marked her own place of honor among an elite community of British writers.

Notes

1. A.N.L. Munby, *The Cult of the Autograph Letter in England* (London: University of London, Athlone Press, 1962).
2. Thomas Frognall Dibdin, as quoted in Munby, *Cult of the Autograph Letter*, 8.
3. Various sources attribute this phrase to Washington Irving, James Russell Lowell, and Horace Greely, with Irving cited most frequently.
4. For an interesting discussion of Gaskell's various names, E.C. Stevenson, E.C. Gaskell, and Mrs Gaskell, I recommend Dierdre D'Albertis's chapter, "The Life and Letters of E.C. Gaskell," in *The Cambridge Companion to Elizabeth Gaskell*, ed. Jill Matus, 10–26 (Cambridge: Cambridge University Press, 2007).
5. Elizabeth Gaskell to an unknown correspondent, September 2, 1857, in J.A.V. Chapple and Arthur Pollard, eds., *The Letters of Mrs. Gaskell* (Cambridge, MA: Harvard University Press, 1967).
6. The Gaskell Manuscripts include *Letters to E.C. and W. Gaskell*, 2 volumes, *Miscellaneous Letters*, 3 volumes, Letters from W.S. Landor; Letters from Dickens. This essay focuses largely on the first five volumes.
7. Gaskell to Henry Bright, March 14, 1854, in John Chapple and Alan Shelston, eds., *Further Letters of Mrs. Gaskell* (Manchester: Manchester University Press, 2000), 108.
8. Gaskell to Frederick Chapman, August 22, 1860, *Further Letters*, 213.
9. Gaskell to Mrs Susan Deane, May 7, 1855, *Further Letters*, 136.
10. I am indebted to the introduction of Maggie Humm's *Snapshots of Bloomsbury: The Private Lives of Virginia Woolf and Vanessa Bell* (New Brunswick: Rutgers University Press, 2006) for this insight.
11. Ross D. Waller, *Letters Addressed to Mrs. Gaskell by Celebrated Contemporaries* (Manchester: Manchester University Press, 1935).
12. Ibid., 148.
13. Gaskell to unknown, March 8, 1849, *Further Letters*, 71.
14. Gaskell to Edward Chapman, December 5, 1848, *Further Letters*, 64.
15. See Margaret D. Stetz, "Selling Literary Tourism in *The Bookman*," in *Literary Tourism and Nineteenth-Century Culture*, ed. Nicola Watson (Basingstoke: Palgrave Macmillan, 2009), for further information on the early periodicals promoting the book publishing industry.
16. Alexis Easley, *First Person Anonymous* (Aldershot: Ashgate, 2004).
17. Gerard Curtis, *Visual Words: Art and the Material Book in Victorian England* (Aldershot: Ashgate, 2002), 155.
18. Gaskell to Eliza Fox, May 1852, *The Letters of Mrs. Gaskell*, 188.
19. Gaskell to Marianne Gaskell, March 10, 1851, *The Letters of Mrs. Gaskell*, 831.
20. Gaskell to George Smith, August 4, 1959, *The Letters of Mrs. Gaskell*, 566.
21. Gaskell to George Smith, November 2, 1859, *The Letters of Mrs. Gaskell*, 586.
22. Gaskell to Martineau, October 29, 1859, *The Letters of Mrs. Gaskell*, 585.
23. Ibid., 586.
24. Gaskell to Marian Evans (George Eliot), November 10, 1859, *The Letters of Mrs. Gaskell*.
25. George Eliot to Elizabeth Gaskell, November 11, 1859, MS 730, *The Letters of Mrs. Gaskell*, 69.
26. Letter from Marian Evans Lewes to Elizabeth Gaskell, November 11, 1859, vol 1, Gaskell Manuscript Collection. Reproduced by courtesy of the University Librarian and Director, the John Rylands University Library, the University of Manchester.
27. Benedict Anderson, *Imagined Communities: Reflections on the Spread and Origins of Nationalism* (London: Verso, 2006), 6.
28. Ibid., 7.

29. Loren Glass, *Author's Inc: Literary Celebrity in the United States, 1880–1980* (New York: New York University Press, 2004), 11.

30. Allan Axelrad, "The Lumley Autograph and the Great Literary Lion: Authenticity and Commodification in Nineteenth-Century Autograph Collecting," in *Susan Fenimore Cooper: New Essays on Rural Hours and Other Works*, eds. Rochelle Johnson and Daniel Patterson (Athens: University of Georgia Press, 2001), 35.

31. Gaskell to Mrs Spencer, undated 1856, *Further Letters*, 163.

32. Elizabeth Gaskell, *The Life of Charlotte Bronte* (London and New York: Penguin, 1998), 17.

33. Many of her family letters and nearly all of her correspondence with her husband were destroyed as she instructed. Luckily for literary historians, not all of them were. Nearly 900 survive to exhibit her lively mind, writing process, and extensive network of personal and professional alliances.

34. Gaskell to unknown correspondent, June 4, 1865, *The Letters of Mrs. Gaskell*, 761.

35. Ibid.

36. Gaskell to Anne Robson, May 10, 1865, Letter 570, *The Letters of Mrs. Gaskell*, 761.

37. Stephen Raab, "A Short History of Collecting Autographs," Raab Collection webpage: <http://www.raabcollection.com/dynamicContent.aspx?key=pliny>.

38. Henry T. Scott, *A Guide to the Collector of Historical Documents, Literary Manuscripts, and Autograph Letters* (London: S.J. Davey, 1891), 11.

39. See Raab.

40. Munby, *Cult of the Autograph Letter*, 1.

41. In addition to Munby and Scott, another useful and entertaining history of autograph collecting is Thomas F. Madigan's *Word Shadows of the Great: The Lure of Autograph Collecting* (New York: Frederick A. Stokes Company, 1930).

42. As quoted in Munby, *Cult of the Autograph Letter*, 10.

43. Quoted in Christopher Fletcher, "Lord Byron's Unrecorded Autograph Poems," *Notes and Queries* 43 (December 1996): 426.

44. James Fennimore Cooper to Laura Jewett, January 5, 1850, *Letters and Journals of James Fennimore Cooper*, 6 volumes (Cambridge: MA: Harvard University Press, 1960–68), 6: 210.

45. Josh Lauer, "Traces of the Real: Autographomania and the Cult of the Signers in Nineteenth-Century America," *Text and Performance Quarterly* 27, no. 2 (April 2007): 143–63.

46. Ibid., 146.

47. Jacques Derrida, "Signature Event Context," trans. Samuel Weber and Jeffrey Mehlman, *Limited Inc.* (Evanston, IL: Northwestern University Press, 1988), 20.

48. Ibid., 107.

49. Lauer, "Traces of the Real," 144–5.

50. Pierre Nora, "Between Memory and History" [*Les lieux de memorie*], trans. Marc Roudebush, *Representations* 26 (1989): 7–24.

51. See Samantha Matthews, "Making Their Mark: Writing the Poet's Grave," in *Literary Tourism and Nineteenth-Century Culture*, ed. Nicola Watson, 34–5 (Basingstoke: Palgrave Macmillan, 2009).

52. Lauer, "Traces of the Real," 145 and 149.

53. Gaskell to Henry Bright, March 14, 1854, *Further Letters*, 108.

15

The Women of Liulichang: Female Collectors and Bibliophiles in the Late Qing

Shana J. Brown

In her widely known essay "On Not Knowing Greek," Virginia Woolf vividly describes the "sneering, laughing, nimbleness of wit and tongue" of ancient Greek, a language she read fluently.[1] Woolf's original-language quotations by Sophocles and other Greek and Roman writers suggests that her claim to "not know Greek" refers not to ability with the language, but rather to the unbridgeable distance between the modern age and the ancients. For women, rarely schooled in the Classics, this distance was even greater. Nevertheless, to try to understand the Greek world—however difficult that might be—inspired a number of nineteenth-century female writers, from Elizabeth Barrett Browning to George Eliot.[2] By studying Greek these women claimed intellectual parity with men, for whom learning in the Classics was a mark of intelligence and cultural fluency.

Of course, the England of Woolf's generation was not the only society with a passionate interest in antiquity; Chinese scholars of the same generation were enamored of their own ancient past, as they had been for centuries. Even after the eradication of the imperial civil service examination system in 1905, which tested the Confucian Classics almost exclusively, Chinese scholars continued to believe that immersion in ancient literature nurtured critical reasoning skills and the moral senses of young students. Such was the enduring allure of their own ways of "knowing Greek" that classical learning brought great cultural prestige, even after it no longer provided an immediate career benefit.[3]

For Chinese women of the Qing Dynasty (1644–1911), the struggle to earn the educational opportunities more readily afforded to their male counterparts invited an immersion in the same classical curriculum.[4] Beginning in the early nineteenth century, and continuing into the early twentieth (the period defined here as "late Qing"), elite Chinese women were newly assertive of their rights to seek educations and express themselves through literature. Just like Woolf and some of her contemporaries, they did so by appropriating elements of a hitherto largely male scholarly tradition. They might have sympathized with Woolf's enthusiasm for the Classics, and fully understood its implicit statement about the right of a woman writer to claim critical judgment about the most revered texts of the canon. By taking pleasure in antiquity through collecting artifacts and then writing poems about them, late-Qing women claimed for themselves increasingly greater participation in public life.

Chinese women at the turn of the century demonstrated erudition and social status not only by fluency in the textual tradition, but by participation in the genteel social activities that gave flavor to classical learning for their male counterparts, like enjoying poetry games with close friends, or collecting books and art objects. Late-Qing men boasted of their obsessions for ancient bronze vessels and coins, rubbings of stelae inscriptions, and other artifacts. As the painter Li Youxian (1807–76) wrote:

> in my generation, men of the last fifty years, whenever we find something
> like a coin as small as an elm seed, we pass it around to profuse admiration,
> so pleased to have found something unusual. Onlookers must have
> a good laugh to see our obsessions. Non-collectors can never really
> understand what it means to experience this kind of pleasure.[5]

As this essay will discuss, Li Youxian's female contemporaries followed suit, using the practices of collecting and connoisseurship to further demonstrate fluency in classical learning. For many women, this sense of cultural literacy could forge a more companionate bond with their collector husbands, in contrast to a more typical family relationship where the most intimate relationships a woman could enjoy were with her children, particularly her sons, and her female relations.[6] The most famous historical example of a romantic marriage created through shared collecting practices was the union of the Northern Song poet Li Qingzhao (1084–1151?) and her husband.[7] In asserting their own identities as writers and collectors, late-Qing women drew upon Li Qingzhao's legacy as a collector. An example is the reformist intellectual Xue Shaohui (1855–1911), a poet and translator who enjoyed collecting and appreciating rare paintings and artifacts with her diplomat husband.[8]

For many women, the practices of reading and collecting did not just open intellectual doors; they opened their household doors, as well. During Xue Shaohui's lifetime, there is evidence of increasing physical participation of women in spaces generally reserved for male collectors, such as bookstores and art markets. By becoming consumers of these luxuries, Chinese women could experience the pleasures of the *flâneuse*, a role that in nineteenth-century Europe, particularly via the newly developed department store, gave women more opportunities to (in Balzac's words) "promenade on the boulevards" and "amuse themselves by shopping."[9] In particular, by visiting the book and antiques market of large Chinese cities, like the Liulichang neighborhood in Beijing, women were given the chance to experience "empowerment in the relation between looking and having," in Anne Friedberg's view, by enjoying the "diversion, self-gratification, expertise, and physical activity" of shopping.[10]

The presence of women in literary neighborhoods of late-Qing cities prefigures the wider entry of women into Chinese public life. At a time when women were still expected to be sequestered in the "inner chambers" of the domestic sphere, book- and art-collecting offered a rare opportunity to enter urban public space. This was particularly significant during the late nineteenth and early twentieth centuries, a time when women were seeking greater political rights and social participation across the board. Perhaps not even women's education, becoming more widespread in the same period—single-sex and taking place in enclosed, controlled spaces—could offer quite the same potential for women to assert their physical presence in the public world. Hence my argument that late-Qing collecting and writing practices, by giving women an intellectual and social justification to enter male literary space—literally and figuratively—were a critical process by which Chinese women became more actively engaged with the emerging Chinese public sphere.

This is not to say that Chinese women were never scholars or collectors until Xue Shaohui and her contemporaries in the late nineteenth century; on the contrary, the elite female artist, poet, and collector was a well-established role, if small in actual number. As mentioned above, perhaps the most famous female collector was Li Qingzhao, whose biographical addendum to her husband's catalog of bronze artifacts described their shared obsession with antiquities.[11] As this essay will discuss, Li Qingzhao's example held out hope to many elite women that they, too, could achieve "a companionate marriage that included intellectual exchange and shared aesthetic experiences," to use Susan Mann's words.[12] Models of famous female poets were even more plentiful. The literary production of women bloomed in the late eighteenth and early nineteenth centuries (we have works from several thousand female writers from the Qing period overall), when classical scholarship and literary activity were well supported by the imperial state as well as nurtured through private publication. It was during this period that the poet Yun Zhu (1771–1833), with help from her devoted son, compiled an ambitious anthology of women's poetry in 1836.[13] Over the next several decades, there appeared many more anthologies of women's poems, as well as single-author works by female poets, including Xue Shaohui's posthumous *Poetry Collection from the Tower of Somber Rhymes*, printed by her husband in 1911. The attention paid to female poets during the Qing period is itself a significant cultural formation, one that continued well into the Republican period, when more and more anthologies of female poets were issued and a number of studies of female poets were established.[14]

The late eighteenth and early nineteenth centuries witnessed a boom in antiquarian collecting by male scholars, and not surprisingly, we see more examples of women interested in collecting art and antiquities, including the epigraphic rubbings so prized by their male contemporaries. Feng Sihui (1748–74) wrote poetry about buying books.[15] Wang Duan (1793–1838) celebrated a rubbing taken from a famous sculpture of a Buddhist deity, the Jade Maiden or Bixia Fairy, located at the goddess's temple complex on Mount Tai in Shandong.[16] Wu Zao (1799–1862) commemorated an epigraphic rubbing of a Jin Dynasty stele, the "Mrs Sun" inscription, discovered in 1793 by the calligrapher Jiang Fengyi.[17] And the Qing poetess Zhang Xiuduan (dates unknown) enjoyed viewing bronze vessel inscriptions with friends, which inspired "the minds of antiquarians to turn together to write verse," recording the "fragrance of the old articles" in poetry.[18] Collecting books, poring over epigraphical rubbings, and admiring bronze vessels with friends, these women collectors were laying claim to an elite and largely male form of knowledge—expertise in the material culture of Classics and the ancient past. To use Virginia Woolf's phrase, they knew their Greek.

The collecting practices commemorated in these poems had a geographical as well as literary nexus. For both men and women, the primary antique and book markets of the empire were located in the capital city (modern Beijing), in the neighborhood called Liulichang. A commercial and manufacturing area even during the medieval period (the district, located just to the south of the Forbidden City, housed the imperial tile works that helped build the Ming-era palaces), Liulichang developed rapidly as a book market during the late eighteenth century, when a series of imperially sponsored book compilation projects, undertaken nearby, encouraged officials to frequent the neighborhood in search of rare texts. Whereas Liulichang had some 30 booksellers in the late eighteenth century, a hundred years later that number had almost tripled, accommodating a growing appetite for books, stationery, and curios.[19] Permanent storefronts competed with weekly markets which offered flowers, candy, and toys to shoppers, as well as annual markets timed to celebrate the lunar New Year. The city telephone bureau was established in Liulichang, as were modern schools, exhibition halls, and the city's first photography studio, the Fengtai.[20] Xue Shaohui's photograph survives—as do several of her female contemporaries—and they may have been taken in Liulichang, or in similar shopping districts in other major cities. Liulichang was a place to see and be seen, in many respects.

With its proximity to the imperial offices, Liulichang became a place for scholar-officials to visit bookstores, purchase artworks, and buy their brushes, ink, and blank examination papers. In a city with no public libraries or universities, Liulichang fulfilled an important social function, with genteel proprietors hosting informal gatherings of browsing scholars. Perhaps more surprisingly, nineteenth-century Liulichang was regularly visited by women, as this undated poem describes:

> The Liulichang market is open once again.
> Rare treasures are lined up everywhere.
>
> Women rub shoulders and carts jam the
> streets, everyone saying they will just take a
> quick look and return early.[21]

Why were there so many women in Qing Liulichang, and who were they? The question why there were so many literate women is complex, but as stated before, the late eighteenth and early nineteenth centuries saw a boom in publication projects by and about literate women, for whom literary activities like writing poetry were increasingly common. Although probably no more than 10 percent of Chinese women overall during the period could read and write, those women who were lucky enough to attain literacy were increasingly active in publishing their own works and those of their contemporaries.[22] Like their male counterparts, these increasingly large numbers of literate women would have gravitated to Liulichang as the natural place to buy books, many of them by or about women.

Educated women may have felt particularly comfortable in the neighborhood because it was adjacent to several large temple complexes, including the Fire God temple. Qing women were known to enjoy visiting temples. The prominent Confucian writer Chen Hongmou (1696–1771) had fretted over the corrupting influence of temple life on otherwise staid women, who could be found "parading around visiting temples and monasteries, burning incense and holding services, kneeling to listen to the chanting of the sutras. In the temple courtyards and in the precincts of the monasteries, they chat and laugh freely."[23] But despite Confucian disapproval, women continued to go to temples and their fairs, and by the end of the dynasty, as Madeleine Dong writes, Beijing residents called some "temple markets 'fairs for the ones-in-the-house' (wives) to go to."[24] These temples sometimes held markets as often as once every ten days (the traditional Chinese week), offering retail goods for sale, theatrical performances, street snacks, and other entertainments. Markets attracted visitors eager to "see the hot and noisy spectacle," as Jianfei Zhu writes, which "constituted some of the most exciting moments in the public life of the population of Beijing."[25] Respectable women would not have patronized theaters and teahouses (sites of drinking and carousing) in the adjacent neighborhood of Dashalar, but they could see opera performed at temples, which considerately offered separate seating for male and female audience members.[26]

The answer to *who* they were is more complex. Many of them were genteel wives and daughters of wealthy houses, who, like the anthologist Yun Zhu, married into aristocratic families.[27] Many texts specify that *shinü*, or elite females, often visited Liulichang, at least during the all-important New Year's season. "In the first month of the year," remarked the turn-of-the-century visitor Ma Jiongzhang, who dallied in the area with friends during the festival season, "female gentry (*shinü*) poured out into the city, like tea or clouds."[28] Likewise, an early twentieth-century visitor noted the prevalence of *shinü* during the New Year. He commented that teashops in the area now served men and women, seated at separate tables, an arrangement that was attracting more female customers.[29] Women were becoming more visible in provincial capitals as well; after 1906, teahouses in Chengdu began to allow women customers. Although they attempted to attend performances in commercial theaters, Chengdu women were forcibly expelled by police, who feared the social chaos when respectable women were allowed to inhabit the same social space as prostitutes and their customers.[30]

Many of the women visiting Liulichang were probably concubines (secondary wives) and courtesans, who were often well-educated artists and poets. In the early decades of the twentieth century, the museum professional Zhou Zhaoxiang (1880–1954), who founded several associations devoted to collecting art and antiques, training painters, and publishing art-related journals, commented on the presence of concubines in Liulichang. As he remembered his first visit to the capital in 1899, carts and horses crowded before the gates to the neighborhood, which was full of "rich men's concubines, upper-class men of letters, pretty-boy servants, the red wheels and carved saddles [of nobility], embroidered clothes and pearl buttons, all making a gracefully fluttering scene, wild as a dreamscape."[31] However, the secondary wives seen by Zhou Zhaoxiang in the neighborhood might still have been elite and educated; genteel concubines were increasingly active in many areas of late-Qing public life.[32]

Whether first or secondary wives, the women who ventured into Liulichang took advantage of one of the few public spaces that accommodated women without undue scandal.[33] Liulichang harbored gender transgression of several kinds, as a late nineteenth-century poem makes clear:

Narrow sleeves, long gowns are bound together in new fashions.
Fine slivers of dancing shoes are wrinkled with fragrant dust.
Girls love to act like boys.
It is not possible to distinguish male from female, true from false.[34]

Zhou Zhaoxiang's reference to "pretty-boy servants"—possibly male prostitutes—highlights the sexually ambiguous nature of the neighborhood's *flâneurs* and *flâneuses*. We note Liulichang's proximity to the nearby theater district in Dashalar, where young female-role actors (*dan*) were frequently invited to entertain elite male patrons, remaining in female costume as they did so.[35] The two adjacent pleasure quarters—literary and theatrical—thus offered alternatives to conventional gender roles, a liberating quality of the neighborhood for aspiring female writers and collectors. For women, the transgression consisted in simply being active in the public space, particularly in ways usually reserved for educated men.

Of course, many of the women who visited Liulichang browsed conventionally feminine markets. Li Ciming (1829–94), a comprehensive diarist of capital life, noted that women and children were particularly common in the market during the New Year, shopping for toys.[36] This might seem to lead to the conclusion that women in Liulichang, while enjoying the freedom of the public space, still went there to pursue typically "female" consumer activities, rather than buying books and artworks like male scholars. A female character in the turn-of-the-century novel *The Sea of Regret*, set in Beijing, visits "a cosmetics shop in Dashalar" and ends up buying "two sandalwood rosaries and a pair of incense sachets," no doubt intended for private devotions, as well as a pet squirrel.[37] Perhaps like the nineteenth-century European women who shopped in department stores, "knowing that nothing would jar with their feminine sensibility and moral uprightness," the tastes of Chinese women were marked by gender identities.[38] Certainly in succeeding decades, Chinese women would be bombarded with advertisements enticing them to purchase cosmetics, clothing, and the latest hairstyles in order to be at once modern, fashionable, and feminine.[39]

Yet period magazines suggest that it was not uncommon for women to be found in bookstores. The vernacular journal, the *Capital Pictorial to Awake the World* (Jiujing xingshi huabao, published between 1908 and 1909), includes an illustration entitled "The Education of Women." The picture shows a woman dressed in a long plain gown and short vest like a male scholar, sitting and reading at a bookstore table while two clerks assist her. Prominently visible are her feet, soberly shod in plain black shoes and seemingly unbound. A young boy, possibly her son, looks on. The caption reads:

> Bookstores in the Donghuamen neighborhood [just outside the east gate of the Forbidden City] frequently have educated women in their shops buying all kinds of books. One hears that they buy them and bring them home to read aloud to illiterate women of the household. They can all expound [on ideas] like this women [in the illustration]! How can women's education not succeed in China?[40]

The focus on educating children is not surprising; the literate mother, who could nurture intellectual talent in her sons, is another trope of the traditional Chinese woman. And it is true that even when the Qing state and its successors encouraged more educational opportunities for women, they often couched their programs in the traditional language of the need to educate mothers for the good of their sons.[41] Yet the educated, non-traditional woman was emerging too, as we see from the famous example of Qiu Jin (1875–1911), who left her husband and children to study in Japan, eventually embracing revolutionary politics; and the wealthy entrepreneur and famous poet Lü Bicheng (1883–1943), who began her career as a reporter for a prominent Tianjin newspaper and remained single throughout her life.[42] Hence educated women of the period could refer to a spectrum of female identities, with different visions of how modernity and traditional gender roles (motherhood, marriage, and other family responsibilities) could coincide.

In the same year that the "Education of Women" illustration appeared, a remarkable female writer, reformist intellectual, poet, and connoisseur visited Liulichang with her husband. This was Xue Shaohui, a Fuzhou native who lived in the capital for a brief time at the end of her life. Xue Shaohui was the author of the *Biographies of Exemplary Foreign Women* (Waiguo lienu zhuan) and the first Chinese translator of Jules Verne's *Around the World in Eighty Days*, completed while accompanying her husband Chen Shoupeng (1857–?) on a diplomatic posting in France. She was born into a cultivated family; her mother was a poet and painter, and she and her sisters delighted in poetic competitions. She was active in reformist politics during the late 1890s, particularly in the movement to establish the first modern women's academy in Shanghai. The inaugural meeting of the Women's Study Society, held in Shanghai in December 1897, was co-chaired by Xue Shaohui's French sister-in-law, Lai Mayi. Xue Shaohui herself was a frequent contributor to the Society's journal *Chinese Girl's Progress* (Nü xuebao), whose illustrations were provided by a female artist, Liu Jing.[43]

Among Xue Shaohui's extensive poems and essays we find a number of pieces reflecting on Li Qingzhao who, along with her first husband Zhao Mingcheng (1081–1129), amassed a famous collection of paintings, bronze vessels, rare books, and other treasures before the fall of the Song Dynasty to northern invaders. Throughout most of the Late Imperial period, Li Qingzhao was esteemed primarily as a writer of lyric (*ci*) poetry, a format particularly popular with female writers. Her manner of poetry, called the "Yi'an style" after her courtesy name, was widely emulated until the end of the Qing Dynasty. Perhaps because of her remarkable accomplishments as a poet and collector, Li Qingzhao's gender sat uncomfortably with scholars. One important question for later Chinese scholars was how to interpret her exceptionality, as a woman whose poetry surpassed many of her male contemporaries. Late-Ming biographies, for example, begin with the statement that Li Qingzhao "was not a woman" and end by praising her as one of the only two Song women who could write.[44] Even complimentary scholars suggested that there was something non-feminine about her achievements.[45] An early nineteenth-century compendium of female painters, *Yutai huashi* (the History of painters from the jade terrace) by Tang Shuyu (1789–1835), describes Li Qingzhao as a "calligrapher, painter, and *ci* poet, excellent at literary description." The text then praises her memoir of collecting, noting that "up to the present day, whenever scholars read her preface to *Jinshi lu*, their spirits are immediately refreshed." Yet the entry continues: "What kind of an old hag was she, to create such a surprising fragrance?"[46] That typical note of misogynistic surprise—an insult to mask a compliment, in this case on her ability to write movingly as a collector of antiques—implies that few women could have emulated her diverse literary and scholarly accomplishments.

Despite such mixed responses to Li Qingzhao by male biographers, a number of nineteenth-century writers reengaged with her legend, although with cautious sentiments regarding her unusual biography: Li Qingzhao, after being widowed by her beloved first husband, remarried (unchaste) and then sought a divorce from her new husband (unvirtuous). Yet the harmonious intellectual companionship Li Qingzhao enjoyed with Zhao Mingcheng remained a potent role-model. For the female poet Gu Taiqing (1799–1876), Li Qingzhao's relationship with her husband was notable for its harmony and equality of interests; both spouses were connoisseurs of antiques like ancient bronze vessels.[47] Huang Youqin (courtesy name Meixin) had more reservations about the morality of Li Qingzhao's remarriage, but nevertheless related to her not only as a poet, but as a scholar of antiquity. Huang Youqin's husband remarked that he "felt happy whenever he could study a graph with Meixin"; their own marriage apparently enjoyed the felicity of a bond built on shared collecting practices.[48] For many of the Qing women who wrote about Li Qingzhao, it is clear that her harmonious and intellectually engaged marriage with her spouse was one of the most affecting elements of her legend.

Xue Shaohui also appreciated Li Qingzhao's model of a wife who enjoyed collecting antiquities with her husband. When she lived in the capital, Xue Shaohui frequented the Liulichang neighborhood to collect books and antiques with her husband, nicknamed Yiru. For example, in a pair of poems from 1908, Xue Shaohui described an outing to Liulichang which reminded her of Li Qingzhao (who lived centuries before the imperial city was even established):

Year wushen [1908], first month of spring. My bronchitis is somewhat better. Yiru says the Liulichang book market has many old block-printed books, so we took a rickshaw together to the Fire God's temple. We saw various antiques stalls, and sets of calligraphy and paintings, but genuine and fake articles were not distinguished. There were not many book stalls, but there were some exceptionally fine rare books. Afterwards in the bookstores we caught a glimpse of a Yuan edition of the Ancient and Modern Discourses on the Source of the River *(Gujin liuyuan zhi lun), and an original edition of the [Qianlong era]* Lyric Poetry Catalog from the Xiqing Palace *(Xiqing cipu). Even though they asked outrageous prices, we could not help but get them. On the way home I composed this poem aloud to Yiru:*

No immortals could yearn more for piles of books, or
desire spoiled fragments saved from disaster.

Nothing can wash away money like a lonely customer, returning from the mountains with empty hands [i.e., having been unsuccessful at business or the market].

The next poem in the pair refers explicitly to Li Qingzhao:

Money for paper and ink, parched [blank] scrolls, and book-
covers, make me smile repeatedly at the bitter cold.

I return to the Su Xi [Five Dynasties artist] painting in the
hall. Mourning, I finally understand Li Yi'an.[49]

Here Li Qingzhao figures in Xue Shaohui's experiences primarily as a collector, and as someone whose experiences of loss and sacrifice in building a collection become a touchstone for Xue Shaohui's own experiences as a consumer in the marketplace. At the same time, Xue Shaohui implicitly positions her own conjugal intimacy with her husband as a modern version of the kind of collectors' partnership that Li Qingzhao enjoyed with Zhao Mingcheng. Thus for a woman collector at the end of the Qing, Li Qingzhao's legacy was not necessarily primarily as a poet, but instead as a connoisseur of art and antiques.

Li Qingzhao's legacy as a collector, however, was bittersweet. In her postface to the *Record of Antiquities* (Jinshi lu), her husband's catalog of bronze artifacts, she conveys the intimacy achieved by conjugal collectors, as well as the sacrifices that such collections required:

On the fifteenth day of every month, my husband would get a short vacation from the Academy; he would "pawn some clothes" for five hundred cash and go to the market in the Xiang-guo Temple, where he would buy fruit and rubbings of inscriptions. When he brought these home, we would sit facing one another, rolling them out before us, examining and munching. And we thought ourselves persons of Ge-tian [i.e., in paradise].

I happen to have an excellent memory, and every evening after we finished eating, we would sit in the hall called "Return Home" and make tea. Pointing to the heaps of books and histories, we would guess on which line of which page in which chapter of which book a certain passage could be found. Success in guessing determined who got to drink his or her tea first. Whenever I got it right, I would raise the teacup, laughing so hard that the tea would spill in my lap, and I would get up, not having been able to drink any of it at all. I would have been glad to grow old in such a world.[50]

However, as Stephen Owen has pointed out, Li Qingzhao's memoir emphasizes the great financial sacrifices required to build the collection. Gradually, too, the conjugal intimacy seems to have faded. At a certain point the collection was locked away by her husband, and Li Qingzhao had to request access. Driven to poverty by her husband's obsession with collecting, Li Qingzhao lived in a state of "nervousness and anxiety," having to "plan how to make do with only one meat dish in our meals and how to do away with all the finery on my dress."[51]

In her own life, Xue Shaohui faced many of the same tensions, familiar to almost all collectors, between the desire to possess beautiful artifacts and the financial difficulties of doing so. An early poem (dated *circa* 1881, when the writer was a teenage bride), recalls a sacrifice to purchase a beautiful but expensive painting for her husband:

Someone wants to sell [a painting] in the manner of "Seventeen Histories from the Old Pavilion" by Chen Gongfu. It is done with cinnabar-lead paint in five colors, with a very antique flavor.[52] *My husband loves it, but bitterly cannot afford the price. So I used a gold bracelet to pay for it, and then composed this poem:*

Why not divide the filigree bracelet in half. White cornelian
of the first rank has a surprising fragrance.

One ought to know if the Zuohai writer [her husband, from
Zuohai in Fuzhou] is depleted. A great elegance is like a spoke
in a wheel, always looking towards the gentleman.[53]

Xue Shaohui was surely aware that her sacrifice echoed the selfless Li Qingzhao. Yet she still saw herself as a "spoke" supporting the "wheel" of her husband—a subordinate role that nonetheless underscores their harmony and interconnectedness. Other poems refer to the pleasures of the conjugal collecting pair, as when her sister brought over a rare gift—some "cliff tea" from Wuyi Mountain in Fujian—and Xue Shaohui enjoyed it with her husband in a special clay teapot he had collected, "as heavy as a barbarian tripod."[54] Li Qingzhao and Xue Shaohui articulated their interest in artifacts as a function of their marital relationship, a way to nurture the conjugal intimacy that educated women prized. But whereas Li Qingzhao remained inside her house, enjoying a collection purchased in the markets by her husband, Xue Shaohui visited the market and selected objects alongside her husband. Her physical mobility echoed her intellectual audacity and broader participation in the public world, including her activities as a proponent of educational reform.

Overall, however, Xue Shaohui emphasized her dependence on her conjugal relationship, demonstrating relatively traditional values in comparison with some of the more radically feminist members of her generation, like Qiu Jin and Lü Bicheng. As Nanxiu Qian has argued, Xue Shaohui was both an exception to, and a representative of, her class and generation. She was granted privileges and opportunities afforded to only the minutest sliver of her generation, and the literary voice she developed is rare even within this elite cohort. Yet along with several other participants in the Women's Study Society group, she defended many aspects of the literary role traditionally fulfilled by elite female women, namely by embracing the traditional concept of the *cainü* or talented woman, a concept that complimented the female scholar for her accomplishments while at the same time emphasizing her gender and overall Confucian role. The *cainü* concept was criticized by Qiu Jin and turn-of-the-century male reformers like Liang Qichao (1873–1929), becoming a focal point of the larger debate over the advisability of change within versus change beyond traditional cultural social roles.[55]

An essay by Xue Shaohui on Li Qingzhao, reflecting on the medieval poet's second marriage and attempt to dissolve that union, is typical of this kind of transitional generation, when debates over how the changing status of women would affect other areas of traditional family life were swirling throughout the intellectual world. Like Gu Taiqing and Huang Youqin a century earlier, Xue Shaohui tried to come to terms with the legacy of Li Qingzhao as poet, antiquarian, and divorcee. Her essay compares Li Qingzhao to another (possibly apocryphal) female poet, Zhu Shuzhen (*circa* 1135–80), who is believed to have had a bad marriage, committed adultery, and then killed herself, whereupon her family destroyed most of her poems.[56] Xue Shaohui is sympathetic to both cases. "Poor women!" she says of the two poets. "Gossiping and trouble-making are the favorite tasks of [male] literati." The criticism of the personal lives of the two writers, she argues, only occurred because "black and white are confused, chastity and lasciviousness are rarely differentiated," and because male critics hold double standards.[57] In utilizing a Confucian vocabulary to criticize male writers, Xue Shaohui further articulates the overall goals of the classically trained woman scholar of the period, namely to transgress her gender by appropriating male intellectual standards knowledge while, at the same time, upholding the image of the loyal and romantic *cainü*. By forgiving Li Qingzhao her lack of chastity, Xue Shaohui prefigures by a generation the obsession that Chinese intellectuals would come to have with Ibsen's Nora, whose sense of self-worth fueled her escape from a disappointing bourgeois marriage.[58]

As Nanxiu Qian and others have argued, Xue Shaohui and her contemporaries were poised on the cusp of a new intellectual world. Although they enjoyed unprecedented opportunities for travel, education, and self-expression, they still seem old-fashioned compared to the perspective of the women who would come after them. For example, her husband Chen Shoupeng portrays Xue Shaohui as exceedingly modest, claiming that her verse is not worthy of publication.[59] If accurate, this kind of reticence might make Xue Shaohui and her generation less interesting as historical actors. But even if Xue Shaohui and her contemporaries seem old-fashioned, their traditionalism fades when we recall how physically and intellectually "out" their passage to modernity had been, incubated by the unique environment of Liulichang and other urban commercial districts. More than any generation in the past, Xue Shaohui and her contemporaries used the intellectual practices of their male counterparts, as writers and collectors, to physically and discursively enter urban public life. Once there, they have never left.

Notes

1. Virginia Woolf, "On Not Knowing Greek," *Collected Essays, Volume One* (London: The Hogarth Press, 1966), 2.
2. Isobel Hurst, *Victorian Women Writers and the Classics: The Feminine of Homer* (Oxford: Oxford University Press, 2006), 220–22.
3. For a discussion of the ongoing importance of classical learning in twentieth-century intellectual life, see Wen-hsin Yeh, *The Alienated Academy: Culture and Politics in Republican China, 1919–1937* (Cambridge, MA: The Council on East Asian Studies, Harvard University and Harvard University Press, 1990), passim.
4. See Dorothy Ko, *Teachers of the Inner Chambers: Women and Culture in Seventeenth-Century China* (Stanford, CA: Stanford University Press, 1994), passim.
5. Li Youxian, "Gu quan hui hou xu" [Postface to compendium of ancient coins]. Reprint. In *Zhongguo qianbi wenxian congshu* [Collection of Chinese literary works on coins] 16:1, edited by Ma Feihai and Wang Guichen (Shanghai: Shanghai guji chubanshe, 1992), 11–12. For a discussion of the "obsessions" felt by collectors, see Judith Zeitlin, *Historian of the Strange: Pu Songling and the Chinese Classical Tale* (Stanford: Stanford University Press, 1993), passim.
6. For a discussion of these kinds of marriages, see Susan Mann, *Precious Records: Women in China's Long Eighteenth Century* (Stanford: Stanford University Press, 1997), 22.
7. Women's writings, particularly poetry, were often concerned with romantic love, but as several studies have indicated, this romantic ideal was only rarely achieved. See Wilt L. Idema, "Male Fantasies and Female Realities: Chu Shu-chen and Chang Yü-niang and their Biographies," in *Chinese Women in the Imperial Past: New Perspectives*, ed. Harriet T. Zurndorfer (Leiden, Boston, Köln: Brill, 1999), passim.
8. Although it may be true that in the Song period, as John Wixted has argued, "there is little critical reference to Li Ch'ing-chao being used as a model by women," my research shows that Li Qingzhao was unambiguously a model for Qing scholars, at least as an antiquarian. See John Timothy Wixted, "The Poetry of Li Ch'ing-chao: A Woman Author and Women's Authorship," in *Voices of the Song Lyric in China*, ed. Pauline Yu (Berkeley: University of California Press, 1994), 147.
9. Ruth E. Iskin, "The *Flâneuse* in French Fin-de-Siècle Posters: Advertising Images of Modern Women in Paris," in *The Invisible Flaneuse?: Gender, Public Space and Visual Culture in Nineteenth Century Paris*, edited by Aruna D'Souza and Tom McDonough (Manchester: Manchester University Press, 2006), 115.
10. Anne Friedberg, *Window Shopping: Cinema and the Postmodern* (Berkeley: University of California Press, 1993), 57.
11. For a discussion of another medieval female collector, see Shen C.Y. Fu, "Princess Sengge Ragi, Collector of Painting and Calligraphy," translated and adapted by Marsha Weidner, in *Flowering in the Shadows: Women in the History of Chinese and Japanese Painting*, edited by Marsha Weidner (Honolulu: University of Hawaii Press, 1990). However, Sengge Ragi, a Yuan (Mongol) princess, seems not to have inspired Qing women in the way Li Qingzhao did.
12. Susan Mann, "The Education of Daughters in the Mid-Ch'ing Period," in *Education and Society in Late Imperial China, 1600–1900*, edited by Alexander Woodside and Benjamin A. Elman (Berkeley: University of California Press, 1994), 23.
13. Mann, *Precious Records*, 19–20. For a discussion of male assistance in the publication of works devoted to women's writings, see Clara Wing-chung Ho, "Encouragement from the Opposite Gender: Male Scholars' Interests in Women's Publications in Ch'ing China—A Bibliographic Study," in *Chinese Women in the Imperial Past: New Perspectives*, edited by Harriet T. Zurndorfer (Leiden, Boston, Köln: Brill, 1999), 308–13.

14. See Chen Shuiyun, "Ershi shiji de qingdai nüxing ci yanjiu" [Research on Qing Dynasty women's ci poems in the 20th century], *Funü yanjiu luncong* 1 (2004): 67–72, passim.

15. Feng Sihui, "Mai shu he yun" [Verse on buying books], in *Xiu yu yin* [Embroidery surplus poems] (China: 1764), 6.3b–6.4a, McGill-Harvard-Yenching Library Ming-Qing Women's Writings Digitization Project, <http://digital.library.mcgill.ca/mingqing/english/>.

16. Wang Duan, "Shu Bixiayuanjun yu yin ta ben hou" [Postface to rubbing of the Bixia Fairy calligraphy], in *Lin xia ya yin ji* [Collection of elegant sounds from beneath the forest], edited by Mao Jun (China: 1884), 2:1a, McGill-Harvard-Yenching Library Ming-Qing Women's Writings Digitization Project. <http://digital.library.mcgill.ca/mingqing/english/>.

17. Wu Zao, "Manjianghong: Jiang Juxiang xue bo xin de Jin Rencheng tai shou Sun fu ren bei ta ben zheng ti wei tian ci jie" [To the tune of "Manjianghong": On the theme of a rubbing of the Jin Dynasty Mrs Sun stele in Rencheng, newly found by Jiang Juxiang], in *Xiao tan luan shi hui ke bai jia guixiu ci* [Compendium of women's ci from the little sandalwood studio], edited by Xu Naichang (China: Nan Lingxu keben, 1896), 19b, <McGill-Harvard-Yenching Library Ming-Qing Women's Writings Digitization Project. http://digital.library.mcgill.ca/mingqing/english/>.

18. Zhang Xiuduan, "Qian diao (Jin lü qu)" [First verse, to the tune of Jin lü qu], in *Guixiu ci chao* [Draft of women's ci poetry], edited by Xu Naichang (China: Xiao tan luan she ke ben, 1909), 14.10a–b, McGill-Harvard-Yenching Library Ming-Qing Women's Writings Digitization Project. <http://digital.library.mcgill.ca/mingqing/english/>.

19. See the list of book and antique stores in Yuan Miao, Zhu Tuo, "Liulichang fang si bian'e lu" [Record of Liulichang market placards], in *Liulichang xiaozhi* [Short gazetteer of Liulichang], edited by Sun Dianqi (Beijing: Beijing chubanshe, 1982), 38–44.

20. Zhang Hanrui, "Liulichang yan ge kao" [Studies on the transformation of Liulichang], in *Liulichang xiaozhi* [Short gazetteer of Liulichang], edited by Sun Dianqi (Beijing: Beijing chubanshe, 1982), 16–17.

21. De Shuoting, "Changdian," [Liulichang], in *Liulichang xiaozhi* [Short gazetteer of Liulichang], edited by Sun Dianqi (Beijing: Beijing chubanshe, 1982), 83.

22. Ho, "Encouragement," 308.

23. Susan Mann, "Grooming a Daughter for Marriage: Brides and Wives in the Mid-Qing Period," in *Chinese Femininities/Chinese Masculinities: A Reader*, eds. Susan Brownell and Jeffrey N. Wasserstrom; foreword by Thomas Laqueur (Berkeley and London: University of California Press, 2002), 110.

24. Madeleine Yue Dong, *Republican Beijing: The City and its Histories* (Berkeley: University of California Press, 2003), 165.

25. Zhu Jianfei, *Chinese Spatial Strategies: Imperial Beijing, 1420–1911* (London and New York: Routledge Curzon, 2004), 84.

26. Ibid., 165.

27. Mann, *Precious Records*, 94.

28. Ma Jiongzhang. "Changdian ji," in *Liulichang xiaozhi* [Short gazetteer of Liulichang], edited by Sun Dianqi (Beijing: Beijing chubanshe, 1982), 45. I am unable to locate biographical information on Ma Jiongzhang, but this dating seems appropriate given the overall tone of the text.

29. Sun Dianqi, *Liulichang xiaozhi* [Short gazetteer of Liulichang] (Beijing: Beijing chubanshe, 1982), 46. This anonymous text would seem to be clearly twentieth-century, since it references the rise of handicrafts in the neighborhood and uses various modern terminologies.

30. Wang Di, *Street Culture in Chengdu: Public Space, Urban Commoners, and Local Politics, 1870–1930* (Stanford: Stanford University Press, 2003), 181.

31. Zhou Zhaoxiang, *Liulichang zaji* [Miscellaneous notes on Liulichang] (Beijing: Beijing Yanshan chubanshe, 1995), 5.

32. Nanxiu Qian, "Revitalizing the Xianyuan (Worthy Ladies) Tradition: Women in the 1898 Reforms," *Modern China* 29, no. 4 (2003): 39.

33. See, for example, the scandal over women shopping in Chengdu, in Wang Di, *Street Culture in Chengdu*, 182.

34. Zhang Hanrui, "Liulichang yan ge kao," 11.

35. Joshua Goldstein, *Drama Kings: Players and Publics in the Re-Creation of Peking Opera, 1870–1937* (Berkeley: University of California Press, 2007), 66.

36. Li Ciming, "Tao hua sheng jie'an riji" [Diary from the Peach-blossom Studio], in *Liulichang xiaozhi* [Short gazetteer of Liulichang], edited by Sun Dianqi (Beijing: Beijing chubanshe, 1982), 33.

37. Wu Jianren, "Hen hai," *The Sea of Regret: Two Turn-of-the-Century Chinese Romantic Novels*, translated by Patrick Hanan (Honolulu: University of Hawai'i Press, 1995), 57.

38. Pamela Pilbeam, "Bourgeois Society," in *A Companion to Nineteenth-Century Europe, 1789–1914*, edited by Stefan Berger (Malden, MA: Blackwell Publishers, 2006), 94.

39. Carlton Benson, "The Manipulation of *Tanci* in Radio Shanghai During the 1930's," *Republican China* 20, no. 2 (April): 134, 135; Louise Edwards, "Policing the Modern Woman in Republican China," *Modern China* 26 (2000): 123.

40. *Jiujing xingshi huabao* [The capital periodical to awaken the world], published 1908–09. Reprint. *Jiujing xingshi huabao: wan Qing shijing baitai* [The capital periodical to awaken the world: Opinions from the late-Qing city], edited by Zhang Fenggang (Beijing: Zhongguo wenlian chubanshe, 2003), 288.

41. Wendy Larson, *Women and Writing in Modern China* (Stanford: Stanford University Press, 1998), 55–6.

42. Grace S. Fong, "Alternative Modernities, or a Classical Woman of Modern China: The Challenging Trajectory of Lü Bicheng's (1883–1943) Life and Song Lyrics," in *Beyond Tradition and Modernity: Gender, Genre, and Cosmopolitanism in Late Qing China*, edited by Grace S. Fong, Nanxiu Qian, and Harriet T. Zurndorfer (Leiden and Boston: Brill, 2004), 13–14.

43. Qian, "Revitalizing the Xianyuan (Worthy Ladies) Tradition," 5–6, 18–19.

44. See the almost identical texts in Zhao Shijie, "Li Qingzhao," in *Gu jin nü shi* [Ancient and modern educated women] (China: Wen qi ke ke ben, *circa* 1628–44), 73a–b, McGill-Harvard-Yenching Library Ming-Qing Women's Writings Digitization Project, <http://digital.library.mcgill.ca/mingqing/english>; and Zhong Xing, "Li Qingzhao," in *Ming yuan shi gui* [Poems by famous beauties] (China: *circa* 1621–44), 18.1b, McGill-Harvard-Yenching Library Ming-Qing Women's Writings Digitization Project, <http://digital.library.mcgill.ca/mingqing/english/>.

45. Lu Chang, "Li Qingzhao," *Li chao ming yuan shi ci* [Poems of famous historical beauties] (China: Hongshulou ke ben, 1772), 7:19a–b, McGill-Harvard-Yenching Library Ming-Qing Women's Writings Digitization Project, <http://digital.library.mcgill.ca/mingqing/english/>.

46. Tang Shuyu, *Yutai huashi* [History of painters from the jade terrace] (China: Qiantang Wang shi Zhenyitang, 1824). Reprint. *Xuxiu Siku quanshu* [Additions to the complete library of the four treasuries] (Shanghai: Shanghai guji chubanshe, 1995–2002), 1084:347.

47. Gu Taiqing, "Jin lü qu: Yuntai xiangguo shuti Song ben 'Jinshi lu'" [To the tune of 'Jin lü qu': A Song edition Jinshi lu inscribed by Yuntai xiangguo], in *Donghai yu ge* [Songs of fishing in the Eastern sea], edited by Gu Chun (China: 1913), 48a, McGill-Harvard-Yenching Library Ming-Qing Women's Writings Digitization Project, <http://digital.library.mcgill.ca/mingqing/english/>. Gu Taiqing's writings about Li Qingzhao have a certain *frisson*, as there were rumors for a century of an adulterous affair between Gu and a famous antiquarian, Gong Zizhen (1792–1841), subsequently disproved. See Geremie R. Barmé, *Gong Xiaogong: A Case of Mistaken Identity*, Asian Studies Institute Occasional Lecture 1 (Wellington, NZ: Asian Studies Institute, Victoria University of Wellington, 1999), 8–9.

48. Huang Youqin, "Shu ya liang tang zhong kan Jinshi lu" [Afterword to the Records of Metal and Stone from the Elegant Book Studio], in *Guochao weixiu zheng shi ji* [Collected works of Qing cultivated ladies] (China: 1831), 19.1a–19.1b, McGill-Harvard-Yenching Library Ming-Qing Women's Writings Digitization Project, <http://digital.library.mcgill.ca/mingqing/english/>.

49. Xue Shaohui, *Xue Shaohui ji* [Collected works of Xue Shaohui] (Beijing: Fangzhi chubanshe, 2003), 45.

50. Li Qingzhao, "Interlude: Li Qing-zhao's Epilogue to *Records on Metal and Stone*," in *Anthology of Chinese Literature, Beginnings to 1911*, edited and translated by Stephen Owen (New York: W.W. Norton & Company, 1997), 592–3.

51. Ibid., 593.

52. Chen Gongfu (1771–1834) was a painter from Fujian.

53. *Xue Shaohui ji*, 7.

54. *Xue Shaohui ji*, 87.

55. Amy D. Dooling and Kristina M. Torgeson, "Introduction," in *Writing Women in Modern China: An Anthology of Women's Literature from the Early Twentieth Century*, edited by Amy D. Dooling and Kristina M. Torgeson (New York: Columbia University Press, 1998), 4.

56. Sophie Volff, "Zhu Shuzhen," in *Women Writers of Traditional China: An Anthology of Poetry and Criticism*, edited by Kang-i San Chang and Haun Saussy; Charles Kwong, associate editor; Anthony C. Yu and Yu-kung Kao, consulting editors (Stanford: Stanford University Press, 1999), 100.

57. *Xue Shaohui ji*, 146–7.

58. Elizabeth See Eide, *China's Ibsen: From Ibsen to Ibsenism* (London: Curzon, 1987), passim.

59. Chen Shoupeng, "Xu" [Remembrance], in *Xue Shaohui ji* [Collected works of Xue Shaohui], by Xue Shaohui (Beijing: Fangzhi chubanshe, 2003).

Japanese Objects in Impressionist Women's Art: Collecting Culture and Creating Identity

Jennifer T. Criss

Between 1870 and 1894, the French artist Berthe Morisot and her American colleague Mary Cassatt created a series of paintings and prints showing either upper-middle-class women or high-bourgeois interiors where a specific decorative attribute, a Japanese fan known as an *uchiwa*, played a key role in each image's connotation.[1] *Uchiwa* fans were a type of flat, circular fan with a slender bamboo frame and handles and a silk center often painted with a floral motif.[2] These female-associated products first began to reach Europe in significant numbers following Japan's official opening to the West in 1854 after two and a half centuries of self-imposed closure. Although *uchiwa* were more expensive and less easily obtained than the widely available, popular, and economical folding fans also imported from Japan, they were considered more exotic and therefore became more prized within a European context.[3]

Uchiwa fans formed part of what were collectively known in nineteenth-century France as *japonaiseries*. This term, coined in 1867 by the brothers Edmond and Jules de Goncourt, included a wide variety of Japanese and Japanese-inspired items that ranged from fans and silks to dolls and parasols to ceramics and even *ukiyo-e* woodblock prints.[4] By the time of the 1867 Exposition Universelle in Paris, when Japanese arts were first presented on a large scale to an international audience, *japonaiseries* had captured the interest of progressive French culture.[5] Within a decade, Japanese products of all types and all price ranges had become absorbed into the aesthetic sensibilities of both the middle and upper classes in France. These diverse objects became directly associated with the female-dominated realm of household and sartorial consumption and were prominently displayed in the equally female-controlled domestic interior. By the 1890s, *japonaiseries* and particularly *uchiwa* had become fully engrained within French culture and considered essential elements for domestic décor and elegant fashion.[6]

For the female consumer of the upper bourgeoisie, the ownership of any type of *japonaiserie* held a distinctly elevated significance within her Parisian social sphere. These prized possessions not only reflected their purchasers' cultural awareness of Japan, but their display also reflected patrons' social status as part of a class wealthy enough to buy these decorative items. Since aesthetic value became the primary purpose for these works when displayed in the West, in both Europe and America, their presentation typically occurred with little understanding of the objects' meanings in their original contexts. Surprisingly, though many of these items were imported directly from Japan, others were in fact European fabrications mimicking the shapes of the originals; Western consumers did not differentiate between these sources or qualities and called them all collectively *japonaiseries*.[7] Consequently, it was not the *japonaiseries'* former function or authenticity that mattered to a European bourgeois audience, but rather the symbolic role these items held as cultural signifiers of popular fashion for upper-middle-class women and their domestic sphere.

As women fully integrated into their gendered high-bourgeois society, the avant-garde artists Berthe Morisot and Mary Cassatt could not escape the cultural fascination with *japonaiseries*, especially that of the *uchiwa* fans that became essential attributes for their class and gender. The appearance of a variety of these objects within paintings and prints that the artists created between the 1870s and 1890s instead suggests that both women embraced the artistic as well as decorative fashion for all things Japanese signified by the *uchiwa*. Given their original association with the elite avant-garde and their later connotation as elements of popular fashion, the display of *uchiwa* within Cassatt and Morisot's works of art shows how the artists both responded pictorially to the interests and fashions relative to their contemporary societies. As will be shown, the prominence of the women Impressionists' own *uchiwa* fans in their art reveals the pair's dual identities as modern painters who embraced the novelty of Japanese aesthetics and as proper women who were equally swayed by the cultural value of *japonaiseries* within a feminized, domestic, and fashionable context.

Uchiwa Fans as *Japonaiseries* in Nineteenth-Century Art and Society

Cassatt and Morisot each maintained an unusual relationship with Japanese art, one based on their distinct roles within their late-nineteenth-century society. As the two major women of the Impressionist circle, they continually chose to affiliate themselves with the artistic, mixed-gendered avant-garde throughout their careers.[8] Yet they were also high-bourgeois ladies who adhered to the social codes and restrictions faced by their sex and class. Thus, while they recognized *japonaiseries* as important cultural referents of contemporary fashions, their interest in the foreign objects also spoke to their membership in elite artistic society. They, like other members of the cultural vanguard in the late nineteenth century, and like few other women, had earlier and broader exposure to Japanese goods than French society did as a whole. Importantly, Cassatt and Morisot both owned extensive collections of *ukiyo-e* prints as well as Japanese fans that they hung in their homes.[9] They also had regular access to high quality Japanese goods through visits to the collections of their fellow artists and other collectors starting in the 1860s. By the next decade, they, like other members of their social class and gender, could also purchase *japonaiseries* at a variety of specialty shops and department stores within the city of Paris, many of which catered to a female audience.[10] Consequently, in analyzing each artist's incorporation of *uchiwa* fans as visual props within painted and print representation, it is necessary to consider these concurrent facets of Cassatt and Morisot's identities as equally significant to their approach not only to collecting but also to depicting *japonaiseries*.

The decision to include *uchiwa* within their works of art was not an innovation of either individual. Since the 1860s, male artists including James McNeill Whistler, Claude Monet, and Édouard Manet had incorporated *uchiwa* as props into paintings showing female sitters within studio spaces.[11] Among these images was one that directly influenced Morisot: Manet's exploration of the woman-Japan-interior topos in his 1873–74 *Lady with Fans* (Figure 16.1). This work, showing the socialite Nina de Callias reclining on a sofa and surrounded by a wall of *uchiwa* fans, came into Morisot's possession in 1885 and hung prominently within her home, where it presumably served as inspiration for both her art and her home décor.[12]

What distinguishes this work from the paintings and prints showing *uchiwa* that Morisot and Cassatt produced are the spaces in which the works were all created. Whistler, Monet, and Manet created their scenes showing *uchiwa* within studios, where the fans functioned as temporary props that could be placed and removed at will. During this period, however, women artists did not and could not possess the same type of artistic atelier outside the home that was the privilege of their male colleagues. Instead, Cassatt and Morisot had to work within their own residences for the majority of their careers, rarely enjoying a space dedicated entirely to their profession. Morisot had to paint in her parlor for many years, which required her to pack up her painting materials when visitors would arrive.[13] While Cassatt did maintain at least one studio outside her home from the late 1870s to around 1882, she still required chaperoning to and from the space, as

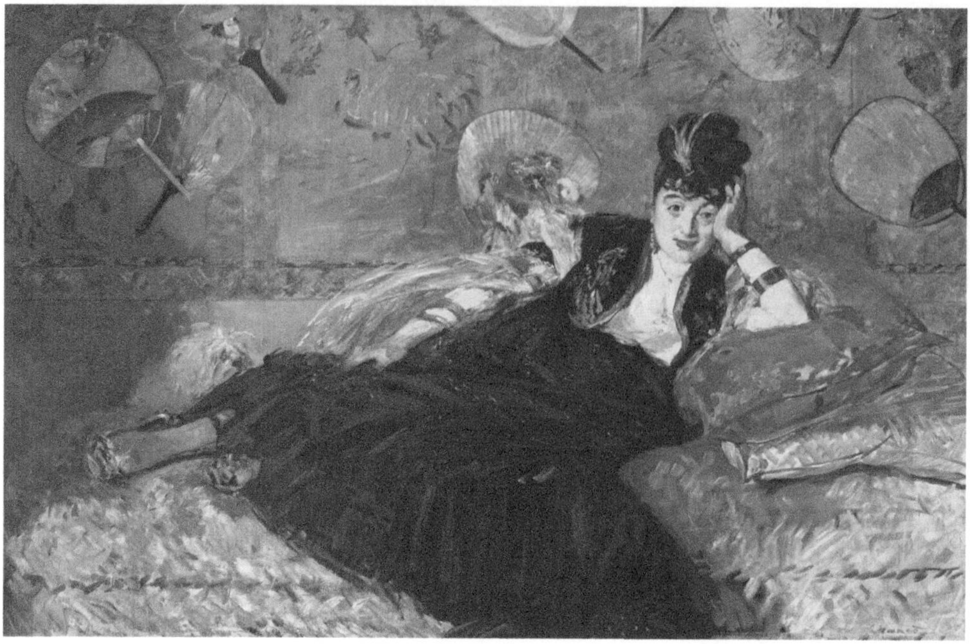

16.1 Édouard Manet, *Lady with Fans: Portrait of Nina de Callias*, 1873–74. Oil on canvas, $44^{11}/_{16} \times 65^{11}/_{32}$ in. (113.5 × 166.5 cm). Paris, Musée d'Orsay. Erich Lessing/Art Resource, New York

required by societal convention; despite her access to a studio, she still created a significant portion of her artwork in her own domestic interior.[14] Importantly, these personal settings appear in numerous compositions of both artists. Overall, their female-oriented, domestic ateliers correspond to Griselda Pollock's "spaces of femininity" and maintained none of the independence and modernity associated with the nineteenth-century male artist's studio.[15]

Given the fact of where these women were relegated to paint within residential spaces that helped to frame pictorial scenes, it follows that their own home furnishings and decorations, including their own personal collections of *uchiwa* fans, appear in the backgrounds of their works of art. Although Cassatt and Morisot must have manipulated the precise placement of their possessions for compositional effect, the *uchiwa* that appear within their pictorial *oeuvres* were not simply props that served to create an intentional and changeable theatrical studio ambiance. Instead, they were objects the artists had purchased and that were most likely already on display in their homes. Consequently, Cassatt and Morisot's intentional incorporations of *uchiwa* fans as prominent components within painted and printed scenes help to invoke a conceptualization of "Japan" that held distinct connotations as signifiers of both the progressive artistic world and the high-bourgeois feminine social sphere to which both women belonged.

Morisot's Painted *Japonaiserie* Fans

Of all the female artists of the nineteenth-century avant-garde, Berthe Morisot revealed the strongest attachment to *uchiwa* fans as decorative and utilitarian objects.[16] These fans appear in several canvases from 1870 to 1894 that reflect the ever-changing views of *uchiwa* for the artist and her contemporary society. With only one exception, Morisot depicted these fans as part of her own interior decoration in three separate homes inhabited during her adult life. Considering that Morisot collected a variety of French and Japanese fans, along with the knowledge that she painted primarily in her own domestic interiors, it is therefore likely that the artist's own pieces appear as objects in the personal spaces captured in her canvases. Within her collection of Japanese and European fans, no detailed record of which exists today, were at least a few *uchiwa* that originally belonged to Manet and appeared in the background of his *Lady with Fans*.[17]

The earliest known inclusion of an *uchiwa* within a composition created in Morisot's personal residence was her *Woman with a Fan* of *circa* 1877.[18] This particular work shows a theme common to the artist: a woman wearing the garments of the upper middle class placed within a fashionable interior. The unidentified figure, who may have been a hired model, reclines slightly on a couch with a panel fan propped against her side. Morisot painted this work in the parlor-studio of her home on the avenue d'Eylau (now avenue Victor Hugo) during the high point of French cultural interest in *japonaiseries* among members of the female bourgeoisie surrounding the 1878 Exposition Universelle. Given the fact that the *uchiwa* is the primary decorative object in this canvas, it is clear that the fan must have held great value for the artist in the conception of her composition. Most significantly, because the particular space shown in the painting is Morisot's own domestic space, *Woman with a Fan* serves as a visual acknowledgement of her possession of these commercial goods.

Given the absence of the name of Morisot's sitter, the prominent inclusion of the *japonaiserie* shows Morisot's own understanding of modern fashion and aesthetics more than revealing a cultural elitism specific to her sitter. In this regard, *Woman with a Fan* differs significantly from Morisot's first known work to include an *uchiwa*, *The Pink Dress* of *circa* 1870 (Metropolitan Museum of Art, New York). In the earlier piece, Morisot depicted one of these fans in the background of a portrait of a family friend that was painted inside the sitter's home.[19] In that instance, the emphasis on the *uchiwa* at a relatively early date within the history of *japonaiseries* alludes to the elevated status of the sitter's family as well as of the artist, who had the forbearance to emphasize the fan as one of the only decorative elements in the portrait.

In *Woman with a Fan*, however, the depiction of Morisot's own domestic space along with the unidentified sitter places all the emphasis on the painter and her personal understanding of the importance of *uchiwa* fans within her high-bourgeois society. The composition reflects Morisot's ownership of *uchiwa* and her desire to utilize the fan as a cultural and aesthetic signifier. Overall, this scene can be read as a compilation of elegant and decorative sartorial as well as domestic attributes, which, as an ensemble, place the figure within the elevated classes of French society. Even if that were not the true social position to which Morisot's model belonged, that fact would have mattered less than her appearance in the composition: nineteenth-century viewers would have understood the elevated connotation of clothing, setting, and decorations specific to this scene. In this respect, *Woman with a Fan* demonstrates how Morisot visually manipulated her collection of Japanese art to create, and not simply to reinforce, social class.

In addition to crafting portraits of fashionable women with *uchiwa*, Morisot also incorporated the round fans as domestic props within her architectural décor. A work entitled *The Mantle* of 1885 shows the display of an *uchiwa* precisely positioned above a chimney in Morisot's salon in her home on the rue de Villejust.[20] The artist's use of the Japanese fan next to a pot of flowers and in front of a large mirror removed the object from its sartorial associations and placed it within the realm of the decorative. Perhaps this shift in her conceptualization of *uchiwa*, years after their 1878 climax as signs of the exotic and the foreign, was triggered by Manet, whose *Lady with Fans* she came to possess in the same year she painted *The Mantle*. Rather than simply displaying her *uchiwa* on the wall, as appeared in the painting of Nina de Callias, however, Morisot chose to adapt Manet's pairing of woman and Japanese fan into an emphasis on the intimate setting of her piece. The angled placement of an *uchiwa* on a mantelpiece had in fact been a stylistic convention for years at the time Morisot produced her painting. A clothing advertisement from the Parisian periodical *La Mode Illustrée* from November 1871 (Figure 16.2) mirrors nearly exactly *The Mantle*, or rather Morisot's painting imitates a detail of the journal's illustration. This comparison is not to say that the artist copied the periodical's image or even used it as a model, but rather that her painting epitomized a national passion for *japonaiseries* as presented in fashionable and feminine domestic space throughout the 1870s and 1880s. Consequently, in *The Mantle*, Morisot sought inspiration for her depiction of *uchiwa* from two distinct sources that exemplify the duality of her own identity: avant-garde artistic, via Manet, and feminized domestic, through the affiliation with décor and fashion.

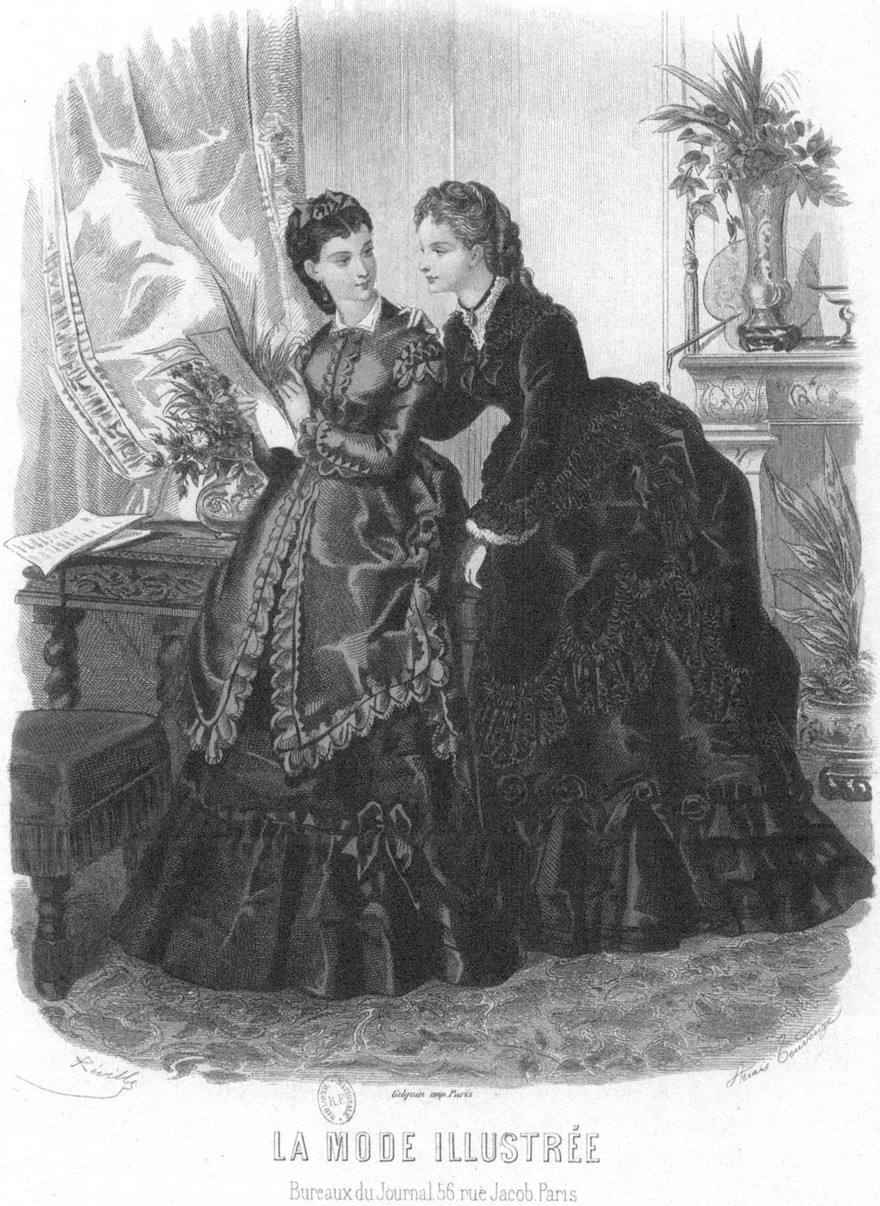

16.2 *La Mode Illustrée*, vol. 16 (November 5, 1871), illustration 45. Paris, Bibliothèque nationale de France, Imprimés Tolbiac, FOL-LC14-130

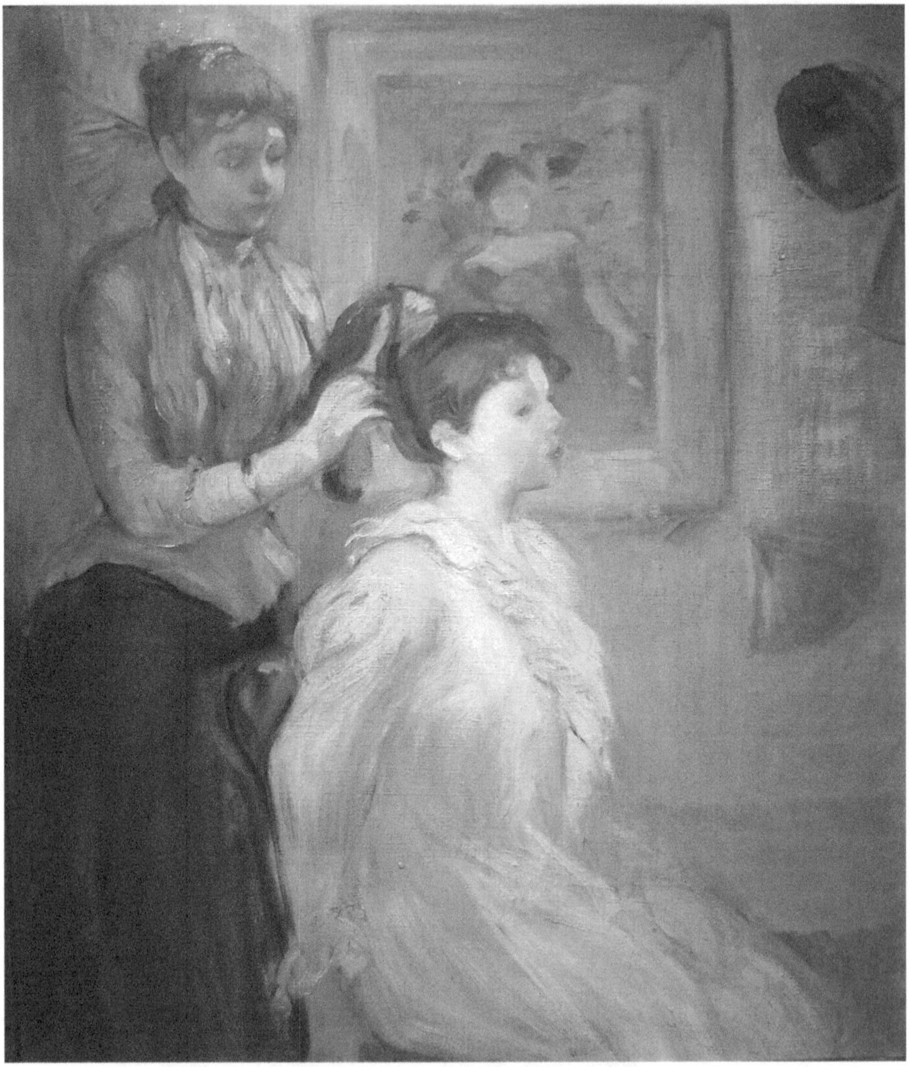

16.3 Berthe Morisot, *The Coiffure*, 1894. Oil on canvas, 21 5/8 × 18 1/8 in. (55 × 46 cm). Buenos Aires, Museo Nacional de Bellas Artes

Nearly a decade later, Morisot once again emphasized an *uchiwa* fan in a painting that in many ways represents the culmination of the artist's career. *The Coiffure* of 1894 (Figure 16.3) shows two female models, where one stands and fixes her seated companion's hair.[21] Morisot produced this painting in a small studio she created in the upper floor of a home on the rue Weber where she moved following her husband's death.[22] Importantly, this space was the only dedicated atelier of Morisot's professional career, though it still retained the feeling of intimacy incorporated into her other salon-studios. In this painting, the models pose before a wall decorated with several different types of fans. Morisot painted three folding fans in black, red, and grey, along with one round Japanese fan that she cropped by the edge of her composition.[23] The latter is painted with what appears to be the horizontally aligned image of a female Japanese figure seen from the back or side; she is dressed in a pink garment and has her hair in an up-do.[24] The pairing of the Asian figure and the European models at their toilette emphasizes the scene's overall theme of the creation of femininity. Thus, by visually reinforcing the subject of the *uchiwa* within her composition, Morisot fully appropriated it to serve her own pictorial and aesthetic purposes.

Beyond simply focusing on the *uchiwa, The Coiffure* also reveals how Morisot perceived her own status within the avant-garde art world. Behind the two models is a copy of Morisot's 1877 *The Black Bodice* (National Gallery of Ireland, Dublin), a work probably shown at the Third Impressionist exhibition in the year of its execution. In this painting within a painting, a well-dressed woman, who may be on her way to the theater or other evening outing, looks directly out at the viewer, engaging the spectator with her compelling gaze. The figure in *The Black Bodice* may have even posed in front of a Japanese silk six-panel screen covered with a floral motif, thereby reinforcing the work's avant-garde connotations.[25] Yet despite the artistic success of *The Black Bodice,* its appearance in the background of a painting created 17 years later was unusual for an artist who very rarely displayed her own paintings in her home, let alone showed them as props in other compositions.[26]

Given these facts, it is necessary to question why Morisot wished to incorporate *The Black Bodice* into her later painting. Scholars have discussed *The Coiffure* as a nostalgic image "about the dialogue of art and life," in which the models shown in the act of preparing for an outing allude to the finished product of the polished, well-dressed woman seen behind them.[27] Nostalgia seems to have no role in this painting, however, and it appears that Morisot instead celebrates her career as a member of the Impressionist group by reproducing *The Black Bodice* so prominently and with such clarity. Additionally, despite the small scale of her final studio, it produced a feeling of warmth and protection, as captured in the female-only space of *The Coiffure*. This sensation is reinforced by the pictorial elegance of *The*

Black Bodice. Overall, *The Coiffure* demonstrates that the very self-critical artist finally attained the confidence one year before her death to allow her own Impressionist art to take the place of honor in the background of her painting.[28]

It seems, therefore, that Japanese art, in the form of the *uchiwa* fan, was the required intermediary to help Morisot reach the level of self-assurance captured in this late composition. The linking of Japanese and European women at their toilette, the feminine association of Asian and European fans, and the avant-garde formal qualities of the canvas, as well as the painting within the painting, all show Morisot's diverse artistic interests.[29] As Jean Baudrillard has argued, collected objects such as the variety of those appearing in *The Coiffure* should be viewed as a system relating to the individual because "it is invariably *oneself* that one collects."[30] In all, therefore, *The Coiffure* and her other paintings showing *uchiwa* reveal Morisot's diverse yet concurrent personae: Impressionist painter, collector of avant-garde as well as fashionable sartorial and domestic attributes, and nineteenth-century high-bourgeois woman.

Fan *Japonaiseries* in Mary Cassatt's Prints

Much like her colleague, Mary Cassatt also had an extensive relationship with Japanese art. Not only did she own *ukiyo-e* prints as well as ceramics and Japanese screens, she also incorporated aspects of Japanese aesthetics into many paintings and especially her celebrated set of ten color aquatints from 1890.[31] Significantly, Cassatt probably also possessed *uchiwa* fans. When they appear within her art, specifically two prints from 1880 and 1890, they reflect how the American artist perceived these domesticated Japanese objects, as well as reveal the elevated European social status she associated with them.

Cassatt's first inclusion of a Japanese fan occurred in her *Woman Seated in a Loge* of *circa* 1880 (Figure 16.4). This lithograph was part of a larger group of paintings and prints that Cassatt produced between 1879 and 1882 showing fashionably dressed upper-middle-class women in the balcony of a theater.[32] The unidentified figure in this print reclines in her chair in a loge while raising her opera glasses to her eyes, thus engaging with the performance without ignoring the important social spectacle of attending the theater. The model wears a sleeveless dress with bows at the shoulders and with a collar that modestly shows only part of her neck and hides her décolletage. Her upswept hair is uncovered, and in her gloved left hand she holds a fan.

It is the specific fan that Cassatt depicted that makes this composition vastly different from all her other theater pictures. Here, rather than carrying

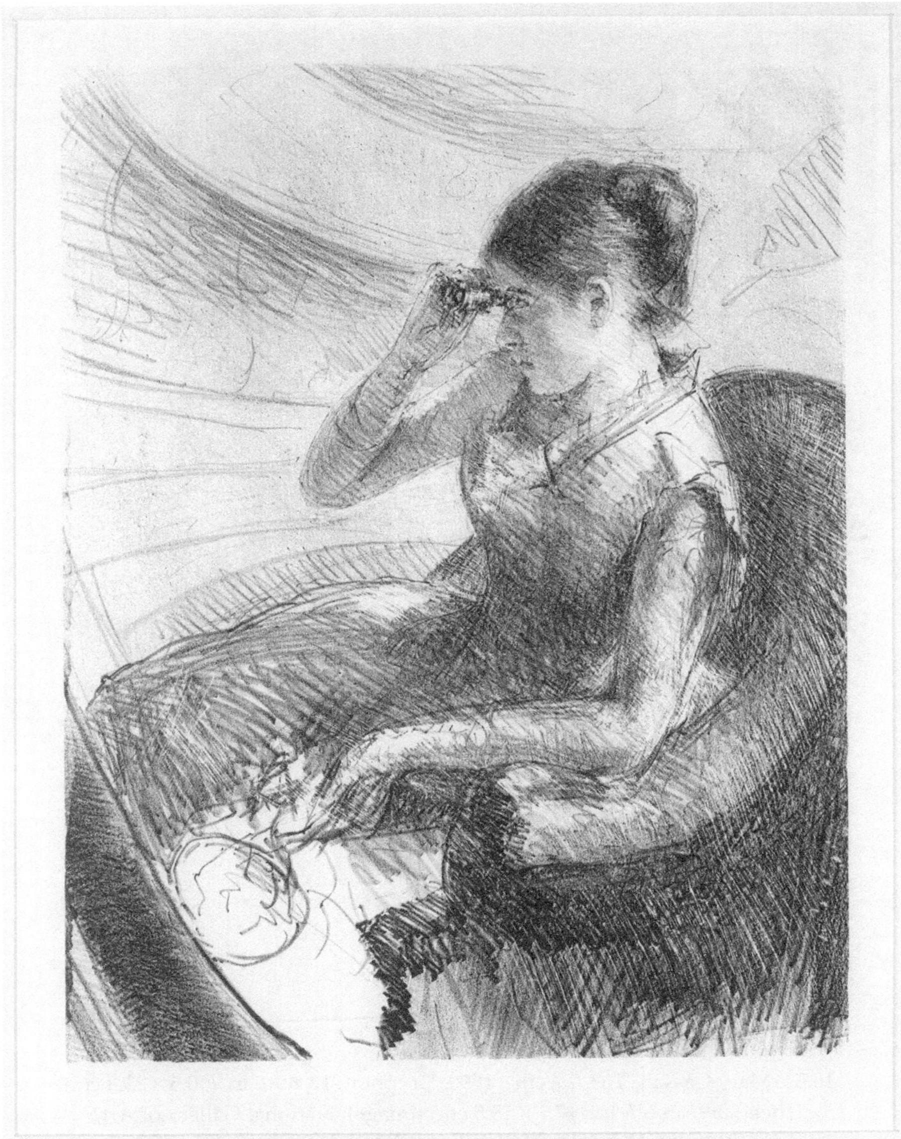

16.4 Mary Stevenson Cassatt, *Woman Seated in a Loge, circa* 1880. Lithograph, $17^{11}/_{16} \times 12^{1}/_{2}$ in. (45 × 31.8 cm) (sheet), $11^{1}/_{8} \times 8^{5}/_{8}$ in. (28.3 × 21.9 cm) (image). Museum of Fine Arts, Boston. Bequest of W.G. Russell Allen, 63.309. Photograph © 2009, Museum of Fine Arts, Boston

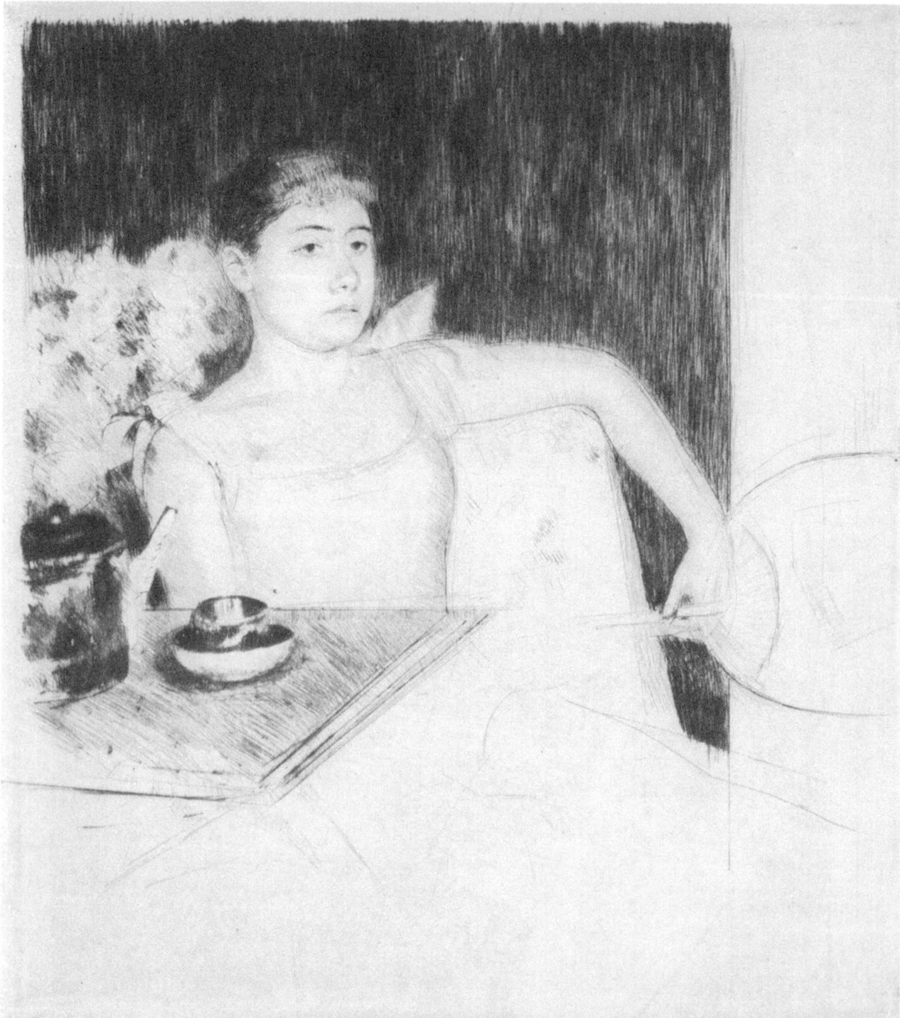

16.5 Mary Cassatt, *The Tea*, *circa* 1890. Drypoint, 12 × 9$^{3}/_{8}$ in. (30.5 × 23.8 cm) (sheet), 6$^{15}/_{16}$ × 6$^{1}/_{8}$ in. (17.7 × 15.5 cm) (image). National Gallery of Art, Washington, DC, Ailsa Mellon Bruce Fund. Image courtesy of the Board of Trustees, National Gallery of Art, Washington DC

a traditional European folding fan, the model grasps a Japanese *uchiwa* in her left hand, allowing it to fall below the edge of the balcony railing and away from the eyes of other spectators. Despite the unfinished quality of the lithograph, it is certain that she holds an *uchiwa* fan from what is visible of its shape and its specific frame and handle. Most male and female viewers of this print would have recognized the *uchiwa* from its newfound public significance following the 1878 Exposition Universelle. Importantly, Cassatt placed the *uchiwa* not prominently on display in the print but instead showed it as visible only to the select few individuals who would have shared the woman's box. Consequently, it becomes a private sign of the utmost social privilege in an otherwise public depiction of high-bourgeois fashions.

Cassatt also showed her own attachment to the world of modern art in this composition beyond the use of the *uchiwa*: the work is one of only two surviving lithographs in the artist's hand and was part of her first experimental series of prints begun in 1879.[33] Cassatt probably created this print for the journal *Le Jour et la Nuit*, which her colleague Edgar Degas had envisioned in 1879 but which never came to fruition. Significantly, Cassatt's choice of subject matter for this print points to her understanding of the place of *uchiwa* within upper-middle-class female circles as well as the male-dominated art world she frequented. *Woman Seated in a Loge* makes reference to the artist's own dual affiliations with modern art and modern life in the combination of the theme, the sitter, her accessories, and the artist's stylistic innovations working in lithography. Moreover, the fact that this work was not a painting or pastel but a print meant to be reproduced and published as part of a progressive art journal establishes Cassatt's association of *japonaiseries* with the avant-garde.[34]

Despite her initial enthusiasm and intention for publication, however, Cassatt did not display *Woman Seated in a Loge* until a retrospective of her work held at Durand-Ruel's Parisian gallery in 1893. Alongside this early depiction of an *uchiwa*, she showed at least one additional print showing a similar fan, *The Tea* of 1890 (Figure 16.5). This drypoint was one of a set of twelve that Cassatt had first exhibited in March 1890 at the Second Exhibition of Painter-Engravers.[35] Half of this series shows Cassatt's archetypal theme of mothers and children, while the remaining works depict women in domestic settings. Overall, each of the drypoints shows aesthetic qualities that Cassatt imitated from the many Japanese woodblock prints that decorated her home, particularly the sharp outlining, lack of shading, and reduction of form to the most essential lines and shapes.

Of the entire set of twelve, *The Tea* is the only image to show *japonaiseries* and to emphasize an *uchiwa* fan. The model wears an elegant sleeveless gown tied with bows at the shoulders and sits on a floral-patterned couch in a space reminiscent of the parlor of an upper-middle-class French home. On a table before her sit parts of a porcelain tea set. She drapes her arm over the top edge of the sofa and holds a large *uchiwa* in her left hand. For *The Tea* and its two surviving print studies,[36] the *uchiwa* functions both as a sartorial attribute and as part of a larger decorative display. While her *uchiwa* is not itself painted, that may have been an intentional decision on the part of the artist: it allowed female viewers of the print, many of whom probably owned *uchiwa*, to imagine themselves and their own possession as participants within the scene. Cassatt also intentionally cropped the fan by the right border of the print, a device reminiscent of Japanese art. This technique also served to emphasize the foreign as well as modern connotations of the *uchiwa* itself. Similarly, the dark background contrasts with the empty space on the right edge of *The Tea* that, along with the outlining, flatness, and lack of shading, help to emphasize the "Japaneseness" of the composition. Thus, Cassatt intentionally combined elements of artistic *japonisme* with *japonaiseries* in this unusual drypoint.

Cassatt further encouraged the atmosphere of fashionable elegance and wealth in *The Tea* by also showing part of a prized porcelain tea set. This set, made famous in Cassatt's portrait of her cousin Mrs Mary Dickinson Riddle, entitled *Lady at the Tea Table* (1883, Museum of Fine Arts, Boston), was part of her own collection and had been a gift of Mrs Riddle. Cassatt and her family believed the set to be Japanese, though more recent research has identified the cream and blue decoration with gilded rims as high quality Chinese export porcelain.[37] Regardless of its actual origins, the set's exclusivity, its prominence in the painting, and the inclusion of "Japanese" ceramics in addition to the *uchiwa* fan all reinforce the refined taste and aesthetic awareness Cassatt captures in this print.

For *The Tea*, then, Cassatt's depiction of her own *japonaiseries* as the only attributes in the print helped to evoke a scene interesting to both Paris's fashionable social elite and its artistic avant-garde. Given that Cassatt possessed her own collection of *ukiyo-e* and other Japanese objects, the artist clearly knew the role *uchiwa* played in both popular consumer culture and modern artistic society during this period. Significantly, this drypoint unites the artist's interests in pictorial *japonisme* with fashionable *japonaiseries* in the world of the female high bourgeoisie. Cassatt herself was part of this elevated French society, despite her American nationality, and followed every formality that her social position required. All together, in *The Tea*, Cassatt captured her own understanding of the importance of *japonisme* in late-nineteenth-century French art and culture. By coupling the Japanese *uchiwa* with the prized porcelain tea set in a Japanese-inspired composition, Cassatt created a pictorial scene where *japonaiseries* symbolized her own selective, female, and fashionable, as well as avant-garde, worlds.

Together, *The Tea* and *Woman Seated in a Loge* unite *japonaiseries* with other elements of high fashion specific to Cassatt's own social class. According to Rémy Saisselin, these particular interior spaces and their décor "expressed the general if at times unconscious or at least unstated values of bourgeois society, but also, the true status or situation of the art object in that society."[38] In these images, therefore, Cassatt demonstrates how her own gender and class created social identity and, most importantly, the role *uchiwa* played within that process of self-fashioning for women in the 1880s and 1890s. Moreover, the *japonaiseries* in her prints simultaneously reinforce Cassatt's own role as the creator of these scenes and the collector of the objects displayed. Because the sitters cannot be identified in these works beyond their decorative attributes, the intentionally incorporated *japonaiseries* should be seen as a reflection of the artist herself. In all, by prominently including and pictorially emphasizing these foreign signifiers within two separate scenes, Cassatt created prints demonstrating her own identity as a collector of an elite and a popular Japan that equally influenced French art and French high society in the late nineteenth century.

Conclusion: *Japonaiseries* as Cultural Signifiers

From the earliest days of interest in the commercialization of Japanese art to years past its peak as the most fashionable foreign culture the West wished to possess, *japonaiseries* in the form of round *uchiwa* fans played a key role in European art. The appearance of these fans in the images of Morisot and Cassatt specifically linked upper-middle-class French women with Japanese-inspired domestic and sartorial attributes through visual representation and repetition. Importantly, it is the artists' attention to *japonaiseries* that reveals how nineteenth-century upper-middle-class women, not simply women artists, made these objects an intrinsic part of their lives. The pictorial representations of *japonaiseries* in Morisot and Cassatt's imagery show how these items became fully integrated into their home décor, their dress, even their overall identities as members of a privileged class of art collectors. These images prove that, by the 1890s, *japonaiseries* had lost their novelty and purely avant-garde status. By then, they had transformed into thoroughly French elements of woman's culture, where the once-exotic objects had become *de rigueur* components of French female bourgeois domesticity.

As a whole, this selection of images acknowledges how deeply Japanese art objects appealed to these artists for both their aesthetic and cultural values. Their concentration on *japonaiseries* within paintings and prints themselves created in modern visual language reveals how Morisot and Cassatt created an adaptation of *japonisme* that spoke to both their artist colleagues and to their female social peers. By showing these items as fully integrated into their homes and personal lives, rather than used as simple studio props, therefore, the women artists turned *japonaiseries* into items that would have provided different, though equally demonstrative, messages to audiences of men and women, artists and non-artists alike. It is the simple fact that both the progressive and fashionable elements of *uchiwa* appear in all of these works that reveals how each artist placed equal weight on both connotations within her compositions; one evocation does not take precedence over the other, and it is their continual combination within subject and form that creates the overarching significance of this group of images. For the women Impressionists, therefore, depicting Japanese *uchiwa* fans from their own personal collections within two-dimensional pictorial renderings of their private domestic spaces became an essential means to express their dual affiliations with modern art and modern society in the late nineteenth century.

Notes

1. This essay stems from part of the author's dissertation, "*Japonisme* and Beyond in the Art of Marie Bracquemond, Mary Cassatt, and Berthe Morisot, 1867–1895," PhD Dissertation, University of Pennsylvania, 2007. I would like to thank Larry Silver, Susan Sidlauskas, and Suzanne Lindsay for their insightful comments in helping to shape the extended version of this text.

2. In her glossary, Koyama-Richard describes an *uchiwa* as "Eventail rigide, de forme presque circulaire, qui fut très à la mode en Europe entre les années 1880 et 1900 et fut souvent représenté dans les tableaux impressionnistes." See Brigitte Koyama-Richard, *Correspondance adressée à Hayashi Tadamasa* (Tokyo: Institut de Tokyo, Institution Administrative Indépendante, Centre National de Recherche pour les Propriétés Culturelles; Kokushokankôkai, 2001), 606.

3. Marc Gerstein, "Impressionist and Post-Impressionist Fans," PhD Dissertation, Harvard University, 1978, xxi: "In 1888, 2,442,478 Japanese folding fans and 129,446 screen fans were imported into France."

4. On August 1, 1867, the writers Edmond and Jules de Goncourt concluded a letter to the collector and art critic Philippe Burty with the phrase in English, "*Japonaiseries* for ever!" Jules de Goncourt, "Philippe Burty, August 1, 1867," *Lettres de Jules de Goncourt* (Paris: G. Charpentier, 1885), 265.

5. The 1867 exhibition was the first opportunity for continental Europe to experience Japanese arts, in the form of an official exhibition organized by the Tokugawa Shogunate displaying metalwork, ceramics, lacquerware, bronzes, screens, *ukiyo-e* woodblock prints, and even furniture and books. On Japan's role in Western international exhibitions, see *Japan Goes to the World's Fairs: Japanese Art at the Great Expositions in Europe and the United States 1867–1904* (Los Angeles: Los Angeles County Museum of Art, 2005).

6. These ideas are explored more fully in Chapters One and Two of the author's doctoral thesis. See Criss, "*Japonisme* and Beyond," 24–210.

7. It is impossible to determine a precise meaning of "*japonaiseries*" in the nineteenth century. Some of these goods were created in Japan for internal consumption, of which only a small percentage was exported overseas. Generally, the cost of such items was higher, since the quality of these pieces was superior to that of other export wares. Many *japonaiseries* were mass-produced in Japan for an entirely Western market; these goods, which often incorporated Western perspective or subjects, were less expensive than the rare and individualized pieces exported by Japan. Additionally, many of what are traditionally labeled *japonaiseries* were actually fabricated on French soil or elsewhere within Europe for domestic satisfaction.

8. In addition to Cassatt and Morisot, Marie Bracquemond exhibited at three of the Impressionist exhibitions; Eva Gonzalès, a student of Édouard Manet's and rival of Morisot's, never showed with the group but is typically considered the fourth woman Impressionist for her adherence to her teacher's progressive approach to painting. After earlier participation at the Salon, Cassatt showed at four of the Impressionist exhibitions, and Morisot at seven of the eight. Neither artist chose to affiliate with any of the female artist organizations gaining popularity in France at that time and instead continually exhibited in mixed-gender venues.

9. The exact pieces that comprised these two collections are today unfortunately unknown, with the Japanese objects having been lost, sold, or otherwise distributed since each artist's death.

10. Locales offering *japonaiseries* for sale ranged from art galleries like that of Siegfried Bing to stores, such as La Porte Chinoise, to new department stores like Le Bon Marché, which opened in 1852. For a thorough compilation of venues selling East Asian objects during the second half of the nineteenth century, see Phyllis Anne Floyd, "*Japonisme* in Context: Documentation, Criticism, Aesthetic Reactions," PhD Dissertation, University of Michigan, 1983, Appendix B, "Dealers of *Japoneries*," 379–427.

11. Consider, for example, Whistler's *Princess of the Land of Porcelain* (1863–64, Freer Gallery of Art, Washington, DC), with the inclusion of one *uchiwa* held as a prop in the model's hand and another hanging on the wall behind her; and Monet's *La Japonaise* (1876, Museum of Fine Arts, Boston), where his kimono-clad wife stood before a wall of *uchiwa* in a work that visually mocks the role these fans in particular and *japonaiseries* in general had come to play within feminized domestic fashions in France.

12. Morisot purchased this painting at the estate sale of Manet's art two years after his death; she listed it as number 3 of her collection of Manet works in her diary from 1885–86 and described it as "Mme de Callias exposée à la vente sous le titre de la dame aux éventails—fait avec le plus grand soin en vue d'une exposition.—Nina de Callias vivait alors avec Charles Cross, ce fantaisiste de tant de talent. M. de Callias vint faire une visite à Manet le priant de ne pas mettre le nom de la personne de sa femme en évidence et Ed. avec beaucoup de courtoisie retourne la toile." Berthe Morisot, unpublished notebook known as the "Carnet 1885–86," 27–28, transcription from the Musée Marmottan-Monet, 6–7. Morisot, who first met Manet in 1869 and sat for numerous portraits over the next five years, became his sister-in-law in 1874 when she married his younger brother Eugène.

13. During her early years of study, Morisot shared with her sister Edma, also a promising artist, a studio that their father built for them in the yard of the family's home. This studio was destroyed during its occupation by troops during the Franco-Prussian War and subsequent Commune of 1870–71.

14. The annotated map "Mary Cassatt's Paris," lists 2, rue Duperré, off of place Pigalle, as Cassatt's studio in 1882. See Judith A. Barter, ed., *Mary Cassatt: Modern Woman* (Chicago: The Art Institute of Chicago in association with Harry N. Abrams, Inc., 1998), 354–5. The catalog's chronology, 337, notes that she might have rented this space as early as 1878.

15. Griselda Pollock, "Modernity and the Spaces of Femininity," in *Vision and Difference: Femininity, Feminism and the Histories of Art* (London: Routledge, 1988), 50–90.

16. Morisot even appeared holding an *uchiwa* in her portrait by Marcellin Desboutin, *Portrait of Berthe Morisot*, 1876. One version of this etching is in the collection of the Bibliothèque Nationale de France, Paris.

17. Morisot, "Carnet 1885–86," 28, transcription from the Musée Marmottan-Monet, Paris, 7: "Je conserve quelques écrans ayant servis pour les fonds entre autres celui représentant la pêche à la baleine." It is known that Morisot collected various objects, including *ukiyo-e* and decorative fans. She also inherited some of the Manet family's collection of eighteenth-century European fans, some of which appear in her paintings including *Femme à l'éventail* or *Au bal* of 1875, painted the year after her marriage into the Manet family. Today, all of these undocumented items are dispersed, lost, or destroyed. According to information gathered in conversations between the author and scholars William Scott and Hugues Wilhelm, many of these Japanese and japonist works had been kept at the family home at the Château de Mesnil and were ruined in flooding or otherwise lost over the years.

18. Berthe Morisot, *Woman with a Fan*, 1877. Oil on canvas, 19 ¼ × 23 ¼ in. (49 × 59 cm). Private location. For a reproduction, see Alain Clairet, Delphine Montalent, and Yves Rouart, *Berthe Morisot 1841–1895: Catalogue raisonné de l'œuvre peint* (Montolivet, France: CÉRA-nrs, 1997), figure 69, p. 147.

19. There is some discrepancy as to which of the Carré sisters is depicted in this portrait, Marguerite or Valentine, and it has been dated anywhere from 1868 to 1873. It is possible that this painting was commissioned as an engagement or wedding portrait of the young woman, given the prominently displayed ring on her left hand. Were that the original purpose for the work, the emphasis on the *uchiwa* would have reinforced the elevated social status of Mademoiselle Carré and her family.

20. Berthe Morisot, *The Mantle*, 1885. Oil on canvas, 21 ⅝ × 25 ½ in. (55 × 65 cm). Private collection. For a reproduction, see Clairet et al., *Berthe Morisot 1841–1895: Catalogue raisonné*, figure 190, p. 207.

21. Clairet et al., *Berthe Morisot 1841–1895: Catalogue raisonné*, 292, identifies the models as Jeanne-Marie and Marthe.

22. Anne Higonnet, *Berthe Morisot* (Berkeley: University of California Press, 1990), 213, notes: "her new home included a studio, made by joining together two or three maids' rooms on the building's top story."

23. Wilhelm describes these fans as "deux écrans japonais, deux éventails," meaning two *uchiwa* and two folding fans. It appears, however, that there are three European-style and one Japanese fan shown here. See Hugues Wilhelm, "La Coiffure, 1894," in Sylvie Patry, Hugues Wilhelm, and Sylvie Patin, with the assistance of Michèle Moyne, *Berthe Morisot 1841–1895* (Paris: Éditions de la Réunion des musées nationaux, 2002), 420.

24. It is difficult to ascertain the true subject of this painted *uchiwa*, and it would have been highly unusual for *uchiwa* to be decorated horizontally rather than vertically. Regardless of the fan's actual subject, it is clear that Morisot manipulated her rendering of the *uchiwa* to evoke the image of a woman fixing her hair.

25. Clairet et al., *Berthe Morisot 1841–1895: Catalogue raisonné*, 149.

26. With the exception of *The Goose* of 1885/91 (Private Collection) and her copy of Boucher's *Venus at Vulcan's Forge* of 1884 (Private Collection), the artist relegated her own works to private rooms within her homes where only the most intimate circle of women and almost no visitors would see them. On the main floor of her home she preferred to show her collection of art by other members of the avant-garde, including Manet, Monet, and Edgar Degas.

27. Charles F. Stuckey and William P. Scott, with the assistance of Suzanne G. Lindsay, *Berthe Morisot, Impressionist* (New York: Hudson Hills Press, 1987), 170.

28. Works by other artists appear in the background of several Morisot compositions, including: *Two Sisters* (1869, National Gallery of Art, Washington, DC), with one of Degas's painted fan-shaped silk canvases entitled *Spanish Dancers and Musicians*; *Before the Mirror* (1890, Fondation Pierre Gianadda, Martigny, Switzerland), with Manet's *Portrait of Berthe Morisot Reclining*; *The Violin Lesson* (1893, Private Collection), with Manet's portrait *Isabelle Lemonnier*; and *Julie Playing the Violin* (1893, Collection Herman Mayer), that shows both Manet's *Berthe Morisot Reclining* and Degas's *Portrait of Eugène Manet*.

29. Again, Morisot may have altered the actual layout of her studio space in order to create the specific groupings perceptible in her paintings. Yet it is likely that the artist hung these fans for at least a short period of time on her walls alongside her own painting.

30. Jean Baudrillard, "The System of Collecting," in *The Cultures of Collecting*, eds. John Elsner and Roger Cardinal, trans. Roger Cardinal (London: Reaktion Books, 1994), 12.

31. Cassatt owned a significant collection of *ukiyo-e*, much of which was sold in 1950. The artists of her prints included Hiroshige, Yeisen, Hokusai, Kiyonaga, Shunjo, Shunzan, Harunobu, Utamaro, Yeishi, and Yeizan, as listed in *Rare Japanese Prints*, Kende Galleries, Inc., April 21–22, 1950, lots 56–89. See discussion in Nancy Mowll Mathews and Barbara Stern Shapiro, *Mary Cassatt: The Color Prints* (New York: Harry N. Abrams, Inc., in association with Williams College Museum of Art, 1989), 54, n. 39.

32. In these images, women are sometimes alone and sometimes in the company of a female companion. Two of the most famous images from this series are *Woman with a Pearl Necklace* (1879, Philadelphia Museum of Art) and *In the Loge* (1879, Museum of Fine Arts, Boston).

33. The other prints Cassatt created in 1879–80 were softground etchings with aquatint. It is likely that Cassatt learned the lithography technique from Edgar Degas. See Adelyn Dohme Breeskin, *Mary Cassatt: Graphic Art* (Washington, DC: Published for Smithsonian Institution Traveling Exhibition Service by Smithsonian Institution Press, 1981), 38.

34. Interestingly, the importance of this print existed for Degas as well; one of the two surviving impressions of the second state of this lithograph, now in the collection of the Museum of Fine Arts in Boston (accession number 63.309), was in Degas's possession, presumably from the time of its printing until his death in 1917, where it was counted among the works in his atelier. Degas must have appreciated not only Cassatt's experiments with the medium in this work, but also the sitter's overt interest in Japanese art.

35. Cassatt printed these herself in a set of 25. Their success was so great that her dealer, Durand-Ruel, sold them in sets rather than individually. See Nancy Mowll Mathews, *Mary Cassatt: A Life* (New York: Villard Books, 1994), 193–4. According to Breeskin, at least two of the five states of this print were shown in 1893 as numbers 66 and 92. Numerous examples of the various states of *The Tea*

survive today. See Adelyn Dohme Breeskin, *Mary Cassatt: A Catalogue Raisonné of the Graphic Work* (Washington, DC: Smithsonian Institution Press, 1979), 59.

36. Cassatt refined her choice of theme in two preliminary drypoints related to the final composition, *Mimi as a Brunette* and *Mimi Holding a Japanese Fan*, both of 1889. Examples of these study prints exist in the collection of the National Gallery of Art in Washington, DC.

37. Mathews, *Mary Cassatt: A Life*, 165; Barter, *Mary Cassatt: Modern Woman*, 58.

38. Rémy G. Saisselin, *Bricabracomania: The Bourgeois and the Bibelot* (London: Thames and Hudson, 1985), 63.

17

The Female Past and Modernity: Displaying Women and Things in New Zealand Department Stores, Expositions, and Museums, 1920s–1960s[1]

Bronwyn Labrum

In 1968, Roger Duff, the Director of the Canterbury Museum in Christchurch, New Zealand's third largest city, remarked on the popularity of his institution's "Colonial Street" exhibition. Installed nine years earlier, it was one of four areas that made up the "Canterbury Colonists Galleries," along with a suite of Victorian and pre-colonial period rooms; furniture and armor cases; and a costume gallery spanning the years 1800–1927. The "Street" was, in fact, a misnomer. It was an L-shaped configuration of two streets, a square and a place, which together contained recreations of twelve shops and a three-roomed cob house complete with a cab and horse at one end.[2] Duff observed that "it gives great pleasure to the many visitors of all ages who enjoy 'window-shopping' there." By avoiding "labelling any of the articles exhibited," Duff believed that staff had created a "realistic atmosphere," thereby further emphasizing the mercantile spectacle.[3] The notion of window-shopping amongst the exhibits is a fascinating echo of the way that the modern museum developed in tandem with the department store in the nineteenth century: architecture, styles of display, and interpretation owed as much to commerce as to culture.[4] This chapter shows how this phenomenon was still current a century later, in the period before the much derided commercialism of the "new museology" in the late twentieth and early twenty-first century.[5] It does this through a case study of a group of key institutions in New Zealand that were formative in the development of history as a museum discipline, as distinct from the earlier establishment of the disciplines of science and art in the first "museum period" of the nineteenth century. In the mid-twentieth century key staff and practices associated with the department store, the exposition, and the museum combined, across material culture and genres usually thought to be discrete, to construct new representations of women and of material culture. I argue that these interpretations rested on particular notions of the female colonial past and also, paradoxically, of modernity, articulated through the consumption of parallel and contrasting female identities, roles, and modes of representation. This study analyzes both the subject and content of objectified femininity which resulted from the construction of a particular "gaze," the form of "the view," and what was being looked at.

In this chapter an emphasis on cultural history—how New Zealanders became interested in their colonial past and what form that interest took—intersects with a preoccupation with a key aspect of museum studies, in particular, the twentieth-century development of the institutional collecting and display of those objects deemed to be "historical." This phenomenon cannot be fully understood, however, without attention to key insights of material culture studies. As Beth Fowkes Tobin notes in the introduction, "consumption and collecting [are] social practices that are productive of social and cultural meanings and effects." Contemporary scholars focus on how "objects … participate in the formation of identities and the constitution of embodied subjectivities, [how] subjects can endow objects with subjectivity, and furthermore, objects can act with a kind of agency we tend to think should be reserved for human subjects." As well as describing the exhibited objects in my chosen case studies, archival material from the museums in which they were displayed is fundamental to understanding why and how they were collected and exhibited. Using the papers of one of the museum professionals in particular has afforded an insight into the way that subjects and objects mutually constructed each other and enabled me to create a cultural biography of the objects, tracing how they moved in and out of consumption circles from the commercial sphere to becoming museum pieces. Above all, the highly gendered nature of this endeavor, and the links between different spheres and modes of collecting and display, are only fully revealed if objects, archives, and images are brought together with theoretical insights.

The Canterbury Museum's street was one of at least three "impressions" of an historical commercial streetscape in New Zealand museums at this time.[6] These included the Auckland War Memorial Museum's "Centennial St," which opened in 1967 in the nation's largest city, and the Whanganui Regional Museum's early twentieth-century street, established in 1973 in the small city on the North Island's west coast. Local museums in a variety of smaller towns and settlements also had their own versions. The local antecedents of these streetscapes lay in the displays of merchandise aimed at women in the nation's burgeoning department stores, and, more immediately, in two international expositions, or world's fairs, mounted in 1925 and 1940. Other influences reflected the international trade in ideas and practices amongst all these institutions over the same period.

Browsing in an Elegant Environment

New Zealand department stores had undergone expansion and consolidation and emerged as major retailers by the mid-1920s, slightly later than similar developments in Britain, Europe, North America, and Australia, largely because of the relatively late date of European colonization. From their humble beginnings as drapery stores, evident in most of the main centers in the late 1860s, they had reached their "golden age" in the first decades of the twentieth century. In the process they were transformed into American-style "department stores," rather than the "emporium" of the colonial age. "Modern and up to date with fashion, brimming with color and light, bustling with purposeful shoppers and courteous staff," historian Helen Laurenson notes that: "they were pivotal centers of interest around which much of the life of cities and towns … revolved. They offered a glimpse of the exotic 'other'—the world of the great metropolis."[7] By the 1960s, however, the impressive city had an energetic rival in the expanding and celebrated suburb. The first suburban shopping mall was constructed in Auckland in 1963, as New Zealand again followed "novel and enlivening" international trends.[8]

Yet in their heyday, department stores offered many enticements. You did not have to pay to enter and you were under no compulsion to buy. If you did want to purchase goods, you experienced "service, comfort and [an] amazing selection"[9] in new or newly refurbished, grand, multi-level buildings that had "facades of colour, glass and light."[10] The department store frontage, specifically the growing and more sophisticated use of window displays, in effect "3D catalogues, crammed with goods,"[11] acted like a magnet. The huge numbers who flocked to look were unfamiliar with such a visual feast outside show business. Following American trends, these presentations (often the most effective in the whole store) had became more restrained and controlled by the 1920s. According to Helen Laurenson, "they reinforced links with modernity as they presented a glimpse of things to come, constantly changing with the seasons, and presenting the latest in fashion."[12]

The layout of stores had also settled into a pattern of clearly defined spaces according to gender and age, although this did not cut across the notion that departments stores were for everyone. The ground floor contained "glamour and impulse items to waylay women on their way to the upper floors" and "clothing and furnishing for men who were presumed too timid to venture further into the store."[13] Spaces for children were on upper floors, including rooftop play areas. In between were more floors aimed at women. The crowning glory, literally, of many departments stores was the tearoom, usually accessed via the modern miracle of elevators, and a haven for tired and thirsty shoppers and families.

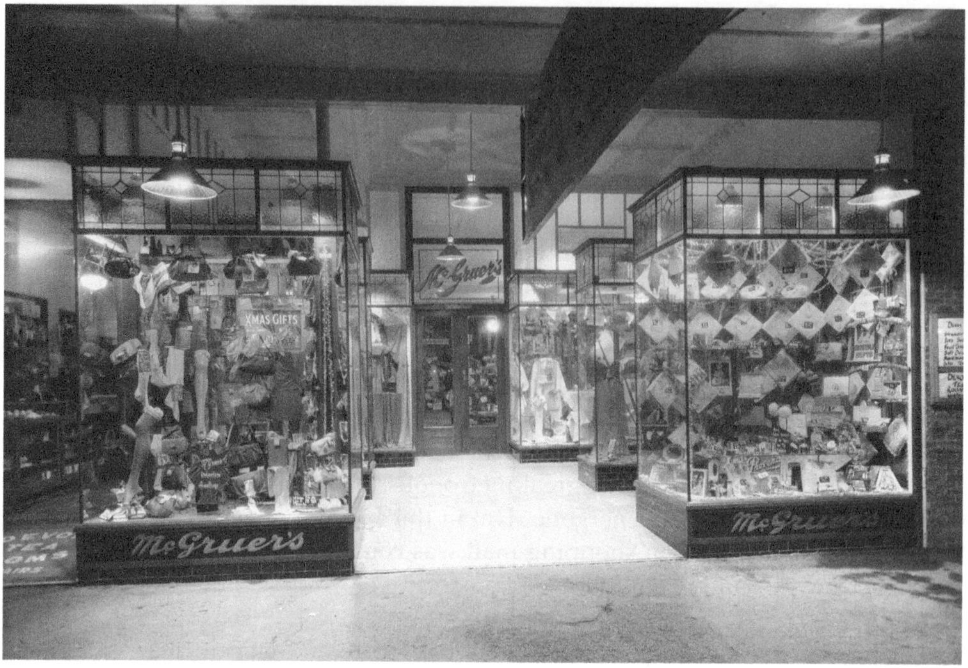

17.1 Even small towns had impressive glass-fronted retailers. Here McGruer's household drapery and apparel store, in Devon Street, New Plymouth, is decorated for the Christmas period, *circa* 1920s. Photographer: William Stanley Oakley, F-21724-1/1, W.S. Oakley Collection, Alexander Turnbull Library, Wellington, New Zealand

Over time, department store interiors were more spaciously arranged and this allowed the customer more freedom of movement. Time and money were lavished on display furniture, such as tables with stands, glass-sided showcases, "exquisitely turned out mannequins," sleek and stylish cabinets with chrome fittings, and modern and less elaborately patterned carpets. As Fiona McKergow has argued, the stores were more attuned to the personal pleasures of browsing in an elegant environment, with good sightlines, and beautiful tables and showcases.[14] "The magic strand of fashion," evident in the store's window displays, its elegantly arranged stock, and modish advertising, was combined with female sociability in the mannequin parades.[15] These had become omnipresent by the 1920s. Afternoon and, sometimes, evening parades for "devotees" rather than "customers" were recreational outlets that combined sensual and social pleasures. At these events, women could "share anecdotes and intimacies, or laugh and grumble as they chose," whether they purchased garments or not.[16]

Modern Objects and "the Glamour of Age"

The new urban visual culture being constructed in and around department stores had its counterpart in international expositions. In this period, there were two major world's fairs: the 1925–26 New Zealand and South Seas International Exhibition in the southern city of Dunedin, the country's largest center at the time, and the 1939–40 New Zealand Centennial Exhibition in the capital city of Wellington, in the North Island. Both expositions utilized techniques and themes from department stores, and both made direct appeals to female visitors and a perceived female constituency.

The "southern hemisphere's greatest exhibition" at Dunedin was open for six months from spring to autumn and attracted over 3.2 million visitors from a population of just over 1.4 million.[17] As with every world's fair since the Great Exhibition at Hyde Park in London in 1851, it functioned as "a machine for progress," to show off the nation's achievements across technology, trade, industry, arts, and science.[18] Visitors of both sexes and all ages, and many in family groups, flocked to the Exhibition. Yet males and females did not always attend the same courts and even when they did, they often took away different experiences and ideas from them.[19]

The "women's section," a brand new feature of the Exhibition, encouraged this pattern of activity and response. It was "so successful it will be a necessary adjunct to all future undertakings."[20] At the urging of the Exhibition's Director General, who wanted the already established Women's Rest Room Committee to widen its ambit, a central committee of prominent women leaders and representatives from the key women's organizations in the city was formed.[21] Its goal was to:

> represent and co-ordinate all women's interests and activities in connection with the Exhibition, especially in the direction of housing and hospitality, providing lectures on subjects interesting to women, and assisting the Directorate in all matters relating to the welfare of women visitors to the Exhibition and of women working therein.[22]

A range of displays occupied over 4,500 square feet in a prominent position in the No. 4 Pavilion on the east side of the Australian Court and north of the Canadian Court. There were three key areas. The first was "a miniature Exhibition in itself" of women's arts (fine and applied), crafts, and literature from many countries including Australia, the United States, and Great Britain. This included three bays of live demonstrations of spinning, weaving, lacemaking, pottery, illuminating and lettering, batik dying, bookbinding, color process printing, and sealing wax work. Themed "special week" exhibits encouraged women to send in items of handiwork from all over New Zealand, in an increasingly competitive series of displays. This was definitely a female "dream world of consumption"[23] with its chic, modern entrance and elegant internal layout.

The other two areas consisted of a "Loan Section" and the Lecture Hall program. The former illustrates how important the display of material culture was to the Women's Committee in creating a sense of women's history and women's values, alongside their manifest achievements in the arts. The following inscription appeared above the entrance to this section, which contained modern objects and many more "enveloped in the glamour of age":

> This little nook is devoted to the memory of things as they used to be long ago. Many of the exhibits are beautiful and valuable; but they have their place here not on account of their beauty and value, but for their connection with the lives of our mothers and grandmothers. Costly and beautiful, or merely homely and quaint, we, the women of Dunedin, have collected them here in the hope that they may bring back pleasant memories of bygone days to many others.[24]

In separate areas, also coordinated by the women's committee, visitors could view the Plunket Society's exhibition in pavilion no. 6,[25] or take advantage of the women's rest rooms and crèche, which were close to the Fernery and Art Gallery.

The rest rooms were made possible through funds raised by local women. They contained a women-only lounge, a nursery, an office, kitchenette, and cloakrooms. Two paid attendants dealt with 36,000 visitors, with an average weekly attendance of 1,500. The crèche was "one of the most popular and serviceable adjuncts to the Exhibition."[26] Over 3,000 infants passed through it, and parents paid one shilling for three hours' care given by volunteers, mostly from the Women's Christian Temperance Union. Students from the Home Science Department of Otago University, who learnt the basics of domestic architectural design with a concentration on planning and interior decorating, designed a modern kitchen in a "Home Science Cottage," which proved a very popular display. There was also a Girls Club Room managed by the Young Women's Christian Association for female employees at the Exhibition.[27] Last, but not least, there was a Women's Section Grand Poster and Fancy Dress Ball.[28]

By the time of the last world's fair in New Zealand in 1939–40, the "pleasant memories of bygone days" had come to the forefront of national consciousness. Before then, the primary cultural reference point had been the United Kingdom, from which many settlers had migrated from the mid-nineteenth century onwards to found the newest British colony. The society at large saw itself as British and white, for the most part ignoring its own human history, or if it was acknowledged, seeing it in imperial terms. Pakeha (European/non-indigenous) New Zealanders contented themselves with being "better Britons of the South Pacific" and this contributed to the belated discovery that they had a history of any significance.[29] A number of related events and activities helped overturn the "general absence, or at least a narrow sense, of national and historical consciousness" among twentieth-century New Zealanders.[30] During the 1930s, centennials of European settlement were "thick on the ground", with re-enactments of the landing of the first whalers, settlers and so forth, plaques and markers.[31] The year 1940 was the centenary of the signing of the Treaty of Waitangi between iwi (Maori tribes) and the British Queen Victoria, which facilitated settler colonization.[32] The government sponsored an enormous range of historical commemorations, celebrations, and publications throughout the country. City and town councils and local organizations enthusiastically participated in the nationwide festivals and mounted tributes in subsequent years as their own centenaries came round.[33]

The New Zealand Centennial Exhibition was the national centerpiece of the 1940 celebrations. Erected in the suburb of Rongotai in Wellington, the capital city, it contained a huge range of displays over its 55 acres. These exhibits included a large government contribution, which commemorated the material progress of New Zealand, innovations in technology, the pioneering spirit of its inhabitants and its famed natural beauty. Although it coincided with wartime restrictions and privations, over 2.6 million people (in a total population of just over 1.6 million) went through the turnstiles during its five-month run.[34]

Mindful that New Zealand was the first nation-state in the world to grant women the vote in 1893, and wanting to show how forward-looking and progressive the government was, the Exhibition also included a substantial 8,000 square foot women's section.[35] The directors' "appreciation of the importance of having the co-operation of women and a representation of their work and its part in the national life of New Zealand was well justified. From the very first visitors thronged [this section], in which all aspects of women's interests in the home and of their part in the earliest days of the Dominion were on view."[36] Coordinated once again by an executive committee of leading female civic, political, and community leaders,[37] this women's section was more ambitious and wide-ranging. Subcommittees covered more areas, such as professional women's interests, music, drama, sociology and psychology, medicine, electricity, horticulture, and science. There was also a determined and successful effort to cater for rural women around New Zealand through the Women's Institute and the Women's Division of the Farmer's Union.

The organizers devised the displays and activities in a broadly similar fashion to the 1925 Exhibition. Continuing the established tradition, there was a display of women's fine arts and arts and crafts, ranging from drawing and painting to needlework and designs for fabrics, textiles, and wallpapers. Combining local and representative work from the Dominions of Australia, Canada, and Great Britain, it offered "a comprehensive impression of the creative ability of New Zealand women in various media."[38] Once again, there were live demonstrations of pottery making, spinning, and weaving.

Visitors to the women's section could also attend the very popular daily program of talks in the 200-seat lecture hall, by "experts in domestic science and professional callings from all over the Dominion."[39] The New Zealand Free Kindergarten Union Incorporated managed the presentation of a kindergarten building, adjacent to the children's play area, designed and furnished along "modern lines," complete with a display of children's toys and with trained staff on hand to provide advice. The countrywomen's section had its own loans section, crafts, lectures, and demonstrations. A special portion was devoted to the display and sale of the work of Maori members of the Women's Institute and the Women's Division of the Farmer's Union. Maori were predominantly rural dwellers until rapid mass urban migration, stimulated by the industrial demands of World War II and the economic and social opportunities of the growing cities in the 1950s and 1960s, encouraged many to shift and permanently reside in towns and cities.

The elaborate, largely historical, loan sections owed much to department store practices and presaged the content of museum presentations. The Exhibition's future-oriented themes of progress and modernity were not inconsistent with a strong emphasis on heritage. As several scholars have recognized, heritage is "ironically, a sign of modernity not only because it recognizes the past as past but recycles it as a regenerative resource."[40] At the Exhibition, claims to a place in the present and therefore in the future were based on the strength of past triumphs, which were materialized for a largely female audience in particular ways.

The loans section contained two nineteenth-century domestic "period rooms," a familiar museum exhibition technique. The first was a North Island pioneer hut *circa* 1840 and next door to it was an "Early Pioneers Room" from the South Island *circa* 1850–60, reflecting the relative states of colonization and "development" of the two islands.[41] The hut was suitably rough and ready, with the bare essentials, while the other room was elaborately framed by its title and reproductions of emigration posters. It showed a prosperous family in their parlor. The wife sits with her needlework and the daughter plays with her doll, while the husband has just arrived, still clutching his top hat and with his traveling bag at his feet. The comfortably appointed room contains a piano, a harp, table and chairs, chaise longue, and other furniture, and a woman's workbox on a stand. There is a lamp on the table and many pictures on the wallpapered walls, including a silhouette and a sampler. The mannequins are dressed very well and fashionably, if not quite all in the appropriate period. It is as if the visitor in front of the ropes comes upon the scene in mid-action.

The two rooms were "without doubt the most striking historical displays in the whole Exhibition."[42] They were "finished in faithful detail" with family treasures lent specifically for the occasion. Because the rooms and

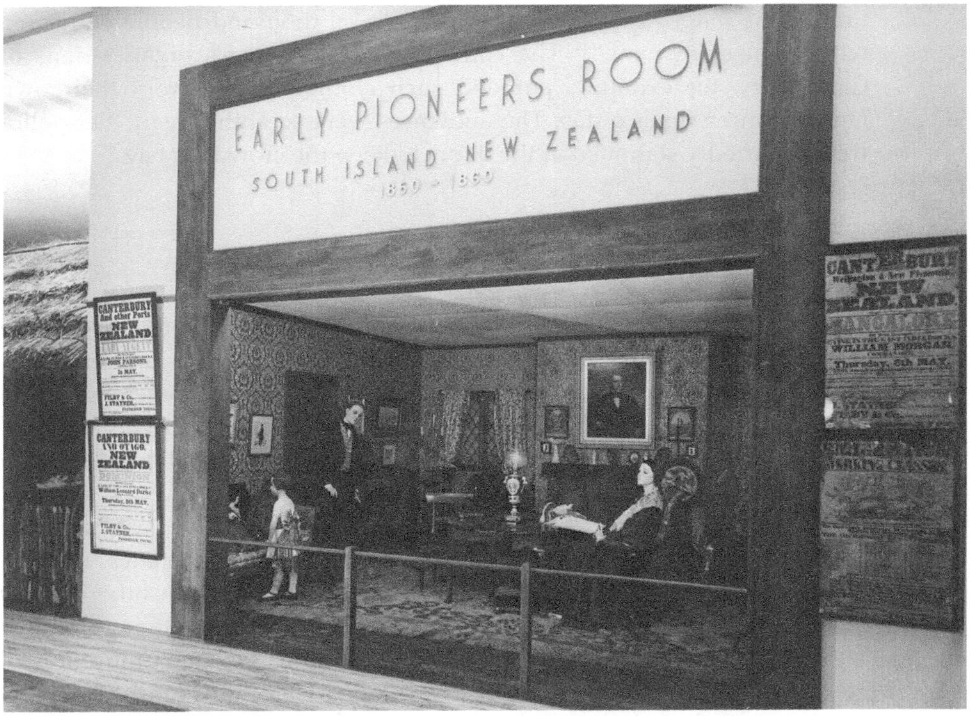

17.2 The elaborate "South Island Pioneer" period room with the North Island "pioneer hut" just visible on the left in the women's section, at the New Zealand Centennial Exhibition, 1940. 1/2-036211-F, PAColl 3036, Eileen Deste Collection, Alexander Turnbull Library, Wellington, New Zealand

articles within them were "rich in storied associations," with an undoubted air of authenticity, it was as if they were indeed collections on display in a museum.[43] Completing the museological aura but, it must also be said, imparting a commercial flavor, each individual exhibit was numbered. The Women's Court Catalogue gave the history of each article and the name of its owner. The museum conceit continued with the display of antiques and other historical objects in neighboring glass cases as general loan exhibits.

As well as the worthy advice and the more intimate and personal gratification in seeing the period rooms and the treasures in them bring history alive, there was one more obvious borrowing from commerce. This time it echoed the department store's sensual and social pleasures more unambiguously. Although few historians have paid much attention, the official history of the Exhibition acknowledged that: "An outstanding feature were the Dress Parades of Period Frocks which were staged from time to time in the main Assembly Hall [that] several thousand people witnessed with great enjoyment."[44] The combined rural women's organizations of Canterbury, for example, paraded such clothing, often from their own families, three times a day. The audiences were so enthusiastic that police were reportedly stationed at the doors to keep the crowds at bay.[45]

Materializing the Pioneer Past in Museums

The 1940 Centennial Exhibition and the anniversaries of the previous decade stimulated a growing interest by Pakeha in their history and heritage. Over the next two decades there were several interrelated developments: a myriad of local historical societies were either established or re-invigorated; the Historic Places Trust, the government-supported national heritage organization, was established; universities began to teach New Zealand history for the first time; and communities founded or revived a remarkable number of museums, often in tandem with historical societies.[46] Before World War II, New Zealand museums, along with those in other former British settler colonies, were devoted to natural history, ethnography or art rather than "history" per se. These institutions began as museums of geology, flora, and fauna and then developed collections and displays in ethnographic material. They contained very few non-indigenous historical collections. Art collections were increasingly housed in art galleries, rather than museums. The number of art galleries and museums officially listed grew rapidly from just 38 institutions in 1958 to 112 ten years later, and they kept on growing in number.[47] Unsurprisingly, the most notable increase was "especially in collections made on the occasion of the celebration of a local centenary or on the preservation of a house or cottage of some historical merit."[48] Developments at the Dominion Museum reflect this overall pattern. The first temporary exhibition of early colonial history opened in 1954 and an honorary curator of cultural history was appointed four years later. The first curator of colonial history began work in 1968 and the following year the Colonial History Gallery was established.

Some contemporaries believed that the boom in museums and historical collections "has been more apparent than real however, as intentions have not always been realised … The rosy rhetoric of proud celebrants is more likely to be commemorated in newspaper files than in a rainproof roof sheltering instructive and intriguing exhibits."[49] Yet the sense of having an interesting, localized past that is worth representing and preserving in a museum had clearly come into being. According to W.H. Oliver, the author of *The Story of New Zealand* (1960), one of the first general national histories to be published, his generation of New Zealanders was involved in "the project of finding a country by thinking about it."[50] Individuals and groups were contributing to the construction of "New Zealand" through a discourse of cultural languages—literature, painting, architecture, decorative arts, music, and popular culture.[51] As Chris Healy's examination of history, social memory, and colonialism in Australia argued, the way in which the past is constructed in the public imagination produces something called "Australian history."[52] From a slightly different perspective, Amiria Henare refers to the way that regional history museums and historical/heritage sites are part of "cultural landscapes," and how they provide evidence of history making in many different settings. Henare argues that historical collections and displays functioned as memory places for Pakeha, and formed whiggish, largely triumphalist, and laudatory accounts of settler pioneers, who broke in the land and built up the country into what it had become today.[53] Yet a careful examination of the display of women and things in museums in the 1950s and 1960s uncovers an intriguing and significant set of processes. These exemplify the active production of meaning through popular forms of history and heritage, which, rather than distorting them, materialized certain styles of women's history in ways that made sense to large audiences, and which acted as a foil to the production of a modern female present. As scholars of museums and heritage have concluded: "Museums and 'heritage' create modern culture by providing a space where the present can mark off the past as 'a foreign country'."[54]

Women Walk Colonial Streets

At the same time as a pioneer history was being reconstructed and celebrated, the female past was shifting further towards center stage. It was helped by the activities of key individuals, but also resulted from the confluence of aspects of contemporary feminine popular culture, which answered the increasing clamor within communities for historical representation and their desire to donate historical material culture to local museums. Museums, bastions of scientific, ethnographic or art historical enquiry, and slow to recognize history officially, now reflected the rise in popular interest in history in this period, which seeped in from adjacent cultural fields such as heritage, costume appreciation, and historical societies. The Canterbury Museum is my exemplar, although its experience was not unique. Similar developments, but over different periods, occurred at other metropolitan and regional museums around New Zealand.

The Canterbury Museum was established in 1867 in Christchurch, the main city of the Canterbury Province in the South Island. It was the most English center in the colony, the epitome of this "Better Britain." The Museum's history follows the general trajectory of interest in New Zealand history that I have already outlined. The first late-nineteenth-century phase of historical awareness can be seen in the establishment of an "Early Colonists Room" in the north end of the gallery of the New Zealand Room from 1910, which was a response to the Board of Governors' stated desire for a history department the previous year.[55] During the 1940s, the Museum's annual reports referred to "antiquities," "Early Colonist," and "historical" collections.

In 1947, the Museum was transferred from University College control through a Board of Governors to local body control in the form of a Trust Board. Members of the Trust Board included a representative of the City Pilgrim and Early Settlers Association, which had formed in 1923.[56] Although there was as yet no colonial history curator, the sense of historical interest was remarked upon: the Museum's mandate was to illustrate "the story of its own growth since the settlement of the Province, and no less the more general story of Nature and Man, with special reference to our own Province, New Zealand and the Pacific Basin".[57] There was a temporary display of "period costume" and the 1948–49 Annual Report commented that "numerous accessions reflect the growing interest of the public as a natural centre of historical displays, and a repository of archives."[58] Indeed, most of the historical items came into the collection, through donation, after 1950.

The preparations for the 1950 Provincial Centennial Celebrations provided the specific catalyst for the development of colonial history in the Museum. These celebrations, like those around the rest of the country, included re-enactments, historical pageants, dedicated church services, the erection of memorials and plaques, music, artistic and literary endeavors. That same year an "Early Colonists Exhibition" opened in the Museum's "Early Canterbury Hall." Approaching the hall, the visitor's eye was drawn first to a large mural painting, complete with satirical replica 1848 *Punch* cartoons and Canterbury Association handbills enticing migrants. They then moved on to a scale diorama of the first four ships at Lyttleton, the embarkation port. Proceeding down the left of the hall, a sense of the three-month voyage out was brought home by the recreation of first class emigrants' quarters aboard the *Charlotte Jane*, complete with authentic furniture. Then in the middle of the hall, the visitor would see Dr A.C. Barker's V-hut or tent in wood and thatch, covered in a discarded studding sail, which he set up a week after arriving in 1850. This was so roomy it had full-size furniture in it and was used mainly by Mrs Barker and her companion, Miss Letitia Bowen. They are shown as fully costumed mannequins sitting sewing with Master Barker, also appropriately attired, looking on. Walking around the rest of the hall clockwise, the visitor would pass the reconstruction of an early two-roomed cob cottage, again quite elaborately furnished with resident figures; the bedroom and sitting room of a Christchurch house, 1850–60; an 1890s Victorian Room representing "a new house and a new generation." Six cases down the right-hand side of the hall contained numerous examples of "colonial silver," "costumes and textiles," "china and bric-a-brac," and "hardware and kitchen" ware.[59]

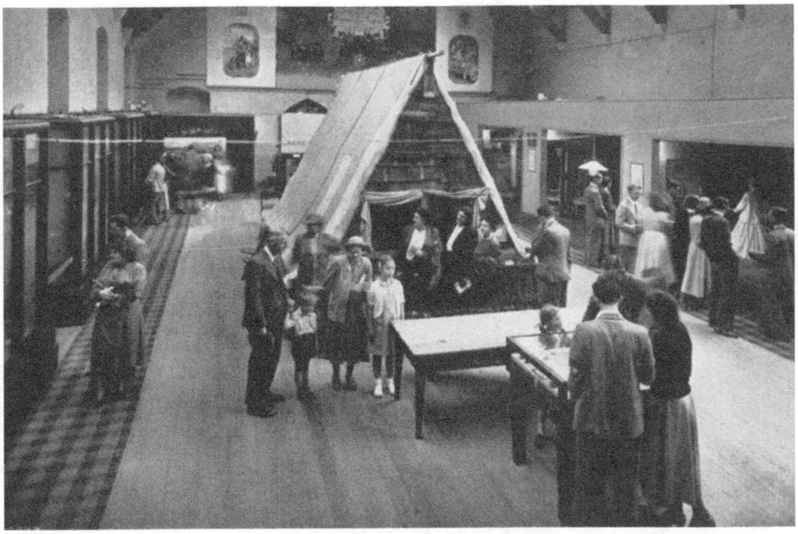

17.3 Visitors throng the Canterbury Colonists Exhibition, 1950–51. The conventional long rectangular gallery space has a high ceiling with period room displays around the perimeter for promenade viewing. Dr Barker's roomy V-hut with vitrine and map displays dominate the center of the gallery. *Canterbury Colonists Exhibition, 1950–51*, The Friends of the Canterbury Museum, Christchurch, 1951, p. 29

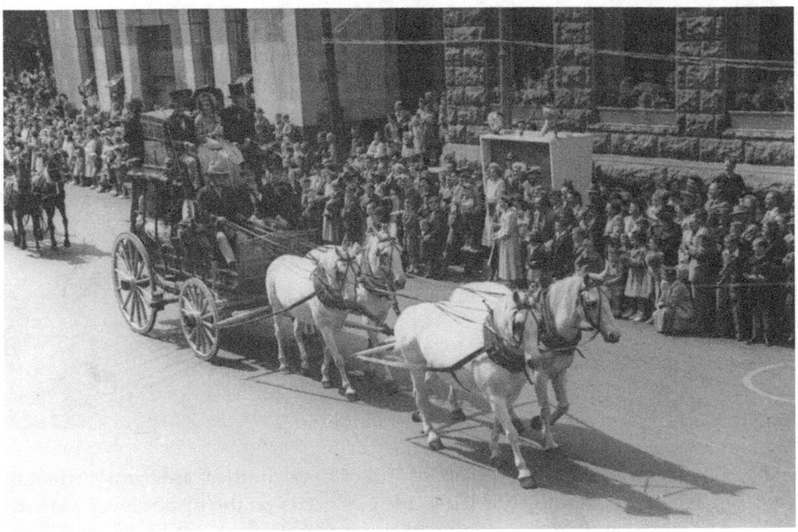

17.4 A costumed historical procession, part of the Canterbury centenary celebrations in Christchurch city, December 1950. 19XX.2.55, Leicagraph Studio photograph, Canterbury Museum

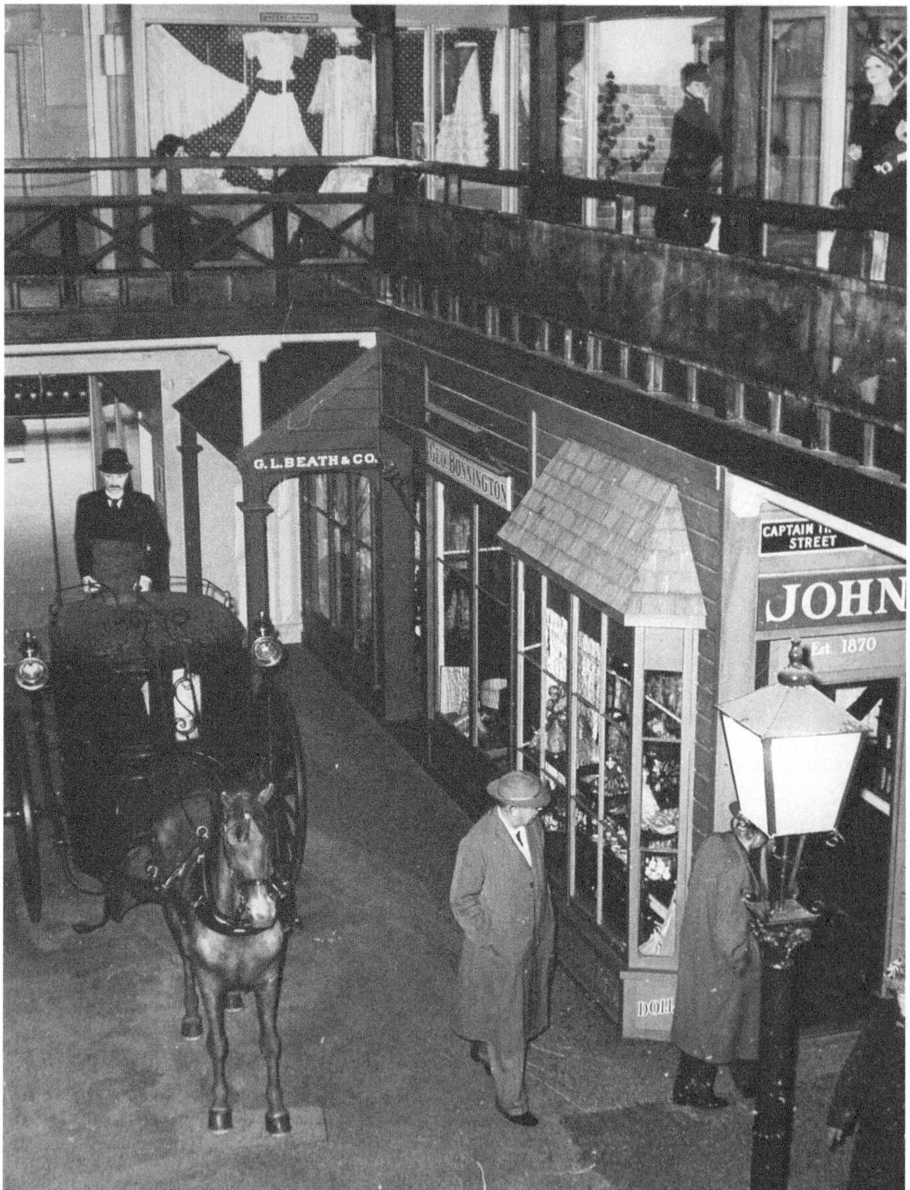

17.5 Even men came to look at the horse and carriage in the Canterbury Street in this view from 1960. The arcade-style Costume Gallery is on the upper level. Garments similar to those on display, and the fabric and trimmings, could be seen in the shops in the street, which were based on actual stores and establishments in Christchurch city. 1990.358.902, unknown photographer, Rose Josephine Reynolds Collection, Canterbury Museum

It was "without doubt the most successful exhibition in the Museum's history," attended over nine months by 77,000 paying visitors, in a total regional population of 282,571. It earned over £3,500 in one shilling and six penny admissions. The Museum felt that it showed the public "the vivid possibilities of the museum reconstruction of Colonial history by period room and habitat settings," and it was the most ambitious attempt yet of any museum to do that.[60] As with the international expositions, over a hundred families from the province lent or donated objects for the display, including "heirloom furniture, utensils, silver and china-ware."[61] According to visitors, it was "history made to live" and the "most interesting part of the centennial." One sightseer was "thankful to live in 1950."[62] Others wrote "3rd visit (still interested)" and thought "the curtain had been raised"—an interesting theatrical metaphor.[63]

Buoyed by this success, the Museum opened a Hall of Folk Culture in the former Ethnological Hall the following year, in order to embrace the themes of Colonial and South Seas Folk Arts.[64] The new Canterbury Colonists section had a ship cabin, two cottage rooms, two rooms for period costume, English fashion plates and a scale model of the Ferrymead Railway Station. Although it closed in 1955, it provided a preview of the permanent Colonists Hall planned for the new Centennial Memorial wing, which opened three years later.

The inspiration for the Street came from a number of sources in New Zealand and England: the women's section of the 1940 Centennial Exhibition, specifically the South Island Pioneer Room 1850–60; the Folk Museum of Yorkshire Life with its reconstructed street of Kirkgate; and the Folk Museum at Kirkstall Abbey in Leeds.[65] The Museum Director regarded this display "as a permanent memorial to the domestic customs of our colonial ancestors for the inspiration of their descendants."[66] In 1965, the Museum began a major project focused on the more usual tropes and narratives of Pakeha pioneer history, which did not include women in quite the same way as the Street and the costume gallery. The south end of the Hall of Transport would be altered to "serve as an introduction to the European settlement of Canterbury" with a section on whaling; a reconstructed cabin interior with diorama of one of the first four emigrant ships, the *Charlotte Jane*; a reconstruction of the blockhouse from Akaroa; and a gold-mining diorama complete with mining objects.[67] A blacksmith's forge and bullock's dray followed.

Extending the Space for a Female Past

As well as the more general interest in New Zealand history and the stimulus of the provincial centennial, more room for a female past was made by the redoubtable Rosa (Rose) Reynolds (1907–1994). She became the "honorable custodian of colonial exhibits" in 1958, after a decade's association with the Museum, stemming from her "lifetime's interest in an honorary capacity in the material record of Victorian Canterbury."[68] She continued as honorary curator of colonial history through to 1977. Reynolds was one of a number of hitherto overlooked women who helped to carve out a female sphere, which ultimately led to the development of history in museums on a broader and more thoroughgoing scale.[69]

Reynolds had long-standing links with the early settlers association, local theater, and other performing arts, through costume design and display. She had dressed the performers in the pioneer colonial sequences in the *Canterbury Centennial Celebrations* (1950), produced by the New Zealand National Film Unit. She was an advisor to another key centennial event: the first four ships arrival reenactment, including the farewell breakfast for departing colonists and ball on board the *Randolph*, for which she designed all the costumes. She was also instrumental in developing the Gallery of Period Costume.

An effective and assiduous publicist amongst her local historical and heritage networks, Reynolds belonged to many key organizations in the city, including the Christchurch Civic Trust, the Historic Places Trust, the Christchurch Cathedral Association, and the friends' organizations of the Museum and the Robert McDougall Art Gallery. She was also diligent in writing for the "News for Women" and the "Women's news and views" sections of the local newspaper, thereby building a female audience for her galleries. She even used the "Museum of Nature" page, contributed by a range of Canterbury Museum staff, to publicize the clothing and textile collections. She wrote pieces on "Fashions in Wigs"; umbrellas and parasols; embroidered samplers; work tables and workboxes; programmes printed on silk; Peddler dolls; and sailor suits.[70] An article by her about the Colonist Galleries appeared in the October 1968 issue of the national circulation magazine, *Family Circle*. Given her good international contacts, it is not surprising that there was a one and a half-page spread in the English magazine, *Country Life*, in 1951.[71]

Like women active in the other main centers, she also gave numerous radio talks locally and nationally. Rosa spoke about the new costume gallery on the "women's session" program in March 1957, and about the Museum on the "city roundabout" show the following month. In 1959, she was invited to contribute to a series on the national YC network on New Zealand colonial architecture and decoration for the period to 1879, and to give her opinions on early colonial museums the same year. A lively and authoritative commentator, she called for curatorial training and greater knowledge of colonial New Zealand history, supported the preservation of old homesteads, and urged provincial museums to have "early colonial" or "colonial history" sections, "otherwise with the passing of years it will be too late." Acknowledging

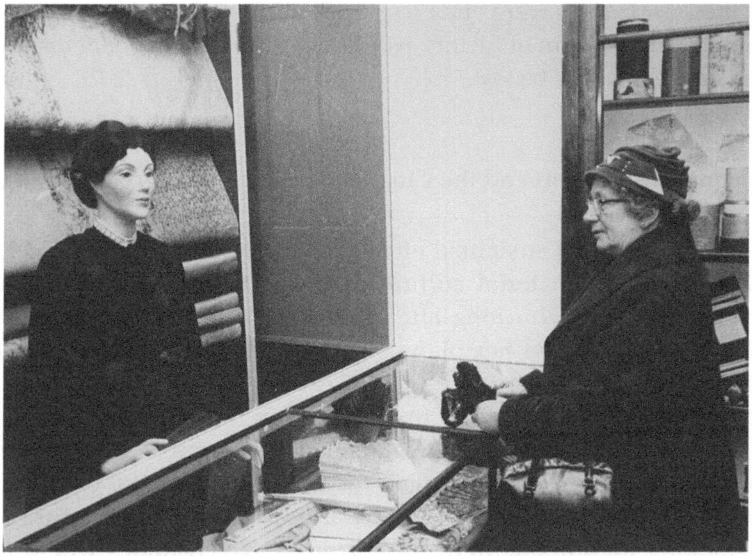

17.6 A female visitor prepares to be served in the J Ballantyne shop, Canterbury Street, Canterbury Museum, 1960. Ballantynes later became a well-known department store in the city. 1990.358.923, unknown photographer, Rose Josephine Reynolds Collection, Canterbury Museum

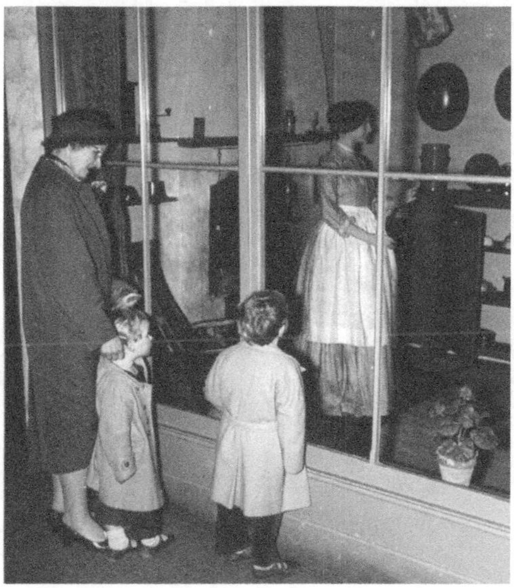

17.7 Visitors young and old peer into the Cob Cottage, Canterbury Street, Canterbury Museum, 1960. 1990.358.950, unknown photographer, Rose Josephine Reynolds Collection, Canterbury Museum

that these endeavors were "tied to parochialism and local values," Reynolds thought that this form of history would not work in a national institution, as "the keenness would be lost."[72]

"Personal Adornment and the Close Association of Everyday Things"

Reynolds' huge and sustained efforts to collect and preserve local history and to highlight material culture of interest to women reflected long-standing interests. Not long after she began at the Canterbury Museum in 1948, she explained her plans for a new costume gallery in a letter to Miss Buck, at the Gallery of English Costume in Rushholme, Manchester. Reynolds had been interested in stage design for many years and she had "assisted shops in period costume displays from time to time." She wanted to collect and preserve costumes for the period up to 1900 and "only wished she had started rescue work a little earlier." It appears that she was looking for suitable items to borrow—"No costumes would be worn by people only on lay figures"—and she specified those that were always difficult to procure, such as male working clothes and a children's box. The

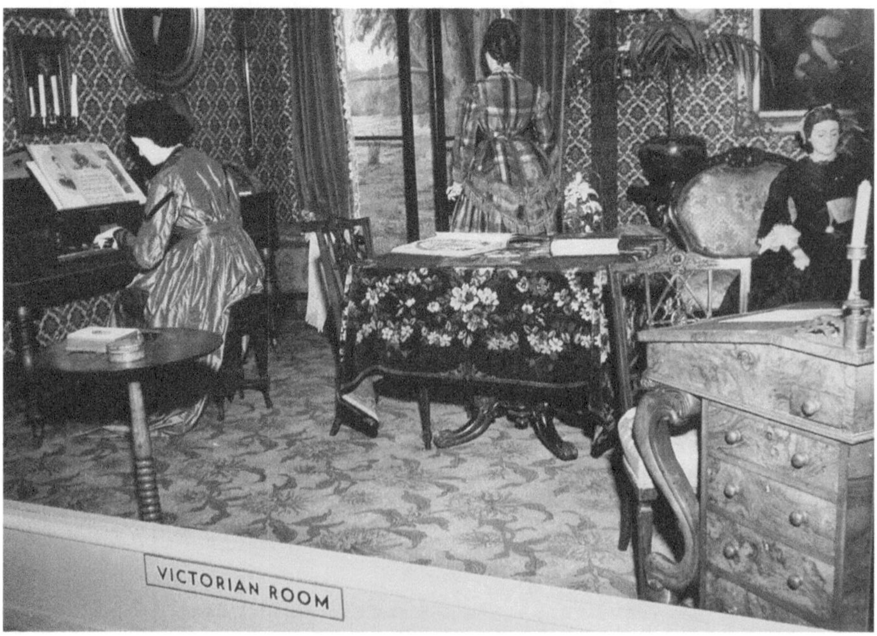

17.8 The Victorian Room display, Canterbury Museum, 1960. 1990.358.950, unknown photographer, Rose Josephine Reynolds Collection, Canterbury Museum

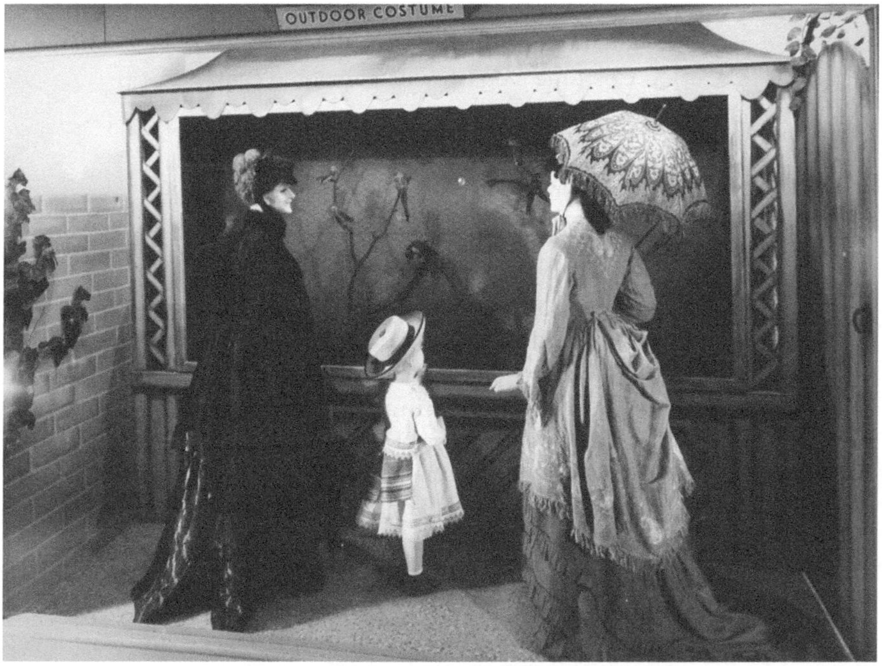

17.9 Extensive use of elaborately dressed mannequins and mural settings were a feature of the Costume Gallery, Canterbury Museum, shown here in 1960. 1990.358.979, unknown photographer, Rose Josephine Reynolds Collection, Canterbury Museum

local up-market department store, Ballantynes, had loaned mannequins and Reynolds borrowed from London's Victoria and Albert Museum, the premiere decorative arts institution in the Commonwealth.[73]

Reynolds was also involved in pageants and fashion parades in the centennial year. The DIC department store and Ellesmore Plunket Society presented a fundraiser, "Family Album of the Canterbury Plains," from October 9 to 12, at afternoon and evening (formal dress) sessions. A presentation in "Story, Fashion and Music," it featured "Old Time Models, some over 100 years old, and their modern counterparts, worn by Descendants and other Ladies of the district."[74] Similarly, Reynolds helped organize and provided commentary at an evening "Cavalcade of Fashion" at the Wentworth Hotel over three nights in December, sponsored by the Canterbury Pilgrim and Early Settlers Association in cooperation with the Repertory Theatre and the Women's Centennial Pageantry Sub-committee. The program itself was an object of wonder and delight. In the shape of a fold-out fan, with pink and white lace, it was printed by the local and renowned Caxton Press.

Reynolds was clearly not preoccupied with strict notions of authenticity in the way that professional museum staff would be today. In her 1953 annual report for the Period Costume Department, she noted that:

> Unlike the older settled countries, New Zealand is limited to a more recent period for displaying genuine local costumes and for some time I have felt that in addition to showing all early colonial examples, faithful reproductions of pre-colonial periods would enable the children to visualise more clearly the dress and manners of historical times.[75]

That same year she prepared the Ballantynes' Elizabethan window display for the coronation of Queen Elizabeth II. The Museum received the costumes and drop scenes afterwards, which she immediately put on display.

In the 1960s, her efforts were bearing fruit and she had acquired the taste for authenticity, while extending the temporal boundaries of what constituted Canterbury history in the Museum through to the period immediately after 1900. Because she was not able to buy dresses of that period, she happily received a wide range of donations. She observed that "through the medium of personal adornment and the close association of everyday things," donations "provide a wide and varied panorama of our colonial and early post-colonial life. Carefully preserved and displayed in the right setting, they should give endless delight and satisfaction for generations to come."[76] The Museum's non-commercial character was preserved in the Christchurch Street, so that the shops carried no contemporary advertising. Instead, all the shops were individually sponsored—another feat of organization and marketing. Individual objects displayed in the front windows, and the few shops you could enter, bore no object labels. An accompanying booklet provided information and interpretation, as had been provided at the 1940 Centennial Exhibition.

The intersection of historical costume, pageants, and departments stores that Reynolds' interests represent was replicated elsewhere in New Zealand as she corresponded with and assisted female museum staff at other institutions, who followed her lead. Edna M. Stephenson at the Auckland Museum was very grateful. She led the installation of the northern city's "Centennial Street," which was a scaled-down series of streets based loosely on mid-nineteenth-century Auckland that had first been paid for by Milne & Choyce, a leading local department store. She declared: "I can now really understand your interest in and love of costume … [we are] gradually building up quite a good collection. It is very humble compared to your collection but a good basis to start from." She also acknowledged ruefully that Reynolds made all the wigs for display.[77]

The successful efforts of Reynolds and others to collect and display the female past in this period, albeit in an imperial and "pioneer" framework and in the mode of "period rooms," require us to reevaluate the importance of fashion, clothing, and dressing up in the construction of the female past. Their efforts are a key example of the materialization of history that is easy to overlook as ephemeral and middlebrow. Yet the collections and galleries that she and others were responsible for demonstrate that, despite their elite background and the way they drew upon notions of "founders" and "founding families," their appeal was much wider across gender and age groups, and particularly with women. These efforts were instrumental in creating a Pakeha female past through objects and spaces, which literally embodied history for contemporary audiences by marking them off from the present. It would take the influence of women's liberation and the "new" social history from the 1970s, as well as different exhibition technologies, for a different conception of a female past and of late modernity to emerge.

Conclusion: A Modern Female Exhibitionary Complex

Shoppers and the visitors to expositions and museum exhibitions were making history when they browsed in their different versions of the "temple of things."[78] People, and especially women, came in large numbers to look at visual displays that created a modern female present by materializing a female past. This chapter has charted the shifts in representational practices and modes of observation[79] over time, but has also argued that there are clear analogies in material culture across a number of fields that are normally thought of as being distinct and unrelated. For some time now, scholars have made persuasive arguments for the all-encompassing social embrace of material culture both in and outside of Western, industrialized societies. They argue that material objects matter because "the meanings people give to objects, the whole process of acquisition, notions of taste, style, social competition, the emotional pleasure derived from material objects, and the symbolic product values ... help us examine the shifts in intellectual feelings about the core relationships between humans, goods, and society."[80] In early to mid-twentieth-century New Zealand, the sensual and social pleasures of seeing objects from mothers and foremothers and of attending fashion parades, and the familiar and inextricably linked cultural spaces of the department store, exhibition, and museum, produced a twentieth-century version of the "exhibitionary complex"[81] that opened up a space for female interests and values. Rather than being principally a regulating or oppressive site, or only a memory place for congratulatory and triumphant colonialism, it was also constitutive, producing a novel way of seeing one's historical self, in the innovative form of shops and fashion parades, and revealing a new present. When visitors, and particularly

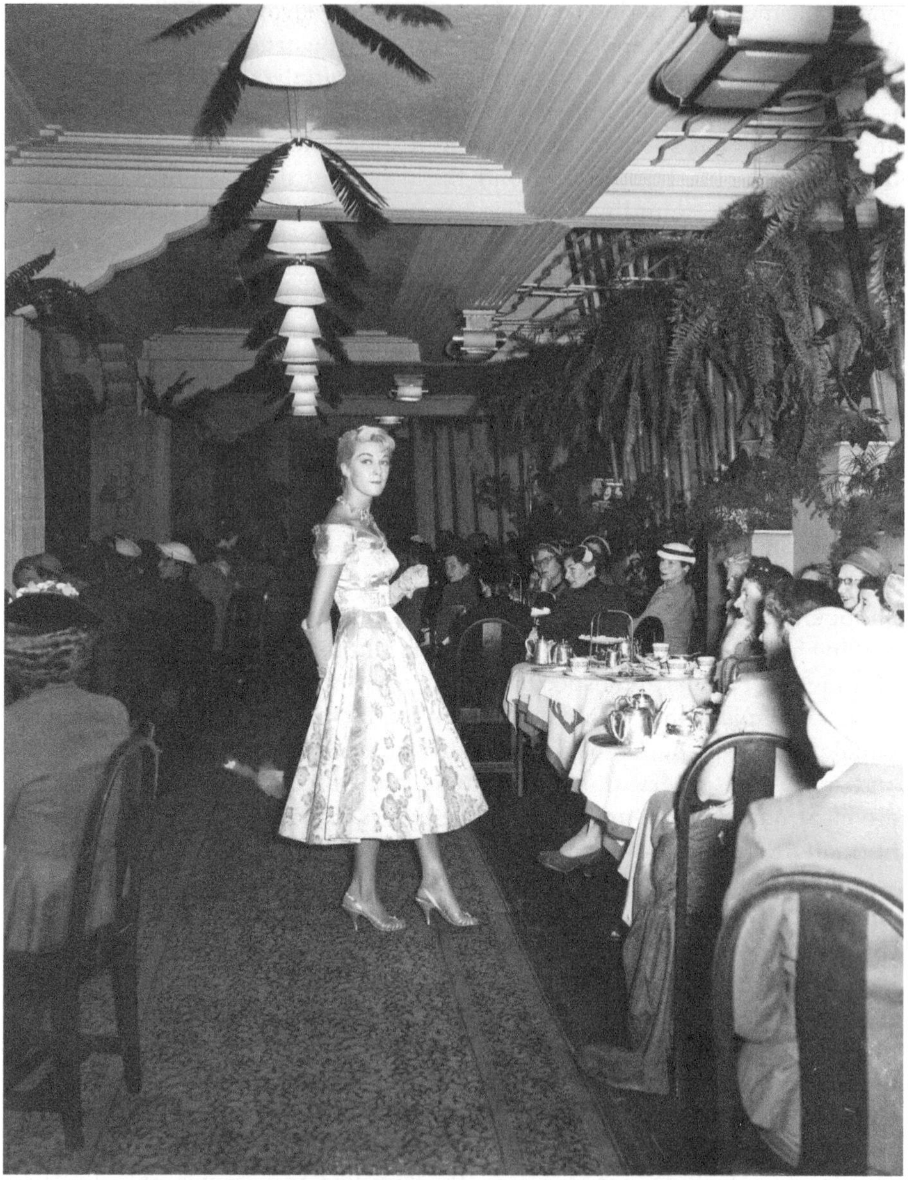

17.10 Fashion show, James Smith's department store, Wellington, *circa* 1953. PAColl-3332-03-15, James Smith Ltd Collection, Alexander Turnbull Library, Wellington, New Zealand

women, saw objects on display in this way, it was not simply the object nor only the viewer that mattered, but the relations between them that created new experiences and new understandings.

Notes

1. My grateful thanks to the Information Manager/Curator of Manuscripts Joanna Condon and the desk staff, especially Eva Sullivan, at the Documentary Research Centre at the Canterbury Museum, and History Curator Rose Young and staff of the Auckland War Memorial Museum Library, for their helpful assistance. I have benefited enormously from many conversations on this and related subjects with Conal McCarthy, who also read and commented on an earlier draft. This research was supported by a Massey University Research Fund grant and the School of Visual and Material Culture.

2. For further detail and interpretation, see *Canterbury Colonists Galleries: A Guide* (Christchurch: Canterbury Museum, 1960).

3. Roger Duff to Clarice Lorgelly, [?] 1968. Series 6/6 Canterbury History (Early Colonial), folder 13, Canterbury Museum Records (hereafter CMR), Documentary Research Centre, Canterbury Museum.

4. The large literature includes Carol Duncan, "Museums and Department Stores: Close Encounters," in *High-Pop: Making Culture into Popular Entertainment*, ed. Jim Collins, 129–54 (Malden and Oxford: Blackwell Publishers, 2002). For a more recent statement in terms of the wider nineteenth-century urban visual culture, see "Part Four: Practices of Display and the Circulation of Images," in *The Nineteenth-Century Visual Culture Reader*, eds. Vanessa R. Schwartz and Jeannene M. Przyblyski (New York and London: Routledge, 2004), 115–16. See also Tony Bennett, *The Birth of the Museum: History, Theory, Politics* (London and New York: Routledge, 1995); Patricia Mainardi, *The End of the Salon: Art and the State in the Early Third Republic* (Cambridge: Cambridge University Press, 1993); and Erika Rappaport, *Shopping for Pleasure: Women in the Making of London's West End* (Princeton: Princeton University Press, 2000).

5. The classic work is Peter Vergo, ed. *The New Museology* (London: Reaktion Books, 1989). For an example of anti-commercialism, see also Charles Saumarez Smith, "The Future of the Museum," in *A Companion to Museum Studies*, ed. Sharon Macdonald, 543–54 (Malden, MA: Blackwell, 2006).

6. The exhibition "recreates the impression of early 20th century Wanganui businesses from this prosperous time." The Whanganui Regional Museum, "The Street—Wanganui 1900–1920," Whanganui Regional Museum, <http://www.wanganui-museum.org.nz> (click on "exhibitions" then "on view," accessed April 18, 2008).

7. Helen B. Laurenson, *Going Up Going Down: The Rise and Fall of the Department Store* (Auckland: Auckland University Press, 2005), 6–7. See also Julia Millen, *Kirkcaldie & Stains: A Wellington Story* (Wellington: Bridget Williams Books, 2000).

8. Laurenson, *Going Up Going Down*, 12.

9. Ibid., 12.

10. Ibid., 12–13.

11. Louise Shaw, "Hallenstein Brothers and Company 1876–1906, the Early Years of Mass Retailing in New Zealand," PGDipAAs, University of Otago, 1994, 43, cited in Laurenson, *Going Up Going Down*, 14.

12. Laurenson, *Going Up Going Down*, 23.

13. Susan Porter Benson, *Counter Cultures: Saleswomen, Managers, and Customers in American Department Stores* (Urbana: University of Illinois Press, 1986), 44, cited in Laurenson, *Going Up Going Down*, 33.

14. Fiona McKergow, "'Just the Thing': Shopping for Clothes in Palmerston North," in *Looking Flash: Clothing in Aotearoa New Zealand*, eds. Bronwyn Labrum, Fiona McKergow, and Stephanie Gibson (Auckland: Auckland University Press, 2007), 145.

15. Laurenson, *Going Up Going Down*, 55; McKergow, "'Just the Thing'," 147.

16. McKergow, "'Just the Thing'," 148.

17. The subtitle of the official pictorial history, published in 1926 under the authority of the New Zealand Government Publicity Board, assisted by the Exhibition Company; "Population," from *An Encyclopaedia of New Zealand*, ed. A.H. McLintock, originally published in 1966, Te Ara—The Encyclopedia of New Zealand, <http://www.TeAra.govt.nz/1966/P/Population/en> (accessed April 10, 2008).

18. Bennett, *The Birth of the Museum*, 10.

19. Barbara Brookes, Erik Olssen, and Emma Beer, "Spare Time? Leisure, Gender and Modernity," in *Sites of Gender: Women, Men and Modernity in Southern Dunedin, 1890–1940*, eds. Barbara Brookes, Annabel Cooper, and Robin Law (Auckland: Auckland University Press, 2003), 171.

20. G.E. Thompson, *Official Record of the New Zealand and South Seas International Exhibition, Dunedin, 1925–26* (Dunedin: Coulls Somerville Wilkie Ltd, 1926), 117.

21. See the photograph of the committee in Thompson, *Official Record*, opposite p. 120 and the list of names on p. 136.

22. Thompson, *Official Record*, 117.

23. Rosalind Williams, "Dream Worlds of Consumption," in *Communication in History: Technology, Culture, Society*, eds. David Crowley and Paul Heyer, 179–85 (Boston: Allyn & Bacon, 2003).

24. Thompson, *Official Record*, 120.

25. The Royal New Zealand Plunket Society (1907–) is an incorporated society which provides a range of non-institutional health and welfare services to babies and young children, and advice and services for their parents.

26. Thompson, *Official Record*, 35–6.

27. See Gladys McGill, "House Planning and Interior Decoration," *University of Otago Home Science Department Bulletin* 4 (1925); Thompson, *Official Record*, 118.

28. Thompson, *Official Record*, 128.

29. James Belich, *Paradise Reforged: A History of the New Zealanders from the 1880s to the Year 2000* (Auckland: Penguin, 2001), passim.

30. J.M. Gore, "Representations of History and Nation in Museums in Aotearoa and New Zealand—The National Museums of Australia and The Museum of New Zealand Te Papa Tongarewa," PhD Dissertation, University of Melbourne, 2002, 19–20. In the 1890s there was also a keen sense of the past as many regions celebrated settlement jubilees, established organizations of "Old Colonists" and produced "pioneer history." See Gavin McLean, "Where Sheep May Not Safely Graze: A Brief History of New Zealand's Heritage Movement 1890–2000," in *Common Ground? Heritage and Public Places in New Zealand*, ed. Alexander Trapeznik (Dunedin: University of Otago Press, 2000), 27.

31. McLean, "Where Sheep May Not Safely Graze," 30.

32. See, for example, Claudia Orange, *The Treaty of Waitangi* (Wellington: Bridget Williams Books with the assistance of the Historical Branch, Department of Internal Affairs, 1992).

33. See William Renwick, ed. *Creating a National Spirit: Celebrating New Zealand's Centennial* (Wellington: Victoria University Press, 2004).

34. Conal McCarthy, "New Zealand Centennial Exhibition, Wellington, 1940," in *Encyclopedia of World's Fairs and Expositions*, eds. J. Findling and K. Pelle (North Carolina: McFarlane Press, 2008). See also Renwick, *Creating a National Spirit.*

35. The early attainment of female suffrage was far from straightforward, nor was it an unequivocally progressive event. It did not lead to early gains in other areas, such as being elected to parliament, on juries or entry into the police force, or other positions of professional prominence. See Patricia Grimshaw, *Women's Suffrage in New Zealand*, revised edition (Auckland: Auckland University Press, 1987); Charlotte Macdonald, *The Vote, the Pill and the Demon Drink: A History of Feminist Writing in New Zealand, 1869–1993* (Wellington: Bridget Williams Books, 1993).

36. N.B. Palethorpe, *Official History of the New Zealand Centennial Exhibition, Wellington, 1939–40* (Wellington: The New Zealand Centennial Exhibition Company Ltd, 1940), 104.

37. The list is in Palethorpe, *Official History*, 107–8.

38. Ibid., 105.

39. Ibid., 106.

40. Conal McCarthy, *Exhibiting Maori: A History of Colonial Cultures of Display* (Oxford: Berg, 2007), 58, 69; Barbara Kirchenblatt-Gimblett, *Destination Culture: Tourism, Museums and Heritage* (Berkeley: University of California Press, 1998), 149–50; Nick Prior, *Museums and Modernity: Art Galleries and the Making of Modern Culture* (Oxford: Berg, 2002), 9–10.

41. Jock Phillips, "Afterword—Reading the 1940 Centennial," in Renwick, *Creating a National Spirit*, 279.

42. Palethorpe, *Official History*, 105.

43. Ibid., 104–5.

44. Ibid., 106.

45. Nadia Gush, "Cultural Fields of the Canterbury Plains: Women and Cultural Citizenship in Canterbury, c.1890–1940," PhD Dissertation, Victoria University of Wellington, 2007, 1–2.

46. McLean, "Where Sheep May Not Safely Graze."

47. Athol McCredie, "Going Public: New Zealand Art Museums in the 1970s," Master's Thesis, Massey University, 1999, 14.

48. B. Gamble and R. Cooper, *Art Galleries and Museums of New Zealand* (Auckland: Art Galleries and Museums Association of New Zealand, 1969), 5.

49. Keith W. Thomson, *Art Galleries and Museums of New Zealand* (Wellington: Reed, 1981), 1.

50. W.H. Oliver, *Looking for the Phoenix: A Memoir* (Wellington: Bridget Williams Books, 2002), chapter seven.

51. McCarthy, *Exhibiting Maori*, 116–17. I have discussed the development of "history" as a discipline and the historical collections and displays that constituted it in Bronwyn Labrum, "Making Pakeha History in New Zealand Museums: Community and Identity in the Post-War Period," in *Museum Revolutions: How Museums Change and Are Changed*, eds. Simon J. Knell, Suzanne MacLeod, and Sheila Watson (London and New York: Routledge, 2007), 149–59.

52. Chris Healy, *From the Ruins of Colonialism: History as Social Memory* (Melbourne: Cambridge University Press, 1997).

53. Amiria Henare, *Museums, Anthropology and Imperial Exchange* (New York: Cambridge University Press, 2005). Sociologist Claudia Bell visited many New Zealand museums in the first half of the 1990s. She saw a Pakeha "folk-history" in displays that "appear determined to bowdlerize political issues, offering 'untainted' myths of colonial life." Furthermore, "preference stays with a decorative version of the past." She concluded that the "experience at museums offers a conservative history for undemanding consumers." Claudia Bell, *Inventing New Zealand: Everyday Myths of Pakeha Identity* (Auckland: Penguin, 1996), 68, 69, 73, 81.

54. McCarthy, *Exhibiting Maori*, 12. See also Kirchenblatt-Gimblett, *Destination Culture*, and Prior, *Museums and Modernity*.

55. "Collection and Allied Policies of the Canterbury Museum," 1994, 9, Series 7/4 Museum Publications, Box 5, CMR; *Annual Report 1959–60*, Canterbury Museum (hereafter AR), 10.

56. The first members were from the remaining settlers who came in the "First Four Ships" (arriving in Lyttelton, December 1850) and descendants of early settlers who had arrived on Canterbury Association ships up until October 31, 1876. Current members consist of descendants of those early pioneers and others who have an interest in that period of Canterbury's formation. The Association promotes and preserves the history of that early settlement and of those early pioneers, who they see as laying the foundations of Christchurch city. Canterbury Pilgrims and Early Settlers Association, <http://www.pilgrims.co.nz> (accessed April 10, 2008).

57. AR, 1948–49, 5.

58. AR, 1948–49, 14.

59. For further details, see the exhibition guidebook, *Canterbury Colonists Exhibition at the Canterbury Museum on the Occasion of the Centenary of the Province* (Christchurch: The Friends of the Canterbury Museum, 1950).

60. AR, 1950–51, 5; "Canterbury and Christchurch Region," from *An Encyclopaedia of New Zealand*, ed. A.H. McLintock, originally published in 1966, Te Ara—The Encyclopedia of New Zealand, <http://www.TeAra.govt.nz/1966/P/Population/en> (accessed April 10, 2008).

61. AR, 1950–51, 10.

62. Series 7/4 Box 5, Early Colonists Display Visitors Book 1950, No. 1, CMR.

63. Series 7/4 Box 5, Early Colonists Display Visitors Book 1950, No. 2, CMR.

64. AR, 1951–52, 7.

65. "Canterbury Museum Canterbury Colonial Galleries," 97/91, Box 21, folder 176, Rosa Josephine Reynolds Papers 1801–1990, ARC 1994.42 (hereafter RR Papers), Manuscripts Collection, Canterbury Museum.

66. Typescript of "Introduction to Canterbury Colonists Gallery," 3, Series 6/6, Folder 17 – Undated correspondence and information, CMR.

67. AR, 1965–66, 11.

68. AR, 1958–59, 19.

69. For example, at the National Museum, botany expert and illustrator Nancy Adams started cataloguing and exhibiting textiles and clothing in the early 1950s. At the Auckland War Memorial Museum, Edna M. Stephenson was the Recorder (Old Colonists) from 1965 and the Librarian, Miss Evans, also played a pivotal role in the development of its "Centennial St." After Stephenson's departure in 1970, Audrey McBirney took over as the Recorder (Colonial Section).

70. See "Canterbury Museum Scrapbook—Newspaper Clippings 1957–74," Box 22, folder 182A, RR Papers.

71. *Family Circle*, October 1968, 29—31; and *Country Life*, August 10, 1951, Art Galleries and Museums Association of New Zealand mixed file, Box 26, folder 204, RR Papers.

72. "Notes and Comments on Early Colonial Museums," April 20, 1959, Box 30, folder 223, RR Papers.

73. Rose Reynolds to Miss Buck, July 3, 1949, Series 6/6, folder 6, Canterbury History (early Colonial) 1949–59, Correspondence (Period Costume), RR Papers.

74. "Canterbury Centennial mixed file," Box 25, folder 195, RR Papers.

75. AR, 1952–53, 21.

76. Typescript of Reynolds' 1963 annual report, 3, Series 2/5, Folder 4 "Other Reports to Trust Board—Departmental 1958–1983," CMR.

77. Edna Stephenson to Rose Reynolds, July 4, 1967, 'Centennial Street', MA 2004/6, Auckland Museum archives.

78. Bennett, *The Birth of the Museum*, 48.

79. Schwartz and Przyblyski, *The Nineteenth-Century Visual Culture Reader*, 7.

80. Ann Smart Martin, cited in Lou Taylor, *The Study of Dress History* (Manchester: Manchester University Press, 2001), 72.

81. The influential title of a key chapter in Bennett, *The Birth of the Museum*.

Bibliography

Manuscripts and Archives

Archives Privées (Gramont, Mackau, Maréchal Berthier, Massa, Maison de France, Montebello, Mugnier, Murat) held at the Archives Nationales de France, Paris.

AT&T Publications and Vertical Files Collections. AT&T Archives and History Center. San Antonio, TX.

BBC Written Archives Centre, File R51/225/1 (Venereal Disease 1A 1942–43).

BBC Written Archives Centre, File R51/225/2 (Venereal Disease 1B 1944–45).

BBC Written Archives Centre. Radio transcripts. microfilm T664.

Canterbury Museum Records, Documentary Research Centre, Canterbury Museum, Christchurch, New Zealand.

Hansard's *Parliamentary Debates*. 3rd Ser.ccxxvii, 1876.

India Office Records. E218/518/1. British Library.

Mass Observation Archive. University of Sussex.

Ministry of Food (Great Britain). *Food Control (National Rationing); Instructions to Food Control Committees; Part I; October 1939.*

Ministry of Health. "Campaign Memorandum of V.D. Propaganda for the Ministry of Health." April 3, 1944.

Ministry of Health. "Campaign Memorandum of V.D. Propaganda for the Ministry of Health." January 25, 1943.

MS Catalogue of British Shells in the Possession of J.T. Swainson. Zoology Library. Natural History Museum, London.

Mss Relative to British Testacea. Zoology Library. Natural History Museum, London.

Museum archives. Auckland War Memorial Museum. Auckland, New Zealand.

N.W. Ayer Advertising Agency Records, Archives Center. National Museum of American History. Smithsonian Institution. Washington, DC.

Pacific Bell Publications and Vertical Files Collections. AT&T Archives and History Center. San Antonio, TX.

Pennant Correspondence. Warwickshire County Record Office, England.

Portland Papers, Longleat, England.

Pulteney Correspondence. Linnean Society, London.

Reynolds, Rosa Josephine, Papers 1801–1990, ARC 1994.42, Manuscripts Collection, Canterbury Museum, Christchurch, New Zealand.

Swainsoniana. Zoology Library. Natural History Museum, London.

Warshaw Collection of Business Americana—Telephone. Archives Center. National Museum of American History. Smithsonian Institution. Washington, DC.

Printed Sources

Ackermann Repository of Arts, Literature, Commerce, Fashions, and Politics. London: Rudolf Ackermann. Vol. I (January 1809) and Vol. XIV (September 1815).

Adamson, John and Katherine Prior. *Maharajas' Jewels*. New York: Vendome Press, 2000.

Adamson, Natalie. "'Circles of Belief': Patronage, Taste and Shared Creativity in Odilon Redon's Decorative Painting." *Studies in the Decorative Arts* (1996): 107–30.

Adolph, Andrea. "Luncheon at 'The Leaning Tower': Class and Consumption in Virginia Woolf's *Between the Acts*." *Women's Studies: An Interdisciplinary Journal* 34, no. 6 (2005): 439–59.

Adorno, Theodor. *The Culture Industry: Selected Essays on Mass Culture*. Edited by J.M. Bernstein. London: Routledge, 1990.

Agay, Cécile. "Le boy américaine à l'école." *Marie-France* 8 (1945): 5.

Alary, Éric and Dominique Veillon. "L'Après-guerre de Femmes: 1947, un Tournant?" In *L'Année 1947*. Edited by Serge Bernstein and Pierre Milza, 487–511. Paris: Presses de la Fondation Nationale des Sciences Politiques, 2000.

Allen, Charles and Sharada Dwivedi. *Lives of the Indian Princes*. New York: Crown Publishers, 1984.

Allen, Charles Dexter. *Ex Libris: Essays of a Collector.* Norwood, MA: Norwood Press, 1896.

Allen, David Elliston. "Tastes and Crazes." In *Cultures of Natural History*. Edited by N. Jardine, J.A. Secord, and E.C. Spary, 394–407. Cambridge: Cambridge University Press, 1996.

——. *Naturalists and Society: The Culture of Natural History in Britain, 1700–1900.* Aldershot: Ashgate Variorum, 2001.

——. *The Naturalists in Britain: A Social History* [1976]. Princeton: Princeton University Press, 1995.

Anderson, Benedict. *Imagined Communities: Reflections on the Spread and Origins of Nationalism*. London: Verso, 2006.

Anderson, K.G.W., ed. *Enlightening the British: Knowledge, Discovery and the Museum in the Eighteenth Century*. London: British Museum Press, 2003.

Anderson, Patricia. *The Printed Image and the Transformation of Popular Culture 1790–1860*. Oxford: Clarendon Press, 1991.

Annual Report, 1940–78, Canterbury Museum, Christchurch, New Zealand.

Anon. "Cette Parfaite Domestique: l'Electricité." *La Femme* 64 (1946): 4–5, 19.

Anon. "De la Resistance à la Reconstruction" *Marie-France* 4 (1944): 1.

Anon. *Etiquette for Ladies and Gentlemen*. London: Frederick, Warne and Co., 1876.

Anon. "Le Pays des Stars est aussi le Paradis Terrestre: La Vie de Trois Ménages en Californie." *La Femme* 30 (1946), 4–6.

Anon. "Les GIs Adressent 112 Reproches aux Français." *La Femme* 36 (1946): 8–9, 19.

Anon. "Premières Images de la Nouvelle Existence de Mesdames GIs, Le Bonheur à l'Américaine." *La Femme* 46 (1946): 3–4.

Anon. (George Annesley, Earl of Montmorris?). "Short Instructions for Collecting Shells" [1815?].

Anon. *The Ladies' Hand-Book of the Toilet: A Manual of Elegance and Fashion*. London: H. Gt. Clarke and Co., 1843.

Anon. "Voila comment on s'Habille à Hollywood." *Elle* 18 (1946): 6–7.

Appadurai, Arjun. "Introduction: Commodities and the Politics of Value." In *The Social Life of Things: Commodities in a Cultural Perspective*, 3–63. Cambridge: Cambridge University Press, 1986.

Ashton, S.R. *British Policy Towards the Indian States, 1905–1909.* London: Curzon Press, 1982.
Atkinson, Diane. *Love and Dirt: The Marriage of Arthur Munby and Hannah Cullwick.* London: Macmillan, 2003.
Auslander, Leora. "The Gendering of Consumer Practices." In *The Sex of Things: Gender and Consumption in Historical Perspective*. Edited byVictoria de Grazia with Ellen Furlough, 79–112. Berkeley: University of California Press, 1996.
___. *Taste and Power: Furnishing Modern France*. Berkeley: University of California Press, 1996.
Austen, Jane. *Jane Austen's Letters*. Edited by Deirdre Le Faye. Oxford: Oxford University Press, 1995.
___. *Letters 1796–1817*. Edited by R.W. Chapman. Oxford: Oxford University Press, 1978.
___. *Persuasion*. Edited by Linda Bree. Ontario, Canada: Broadview Literary Texts, 2000.
Axelrad, Allan. "The Lumley Autograph and the Great Literary Lion: Authenticity and Commodification in Nineteenth-Century Autograph Collecting." In *Susan Fenimore Cooper: New Essays on Rural Hours and Other Works.* Edited by Rochelle Johnson and Daniel Patterson. Athens: University of Georgia Press, 2001.
Ayer, N.W. and Sons. *Fifty Years of Telephone Advertising, 1908–1958*. New York: N.W. Ayer and Sons, n.d.
Baker, Naimh. *Happily Ever After? Women's Fiction in Postwar Britain 1945–60*. New York: St Martin's, 1989.
Baker, Thomas N. *Sentiment and Celebrity: Nathaniel Parker Willis and the Trials of Literary Fame*. New York: Oxford University Press, 1999.
Balzac, Honoré de. "Traité de la vie élégante." In *Oeuvres complètes, oeuvres diverses, Paris*, vol. 2. Paris: Louis Conard, 1938.
Bao, Mingxin. "Chinese Lady's Daily Wear in Late Qing Dynasty and Early Republic Period." *Journal of China Textile University* (English edition) 8, no. 3 (1991): 9–21.
Barmé, Geremie R. *Gong Xiaogong: A Case of Mistaken Identity*. Asian Studies Institute Occasional Lecture 1. Wellington, NZ: Asian Studies Institute, Victoria University of Wellington, 1999.
Barnes, Ruth and Joanne B. Eicher, eds. *Dress and Gender: Making and Meaning*. New York: Berg, distributed by St Martin's Press, 1992.
Barrett, R.T. "Jack and Jill Build a Home." *Pacific Bell Magazine* 22 (January 1929): 8–9.
Barringer, Tim and Tom Flynn, eds. *Colonialism and Its Objects: Empire, Material Culture, and the Museum*. New York: Routledge 1998.
Barter, Judith A., ed. *Mary Cassatt: Modern Woman*. Chicago: The Art Institute of Chicago in association with Harry N. Abrams, Inc., 1998.
Bartillat, Christian de. *Histoire de la noblesse française: de 1789 à nos jours*. Vol. 2: *Les nobles du Second Empire à la fin du XXe siècle*. Paris: Albin Michel, 1991.
Batchelor, Jennie and Cora Kaplan, eds. *Women and Material Culture, 1660–1830.* Basingstoke: Palgrave Macmillan, 2007.
Baudelaire, Charles. "Some French Caricaturists." In *The Painter of Modern Life*. Edited and translated by J. Mayne, 166–86. London: Phaidon, 1965.
Baudrillard, Jean. "The Art Auction: Sign Exchange and Sumptuary Value." In *For a Critique of the Political Economy of the Sign*, 112–22. Translated by Charles Levin. St Louis, MO: Telos Press, 1981.
___. "The System of Collecting." In *The Cultures of Collecting*. Edited by John Elsner and Roger Cardinal, 7–24. Translated by Roger Cardinal. London: Reaktion Books, 1994.

Bayly, C.A. *Indian Society and the Making of the British Empire.* Cambridge: Cambridge University Press, 1988.

Bazin, Nancy Topping and Jane Hamovit Lauter. "Virginia Woolf's Keen Sensitivity to War: Its Roots and Its Impact on Her Novels." In *Virginia Woolf and War.* Edited by Mark Hussey, 14–39. Syracuse: Syracuse University Press, 1991.

Beamish, Richard. *The Psychonomy of the Hand; or, the Hand an Index of Mental Development.* London: Frederick Pitman, 1865.

Beaudry, Mary C. *Findings: The Material Culture of Needlework and Sewing.* New Haven: Yale University Press, 2006.

Beckman, Thomas. "American Diesinkers and Their Cameo Stamps, 1850–1880: A Researcher's Discoveries and Survey." *Maine Antique Digest* (May 1999): 45b–46b.

Beetham, Margaret. *A Magazine of Her Own? Domesticity and Desire in the Women's Magazine, 1800–1914.* London and New York: Routledge, 1996.

Belich, James. *Paradise Reforged: A History of the New Zealanders from the 1880s to the Year 2000.* Auckland: Penguin, 2001.

Belk, Russell W. and Melanie Wallendorf. "Of Mice and Men: Gender Identity in Collecting." In *The Material Culture of Gender: The Gender of Material Culture.* Edited by Kenneth Ames and Katherine Martinez, 7–27. Ann Arbor, MI: University of Michigan Press, 1997.

Bell, Claudia. *Inventing New Zealand: Everyday Myths of Pakeha Identity.* Auckland: Penguin, 1996.

Bennett, Tony. *The Birth of the Museum: History, Theory, Politics.* London and New York: Routledge, 1995.

Benson, Carlton. "The Manipulation of *Tanci* in Radio Shanghai During the 1930's." *Republican China* 20, no. 2 (April): 117–46.

Berger, John. *Ways of Seeing.* New York: Penguin, 1973.

Bermingham, Ann and John Brewer. *The Consumption of Culture, 1600–1800: Image, Object, Text.* New York: Routledge, 1995.

Bernage, Berthe. "Recevrons-nous Quand Même?" *Le Petit Echo de la Mode* 40 (1947): 2.

Bernard, Malcolm. *Fashion as Communication.* London and New York: Routledge, 1996.

Beshero-Bondar, Elisa E. "Eliza Leslie." In *Dictionary of Literary Biography, Volume 202: Nineteenth-Century American Fiction Writers.* Edited by Kent P. Ljungquist, 166–72. Detroit: Gale Research Co., 1989.

Bess, Michael. *Ecology and Technological Modernity in France, 1960–2000.* Chicago: University of Chicago Press, 2003.

Bian, Xiangyang. "Origin of Qipao Fashion in Early Republic Period." *Journal of Donghua University* (English edition) 20, no. 4 (2003): 21–6.

Bingo 20 (1954).

Bingo 63 (1958).

Blake, David Haven. *Walt Whitman and the Culture of American Celebrity.* New Haven: Yale University Press, 2006.

Blank, Antje. "Dress." In *Jane Austen in Context.* Edited by Janet Todd, 234–51. Cambridge: Cambridge University Press, 2005.

Blessington, Marguerite. *The Idler in Italy,* vol. 2. Philadelphia: Carey & Hart, 1839.

Blodgett, Harriet. "Food for Thought in Virginia Woolf's Novels." *Woolf Studies Annual* 3 (1997): 45–60.

Bonneville, Françoise de. *Le livre du bain.* Paris: Flammarion, 1997.

Bonvoisin, Samra-Martin and Michèle Maignien. *La Presse Féminine.* Paris: Presses Universitaires de France, 1986.

Boone, Catherine. *Merchant Capital and the Roots of State Power in Senegal, 1930–1985.* New York: Cambridge University Press, 1992.

Bordo, Susan. *Unbearable Weight: Feminism, Western Culture, and the Body*. Berkeley: University of California Press, 1993, 2003.

Bore, Henry. *The Story of the Invention of Steel Pens*. New York: Ivison, Blakeman & Company, 1890.

Bourdieu, Pierre. *Distinction: A Social Critique of the Judgment of Taste*. Translated by Richard Nice. Cambridge: Harvard University Press, 1984.

___. *Distinction: A Social Critique of the Judgement of Taste* [1984]. Translated by Richard Nice. London: Routledge, 2000.

___. *Masculine Domination*. Translated by Richard Nice. Cambridge: Polity Press, 2001.

___. *Outline of a Theory of Practice*. Cambridge: Cambridge University Press, 1977.

___. "The Production of Belief: Contribution to an Economy of Symbolic Goods." In *The Field of Cultural Production: Essays on Art and Literature*, 74–80. New York: Columbia University Press, 1993.

Branca, Patricia. "Image and Reality: The Myth of the Ideal Victorian Woman." In *Clio's Consciousness Raised: New Perspectives on the History of Women*. Edited by Mary S. Hartman. New York: Octagon Books, 1976.

Braudel, Fernand. *Civilization and Capitalism, 15th–18th Century*. 3 volumes. New York: Harper & Row, 1982–84.

Braun-Ronsdorf, Margarete. *The History of the Handkerchief*. Leigh-on-Sea, England: F. Lewis, 1967.

Breen, T.H. "The Meaning of Things: Interpreting the Consumer Economy in the Eighteenth Century." In *Consumption and the World of Goods*. Edited by John Brewer and Roy Porter, 249–60. New York: Routledge, 1994.

Breeskin, Adelyn Dohme. *Mary Cassatt: A Catalogue Raisonné of the Graphic Work*. Washington, DC: Smithsonian Institution Press, 1979.

___. *Mary Cassatt: Graphic Art*. Washington, DC: Published for Smithsonian Institution Traveling Exhibition Service by Smithsonian Institution Press, 1981.

Breward, Christopher. *The Hidden Consumer: Masculinities, Fashion and City Life 1860–1914*. Manchester: Manchester University Press, 1988.

Brewer, John and Frank Trentmann, eds. *Consuming Cultures, Global Perspectives: Historical Trajectories, Transnational Exchanges*. Oxford: Berg, 2006.

Brewer, John and Roy Porter, eds. *Consumption and the World of Goods*. New York: Routledge, 1994.

"Bridal Bouquet Bloom." In *Beauty Parlour Box 1, Advertisements Beauty Parlour–Hairdressers' Advertisements*. Edited by John Johnson Collection, 1892.

Brigham, David R. *Public Culture in the Early Republic: Peale's Museum and Its Audience*. Washington, DC: Smithsonian Institution Press, 1995.

Brillat-Savarin, Jean Anthelme. *The Physiology of Taste: Or, Meditations on Transcendental Gastronomy*. Translated by M.F.K. Fisher. New York: Harcourt, 1978.

Broido, Lucy. *The Posters of Jules Chéret*, Catalogue Raisonné. 2nd ed. New York: Dover, 1992.

Bromberger, Merry. "24 heures avec Barbara et Teddy à Paris (Texas)." *La Femme* 11 (1945): 2–11.

Brookes, Barbara, Erik Olssen, and Emma Beer. "Spare Time? Leisure, Gender and Modernity." In *Sites of Gender: Women, Men and Modernity in Southern Dunedin, 1890–1940*. Edited by Barbara Brookes, Annabel Cooper, and Robin Law, 151–89. Auckland: Auckland University Press, 2003.

Brown, Bill, ed. "Thing Theory." *Critical Inquiry* 28 (2001): 1–22.

Buckley, Cheryl. "On the Margins: Theorizing the History and Significance of Making and Designing Clothes at Home." In *The Culture of Sewing: Gender, Consumption and Home Dressmaking*. Edited by Barbara Burman. Oxford: Berg Press, 1999.

Bushman, Richard L. *The Refinement of America: Persons, Houses, Cities*. New York: Random House Inc., 1993.

Butler, Judith. *Bodies That Matter: On the Discursive Limits of Sex*. New York: Routledge, 1993.

——. *Gender Trouble: Feminism and the Subversion of Identity*. New York: Routledge, 1990.

——. "Performative Acts and Gender Constitution: An Essay in Phenomenology and Feminist Theory." In *Performing Feminisms: Feminist Critical Theory and Theatre*. Edited by Sue Ellen Case, 270–82. Baltimore: Johns Hopkins University Press, 1990.

Cahiers de l'Institut Français de Presse. Paris: Institut Français de Presse et des Sciences de l'Information, 1989.

Caine, Barbara. *Victorian Feminists*. Oxford: Oxford University Press, 1992.

Callahan, Genevieve A. "Fourteen Pages of Household Helpfulness." *Sunset* 72, no. 3 (March 1934): 18–22.

Callvert, R.S. "Telephone Conveniences in Your New Home." *Bell Telephone Magazine* 33, no. 3 (Autumn 1954): 165–8.

Campbell, Colin. "Understanding Traditional and Modern Patterns of Consumption in Eighteenth-century England: A Character-Action Approach." In *Consumption and the World of Goods*. Edited by John Brewer and Roy Porter, 40–57. New York: Routledge, 1994.

Cannadine, David. *Aspects of Aristocracy*. New Haven: Yale University Press, 1994.

——. *Ornamentalism: How the British Saw Their Empire*. Oxford: Oxford University Press, 2001.

"Canterbury and Christchurch Region," from *An Encyclopaedia of New Zealand*. Edited by A.H. McLintock, originally published in 1966. Te Ara—The Encyclopedia of New Zealand. <http://www.TeAra.govt.nz/1966/P/Population/en>.

Canterbury Colonists Exhibition at the Canterbury Museum on the Occasion of the Centenary of the Province. Christchurch: The Friends of the Canterbury Museum, 1950.

Canterbury Colonists Galleries: A Guide. Christchurch: Canterbury Museum, 1960.

Canterbury Pilgrims and Early Settlers Association. <http://www.pilgrims.co.nz>.

Carine. "Le système Taylor à La Cuisine." *La Femme Nouvelle* 27 (1946): 15.

Carroll, Peter. "Refashioning Suzhou: Dress, Commodification, and Modernity." *Positions: East Asia Cultures Critique* 11, no. 2 (2003): 443–78.

Casey, Emma and Lydia Martens. *Gender and Consumption: Domestic Cultures and the Commercialisation of Everyday Life*. Aldershot: Ashgate, 2007.

Castellane, Boni de. *Mémoires*. Paris: Perrin, 1986.

Castries, René de La Croix de. *Papiers de famille*. Paris: Éditions France-Empire, 1977.

Catalogue of the Portland Museum. London, 1786.

Centorame, Bruno. "Les Grands Magasins Crespin-Dufayel." In *Les Cathédrales du Commerce Parisien: Grands Magasins et Enseignes*. Edited by Béatrice De Andia and Caroline François, 81–4. Paris: Action Artistique de la Ville de Paris, 2006.

Certeau, Michel de. *The Practice of Everyday Life*. Translated by Steven Rendall. Berkeley and London: University of California Press, 1984.

Chabot, Michel. *Histoire de Jean et Yvonne domestiques en 1900. Racontée par Paul, leur fils, à Michel, son petit-fils*. Paris: Les Editions 1900, 1988.

Chakrabarty, Dipesh. *Provincializing Europe: Postcolonial Thought and Historical Difference*. Princeton: Princeton University Press, 2000.

Chalmers-Hunt, J.M. *Natural History Auctions, 1700–1972: A Register of Sales*. London: Sotheby-Park Bernet, 1976.

Champsaur, Florence Brachet. "Les Grands Magasins et la mode." In *Les Cathédrales du Commerce Parisien: Grands Magasins et Enseignes*. Edited by Béatrice De Andia and Caroline François, 143–8. Paris: Action Artistique de la Ville de Paris, 2006.

Chang, Eileen (Zhang, Ailing). "A Chronicle of Changing Clothes." Translated by Andrew F. Jones. *Positions: East Asia Cultures Critique* 11, no. 2 (2003) [1943]: 427–41.

Chapple, J.A.V. and Arthur Pollard, eds. *The Letters of Mrs. Gaskell*. Cambridge, MA: Harvard University Press, 1967.

Chapple, John and Alan Shelston, eds. *Further Letters of Mrs. Gaskell*. Manchester: Manchester University Press, 2000.

Charle, Christophe. "Noblesse et élites en France au début du XXe siècle." In *Les noblesses européennes au XIXe siècle*, 407–33. Milan: Università di Milano and Rome: École Française de Rome, 1988.

Charney, Leo and Vanessa Schwartz, eds. *Cinema and the Invention of Modern Life*. Berkeley: University of California Press, 1995.

Charnwood, Dorothea Mary Roby Thorpe. *An Autograph Collection and the Making of It*. London: E. Benn Ltd., 1930.

Chatterjee, Partha. *The Nation and Its Fragments: Colonial and Postcolonial Histories*. Princeton: Princeton University Press, 1993.

Chee Dimock, Wai and Michael T. Gilmore. *Rethinking Class: Literary Studies and Social Formations*. New York: Columbia University Press, 1994.

Chen Shoupeng. "Xu" [Remembrance]. In *Xue Shaohui ji* [Collected works of Xue Shaohui], by Xue Shaohui. Beijing: Fangzhi chubanshe, 2003.

Chen Shuiyun. "Ershi shiji de qingdai nüxing ci yanjiu" [Research on Qing Dynasty women's ci poems in the 20th century]. *Funü yanjiu luncong* 1 (2004): 67–72.

Cheuk, Pak-Tong. "A History of the Calendar Poster." In *Chinese Women and Modernity: Calendar Posters of the 1910s–1930s*. Edited by Ng Chun Bong, Cheuk Pak-Tong, Wong Ying, and Yvonne Lo, 8–15. Hong Kong: Joint Publishing Co. Ltd, 1996.

Childers, Kristen Stromberg. *Fathers, Families, and the State in France, 1914–1945*. Ithaca: Cornell University Press, 2003.

Clairet, Alain, Delphine Montalent, and Yves Rouart. *Berthe Morisot 1841–1895: Catalogue raisonné de l'œuvre peint*. Montolivet, France: CÉRA-nrs, 1997.

Clark, William, Jan Golinski, and Simon Schaffer, eds. *The Sciences in Enlightenment Europe*. Chicago: University of Chicago Press, 1999.

Clermont-Tonnerre, Élisabeth de. *Au temps des équipages*. Paris: Grasset, 1928.

Clunas, Craig. "Modernity Global and Local: Consumption and the Rise of the West." *American Historical Review* 104 (1999): 1497–1511.

Cohn, Bernard. "Representing Authority in Victorian India." In *An Anthropologist among the Historians and Other Essays*. Delhi: Oxford University Press, 1987.

Colbert, Benjamin. *Shelley's Eye: Travel Writing and Aesthetic Vision*. Aldershot, Hants, England and Burlington, VT: Ashgate Publishing, 2005.

Colley, Linda. *Britons: Forging the Nation, 1707–1837*. New Haven: Yale University Press, 1992.

Collingham, E.M. *Imperial Bodies: The Physical Experience of the Raj, c.1800–1947*. Cambridge: Polity Press, 2001.

Collins, Bradford R. "The Poster as Art: Jules Chéret and the Struggle for the Equality of the Arts in Late Nineteenth-Century France." *Design Issues* 2 (1985): 41–50.

Colquhon, Kate. *Taste: The Story of Britain Through its Cooking*. New York: Bloomsbury USA, 2007.

Conklin, Alice C. *A Mission to Civilize: The Republican Idea of Empire in France and West Africa, 1895–1930*. Stanford: Stanford University Press, 1997.

Conrad, Joseph. *Heart of Darkness*. Harmondsworth: Penguin, 1988.

Cook, James W. *The Arts of Deception: Playing with Fraud in the Age of Barnum*. Cambridge: Harvard University Press, 2001.
Cooper, James Fennimore. *Letters and Journals of James Fennimore Cooper*. 6 volumes. Cambridge: MA: Harvard University Press, 1960–68.
Cooter, Roger. *The Cultural Meaning of Popular Science: Phrenology and the Organization of Consent in Nineteenth-Century Britain*. Cambridge: Cambridge University Press, 1984.
Copland, Ian. *The Princes of India in the Endgame of Empire, 1917–1947*. Cambridge: Cambridge University Press, 1997.
Coquart, Elizabeth. *La France des G.I.'s: Histoire d'un Amour Déçu*. Paris: Albin Michel, 2003.
Cowan, Ruth Schwartz. *More Work for Mother: The Ironies of Household Technology from the Open Hearth to the Microwave*. New York: Basic Books, Inc., 1984.
Cowdrey, Mary Bartlett. *American Academy of Fine Arts and the American Art-Union 1816–1852*. New York: New York Historical Society, 1963.
Crane, Diana. *Fashion and Its Social Agenda: Class, Gender and Identity in Clothing*. Chicago: University of Chicago Press, 2000.
Criss, Jennifer T. "*Japonisme* and Beyond in the Art of Marie Bracquemond, Mary Cassatt, and Berthe Morisot, 1867–1895." PhD Dissertation, University of Pennsylvania, 2007.
Croll, Elisabeth. *Changing Identities of Chinese Women: Rhetoric, Experience, and Self-Perception in Twentieth-century China*. Hong Kong: Hong Kong University Press, 1995.
Crowley, John. *The Invention of Comfort: Sensibilities and Design in Early Modern Britain and Early America*. Baltimore: Johns Hopkins University Press, 2001.
Cumming, Valerie. *Gloves*. Edited by Aileen Ribeiro. *The Costume Accessories* series. London: B.T. Batsford Ltd., 1982.
Cunnington, C. Willett. *English Women's Clothing in the Nineteenth Century*. London: Faber & Faber, 1937.
———. *English Women's Clothing in the Nineteenth Century*. New York: Dover Publications, 1990.
Cunnington, Phillis Emily. *The History of Underclothes*. London: Courier Dover Publications, 1992.
Curtin, Michael. *Propriety and Position: A Study of Victorian Manners*. New York: Garland, 1987.
Curtis, Gerard. *Visual Words: Art and the Material Book in Victorian England*. Aldershot: Ashgate, 2002.
D., C. "Une Politique de la Famille est Nécessaire." *La Femme Nouvelle* 10 (1945): 4.
D'Albertis, Dierdre. "The Life and Letters of E.C. Gaskell." In *The Cambridge Companion to Elizabeth Gaskell*. Edited by Jill Matus, 10–26. Cambridge: Cambridge University Press, 2007.
D'Avenel, Vicomte Georges. "Mécanisme de la vie moderne: Les Grands Magasins." *Revue des Deux Mondes* (July 1, 1894): 329–69.
Da Silveira, Piedade. "Les magasins de nouveautés (1800–1850)." In *Les Cathédrales du Commerce Parisien: Grands Magasins et Enseignes*. Edited by Béatrice De Andia and Caroline François, 33–43. Paris: Action Artistique de la Ville de Paris, 2006.
Dance, S. Peter. "The Authorship of the *Portland Catalogue*." *Journal of the Society for the Bibliography of Natural History* 4 (1962): 30–34.
———. *A History of Shell Collecting*. Leiden: Brill, 1986.
———. *Shell Collecting: An Illustrated History*. Berkeley: University of California Press, 1966.

Daston, Lorraine and Katharine Park. *Wonders and the Order of Nature, 1150–1750.* New York: Zone Books, 1998.
Daudet, Julia. *Journées de femme.* Paris: E. Fasquelle, 1898.
___. *Souvenirs autour d'un groupe littéraire.* Paris: Charpentier, 1910.
Daumard, Adeline. *Les bourgeois et la bourgeoisie en France depuis 1815.* Paris: Aubier, 1987.
___. *Les fortunes françaises au XIXe siècle.* Paris: Mouton, 1973.
Davidoff, Leonore. "Class and Gender in Victorian England: The Diaries of Arthur J. Munby and Hannah Cullwick." *Feminist Studies* 5, no. 1 (1979): 87–141.
Davidoff, Leonore and Catherine Hall. *Family Fortunes: Men and Women of the English Middle Class, 1780–1850.* Women in Culture and Society series. Chicago: University of Chicago Press, 1987.
Davies, Philip. *The Penguin Guide to the Monuments of India.* Middlesex: Penguin, 1989, II.
Day, Angélique, ed. *Letters from Georgian Ireland: The Correspondence of Mary Delany, 1731–68.* Belfast: Friar's Bush Press, 1991.
De Andia, Béatrice and Caroline François, eds. *Les Cathédrales du Commerce Parisien: Grands Magasins et Enseignes.* Paris: Action Artistique de la Ville de Paris, 2006.
De Shuoting. "Changdian" [Liulichang]. In *Liulichang xiaozhi* [Short gazetteer of Liulichang]. Edited by Sun Dianqi. Beijing: Beijing chubanshe, 1982.
Dear, Peter. *The Intelligibility of Nature: How Science Makes Sense of the World.* Chicago: University of Chicago Press, 2006.
Delany, Mary. *The Autobiography and Correspondence of Mary Granville, Mrs. Delany: with Interesting Reminiscences of King George III and Queen Charlotte.* Edited by Lady Llanover. 6 volumes. London: R. Bentley, 1861, 1862.
Derrida, Jacques. "Signature Event Context." Translated by Samuel Weber and Jeffrey Mehlman. In *Limited Inc.*, 1–23. Evanston, IL: Northwestern University Press, 1988.
Development. London: Frederick Pitman, 1865.
Devi, Gayatri. *A Princess Remembers.* Calcutta: Rupa & Co., 1995.
Devi, Sunity. *Autobiography of an Indian Princess: Memoirs of Maharani Sunity Devi of Cooch Behar.* New Delhi: Vikas Publishing House, 1995.
Devon, James. *Let's Eat!* London: War Facts Press, 1944.
Diallo, Nafissatou. *De Tilène au Plateau: une enfance dakaroise.* Dakar: Les Nouvelles Editions Africaines du Sénégal, 1997.
Diamond, Hanna. "Gaining the Vote: A Liberating Experience?" *Modern and Contemporary France* 3 (1995): 129–48.
___. *Women and the Second World War in France, 1940–1948: Choices and Constraints.* Essex: Pearson Education Unlimited, 1999.
Dickens, Charles. *Hard Times.* New York: Pearson Longman, 2004.
Dimen, Muriel. *Sexuality Intimacy Power.* Hillsdale, NJ: The Analytic Press, 2003.
Dogan, Mattei and Jacques Narbonne. *Les Françaises Face à la Politique.* Paris: Cahiers de la Fondation Nationale des Sciences Politiques, 1955.
Donald, Diana. *Followers of Fashion: Graphic Satires of the Georgian Period.* London: Hayward Gallery Publishing, 2002.
Dong, Madeleine Yue. *Republican Beijing: The City and its Histories.* Berkeley: University of California Press, 2003.
Donovan, Edward. *Instructions for Collecting and Preserving Various Subjects of Natural History* (London, 1794).
___. *Natural History of British Shells.* 5 volumes. London, 1799–1803.
Dooling, Amy D. and Kristina M. Torgeson. "Introduction." In *Writing Women in Modern China: An Anthology of Women's Literature from the Early Twentieth Century.*

Edited by Amy D. Dooling and Kristina M. Torgeson. New York: Columbia University Press, 1998.

Doutreuve, Marthe. "Politique Féminine." *Marie-France* 19 (1945): 5.

Dube, Saurabh. *Stitches on Time: Colonial Textures and Postcolonial Tangles*. Durham: Duke University Press, 2004.

Duchen, Claire. "Une Femme Nouvelle pour une France Nouvelle." *Clio* 1 (1995): 151–64.

——. *Women's Rights and Women's Lives in France, 1944–1968*. New York: Routledge, 1994.

Duncan, Carol. "Museums and Department Stores: Close Encounters." In *High Pop: Making Culture into Popular Entertainment*. Edited by Jim Collins, 129–54. Malden and Oxford: Blackwell Publishers, 2002.

Eagle Russett, Cynthia. *Sexual Science: The Victorian Construction of Womanhood*. Cambridge: Harvard University Press, 1989.

Easley, Alexis. *First Person Anonymous*. Aldershot: Ashgate, 2004.

Editors' Preface. *Journal of Material Culture* 8, no. 3 (2003): 243–4.

Edwardes, M. *Modes and Manners of the Nineteenth Century*. London: J.M. Dent and Company, 1909.

Edwards, Louise. "Policing the Modern Woman in Republican China." *Modern China* 26, no. 2 (2000): 115–47.

Edwards, Michael M. *The Growth of the British Cotton Trade*. New York: A.M. Kelley, 1967.

Eide, Elizabeth. *China's Ibsen: From Ibsen to Ibsenism*. London: Curzon, 1987.

Elias, Norbert. *The Civilising Process*. Vol. 2: *State Formation and Civilisation*. Translated by Edmund Jephcott. Oxford: Basil Blackwell, 1982.

Ellenberger, Nancy W. "The Transformation of London 'Society' at the End of Victoria's Reign: Evidence from the Court Presentation Records," *Albion* 22 (1990): 633–53.

Ellis, B. Eldred. *Gloves and the Glove Trade*. London: Sir Isaac Pitman & Sons, Ltd., 1921.

Etienne, Mona. "Women and Men. Cloth and Colonization: The Transformation of Production Distribution Relations among the *Baule* (Ivory Coast)." *Cahiers d'Etudes Africaines* 65 (1999): 41–64.

Fair, Laura. "Dressing up: Clothing, Class and Gender in Post-Abolition Zanzibar." *Journal of African History* 39 (1998): 63–94.

Fairholt, Frederick William. *Costume in England: A History of Dress from the Earliest Period Till the Close of the Eighteenth Century*. London: Chapman and Hall, 1846.

Faye, Cheikh F. "Opinion publique et animation politique: permanence des moyens traditionels dans un contexte colonial." *Historiens Géographes du Sénégal* 6 (1991).

Faye, Ousseynou. "L'habillement et ses accessoires dans les millieux Africains de Dakar, 1857–1960." *Revue Sénégalaise d'Histoire* 1 (1995): 69–86.

Feng Sihui. "Gu yan [Ancient inkstone]," *Xiu yu yin* [Embroidery surplus poems]. China: 1764. McGill-Harvard-Yenching Library Ming-Qing Women's Writings Digitization Project. <http://digital.library.mcgill.ca/mingqing/english/>.

——. "Mai shu he yun" [Verse on buying books]. In *Xiu yu yin* [Embroidery surplus poems]. China: 1764. McGill-Harvard-Yenching Library Ming-Qing Women's Writings Digitization Project. <http://digital.library.mcgill.ca/mingqing/english/>.

Ferragamo, Salvatore. *Shoemaker of Dreams*. London: George G. Harrap & Co., 1957.

Festing, Sally. "Rare Flowers and Fantastic Breeds: The 2nd Duchess of Portland and Her Circle." *Country Life* 12 (June 1986): 1684–6, and 19 (June 1986): 1772–4.

Field, Andrew. "Selling Souls in Sin City: Shanghai Singing and Dancing Hostesses in Print, Film and Politics, 1920–49." In *Cinema and Urban Culture in China, 1922–1943*. Edited by Yingjin Zhang. Stanford: Stanford University Press, 1999.

Findlen, Paula. *Possessing Nature: Museums, Collecting, and Scientific Culture in Early Modern Italy*. Berkeley: University of California Press, 1994.

Finkelstein, Joanne. *The Fashioned Self*. Cambridge: Polity Press, 1991.

Finnane, Antonia. *Changing Clothes in China*. New York: Columbia University Press, 2008.

___. "What Should Chinese Women Wear? A National Problem." *Modern China* 22, no. 2 (1996): 99–131.

Fischer, Claude S. *America Calling: A Social History of the Telephone to 1940*. Berkeley: University of California Press, 1992.

Fischer, Claude S. and Glenn Carroll. "Telephone and Automobile Diffusion in the United States, 1902–1937." *American Journal of Sociology* 93 (March 1988): 1153–78.

Fisher, Michael. *Indirect Rule in India: Residents and the Residency System, 1764–1858*. Delhi: Oxford University Press, 1991.

Fiske, John. *Understanding Popular Culture*. Boston: Unwin Hyman, 1989.

Fitzroy, Yvonne. *Courts and Camps in India, Impressions of Viceregal Tours, 1921–1924*. London: Methuen & Co., 1926.

Fletcher, Christopher. "Lord Byron's Unrecorded Autograph Poems." *Notes and Queries* 43 (December 1996): 425–8.

Flint, Janet. "The American Painter-Lithographer." In *Art and Commerce: American Prints of the Nineteenth Century*, 126–42. Charlottesville: University Press of Virginia, 1978.

Floyd, Phyllis Anne. "*Japonisme* in Context: Documentation, Criticism, Aesthetic Reactions." PhD Dissertation, University of Michigan, 1983.

Foley, Susan K. *Women in France since 1789*. New York: Palgrave, 2004.

Fong, Grace S. "Alternative Modernities, or a Classical Woman of Modern China: The Challenging Trajectory of Lü Bicheng's (1883–1943) Life and Song Lyrics." In *Beyond Tradition and Modernity: Gender, Genre, and Cosmopolitanism in Late Qing China*. Edited by Grace S. Fong, Nanxiu Qian, and Harriet T. Zurndorfer. Leiden and Boston: Brill, 2004.

Foster, Robert J. "Tracking Globalization: Commodities and Value in Motion." In *Handbook of Material Culture*. Edited by Christopher Tilley, Webb Keane, Susanne Küchler, Michael Rowlands, and Patricia Spyer, 285–302. London and Thousand Oaks: Sage, 2006.

Foster, Vanda. *A Visual History of Costume: The Nineteenth Century*. London: B.T. Batsford Ltd., 1984.

Foucault, Michel. *The History of Sexuality: An Introduction*. New York: Pantheon Books, 1978.

Fouquières, André de. *Cinquante ans de panache*. Paris: Horay, 1951.

Fourastié, Jean and Françoise Fourastié. *Histoire du Confort*. 2nd edition. Paris: Presses Universitaires de France, 1962.

Frazier, Arthur H. "Joseph Saxton and His Contributions to the Medal Ruling and Photographic Arts." Edited by Smithsonian Institution. Washington, DC: Smithsonian Institution Press, 1975.

Frederick, Christine. *Household Engineering: Scientific Management in the Home*. Chicago: New School of Home Economics Press, 1915.

Friedberg, Anne. *Window Shopping: Cinema and the Postmodern*. Berkeley: University of California Press, 1993.

Frisby, David. "Introduction to the Texts." In *Simmel on Culture, Selected Writings*. Edited by David Frisby and Mike Featherstone, 1–31. London: Sage Publications, 1997.

Frost, Robert L. "Machine Liberation: Inventing Housewives and Home Appliances in Interwar France." *French Historical Studies* 18 (1993): 109–30.

Froula, Christine. "Rewriting Genesis: Gender and Culture in Twentieth-Century Texts." *Tulsa Studies in Women's Literature* 7, no. 2 (Autumn 1998): 197–220.

Fu, Shen C.Y. "Princess Sengge Ragi, Collector of Painting and Calligraphy." Translated and adapted by Marsha Weidner. In *Flowering in the Shadows: Women in the History of Chinese and Japanese Painting*. Edited by Marsha Weidner. Honolulu: University of Hawaii Press, 1990.

Gaillard, Marc. *Les belles heures des Champs-Élysées.* Amiens: Martelle, 1990.

Gamble, B. and R. Cooper. *Art Galleries and Museums of New Zealand*. Auckland: Art Galleries and Museums Association of New Zealand, 1969.

Garrett, Valery M. *Chinese Clothing: An Illustrated Guide*. Hong Kong: Oxford University Press, 1994.

Gascoigne, Bamber. *How to Identify Prints: A Complete Guide to Manual and Mechanical Processes from Woodcut to Inkjet*. 2nd ed. London: Thames & Hudson, 2004.

Gascoigne, John. *Joseph Banks and the English Enlightenment: Useful Knowledge and Polite Culture.* New York: Cambridge University Press, 1994.

Gaskell, Elizabeth. *The Life of Charlotte Bronte.* London and New York: Penguin, 1998.

Gell, Alfred. *Art and Agency: A New Anthropological Theory.* New York: Oxford University Press, 1998.

Gerstein, Marc. "Impressionist and Post-Impressionist Fans." PhD Dissertation, Harvard University, 1978.

Ghosh, Durba. *Sex and the Family in Colonial India.* Cambridge: Cambridge University Press, 2006.

Gienow-Hecht, Jessica C.E. "Shame on US? Academics, Cultural Transfer, and the Cold War—A Critical Review." *Diplomatic History* 24 (2000): 465–94.

Gifford, Harry, Fred E. Cliffe and George Arthurs. "Rotten Cotton Gloves." London: Montgomery & Company, 1928.

Gilbreth, Lillian. *The Home-maker and Her Job*. New York: D. Appleton, 1927.

Gilman, Sander. *The Jew's Body.* New York: Routledge, 1991.

Gilmartin, Christina Kelly. "Gender in the Formation of a Communist Body Politic." *Modern China* 19, no. 3 (1993): 299–329.

Girouard, Mark. *Life in the French Country House*. London: Cassell and Co., 2000.

Giroud, Françoise with Claude Glayman. *Si je Mens … Conversations avec Claude Glayman.* Paris: Société Express-Union et Éditions Stock, 1972.

Glass, Loren. *Author's Inc: Literary Celebrity in the United States, 1880–1980.* New York: New York University Press, 2004.

Godelier, Maurice. *The Enigma of the Gift* [1996]. Translated by Nora Scott. Chicago: University of Chicago Press, 1999.

Goldstein, Joshua. *Drama Kings: Players and Publics in the Re-Creation of Peking Opera, 1870–1937*. Berkeley: University of California Press, 2007.

Golinski, Jan. *Science as Public Culture: Chemistry and Enlightenment in Britain, 1760–1820*. Cambridge: Cambridge University Press, 1992.

Goncourt, Jules de. *Lettres de Jules de Goncourt*. Paris: G. Charpentier, 1885.

Gondola, Charles D. "Dream and Drama: The Search for Elegance among Congolese Youth." *African Studies Review* 42 (1999): 23–48.

Gore, J.M. "Representations of History and Nation in Museums in Aotearoa and New Zealand—The National Museums of Australia and The Museum of New Zealand Te Papa Tongarewa." PhD Dissertation, University of Melbourne, 2002.

de Grazia, Victoria. *Irresistible Empire: America's Advance through Twentieth-Century Europe.* Cambridge: The Belknap Press of Harvard University Press, 2005.

___. "Mass Culture and Sovereignty: The American Challenge to European Cinemas, 1920–1960." *Journal of Modern History* 61 (1989): 53–87.

Green, Reina. "Open Ears, Appetite, and Adultery in *A Woman Killed with Kindness*." *English Studies in Canada* 31, no. 4 (December 2005): 53–74.

Grier, Katherine C. *Culture and Comfort: Parlor Making and the Middle-Class Identity, 1850–1930*. Washington and London: Smithsonian Institution Press, 1988.

Griffiths, Antony. *Prints and Printmaking: An Introduction to the History and Techniques*. New York: Alfred Knopf, 1980.

Grimshaw, Patricia. *Women's Suffrage in New Zealand*. Revised edition. Auckland: Auckland University Press, 1987.

Groce, George C. and David H. Wallace. *The New-York Historical Society's Dictionary of Artists in America 1564–1860*. New Haven: Yale University Press, 1957, 1979.

Groom, Gloria. *Édouard Vuillard Painter-Decorator: Patrons and Projects, 1892–1912*. New Haven: Yale University Press, 1993.

Grosz, Elizabeth. *Volatile Bodies: Toward a Corporeal Feminism*. Bloomington: Indiana University Press, 1994.

Gu Taiqing. "Jin lü qu: Yuntai xiangguo shuti Song ben 'Jinshi lu'" [To the tune of 'Jin lü qu': A Song edition Jinshi lu inscribed by Yuntai xiangguo]. In *Donghai yu ge* [Songs of fishing in the Eastern sea]. Edited by Gu Chun. China: 1913. McGill-Harvard-Yenching Library Ming-Qing Women's Writings Digitization Project. <http://digital.library.mcgill.ca/mingqing/english/>.

Gush, Nadia. "Cultural Fields of the Canterbury Plains: Women and Cultural Citizenship in Canterbury, c.1890–1940." PhD Dissertation, Victoria University of Wellington, 2007.

Gyp, *Les moins de vingt ans*. Paris: Calmann-Lévy, 1930.

Haddow, Robert. *Pavilions of Plenty: Exhibiting American Culture Abroad in the 1950s*. Washington, DC: Smithsonian Institution Press, 1997.

Haller, Evelyn. "The Anti-Madonna in the Work and Thought of Virginia Woolf." In *Virginia Woolf: Centennial Essays*. Edited by Elaine K. Ginsberg and Laura Moss Gottleib, 93–109. Troy, NY: Whitson, 1983.

Hansen, Karen T. "Transnational Biographies and Local Meanings: Used Clothing Practices in Lusaka." *Journal of Southern African Studies* 21 (1995): 131–45.

Harcourt, François-Charles de. *Regards sur un passé*. Paris: Robert Laffont, 1989.

Harris, Elizabeth M. *The Art of Medal Engraving: A Curious Chapter in the Development of 19th Century Printing Processes*. Newtown, PA: Bird & Bull Press, 1991.

Harris, Kristine. "The New Woman: Image, Subject, and Dissent in 1930s Shanghai Film Culture." *Republican China* 20, no. 2 (1995): 55–79.

Harris, Russell. *The Lafayette Studio and Princely India*. New Delhi: Lustre Press/Roli Books, 2005.

Harrison, Hanrietta. *The Making of the Republican Citizen: Political Ceremony and Symbols in China, 1911–1929*. Oxford and New York: Oxford University Press, 2000.

Hart, John S. *Female Prose Writers of America*. Philadelphia: E.H. Butler, 1852.

Hartmann, Susan M. *The Home Front and Beyond: American Women in the 1940s*. New York: Macmillan, 1982.

Healy, Chris. *From the Ruins of Colonialism: History as Social Memory*. Melbourne: Cambridge University Press, 1997.

Heather-Bigg, Ada. "Women and the Glove Trade." *Nineteenth Century* 30, no. 178 (1891): 939–51.

Henare, Amiria. *Museums, Anthropology and Imperial Exchange*. New York: Cambridge University Press, 2005.

Henderson, Harry. "The Mass-Produced Suburbs, I." *Harpers* 207, no. 1242 (November 1953): 25–32.
Hendrickson, Hildi. "Bodies and Flags: The Representation of Herero Identity in Colonial Namibia." In *Clothing and Difference: Embodied Identities in Colonial and Post-Colonial Africa*. Edited by Hildi Hendrickson, 213–44. Durham and London: Duke University Press, 1996.
Henkins, David M. *City Reading*. New York: Columbia University Press, 1998.
Heydt, Stephanie Mayer. "The Art of *The Gift*: William Sidney Mount, Daniel Huntington, and the Antebellum Gift Book Industry." PhD Dissertation, Boston University, 2008.
Higgs, David. *Nobles in Nineteenth-Century France: The Practice of Inegalitarianism*. Baltimore: Johns Hopkins University Press, 1987.
Higonnet, Anne. *Berthe Morisot*. Berkeley: University of California Press, 1990.
Hill, Constance. *Jane Austen: Her Home and Her Friends*. Whitefish, MT: Kessinger Publishing, 2004.
Hillel, Marc. *Vie et Mœurs des GIs en Europe: 1942–1947*. Paris: Balland, 1981.
Hixson, Walter. *Parting the Curtain: Propaganda, Culture, and the Cold War 1945–1961*. New York: St Martin's Griffin, 1997.
Ho, Clara Wing-chung. "Encouragement from the Opposite Gender: Male Scholars' Interests in Women's Publications in Ch'ing China—A Bibliographic Study." In *Chinese Women in the Imperial Past: New Perspectives*. Edited by Harriet T. Zurndorfer. Leiden, Boston and Köln: Brill, 1999.
Hoganson, Kristin. "The Fashionable World: Imagined Communities of Dress." In *After the Imperial Turn: Thinking with and through the Nation*. Edited by Antoinette Burton. Durham and London: Duke University Press, 2003.
Holland, Vivian. "On Collecting Fashion Plates." *The Book-Collector's Quarterly* 2 (1951): 10–28.
Hollander, Anne. *Seeing through Clothes*. New York: Penguin Books, 1988.
——. *Sex and Suits*. New York: A.A. Knopf, 1994.
Holmes, Jeremy. Afterword to *Saplings*, by Noel Streatfeild, 363–77. London: Persephone Books, 2000.
Honey, Maureen. *Creating Rosie the Riveter: Class, Gender, and Propaganda During World War II*. Boston: University of Massachusetts Press, 1985.
Hoskins, Janet. "Agency, Biography and Objects." In *Handbook of Material Culture*. Edited by Christopher Tilley, Webb Keane, Susanne Küchler, Michael Rowlands, and Patricia Spyer, 74–84. London and Thousand Oaks: Sage, 2006.
——. *Biographical Objects: How Things Tell the Stories of People's Lives*. London: Routledge, 1998.
Houdeville, Louis. *Pour une Civilisation de l'Habitat*. Paris: Éditions Ouvrières, 1960.
Howard, Seymour. "The Steel Pen and the Modern Line of Beauty." *Technology and Culture* 26, no. 4 (October 1985): 785–98.
Huang Youqin. "Shu ya liang tang zhong kan Jinshi lu" [Afterword to the Records of Metal and Stone from the Elegant Book Studio]. In *Guochao weixiu zheng shi ji* [Collected works of Qing cultivated ladies]. China: 1831. McGill-Harvard-Yenching Library Ming-Qing Women's Writings Digitization Project. <http://digital.library.mcgill.ca/mingqing/english/>.
Hudson, Derek. *Munby, Man of Two Worlds: The Life and Diaries of Arthur J. Munby 1828–1910*. London: William Clowes & Sons, Ltd., 1972.
Humble, Nicola. *Culinary Pleasures: Cookbooks and the Transformation of British Food*. London: Faber and Faber, 2005.

Humm, Maggie. *Snapshots of Bloomsbury: The Private Lives of Virginia Woolf and Vanessa Bell*. New Brunswick: Rutgers University Press, 2006.

Hunnisett, Basil. *Engraved on Steel: The History of Picture Production Using Steel Plates*. Aldershot: Ashgate, 1998.

——. *Steel-Engraved Book Illustration in England*. Boston: David R. Godine, 1980.

Hurst, Isobel. *Victorian Women Writers and the Classics: The Feminine of Homer*. Oxford: Oxford University Press, 2006.

Huse, Nancy. *Noel Streatfeild*. New York: Twayne Publishers, 1994.

Idema, Wilt L. "Male Fantasies and Female Realities: Chu Shu-chen and Chang Yü-niang and their Biographies." In *Chinese Women in the Imperial Past: New Perspectives*. Edited by Harriet T. Zurndorfer. Leiden, Boston and Köln: Brill, 1999.

Idowu, H.O. "The Establishment of Elective Institutions in Senegal." *Journal of African History* IX (1968): 261–77.

Irvine, William B. *On Desire*. Oxford: Oxford University Press, 2005.

Iskin, Ruth E. "The *Flâneuse* in French Fin-de-Siècle Posters: Advertising Images of Modern Women in Paris." In *The Invisible Flaneuse?: Gender, Public Space and Visual Culture in Nineteenth Century Paris*. Edited by Aruna D'Souza and Tom McDonough. Manchester: Manchester University Press, 2006.

——. *Modern Women and Parisian Consumer Culture in Impressionist Painting*. Cambridge: Cambridge University Press, 2007.

——. "The Pan-European *Flâneuse* in Fin-de-Siècle Posters: Advertising Modern Women in the City." *Nineteenth-Century Contexts* 25 (2003): 333–56.

——. "Popularizing New Women in Belle Époque Advertising Posters." In *A Belle Époque? Women and Feminism in French Society and Culture 1890–1910*. Edited by Diana Holmes and Carrie Tarr, 95–112. Oxford and New York: Berghahn Books, 2006.

Jack, Florence B. and Rita Strauss. *The Woman's Book: Contains Everything a Woman Ought to Know*. London: T.C. & E.C. Jack, 1911.

Jaffer, Amin. *Made for Maharajas: A Design Diary of Princely India*. New Delhi: Lustre Press/Roli Books, 2007.

Japan Goes to the World's Fairs: Japanese Art at the Great Expositions in Europe and the United States 1867–1904. Los Angeles: Los Angeles County Museum of Art, 2005.

Japonisme et mode Exhibition Catalogue. Paris: Les Musées de la Ville de Paris, 1996.

Jardine, Nicholas, J.A. Secord, and E.C. Spary, eds. *The Cultures of Natural History*. Cambridge: Cambridge University Press, 1996.

Jasanoff, Maya. *Edge of Empire: Lives, Culture and Conquest in the East, 1750–1850*. New York: Knopf, 2005.

Jenkins, Henry. *Textual Poachers: Television Fans and Participatory Culture*. New York: Routledge, 1992.

Jensen, Robert. *Marketing Modernism in Fin-de-Siècle Europe*. Princeton: Princeton University Press, 1994.

Jenson, Jane. "The Liberation and New Rights for French Women." In *Behind the Lines: Gender and the Two World Wars*. Edited by Margaret Randolph Higgonet, Jane Jenson, Sonya Michel, and Margaret Collins Weitz, 272–84. New Haven: Yale University Press, 1987.

Jhally, Sut. *The Codes of Advertising: Fetishism and the Political Economy of Meaning in the Consumer Society*. New York: Routledge, 1990.

Jiujing xingshi huabao [The capital periodical to awaken the world], published 1908–09. Reprint. *Jiujing xingshi huabao: wan Qing shijing baitai* [The capital periodical to awaken the world: Opinions from the late-Qing city]. Edited by Zhang Fenggang. Beijing: Zhongguo wenlian chubanshe, 2003.

Johnson, Marian Ashley. "Gold Jewelry of the Wolof and Tukolor of Senegal." *African Arts* 27 (1994): 36–49, 94–5.

Joline, Adrian H. *Meditations of an Autograph Collector.* New York: Harper and Bros. Publishers, 1902.

Jones, Gareth Stedman. *Outcast London: A Study in the Relationship between Classes in Victorian Society*. London: Penguin Books, 1992.

Jones, Sir Thomas G. *The Unbroken Front, Ministry of Food, 1916–1944: Personalities and Problems*. London: Everybody's Books, 1944.

Joshi, Sanjay. *Fractured Modernity: Making of a Middle Class in Colonial North India*. New Delhi: Oxford University Press, 2001.

Joshi, Varsha. *Polygamy and Purdah.* Jaipur: Rawat Publications, 1995.

Jouvin's Glove Manufactory. "Jouvin's Glove Manufactory." In *Women's Clothes and Millinery Box 3; Advertisements–Gloves*. Edited by John Johnson Collection. Paris: Jouvin's Glove Manufactory, 1862.

Keane, Webb. "Introduction: Subject and Objects." In *Handbook of Material Culture*. Edited by Christopher Tilley, Webb Keane, Susanne Küchler, Michael Rowlands, and Patricia Spyer, 197–202. London and Thousand Oaks: Sage, 2006.

Keller, Alexandra. "Disseminations of Modernity: Representation and Consumer Desire in Early Mail-Order Catalogs." In *Cinema and the Invention of Modern Life*. Edited by Leo Charney and Vanessa Schwartz, 156–82. Berkeley: University of California Press, 1995.

Kelly, Gary. "Education and Accomplishments." In *Jane Austen in Context*. Edited by Janet Todd, 252–61. Cambridge: Cambridge University Press, 2005.

Kennett, Lee. *GI: The American Soldier in World War II.* New York: Charles Scribner's Sons, 1987.

Kingery, David, ed. *Learning from Things: Method and Theory of Material Culture Studies.* Washington, DC: Smithsonian Institution Press, 1995.

Kirchenblatt-Gimblett, Barbara. *Destination Culture: Tourism, Museums and Heritage.* Berkeley: University of California Press, 1998.

Klein, Lawrence. "Politeness for Plebes: Consumption and Social Identity in Early Eighteenth-Century England." In *The Consumption of Culture, 1600–1800: Image, Object, Text*. Edited by Ann Bermingham and John Brewer, 362–82. New York: Routledge, 1995.

Ko, Dorothy. *Teachers of the Inner Chambers: Women and Culture in Seventeenth-Century China*. Stanford, CA: Stanford University Press, 1994.

Kopytoff, Igor. "The Cultural Biography of Things: Commoditization as Process." In *The Social Life of Things: Commodities in a Cultural Perspective.* Edited by Arjun Appadurai, 64–93. Cambridge: Cambridge University Press, 1986.

Koyama-Richard, Brigitte. *Correspondance adressée à Hayashi Tadamasa.* Tokyo: Institut de Tokyo, Institution Administrative Indépendante, Centre National de Recherche pour les Propriétés Culturelles; Kokushokankôkai, 2001.

Krill, John. *English Artists' Paper: Renaissance to Regency.* 2nd revised and expanded edition. New Castle, DE: Oak Knoll Press, 2001.

Kristeva, Julia. *Powers of Horror: An Essay on Abjection*. Translated by Leon S. Roudiez. New York: Columbia University Press, 1982.

Kuisel, Richard. "Americanization for Historians." *Diplomatic History* 24 (2000): 509–15.

———. *Seducing the French: The Dilemma of Americanization.* Berkeley: University of California Press, 1993.

Kuper, Hilda. "Costume and Identity." *Comparative Studies in Society and History* 15 (1973): 348–67.

Kutcha, David. "The Making of the Self-Made Man: Class, Clothing, and English Masculinity, 1688–1832." In *The Sex of Things: Gender and Consumption in Historical Perspective*. Edited by Victoria de Grazia and Ellen Furlough. Berkeley: University of California Press, 1996.

Labrum, Bronwyn. "Making Pakeha History in New Zealand Museums: Community and Identity in the Post-War Period." In *Museum Revolutions: How Museums Change and Are Changed*. Edited by Simon J. Knell, Suzanne MacLeod, and Sheila Watson, 149–59. London and New York: Routledge, 2007.

Lacroix, Jean-Bernard and Saliou Mbaye. "Le vote des femmes au Sénégal." *Ethiopiques* 6 (1976): 26–43.

Laing, Ellen Johnston. "Visualising Evidence for the Evolution of 'Politically Correct' Dress for Women in Early Twentieth Century Shanghai." *Nan Nü* 5, no. 1 (2003): 69–114.

Lal, Ruby. "The 'Domestic World' of the Mughals in the Reigns of Babur, Humayan and Akbar, c. 1500–1605." Unpublished PhD Thesis, University of Oxford, 2000.

Lamont, Michèle. *Money, Morals, and Manners: The Culture of the French and American Upper-Middle Class*. Chicago: University of Chicago Press, 1992.

Lancaster, William. *The Department Store: A Social History*. London: Leicester University Press, 1995.

Langley Moore, Doris. *Fashion through Fashion Plates, 1771–1970*. New York: Clarkson N. Pooter Inc., 1971.

Larousse, Pierre. *Grand Dictionnaire Universel du XIXe Siècle* (1866–79). Vol. 10. Reprint. Geneva and Paris: Slatkine, 1982.

Larson, Wendy. *Women and Writing in Modern China*. Stanford: Stanford University Press, 1998.

Lassner, Phyllis. *British Women Writers of World War II: Battlegrounds of Their Own*. New York: St Martin's, 1998.

Latour, Bruno. "The Berlin Key or How to Do Words with Things." In *Matter, Materiality, and Modern Culture*. Edited by P.M. Graves-Brown. London: Routledge, 2000.

___. "Visualization and Cognition: Thinking with Eyes and Hands." *Knowledge and Society* 6 (1986): 1–40.

Lauer, Josh. "Traces of the Real: Autographomania and the Cult of the Signers in Nineteenth-Century America. *Text and Performance Quarterly* 27, no. 2 (April 2007): 143–63.

Laurenson, Helen B. *Going Up Going Down: The Rise and Fall of the Department Store*. Auckland: Auckland University Press, 2005.

Lavater, John Casper. *Essays on Physiognomy: Designed to Promote the Knowledge and the Love of Mankind*. Translated by Thomas Holcroft. 12th edition. London: William Tegg, 1862.

Law, John and Michael Lynch. "Lists, Field Guides, and the Descriptive Organization of Seeing; Birdwatching as an Exemplary Observational Activity." *Human Studies* 11, nos. 2/3 (1988): 271–304.

Le Wita, Béatrix. *French Bourgeois Culture*. Cambridge: Cambridge University Press, 1994.

Lee, Leo Oufan. *Shanghai Modern: The Flowering of a New Urban Culture in China 1930–1945*. Cambridge, MA: Harvard University Press, 1999.

Leenhardt, M. "Pourquoi se vêtir?" *L'Amour de l'Art* 1 (1952).

Lee-Warner, William. "The Native States of India." In *British Empire Series, Volume 1: India, Ceylon, Straits Settlements, British Northern Borneo, Hong-Kong*. London: Kegal Paul, Trench, Trubner & Co, 1899.

Lehmann, René. "Elle et Lui." *La Femme Nouvelle* 1 (1945): 2.

Lehuu, Isabelle. *Carnival on the Page: Popular Print Media in Antebellum America*. Chapel Hill: University of North Carolina Press, 2000.
Lemire, Beverly. *Dress, Culture, and Commerce: The English Clothing Trade Before the Factory, 1660–1800.* Basingstoke, Hampshire: Macmillan, 1997.
Leppert, Richard. "Social Order and the Domestic Consumption of Music: The Politics of Sound and the Policing of Gender Construction in Eighteenth-Century England." In *The Consumption of Culture, 1600–1800: Image, Object, Text*. Edited by Ann Bermingham and John Brewer, 514–34. New York: Routledge, 1995.
Li Ciming, "Tao hua sheng jie'an riji" [Diary from the Peach-blossom Studio]. In *Liulichang xiaozhi* [Short gazetteer of Liulichang]. Edited by Sun Dianqi. Beijing: Beijing chubanshe, 1982.
Li Qingzhao. "Interlude: Li Qing-zhao's Epilogue to *Records on Metal and Stone*." In *Anthology of Chinese Literature, Beginnings to 1911*. Edited and translated by Stephen Owen. New York: W.W. Norton & Company, 1997.
Li Youxian. Postface to *Gu quan hui* [Compendium of ancient coins] by Weng Shupei. Reprint. In *Zhongguo qianbi wenxian congshu* [Collection of Chinese literary works on coins] 16:1. Edited by Ma Feihai and Wang Guichen. Shanghai: Shanghai guji chubanshe, 1992.
Liangyou huabao [The Young Companion] *Sun Chuanfang jinzhi nüzi chuan qipao.* Shanghai, March 2 (1926): 7.
Lichtenberger, Marguerite. "Notre ami Jack." *Marie-France* 77 (1946): 12–13.
Lightfoot, John. *Philosophical Transactions of the Royal Society* 76 (1786): 160–70.
Lin, Yutang. "*Lun xizhuang*". In *Lin Yutang zuanza, Shangjuan*. Fuzhou: *Haixia wenyi chubanshe*, 1988 [1934].
Ling, Wessie. *Fusionable Cheongsam*. Hong Kong: Hong Kong Arts Centre, 2007.
Linglong. Shanghai, 1931–37.
Linton, Eliza Lynn. *The Girl of the Period and Other Social Essays.* 2 volumes. London: Richard Bentley & Son, 1883.
Livre d'or 1900. Paris: Bender, 1900.
Lu Chang. "Li Qingzhao." *Li chao ming yuan shi ci* [Poems of famous historical beauties]. China: Hongshulou ke ben, 1772. McGill-Harvard-Yenching Library Ming-Qing Women's Writings Digitization Project. <http://digital.library.mcgill.ca/mingqing/english/>.
Lyon, George Ella. "Virginia Woolf and the Problem of the Body." In *Virginia Woolf: Centennial Essays*. Edited by Elaine K. Ginsberg and Laura Moss Gottleib, 111–26. Troy, NY: Whitson, 1983.
Macdonald, Charlotte. *The Vote, the Pill and the Demon Drink: A History of Feminist Writing in New Zealand, 1869–1993*. Wellington: Bridget Williams Books, 1993.
Macknight, Elizabeth C. "Cake and Conversation: The Women's *jour* in Parisian High Society, 1880–1914." *French History* 19 (2005): 342–63.
——. "A 'Theater of Rule'? Domestic Service in Aristocratic Households under the Third Republic." *French History* (forthcoming).
Madigan, Thomas F. *Word Shadows of the Great: The Lure of Autograph Collecting.* New York: Frederick A. Stokes Company, 1930.
Mainardi, Patricia. *The End of the Salon: Art and the State in the Early Third Republic.* Cambridge: Cambridge University Press, 1993.
Malinowski, Bronislaw. *Argonauts of the Western Pacific* [1922]. Prospect Heights, IL: Waveland Press, 1984.
Mann, Susan. "The Education of Daughters in the Mid-Ch'ing Period." In *Education and Society in Late Imperial China, 1600–1900*. Edited by Alexander Woodside and Benjamin A. Elman. Berkeley: University of California Press, 1994.

___. "Grooming a Daughter for Marriage: Brides and Wives in the Mid-Qing Period." In *Chinese Femininities/Chinese Masculinities: A Reader*. Edited by Susan Brownell and Jeffrey N. Wasserstrom. Foreword by Thomas Laqueur. Berkeley and London: University of California Press, 2002.

___. *Precious Records: Women in China's Long Eighteenth Century*. Stanford: Stanford University Press, 1997.

Mantegazza, Paolo. *Physiognomy and Expression*. London: Walter Scott, 1890.

Marchand, Roland. *Advertising the American Dream: Making Way for Modernity, 1920–1940*. Berkeley: University of California Press, 1985.

Marcus, Sharon. "Reflections on Victorian Fashion Plates." *Differences: A Journal of Feminist Cultural Studies* 14, no. 3 (2003): 4–33.

Martin, Ann Smart. "Material Things and Cultural Meanings: Notes on the Study of Early American Material Culture." *The William and Mary Quarterly* 53 (1996): 5–12.

Martin, Michèle. *"Hello Central?" Gender, Technology, and Culture in the Formation of Telephone Systems*. Montreal: McGill-Queen's University Press, 1991.

Martin, Phyllis M. "Contesting Clothes in Colonial Brazzaville." *Journal of African History* 35 (1994): 401–26.

___. *Leisure and Society in Colonial Brazzaville*. Cambridge: Cambridge University Press, 1995.

Martine, Claude. "Histoire de Thé." *La Femme Nouvelle* 10 (1945): 11.

Martinez, Katharine. "John Sartain (1808–1897): His Contribution to American Printmaking." *Imprint* 8, no. 1 (1983): 1–12.

___. "Portrait Prints by John Sartain." In *American Portrait Prints: Proceedings of the Tenth Annual American Print Conference*. Edited by Wendy Wick Reaves, 135–93. Charlottesville: University Press of Virginia, 1984.

Martinez, Katharine and Page Talbott, eds. *Philadelphia's Cultural Landscape: The Sartain Family Legacy*. Philadelphia: Temple University Press, 2000.

Martyn, Thomas. *The Universal Conchologist*. London, 1784–92.

Marvin, Carolyn. *When Old Technologies Were New: Thinking About Communication Technologies in the Late Nineteenth Century*. New York: Oxford University Press, 1988.

Marzio, Peter C. "The Democratic Art of Chromolithography in America: An Overview." In *Art and Commerce: American Prints of the Nineteenth Century*, 76–102. Charlottesville: University Press of Virginia, 1978.

Masquelier, Adeline. "Mediating Threads: Clothing and the Texture of Spirit/Medium Relations in Bori (Southern Niger)." In *Clothing and Difference: Embodied Identities in Colonial and Post-Colonial Africa*. Edited by Hildi Hendrickson, 66–94. Durham and London: Duke University Press, 1996.

Mathews, Nancy Mowll. *Mary Cassatt: A Life*. New York: Villard Books, 1994.

Mathews, Nancy Mowll and Barbara Stern Shapiro. *Mary Cassatt: The Color Prints*. New York: Harry N. Abrams, Inc., in association with Williams College Museum of Art, 1989.

Mathur, L.P. and Laxmi Sukhwal. "British Interference in the Internal Sovereignty of Princely States (1858–1885)." In *British Policy Towards Princely States of India*. Edited by R.P. Vyas. Jodhpur: Rajasthan-Vidya Prakashan, 1991.

Matthews, Samantha. "Making Their Mark: Writing the Poet's Grave". In *Literary Tourism and Nineteenth-Century Culture*. Edited by Nicola Watson, 34–5. Basingstoke: Palgrave Macmillan, 2009.

Mauss, Marcel. *The Gift: The Form and Reason for Exchange in Archaic Societies* [1925]. Translated by W.D. Hall. New York: Norton, 1990.

McCann, Andrew. *Cultural Politics in the 1790s: Literature, Radicalism, and the Public Sphere*. New York: St Martin's Press, 1999.
McCarthy, Conal. *Exhibiting Maori: A History of Colonial Cultures of Display*. Oxford: Berg, 2007.
——. "New Zealand Centennial Exhibition, Wellington, 1940." In *Encyclopedia of World's Fairs and Expositions*. Edited by J. Findling and K. Pelle. North Carolina: McFarlane Press, 2008.
McClintock, Anne. *Imperial Leather: Race, Gender and Sexuality in Colonial Conquest*. New York: Routledge, 1995.
McCredie, Athol. "Going Public: New Zealand Art Museums in the 1970s." Master's Thesis, Massey University, 1999.
McGill, Gladys. "House Planning and Interior Decoration." *University of Otago Home Science Department Bulletin* 4 (1925).
McKendrick, Neil, John Brewer, and J.H. Plumb. *The Birth of the Consumer Society: The Commercialisation of England*. Bloomington: University of Indiana Press, 1982.
McKergow, Fiona. "'Just the Thing': Shopping for Clothes in Palmerston North." In *Looking Flash: Clothing in Aotearoa New Zealand*. Edited by Bronwyn Labrum, Fiona McKergow, and Stephanie Gibson, 132–53. Auckland: Auckland University Press, 2007.
McLean, Gavin. "Where Sheep May Not Safely Graze: A Brief History of New Zealand's Heritage Movement 1890–2000." In *Common Ground? Heritage and Public Places in New Zealand*. Edited by Alexander Trapeznik, 25–44. Dunedin: University of Otago Press, 2000.
McMichael, Morton. "An Address Delivered before the Northern Lyceum of the City and County of Philadelphia." In *Historical Society of Pennsylvania Closed Stacks*. Philadelphia, 1839.
McMillan, Nora F. "William Swainson (1789–1855) and his Shell Collections." *Journal of the Society for Bibliography of Natural History* 9 (1980): 427–34.
Mendes da Costa, Emanuel. *Elements of Conchology: Or, an Introduction to the Knowledge of Shells*. London, 1776.
Mension-Rigau, Éric. Aristocrates et grands bourgeois: education, traditions, valeurs. Paris: Pluriel, 1994.
Merish, Lori. *Sentimental Materialism: Gender, Commodity Culture, and Nineteenth-Century American Literature*. Durham: Duke University Press, 2000.
Metcalf, Thomas. *Ideologies of the Raj*. Cambridge: Cambridge University Press, 1995.
Michel, Adolph F. and T. Hunt Clark. "Advance Arrangements for Telephone Convenience." *Bell Telephone Magazine* 28, no. 4 (Winter 1949–50): 217–26.
Mille, Pierre. "The Black Vote in Senegal." *Journal of African Sociology* 1 (1901): 64–79.
Millen, Julia. *Kirkcaldie & Stains: A Wellington Story*. Wellington: Bridget Williams Books, 2000.
Miller, Daniel. *Acknowledging Consumption*. New York: Routledge, 1994.
——. "Coca-Cola: A Black Sweet Drink from Trinidad." In *Material Cultures*. Edited by Daniel Miller, 169–87. Chicago: University of Chicago Press, 1997.
——. *Material Culture and Mass Consumption*. Oxford: Blackwell, 1987.
——. *Material Cultures: Why Some Things Matter*. Chicago: University of Chicago Press, 1998.
——. *A Theory of Shopping*. Ithaca, NY: Cornell University Press, 1998.
Miller, Michael. *The Bon Marché: Bourgeois Culture and the Department Store, 1869–1920*. Princeton NJ: Princeton University Press, 1981.

Mittler, Barbara. "Of Elegance and Eloquence: *Linglong* and the Art of Being a 'New Woman' in 1930s China." Paper presented at the AAS Annual Conference, San Diego, March 12, 2000.

Molineux, Thomas. *An Introduction to Byrom's Universal Short-hand.* 6th edition. London: Longman, Hurst, Rees, Orme and Browne, 1823.

Monnickendam, A. *Secrets of the Diamond.* London: Frederick Muller Ltd., 1941.

Moore, Lisa L. "Queer Gardens: Mary Delany's Flowers and Friendships." *Eighteenth-Century Studies* 39 (2005): 49–70.

Moore, Lucy. *Maharanis: The Lives and Times of Three Generations of Indian Princesses.* London: Viking, 2004.

Morgan, Marjorie. *Manners, Morals and Class in England, 1774–1858.* Houndmills: Macmillan, 1994.

Morgenthau, Ruth Stachtcher. *Political Parties in French-Speaking West Africa.* Oxford: Clarendon Press, 1964.

Mott, Frank Luther. *A History of American Magazines.* 5 volumes. Cambridge: Harvard University Press, 1957–58.

Mulvey, Laura. "Visual Pleasure and Narrative Cinema" [1975]. In *Art after Modernism: Rethinking Representation.* Edited by Brian Wallis, 360–73. New York: New Museum of Contemporary Art; Boston: D.R. Godine, 1984.

Munby, A.N.L. *The Cult of the Autograph Letter in England.* London: University of London, Athlone Press, 1962.

Munby, Arthur. "Munby Diary." In *Munby, Man of Two Worlds: The Life and Diaries of Arthur J. Munby, 1812–1910.* Edited by Derek Hudson. Cambridge: Gambit, 1974.

Mustapha, Hudita Nura. "Portraits of Modernity: Fashioning Selves in Dakarois Popular Photography." In *Images and Empires: Visuality in Colonial and Postcolonial Africa.* Edited by Paul S. Landau and Deborah D. Kaspin, 172–92. Berkeley and Los Angeles: University of California Press, 2002.

Myers, Fred R., ed. *The Empire of Things: Regimes of Value and Material Culture.* Santa Fe: School of American Research Press, 2001.

Myers, Sylvia H. *The Bluestocking Circle: Women, Friendship, and the Life of the Mind in Eighteenth-Century England.* Oxford: Oxford University Press, 1990.

National Portrait Gallery. Research. "British Painters and Artists' Suppliers." National Portrait Gallery. <http://www.npg.org.uk/live/artistsupp.asp>.

Naudin, Jean-Bernard and Christiane de Nicolay-Mazery. *Visite privée: hôtels particuliers de Paris.* Paris: Chêne, 1999.

Ndiaye, Adja NDeye B. *Collier de Cheville.* Dakar: Nouvelles Editions Africaines, 1983.

Newsome, W. Brian. "The Struggle for a Voice in the City: The Development of Participatory Architectural and Urban Planning in France, 1940–1960." PhD Dissertation, University of South Carolina, 2002.

Ng, Hao. *Duhui yunshang. Xishuo zhongguo funü fushi yu shenti geming (1911–1935).* Hong Kong: Joint Publishing Co. Ltd, 2006.

Niang, Fatou Siga Niang. *Reflets de modes et traditions Saint-Louisiennes.* Dakar: Editions Khoudia, 1990.

Nichols, Heidi Lynne. *The Fashioning of Middle-Class America: Sartain's Union Magazine of Literature and Art and Antebellum Culture.* New York: Peter Lang, 2004.

Nipps, Karen. "Charles Jacobs Peterson." In *Dictionary of Literary Biography, Volume 79: American Magazine Journalists, 1850–1900.* Edited by Sam G. Riley, 236–41. Detroit: Gale Research Co., 1989.

———. *Naturally Fond of Pictures: American Illustration of the 1840s and 1850s.* Philadelphia: Library Company of Philadelphia, 1989.

Nixon, Sean. "Exhibiting Masculinity." In *Representation: Cultural Representations and Signifying Practices*. Edited by Stuart Hall. London: Sage Publications, 2000.
Noailles, Anna de. *Le livre de ma vie.* Paris: Mercure de France, 1976.
Noble, Mrs Robert. *Every Woman's Toilet Book.* London: George Newnes, Limited, 1908.
Nochlin, Linda and Tamar Garb, eds. *The Jew in the Text: Modernity and the Construction of Identity*. London: Thames and Hudson, 1995.
Nolan, Mary. "Consuming America, Producing Gender." In *The American Century in Europe.* Edited by R. Laurence Moore and Maurizio Vaudagna, 243–61. Ithaca: Cornell University Press, 2003.
Nora, Pierre. "Between Memory and History" [*Les lieux de memorie*]. Translated by Marc Roudebush. *Representations* 26 (1989): 7–24.
Nord, Philip G. *Paris Shopkeepers and the Politics of Resentment*. Princeton, NJ: Princeton University Press, 1986.
Okker, Patricia. *Our Sister Editors: Sarah J. Hale and the Tradition of Nineteenth-Century American Women Editors*. Athens: University of Georgia Press, 1995.
Oliver, W.H. *Looking for the Phoenix: A Memoir.* Wellington: Bridget Williams Books, 2002.
Olney, R.J. "The Portland Papers." *Archives* XIX (no. 82) 1989: 78–87.
Olsen, Kirstin. *Daily Life in 18th-Century England.* Westport, CT: Greenwood Press, 1999.
Orange, Claudia. *The Treaty of Waitangi*. Wellington: Bridget Williams Books with the assistance of the Historical Branch, Department of Internal Affairs, 1992.
Outram, Dorinda. *Enlightenment*. Cambridge: Cambridge University Press, 1995.
Palethorpe, N.B. *Official History of the New Zealand Centennial Exhibition, Wellington, 1939–1940*. Wellington: The New Zealand Centennial Exhibition Company Ltd, 1940.
Pange, Comtesse Jean de. *Comment j'ai vu 1900.* Paris: Grasset, 1962.
Parkins, Wendy, ed. *Fashioning the Body Politic: Dress, Gender, Citizenship*. Oxford: Berg, 2002.
Parry, Jonathan P. "The *Gift*, the Indian Gift, and the 'Indian Gift'." *Man* 21 (1986): 453–73.
Patry, Sylvie, Hugues Wilhelm, and Sylvie Patin, with the assistance of Michèle Moyne. *Berthe Morisot 1841–1895*. Paris: Éditions de la Réunion des musées nationaux, 2002.
Pearce, Susan. *Museums, Objects, and Collections*. Washington, DC: Smithsonian Institution Press, 1993.
———. *On Collecting: An Investigation into Collecting in the European Tradition*. New York: Routledge, 1995.
Pedersen, Susan. *Family, Dependence, and the Origins of the Welfare State: Britain and France, 1914–1945*. Cambridge: Cambridge University Press, 1993.
Peiss, Kathy. *Hope in a Jar: The Making of America's Beauty Culture*. New York: Metropolitan Books, 1998.
Pells, Richard. *Not Like Us: How Europeans Have Loved, Hated, and Transformed American Culture Since World War II.* New York: Basic Books, 1997.
Pennsylvania Academy of the Fine Arts. *Catalogue of the Exhibition of Paintings and Drawings*. Philadelphia: T.K. and P.G. Collins, Printers, 1843.
Perrot, Michelle, ed. *A History of Private Life*. Vol. 4. *From the Fires of Revolution to the Great War*. Translated by Arthur Goldhammer. Cambridge, MA: The Belknap Press, 1990.
Perrot, Philippe. *Fashioning the Bourgeoisie: A History of Clothing in the Nineteenth Century*. Translated by Richard Bienvenu. Princeton: Princeton University Press, 1981, 1994.

———. "Quand le tabac conquit la France." *Histoire* (1982): 98–104.
Petroski, Henry. *The Pencil: A History of Design and Circumstance.* New York: Knopf, 1990.
Phillips, Peggy A. *Modern France: Theories and Realities of Urban Planning.* Landham: University Press of America, Inc., 1987.
Pierrot, Henriette. "Trois Mille Françaises au Paradis des Femmes." *La Femme* 41 (1946): 3, 19.
Pilbeam, Pamela. "Bourgeois Society." In *A Companion to Nineteenth-Century Europe, 1789–1914.* Edited by Stefan Berger. Malden, MA: Blackwell Publishers, 2006.
Plain, Gill. *Women's Fiction of the Second World War: Gender, Power and Resistance.* New York: St Martin's, 1996.
Poiger, Uta. "Beyond 'Modernization' and 'Colonization'." *Diplomatic History* 23 (1999): 45–56.
Pointon, Marcia. *Strategies for Showing: Women, Possession, and Representation in English Visual Culture, 1665–1800.* Oxford: Oxford University Press, 1997.
Pollard, Miranda. *Reign of Virtue: Mobilizing Gender in Vichy France.* Chicago: University of Chicago Press, 1998.
Pollock, Griselda. "Modernity and the Spaces of Femininity." In *Vision and Difference: Femininity, Feminism and the Histories of Art*, 50–90. London: Routledge, 1988.
"Population," from *An Encyclopaedia of New Zealand.* Edited by A.H. McLintock, originally published in 1966. Te Ara—The Encyclopedia of New Zealand. <http://www.TeAra.govt.nz/1966/P/Population/en>.
Porter Benson, Susan. *Counter Cultures: Saleswomen, Managers, and Customers in American Department Stores.* Urbana: University of Illinois Press, 1986.
Prior, Nick. *Museums and Modernity: Art Galleries and the Making of Modern Culture.* Oxford: Berg, 2002.
Proust, Marcel. *In Search of Lost Time.* Translated by C.K. Scott Moncrieff and Terence Kilmartin. Revised by D.J. Enright. London: Vintage, 1996.
Prown, Jules. "Mind in Matter: An Introduction to Material Culture Theory and Method." *Winterthur Portfolio* 17 (1982): 1–19.
Prown, Jules David and Kenneth Haltman. *American Artifacts: Essays in Material Culture.* East Lansing, MI: Michigan State University Press, 2000.
Pulju, Rebecca. "Consumers for the Nation: Women, Politics and Consumer Organization in France, 1944–1965." *Journal of Women's History* 18 (2006): 68–90.
Qian, Nanxiu. "Revitalizing the Xianyuan (Worthy Ladies) Tradition: Women in the 1898 Reforms." *Modern China* 29, no. 4 (2003): 399–454.
Queen Victoria's Proclamation, November 1, 1858. In *Imperialism and Orientalism: A Documentary Sourcebook.* By Barbara Harlow and Mia Carter. New York: Methuen, 1987.
Raab, Stephen. "A Short History of Collecting Autographs." Raab Collection Webpage: <http://www.raabcollection.com/dynamicContent.aspx?key=pliny>. Last consulted: June 15, 2008.
Rai, Mridu. *Hindu Rulers, Muslim Subjects: Islam, Rights and the History of Kashmir.* Princeton: Princeton University Press, 2004.
Rakow, Lana F. *Gender on the Line: Women, the Telephone, and Community Life.* Champaign: University of Illinois Press, 1991.
Ramusack, Barbara. *The Indian Princes and Their States.* Cambridge: Cambridge University Press, 2004.
———. *The Princes of India in the Twilight of Empire: Dissolution of a Patron–Client System, 1914–1939.* Columbus: University of Cincinnati Press, 1978.
Rappaport, Erika Diane. "'A New Era of Shopping': The Promotion of Women's Pleasure in London's West End, 1909–1914." In *Cinema and the Invention of Modern*

Life. Edited by Leo Charney and Vanessa R. Schwartz, 130–55. Berkeley: University of California Press, 1995.
——. *Shopping for Pleasure: Women in the Making of London's West End*. Princeton: Princeton University Press, 2000.
Reaves, Wendy Wick, ed. *American Portrait Prints: Proceedings of the Tenth Annual American Print Conference*. Charlottesville: University Press of Virginia, for the Smithsonian Institution, 1984.
Reay, Barry. *Watching Hannah: Sexuality, Horror and Bodily De-Formation in Victorian England*. London: Reaktion Books Ltd., 2002.
Reddy, William M. "The Concept of Class." In *Social Orders and Social Classes in Europe since 1500: Studies in Social Stratification*. Edited by M.L. Bush, 13–25. London: Longman, 1992.
Régnier, Henri de. *Images Venitiennes*. Paris: Fontemoing, 1912.
Renwick, William, ed. *Creating a National Spirit: Celebrating New Zealand's Centennial*. Wellington: Victoria University Press, 2004.
Rhys, Grace. "Introduction." In *Modes and Manners of the Nineteenth Century*. By M. Edwardes. London: J.M. Dent and Company, 1909.
Ribeiro, Aileen. *The Art of Dress: Fashion in England and France 1750 to 1820*. New Haven: Yale University Press, 1995.
——. *Dress in Eighteenth Century Europe 1715–1789*. New Haven: Yale University Press, 2002.
Richards, Thomas. *The Commodity Culture of Victorian England: Advertising and Spectacle, 1851–1914*. Stanford: Stanford University Press, 1990.
Richardson, Joanna. *Portrait of a Bonaparte: The Life and Times of Joseph-Napoleon Primoli 1851–1927*. London: Quartet Books, 1987.
Rickford, Kathleen E. "The ABC's of Cloth and Politics in Ivory Coast." *Afrika Today* 41 (1994): 5–25.
Roberts, Mary-Louise. *Civilization without Sexes: Reconstructing Gender in Postwar France, 1917–1927*. Chicago: University of Chicago Press, 1994.
——. "Samson and Delilah Revisited: The Politics of Women's Fashion in 1920s France." *The American Historical Review* 98 (1993): 657–84.
Roger, Philippe. *The American Enemy: The History of French Anti-Americanism*. Chicago: University of Chicago Press, 2005.
Rosenberg, Emily. "Consuming Women: Images of Americanization in the 'American Century'." *Diplomatic History* 23 (1999): 479–97.
Ross, Ellen. *Love and Toil: Motherhood in Outcast London, 1870–1918*. New York: Oxford University Press, 1993.
Rousset-Charny, Gérard. Les palais parisiens de la belle époque. Paris: Délégation à l'Action Artistique de la Ville de Paris, 1990.
Royal Society for the Encouragement of Arts, Manufactures and Commerce. "The British Empire and Commonwealth Museum." Item 5: Chip Hats. <http://www.rsa.org.uk/250/empire.asp>.
Rudolph, Lloyd and Susanne Rudolph. *Essays on Rajputana*. New Delhi: Concept Publishing Company, 1984.
——. *The Modernity of Tradition: Political Development in India*. Chicago: University of Chicago Press, 1967.
Said, Edward. *Orientalism*. New York: Vintage Books, 1979.
Saisselin, Rémy G. *Bricabracomania: The Bourgeois and the Bibelot*. London: Thames and Hudson, 1985.
——. *The Bourgeois and the Bibelot*. New Brunswick: Rutgers University Press, 1984.

Saumarez Smith, Charles. "The Future of the Museum." In *A Companion to Museum Studies*. Edited by Sharon Macdonald, 543–54. Malden, MA: Blackwell, 2006.
Schaffer, Frederick C. *Democracy in Translation: Understanding Politics in an Unfamiliar Culture*. Ithaca: Cornell University Press, 1998.
Scheper-Hughes, Nancy. Introduction to *Child Survival: Anthropological Perspectives on the Treatment and Maltreatment of Children*. Edited by Nancy Scheper-Hughes. Dordrecht, Holland: D. Reidel, 1987.
Schiebinger, Londa. *Nature's Body: Gender in the Making of Modern Science*. Boston: Beacon Press, 1993.
Schlote, Werner. *British Overseas Trade from 1700 to the 1930s*. Oxford: Blackwell, 1952.
Schlumberger, Gustave. *Mes souvenirs 1844–1928*. Paris: Plon, 1934.
Schmidt, Leigh Eric. *Consumer Rites: The Buying and Selling of American Holidays*. Princeton: Princeton University Press, 1995.
Schneider, Karen. *Loving Arms: British Women Writing the Second World War*. Lexington: University Press of Kentucky, 1997.
Schwartz, Vanessa. *It's So French: Hollywood, Paris, and the Making of Cosmopolitan Film Culture*. Chicago: University of Chicago Press, 2007.
Schwartz, Vanessa R. and Jeannene M. Przyblyski, eds. *The Nineteenth-Century Visual Culture Reader*. New York and London: Routledge, 2004.
Scindia, Vijaya Raje. *The Last Maharani of Gwalior: An Autobiography*. Albany: State University of New York, 1987.
Scott, A.C. *Chinese Costume in Transition*. Singapore: Donald Moore, 1958.
Scott, Henry T. *A Guide to the Collector of Historical Documents, Literary Manuscripts, and Autograph Letters*. London: S.J. Davey, 1891.
Sears, Sallie. "Theater of War: Virginia Woolf's *Between the Acts*." In *Virginia Woolf: A Feminist Slant*. Edited by Jane Marcus, 212–35. Lincoln: University of Nebraska Press, 1983.
Seck, Djibril. "Histoire des modes vestimentaires chez les jeunes filles à Dakar 1945–1960." Mémoire de Maîtrise, Université Cheikh Anta Diop, 2000.
Seguy, Philippe. "Costume in the Age of Napoleon." In *The Age of Napoleon: Costume from Revolution to Empire*. Edited by Katell le Bourhis. New York: The Metropolitan Museum of Art/Harry N. Abrams, 1989.
Seymour, Miranda. *Mary Shelley*. London: John Murray, 2000.
Shapin, Steven. *The Social History of Truth: Civility and Science in Seventeenth-Century England*. Chicago: University of Chicago Press, 1994.
Shapin, Steven and Christopher Lawrence. "Introduction: The Body of Knowledge." In *Science Incarnate: Historical Embodiments of Natural Knowledge*. Edited by Christopher Lawrence and Steven Shapin, 1–19. Chicago: University of Chicago Press, 1998.
Shapin, Steven and Simon Schaffer. *Leviathan and the Air-Pump: Hobbes, Boyle, and the Experimental Life*. Princeton: Princeton University Press, 1985.
Shelley, Mary Wollstonecraft. *The Journals of Mary Shelley 1814–1844*. Edited by Paula R. Feldman and Diana Scott-Kilvert. Baltimore: Johns Hopkins University Press, 1987.
———. *The Letters of Mary Wollstonecraft Shelley*. Vol. 1. Edited by Betty T. Bennett. Baltimore: Johns Hopkins University Press, 1980.
Shelley, Percy Bysshe. *The Letters of Percy Bysshe Shelley*. Edited by Frederick L. Jones. 2 volumes. Oxford: Clarendon Press, 1964.
Shteir, Ann. *Cultivating Women, Cultivating Science: Flora's Daughters and Botany in England, 1760–1860*. Baltimore: Johns Hopkins University Press, 1996.

Silverman, Willa Z. "Gyp et l'Affaire Dreyfus." *Modern and Contemporary France* 43 (1990): 5–16.

Simmel, Georg. "The Philosophy of Fashion" [1905]. Translated by Mark Ritter and David Frisby. In *Simmel on Culture, Selected Writings*. Edited by David Frisby and Mike Featherstone, 187–205. London: Sage Publications, 1997.

Simon, Marie. *Fashion in Art: The Second Empire and Impressionism.* Translated by Edmund Jephcott. London: Zwemmer, 1995.

Sinclair, Bruce. *Philadelphia's Philosopher Mechanics: A History of the Franklin Institute 1824–1865.* Baltimore: Johns Hopkins University Press, 1974.

Sloan, Kim, ed. *Enlightenment: Discovering the World in the Eighteenth Century*. London: British Museum Press, 2003.

Smith, Bonnie G. *Ladies of the Leisure Class: The Bourgeoises of the Nord in the Nineteenth Century*. Princeton: Princeton University Press, 1981.

Smith, Ophia. "Charles and Eliza Leslie." *Pennsylvania Magazine of History and Biography*, 1950, 512–27.

Smith, Shawn Michelle. *American Archives: Gender, Race, and Class in Visual Culture*. Princeton: Princeton University Press, 1999.

Smith, William M. *Gloves Past and Present*. New York: The Sherwood Press, Inc., 1917.

Southey. Robert. *Letters From England: By Don Manuel Alvarez Espriella*. 3 volumes. London: Longman, 1808.

Sowerwine, Charles. *France since 1870: Culture, Politics and Society*. New York: Palgrave, 2001.

Spain, Daphne. *Gendered Spaces*. Chapel Hill: University of North Carolina Press, 1992.

Spary, Emma C. "Codes of Passion." In *Wissenschaft als Kulturelle Praxis, 1750–1900*. Edited by H.E. Bodecker, P.H. Reill, and J. Schlumbohm. Gottingen: Vandenhoeck and Ruprecht, 1999.

——. "Scientific Symmetries." *History of Science* 42 (2004): 1–46.

Spence, Jonathan. *The Search for Modern China*. New York: W.W. Norton & Co., 2000.

Spencer, Anne M. "In Praise of Heroes: Contemporary African Commemorative Cloths." *African Arts* 16 (1982): 84–5.

Spigel, Lynn. *Make Room for TV: Television and the Family Ideal in Postwar America*. Chicago: University of Chicago Press, 1992.

Spivak, Gayatri. "Can the Subaltern Speak?" In *Marxism and the Interpretation of Culture*. Edited by Cary Nelson and Lawrence Grossberg. Champagne-Urbana, IL: University of Illinois Press, 1988.

St George, Robert. *Conversing by Signs: Poetics of Implication in Colonial New England Culture*. Chapel Hill: University of North Carolina Press, 1998.

Staffe, Baronne de. *Le cabinet de toilette*. Paris: Havard, 1903.

Staves, Susan. "'Books without which I cannot write': How Did Eighteenth-century Women Writers Get the Books They Read?" In *Women and Material Culture, 1660–1830*. Edited by Jennie Batchelor and Cora Kaplan, 192–208. Basingstoke: Palgrave Macmillan, 2007.

Steele, Valerie. *Fashion and Eroticism: Ideals of Feminine Beauty from the Victorian Era to the Jazz Age*. New York: Oxford University Press, 1985.

——. *Paris Fashion: A Cultural History*. New York: Oxford University Press, 1988.

Stetz, Margaret D. "Selling Literary Tourism in *The Bookman*." In *Literary Tourism and Nineteenth-Century Culture*. Edited by Nicola Watson. Basingstoke: Palgrave Macmillan, 2009.

Stott, Rebecca. "Duchess of Curiosities: The Life of Margaret, Duchess of Portland." Welbeck: Pineapple Press for the Harley Gallery, 2006.

Strathern, Marilyn. *The Gender of the Gift*. Berkeley: University of California Press, 1988.

Streatfeild, Noel. *Saplings* [1945]. London: Persephone Books, 2000.
Stuckey, Charles F. and William P. Scott, with the assistance of Suzanne G. Lindsay. *Berthe Morisot, Impressionist*. New York: Hudson Hills Press, 1987.
Sullerot, Evelyn. *La Presse Féminine*. Paris: Armand Colin, 1963.
Sun Dianqi. *Liulichang xiaozhi* [Short gazetteer of Liulichang]. Beijing: Beijing chubanshe, 1982.
Sunstein, Emily W. *Mary Shelley: Romance and Reality*. Boston, Toronto and London: Little, Brown, 1989.
Sutton, Geoffrey. *Science for a Polite Society: Gender, Culture, and the Demonstration of Enlightenment*. Boulder, CO: Westview Press, 1995.
Swainson, William. *Taxidermy: Bibliography and Biography*. London: Longman, 1840.
Swann, Marjorie. *Curiosities and Texts: The Culture of Collecting in Early Modern England*. Philadelphia: University of Pennsylvania Press, 2001.
Tang Shuyu. *Yutai huashi* [History of painters from the jade terrace]. China: Qiantang Wang shi Zhenyitang, 1824. Reprint. *Xuxiu Siku quanshu* [Additions to the complete library of the four treasuries] 1084. Shanghai: Shanghai guji chubanshe, 1995–2002.
Taylor, Lou. *The Study of Dress History*. Manchester: Manchester University Press, 2001.
Tëmkin, Ilya. "Linnaeus, Solander, and Conchology." Unpublished paper. 2006.
Tétart-Vittu, Françoise. "Catalogues et Affiches." In *Les Cathédrales du Commerce Parisien: Grands Magasins et Enseignes*. Edited by Béatrice De Andia and Caroline François, 135–42. Paris: Action Artistique de la Ville de Paris, 2006.
Thane, John. *British Autography. A Collection of Fac-similes of the Hand-writing of the Royal and Illustrious Personages with their Authentic Portraits*. 3 volumes. London, 1793–98.
The Times of India, November 19, 1929.
Thiam, Bodiel. "Coloration des bijoux ouolof en or de basse qualité." *Notes Africaines* 46 (1950): 45.
Thiam, Bodiel. "La coiffure 'gossip' et les bijoux qui lui sont assortis." *Notes Africaines* 45 (1950): 9–11.
Thomas, Nicholas. *Entangled Objects: Exchange, Material Culture, and Colonialism in the Pacific*. Cambridge: Harvard University Press, 1991.
Thompson, G.E. *Official Record of the New Zealand and South Seas International Exhibition, Dunedin, 1925–26*. Dunedin: Coulls Somerville Wilkie Ltd, 1926.
Thomson, Keith W. *Art Galleries and Museums of New Zealand*. Wellington: Reed, 1981.
Thornton, Tamara Plakins. *Handwriting in America: A Cultural History*. New Haven: Yale University Press, 1996.
Tickner, Lisa. *The Spectacle of Women: Imagery of the Suffrage Campaign, 1907–14*. London: Chatto & Windus, 1987.
Tiersten, Lisa. *Marianne in the Market: Envisioning Consumer Society in Fin-de-Siècle France*. Berkeley: University of California Press, 2001.
Tilley, Christopher. *Metaphor and Material Culture*. Oxford: Blackwell, 1999.
___. "Objectification." In *Handbook of Material Culture*. Edited by Christopher Tilley, Webb Keane, Susanne Küchler, Michael Rowlands, and Patricia Spyer, 60–73. London and Thousand Oaks: Sage, 2006.
Tilley, Christopher, Webb Keane, Susanne Küchler, Michael Rowlands, and Patricia Spyer, eds. *Handbook of Material Culture*. London and Thousand Oaks: Sage, 2006.
Todd, Janet, ed. *Jane Austen in Context*. Cambridge: Cambridge University Press, 2005.
Tosh, John. "New Men? Bourgeois Cult of Home." In *Victorian Values: Personalities and Perspectives in Nineteenth-Century Society*. Edited by Gordon Marsden, 77–88. London: Longman, 1998.

Tripp, Aili M., Dior Konaté, and Colleen Lowe-Morna. "Sub-Saharan Africa: On the Fast Track to Women's Political Representation." In *Women, Quotas and Politics*. Edited by Drude Dahlerup, 112–37. Oxon and New York: Routledge, 2006.

Troy, Nancy J. *Modernism and the Decorative Arts in France: Art Nouveau to Le Corbusier*. New Haven: Yale University Press, 1991.

Twyman, Michael. *Lithography 1800–1850*. London: Oxford University Press, 1970.

Veblen, Thorstein. *The Theory of the Leisure Class: An Economic Study of Institutions*. New York: Vanguard Press, 1899; New York and London: The Macmillan Company, 1899; New York: New American Library, 1953.

Veillon, Dominique. *Vivre et Survivre en France, 1939–1947*. Paris: Éditions Payot et Rivages, 1995.

Veillon, Dominique and Éric Alary. "L'Après-guerre de Femmes: 1947, un Tournant?" In *L'Année 1947*. Edited by Serge Bernstein and Pierre Milza, 487–511. Paris: Presses de la Fondation Nationale des Sciences Politiques, 2000.

Vergo, Peter, ed. *The New Museology*. London: Reaktion Books, 1989.

Vickery, Amanda. "Golden Age to Separate Spheres? A Review of the Categories and Chronology of English Women's History." *The Historical Journal* 36, no. 2 (1993): 383–414.

——. "Women and the World of Goods: A Lancashire Consumer and her Possessions, 1751–81." In *Consumption and the World of Goods*. Edited by John Brewer and Roy Porter, 274–301. New York: Routledge, 1994..

Voldman, Danièle. *La Reconstruction des Villes Françaises de 1940 à 1954: Histoire d'une Politique*. Paris: Éditions l'Harmattan, 1997.

Volff, Sophie. "Zhu Shuzhen." In *Women Writers of Traditional China: An Anthology of Poetry and Criticism*. Edited by Kang-i San Chang and Haun Saussy; Charles Kwong, associate editor; Anthony C. Yu and Yu-kung Kao, consulting editors. Stanford: Stanford University Press, 1999.

Volpe, Andrea. *The Middling Sorts: Explorations in the History of the American Middle Class*. New York: Routledge, 2001.

Vyas, R.P. "Introduction." In *British Policy Towards Princely States of India*. Jodhpur: Rajasthan-Vidya Prakashan, 1991.

Wainwright, Nicholas B. *Philadelphia in the Romantic Age of Lithography*. Philadelphia: The Historical Society of Pennsylvania, 1958.

Walkowitz, Judith R. *City of Dreadful Delight: Narratives of Sexual Danger in Late-Victorian London*. Women in Culture and Society series. Chicago: University of Chicago Press, 1992.

Waller, Ross D. *Letters Addressed to Mrs. Gaskell by Celebrated Contemporaries*. Manchester: Manchester University Press, 1935.

Walpole, Horace. *The Duchess of Portland's Museum*. New York: Grolier Club, 1936.

Walton, Whitney. *France at the Crystal Palace: Bourgeois Taste and Artisan Manufacture in the Nineteenth Century*. Berkeley: University of California Press, 1992.

Wang Di. *Street Culture in Chengdu: Public Space, Urban Commoners, and Local Politics, 1870–1930*. Stanford: Stanford University Press, 2003.

Wang Duan. "Shu Bixiayuanjun yu yin ta ben hou" [Postface to rubbing of the Bixia Fairy calligraphy]. In *Lin xia ya yin ji* [Collection of elegant sounds from beneath the forest]. Edited by Mao Jun. China: 1884. McGill-Harvard-Yenching Library Ming-Qing Women's Writings Digitization Project. <http://digital.library.mcgill.ca/mingqing/english/>.

Wang, Xing. *Bainian fushi chaoliu yu shibian*. Hong Kong: Commercial Press, 1992.

Wang, Zheng. *Women in the Chinese Enlightenment, Oral and Textual Histories*. Berkeley: University of California Press, 1999.

Weatherill, Lorna. "The Meaning of Consumer Behaviour in Late Seventeenth- and Early Eighteenth-Century England." In *Consumption and the World of Goods*. Edited by John Brewer and Roy Porter, 206–27. New York: Routledge, 1994.

Weiner, Annette B. *Inalienable Possessions: The Paradox of Keeping-While-Giving*. Berkeley: University of California Press, 1992.

Weiner, Annette B. and Jane Schneider, eds. *Cloth and the Human Experience*. Washington, DC: Smithsonian Institution Press, 1989.

Weitenkampf, Frank. *American Graphic Art*. With a new introduction by E. Maurice Bloch. Grunwald Graphic Arts Foundation, University of California, Los Angeles. New York: Johnson Reprint Corporation, 1970.

West, Candace and Don H. Zimmerman. "Doing Gender." *Gender and Society* 1, no. 2 (1987): 125–51.

Whanganui Regional Museum. "The Street—Wanganui 1900–1920." <http://www.wanganui-museum.org.nz>.

Whitehead, P.J.P. "A Guide to the Dispersal of Zoological Material from Captain Cook's Voyages." *Pacific Studies* (1978): 52–93.

___. "Zoological Specimens from Captain Cook's Voyages." *Journal of the Society for the Bibliography of Natural History* 5 (1969): 161–201.

Wilkins, Guy L. "A Catalogue and Historical Account of the Banks Shell Collection." *Bulletin of the British Museum of Natural History* 1 (1955): 71–119.

___. "The Cracherode Shell Collection." *Bulletin of the British Museum of Natural History* 4 (1957): 121–84.

Williams, Raymond. *Television, Technology, and Cultural Form*. New York: Schodken, 1975.

Williams, Rosalind. *Dream Worlds: Mass Consumption in Late Nineteenth-Century France*. Berkeley: University of California Press, 1982.

___. "Dream Worlds of Consumption." In *Communication in History: Technology, Culture, Society*. Edited by David Crowley and Paul Heyer, 179–85. Boston: Allyn & Bacon, 2003.

Williamson, Judith. *Decoding Advertisements: Ideology and Meaning in Advertising* [1978]. London: Marion Boyars, 1990.

Wilson, Bee. "Thick and Thin." *New Statesman* 14 (October 29, 2001): 47.

Wilson, Elizabeth. *Adorned in Dreams: Fashion and Modernity*. London: Tauris, 2005.

Wilson, Kathleen. "The Good, the Bad, and the Impotent: Imperialism and the Politics of Identity in Georgian England." In *The Consumption of Culture, 1600–1800: Image, Object, Text*. Edited by Ann Bermingham and John Brewer, 237–62. New York: Routledge, 1995.

Wilson, Verity. *Chinese Dress*. London: The Victoria and Albert Museum, 1996.

Wiltshire, John. "Medicine, Illness and Disease." In *Jane Austen in Context*. Edited by Janet Todd, 306–16. Cambridge: Cambridge University Press, 2005.

Wirth-Nesher, Hana. "Final Curtain on the War: Figure and Ground in Virginia Woolf's *Between the Acts*." *Style* 28, no. 2 (Summer 1994): 183–200. Academic Search Complete (accessed November 23, 2007).

Wixted, John Timothy. "The Poetry of Li Ch'ing-chao: A Woman Author and Women's Authorship." In *Voices of the Song Lyric in China*. Edited by Pauline Yu. Berkeley: University of California Press, 1994.

Woman's Own, September 14, 1940.

Wong, Yuching. *Lidai funü paofu kaojiu* [*The Research and Examination of Chinese Women's Gown in Successive Dynasties*]. Taipei: *Zhongguo qipao yanjiu xiehui* [Chinese Chi Pao Research Association], 1975.

Wood, James Playsted. *Magazines in the United States*. New York: The Ronald Press Co., 1971.

Woolf, Virginia. *Between the Acts* [1941]. New York: Harcourt Brace Jovanovich, 1985.

——. *The Diary of Virginia Woolf, Volume Five, 1936–1941*. Edited by Anne Olivier Bell. New York: Harcourt Brace Jovanovich, 1984.

——. *The Letters of Virginia Woolf, Volume Six, 1936–1941*. Edited by Nigel Nicholson and Joanne Trautmann. New York: Harcourt Brace Jovanovich, 1980.

——. "On Not Knowing Greek." *Collected Essays, Volume One*. London: The Hogarth Press, 1966.

——. *Pointz Hall: The Earlier and Later Typescripts of* Between the Acts. Edited by Mitchell Leaska. New York: University Publications, 1983.

Wright, Gwendolyn. *Building the Dream: A Social History of Housing in America*. Cambridge: MIT Press, 1983.

Wu Jianren, "Hen hai." *The Sea of Regret: Two Turn-of-the-Century Chinese Romantic Novels*. Translated by Patrick Hanan. Honolulu: University of Hawai'i Press, 1995.

Wu Zao. "Manjianghong: Jiang Juxiang xue bo xin de Jin Rencheng tai shou Sun fu ren bei ta ben zheng ti wei tian ci jie" [To the tune of "Manjianghong": On the theme of a rubbing of the Jin Dynasty Mrs Sun stele in Rencheng, newly found by Jiang Juxiang]. In *Xiao tan luan shi hui ke bai jia guixiu ci* [Compendium of women's ci from the little sandalwood studio]. Edited by Xu Naichang. China: Nan Lingxu keben, 1896. McGill-Harvard-Yenching Library Ming-Qing Women's Writings Digitization Project. <http://digital.library.mcgill.ca/mingqing/english/>.

Xue Shaohui. *Xue Shaohui ji* [Collected works of Xue Shaohui]. Beijing: Fangzhi chubanshe, 2003.

Yeh, Wen-hsin. *The Alienated Academy: Culture and Politics in Republican China, 1919–1937*. Cambridge, MA: The Council on East Asian Studies, Harvard University and Harvard University Press, 1990.

Yen, Hsiao-pei. "Body Politics, Modernity and National Salvation: The Modern Girl and the New Life Movement." *Asian Studies Review* 29 (2005): 165–86.

Yeo, Richard. *Science in the Public Sphere: Natural Knowledge in British Culture, 1800–1860*. Aldershot: Ashgate, 2001.

Yuan Miao, Zhu Tuo. "Liulichang fang si bian'e lu" [Record of Liulichang market placards]. In *Liulichang xiaozhi* [Short gazetteer of Liulichang]. Edited by Sun Dianqi. Beijing: Beijing chubanshe, 1982.

Zakim, Michael. *Ready-Made Democracy: A History of Men's Dress in the American Republic*. Chicago: University of Chicago Press, 2003.

Zboray, Ronald J. *A Fictive People: Antebellum Economic Development and the American Reading Public*. New York: Oxford University Press, 1993.

Zeitlin, Judith. *Historian of the Strange: Pu Songling and the Chinese Classical Tale*. Stanford: Stanford University Press, 1993.

Zeldin, Theodore. *France 1848–1945*. Vol. 1: *Ambition, Love, and Politics*. Oxford: Oxford University Press, 1973.

Zhang Hanrui. "Liulichang yan ge kao" [Studies on the transformation of Liulichang]. In *Liulichang xiaozhi* [Short gazetteer of Liulichang]. Edited by Sun Dianqi. Beijing: Beijing chubanshe, 1982.

Zhang Xiuduan. "Qian diao (Jin lü qu)" [First verse, to the tune of Jin lü qu]. In *Guixiu ci chao* [Draft of women's ci poetry]. Edited by Xu Naichang. China: Xiao tan luan she ke ben, 1909. McGill-Harvard-Yenching Library Ming-Qing Women's Writings Digitization Project. <http://digital.library.mcgill.ca/mingqing/english/>.

Zhao Shijie. *Gu jin nü shi* [Ancient and modern educated women]. China: Wen qi ke ke ben, *circa* 1628–44. McGill-Harvard-Yenching Library Ming-Qing Women's Writings Digitization Project. <http://digital.library.mcgill.ca/mingqing/english/>.

Zhong Xing. *Ming yuan shi gui* [Poems by famous beauties]. China: *circa* 1621–44. McGill-Harvard-Yenching Library Ming-Qing Women's Writings Digitization Project. <http://digital.library.mcgill.ca/mingqing/english/>.

Zhou Zhaoxiang. *Liulichang zaji* [Miscellaneous notes on Liulichang]. Beijing: Beijing Yanshan chubanshe, 1995.

Zhu Jianfei. *Chinese Spatial Strategies: Imperial Beijing, 1420–1911*. London and New York: Routledge Curzon, 2004.

Zola, Emile. *Au Bonheur des Dames* [1883]. Paris: Fasquelle, 1970.

——. *The Belly of Paris* [*Le Ventre de Paris*] [1873]. Translated by Ernest Alfred Vizetelly. Los Angeles: Sun and Moon Press, 1996.

——. *The Ladies' Paradise*. Translated by Henry Vizetelly's firm, 1886. Introduction by K. Ross. Berkeley: University of California Press, 1992.

Zweiniger-Bargielowska, Ina. *Austerity in Britain: Rationing, Controls, and Consumption 1939–1955*. Oxford: Oxford University Press, 2000.

Zwerdling, Alex. "*Between the Acts* and the Coming of War." *NOVEL: A Forum on Fiction* 10, no. 3 (Spring 1977): 220–36.

Index

Page numbers in *italics* refer to figures.

For Product Safety Concerns and Information please contact our
EU representative GPSR@taylorandfrancis.com Taylor & Francis
Verlag GmbH, Kaufingerstraße 24, 80331 München, Germany